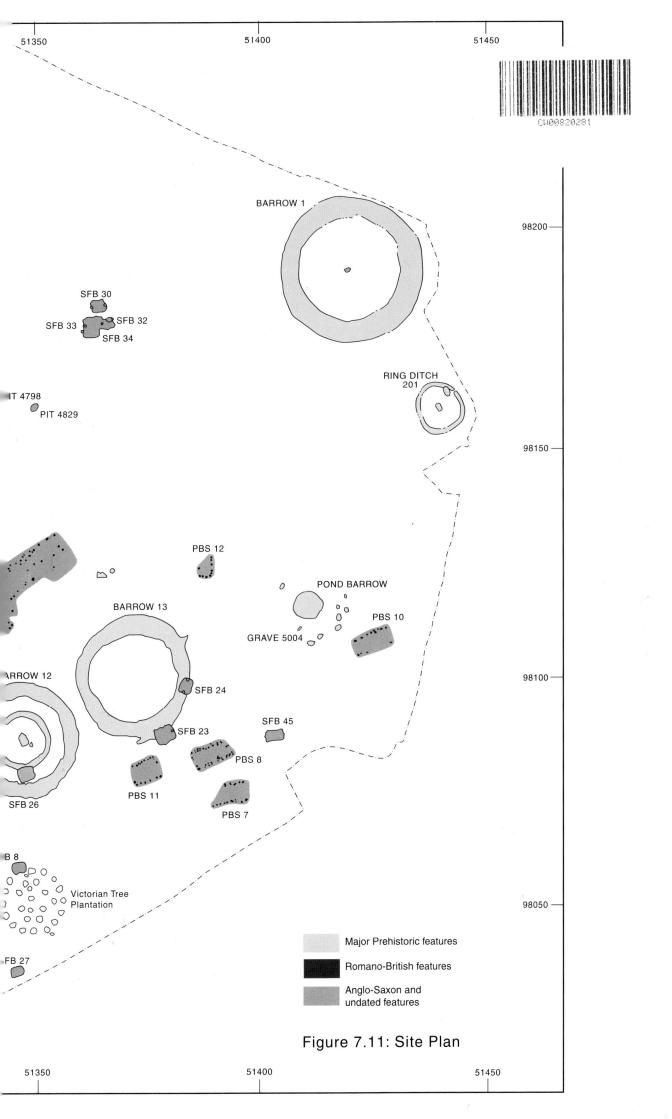

Figure 7.11: Site Plan

with very best wishes from SPARKY

all the best Nats? Icky R.

Thinking of you Take care. Nats x

Best wishes Carl.

Best wishes Graham we are thinking of you

Thinking about you! All the best Stueb.

Give your illness hell! Mark

Best wishes Kev.

Jeve All the Best thge

Missing you Graham David & Ben

ALL THE BEST Drs S.

Thinking All the best, L

We're all thinking of you. Lots of lar Kieron x

CHEERS! GRLS?

It's just not the same without you here! Take care Anne

DUDE I HOPE THIS BOOK HELPS I COULDN'T READ IT DAN D

Sending you massive get well and heal wishes come back soon Kate x

All the best, Edward

Best wishes Shelley.

None of this would've been possible without you, dear soul. Love

Best wishes, Jane xx

Hi Graham we need you come back Take care lots of love

You're missed very much! Come back soon, Graham.

Best wishes Chris

Love Anna R.

Not the same without you. Jill

all the best! Markos

Dear Graham I hope the hospital walls are ringing with your blue dulcet tones... we're missing you! lots of love, Sarah x x

We hope to see you around soon. We miss you keep the spirit up. Nicholas M-G

Missing you + thinking of you. Lots of love Rose

Best wishes, Leo

BEST WISHES Omma

Dear Graham missing you loads & sending you very best wishes Anna K

All the best DANNI!

All the best, George

Dear Graham, You've got to come back to teach Sparky to cuss and swear like a trooper! Missing your voice T.-H.

The old place isn't the same without you Good luck mate - Jon G.

Thinking of you! Winter x

All the best! Anna

keep your chin up! graham, love, Sue.

Keep fighting Graham! My thoughts are with you Lorraine

All the best Sophie x

Good Luck Matt.

Take care Graham we're thinking of you Robin + Greg

EXCAVATIONS AT BARROW HILLS, RADLEY, Oxfordshire, 1983–5

Volume 2: The Romano-British cemetery and Anglo-Saxon settlement

By Richard Chambers and Ellen McAdam

with contributions by

Lyn Barnetson, Paul Blinkhorn, Paul Booth, Angela Boyle, P D C Brown, Anne Dodd,

Barbara Ford, Guy Grainger, Mary Harman, David Miles, Lisa Moffett and Chris Salter

Illustrations by

Danny Hacker, Amy Hemingway, Paul Hughes,

Sarah Lucas, Danyon Rey and Georgina Slater

Oxford Archaeology

Thames Valley Landscapes Monograph No. 25

2007

The publication of this volume has been generously funded by English Heritage

Published for Oxford Archaeology by Oxford University School of Archaeology as part of the Thames Valley Landscapes Monograph series

Designed by Oxford Archaeology Graphics Office

Edited by Philippa Bradley and Chris Hayden

This book is part of a series of monographs about the Thames Valley Landscapes – which can be bought from all good bookshops and internet bookshops. For more information visit thehumanjourney.net

Figures 1.1, 1.5, 1.6 are reproduced from the Ordnance Survey on behalf of the controller of Her Majesty's Stationery Office, © Crown Copyright, AL100005569

Fig. 1.2 British Geological Survey. © NERC. All rights reserved

ISBN 978-0-947816-73-5

Typeset and printed in Europe by the Alden Group, Oxfordshire

Contents

Figures

CHAPTER 4

CHAPTER 6

CHAPTER 7

Plates

Tables

CHAPTER 5

CHAPTER 6

CHAPTER 7

Summary

Between 1983–5 excavation of 3.5 ha of gravel terrace at Barrow Hills, Radley, recorded three distinct phases of activity on a site whose existence was known from aerial photography: a prehistoric monument complex, a Romano-British cemetery and an early Anglo-Saxon settlement. The prehistoric features are reported on in Volume 1 (Barclay and Halpin 1999). This report, Volume 2, deals with the Romano-British cemetery and Anglo-Saxon settlement. The Romano-British cemetery consisted of 69 burials dating to the 3rd and 4th centuries and occurring as both distinct burials groups and isolated graves. There were 57 inhumations and 12 cremations, 6 of which were within a square ditched enclosure. The skeletal assemblage was well preserved. The report considers the evidence for the organisation of the cemetery, orientation, age and sex, body position, decapitation, coffins, inhumation versus cremation, grave goods, chronology and location. It is likely that the area of the prehistoric barrow cemetery was not cultivated in the Romano-British period, and the cemetery may have been laid out along the line of a north-south trackway. It probably served as the cemetery for the adjacent settlement site of Barton Court Farm (Miles 1986), and the cemetery groupings are compared with the population models postulated for that site.

The Anglo-Saxon settlement was represented by 22 post-built structures, 45 sunken-featured buildings, 2 inhumations, pits, fills of prehistoric barrow ditches and various other features. The settlement is dated by finds evidence to the 4th to early 7th centuries. The Anglo-Saxon features at Barton Court Farm, previously published in fiche, are also listed here. Chapter 3 describes the features and the evidence for their construction and use. Chapter 4 discusses the pottery assemblage, one of the largest excavated in England with a total weight of 127.62 kg. Chapter 5 deals with the small finds, and the environmental evidence is described in Chapter 6. Chapter 7 discusses the evidence for the settlement. It is suggested that the sunken-featured buildings and barrow ditches were backfilled deliberately using tertiary midden material, and that this makes dating individual features and hence phasing the site difficult. The Anglo-Saxon features at Barton Court Farm may have been part of the same settlement. It is posited that the central cluster of buildings at Barrow Hills, with a hall positioned end-on to buildings arranged around three sides of an open space in a grouping reminiscent of Chalton and Cowdery's Down, was located in relation to the Romano-British cemetery and its trackway. The barrow ditches, in contrast, were deliberately filled with rubbish. There is some evidence for variation in function between different parts of the site, with a higher proportion of butchery waste from the ditches of barrows 12 and 13.

Zusammenfassung

Von 1983–1985 wurde eine 3.5 ha große Fläche auf der Schotterterrasse bei Barrow Hills, Radley ausgegraben. Bei den Ausgrabungen konnten drei verschiedene Nutzungsphasen der bereits durch Luftbilder bekannten Fundstelle festgestellt werden: eine Anlage mit prähistorischen Denkmälern, ein Romano-Britisches Gräberfeld und eine frühe Angelsächsische Siedlung. Die prähistorischen Denkmäler wurden in Band 1 (Barclay and Halpin 1999) vorgelegt. Dieser Bericht, Band 2, behandelt die Romano-Britischen Gräber und die Angelsächsische Siedlung. Das Romano-Britische Gräberfeld bestand aus 69 Gräbern, die in das 3. und 4. Jh. n. Chr. datieren und die sowohl als Grabgruppen, aber auch als isolierte Gräber auftraten. Es waren insgesamt 57 Körperbestattungen und 12 Brandbestattungen, von denen 6 mit rechtwinkeligen Grabgärten umgeben waren. Der Erhaltungszustand der Skelette war sehr gut. Der vorliegende Bericht legt die Befunde für den Belegungsablauf des Gräberfeldes, Orientierung, Alter und Geschlecht, Bestattungslage, Enthauptungen, Särge, Körperbestattung versus Brandbestattung, Grabbeigaben, Chronologie und Chorologie vor. Es ist anzunehmen, dass der Bereich der prähistorischen Hügelgräber in Romano-Britischer Zeit noch nicht kultiviert war, und dass das Gräberfeld entlang eines von Norden nach Süden verlaufenden Weges angelegt wurde. Das Gräberfeld gehörte wahrscheinlich zur angrenzenden Siedlung Barton Court Farm (Miles 1986) und die Grabgruppierungen im Gräberfeld werden den für diese Fundstelle aufgestellten Bevölkerungsmodellen gegenübergestellt.

Die Angelsächsische Siedlung war durch 22 Pfostenbauten, 45 Grubenbauten, 2 Körperbestattungen, Gruben, die Verfüllungen der Gräben der prähistorischen Grabhügel und verschiedene andere Befunde belegt. Die Datierung der Siedlung ist durch Fundmaterial, das vom 4. bis in das frühe 7. Jh. datiert, gesichert. Die Angelsächsischen Befunde in Barton Court Farm, die bereits auf Mikrofiche publiziert worden sind, werden hier ebenfalls aufgelistet. Kapitel 3 beschreibt die Anlage, sowie die Belege für deren Konstruktion und Nutzung. Kapitel 4 behandelt die Keramik, eine der größten jemals in England ausgegrabenen Mengen, mit einem Gesamtgewicht von 127.62 kg. In Kapitel 5 werden die Kleinfunde vorgelegt, und die Befunde zur Umwelt der Fundstelle werden in Kapitel 6 beschrieben. In Kapitel 7 werden die Siedlungsbefunde abgehandelt. Vieles weist darauf hin, dass die Wiederverfüllung der Grubenbauten und der Gräben der Grabhügel mit tertiärem Abfallmaterial absichtlich erfolgte. Die

Datierung einzelner Strukturen und die Ermittlung der verschiedenen Siedlungsphasen werden dadurch erschwert. Die Angelsächsischen Befunde in Barton Court Farm könnten Teil der gleichen Siedlung gewesen sein. Es wird angenommen, dass die Anlage der zentralen Gebäudegruppe in Barrow Hills in Bezug zum Romano-Britischen Gräberfeld und dem dazugehörigen Weg erfolgte. Die Anordnung der zentralen Gebäudegruppe, mit den Gebäuden die sich um einen offenen Platz gruppieren und dem daran anschließenden Saalbau, erinnert an Chalton und Cowdery's Down.

Acknowledgements

Scheduled monument consent for the development of this site was granted subject to the site being available for excavation for two years from the granting of outline planning permission. The excavation was undertaken by the Oxford Archaeological Unit for English Heritage with labour supplied by the Manpower Services Commission. For permission to excavate the Unit is grateful to the owners of the site, initially Mr W P Docker-Drysdale and later Kibswell Builders Ltd, and to the horticultural tenant, Mr B Ford. The excavation would not have been as successful without the hospitality of Mr and Mrs Docker-Drysdale, and Mr Ford provided assistance on numerous occasions throughout the excavation. The excavation could not have been successfully concluded without the support and interest of various members of the Inspectorate of Ancient Monuments including Mrs G Andrews and Mr A J Fleming in particular.

Many people contributed their time and effort to the excavation and I would like to thank them all, especially the members of the Abingdon Archaeological Society and the Oxford In-Service Training Scheme. Conservation was undertaken by Mrs Gwyn Miles and the laboratory staff of the Ashmolean Museum, Oxford.

The preparation of this report has been very much a corporate effort. I am grateful to all of the contributing authors, who produced their manuscripts speedily and efficiently. Thanks are due to Professor R J C Atkinson for permission to reproduce the plan of the cemetery that he and Mrs Atkinson excavated at Barrow Hills in 1945. Dr Mark Robinson assisted with some of the more difficult botanical identifications. Professor S Frere and Mr D Miles provided many helpful comments. The overall interpretation of the archaeology of the site with all its attendant errors remains the responsibility of the author.

The excavation at Barrow Hills was funded by the Manpower Services Commission and English Heritage, who also funded the first phase of post-excavation.

Richard Chambers

This report would not have been brought to press without the help and advice of many friends and former colleagues at Oxford Archaeology, English Heritage and elsewhere. My thanks are due in particular to all those who worked on the new and revised text and illustrations; particularly the In-service trainees Jane Robertson, who produced the site mosaic, and Alwen Pearson and Julia Wise, who worked on the aerial photographic evidence. I am also grateful to Sheila Raven, who worked on the pottery. From English Heritage, Steve Trow, Jon Humble, Val Horsler, Chris Scull (to whose impeccable context sheets the project owes so much) and Helen Keeley offered advice and support. Thanks are due to the staff of Oxford Archaeology's Finds, Environmental and Archive departments who have provided assistance and support over the years. Dominic Powlesland and Jess Tipper provided practical help and information. My family showed exceptional forbearance throughout. Finally, I should like to thank Mark O'Neill, Head of Glasgow Museums, for allowing me to work on this report as part of my research programme.

The second phase of post-excavation was funded by English Heritage and Oxford Archaeology (formerly the Oxford Archaeological Unit). Chris Hayden is thanked for editorial work on the report.

Ellen McAdam

Chapter 1: Introduction

By Richard Chambers and Anne Dodd

BACKGROUND TO THE EXCAVATION (FIG. 1.1)

This volume forms the second part of the report on the excavations at Barrow Hills, Radley, Oxfordshire, conducted by the Oxford Archaeological Unit with Reading University from 1983 to 1985 in advance of housing development, and deals with the Romano-British cemetery and Anglo-Saxon settlement. The prehistoric monument complex forms the subject of Volume 1 (Barclay and Halpin 1999). The site, centred at SU 51359815, lay 1.5 km north of the river Thames and 2 km north-east of the centre of Abingdon, within the Vale of White Horse (Fig. 1.1). The area is now in Oxfordshire, but until the reorganisation of local government boundaries in 1974 was part of Berkshire.

The site lay within a major concentration of archaeological features on the Second (Summertown/Radley) Gravel Terrace which was discovered by aerial photography in the 1920s by O G S Crawford. This was followed by more detailed work by Major Allen in the 1930s. The history of the aerial photography and investigation of the site is discussed exhaustively in Chapter 1 of Volume 1 (Barclay and Halpin 1999). Further aerial photography in 1959 and 1965 by the Cambridge University Committee for Aerial Photography revealed in more detail the probable existence of a Roman cemetery and a large Anglo-Saxon settlement at the south-west end of the prehistoric monument complex at Barrow Hills. Saxon pottery was collected by Leeds from gravel pits to the north of the present excavations (Leeds and Harden 1936, fig. 1), and in 1963 limited salvage excavation confirmed the presence of early Saxon occupation to the west, south of the causewayed enclosure (Avery and Brown 1972). In 1974, Benson and Miles drew attention to the archaeological importance of the area (1974, 87–90) and called for a programme of rescue and research excavation to counter the threat which economic and social pressures were posing to what they described as 'one of the finest sequences of continuous land use in the Upper Thames'. Figures 1.3–4 and Plate 1.1 summarise the aerial photographic evidence for the Romano-British and Anglo-Saxon features.

From the early 1970s onwards the area has been rapidly and extensively developed, with the creation of suburban housing and a peripheral road. A number of excavations, beginning with Barton Court Farm (Miles 1986) and including Barrow Hills, Radley, have been undertaken in response to this growth, and continue to the time of writing with the phased redevelopment of Abingdon's former cattle market (the Vineyard site) and its disused railway.

RELIEF AND GEOLOGY (FIG. 1.2)

The site lay on level ground some 60 m above sea level and about 8 m above the level of the river Thames, 1.5 km from the right or Wessex bank. The character and topography of the area are chiefly governed by the location of Late Pleistocene sand and gravel deposits, and the site lay towards the south end of the Second (Summertown/Radley) Gravel Terrace, which is the most extensive of the four gravel terraces flanking the Upper Thames. The gravel overlies impermeable Kimmeridge clay and the site had free-draining, thin soil (generally 0.15–0.30 m thick), prone to leaching and drought. To the west of the site springs rise from the base of the gravel, along the edge of a broad stream channel known as Daisy Banks, and to the south and south-east a line of springs occurs along the belt of heavy land between the Second and First Gravel Terraces.

The Second Terrace is approximately 1 km wide at this point, and to its north clay soils gradually give way to the sands and limestones of the Corallian Ridge, rising to a height of 165 m at Bagley Wood, a little to the south-west of Oxford. To the south of Barrow Hills, the opposite or left bank of the Thames is marked by low partly-wooded hills beyond which lie the Chiltern plain and the prominent scarp of the chalk downs. To the south and east the site is bordered by a fairly steep drop of about 2 m, after which the ground slopes down by about 5 m over a distance of 300 m towards the First Gravel Terrace and the edge of the Thames floodplain.

The environment around Barrow Hills has changed drastically since later prehistoric and historic times (Lambrick 1992; Robinson 1992), and since the last war the pace of change has been particularly rapid. From at least the 14th century, the gravel terraces had been used primarily for cereal production. Until the early 1970s, the land between Abingdon, Radley and the river Thames remained farmland, penetrated only by ribbon development along the Radley Road and the construction of the Didcot to Oxford railway line in 1844, with a branch line to Abingdon added in 1856. Along the edge of the floodplain, the First Gravel Terrace has been extensively quarried; although some pits have been backfilled for agricultural or building use many have been left as areas of open water, creating a wetter environment than for several thousand years. The clay belt along the south edge of the Second Terrace has largely been drained and the ancient permanent pasture has been ploughed up, as has much of the floodplain beside the river. The ground immediately to the south and east of the housing development that now occupies the site, which is clear in the photographs taken during the 1983–5

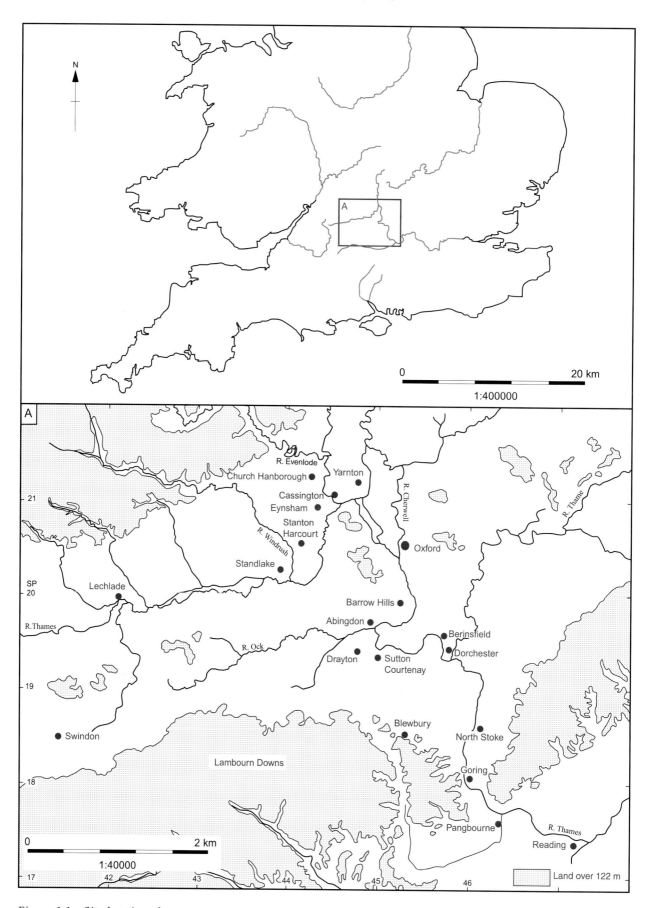

Figure 1.1   Site location plan.

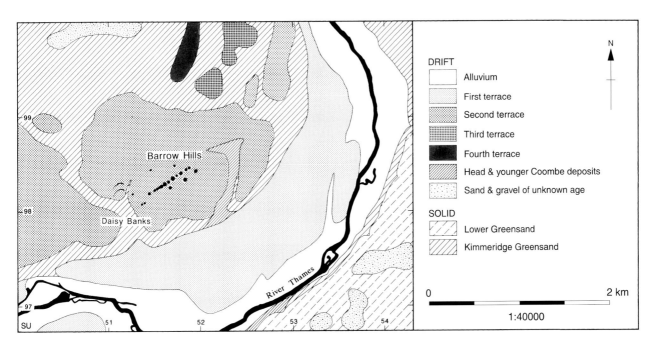

Figure 1.2   Solid and drift geology of the Radley area.

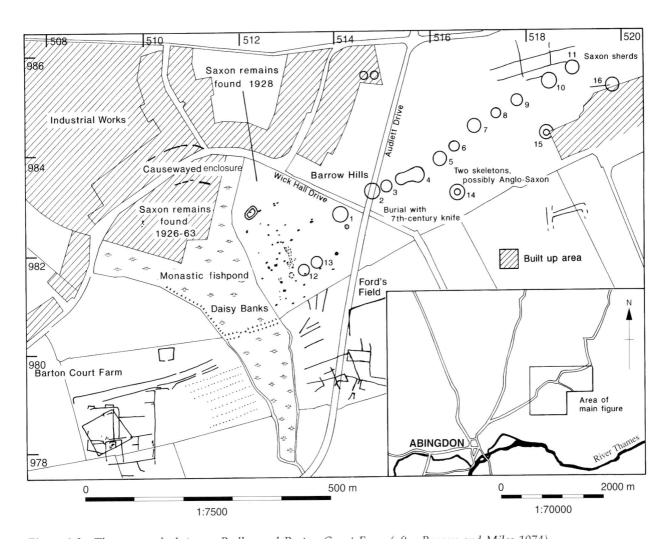

Figure 1.3   The cropmarks between Radley and Barton Court Farm (after Benson and Miles 1974).

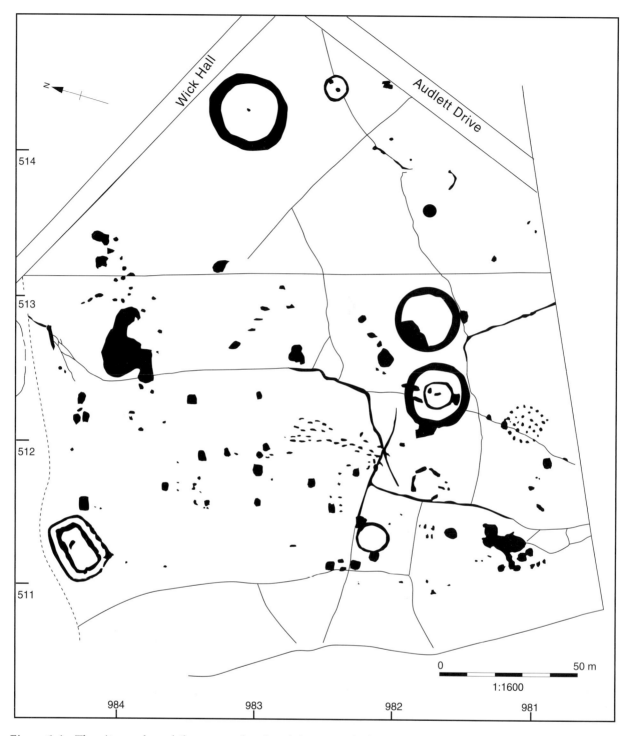

Figure 1.4 The site: a plan of the cropmarks plotted from aerial photographs (see Figure 1.3). The irregular lines represent natural periglacial features.

excavations, was thickly overgrown with hawthorn, elder and brambles by 1998.

ARCHAEOLOGICAL BACKGROUND

The confluences of the Thames and its tributaries, combined with broad gravel terraces, have attracted notable foci of settlement (Miles 1986, 1) and survey and archaeological investigation have demonstrated a complex network of settlement in this part of the Upper Thames Valley. The confluence of the Ock and the Thames at Abingdon had a Neolithic focus at the Abingdon causewayed enclosure, adjacent to the Barrow Hills site. The area continued to be a focus for burial and other purposes throughout the Bronze Age and the evidence for prehistoric activity in the area is considered in detail in Volume 1 of this report (Barclay and Halpin 1999).

4

Plate 1.1   Aerial photograph of the cropmarks at Barrow Hills taken on 9 June 1959. The marshy area of Daisy Banks is off the bottom of the photograph, to the left is the Neolithic oval barrow and to the right the circular ditches representing the west end of the Bronze Age barrow cemetery. The sunken-featured buildings of the early Anglo-Saxon settlement appear as dark rectangles. Cambridge University collection.

The Romano-British landscape (Fig. 1.5)

By the end of the Iron Age, if not earlier, the landscape was well populated and very fully exploited. Late Roman coins and pottery were found during the 1928 excavations of Abingdon Abbey, south of the Vineyard site, and intensive occupation continued well into the 4th century. Recent excavations at the Vineyard site in the centre of Abingdon, SU 499972 (Allen 1990a; 1990b; 1991), have revealed extensive evidence of occupation from the middle and late Iron Age and early Roman period. The site was enclosed by a defensive ditch and bank and may have functioned as a local market centre. Intensive occupation ended in the early to mid 2nd-century AD, and was succeeded by a single masonry building with a well, which continued in use into the 4th century. Another masonry building, in East St Helen Street, was investigated by Akerman in the 19th century. He recorded the presence of massive foundations and a herringbone tiled floor, in association with pottery, coins and a great quantity of animal bones (1865, 145, 202–3); the nature of the remains inclined him to believe that there had been a temple on the site. Walls of a building constructed in the late 1st or early 2nd century have been found in recent work on a site some 40 m to the south-west (Wilson and Wallis 1991). A third masonry building, apparently including a hypocaust, was reportedly found when the Stratton Way Inner Ring Road was constructed. Similar evidence of occupation in the Roman period has frequently been noted from small-scale work elsewhere in the centre of Abingdon (eg Wilson 1991 and Miles 1973, where the excavators noted a concentration of occupation in the 1st-2nd centuries AD which diminished thereafter, as at the Vineyard).

To the north-west of the town centre, Chambers (1980) noted settlement features and domestic refuse at the site of Abingdon School (SU 49459532), and deposits from the later Roman period were recorded at Bath Street, SU 49529728 (Ainslie 1991). To the north-east, at Boxhill (SU 499979), seven burials were cut through late Romano-British settlement features (Wilson 1980). To the south of Abingdon, part of a

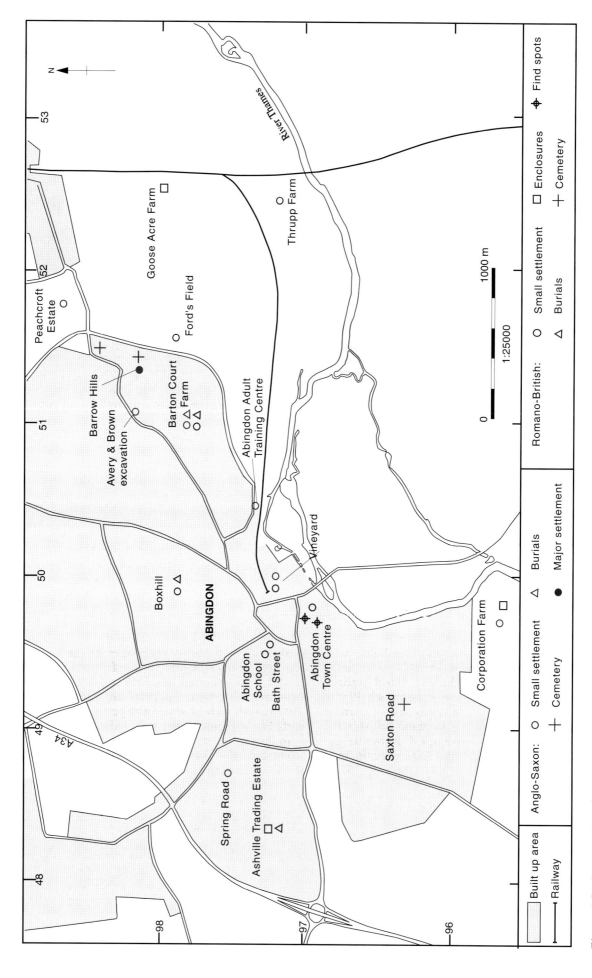

Figure 1.5 Romano-British and early Anglo-Saxon sites in Abingdon.

mid 2nd-century Romano-British enclosure ditch was excavated at the Corporation Farm site, SU 497957-SU 497970 (Abingdon and District Archaeological Society 1973).

Excavations in the west of the town at the Ashville Trading Estate (SU 483973) revealed part of an Iron Age settlement succeeded in the Romano-British period by a field system, pits and wells representing a system of small paddocks, in use from the 1st to the 3rd centuries (Parrington 1978, 36). Part of a small Romano-British cemetery was found *c* 200 m south of the site, adding weight to the suggestion that a significant Romano-British settlement site lay in the vicinity (Parrington 1978, 36). Subsequent work at the adjacent MG car factory site (Halpin 1982) revealed further Romano-British field ditches, one of which contained large quantities of Roman pottery, and further excavation on the site in 1995 recovered Saxon pottery (M Roberts pers. comm.).

To the east and north-east of Abingdon, the area around Barrow Hills has also revealed evidence of widespread occupation and use in the Romano-British period. At Barton Court Farm, approximately 300 m south-west of Barrow Hills, at SU 510978 (Miles 1986), the first enclosed farmstead dated to the late Iron Age was succeeded by a second farmstead which was in use from the later 1st century to the mid 2nd century AD. Following a gap in the settlement sequence, a modest villa farmhouse was built on the site in the latter part of the 3rd century, and at its peak in the late 4th century it was surrounded by a ditched enclosure and a regular grid of ditched paddocks and yards extending to 1.4 ha. In the extreme south-east of the paddock system was an area devoted to the burial of newborn and very young infants. The main villa farmhouse was systematically demolished towards the end of the 4th century, although Romano-British occupation probably continued on the site in a secondary cottage building well into the 5th century.

Approximately 200 m south of Barrow Hills, at Ford's Field (SU 514979), a Romano-British date was established for two ditches by trenching and field-walking. Finds from the site included a coin of Gratian, AD 375–378, and a Roman bronze knee brooch (Wallis 1981a). Approximately 500 m north-east of Barrow Hills, at SU 518987, a 'humble' Romano-British farm was excavated, apparently occupied from the 1st century BC to the mid 2nd century AD and again from the late 3rd into the 4th century AD (Spickett 1975). Between this farm and Barrow Hills lay a Romano-British cemetery, at SU 515984, recorded by Atkinson in a partial salvage excavation in 1945 (Atkinson 1952–3) and consisting of 35 adult inhumations arranged in regular rows.

At Thrupp Farm, approximately 1 km south of Barrow Hills at SU 525972, a small settlement dating from the 2nd century BC into the early Roman period was found (Jones *et al.* 1980; Wallis 1981b). Goose Acre Farm, approximately 1 km east of Barrow Hills, has revealed extensive networks of features in aerial photographs, and several sites have been investigated. Evidence of ubiquitous Romano-British field enclosures has been noted in recent excavations of Iron Age sites at Eight Acre Field, SU 525980, and the field immediately to the south-west (Mudd 1995). The Barrow Hills cemeteries may have occupied marginal land between the Barton Court estate and the Gooseacre Farm settlement.

Saxon settlement (Figs 1.5–6)

The importance of the Abingdon area as a focus of early Anglo-Saxon settlement has been recognised since the excavation there in 1934–5 of a major pagan Anglo-Saxon cemetery at Saxton Road, SU 490963 (Leeds and Harden 1936). Including more recent finds of burials in the area, the cemetery is known to have contained 128 inhumations and 99 cremations and is considered by Dickinson to date from the early 5th to the early 7th centuries (1976, Vol. 2, 3). The cemetery is remarkable in the Upper Thames region for the large number of 5th-century burials it contained (Dickinson 1976, Vol. 1, 403). At Corporation Farm, SU 497957-SU 497970, approximately 1 km south-east of the Saxton Road cemetery, three sunken-featured buildings and two pits containing pottery considered to be of 5th-century date were found (Abingdon and District Archaeological Society 1973). Dickinson (1976, Vol. 2, 3) has noted the proximity of the two sites and it seems likely from their dating that they should be associated.

Further early Anglo-Saxon remains have been recovered approximately 1 km to the north of Saxton Road, at the modern town cemetery at Spring Road, SU 488975, where an evaluation carried out by the Oxford Archaeological Unit in 1990 revealed traces of a sunken-featured building and two lines of post-holes. Remains of a further sunken-featured building, and concentrations of early Anglo-Saxon pottery, some decorated, have also been recorded during grave-digging at the site (Allen and Kamash in prep.).

On the east of the town centre, early Anglo-Saxon settlement evidence was recovered at the Vineyard site (see above) in the form of two 6th-century sunken-featured buildings, both containing weaving equipment, domestic pottery and animal bones. They may represent settlement peripheral to a main early Saxon focus further west (Allen 1990a; 1990b).

In the area around Barrow Hills, substantial early Anglo-Saxon settlement evidence has been recovered at three other sites. Excavation at the site of Abingdon Adult Training Centre, SU 505973, revealed three sunken-featured buildings which contained large quantities of pottery and animal bone, and individual finds of spinning and weaving equipment, worked bone, jewellery, quern fragments and whetstones (Keevill 1992). The site was in use from the 6th to the 7th century.

At Barton Court Farm, early Anglo-Saxon occupation of the Romano-British villa farmstead appeared to have followed rapidly after the demolition of the main villa building. The Saxon settlement consisted of seven sunken-featured buildings, several

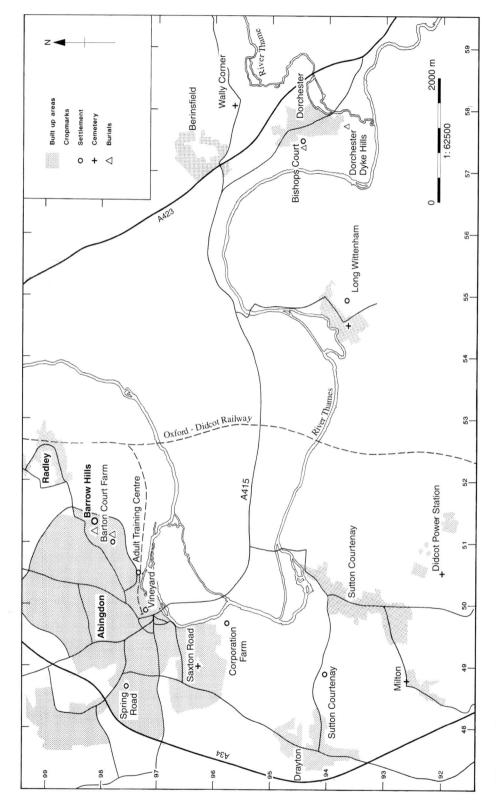

Figure 1.6 Major Anglo-Saxon sites between Dorchester and Radley.

post-built structures, fence lines, a pit, a wicker-lined well within a Romano-British ditch, four (possibly five) human burials and debris deposited in ditches (Miles 1986, 35; Fig. 7.5). Details of the features hitherto published only in fiche are given in Chapter 3. The settlement was in use from the mid 5th century to the mid 6th century (1986, 19), and thus overlapped with Barrow Hills. Its relationship to Barrow Hills is discussed at greater length in Chapter 7.

Salvage excavation in 1963 at the Abingdon Neolithic causewayed enclosure, immediately to the northwest of the Barrow Hills site at SU 511983, revealed two pits of Saxon date which are almost certainly associated with the main settlement to the south-east (Avery and Brown 1972). The excavator was unable to offer any definite interpretation of either feature, but noted that pit 1 contained two postholes of probable Saxon date, and that both pits were used for the dumping of contemporary refuse moved from elsewhere. These and other Anglo-Saxon features in the area of Barrow Hills are listed in Chapter 3.

In sharp contrast to the Romano-British and early Saxon periods, there is very little evidence for the use of the land around Barrow Hills from the mid Saxon period onwards. The early Saxon settlements all appear to have gone out of use in the 7th century, and this may be associated with the foundation of Abingdon Abbey. Barton Court, Thrupp, Northcourt Grange, Wick and Radley were all estates of Abingdon Abbey in the later medieval period (Bond 1979, fig. 2), but the place name Barrow Hills is first recorded in Land Revenues of 1547 (Gelling 1974, 437, 456–7).

GEOPHYSICAL SURVEY

Prior to excavation, selected areas of the field south of Wick Hall Drive were subjected to a magnetometer survey in 1983 to ensure the precise location of the cropmarks on the ground (Ancient Monuments Laboratory 1983). The results were particularly clear, even locating inhumation graves within the Roman period cemetery, but no new features were added to the cropmark survey. The smaller area to the north of Wick Hall Drive was surveyed in January 1985. The survey has been discussed by David (1994, 6–7 and figs 1–2) and full details are given in Volume 1 (Bartlett 1999, 11–14).

THE EXCAVATIONS

The excavations took place from 1983–5 in advance of housing development and were conducted by the Oxford Archaeological Unit, now Oxford Archaeology, with funding from English Heritage. Labour was provided by the Manpower Services Commission, students from the Department of Archaeology of the University of Reading and members of the Abingdon Area Archaeological and Historical Society. Richard Chambers of the Oxford Archaeological Unit directed the topsoil stripping of the main field, after which his team cleaned the stripped surface and planned all features, including natural ones. Responsibility was

then divided by period. Excavation of the Neolithic features was directed by Professor Richard Bradley of the University of Reading and excavation of the Bronze Age features was directed by Claire Halpin of the Oxford Archaeological Unit. The Romano-British cemetery and Anglo-Saxon settlement were excavated under the direction of Richard Chambers. The programme included preliminary fieldwalking, geophysical and contour surveys (see Barclay and Halpin 1999, chapter 2).

The site and excavation strategy

The aims of the excavation which are relevant to this volume were the investigation of later prehistoric and Romano-British land use and of the Romano-British cemetery and Anglo-Saxon settlement, especially in relation to the site at Barton Court Farm and to subsequent developments in local settlement and land use.

The site at Barrow Hills was characterised by an unusually thin layer of topsoil (0.15–0.30 m thick) which generally lay directly on the surface of the gravel terrace. Faint surface traces of ridge and furrow still survived over much of the site, and extensive topsoil stripping before excavation revealed clear traces in the surface of the underlying gravel terrace. The ridge and furrow could not be directly dated by archaeological means, but was presumed to date from the medieval period when the land belonged to Abingdon Abbey. The field had been heavily cultivated for cereals in recent years, and share marks from modern ploughing were also revealed in many parts of the site, running at an angle to the ridge and furrow.

The Anglo-Saxon ground surface did not survive. Generally the features were discrete and shallow, cut into fine sandy gravel. The thin topsoil had caused even small stakeholes to penetrate the gravel, although often only to a depth of a few centimetres, and it was not always easy to differentiate between postholes and burrows left by widespread animal activity on the site. During the early months of the excavation, soil samples were taken from both natural and man-made features in an attempt to detect any general distinguishing attributes such as a difference in texture or colour caused by leaching over different periods of time. However, no such differences were detected.

Richard Chambers directed the topsoil stripping, after which his team cleaned the stripped surface and planned all features, including natural ones, at 1:50 (the 'B' plans). Responsibility was then divided by period (see above). The 'henge' observed on aerial photographs proved to be a 19th-century tree plantation. The area north of Wick Hall drive was stripped and investigated in 1985, but the dark shapes visible on the aerial photographs (Fig. 1.4) proved to be tree-throw holes, and no Anglo-Saxon features or artefacts were recorded in this area.

Over the first *c* 1.5 ha of the site, all features were sectioned. Following a reduction in funding and manpower from April 1984, it became necessary to adopt a more selective excavation strategy towards the remaining 2 ha, although owing to the difficulty of distinguishing animal burrows and man-made features, every pit- or posthole-like structure with the exception of several small areas of soft sand in which there was intense animal activity was excavated.

Recording system

The national grid served as the site grid. Features were recorded according to the then standard Oxford Archaeological Unit system; each feature was given a number in a continuous sequence, and each excavated segment of a feature (for example a quadrant of a sunken-featured building) was given a letter, starting from A in each feature; each layer within a segment was numbered in a continuous sequence starting from 1. For the sunken-featured buildings, the south-west quadrant was A, the south-east B, the north-east C and the north-west D (Fig. 1.7). The three elements of the notation were separated by oblique strokes; the complete context reference for layer 3 of quadrant C of SFB 1055 would be 1055/C/3.

The Romano-British graves were excavated in plan and planned on graph paper at 1:10. sunken-featured buildings were excavated and recorded in quadrants; postholes were half-sectioned and were usually recorded separately. During the excavation, plans and sections of individual sunken-featured buildings were drawn during or immediately after excavation on graph paper or drawing film at 1:20, and the sections of most postholes were also drawn on graph paper at 1:20. Excavated areas were planned on A4 sheets of tracing film at 1:50, and these plans (the 'C' plans) were amalgamated and traced on Al sheets of film to produce 1:50 area plans. It is from these area plans that the site mosaic has been drawn. Information is

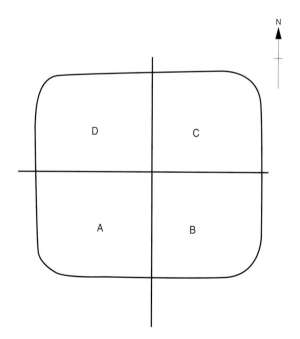

Figure 1.7 Diagram showing the position of the quadrants in a sunken-featured building.

missing for the grid square to the north-east of SFB 2. There are no original A4 'C' plans for this area in the archive and the existence of one or two postholes is known only from overlaps with other plans. Over the rest of the site the 'C' plans form a complete and reliable record.

During excavation, each small find was allocated a number in a running sequence. In the course of the first phase of post-excavation analysis, however, the finds were renumbered and a new finds catalogue was prepared by John Hedges. In this catalogue, a copy of which has been lodged with the archive, the finds from the Romano-British cemetery appear first as numbers 1 to 135, followed by the objects from the Anglo-Saxon settlement, including Romano-British and post-medieval finds, as numbers 136 to 625. Within these divisions the finds are grouped firstly by material and secondly by a ranking system which runs from personal items to manufacturing debris. Both numbering systems have been retained in this report: the original small find numbers are preceded by the letters SF.

Post-excavation analysis
by Ellen McAdam

The post-excavation analysis was funded by English Heritage and took place in three stages. Richard Chambers prepared the first draft of this report between 1985–91. The reports on the faunal and plant remains, human remains, slags and knives and razors were completed in their present forms by 1987, as were many of the illustrations. On the retirement of Mr Chambers from archaeology in 1991 responsibility for managing the publication of the completed report was assumed by Ellen McAdam. The following tasks were undertaken and a draft for refereeing was prepared by May 1996:

1 All illustrations were checked against the archive and corrected, redrawn or supplemented as necessary.
2 The text for all Romano-British and Anglo-Saxon features was checked against the archive and corrected, reformatted or supplemented as necessary.
3 The Anglo-Saxon small finds (with the exception of burnt clay and querns) were recatalogued and analysed.
4 The Romano-British pottery was reanalysed and a selected group of the Anglo-Saxon pottery was reanalysed.
5 The introduction was revised in the light of recent work.
6 Discussions of the Romano-British and Anglo-Saxon settlements were written.
7 The site archive was security copied.

During pre-refereeing consultation in 1997 the partial analysis of the Anglo-Saxon pottery assemblage was considered to represent an omission, and English Heritage agreed to fund a full reanalysis. This was completed in 2001 and the results incorporated into the present report in 2002–3.

This report describes the 1983–5 excavations and appraises them in the light of other discoveries in the area. Features are described in a series of gazetteers. The Romano-British cemetery is described and discussed in Chapter 2 and the Anglo-Saxon sunken-featured buildings, post-built structures and other features in Chapter 3. Details of the Anglo-Saxon features at Barton Court Farm, hitherto published only in fiche (Miles 1986), are included by kind permission of David Miles. Chapters 4, 5 and 6 discuss the Anglo-Saxon pottery, other finds and environmental evidence, and Chapter 7 summarises the evidence for the site and seeks to place it in context.

The difficulties attending backlog post-excavation projects are well known. It is a tribute to the consistent and thorough recording of the original excavator and his team that it has been possible to publish this site. A report prepared over such a time-span by different hands inevitably contains errors of omission and commission, and with limited resources it has not been feasible to rectify all these. Much of the preparation of this draft has taken place in the co-author's spare time. The reader is asked to remember the age and history of this report, and to regard its imperfections with tolerance. The primary concern throughout has been to publish an accurate account of this important site without further unnecessary delay.

Location of archive

The archive has been deposited with the Ashmolean Museum, Oxford, accession number 1995.113, and a copy of the archive is held by the National Archaeological Record. The finds have also been deposited with the Ashmolean Museum, with the exception of the human remains, which are held by the Natural History Museum, London.

Chapter 2:   The Romano-British Cemetery

By Richard Chambers and Angela Boyle

INTRODUCTION

The 69 archaeologically detectable Romano-British burials on this site belonged to the 3rd and 4th centuries and occurred both as distinct burial groups and as isolated graves (Fig. 2.1, Pl. 2.1, Table 2.1). There were 57 inhumations and 12 cremations, 6 of which were located within a square ditched enclosure. The human skeletal assemblage was extremely well preserved due to the alkaline nature of the Thames Valley gravels upon which the site was located. Cremation deposits had suffered as a result of repeated ploughing, and although some were afforded protection by the ridges of the former open field system, an unknown number may have been lost. Most cremation burial pits stopped at the surface of the gravel terrace, as had the ploughing. Several pottery fragments from the topsoil may have represented ploughed-out burials, but unaccompanied shallow bone deposits would have left no trace.

An inhumation cemetery was excavated in 1945 some 300 m to the north of the present burial area (Atkinson 1952–53). The cemetery comprised a distinct burial group of 35 inhumations, all orientated north-south and apparently arranged in rows running in a west-east direction (see Fig. 2.5). Excavations to the north of Wick Hall Drive during 1983–5 did not reveal any further burials in the intervening area. Atkinson's cemetery will be referred to in the text as Radley I and the present cemetery as Radley II.

CEMETERY ORGANISATION (Figs 2.1–4)

As with the site excavated by Atkinson (1952–3) the full extent of the cemetery seems to have been revealed. The main area of the cemetery was formed by a discrete group of 49 inhumations and 11 cremations within which three distinct 'plots' could be identified. A fourth 'plot' of five inhumations lay 20 m to the SW. Three outlying inhumations and one cremation were also uncovered close to the S edge of the excavated area. The 'plots' have been defined as follows (see Fig. 2.4):

Group A

A linear group of 37 north-south aligned inhumations arranged in rows: 1008–1015, 1017–1020, 1022–1027, 1029, 1037, 1039–1050, 1052, 1093–1094, 1096–1097. Inhumation 1044 is problematic. Although spatially it appears to belong to Group A, its west-east orientation may suggest otherwise.

Group B

A cemetery of nine cremations incorporating a square ditched burial enclosure: 1006–1007, 1203, 1208, 1218, 1233–1235, 1243. Five of these are located within the enclosure (1007, 1218, 1233–35) which is cut at its north-east corner by 1006. The remaining three cremations lie outside the enclosure to the north-west.

Group C

A group of 11 west-east aligned inhumations arranged in a north-south row: 1071, 1090–1092, 1095, 1098–1100, 1102–1103, 1213 and one cremation, 1004. Group C has a distinct west-east orientation and a predominance of infants. The cremation 1004 has a date range equivalent to four of the cremations in Group B and it may well be an outlier belonging to that group.

Group D

A group of five west-east inhumations c 20 m to the south-west of the main agglomeration of burials: 3781–3784, 3786. The group is defined on the basis of its broadly west-east orientation and location at a distance from the main body of the cemetery.

Isolated burials

Isolated burials comprise inhumations 3518, 3521–3522, 4261 and cremation 4614. This is a widely spaced grouping which comprises four outlying inhumations and a cremation. The inhumations are orientated broadly north-south and the cremation has a unique late date range of AD 390–400+.

The pronounced rows within Group A may represent individual linear plots similar to those proposed for the late Romano-British cemeteries at Queensford Farm, Dorchester-on-Thames, Oxon. (Chambers 1987, 66), Curbridge, Oxon. (Chambers 1976, fig. 2; 1978, 252), and for Lankhills, Winchester (Clarke 1979, 185). As Clarke has written, '... often there is a suggestion that graves lay end to end .... There is no reason why lines should have been less satisfactory than rows and it is not therefore implausible to suggest their existence.' This is also broadly true of the burials belonging to Group C though it is not a feature of the other grave groups at Barrow Hills. Radley I (Atkinson 1952–3, fig. 15) may well have been organised on a similar linear basis (see Fig. 2.5).

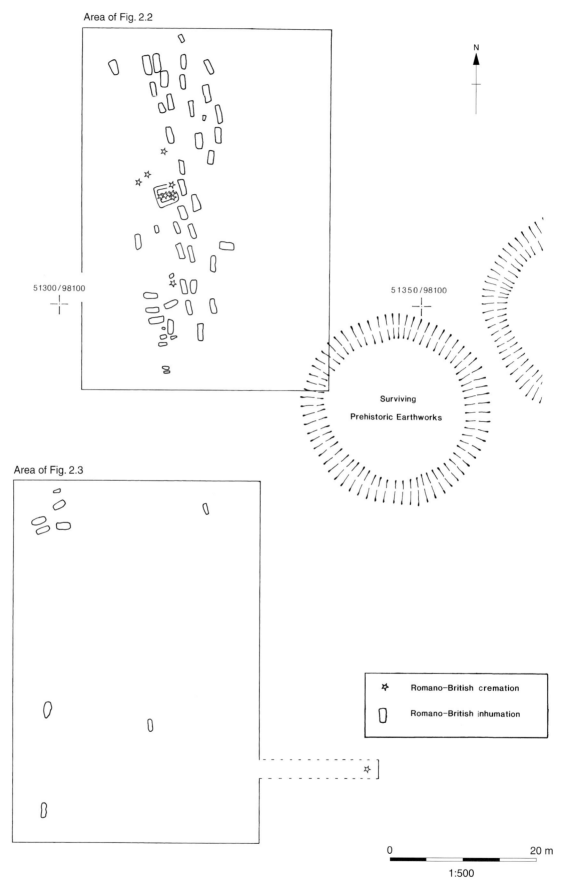

Figure 2.1 The Romano-British burials.

Plate 2.1   The excavator of Barrow Hills, R A 'Charlie' Chambers, photographing a Romano-British grave.

As within the majority of small Romano-British cemeteries in rural areas (Atkinson 1952–3, 32; Chambers 1976, fig. 12; Collis 1977; Chambers 1978, 252; Chambers 1986, 40–41, fig. 1) there was no evidence for boundaries delimiting either the cemetery or individual plots within it, but Radley II was probably laid out along a north-south path leading up from the lower ground to the south (see Romano-British land use and cemetery location below), and the arrangement of the inhumations on the west side of Group A suggests that they respected the small square burial enclosure which appears to have acted as a focus for a number of the cremations in Group B. Hedges or light fences might have been in use, but although they leave few archaeological traces in deep soils, it is likely that such features would have marked the gravel beneath the shallow soil at Barrow Hills.

Overall the graves appear to have been well spaced and none of them intercut. Several of the graves may have been deliberately paired and those whose alignments do not quite match may reflect the inherent difficulty of excavating a rectangular pit accurately aligned upon an earlier grave which was long since infilled and poorly marked. No grave-stones are known from the area but within Group D the west ends of graves 3783 and 3784 were just clipped by postholes 3785 and 3792 (Fig. 2.22). There is no means of dating either posthole, although they do not appear to relate to any of the Anglo-Saxon features in the vicinity. It is possible that they were grave markers, but if so, it is difficult to explain why there were only two in the cemetery.

The absence of intercutting graves and the visible order within the cemetery as a whole does strongly suggest that some form of regulatory system was in operation. Atkinson (1952–3, 32) believed that the ordered layout at Radley I must have been in part due to the existence of markers, perhaps in the form of soil mounds. This was later reiterated by Clarke (1979, 185) who commented that the digging of any grave generates more soil than is required to fill it and suggested that the resulting mound of surplus soil could have provided an adequate marking with which to site the graves accurately, at least in relation to each other. In his discussion of Stanton Harcourt, McGavin (1980, 118) suggested that where a cemetery had a short life span grave fills may have remained visible to act as markers. There was

Table 2.1   The Romano-British inhumations: details of orientation, body position and grave good associations.

Context no.	Orientation	Position	Direction in which skull facing	Grave good details
1008	N-S	on left side	E	coin AD 310–312
1009	NNW-SSE	"	Decapitated, skull beneath left knee	
1010	NNW-SSE	supine	E	pottery beaker
1011	NW-SE	on left side	E	
1012	NNW-SSE	supine	SE	
1013	N-S	"	E	
1014	NNW-SSE	prone	E	
1015	N-S	on left side	E	
1017	N-S	supine	E	
1018	N-S	on left side; legs semi-flexed	Decapitated, skull beneath right knee	
1019	NNW-SSE	"	E	1 R-B sherd in fill
1020	NNW-SSE	supine, turned slightly to left	E	
1022	N-S	supine	E	
1023	NNW-SSE	"	E	
1024	NNE-SSW	"	?	
1025	N-S	prone	E	
1026	N-S	supine	Decapitated, skull to left of body over feet	
1027	N-S	"	E	
1029	N-S	"	E	
1037	N-S	supine, turned slightly to left	E	
1039	NNW-SSE	"	E	
1040	NNW-SSE	supine	E	
1041	NNW-SSE	"	SE	bone pin
1042	NNW-SSE	prone	E	copper-alloy bracelet, shale bracelet, 85 glass beads, 56 hobnails
1043	NNW-SSE	supine	E	
1044	W-E	"	N	
1045	N-S	"	E	
1046	NNW-SSE	"	E	
1047	NNW-SSE	on left side	E	pottery beaker
1048	N-S	supine	E	flint flake
1049	NNW-SSE	prone	E	pottery beaker
1050	N-S	supine	E	
1052	NNW-SSE	on left side, legs semi-flexed	NE	
1071	W-E	supine	?	
1090	W-E	"	NE	
1091	W-E	?	?	
1092	W-E	supine	S	
1093	N-S	prone	E	
1094	N-S	supine	E	
1095	W-E	"	Upwards	
1096	NNW-SSE	"	E	
1097	NNW-SSE	"	Decapitated, head placed below right femur	
1098	WSW-ENE	"	NE	
1099	SW-NE	supine?	?	
1100	W-E	supine	N	
1102	W-E	"	N?	
1103	W-E	?	?	

16

Table 2.1   (Continued)

Context no.	Orientation	Position	Direction in which skull facing	Grave good details
1213	?	?	?	
3518	NNE-SSW	supine, turned slightly to left	E	
3521	N-S	on left side	E	
3522	NNE-SSW	″	SE	tooth
3781	WSW-ENE	supine	W	
3782	WSW-ENE	″	S	
3783	W-E	″	S	
3784	WSW-ENE	?	?	
3786	WSW-ENE	supine	Upwards	
4261	NNE-SSW	″	W	bucket hoop, *c* 40 hobnails

archaeological evidence for one burial having been clearly marked, the 4th-century cremation 1007 which was located at the centre of the small square ditched enclosure 1217. This is discussed in detail below.

The fact that the graves were marked, probably by their mounds, is demonstrated by the fact that they were consistently avoided by the Anglo-Saxon occupants of the site. Only one posthole of PBS 5 clips the northern edge of grave 1013, and the southern half of this building overlies the infant burial 1011, perhaps because it was no longer visible.

The cremation enclosure (Figs 2.2, 2.12–13, Table 2.2)

A shallow gully which cut 0.15 m into the gravel terrace and varied between 0.34–0.6 m in width formed a 3 m enclosure, 1217, around a central 3rd- to 4th-century cremation burial, 1007. Further cremations 1218 and 1233 lay east and west of this central burial. The fragmentary remains of two more cremation burials, 1234 and 1235, also lay within the enclosure. Cremation 1243 lay 5 m north of the enclosure; 1203 and 1208 were located 3 m to the north-west. At some time after the gully had become infilled with gravelly loam the north-east corner was cut by cremation burial pit 1006. The area was heavily affected by animal burrows which masked the true plan of the enclosure (Fig. 2.12). The majority of the cremation deposits had been disturbed and there was a thin scatter of calcined bone over the whole of the immediately surrounding area.

Although similar burial enclosures with central cremations are known to have occurred in large, late Romano-British urban cemeteries outside the Oxford region, notably at Lankhills, Hants., their true distribution is unclear because of the lack of extensively excavated cemeteries on a similar scale to Lankhills (Clarke 1979, 183). Ditched grave enclosures have also been found in small, well regulated cemeteries within the Upper Thames Valley at Claydon Pike, Glos. (Miles *et al.* forthcoming) and Dorchester-on-Thames, Oxon. (Chambers 1987). In each case they also acted as

a focus for later burials. At Lankhills the enclosures were constructed throughout the 4th century to mark and protect what were presumably important graves (all were described as unusual), and Clarke (1979, 183) interpreted them as possible planting trenches, although one such enclosure, F6, was cut by a series of later graves and at Dorchester-on-Thames (Chambers 1987, 45, fig. 3) the insertion of later graves into the ditch fill again suggested that there was no hedge. At Radley II enclosure 1217 was cut by a cremation 1006 after it had silted up.

Orientation (Table 2.1; Figs 2.2–3)

The majority of the inhumations within this cemetery show a strong north-south alignment, placed end to end and side by side as in Group A, where the only exception is grave 1044. With the exception of graves 1100 (south-west – north-east) and 1098 (west-south-west – east-north-east) all those in Group C are orientated on a west-east axis. The five inhumations which make up Group D all lie on a broadly west-east alignment. On the whole, where inhumations are orientated north-south, skulls are turned to face east. It is likely that the influence of local topographical features on burial orientation was a significant factor (Philpott 1991, 1) and the possibility that the linear north-south arrangement of the inhumation burials in Group A may represent an alignment on a single linear feature, perhaps a trackway, has already been mentioned. Radley I also has a strong north-south alignment (Atkinson 1952–3). There was a general move to a west-east orientation in the 4th century and it was seen as initially an urban phenomenon which was not indicative of Christian influence (Thomas 1981, 232).

Age and sex (Tables 2.10–11, 2.13; Figs 2.6–7)

For the purpose of this discussion all the burials within the cemetery are considered to be representative of a homogeneous population, although the different groups are not necessarily contemporary and may

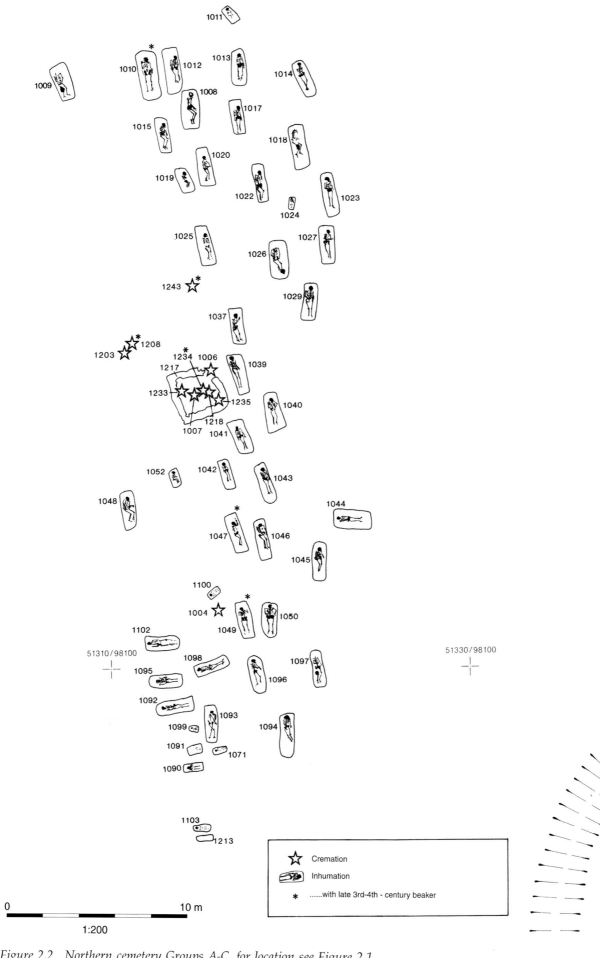

Figure 2.2 Northern cemetery Groups A-C, for location see Figure 2.1.

18

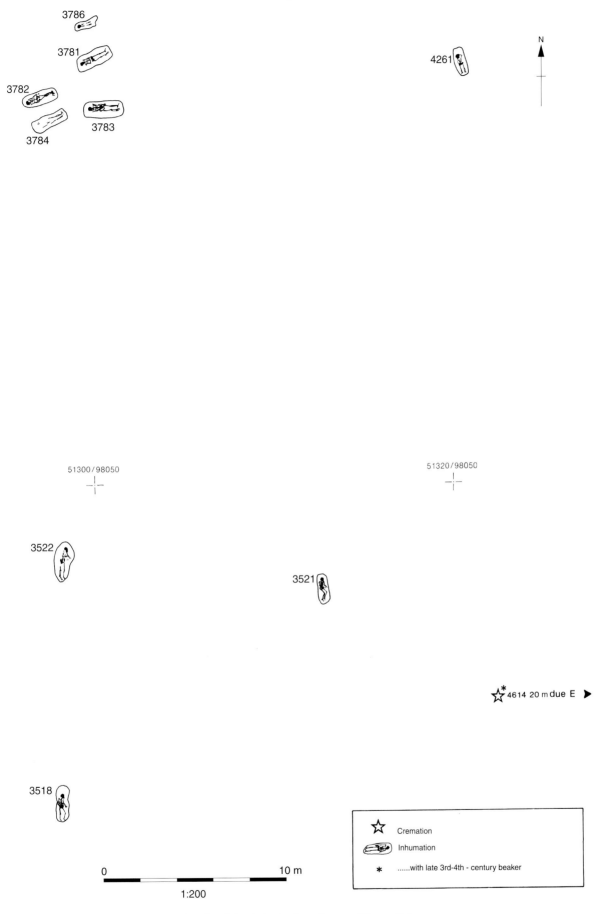

Figure 2.3   Cemetery Group D and isolated burials, for location see Figure 2.1.

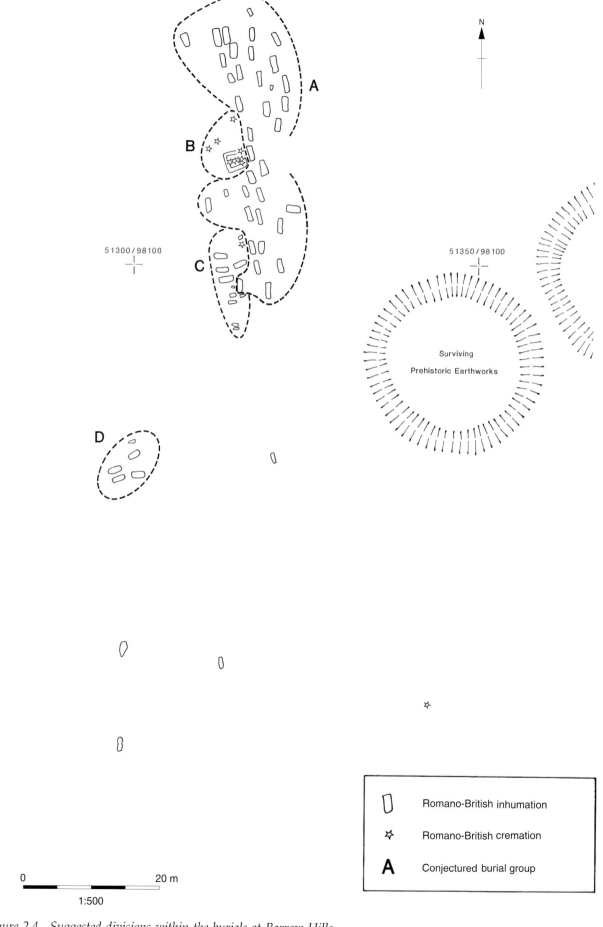

51300/98100

51350/98100

Surviving

Prehistoric Earthworks

N

A

B

C

D

0   20 m

1:500

	Romano-British inhumation
✰	Romano-British cremation
A	Conjectured burial group

Figure 2.4   Suggested divisions within the burials at Barrow Hills.

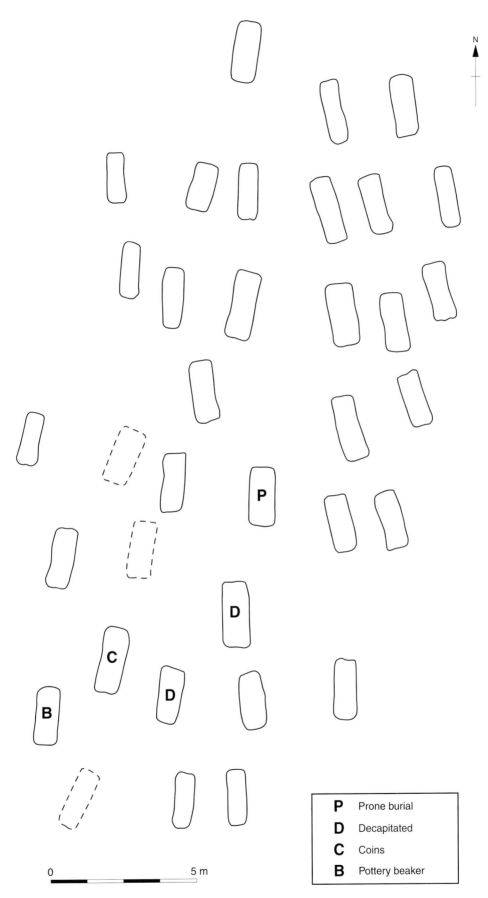

N

P	Prone burial
D	Decapitated
C	Coins
B	Pottery beaker

0   5 m

Figure 2.5   Plan of the late Romano-British inhumation cemetery at Barrow Hills excavated in 1945 (Atkinson 1952).

Table 2.2   The Romano-British cremations: depth, container, associated objects and preservation.

Context no.	Depth of cremation pit (in mm)	Cremation container	Associated objects	Preservation
1001	in topsoil	–	–	–
1004	100	grey ware jar	pottery beaker, fossil sea–urchin	partial
1006	80	''	pottery beaker	''
1007	200	''	colour coat beaker, 2 iron nails	''
1203	60	coarse ware jar	–	''
1208	100	''	pottery beaker, 2 iron nails, calcined bird bone	''
1218	–	coarse ware sherds	–	traces, much animal disturbance
1233	30	–	–	partial
1234	50	–	–	''
1235	–	sherds	fragments of burnt bone and burnt wood	''
1243	220	coarse ware vessel	colour coat beaker	''
4614	100	colour coat beaker	2 nails	''

represent different phases of use rather than different family groupings.

Little can be said about the age and sex of the cremated individuals, as all are unsexed, and only very broad age ranges have been assigned (see Table 2.10 for details). There were 57 inhumations and all were assigned sex and age ranges (see Table 2.11 for details). The group comprised 24 males, 18 females and 15 subadults, who in keeping with usual practice were not assigned sex (see Harman below).

If the composition of the individual groups within the cemetery is considered then certain patterns can be discerned. Group A comprises 18 males, 13 females and 5 subadults, the latter ranging in age from birth to 8 years. Among the adults, males are aged between 18 and upwards of 50 years. Females range between 30 and 50 years of age. Group C comprises 1 male, 3 females and 7 subadults. The single male is aged upwards of 50 years, females range from 30–50 years and subadults are aged from 2 months to 4 years. With the exception of 1213 (?infant) and 1090 (2–4 years) all the children are less than 1 year old. Group D comprises 2 males, 2 females and 1 child aged 2.5–5 years. Men are 35–40 and females are upwards of 40 years. The outlying burials comprise 2 males aged 35 to upwards of 45 years and 2 subadults aged 6–7 and 12–14 years.

Proportionally speaking there are far more children than adults in Group C (7:11) than in any other group within the cemetery. They are also predominantly very young infants. It may be argued that this is because Group A were burying their infants elsewhere. Such a high proportion of child and infant burials is unusual in comparison with other contemporary cemeteries in the region including Radley I (Atkinson 1952–3; Harman *et al.* 1981, 149, table 1). The absence of young women at Radley II is interesting, as one might expect a number to have died in childbirth.

Body position (Table 2.1)

The most common burial position in the rural cemeteries of the later Roman period is a supine extended one; see for example the cemeteries at Stanton Harcourt (McGavin 1980) and Radley I (Atkinson 1952–3). This is also the case at Radley II, where the majority of inhumations are buried in a supine position (24 in Group A, 8 in Group C, 4 in Group D and 2 outliers) and less frequently on the left side in a semi-crouched position (8 in Group A and 2 outliers). Philpott (1991, 71) discusses the possibility that burial in the latter position may be linked to attitude at death and/or deforming disease, which may have impeded the placing of the body in a supine position. However, there does not seem to be any strong correlation between this position and severe skeletal pathology at Radley I. Five individuals, all belonging to Group A, were buried in a prone position. The burial position of 4 individuals is unknown (3 in Group C and 1 in Group D).

In 30 out of the 43 cases in which skull position could be determined, the skull was turned to face east (28 in Group A and 2 outliers). This was not confined to burials with a particular body position or orientation. Three skulls faced south-east (2 in Group A and 1 outlier), 3 faced north (1 in Group A and 2 in Group C), 2 faced west (1 in Group D and 1 outlier), 3 faced north-east (1 in Group A and 2 in Group C) and 2 faced upwards (1 in Group C and 1 in Group D).

Prone burials (Table 2.1; Fig. 2.8)

Burials 1014, 1025, 1042, 1049, 1093 (all belonging to Group A)

Prone burials are considerably rarer than supine or crouched burials but become more common in the 4th century. The examples at Radley II all fall within

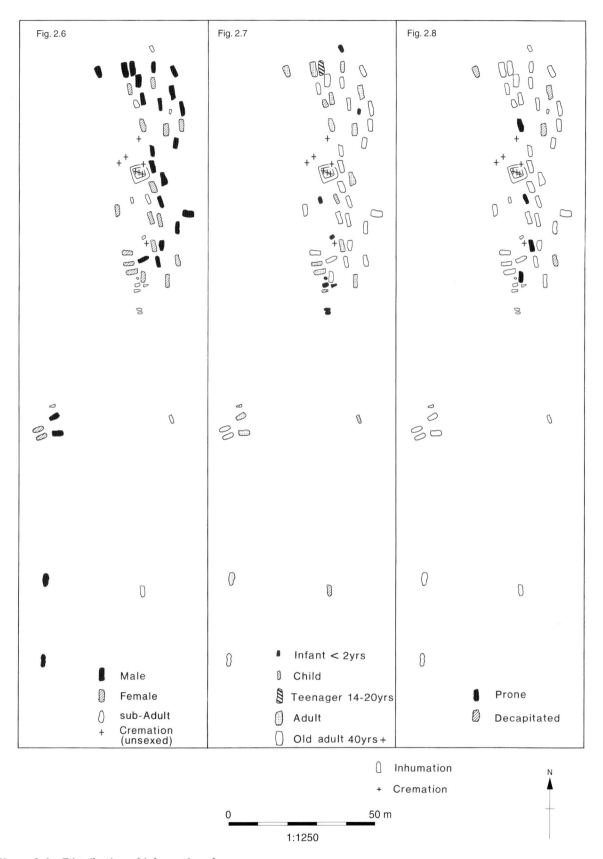

Figure 2.6   Distribution of inhumations by sex.
Figure 2.7   Distribution of inhumations by age.
Figure 2.8   Distribution of prone, semi-prone and decapitated inhumations.

Philpott's 'formal or semi-formal category', that is, burial in a coffin, in association with grave furnishings, within an established cemetery (1991). A total of five prone burials were uncovered, all within Group A and all orientated north-south. Both sexes and a wide age range were represented: one male aged 50+, three females ranging from 30–50 years and a 6–7 year old child. Two of the six graves included grave goods. Skeleton 1042 was a child buried in a coffin with two bracelets, one of copper alloy and one of shale, a necklace comprising 85 glass beads and a pair of shoes, represented by 56 hobnails. A pottery beaker lay to the left of the skull of the man in 1049, The heads of all five burials faced east, as with the majority of the corpses in Group A (Table 2.1).

Like decapitations prone burials commonly occur in both rural and urban extra-mural cemeteries. In the 4th century they appear to be more common in rural or small town cemeteries although they were apparently used to denote 'unusual' burials as early as the 1st century (Philpott 1991, 226). The table published by Harman *et al.* (1981, table 6) indicates that age and sex did not play a major role in determining who was accorded this burial rite. As with decapitated burials, prone corpses appear to have retained the right to an otherwise outwardly normal burial. It may be noteworthy that at Radley II both prone burials and decapitations are confined to Group A. They were not, however, confined entirely to the periphery of the group.

Whatever the motivation behind prone burial, two out of the six inhumation graves in which grave goods were detected were buried prone, in contrast to the general lack of detectable grave goods in the majority of the north-south graves, and two prone burials lay in coffins. A great many of the explanations advanced for the practice of prone burial appear to hinge upon the fact that within urban cemeteries they are almost always located on the peripheries, but this is not at all uniformly true of rural cemeteries, for instance Radley I (Atkinson 1952–3) and Stanton Harcourt (McGavin 1980). It may be that the growing predominance of the practice in the 4th century was related to an increasing concern to differentiate states at death through variation in burial practice (Philpott 1991, 73).

Decapitation (Table 2.1; Pl. 2.2)

Skeletons 1009, 1018, 1026. 1097 (all belonging to Group A)

There was evidence to indicate that four individuals within the cemetery had been decapitated. Although in every case the head had been severed (the osteological evidence is discussed by Harman below) it was always located within the grave, albeit displaced. In three instances the skull was placed under the knees and in the fourth it lay on the feet. In a recent summary of the practice in Roman Britain, details of skull location showed that burial under the knees occurred

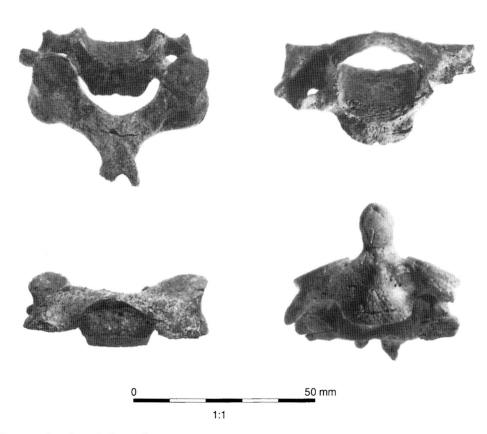

0   50 mm

1:1

Plate 2.2   Photographs of cervical vertebrae cuts.

in 8 out of 123 recorded cases and burial over the feet in 9 cases (Philpott 1991, 78, table 13). This type of burial does not appear to be confined to any particular age or sex group: the examples here comprise two males aged 17–22 years and 18–22 years (1009 and 1018) and two females aged 35–40 years and 40–50 years (1026 and 1097). Two were supine and two lay on their left sides, and all were orientated broadly north-south without any grave furnishings. Evidence for the existence of a coffin was represented in the case of 1097 by a stain in the soil.

Decapitated burials occur in both rural and urban cemeteries, although they are rather more common in the former and are believed to have originated there (Philpott 1991, 83). A survey of the practice in the Oxfordshire region (Harman *et al.* 1981) has shown that decapitation and prone burial were not uncommon among the late Romano-British cemeteries of the Upper Thames; indeed, almost a quarter of the recorded examples for the whole of Britain derive from this area (amalgamation of data from Harman *et al.* 1981 and Philpott 1991). Recent examples include three skeletons from Alchester, Oxon. (Boyle 2001, 386–8) and a single skeleton from the site of the Chemistry Research Laboratory Building, South Parks Road, Oxford (Witkin 2006). Examples are also known from Worton Rectory Farm, Yarnton (Boyle forthcoming) and Crowmarsh (Boyle unpublished). Four 4th-century Roman burials from Abingdon included a decapitation within a lead coffin. It had been buried with six coins dated AD 348–360. In general, age and sex are not seen as a determining factor and the majority of decapitated burials in which the head has been deposited elsewhere in the grave are orientated north-south. The practice declines with the change to west-east burial (Chambers 1976, 30–55; 1978, 252; Harman *et al.* 1981, 148–168).

The motives for this type of burial were discussed in detail with reference to the Lankhills examples (Clarke 1979, 192–3; MacDonald 1979, 414–421), and most recently by Philpott (1991, 77–89), who summarised all the known evidence for Roman Britain. It is clear that whatever the reasons for this particular treatment, the individuals involved often appear to have retained the right to an otherwise outwardly normal burial (cf the example from Abingdon which was accompanied by six coins and buried within a lead coffin). Philpott noted that although grave furniture is not common in decapitations, where it does occur it is broadly consistent with the wider patterns of 4th-century grave furnishings (1991, 73).

As decapitation is geographically so widely distributed, the separation of the head from the remainder of the corpse is likely to have been performed for one or more of a well defined and generally accepted set of motives.

The question of whether or not decapitation was the cause of death is a difficult one to answer. At Lankhills the victims had suffered minimal bone damage and it was therefore suggested (Watt 1979, 342) that the soft tissues in front of the spine were cleared to expose the anterior surfaces of the vertebral bodies. This would have required considerable skill and care and it was deemed likely that the victims were dead prior to the severing of the head. In addition, the totals are thought to reflect the average life expectancy of the Roman population (with the exception of infants and children) and Philpott therefore concluded that there was no reason to suggest that the group who were decapitated were different from those who died in the course of nature (1991, 80).

Where decapitations are associated with datable artefacts in urban cemeteries most can be placed in the second half of the 4th century, and Clarke concluded (1979, 374) that the rite spread from rural to urban sites during this time. This fits well with the dates suggested for the cemetery at Radley II (see Chronology below). Although none of the decapitations is dated *per se,* the general date range for Group A to which they all belong is AD 270–400.

Coffins (Table 2.3; Fig. 2.10, Pl. 2.3)

Graves 1010, 1012, 1013, 1015, 1025, 1042, 1044, 1095, 1097, 1098, 3522, 3781, 3783, 3784, 3786, 4261

Sixteen graves contained evidence for burial in wooden coffins (seven in Group A, three in Group C, four in Group D and two outliers). In addition one coffin is represented by a single nail (1092). Thirteen inhumations contained one or more iron nails and in nine instances the presence of coffins was indicated by soil marks, either as outlines or as differential fillings within and around the container. In six cases the soil marks were accompanied by nails, and in 3783, which contained seven nails, the soil marks clearly represented a rectangular coffin; in three graves, 1015, 1025 and 1097, rectangular soil outlines around or over the body also suggested coffins, although no nails were present. In 3781 the presence of a coffin was suggested by the displacement of the skull. In three graves the jaw had fallen onto the chest, suggesting that the bodies had decayed in a void (Table 2.3). At Dorchester-on-Thames four of the six individuals with fallen jaws were associated with other evidence for coffins (Chambers 1987, 54–7).

As at Lankhills, Dorchester-on-Thames and elsewhere, there was no direct evidence to indicate whether any of the coffins had lids, as has been argued for the Roman period coffins at Mucking (Jones and Jones 1975, 133–87). However, decay of a body in a void and the presence of nails among the bones of the skeleton are suggestive of the presence of lids. In grave 1013 the coffin had been strapped together with ironwork, much of it reused (Fig. 2.24). Apart from several fragments representing one or more plates, parts of hinges and two strips had been re-employed as nailed plates to clamp the coffin boards together. These and an iron corner bracket had been secured with clenched nails, whose protruding ends were bent over to prevent them working loose and falling out.

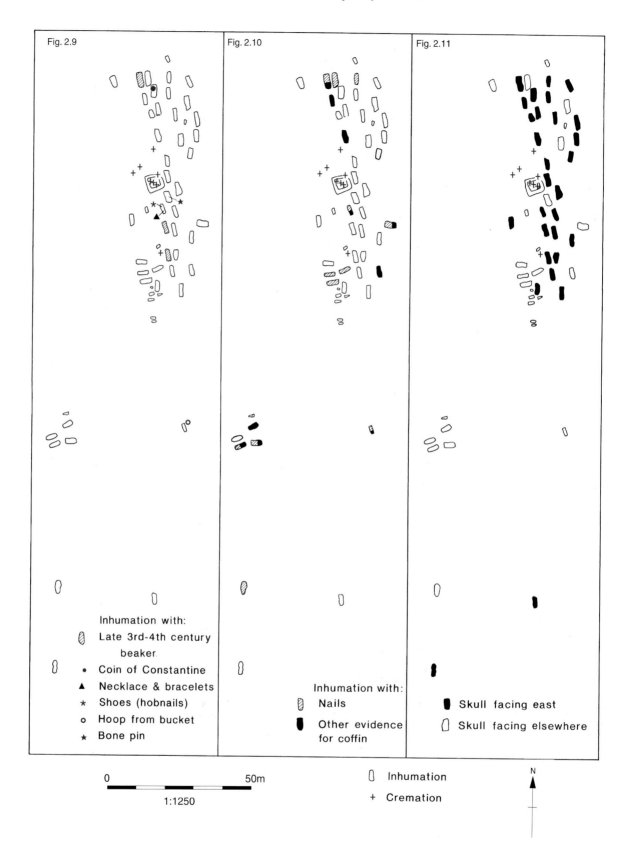

Figure 2.9   Distribution of grave goods accompanying inhumations.
Figure 2.10   Distribution of evidence for inhumations in coffins.
Figure 2.11   Orientation of heads.

Plate 2.3   Grave 1010: Skull and Oxford colour-coated beaker.

Table 2.3   Coffin evidence.

Context No.	Nails and other fittings	Skull/jaw position	Coffin staining.
1010	5		X
1012	11	jaw fallen away, skull rolled away from body	
1013	50		
1015	coffin fittings	jaw fallen away	X
1025		''	X
1042	10		X
1044	2	jaw fallen away	X
1092	1		
1095	4	jaw fallen away	
1097		''	X
1098	2	''	
3522	1		
3781		skull rolled away from body	
3783	7	jaw fallen away	X
3784	2		X
3786	1		
4261	19	jaw fallen away	X

The number of nails within each grave varied widely. Grave 1013 contained 50 nails, but seven other graves yielded fewer than five nails each. In those graves which contained only a few nails, one or two often lay among the bones of the skeleton, perhaps having fallen there when the coffin sides decayed and collapsed. Although traces of miner-alised wood often adhered to the ironwork, the direction of the grain could rarely be distinguished.

The evidence for coffins was less plentiful than in some urban cemeteries such as Lankhills, where they occurred in over 75% of the graves, although their use diminished towards the end of the 4th century (Clarke 1979, 332). On the other hand, relatively few burials in rural late Romano-British cemeteries have produced evidence for burial in coffins and only one of the 35 inhumations in Radley I contained nails (Atkinson 1952–3, 34). At Stanton Harcourt evidence for coffins was recovered from no less than 16 out of 35 graves (McGavin 1980, 118). The fact that there are so few nails in some of the Radley II graves suggests that the coffins must have been dowelled or jointed; well made coffins may have left no trace, and the worst may have been those in which most nails were used.

Cremations (Figs 2.2, 2.12–13; Tables 2.2, 2.4 and 2.10)

Ten of the 12 cremation burials found at Radley II were poorly preserved and only one survived intact. One deposit, 4614, lay 52.5 m south-east of the main body of the cemetery, cremation 1001 was recovered from the topsoil and cremation 1004 appeared within the west-east aligned inhumation Group C. The remaining nine cremation deposits formed burial Group B and were located within and around the square ditched enclosure, 1217, which appears to have served as the focus for the group. All belonged to the later 3rd or 4th centuries, with two (1001 and 4614) perhaps dating to the late 4th century (Tables 2.2 and 2.4). All were placed in shallow pits, which when measurable were never more than 0.40 m in diameter. The majority of the burial pits penetrated the gravel only to a depth of a few centimetres and were later truncated by ploughing.

Five of these cremations were the simple urned type, placed in grey ware or shell-tempered jars. Shell tempering reappeared towards the end of the 4th century at the neighbouring Barton Court villa

Figure 2.12   The cremation enclosure 1217 and surrounding cremation burials.

(Miles 1986). Seven of the cremation burials were placed in, or accompanied by Oxford product colour-coated beakers of the late 3rd or 4th centuries AD, a feature shared with three inhumation graves (Tables 2.1–2, 2.4). All but one of these beakers showed substantial amounts of wear before deposi-

tion in the grave, indicating that they were probably removed from ordinary domestic contexts and that no effort was made to provide new vessels for the purposes of the burial ritual. The beaker in 1007 had been deformed, perhaps due to the intense heat of the funeral pyre, and was used as a container for

1217 Sections

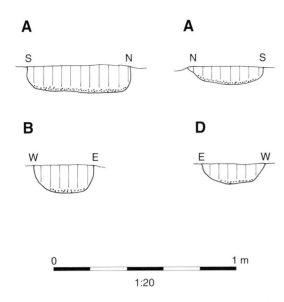

Figure 2.13 Sections across the cremation enclosure 1217.

the ashes. A calcined bird bone was present in cremation 1208, which again was contained within the beaker.

Three widely separated cremation burials each contained fragmentary remains of two iron nails, the significance of which is unclear. Charred wood was not present on any of the nails and their size does not suggest carpentered grave goods. Cremation 1007 had been placed in an approximately square pit, while 1208 and 4614 appear to have been placed in shallower, circular pits.

Only three cremations (1233, 1234 and 1235) appeared to be unurned. They survived as piles of bone located at the base of the topsoil, although it is likely that 1235 was a ploughed out urned cremation (see catalogue below). Similar deposits were identified at Lankhills (Clarke 1979, 350), their survival largely due to the unusual conditions prevailing there. Examples of unenclosed cremations in rural cemeteries are becoming more common and are discussed in detail by Philpott (1991, 45–47)

Seven of the cremations including the small square burial enclosure 1217 lay in a group separated from the inhumations. The enclosure appeared to have been respected by later inhumation graves to the south and east. A cremation lay between graves 1049 and 1100, 20 m to the south, and another isolated cremation 150 m further south again, well away from the cemetery (Fig. 2.1). None of the cremations cut any other burials, and two of the cremations (1006 and 1007) contained the remains of more than one individual.

Clarke was able to identify only 13 4th-century cremation sites from Roman Britain for his discussion of the rite at Lankhills (Clarke 1979, 350–51). Most of

these late cremations occurred within substantial inhumation cemeteries, and only at Winterbourne Down did a substantial number of late Romano-British cremations occur, outnumbering the inhumations by 36:14 (Algar 1961, 470; Philpott 1991, 50).

The isolated cremation 4614 was associated with a colour-coated beaker which has a suggested date range of AD 390–400+. It may therefore represent a slightly later phase of activity, as all other dated cremations are no later than the end of the 3rd century. Unfortunately, the inhumations in Group D and the outlying graves are all undated, although the absence of grave goods and orientation on a west-east alignment may be seen as a general indicator of a later 4th-century date.

Inhumation versus cremation: comparative evidence

Although by the 4th century cremation had been largely superseded by inhumation a small number of late cremations have been identified. Philpott (1991, 50–52) defined three groups within England, one of which, distributed through southern England and the Midlands, incorporates this assemblage. Seven of the cremations were accompanied by colour-coated beakers and assigned a date range of AD 270–400 (for details see Table 2.4. Similarly dated examples from the Midlands have been recovered from Alchester, Oxon. (Booth *et al.* 2001), Asthall, Oxon. (Booth 1997), Barton, Glos. (Heighway 1980, 57) and Bray, Berks. (Wilson 1970, 301–2; Wilson 1972, 349). It has been suggested that 4th-century cremation may be representative of an intrusive Germanic rite (Myres 1973; Clarke 1979) although Philpott (1991, 51–2) argues persuasively that cremations of this date are more likely to represent the survival of a Romano-British rite, particularly among rural populations such as the one served by Radley II in which new influences would have been slow to permeate.

At Radley II colour-coated beakers occurred in both cremation and inhumation graves and the exclusive use of readily available Romano-British wares suggests small closed family, social or religious groups within the indigenous population, reserving their own plots within the burial area. The cremation group in and around the enclosure 1217 may represent religious conservatism in a rural population slow to adopt new ideas.

Grave goods (Pls 2.3–4)

As in Radley I (Atkinson 1952–3), there were few grave goods accompanying the 41 north-south inhumations and all of the 16 west-east inhumations were unfurnished.

Seven north-south aligned inhumation graves contained non-perishable grave goods and seven of the cremation graves contained 3rd- to 4th-century colour-coated drinking beakers similar to those included with three of the inhumations (see Booth, below).

Table 2.4 Pottery dated inhumations and cremations.

Context no.	Young type	Suggested date range	Associated pottery	Burial type
1001	C102	AD 390–400+	Colour coat beaker	Cremation
			Shell tempered jar	
1004	C24	AD 270–400	Colour coat beaker	Cremation
	R24	AD 1st–4th	Grey ware jar	
1006	C23	AD 270–400	Colour coat beaker	Cremation
	–	–	Shell tempered jar	
1007	C23	AD 270–400	Colour coat beaker	Cremation
	R24	AD 1st–4th	Grey ware jar	
1010	C27 or C104	AD 270–400	Colour coat beaker	Inhumation
1047	C29 or C106	AD 270–360	Colour coat beaker	Inhumation
1049	C31	?AD 300–400	Colour coat beaker	Inhumation
1203	–	–	Coarse ware vessel	Cremation
1208	C24	AD 270–400	Colour coat beaker	Cremation
	R24	AD 1st–4th	Grey ware jar	
1218	–	–	Fragments of pot	Cremation
1243	C24	AD 270–400	Colour coat beaker	Cremation
	–	late Roman	Shell tempered jar	
4614	C102	AD 390–400+	Colour coat beaker	Cremation

A child inhumation placed prone within a coffin, 1042, was accompanied by both shale and copper alloy bracelets lying east of the right shoulder, a glass bead necklace by the left shoulder and hobnailed shoes placed between the legs. In Britain shale bracelets are associated chiefly with child graves (Chambers 1986, 37–44) and where dated occur in 4th-century contexts. The copper alloy bracelet may have been manufactured by a local smith and cannot be closely dated. There is as yet no systematic study of copper alloy or shale bracelets, although Clarke has gone some way to remedy this (1979, 301–13). At Wroxton, Oxon., one of the six-year-olds in grave 3 was also associated with a shale and a copper alloy bracelet with a suggested date in the second half of the 4th century (Chambers 1986, 41). At Lankhills eight out of ten shale bracelets were found in child graves and were of an appropriate size. The example from Radley II is of a common type in the form of an unbroken circle, cut from solid shale in such a way that the inner surface is triangular in cross-section. Another child's grave, 4261, also contained hobnailed shoes and an iron hoop, possibly from a small wooden container. No other graves contained evidence for shoes, although footwear without hobnails would have left no trace. The adult grave 1041 contained a bone pin.

An early 4th-century coin of Constantine (AD 310–312) by the left foot of inhumation 1008 was probably intentionally buried, although there were no mineralised traces of a purse or wrapping such as were found with a similarly dated deposit in Radley I (Atkinson 1952–3), where grave 9 contained nine coins sewn up in a piece of linen cloth. It is unlikely that the coin found in 1008 was in circulation much after the mid 4th century. Although grave 3522 contained a tooth and grave 1019 a single abraded pottery sherd, both were probably residual.

The paucity of graves containing contemporary grave goods is paralleled in other later rural cemeteries in the region, such as Radley I (Atkinson 1952–3), Curbridge (Chambers 1976), Stanton Harcourt (McGavin 1980) and Wroxton-St-Mary (Chambers 1986) and increased in frequency as the 4th century proceeded (Clarke 1979, 147).

THE CHRONOLOGY OF THE CEMETERY

Most of the burials excavated at Radley II probably belonged to the 3rd and 4th centuries although the pottery evidence suggests that a date in the early 5th century is not inconceivable in some cases. The colour-coated beakers are all late Roman types and products of the Oxford potteries. In more general terms, various distinctive burial rites such as extended inhumation, prone burial, decapitation, a general decrease in the deposition of grave goods (excepting coins and footwear) and west-east orientation are all consistent with this period. Within the cemetery 12 burials were accompanied by two vessels each. Nine were cremations, which with the exception of the outlier 4614 (with a potentially later date range) belonged to Group B, and three were inhumations, all from Group A. The pottery from 10 of these could be dated and 7 contained at least 1 vessel which belonged to the second half of the Roman period. Seven cremations and three inhumations contained vessels of types which were in production by the late 3rd or the beginning of the 4th century and two cremation burials contained vessels of types which on Young's chronology did not come into production until the end of the 4th century though the evidence from Lower Farm, Nuneham Courtenay (Booth *et al.* 1993) suggests that they also could be dated as early as the early 4th century. While it is possible that some burials were taking

0   50 mm

1:1

Plate 2.4   Grave 1049: Oxford colour-coated beaker.

coin of Constantine with a date range of AD 310–312 which is unlikely to have been in circulation much after the mid 4th century.

ROMANO-BRITISH LAND USE AND THE CEMETERY LOCATION (Fig. 2.14)

In the Roman period the circular ditches of the larger Bronze Age barrows were still discernible as earthworks and remained so until they were infilled with Anglo-Saxon settlement debris (see Chapter 3, Anglo-Saxon fills of prehistoric barrow ditches), and the place-name evidence indicates that the mounds survived into the 16th century AD (Chapter 1, Saxon settlement). Within the prehistoric barrow cemetery there was little evidence for Iron Age or Roman period settlement or cultivation, and this may reflect a surviving folk memory of the ancient use of the area for ritual and burial. The thin leached soil covering the gravel terrace may have ensured that this area remained wasteland or common grazing. There is no environmental evidence for the prevailing land use in the later Roman period but the fact that the land was available for burial suggests that it was permanently out of cultivation and fairly open (although pit 411 contained a substantial amount of pure grain, most of it free-threshing wheat, dated to cal AD 130–510 (1710 ± 70 BP; OxA-1885). The presence of considerable quantities of Romano-British pottery within the Saxon features is indicative of deliberate selection rather than manuring.

Following the extensive excavation of the Barton Court Farm villa, Jones (1986, 38–42) postulated the existence of territorial boundaries between the villa estate and two other less well understood neighbouring settlements at Goose Acre Farm and Thrupp Farm (1986, fig. 25). Excluding the smaller settlement units present in the landscape, about which relatively little is known, Jones derived a gravitational model incorporating a north-south boundary which passed close to the present cemetery. It is more probable that in reality the territorial boundaries respected some major natural feature such as the nearby north-south stream line.

There is cropmark evidence for a trackway leading north-east from Barton Court Farm along the edge of the terrace towards the Daisy Banks stream (Miles 1986, 4, figs 1 and 3; see Figs 1.3 and 2.14). It seems plausible to suggest that on the east side of Daisy Banks this trackway would have encountered a roughly north-south path leading to the smaller contemporary settlement at Ford's Field on the floodplain. If a trackway led northwards from Ford's Field over the First Terrace its most convenient route would have lain east of the marshy ground beside the stream and west of the still standing mounds of barrows 12 and 13 (the smaller ring ditches would no longer have presented significant barriers at this date, although there are signs that ring ditch 801 was deliberately levelled by the Anglo-Saxon inhabitants; see Chapter 3, SFB 14). The existence of such a trackway, on marginal agricultural land and near the probable

place by or soon after AD 270, none of the vessels present in the graves need have been manufactured any earlier than the second half of the 4th century AD (Table 2.4). The distribution of the three pottery-dated inhumations in Group A strongly suggests that the majority of graves within it are likely to belong to the 4th century. Pottery-dated cremations include most of Group B, the cremation 1004 in Group C and the outlier 4614. The large jars containing the cremations, whether in grey or shell-tempered fabrics, are standard late Roman types, which would be equally at home on local occupation sites. It is not, however, possible to determine whether the vessels were manufactured especially for the purpose of burial or whether they were in everyday domestic use, although some of the beakers have worn surfaces suggesting that some time elapsed between manufacture and burial. There is no clue to be gained from their size or decoration as they fall within the normal range recorded for such vessels from other occupation sites such as Barton Court Farm (Miles 1986, 7: C 13, fig. 130).

Of the remaining grave goods, the shale bracelet placed beside the child in grave 1042 is best paralleled in the 4th century at Lankhills, Hants. (Clarke 1979, 301–13), and at Wroxton, Oxon. (Chambers 1987, 42). Inhumation 1008 contained a estate boundary, may explain the location and alignment of the Radley I cemetery. A parallel for this positioning can be found in the cemetery at Stanton Harcourt (McGavin 1980, fig. 2, 117), where the north-south aligned graves appear to have been aligned upon and delimited by a north-south trackway.

It is tempting to relate the burial groups identified at the cemetery to the successive phases of activity at Barton Court Farm. During the phase of use of the infant cemetery within the settlement the burial of adults must have taken place elsewhere. The likely first phase of cemetery activity at Radley II is represented by the large group of 36 north-south inhumations (Group A), only five of whom are subadults, and the cremations whose focus is a rectangular ditched enclosure (Group B). This could represent the peak period of use of the farmstead. If the remaining groups of burials in the cemetery (C and D) represent later phases of use then a decline in the population is indicated. Both of these groups have a west-east orientation and include a much larger proportion of infants. These groups may relate to a decline in the settlement at Barton Court Farm towards the end of the 4th century, perhaps evidenced by the demolition of the farmhouse and the silting up of the main system of paddocks. The use of the smaller two-roomed

'Building 2' may, however, have continued into the 5th century (Miles 1986).

It is interesting to note that the rarer examples of discontinuous traits recorded on the bone, such as retention of metopic suture, separate neural arch of 5th lumbar vertebrae and cleft atlas, occur among all of the burial groups. This may indicate that the different groups represent the successive use of the cemetery by the same family group or groups rather than contemporaneous use by a number of different families.

Radley I (Atkinson 1952–3) and Radley II are almost equidistant from the known major settlement areas to the east and south-west, and both burial areas are separated from the Barton Court Farm villa by the intervening stream and marshy channel now known as Daisy Banks.

The homogeneous burial rites displayed in the largest burial group (Group A, Fig. 2.4) suggest a small, closed, long-lasting social group such as a landowning family. The scatter of small groups and isolated burials to the south of the large burial cluster in the presently excavated area may be associated with the small farmstead further to the south indicated by cropmarks and surface finds during the construction of Audlett Drive in 1981 (Wallis 1981a).

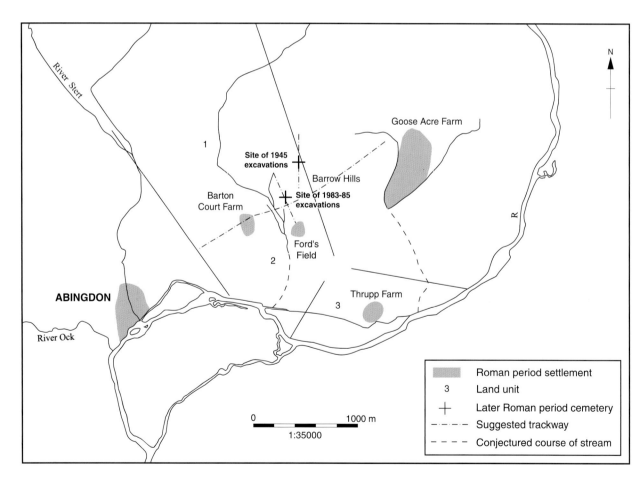

Figure 2.14   Proposed Roman period land divisions in relation to known settlements and cemeteries (after Jones in Miles 1986).

Table 2.5   Summary of the feasibility models for a farmstead based at Barton Court Farm.

Model A	Land unit 1	77 ha	5 working adults	–
Model B	Land units 1 and 2	226 ha	10–12 working adults	+12 at harvest time
Model C	Land units 2 and 3	162 ha	8 working adults	+5 at harvest time
Model D	Land units 1, 2 and 3	311 ha	16 working adults	+16 at harvest time

If Radley II did serve the population of Barton Court Farm then it becomes possible to define more closely two phases of activity within the cemetery. The north-south burials of Group A represent the major phase of cemetery use, probably contemporary with the deposition of cremations in the ditched enclosure (Group B). If the inhabitants of Barton Court Farm were burying their dead in the cemetery then the absence of infants within Group A can be explained by the fact that, as noted above, during this phase of use of the cemetery infants were buried within the settlement. The adjacent Group C with its west-east mainly infant and female burials may be a later addition and the more distant west-east Group D and the other isolated burials later still. Watts has argued (1989) that the presence of discrete west-east neonate graves in a largely adult cemetery may be a pointer to Christianity.

Jones devised a series of models for the population and organisation of the Romano-British farm at Barton Court Farm (1986, 38–42), and it seems appropriate to re-examine these models in the light of the evidence from Radley II. The models are summarised in Table 2.5; Jones considered model C the most convincing on the basis of the available evidence. The cemetery was in use for perhaps 150 years (c AD 270–420), with 41 adults in the first phase, lasting for about 90 years or three generations (assuming 30 years per generation; Arnold 1988) and 11 adults in phase 2, lasting for 60 years or two generations. This indicates a considerable decline in the population, from 13–14 adults per generation to 5–6, even allowing for the fact that these are average figures and that there would have been periods of decline and increase within each phase with corresponding fluctuations in population. Clearly there is no direct correlation with any of the proposed models, but bearing in mind that the cemetery may also have been used by the occupants of the settlement at Ford's Field, the figures for phase 1 are broadly comparable with model C of Jones (1986).

ROMAN POTTERY
by Paul Booth

Introduction

A total of 1124 Roman sherds weighing 21,496 g was recorded from all areas of the site, with roughly equal quantities of sherds coming from Roman burials, Anglo-Saxon sunken-featured buildings and 'other' contexts (the pottery was recorded by Sarah Green). This material was initially divided into fabrics (numbered from 1 to 24). Each context group was recorded

using this fabric series and for vessel forms the type series defined for the Oxfordshire industry by Young (1977). In a few cases other type codes (such as for samian ware) were used, and STJ (undifferentiated storage jar) was also employed. Quantification was principally by sherd count and weight, though EVES were also noted (see below). For the purposes of this report the original fabric numbers have been recoded to bring them into line with the recording system now consistently applied by Oxford Archaeology to all Roman pottery assemblages from the region. One oxidised and three reduced coarse ware fabrics are recoded only in the broadest categories, however, since it was not possible to relocate the original fabric type series. Detailed fabric descriptions are contained in the site archive.

Fabrics and forms

The total quantities of pottery by fabric are given in Table 2.6 together with a common name, published reference or a summary description. The generalised breakdown of pottery (ie combining individual fabrics within the major ware groups, particularly the reduced wares) in relation to context type, ie vessels from graves, from Saxon sunken-featured buildings and from 'other' (undifferentiated) contexts is shown in Table 2.7.

The principal components of the assemblage are Oxfordshire colour-coated ware (F51), reduced coarse wares (R), usually sand-tempered, and shell-tempered (C10) fabrics. The distribution of these is noteworthy, with Oxfordshire colour-coated ware as a major element in the grave groups and in the material from the sunken-featured buildings. Reduced coarse wares were also used in the cemetery and were important in the sunken-featured building groups. Shell-tempered ware, in contrast, occurred almost exclusively in cremation vessels in the cemetery.

The great majority of the pottery was from local sources. Continental imports were represented by samian ware and a single South Spanish amphora sherd, and extra-regional British sources were standard late Roman ones such as the lower Nene Valley and black-burnished (Dorset) industries. The source of the shell-tempered jars is uncertain. They may have originated at the Harrold industry in North Bedfordshire, a major source for such vessels in the late Roman period. If so, they are the only significant non-local product.

Vessel types represented by rims amounted to 12.90 EVEs (estimated vessel equivalents, based on measurement of the surviving percentage of rim

Table 2.6   Quantification of Roman pottery fabrics.

Fabric code	Old no.	Description	No. Sh.	% Sh.	Wt (g)	% Wt
S	8	Samian ware (all sources)	14	1.3	213	1.0
F51	3	Oxfordshire colour-coated ware (Young 1977, 123)	366	52.6	7493	34.9
F52	14	Nene Valley colour coated ware	1	0.1	5	–
F53	21	New Forest colour-coated ware (Fulford 1975, 24–5)	1	0.1	55	0.3
F50	24	Rough cast colour-coated ware from uncertain source	1	0.1	25	0.1
A11	16	South Spanish amphora fabric (form Dressel 20 etc)	1	0.1	140	0.7
M22	13	Oxfordshire white mortarium fabric (Young 1977, 56)	3	0.3	35	0.2
M31	1	Oxfordshire white colour-coated ware (Young 1977, 117)	10	0.9	370	1.8
W12	11	Oxfordshire fine white ware (Young 1977, 93)	8	0.7	87	0.4
W21	18	Oxfordshire coarse white ware (Young 1977, 93)	3	0.3	131	0.6
Q21	7	Oxfordshire white colour-coated ware (Young 1977, 117)	1	0.1	15	0.1
O11	20	Oxfordshire fine oxidised ware (Young 1977, 185)	1	0.1	5	–
O20	22	Coarse oxidised	2	0.2	15	0.1
O	19	Oxidised with grog temper	1	0.1	50	0.2
R11	9	Reduced, very fine	55	4.9	500	2.3
R30	2	Dark grey exterior light grey interior, micaceous	159	14.2	3672	17.1
R30	4	Grey throughout or with red/grey core, cf fabric 2	237	21.1	5562	25.9
R30	6	Grey, hard and coarse with much quartz	11	1.0	150	0.7
R90	5	Grey with coarse quartz and organic temper	8	0.7	312	1.5
R	12	Reduced with oxidised interior, grog temper	4	0.4	16	0.1
R	17	Reduced, grog temper	4	0.4	165	0.8
R	23	Reduced	2	0.2	20	0.1
B11	10	Black-burnished ware (BB1)	6	0.5	116	0.5
C10	15	Shell-tempered, reduced, coarse	218	19.4	2310	10.8
Z	0	Undesignated	7	0.6	34	0.2
TOTAL			1124		21496	

Table 2.7   Distribution of Roman pottery fabrics by context type groupings.

Fabric	Roman Graves		Saxon SFBs		Other contexts		Total sherds	Total weight
	% Sh.	% Wt.	% Sh.	% Wt.	% Sh.	% Wt.		
S	–	–	71.4	77.9	28.6	22.1	14	213
F51	30.6	17.2	38.0	50.7	31.4	32.1	366	7493
Other F	–	–	–	–	100	100	3	85
A11	–	–	–	–	100	100	1	140
M (all)	–	–	76.9	91.4	23.1	8.6	13	405
W (all)	–	–	18.2	66.5	81.8	33.5	11	218
Q21	–	–	–	–	100	100	1	15
O (all)	–	–	50.0	78.6	50.0	21.4	4	70
R (all)	14.6	20.2	32.1	40.0	53.3	39.8	480	10397
B11	–	–	33.3	38.8	66.7	61.2	6	116
C10	99.5	99.1	–	–	0.5	0.9	218	2310
Z	–	–	28.6	50.0	71.4	50.0	7	34
TOTAL							1124	21496

circumference). Non-cemetery material, however, only amounted to 4.91 EVEs. Detailed analysis of the significance of different vessel types based on such a low figure is of little value. The occurrence of types, chiefly using the classification of Young (1977), is presented in Table 2.8 without further comment.

Vessel types recorded as present on the site but unrepresented by rims included samian ware forms 18/31, 31, 37 and Curle 46, Oxfordshire colour-coated types C8, C40, C47, C48, C75, C83 and C97, white wares W14, W15 and ?W53, oxidised coarse ware types O10 and ?O39, and reduced types R52 and R80.

Table 2.8 Quantification of vessel types by EVEs (additional values in brackets represent once-complete vessels known to have been present but with no surviving rim).

Vessel type	EVEs in cemetery contexts	EVEs in other contexts	Total EVEs
Cf C16.2	0.74		0.74
C18		0.15	0.15
C23	1.00 (+ 1)		1.00
C24 miniature	1.00 (+ 2)		1.00
C27	1.00		1.00
C45		0.10	0.10
C46		0.37	0.37
C50		0.22	0.22
C51		0.21	0.21
C52		0.10	0.10
C81		0.17	0.17
C98		0.09	0.09
C100		0.22	0.22
C101/2	1.00		1.00
C106	1.00		1.00
C108	1.00		1.00
WC7		0.40	0.40
R9		0.10	0.10
R15		0.75	0.75
R24	1.15	1.17	2.32
R47		0.67	0.67
R53		0.16	0.16
Jar (reduced)		0.03	0.03
Jar (shell-tempered)	0.10 (+ 5)		0.10
TOTAL	7.99	4.91	12.90

The illustrated vessels are described individually in the grave catalogue. Pottery from the graves is summarised in Table 2.9 below and reused sherds in Anglo-Saxon contexts are dealt with in the section of the report on finds from the Anglo-Saxon structures (Table 5.3).

Discussion

Although the Roman pottery from Barrow Hills was treated as a homogeneous assemblage for the purposes of recording it should be remembered that it is far from being 'normal' occupation debris. The principal components of the assemblage are a group of vessels (some fragmentary) from the Roman burials, and material from the Saxon settlement, much of which derived from the sunken-featured buildings of that settlement.

The vessels associated with the Romano-British burials are noteworthy since they constitute the only significant group of pottery from any late Roman cemetery in the region. The occurrence of one or two vessels with small groups of burials is known, both immediately, in the cemetery at the north-west margin of Barrow Hills (Atkinson 1952–3, 34), at the Old Abbey Grounds, Abingdon (VCH 1906, 202)

Table 2.9 Summary of pottery in graves (note that dates have not been assigned to the coarse ware cremation urns).

Context	Fabric	Type (Young etc)	Possible date range	Burial type
1001	F51	cf C16.2	?AD 300–400	Cremation
	C10	Jar		
1004	F51	C24	AD 270–400	Cremation
	R30	R24		
1006	F51	C23	AD 270–400	Cremation
	C10	Jar		
1007	F51	C23	AD 270–400	Cremation
	R30	R24		
1010	F51	C27	AD 270–400	Inhumation
1047	F51	C106	?AD 350–400	Inhumation
1049	F51	cf C108	?AD 350–400	Inhumation
1203	C10	Jar		Cremation
1208	F51	C24 small	AD 270–400	Cremation
	C10	Jar		
1218	C10	Jar		Cremation
1243	F51	C24 small	AD 270–400	Cremation
	C10	Jar		
4614	F51	C101/2	?AD 325–400	Cremation

and at Ashville (Parrington 1978, 25), and further afield as at Cassington (Case 1982, 147–8), Long Wittenham (Gray 1977, 14), Crowmarsh (Clarke 1996), Roden Downs, Compton, Berks (Hood and Walton 1948, 34) and Fawley, Berks (VCH 1906, 206). In most cases these are colour-coated auxiliary vessels (usually beakers) associated with inhumation burials (the Cassington vessel was a reduced ware bowl or jar). A complete colour-coated beaker of Young type C102 from the Anglo-Saxon settlement at Sutton Courtenay, containing a late 3rd-century coin (Leeds 1947, 85 and 89) may best be explained as having been recovered from a Roman grave. The Barrow Hills group is the only example from the region of a dated late Roman cremation cemetery.

The jars which contained cremated remains were usually in shell-tempered fabrics (six vessels), but reduced coarse wares were also used (two vessels). These vessels are standard late Roman types which would have been equally at home on local occupation sites, though at Barrow Hills only one sherd of the shell-tempered fabric was found outside the cemetery. One cremation was apparently unurned (4614). This and six of the others were accompanied by colour-coated beakers, usually small, of similar character to those found in four of the inhumations.

The colour-coated beakers are all late Roman types and products of the Oxford potteries. The use and possibly the manufacture of some of these vessels into the 5th century might be implied by parallels from some sites. However, it should be noted that the only type (only tentatively identified at Barrow Hills) assigned by Young exclusively to the end of the 4th century (C102) has now been found at the kiln site of Lower Farm, Nuneham Courtenay, in contexts which are very unlikely to date after the mid 4th century at the latest (Booth *et al.* 1993, 163). Nevertheless, a late 4th-century date is quite possible for some of the vessels, perhaps particularly the beaker from inhumation 1049, with its combination of Roman form and 'Saxon' stamps. The character of these stamps is, however, still broadly within the late Oxfordshire tradition, and a single example of such a stamp (from Shakenoak) was used as a potter's mark (Young 1977, 180–181 no. 66), though it is not paralleled amongst the known 'decorative' stamps (cf Young 1977, 130).

It is not possible to determine whether these vessels were manufactured especially for inclusion with burials or whether they were in everyday domestic use. Some of the beakers have worn surfaces, suggesting that some time elapsed between manufacture and burial. One vessel (with cremation 1007) of type C23 was clearly overfired. This may be explained by its having been burnt with the body before being placed in the cremation urn. Alternatively, it may have been a 'second'. The occurrence of such vessels in cremations has been noted from as early as the 1st century AD. The forms and decoration of the vessels do not suggest a specifically funerary function since they fall broadly within the range recorded from occupation sites such as Barton Court Farm (Miles 1986, 7:C 13). However, there is a suggestion that unusually small vessels might have been favoured for inclusion within graves. Four of the six vessels for which measurement is possible were less than 120 mm in height, and this seems certain to have been true of the incomplete vessels from 1001 and 1208 also. A height of about 100 mm is suggested as the maximum for miniature type C101 and *c* 120 mm seems to provide a reasonable dividing line between the miniature beaker C102 (and its related forms) and their larger counterparts (not all the vessels in Young (1977, 172) conform to this definition). While small vessels could occur on domestic sites only one from Barton Court Farm (Miles 1986, 7:C13 no. 74.1) fell within the smaller size category. The high proportion of particularly small vessels in burials at Barrow Hills may therefore be significant.

There is no direct evidence for Roman settlement within the excavated area of Barrow Hills, though such sites do occur in the near vicinity, known both from salvage and large-scale excavation, cropmarks and surface scatters of pottery (see Chapter 1, The Romano-British landscape). Some of the Roman pottery from the Saxon settlement may have been introduced to the site accidentally, possibly as a result of agricultural activities (either within the Roman period or later), but this explanation is unlikely to account for more than a very small proportion of the material. It is noteworthy that there is almost no 'background noise' Roman pottery within the grave fills. This suggests that Roman material was not to be found in the immediate vicinity of the site. It is therefore likely that much of it was 'imported' during the Saxon period. Some support for this suggestion comes from a consideration of the average weight of the Roman sherds. The average figure for the total

assemblage is *c* 19 g. This is towards the high end of the range when compared with data from a selection of recently examined Roman domestic assemblages in the region. These are Asthall (Booth 1997, 104; 11,399 sherds, average weight 12.6 g), Alchester (Booth *et al.* 2001, 263; *c* 46,475 sherds, average weight *c* 13.5 g), Gravelly Guy, Stanton Harcourt (Lambrick and Allen 2004; 14,471 late Iron Age and early Roman sherds, average weight *c* 15 gm), Wally Corner, Berinsfield (Booth 1995, 17; 2319 sherds, average weight *c* 16 g), Wantage (Timby 1996, 135; 3001 sherds, average weight 18.6 g) and Worton Rectory Farm, Yarnton (Hey *et al.* in prep.; 8060 late Iron Age and Roman sherds, average weight *c* 20.6 g.). Unfortunately data for nearby Barton Court Farm are not available. These figures indicate that the average sherd weights at most sites were rather below that at Barrow Hills, though there are a few assemblages in the region which do have closely comparable average weights.

The average sherd weight for Barrow Hills has not been inflated by the presence of substantially complete vessels associated with burials. Since many of these were recovered in a fragmented condition their average sherd weight is in fact lower than the site average, at 14.2 g. Most striking is the average weight of the sherds from sunken-featured buildings. These totalled some 28.6% of all sherds, but 40.8% of weight, with an average of 27.3 g. This figure compares with that for the Anglo-Saxon pottery from the same contexts.

These data suggest that Roman sherds occurring in Saxon features, and particularly those found in the sunken-featured buildings, were deliberately selected, for whatever reason. This is also indicated by the range of material represented in the collection. The total absence of shell-tempered fabrics, widely used in the 4th century (eg at Barton Court Farm) and therefore presumably readily available locally, may be one significant characteristic of the group. 43.3% of the Roman sherds (37.9% by weight) from the sunken-featured buildings were of Oxfordshire colour-coated ware. Directly comparable data from adjacent late Roman sites are lacking, but at Barton Court Farm 'Oxfordshire ware' totalled 20.5% of weight of the late Roman assemblage (recalculated from Miles 1986 fiche 7:C3 omitting Iron Age and Saxon material). The proportion of this total accounted for by colour-coated ware is not known, as the figure also includes mortaria, other white wares and some oxidised coarse wares, but is unlikely to have exceeded 10–15%. There was no significant difference between the proportion of Oxfordshire wares occurring in SFBs and in late Roman features at Barton Court Farm, however, and the Roman material from these features was described as 'smallish worn sherds' (Miles 1986, fiche 7:F3). The only significant difference noted between the composition of the Roman material in late Roman as opposed to Saxon SFB contexts was a marked increase in the incidence of Nene Valley colour-coated ware in the latter. The total quantity of Roman pottery in these contexts, however, was *c* 11.85 kg, of which

Table 2.10   Summary of the cremations.

Group	Context no.	Max. length of fragments (in mm)	Average size of fragments	Identifiable bones	Further comments (inc. age assessment)
–	1001 topsoil	13	S	4 long bone shaft fragments, not all completely calcined	human/animal
C	1004	42	M	skull vault and long bone shaft fragments, part mandible, humerus ends, phalanx	adult
B	1006 cuts cremation enclosure	23	S and M	skull vault and long bone shaft fragments	adolescent/adult
B	1006 SF 6*	19	S	skull vault and long bone shaft fragments	child/adult
B	1006 SF 7*	31	S and M	skull vault and long bone shaft fragments	child/adolescent
B	1007/1*	35	S and M	skull vault and long bone shaft fragments, parts radius head, patella, astragalus	adult
B	1007/2*		S, M and L	skull vault and long bone shaft fragments, parts ulna, femur head, tibia – proximal end	adult? (nuchal crest)
B	1203 adjacent to enclosure	50	M	skull vault and long bone shaft fragments, vertebra	adult
B	1208 adjacent to enclosure	59	S and L	skull vault and long bone shaft fragments, part vertebra, pelvis, patella, phalanx	adult (also fragment bird bone)
B	1218	22	S	skull vault and long bone shaft fragments	?adolescent/adult
B	1233	18	S	long bone shaft fragments	?child/adult
B	1234 within enclosure F1217			charcoal fragments, calcined bone	
B	1235 collapsed animal burrow			calcined bone and pottery fragments	
B	1243 N of enclosure	40	S and L	skull vault and long bone shaft fragments	adult
Isolated	4614			calcined bone, ash and charcoal	

Key
S – small M – medium L – large.
*Deposits 1006 and 1007 were contained within two separate pots, representing at least two individuals in each case.

Nene Valley ware comprised only 3.3% (Miles 1986). It is therefore uncertain that the increase in its representation can be seen as statistically significant.

At Wally Corner, Berinsfield, primarily an assemblage of later 2nd-4th-century date, Oxfordshire colour-coated ware amounted to *c* 7% of the assemblage (by both sherd count and weight; Booth 1995). At Beech House Hotel, Dorchester-on-Thames, Oxfordshire colour-coated ware amounted to 23% (Rowley and Brown 1981, 27 – it is assumed that this figure is based on sherd count, but neither this nor the total quantity of material involved is stated). The representation of colour-coated ware in the Barrow Hills sunken-featured buildings is therefore broadly at least twice that at late Roman sites in the region, and probably exceeds the representation on local rural sites by between three and five times.

The presence of reworked Roman sherds on Saxon settlement sites is a widely known phenomenon, both within the region and beyond. Locally, at Sutton Courtenay, 'several bottoms of Roman vases pared down to form pot-lids' were noted (Leeds 1947, 85) and worn and trimmed fragments (of Oxfordshire colour-coated wares) occurred in sunken-featured buildings at Audlett Drive, Abingdon (Underwood-Keevill 1993, 71–2). The great majority (48, 64%) of the 75 Roman sherds identified as being reused at Barrow Hills were of Oxfordshire colour-coated ware. Three were of samian ware and one in Oxfordshire white ware, the remainder (23, *c* 31%) occurred in a variety of reduced fabrics. With the colour-coated sherds in particular the bases of bowls (including mortaria) were clearly preferred, as at both Sutton Courtenay and Audlett Drive. These lent themselves to conversion into discs, but a variety of shapes occurred, the possible functions of which are discussed below (see Chapter 5, reused Roman pottery). The reasons for the preference for Roman over Saxon pottery for reuse are not certain, but colour was presumably one significant factor (cf Plouviez 1985, 84) and the fine and evenly textured fabrics of some of the selected pieces may have been another.

The Barrow Hills data indicate not only the secondary use of pottery (6.7% of the Roman material bears evidence of physical modification) but on the basis of the evidence of average sherd weight from the sunken-featured buildings a more widespread selective collection and curation of Roman sherds. Some of the apparently unmodifed material may of course have been destined for such treatment, but the purpose behind the collection of the rest is unknown.

Outside the region evidence for comparable sherd collection is found at sites such as West Stow (Plouviez 1985), which produced an assemblage with similar biases to that at Barrow Hills, with an abnormally high proportion of base to body sherds and of fine wares to coarse wares.

Such activity was not a universal phenomenon. The positive absence of evidence for collection and re-use of Roman material is noted at nearby Barton Court Farm, for example (see above) and probably also at Worton Rectory Farm, Yarnton. There are no clear indications why this practice was observed at some sites and not at others, particularly since Roman pottery was readily available in quantity at both Barton Court Farm and Yarnton. As Chapter 5 indicates, other Roman artefacts such as metalwork and glass were also collected and reused at Barrow Hills.

HUMAN BONE
by Mary Harman

Inhumations (Tables 2.1, 2.3, 2.11–13)

This was a rewarding group of skeletons on which to work. Nearly all of the 57 inhumations are in very good condition and almost complete, the only exceptions being 1010 and 1093 (Group A), which are in poor condition, and 1011, 1024 (Group A), 1071, 1091, 1095, 1099 and 1100 (Group C), all of whom, with the exception of the adult 1095 (Group C), are child skeletons in a fair state of preservation. They represent a discrete group, a whole cemetery completely excavated: the only burials which might be missing are those which were so shallow as to be ploughed through and scattered, and any such, if they existed, are perhaps more likely to have been those of small children than older persons.

The sex of adults was determined through examination of the relevant features of the skull and pelvic girdle, and the size and robust or gracile character of the bones; age was assessed from the state of epiphyseal fusion and tooth eruption, attribution of both age and sex being based on the criteria recommended by Ferembach *et al.* (1980, 517–549), the age of adults being assessed also from the degree of wear on the teeth, using Miles's chart (1962, 884). Height was calculated from the total lengths of long bones, using the formulae of Trotter and Gleser

(Brothwell 1981, 101). Table 2.11 gives brief notes on each individual. The completeness of the skeleton is indicated, the sex, age and height are given where possible, and the numbers of carious teeth, abscesses and teeth lost *ante mortem* in the number of teeth and tooth sockets present. The presence of skeletal anomalies and evidence of injury or disease is noted: further details are given below.

There is some difficulty in assessing the age of individuals who lack many of their teeth. None of the skeletons with reasonably complete jaws has lost molars before 30 years. Light wear on the remaining teeth of 1008, 1027 and 1046 (all Group A) suggests that some molar loss occurred in the twenties, though most of the remaining molars in people with many missing show wear consistent with loss of the opposing tooth in the thirties or later. Those people with a considerable proportion of their teeth lost *ante mortem* have therefore been regarded as over 40 years of age, though it is possible that in some cases multiple tooth loss could have occurred earlier. The possibility that when some teeth are lost, wear on those remaining may be more extreme creates a further complication. A number of people have reasonably complete sets of teeth which are worn to such an extent that it seems reasonable to suggest that they may be over 50 years.

The remains from this cemetery may be compared with those from Radley I (Atkinson 1952–3, 32–35) and with others of similar date at Cassington, Curbridge, Queensford Mill and Stanton Harcourt (Harman *et al.* 1981, 145–187).

The number of people involved is quite small and all conclusions should be regarded as tentative. The cemetery may be seen as comprising different contemporary groups or as representative of successive use by one group which gradually went into decline. The choice of interpretation obviously has implications for the conclusions which may be reached regarding population composition. Children under ten comprise about a quarter of the population as a whole; half of these children were babies of six months old or less. This is in contrast to the other cemeteries in the area. Atkinson found no children under 15 in a group of 32 people (Harman *et al.* 1981), and only at Queensford Mill were any number of children found. Here too they formed nearly a quarter of the total population, but there was only one infant, a premature or undersized baby buried with an adult female. Several of the few infants found in the other cemeteries were also in the same grave as adult females, and it is clear that generally they were not buried in the cemeteries, but around the settlements, as at Barton Court Farm (Miles 1986). This cemetery, then, is exceptional in the number of infants found in an area which the community was using to bury all its dead, though neonatal infants are probably underrepresented. However, if one subscribes to the view that the cemetery represents successive use by one group then the situation looks rather different. The majority of children appear within the much smaller Groups

Table 2.11 Summary of the inhumations.

Group	Context no.	Bones present	Sex	Age	Height	Caries	Abscesses	Tooth loss	General comments
A	1008	vc	m	40+	5'7"/1.70 m	05/21	03/25	05/30	pathology: both hips, feet
A	1009	vc	m?	17–22		01/31	00/32	00/32	decapitated; at least 5 lambdoid wormian bones
A	1010	lc	m	20–25		00/29	02/30	00/30	1+ lambdoid wormians; pathology: r ulna
A	1011	lc	–	1–1.5					
A	1012	vc	m	18–20	5'2"/1.57 m	00/27	00/27	01/28	sacralised L6
A	1013	vc	m	25–30	5'6.75"/1.70 m	02/31	01/32	00/32	
A	1014	vc	m	50+	5'5.75"/1.67 m	05/17	05/21	06/28	prone; 10 lambdoid wormians; pathology: spine, r elbow, hips ?rib
A	1015	vc	f?	40+	5'4.5"/1.64 m	01/11	05/15	17/32	pathology: spine
A	1017	vc	f	50+	5'3.5"/1.61 m	04/17	02/27	06/32	pathology: spine, knees, hands, feet
A	1018	vc	m?	18–22		01/32	00/32	00/32	decapitated; 2 lambdoid wormians
A	1019	vc	–	7–8					pathology: skull
A	1020	vc	m	35–40	5'2.75"/1.59 m	09/14	06/23	06/28	metopism; pathology: spine, ribs, clavicle
A	1022	vc	m	50+	5'5.5"/1.66 m	02/10	04/25	08/32	1 lambdoid wormian; pathology: spine, feet
A	1023	vc	m	50+	5'8.75"/1.74 m	02/26	05/30	00/32	9 lambdoid wormians; pathology: spine, ribs, r clavicle
A	1024	lc	–	1–3 m					
A	1025	vc	f	30–35	5'2"/1.57 m	03/13	08/23	06/28	prone; 1 lambdoid wormian; pathology: spine, r clavicle, L3 has cleft neural arch
A	1026	vc	f	35–40	5'1.25"/1.55 m	06/20	10/29	03/32	decapitated; 6 sacral vertebrae, sacrum has cleft neural arches; pathology: spine
A	1027	vc	f	40+	4'11"/1.49 m	00/02	03/06	27/32	3 lambdoid wormians; pathology: spine
A	1029	vc	m	50+	5'8"/1.72 m	01/07	03/19	13/32	4 lambdoid wormians, L5 arch part separate; pathology: spine
A	1037	vc	m	40–50	5'10.25"/1.78 m	08/27	03/29	02/32	4 lambdoid wormians, L5 arch separate; pathology: spine
A	1039	vc	m	40+	5'10.25"/1.78 m	01/08	04/12	21/32	1 lambdoid wormian, inca bone; pathology: spine, r elbow, l hip
A	1040	vc	m?	30–35	5'6"/1.67 m	04/22	01/32	00/32	7+ lambdoid wormians, metopism
A	1041	vc	f	40+	5'3"/1.60 m	04/10	01/15	13/28	9+ lambdoid wormians; pathology: spine, r clavicle, l lower leg
A	1042	lc	–	6–7					prone; 1 lambdoid wormian
A	1043	vc	m	50+	5'9.75"/1.77 m	04/25	01/27	06/32	sacralised L5; pathology: spine, ?ribs
A	1044	vc	m	40–50	5'6.75"/1.69 m	08/21	11/29	02/31	8 lambdoid wormians; pathology: spine, mandible, hands
A	1045	vc	m	50+	5'2.25"/1.58 m	02/12	02/18	06/23	1 ?lambdoid wormian; pathology: spine, mandible, l femur
A	1046	vc	f	40+	5'6.5"/1.68 m	07/13	08/15	11/24	pathology: spine
A	1047	vc	f?	40+	5'0.5"/1.53 m	03/03	03/09	21/30	3 lambdoid wormians, metopism; pathology: spine, l foot

Table 2.11 (Continued)

Group	Context no.	Bones present	Sex	Age	Height	Caries	Abscesses	Tooth loss	General comments
A	1048	vc	f	40+	5'5.25"/1.65 m	01/06	00/09	20/28	3+ lambdoid wormians, metopism, L6; pathology: spine, 1 clavicle, 1 hip
A	1049	vc	f	35–40	5'2"/1.57 m	04/23	06/29	01/30	prone; pathology: spine
A	1050	vc	m	40+	5'8.25"/1.73 m	07/16	07/24	09/32	pathology: spine, ?rib
A	1052	vc	–	c 2					
C	1071	lc	–	4–6 m					pathology: skull, limbs
C	1090	lc	–	2–4					1 parietal wormian
C	1091	legs only	–	4–5 m					
C	1092	vc	f	30–35	5'1.75"/1.57 m	13/29	02/31	00/31	pathology: spine
A	1093	vc	f	40–50	5'4.5"/1.64 m	03/09	09/19	03/22	prone; pathology: spine, ?rib, 1 hand
A	1094	vc	f	35–40	4'11"/1.50 m	00/31	00/32	00/32	L5 cleft neural arch, part separate, sacralised
C	1095	vc	f	35–40	5'1.5"/1.56 m	03/21	04/24	04/28	pathology: spine, r wrist, 1 thumb
A	1096	vc	m	40+	5'4"/1.63 m		04/07	27/32	1+ lambdoid wormians; pathology: spine, 1 humerus, r femur
A	1097	vc	f	40–50	5'2.5"/1.59 m	06/24	01/27	05/32	decapitated, 6 sacral vertebrae, 2 lambdoid wormians; pathology: spine
C	1098	vc	m	50+	5'6.5"/1.69 m	01/30	02/32	00/32	pathology: spine, ribs, 1 scapula
C	1099	–	–	2–4 m					
C	1100	lc	–	9–12 m					pathology: skull, limbs
C	1102	vc	f	40–50	5'7.25"/1.70 m	01/02	00/08	18/26	2+ lambdoid wormians, metopism; pathology: spine, ribs, 1 knee
C	1103	part	–	c 6 m					pathology: skull
C	1213		–	?infant					
Isolated	3518	vc	m	45+	5'1.5"/1.56 m	08/20	04/24	05/29	pathology: severe osteophytes on vertebrae, osteo-arthritis in shoulder and hand; 2+ lambdoid wormians
Isolated	3521	vc	–	12–14		00/24	00/18	00/24	
Isolated	3522	vc	m	35–40	5'7.5"/1.71 m	07/26	02/27	00/32	pathology: slight osteophytes on some lumbar vertebrae, slight periostitis on lower legs
D	3781	vc	m	35–40	5'4.5"/1.64 m	01/16	00/09	00/17	4+ lambdoid wormians, metopic suture, separate neural arch on L5
D	3782	lc	f	40+	5'4.5"/1.64 m	02/25	06/28	05/32	pathology: 1 knee, slight osteophytes
D	3783	vc	m	35–40	5'7.5"/1.71 m	00/27	02/30	02/32	large mandibular torus, sacrum has 6 bodies, slight osteophytes
D	3784	mandible, r arm, legs	f?	40+			02/06	08/16	r femur head diseased
D	3786	lc	–	2.5–5		00/12	00/20		metopic suture, cleft neural arch on atlas
Isolated	4261	vc	–	6–7		02/20	00/22		asymmetric inca bone, cleft neural arch on atlas

C and D as well as among the outliers. It has been argued that the presence of infants and neonates within cemeteries, particularly when associated with west-east orientation, is a feature of the late 4th century and may be related to Christian influences. It may well be that the cemeteries mentioned above are slightly earlier and therefore not directly comparable with this proposed phase of use at Radley II.

Almost half of the population (45.6%) survived beyond the age of 40, some probably well beyond, and there is no obvious difference between males and females in this respect, though in other cemeteries in the area, while half of the men survived beyond 40, only 40% of the women lived beyond this age (Harman *et al.* 1981).

The spatial distribution of the sexes in the cemetery is uneven: within the main body of the cemetery the graves fall into two groups, Groups A and C (Fig. 2.4). Group A respects the square structure associated with the cremations. Just over half (51.3%) of those in Group A are men, while in Group C there are three times as many women as men, though the main body of this group comprises children. These proportions suggest that there may have been a partial segregation of the sexes in death, and a distinction between subadults and adults, though this is only the case if the groups are believed to be contemporary.

The average height of 21 men was 5 ft 6 3/4 ins (1.67 m) and of 17 women was 5 ft 2 1/4 ins (1.57 m); these are precisely the same as the figures for the area as a whole and only slightly less than the modern British averages (Office of Population Census and Surveys 1981).

Lambdoid wormian bones were seen in 23 of the 37 skulls where the feature could be observed (all groups though predominantly A): this represents 62%, which is slightly higher than the frequency observed in other cemeteries in the area (51%). The child in grave 1090 (Group C) had the only example of a parietal wormian bone seen, and the man in grave 1039 (Group A) the only definite inca bone. An open metopic suture was retained by six individuals in whom this could be observed, three men (1020, 1040 (Group A), 3781 (Group D) and three women (1047, 1048 (Group A), 1102 (Group C). A few people had vertebral anomalies and all were in Group A. One man (1037) had a separate neural arch on the 5th lumbar vertebra. Another man (1029) had the arch joined only on one side, and this was also seen in a woman (1094) who had further anomalies. Not only was the arch of the 5th lumbar vertebra half separate from the body, it was also cleft, so that one half was completely free; the body and the other half of the arch were joined to the sacrum, and some of the sacral vertebra had cleft neural arches. Other people exhibited some of these characteristics; one woman (1025) had a cleft neural arch on the 3rd lumbar vertebra, an unusual site. Some cleft neural arches also occurred on the sacra of two men (1018, 1043) and on the entire sacrum of one woman (1026). Extra vertebrae occurred in some people: one

woman (1048) had an extra lumbar vertebra, a man (1013) also had an extra one which was joined to the sacrum, and two women (1026 and 1097) had six sacral vertebrae. It is possible that the people who share these anomalies were related, and if so, this would show that in this cemetery some relations were buried close to one another (1026, 1025, 1029 and 1037, all showing anomalies of the vertebral arch, the last three being particularly similar and also having lambdoid wormian bones), while others were spread over the cemetery (1013, 1026, 1048 and 1097, all with extra vertebrae).

Table 2.12 shows the incidence of caries, abscess and loss in the teeth and tooth sockets present. There is clearly a decline in dental health with increasing age, and the figures are broadly similar to those from other cemeteries in the area (Harman *et al.* 1981). If those over 40 are listed in more closely defined age groups, it appears that those regarded as over 50 had less trouble with caries and abscesses than those in younger age groups, though they had lost more teeth.

One woman, 1092 (Group C), had an abscess at the root of the upper left second molar which had penetrated the maxillary sinus. The crowns of the permanent incisors and first molars of one child of seven to eight years, 1019 (Group C), suggest that there was a serious disturbance to the metabolism at about six months of age, causing malformation of the enamel. This may have been the result of illness or a period of malnutrition.

Degenerative disease of the spine was seen in most of the adults over 30 years of age. There are only slight signs in people aged between 30 and 40 years. One woman, 1049 (Group A) had slight collapsing of the body of the 11th thoracic vertebra. Within the group of five individuals aged between 40 and 50 years all showing degrees of vertebral degeneration, one woman, 1093 (Group A) had eburnation between the atlas and axis, and possibly collapsing of the twelfth thoracic vertebra; one man, 1004 (Group A) had degeneration of the articular facets of most of the cervical and upper thoracic vertebral arches, and severe degeneration of the bodies of the lower cervical vertebrae, the lower thoracic and lower lumbar vertebrae being less severely affected. Of those regarded as over 40 years old, all showed slight signs of degeneration except one man, 1008

Table 2.12 Iincidence of caries, abscesses and antemortem tooth loss in teeth and tooth sockets present, for different age groups.

Age group	Caries	Abscess	Loss
17–30	04/150 (2.7%)	03/153 (2%)	01/154 (0.7%)
30–40	50/242 (20.7%)	41/289 (14.2%)	22/322 (6.8%)
40–50	34/103 (33%)	28/136 (20.6%)	35/172 (20.3%)
40+	31/115 (27%)	46/171 (27%)	184/348 (52.9%)
50+	21/144 (14.6%)	24/199 (12.1%)	45/243 (18.6%)

(Group A); in some individuals, 1041, 1046, 1047, 1050 (Group A) more moderate signs are seen in the cervical, some of the mid thoracic, and the lumbar vertebrae. One of these, 1047 (Group A), has slight collapsing of the bodies of the 4th and 5th lumbar vertebrae. Of those over 50 years, two men, 1023 and 1043 (Group A) are only slightly affected. The women, 1017 and 1045 (Group A) and the other men, 1014, 1022, 1029 (Group A), 1098 (Group C) are all moderately affected in parts of the spine and slightly affected through most of it; both women and one man (1029) have collapsing of some lumbar vertebral bodies.

One man, 1049 (Group A), and one woman, 1015 (Group A), both have two cervical vertebrae joined, possibly through osteo-arthritis, though the fusion may be congenital.

There is evidence of osteo-arthritis in other joints, all in people of 40 years or more except one woman, 1095 (Group C), who was slightly affected in the right wrist and left thumb. One woman, 1045 (Group A), and one man, 1044 (Group A), were slightly affected in the jaw; the latter was also affected in the right wrist, and together with one woman, 1093 (Group A), in the thumbs. One man, 1014 (Group A), was affected in the right shoulder and right wrist; two men, 1039, 1050 (Group A), were affected in the elbow joint. Four people had osteo-arthritis in the hip: one man, 1014 (Group A), was slightly affected; one man, 1008 (Group A) and one woman, 1048 (Group A) were more severely affected, in both hips and the left hip respectively, with erosion and pitting of the articular surfaces and extra bony growth on the margins. One man, 1039 (Group A), was very severely affected in the left hip, with half the head showing severe wear and deterioration, and considerable growth on the other half. One woman, 1017 (Group A), was affected in the knees, and slightly in both hands and feet.

One man, 1098 (Group C), has periostitis on the inner surface of most of the left ribs and two of the right ribs, and had suffered some injury or infection affecting the right shoulder blade. One man, 1096 (Group A), has malformation of the right femoral head, with shortening of the neck and deterioration of the articular surface. One woman, 1045 (Group A), has a low swelling of spongy bone on the medial aspect of the femur, with bone destruction penetrating to the cortex. Another woman, 1041 (Group A), has areas of periostitis on both tibia and fibula near the ankle. Two men, 1008 and 1022 (Group A), had foot problems: the first has mis-shapen joints in both big toes, and the second has mis-shapen ankle and foot bones.

Two infants, 1071 and 1100 (Group C), have periostitis on the skull and on the shafts of some long bones; both femora of the latter are distorted. Another infant, 1103 (Group C), has some spongy bone growth in the orbits. A child of 7–8 years, 1019 (Group A), has periostitis on the skull.

A number of people had suffered fractures. Seven men, 1014, 1029, 1043, 1044, 1050, 1020 and 1023

(Group A), all have healed fractures of the ribs, the last two having multiple fractures, combined in each case with probable fractures of the right clavicle. Three women, 1093, 1094 (Group A), and 1102 (Group C), have healed fractures of the ribs, the last having several fractured on the right side; another woman, 1025 (Group A), probably had a fractured rib, and a fractured right clavicle, while a second woman has a fractured left clavicle. One man, 1096 (Group A), may have had a healed fracture at the proximal end of the right humerus, while another, 1010 (Group A), may have a healing fracture towards the distal end of the ulna shaft.

There were four cases of decapitation (Figs 2.15–18, 2.21, Pl. 2.2). Skeleton 1009 (Group A), probably a young man, had his head buried by the right knee. The neck had been severed between cervical vertebrae 3 and 4: there are cuts on the dorsal surfaces of the arches and also on the inferior surfaces of the bodies of both vertebrae, demonstrating that more than one cut was necessary. Skeleton 1018 (Group A), also probably a young man, lay on his left side with his head buried under his right knee. There are cuts on the inferior surface of the arch of the axis, and also on the ventral surface of the body, and on the ventral surface of the body of the 3rd cervical vertebra, showing that the head was severed between these two vertebrae, in this case probably from the front. Skeleton 1026 (Group A), a woman of 35 to 40 years, was buried with her head over her feet. The neck was cut between cervical vertebrae 5 and 6, there being cuts on the ventral aspect of both vertebrae, suggesting that the head was severed from the front. Skeleton 1097 (Group A), a woman of between 40 and 50 years, was buried with her head under her right femur. There are cuts on the inferior surface of the axis and the superior surface of the third cervical vertebra, showing that at least three cuts were made in severing the head.

The cuts which run across bodies and arches are narrow and not deep, though some have obviously removed slivers of bone from the edges of arches and articular facets, and also from vertebral bodies, generally as thin wedges sliced from the articular surface of the body, in a slightly different plane. At some sites, the head was probably removed by a single blow by an instrument wielded with some force, such as a sword or cleaver, which seems to have been the method used sometimes at Cassington and Stanton Harcourt where the mandible was also cut (Harman *et al.* 1981). The neat character of the marks at Radley II, however, suggests that a fine sharp instrument was used, and once the joint between the two vertebrae was located, several incisions followed the joint until the vertebrae were parted: this is clear in the case of skeleton 1097 (Group A), who has cuts on the ventral surface of the arch of the axis which could not have been made until the neck was partially severed and the gap between the vertebrae widened (Fig. 2.15, Pl. 2.1). Such an operation would require good visibility and involve close work, and although it would not be difficult to carry out on a corpse, it is doubtful whether the cuts observed could have been produced if the decapitation were the cause of death. Similar observations were made in the case of the Lankhills decapitations (Watt 1979, 352).

In other Romano-British and Anglo-Saxon examples, the neck was most commonly cut near the head; in skeleton 1026 (Group A) the cut is lower than usual but well within the recorded range. The position of the heads is interesting: burial beside or between the knees, lower legs and feet is most commonly recorded and three of those at Radley II conform with this.

Five prone burials were excavated; one man over 50 years of age, three of women aged between 30 and 50 years, and one of a child of six to seven years. The burial of children either decapitated or prone is rare, though at Cassington another child of seven to eight years was buried prone.

This cemetery, although it provides further examples of both forms of burial, does not provide reasons for them. Previously it has been impossible to decide whether decapitation took place after death or was the cause of it, but in this cemetery at least it is suggested that the head was removed after death. This cemetery is also important in that it is the first excavated in this area in which numbers of prone and decapitated bodies have been found in a group of people which appears to represent a whole, normal community: the other cemeteries either have very few children in theirs, as at Radley I, or few or no decapitated and prone burials, as at Queensford Mill.

The other Romano-British burials

3781–3784, 3786 *(Group D and isolated burials)*

A small group of five burials to the south-west of the cemetery included coffined burials and all were orientated on a similar axis to the burials in Group C. The group consists of two men, two women and a small child. The age of the child is difficult to assess, as although the state of tooth eruption suggests an age of about five years and wear of the deciduous molars is severe, the length of the long bones suggests an age of 2½–3 years. Possibly growth was seriously retarded, and the closing of the metopic suture may have been temporarily delayed if this was so.

Other isolated burials occur to the south of this group and of the cemetery. Burials 3521 and 3522

both show one of the postures observed in the cemetery, lying on the left side; the latter burial has one nail in the grave. Burial 3518 was not accompanied by any dating evidence, but 4261, a young child, was coffined and wore hobnailed shoes.

Though these people are not necessarily related either to each other or to those buried in the cemetery, it is perhaps worth remarking that several of the rarer anomalies noted in the cemetery (open metopic suture, cleft neural arch on the atlas and separate arch on the fifth lumbar vertebra) also occur in these outlying burials. Evidence of minor osteophytes on some of the vertebrae of these individuals, 3522 (outlier), 3782? and 3783? (Group D), is not unexpected; 3522 (outlier) also had minor areas of periostitis on the shafts of both tibia and fibulae. More serious pathological conditions were observed in 3518 (outlier) in the form of a badly affected spine, shoulders and right finger, 3782 (Group D) in the form of a serious condition affecting the left knee and 3784 (Group D) in the form of an area of degeneration of the right femoral head.

Cremations (Tables 2.2, 2.4, 2.10)

A small number of cremations were found. All were examined and details of maximum length, average size and colour of the fragments recorded. Any pieces which were identifiable were noted together with any evidence concerning the age of the individual, using the age groups recommended by Wells (1960, 29–37). This information is summarised in Table 2.10. Additional details of particular interest are given under the relevant cremations in the inventory below.

INVENTORY OF THE ROMANO-BRITISH BURIALS (FIGS 2.16–24; PLS 2.3–4, TABLES 2.10–11)
by Richard Chambers

Inhumations

This inventory lists the archaeological and osteological details of each grave. The skeletal remains including the pathology are discussed in the section on the inhumations by Mary Harman above. Each grave is defined by the context number allocated to it during the excavation, eg 1058. These context numbers do not run consecutively (Figs 2.2–3). Separate burial numbers have not been allocated. This inventory follows the conventions described in Chapter 1.

Table 2.13   Sex and age of inhumations by group.

Group	Male No.	Age range	Female	Age range	Subadult No.	Age range
A	18	18->50	13	30–50	5	birth-8
C	1	>50	3	30–50	7	2 months-4 years
D	2	35–40	2	>30	1	2.5–5
Outlying	2	35->45	–	–	2	6–7 & 12–14

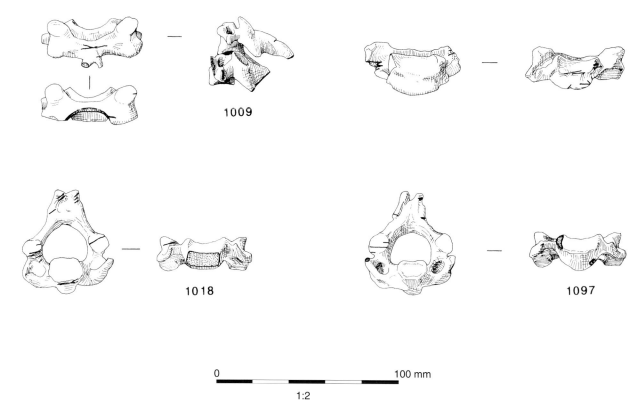

1009

1018   1097

0 ————————————————————— 100 mm

1:2

Figure 2.15   Cut marks on the cervical vertebrae from decapitated Romano-British skeletons.

Each entry begins with a description of the grave pit giving first the shape and then the width and length followed by the depth below the surface of the gravel. The surface of the gravel may be reckoned as 0.2–0.3 m beneath the Roman period ground surface.

Each grave contained a single inhumation unless stated otherwise. Posture, sex and age are given in that order.

The state of preservation of the skeletal remains has been categorised as good, partial, slight or none. Where parts of a skeleton are missing this may in every case be attributable to either natural decay or damage by animals or mechanical means.

The orientation of each extended body has been measured along the longitudinal axis of the grave, ie 270° (magnetic) represents a west-east orientation with the head to the west and the feet to the east. The state of preservation and orientation of the skeletal remains are followed by a detailed description of the skeleton.

The fill of each grave was a mixture of brown loamy subsoil and gravel. As might be expected on a site with only a thin covering of soil over the gravel, the bulk of the filling of each grave was gravel. Details of associated objects and grave goods are given where appropriate. The numbers refer to John Hedges' finds catalogue, now in archive. The original small find numbers assigned in the field are also given, prefixed by SF.

The skeletons were drawn at a scale of 1:20 and were photographed in black and white. The majority of the burials were also recorded on colour slide film. Each burial was described and then photographed through a 0.10 m grid to insure against loss of the detailed plans.

Grave 1008 (Fig. 2.16)

Sub-rectangular, 0.9 m × 2.1 m × 0.25 m deep. On left side, male adult, 40+ years, partial. 4°, facing east. Arms by sides, legs together and slightly flexed. Coin of Constantine I by right foot.

Associated finds:

132 Copper alloy coin of Constantine I (SF 11)
Obv CONSTANTINUS AUG Rev SOLI INV[] PTR Trier AE3 310–312

Grave 1009 (Fig. 2.16)

Rectangular, 0.9 m × 2.0 m × 0.4 m deep. Decapitated, on left side, male? adolescent/adult, 17–22 years, good. 343°, skull upright and facing north. Body lying against west side of grave pit, hands crossed over left hip, legs together, right leg slightly flexed over the skull placed beneath the right knee.

Grave 1010 (Figs 2.16 and 2.23; Pl. 2.3)

Rectangular, 1.16 m × 2.48 m × 0.95 m deep. Supine male adult, 20–25 years, partial. 355°. Skull turned

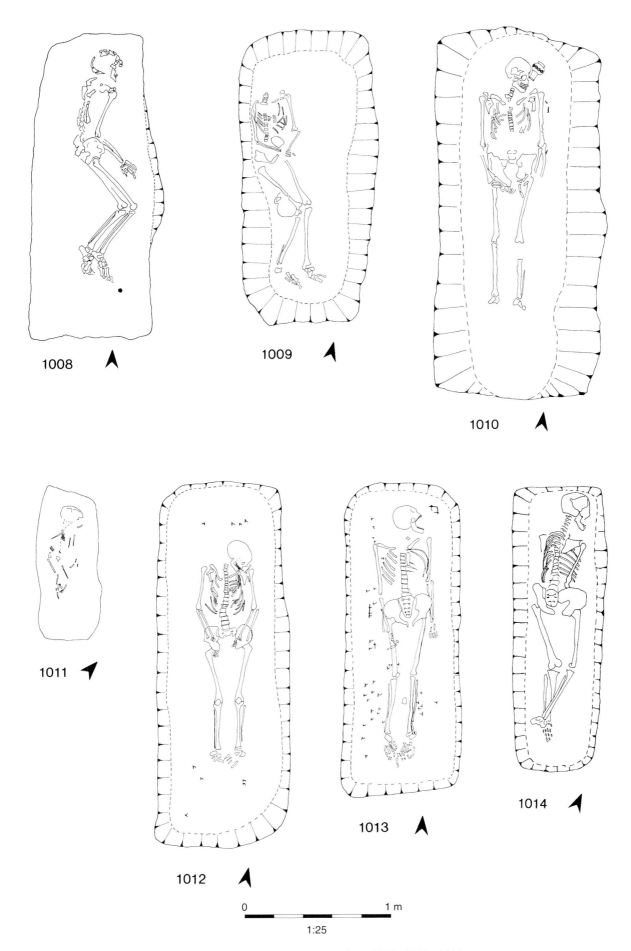

1008

1009

1010

1011

1012

1013

1014

0   1 m

1:25

Figure 2.16   Romano-British inhumations 1008, 1009, 1010, 1011, 1012, 1013, 1014.

45

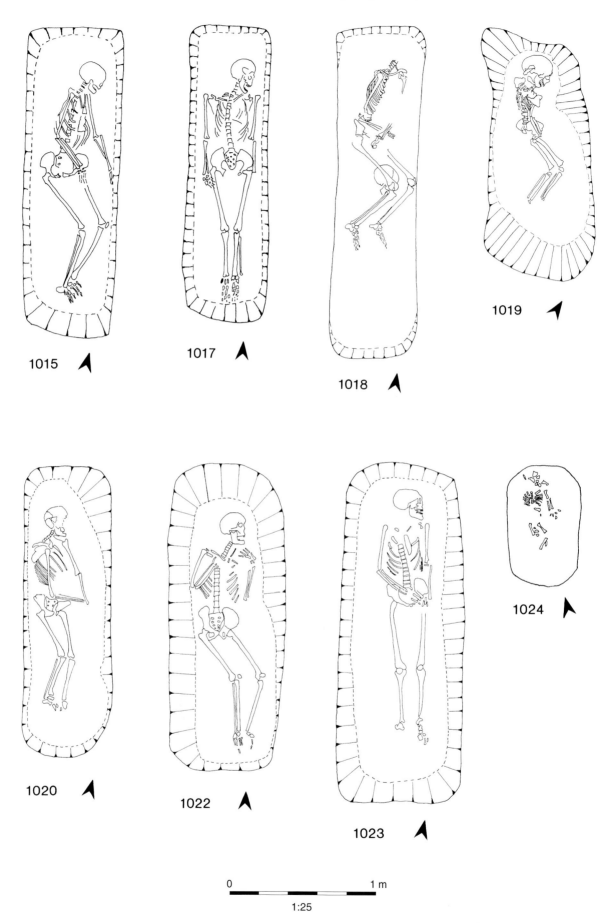

Figure 2.17   Romano-British inhumations 1015, 1017, 1018, 1019, 1020, 1022, 1023, 1024.

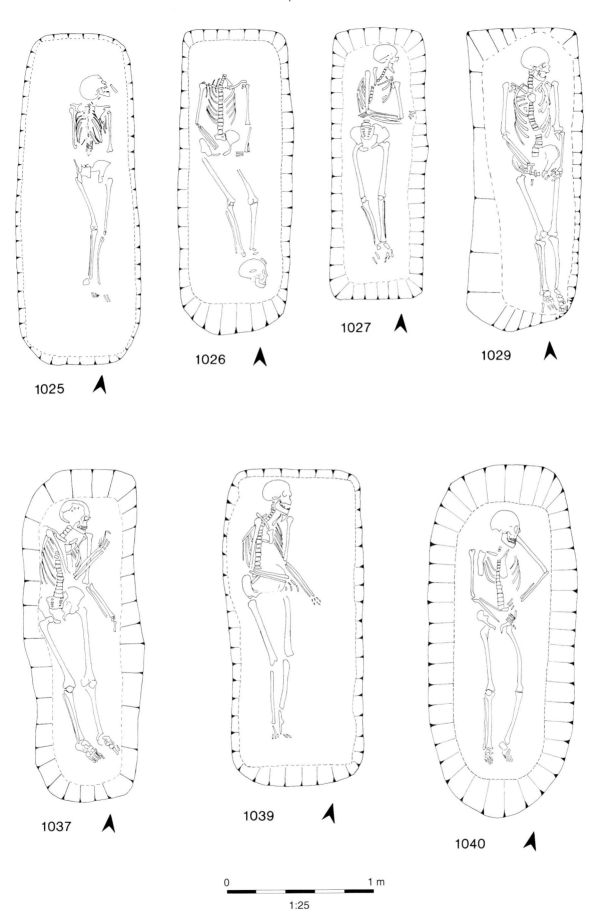

Figure 2.18   Romano-British inhumations 1025, 1026, 1027, 1029, 1037, 1039, 1040.

towards right shoulder, arms by sides, hands on hips, legs straight and parallel. Coffin partially outlined by line of dark soil and higher soil content within the coffin area compared to the gravelly grave filling around the sides. Four iron nails, over right pelvis, under left forearm, by left shoulder and north-west of skull on projected outline of coffin. Oxford product colour-coated beaker by the head.

Associated finds:

Oxford red/brown colour-coated beaker, form C27, AD 270–400 (Young 1977, 153–4). The vessel has white trailed slip decoration over a red/brown slip and bands of rouletting (compare with Atkinson 1952–3, 34).
Also five iron nail fragments representing four nails, one with replaced wood. Not illustrated

13   Fragmentary iron nail. Surviving length 45 mm (SF 13).
14   Fragmentary iron nail. Surviving length 47 mm (SF 14).
15   Fragmentary iron nail. Surviving length 19 mm (SF 17).
16   Fragmentary iron nail. Surviving length 25 mm (SF 21).
17   Fragmentary iron nail. Surviving length 25 mm. Replaced wood. (SF 24).

Grave 1011 *(Fig. 2.16)*

Sub-rectangular, 0.45 m × 1.0 m × 0.26 m deep. On left side, child, 1–1.5 years, slight. 341°, lying on left side facing east. Skull cap, upper arms, fragments of pelvis and legs remained. Possibly disturbed by burrowing animals.

Grave 1012 *(Fig. 2.16)*

Rectangular, 0.96 m × 2.35 m × 0.58 m deep. Supine male, 18–20 years, partial. 356°. Skull tilted towards left shoulder, jaw fallen onto collar bone, arms by sides, legs straight and together. The presence of 11 iron nails at various depths suggests a coffin.

Associated finds:

11   iron nail fragments representing 9 nails, mainly round-headed, a number clearly showing their use in joining coffin boards some 20 mm thick. Not illustrated.
18   Round-headed iron nail. Maximum length 95 mm (SF 87, 89).
19   Round-headed iron nail. Surviving length 65 mm. Replaced wood – board. Maximum thickness (MT) 19 mm (SF 88).
20   Round-headed iron nail. Maximum length 80 mm. Replaced wood – boards at 90° (SF 90).
21   Round-headed iron nail. Surviving length 60 mm. Replaced wood – boards at 90° (SF 91).
22   Round-headed iron nail. Maximum length 85 mm. Replaced wood – board MT 20 mm (SF 92).
23   Fragmentary iron nail. Maximum length 65 mm. Replaced wood – board MT 20 mm. (SF 93)
24   Missing (SF 94).
25   Rectangular-headed iron nail. Surviving length 58 mm. Replaced wood (SF 97).
26   Round-headed iron nail. Maximum length 93 mm min (SF 337).
27   Round-headed iron nail Maximum length 90 mm Replaced wood (SF 337).
28   Round-headed iron nail. Maximum length 85 mm (SF 337).

Grave 1013 *(Figs 2.16 and 2.24)*

Rectangular, 0.75 m × 2.0 m × 0.5 m deep. Supine male adult, 25–30 years, good. 356°. Skull turned to

right, arms by sides, legs straight and together. Fifty iron nails, corner bracket and iron plate with mineralised wood lying at various depths suggest coffin.

Associated finds:

4   Corner bracket; wide rectangular plate bent at slightly acute angle with remains of three nails, two at one end, one at the other, opposite corner missing. Length 72 mm, max. width 72 mm (SF 34).
5   Fitting with turban-shaped end; nail through end. Part of reused hinge. Nail head 17–18 mm in diameter; shank missing Length of fitting 99 mm, max. width 50 mm (SF 84).
6   Fitting with turban-shaped end, tip damaged; nail through end. Part of reused hinge. Nail head 21 mm in diameter. Nail shank 16 mm (incomplete). Length of fitting 91 mm. Width 46 mm (SF 82).
7   Strip with nail at each end. Replaced wood on underside and around nail shanks. Max. depth 14 mm. Length 45 mm. Width *c* 17 mm (SF 42).
8   Rectangular strip with two probable nails; replaced wood on underside. Thickness of wood up to 19 mm (SF 43).
9   Fragment of plate, one corner bent round as a spike – possibly part of a dog. Replaced wood on underside. 37 × 34 mm (SF 81).
10   Fragment of nailed plate. Present length 28 mm (SF 217).
50   nails and fragments, mostly rectangular-headed and occasionally showing replaced wood, many clenched over 15–40 mm.
29   Rectangular-headed iron nail. Surviving length 45 mm. Clenched over 38 mm (SF 35).
30   Rectangular-headed iron nail. Maximum length 54 mm. Clenched over 37 mm (SF 36).
31   Rectangular-headed iron nail. Surviving length 25 mm (SF 37).
32   Rectangular-headed iron nail. Maximum length 50 mm. Clenched over 37 mm (SF 38).
33   Rectangular-headed iron nail. Surviving length 47 mm (SF 39).
34   Fragmentary iron nail. Surviving length 35 mm (SF 40).
35   Fragmentary iron nail. Surviving length 20 mm (SF 41).
36   Fragmentary iron nail. Surviving length 33 mm. Clenched (SF 44).
37   Fragmentary iron nail. Surviving length 25 mm. Clenched (SF 45).
38   Fragmentary iron nail. Surviving length 22 mm (SF 46).
39   Rectangular-headed iron nail. Surviving length 40 mm (SF 47).
40   Rectangular-headed iron nail. Maximum length 67 mm. Clenched over 26 mm (SF 48).
41   Rectangular-headed iron nail. Surviving length 26 mm (SF 49).
42   Fragmentary iron nail. Surviving length 35 mm (SF 50).
43   Fragmentary iron nail. Surviving length 4 mm (SF 51).
44   Round-headed iron nail. Surviving length 35 mm. Clenched over 22 mm (SF 52).
45   Rectangular-headed iron nail. Surviving length 26 mm (SF 53).
46   Rectangular-headed iron nail. Surviving length 40 mm (SF 54).
47   Fragmentary iron nail. Surviving length 30 mm. Clenched (SF 55).
48   Rectangular-headed iron nail. Surviving length 28 mm (SF 56).
49   Fragmentary iron nail. Surviving length 30 mm. Clenched (SF 57).
50   Rectangular-headed iron nail. Maximum length 50 mm. Clenched over 34 mm (SF 58).
51   Fragmentary iron nail. Surviving length 11 mm (SF 59).
52   Rectangular-headed iron nail. Maximum length 30 mm. Clenched over 19 mm (SF 60).
53   Fragmentary iron nail. Surviving length 15 mm (SF 61).
54   Rectangular-headed iron nail. Surviving length 35 mm (SF 62).
55   Fragmentary iron nail. Surviving length 8 mm (SF 63).
56   Rectangular-headed iron nail. Maximum length 54 mm. Clenched over 32 mm (SF 64).
57   Rectangular-headed iron nail. Surviving length 20 mm (SF 65).
58   Rectangular-headed iron nail. Maximum length 50 mm. Clenched over 40 mm (SF 66).

59 Fragmentary iron nail. Surviving length 25 mm. Clenched (SF 67).
60 Fragmentary iron nail. Surviving length 20 mm. (SF 68).
61 Rectangular-headed iron nail. Surviving length 30 mm (SF 69).
62 Fragmentary iron nail. Surviving length 38 mm (SF 71).
63 Rectangular-headed iron nail. Surviving length 34 mm. Clenched over 20 mm (SF 72).
64 Rectangular-headed iron nail. Maximum length 48 mm. Clenched over 20 mm (SF 73).
65 Fragmentary iron nail. Surviving length 14 mm. Clenched (SF 74).
66 Rectangular-headed iron nail. Maximum length 30 mm. Clenched over 15 mm (SF 75).
67 Fragmentary iron nail. Surviving length 20 mm (SF 76).
68 Rectangular-headed iron nail. Surviving length 40 mm (SF 77).
69 Fragmentary iron nail. Surviving length 30 mm. Replaced wood (SF 78).
70 Fragmentary iron nail. Surviving length 17 mm. Replaced wood (SF 79).
71 Fragmentary iron nail. Surviving length 17 mm. Replaced wood (SF 80).
72 Rectangular-headed iron nail. Surviving length 45 mm (SF 83).
73 Fragmentary iron nail. Surviving length 32 mm (SF 85).
74 Fragmentary iron nail. Surviving length 30 mm. Replaced wood (SF 86).
75 Rectangular-headed. Maximum length 48 mm. Clenched over 40 mm (SF 336).
76 Fragmentary iron nail. Surviving length 18 mm (SF 336).
77 Fragmentary iron nail. Surviving length 31 mm. Replaced wood (SF 336).
78 Fragmentary iron nail. Surviving length 31 mm. Replaced wood (SF 336).

Grave 1014 *(Fig. 2.16)*

Rectangular, 0.65 m × 1.85 m × 0.62 m deep. Prone male adult, 50+ years, good. 341°, skull resting on left cheek facing east. Upper arms by sides, forearms beneath stomach, legs together, right foot over left ankle.

Grave 1015 *(Fig. 2.17)*

Rectangular, 0.7 m × 2.0 in × 0.5 m deep. On left side, female ? adult, 40+ years, good. 358°, resting on left shoulder with skull facing east. Arms by sides, pelvis supine, legs together and slightly bent. Higher proportion of brown earth around body than in remainder of grave fill.

Grave 1017 *(Fig. 2.17)*

Rectangular, 0.5 m × 2.0 m × 0.4 m deep. Supine female adult, 50+ years, good. 6°. Skull facing left shoulder, arms by sides, legs straight and together.

Grave 1018 *(Fig. 2.17)*

Rectangular, 0.6 m × 2.2 m × 0.5 m deep. Decapitated, on left side, legs semi-flexed, male, 18–22 years, good. 350°, skull beneath right knee resting on left cheek facing south-east, upper arms by sides, lower arms left over right wrist, legs together and bent up 45°. Space for head left as a void in the top of the grave and 0.6 m left void at the foot of the grave, partly filled with brown earth.

Grave 1019 *(Fig. 2.17)*

Sub-rectangular, 0.7 m × 1.5 m × 0.2 m deep. On left side, legs semi-flexed, child, 7–8 years, partial. 346°, laid on left side in a semi-crouched position facing east. Arms by sides, legs together and bent through 45°. One fragment of Romano-British pottery in the upper filling of the grave.

Grave 1020 *(Fig. 2.17)*

Rectangular, 0.8 m × 2.3 m × 0.4 m deep. Supine male adult, 35–40 years, partial. 358°, skull and shoulders twisted to face eastwards. Body laid against west side of the grave pit, left arm straight, hand 0.15 m in front of body, legs together and slightly flexed.

Grave 1022 *(Fig. 2.17)*

Rectangular, 0.8 m × 2.0 m × 0.34 m deep. Supine male adult, 50+ years, good. 354°, skull on left cheek facing eastwards. Arms by sides but flexed with hands by respective shoulders, legs together and slightly flexed to the east.

Grave 1023 *(Fig. 2.17)*

Rectangular, 0.85 m × 2.22 m × 0.22 m. Supine male adult, 50+ years, good. 349°, skull on left cheek facing east. Left arm by side, right forearm across abdomen with hand on left hip, legs straight and parallel.

Grave 1024 *(Fig. 2.17)*

Sub-rectangular, 0.5 m × 0.8 m × 0.10 m deep. Supine infant, 1–3 months, slight. 8°, body twisted slightly facing east. Skull fragmentary, left arm straight, left forearm crossed over abdomen, legs together, slightly flexed to the east.

Grave 1025 *(Fig. 2.18)*

Rectangular, 0.8 m × 2.15 m × 0.4 m deep. Prone female adult, 30–35 years, partial. 349°, skull on left cheek facing east. Right arm by side and bent up with hand by shoulder, left upper arm by side with forearm beneath abdomen, legs straight and together. Lines of dark soil either side of the skeleton suggested the outline of a coffin.

Grave 1026 *(Fig. 2.18)*

Sub-rectangular, 0.95 m × 1.95 m × 0.5 m deep. Supine decapitated female adult, 35–40 years, good. 360°, skull resting on left cheek facing east between the feet and the end of the grave pit. Upper arms by sides, hands over hips, legs together and flexed slightly to the east.

Grave 1027 (Fig. 2.18)

Rectangular, 0.8 m × 2.0 m × 0.5 m deep. Supine female adult, 40+ years, good. 4°, skull resting on left cheek facing east. Right shoulder propped against conglomerate protrusion on west side of grave, upper arms by sides, forearms crossed over stomach, legs straight and together.

Grave 1029 (Fig. 2.18)

Sub-rectangular, 0.8 m × 2.1 m × 0.4 m deep. Supine male adult, 50+ years, good. 349°, skull resting on left cheek facing east. Upper arms by sides, hands over hips, legs straight and together. Extraneous human bones in the lower grave filling adjacent to upper trunk.

Grave 1037 (Fig. 2.18)

Sub-rectangular, 0.8 m × 2.2 m × 0.35 m deep. Supine, turned slightly to left, male adult, 40–50 years, good. 355°, skull resting on left cheek facing east. Laid against west side of the grave pit, the trunk slightly twisted to face east, arms in front of body, right arm bent up, left arm by side but slightly flexed, legs straight and together.

Grave 1039 (Fig. 2.18)

Rectangular, 0.8 m × 2.15 m × 0.6 m deep. Supine, turned slightly to left, male adult, 40+ years, good. 348°, skull resting on left cheek facing east. Trunk propped against the west side of the grave pit twisted slightly to the east, upper arms by sides, right lower arm across abdomen, left lower arm flexed outwards, legs straight and together.

Grave 1040 (Fig. 2.18)

Sub-rectangular, 0.8 m × 2.2 m × 0.6 m deep. Supine male? adult, 30–35 years, good. 358°, skull resting on left cheek facing east. Body laid against west side of the grave pit, left arm flexed, hand on hip, right forearm over abdomen, legs parallel and straight, foot turned towards the east.

Grave 1041 (Figs 2.19 and 2.25)

Sub-rectangular, 0.8 m × 1.95 m × 0.5 m deep. Supine female adult, 40+ years, good. 349°. Skull tilted towards left shoulder, facing south-east, arms by sides, legs straight and together.

Associated finds:

134 Polished bone pin with a ball head. Length 90 mm (SF 208).

Grave 1042 (Figs 2.19 and 2.25)

Sub-rectangular, 0.64 m × 1.55 m × 0.35 m deep. Prone child, 6–7 years, partial. 348°, skull face down

twisted slightly to face east. Arms by sides, legs straight and together. Dark outline stain of decayed coffin accompanied by four coffin nails, one at each corner. Shale bracelet, copper alloy bracelet and bluish green glass beads by and partly beneath left shoulder. Group of iron hobnails by right foot.

Associated finds:

1   Copper alloy bracelet with flattened terminals decorated with impressed dots. Maximum width 63.5 mm. Thickness 3.5 mm, terminals 6.5 mm (SF 140).

135 Small shale bracelet with sub-circular section and incised rope decoration around outside. Diameter 54 mm, thickness 5–6 mm (SF 139).

85 small transparent and translucent glass beads of three types (SF 111, 115–135, 141–150, 152–204):

(i) 52 conical shaped and of transparent blue colour. Length 5 mm.

(ii) 25 conical, cylindrical or with square sections, of translucent blue-green (turquoise) colour or a mixed blue-green and yellow-green colour. Some are roughly made with irregular extensions. Length 5 mm.

(iii) 8 annular, conical or square-sectioned, of translucent yellow-green colour. Length 4 mm.

c 56 iron hobnails (SF 2)

Ten iron nail fragments, including two rectangular-headed, some with replaced wood and two indicating a board 27 mm thick (79–88)

79 Fragmentary iron nail. Surviving length 24 mm (SF 95).

80 Fragmentary iron nail. Surviving length 31 mm (SF 96).

81 Rectangular-headed iron nail. Surviving length 45 mm. Replaced wood (SF 98).

82 Rectangular-headed iron nail. Surviving length 24 mm. Replaced wood. (SF 99).

83 Fragmentary iron nail. Surviving length 46 mm (SF 100).

84 Fragmentary. Maximum length 70 mm. Replaced wood – board. Maximum thickness 27 mm (SF 103).

85 Fragmentary iron nail. Surviving length 45 mm. Replaced wood – board. Maximum thickness 27 mm (SF 104).

86 Fragmentary iron nail. Surviving length 30 mm. Replaced wood (SF 105).

87 Fragmentary iron nail. Surviving length 27 mm. Replaced wood (SF 106).

88 Fragmentary iron nail. Surviving length 34 mm. Replaced wood (SF 110).

Grave 1043 (Fig. 2.19)

Sub-rectangular, 0.85 m × 2.20 m × 0.53 m deep. Supine male adult, 50+ years, good. 346°. Skull tilted towards left shoulder, right hand over left thigh, left arm by side, legs straight and together.

Grave 1044 (Fig. 2.19)

Rectangular, 1.0 m × 2.3 m × 0.3 m deep. Supine male adult, 40–50 years, good. 282°. Skull tilted slightly towards right shoulder, arms straight, hands over pelvic area, legs straight and together. Two iron coffin nails associated with areas of dark soil above body. Possibly two associated postholes.

Associated finds:

89 Fragmentary iron nail. Surviving length 65 mm (SF 15).

90 Fragmentary iron nail. Length 85 mm. Clenched. Replaced wood (SF 25).

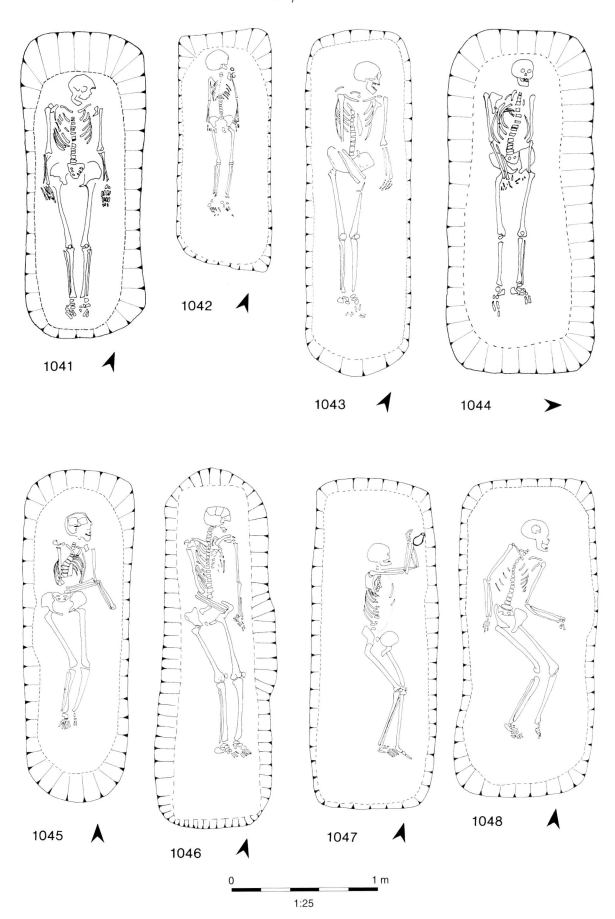

Figure 2.19   Romano-British inhumations 1041, 1042, 1043, 1044, 1045, 1046, 1047, 1048.

Grave 1045 (Fig. 2.19)

Sub-rectangular, 0.86 m × 2.15 m × 0.6 m deep. Supine male adult, 50+ years, partial. 5°, skull resting on left cheek facing east. Left arm straight at 30° to body, right forearm across stomach with hand on left elbow, legs straight and together.

Grave 1046 (Fig. 2.19)

Sub-rectangular, 0.8 m × 2.35 m × 0.46 m deep. Supine female adult, 40+ years, partial. 349°, skull resting on left cheek facing east. Left arm by side, right arm across body with hand on left hip, legs straight and together.

Grave 1047 (Figs 2.19 and 2.23)

Rectangular, 0.85 m × 2.2 m × 0.45 m deep. Supine, on left side, female adult, 40+ years. 346°, skull resting on left cheek facing east. Although supine whole body turned slightly to the east, upper arms extended horizontally towards the east, arms bent 90° at elbows with forearms in front of skull and hands by small pottery beaker, legs slightly flexed. Oxford product colour-coated pottery beaker by hands.

Associated finds:

Oxford red/brown colour-coat beaker, similar to C29, AD 270–360 or C106, undated. (Young 1977, 54, fig. 55, 174, fig. 66). Diagonal comb-stamping

Grave 1048 (Fig. 2.19)

Sub-rectangular, 0.9 m × 2.05 m × 0.4 m deep. Supine female adult, 40+ years, partial. 355°, skull resting on left cheek facing east. Both arms flexed along contour of body, legs slightly flexed.

Associated finds:

Flint flake, probably intrusive

Grave 1049 (Figs 2.20 and 2.23, Pl. 2.4)

Rectangular, 0.6 m × 1.95 in × 0.45 in deep. Prone female adult, 35–40 years, good. 352°, skull resting on left cheek facing east. Left arm beside body with lower arm bent up beneath upper arm, right arm arranged at 30° to body with lower arm bent up and hand by pottery beaker. Oxford product colour-coated pottery beaker by right hand.

Associated finds:

Oxford red/brown colour-coated beaker, similar in form to C31, ? AD 300–400 or C108 undated (Young 1977, 154, fig. 56, 174, fig. 66). This beaker deserves a full description as the impressed decoration appears to be unique. The vessel is similar to the fragments of C31 and C108 published in Young's corpus in having circular indentations of varying size around the circumference (five in this case), but three other decorative motifs appear in random patterns between the dimples and scattered over the neck. The most obvious is the stamped cross-in-circle motif which is quite unlike the rosette stamps commonly found on late Roman colour-coated vessels, though perhaps in that tradition; these are arranged in irregular groups of 3–5 stamps between the dimples. Comb-stamping (found on type C108 between the dimples) is sometimes combined with these circular stamps but is here also found on the neck in no apparent pattern. The third type, triangular stabbed impressions, is less frequent and seems to appear only with one group of the circular stamps; this type has not previously been recorded in Oxford red/brown colour-coated vessels. The colour-coat is very dark brown (unlike the other beakers from the site which are variations on a red/brown colour) and its manufacturing technique is obviously the same as its fellows although it is not quite so well made. The unusual stamped decoration suggests a date after AD 350 (cf Young 1977, 132) if not even later.

Fragments of a similar vessel were recorded from a late context at Barton Court Farm, although only the comb-stamping is present between the indentations. A beaker from Reading of similar appearance and dimensions is published by May (1916, 124, no. 89, plates LII and LIII) although it lacks the random circular stamps and ladder decoration.

Grave 1050 (Fig. 2.20)

Sub-rectangular, 0.8 m × 1.85 m × 0.45 m deep. Supine male adult, 40+ years, good. 3°, skull resting on left cheek facing east. Left arm slightly flexed outwards with hand beneath left pelvis, right lower arm across stomach with hand above left pelvis, legs straight and parallel.

Grave 1052 (Fig. 2.20)

Sub-rectangular, 0.9 m × 0.55 m × 0.26 m deep. Child, *c* 2 years, partial. 344°. Laid on its left side with legs semi-flexed, arms to east of body, right arm flexed, left arm straight, legs together and flexed with knees drawn up by hands.

Grave 1071 (Fig. 2.20)

Rectangular, 0.3 m × 0.8 m × 0.2 m deep. Supine infant, 4–6 months, slight, 256°, skull fragmentary but probably facing north. Right arm parallel to body, left upper arms parallel to body, left lower arm bent up across chest so that hand rests on right shoulder, legs straight and together.

Grave 1090 (Fig. 2.20)

Sub-rectangular, 0.5 m × 1.2 m × 0.25 m deep. Supine child, 2–4 years, partial. 257°. Skull tipped forward so that chin rests on left side of chest, arms straight and by sides, legs straight and together.

Grave 1091 (Fig. 2.20)

Sub-rectangular, 0.4 m × 0.8 m × 0.2 m deep. Infant, 4–5 months, very slight. C 270°. Traces of skull and legs only.

Grave 1092 (Fig. 2.20)

Rectangular, 0.7 m × 2.0 m × ?m deep. Supine female adult, 30–35 years, good. 263°, skull resting on left cheek facing south. Upper arms by sides with hands over pelvic area, legs straight and together. One iron coffin nail.

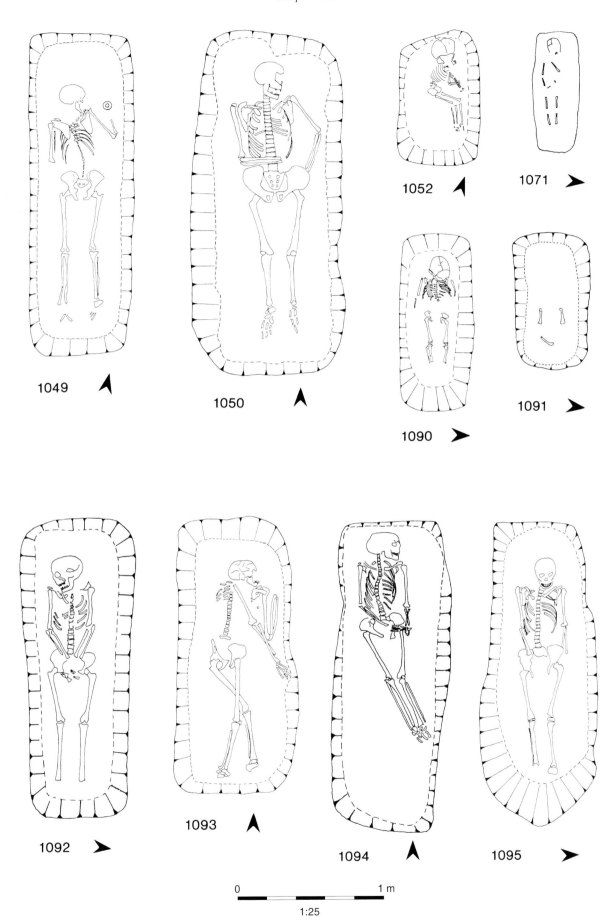

Figure 2.20   Romano-British inhumations 1049, 1050, 1052, 1071, 1090, 1091, 1092, 1093, 1094, 1095.

Associated finds:

91 Round-headed iron nail. Surviving length 21 mm (SF 322)

Grave 1093 (Fig. 2.20)

Sub-rectangular, 0.75 m × 1.85 m × 0.26 m deep. Prone female adult, 40–50 years, good. 3°, skull resting on left cheek facing east. Right upper arm by side with lower arm bent back up with hand by shoulder, left arm laid straight, passing beneath body at an angle with hand on east side of grave pit, legs crossed right over left.

Grave 1094 (Fig. 2.20)

Sub-rectangular, 0.75 m × 2.1 m × 0.45 m deep. Supine female adult, 35–40 years, good. 30°, skull resting on left cheek facing east. Left arm straight by side, right upper arm by side, hand over pelvic area, legs straight and together but at an angle across the grave pit. Large apparently unused area at foot of the grave pit.

Grave 1095 (Fig. 2.20)

Sub-rectangular, 0.75 m × 2.0 m × 0.4 m deep. Supine female adult, 35–40 years, good. 274°. Skull lying face upwards, lower jaw dropped and resting on the neck, arms straight and parallel to body, right hand resting on the pelvis, left hand below pelvis, legs straight and together. Four iron coffin nails.

Associated finds:

92 Round-headed iron nail. Surviving length 23 mm (SF 70).
93 Round-headed iron nail. Surviving length 26 mm (SF 326).
94 Fragmentary iron nail. Surviving length 25 mm. Replaced wood (SF 338).
95 Round-headed iron nail. Surviving length 27 mm (SF 338).

Grave 1096 (Fig. 2.21)

Rectangular, 0.85 m × 2 m × 0.45 m deep. Supine male adult, 40+ years, partial. 353°, skull resting on left cheek facing east. Left arm straight at 30° to body, right arm slightly flexed across chest with hand by left elbow, legs slightly flexed, apart and almost parallel.

Grave 1097 (Fig. 2.21)

Sub-rectangular, 0.63 m × 2.25 m × 0.3 m deep. Decapitated supine female adult, 40–50 years, good. 352°, skull lying on left cheek facing east. Body lying close to west side of grave, skull, decapitated, placed beneath upper right leg, left arm by side, right upper arm by side with forearm across stomach, hand on left forearm, legs together with knees slightly flexed to the east. Soil against the skeleton a dark reddish brown loam possibly produced by a decayed coffin.

Grave 1098 (Fig. 2.21)

Sub-rectangular, 0.7 m × 1.95 m × 0.65 m deep. Supine male adult, 50+ years, good. 262°. Skull tipped forward with jaw resting on the left clavicle, upper arms by sides, hands over right hip, legs straight and together. Two iron nails present in the grave filling suggest a coffin.

Associated finds:

96 Round-headed iron nail. Surviving length 33 mm. Replaced wood board. Surviving thickness 22 mm (SF 102).
97 Fragmentary iron nail. Surviving length 42 mm. Replaced wood (SF 108).

Grave 1099 (Fig. 2.21)

Sub-rectangular, 0.3 m × 0.55 m × 0.5 m deep. Supine infant, 2–4 months, slight. 280°. Fragments of skull, left arm, ribs, spine, pelvis and upper legs remained.

Grave 1100 (Fig. 2.21)

Sub-rectangular, 0.35 m × 0.75 m × 0.1 m deep. Supine infant, 9–12 months, slight, 240°, crushed skull lying on left cheek facing north. Fragmentary arms by sides, legs together with knees slightly flexed to the north.

Grave 1102 (Fig. 2.21)

Rectangular, 0.8 m × 2.0 m × 0.54 m deep. Supine female adult, 40–50 years, partial. 273°, skull turned slightly to the north? Upper arms by sides, left hand beneath pelvis, right hand over left hip, legs straight and together.

Grave 1103 (not illustrated)

Fragmentary remains of infant, c 6 months. 270°. Fragments of skull and long bones remaining.

Grave 1213 (not illustrated)

Sub-rectangular shallow grave-like indentation in the surface of the gravel immediately south of and parallel to the child inhumation 1103. The loam filling contained traces of bone. Probable infant burial heavily affected by animal burrow.

Grave 3518 (Fig. 2.21)

An isolated sub-rectangular grave pit 0.65 m × 1.8 m × 0.3 m deep. Supine, turned slightly to left, male, adult, 45+ years, good. 3°, skull resting on left side facing east. Body laid in grave pit against west side tilting the trunk to face slightly east. Right hand on pelvis, left hand in front of pelvis, right leg straight, left leg slightly flexed.

Grave 3521 (Fig. 2.21)

An isolated sub-rectangular grave pit 0.63 m × 1.52 m × 0.13 m deep. Supine unsexed adolescent, 12–14 years, good. 355°, skull on left side facing south-east. Body laid against west edge of grave tilting the body slightly to face east. Upper arms by sides, hands in front of pelvis, legs together and slightly flexed.

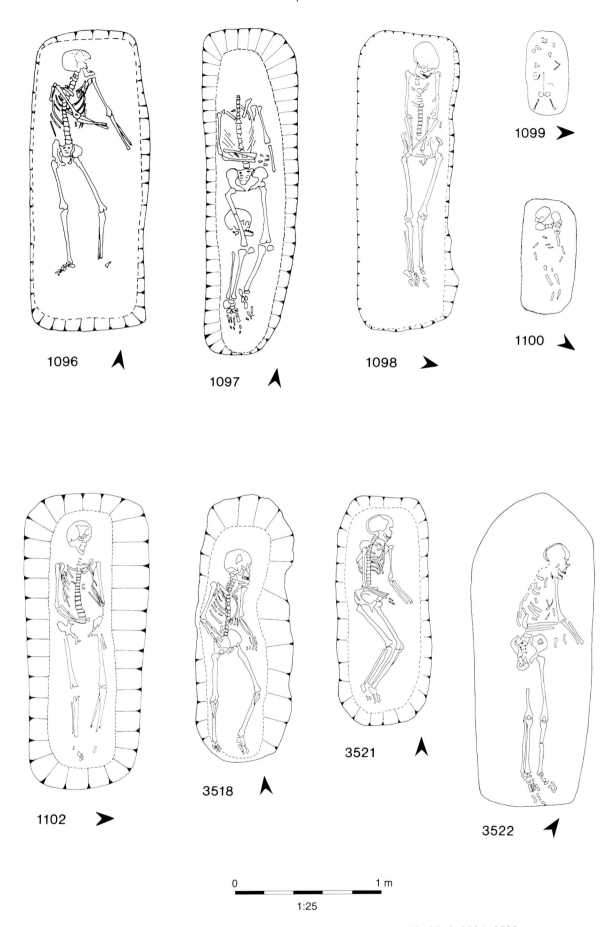

Figure 2.21   Romano-British inhumations 1096, 1097, 1098, 1099, 1100, 1102, 3518, 3521, 3522.

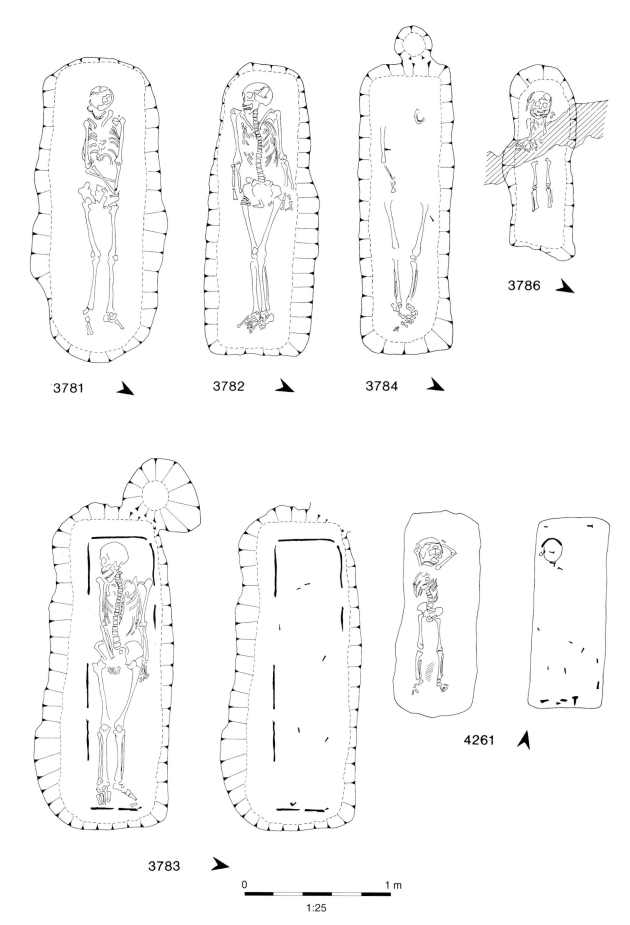

3781

3782

3784

3786

3783

4261

0   1 m

1:25

Figure 2.22   Romano-British inhumations 3781, 3782, 3783, 3784, 3786, 4261.

Grave 3522 *(Fig. 2.21)*

Sub-rectangular grave pit approximately 0.8 m × 2.1 m × 0.2 m deep. On left side, male adult, 35–40 years, good. 340°, skull and trunk lying on left side facing south-east. Upper arms by sides but lower left arm and hand extending away from body against edge of pit, legs parallel and straight. A tooth lay on the left pelvis and one iron nail by the right hand side of the lower jaw.

Associated finds:

100 Fragmentary iron nail. Surviving length 23 mm (SF 1035).

Grave 3781 *(Fig. 2.22)*

One of an isolated group of five burials. Sub-rectangular grave pit, 0.9 m × 2.02 m × 0.45 m deep. Supine male adult, 35–40 years, good. 255°. Skull rolled backwards, neck uppermost but lower jaw resting in a normal position over the neck vertebrae, upper arms by sides, both hands over pelvis, legs together and straight.

Grave 3782 *(Fig. 2.22)*

One of an isolated group of five burials. Sub-rectangular grave pit 0.76 m × 1.93 m × 0.36 m deep. Supine female adult, 40+ years, good. 259°, skull lying on right side facing south. Arms by sides, legs together.

Grave 3783 *(Fig. 2.22)*

One of an isolated group of five burials. Sub-rectangular grave pit, 0.87 m × 2.17 m × 0.60 m deep. Supine male adult. 35–40 years, good. 271°, skull resting on right side facing south. Arms straight, right hand over pelvic area, left hand by side, legs straight and together. Coffin visible as a light grey silty stain in the sandy soil filling. Seven iron nails around and beneath body. A large post pit which cut the north-west corner of this grave may have been a later, unrelated feature.

Associated finds:

101 Fragmentary iron nail. Surviving length 30 mm (SF 1054).
102 Fragmentary iron nail. Surviving length 47 mm. Clenched (SF 1055).
103 Fragmentary iron nail. Surviving length 37 mm (SF 1056).
104 Fragmentary iron nail. Surviving length 32 mm. Replaced wood (SF 1057).
105 Fragmentary iron nail. Surviving length 10 mm (SF 1058).
106 Missing (SF 1059).
107 Fragmentary iron nail. Surviving length 15 mm (SF 1060).

Grave 3784 *(Fig. 2.22)*

One of an isolated group of five burials. Sub-rectangular grave pit 0.66 m × 1.95 m × 0.3 m deep. Supine female? adult, 40+ years, 255°. Remains of lower mandible lying off centre, right arm by side with hand over hip (hand bones missing), legs straight and parallel, feet together. Remainder of skeleton including skull, trunk, pelvis and right arm absent. Two iron nails by right upper arm and left thigh suggest wooden coffin. A posthole 0.3 m in diameter at the head of the grave pit may or may not have been contemporary.

Associated finds:

108 Fragmentary iron nail. Surviving length 62 mm. Replaced wood (SF 1062).
109 Fragmentary iron nail. Surviving length 65 mm. Replaced wood (SF 1063).

Grave 3786 *(Fig. 2.22)*

One of an isolated group of five burials. Sub-rectangular grave pit 0.47 m × 1.22 m × 0.14 m deep. Supine child, 2.5–5 years, remains disturbed by animal burrow cutting across centre of grave. 257°. Skull facing upwards, upper arms by sides, lower arms and trunk disturbed, legs straight and parallel, feet missing. Single iron nail suggests coffin.

Associated finds:

110 Fragmentary iron nail. Surviving length 23 mm. Replaced wood (SF 1061).

Grave 4261 *(Fig. 2.22)*

An isolated grave. Sub-rectangular grave pit 0.54 m × 1.35 m × 0.15 m deep. Supine child, 6–7 years, good. 355°, skull collapsed along sutures and facing west. Arms either side of head, hands behind head pillowing skull, legs straight and parallel. Outline of coffin distinguishable as red-brown loam around body contrasted against dirty gravel packing outside coffin and 19 iron nails with mineralised wood. Over 40 hobnails indicated shoes placed between the legs. Traces of a circular iron feature *c* 160 mm in diameter, possibly the handle and top hoop from a bucket, were recorded on plan above the body but the object was too friable to be lifted without consolidation.

Associated finds:

111 Missing (SF 1106).
112 Missing (SF 1107).
113 Round-headed nail. Maximum length 30 mm (SF 1108).
114 Fragmentary iron. Surviving length 46 mm. Replaced wood (SF 1109).
115 Fragmentary iron nail. Surviving length 30 mm (SF 1110).
116 Fragmentary iron nail. Surviving length 26 mm. Replaced wood (SF 1111).
117 Rectangular-headed iron nail. Surviving length 35 mm (SF 1112).
118 Fragmentary iron nail. Surviving length 40 mm (SF 1113).
119 Fragmentary iron nail. Surviving length 24 mm. Replaced wood (SF 1114).
120 Fragmentary iron nail. Surviving length 50 mm. Replaced wood (SF 1115).
121 Fragmentary iron nail. Surviving length 28 mm. Replaced wood (SF 1116).
122 Rectangular-headed iron nail. Maximum length 29 mm. Replaced wood (SF 1117).
123 Fragmentary iron nail. Surviving length 5 mm (SF 1118).
124 Round-headed iron nail. Surviving length 52 mm. Replaced wood (SF 1119).
125 Fragmentary iron nail. Maximum length 29 mm. Replaced wood (SF 1120).

126 Fragmentary iron nail. Surviving length 35 mm. Replaced wood. (SF 1121).
127 Fragmentary iron nail. Surviving length 32 mm (SF 1122).
128 Round-headed iron nail. Surviving length 24 mm. Replaced wood (SF 1123).
129 Fragmentary iron nail. Surviving length 36 mm. Replaced wood (SF 1125).

3 *c* 40 hobnails

Cremations (Figs 2.26–8)

In this inventory each burial retains the context number allocated to it during the excavation, eg 1058. These context numbers do not run consecutively (Figs 2.2–3). A separate burial number has not been assigned. This inventory follows the conventions described at the beginning of this volume.

Cremation 1001 *(Fig. 2.26)*

Possible remains of cremation in topsoil.

Small Oxford red/brown colour-coated vessel. A possible parallel may be the miniature beaker Young C102 (Young 1977, 174 fig. 66) but the form of the rim and narrow neck suggests a small globular flask, of a type not found in Young's corpus, though perhaps a miniature of a form such as C16.1 (Young 1977, fig 54). Burnt.

Associated with this vessel were fragments of a coarse ware jar in fabric 15, shell-tempered fabric.

Cremation 1004 *(Fig. 2.27)*

Located in the southern end of the inhumation cemetery at the junction between the north-south graves and a group of west-east burials (Fig. 2.12). Cremated bone placed in a grey ware vessel. The remains of a 3rd- to 4th-century Oxford red colour-coated beaker lay on the south-east side of the grave and a small fossil sea urchin was found in soil at the base of the pit. The fossil may have been residual, derived from the local limestone. The pit bottom cut 0.1 m into the gravel terrace. Ploughing had shattered both pottery vessels and an unknown amount of cremated bone was lost. The pit had been dug down to a hard layer of concreted limestone which appears to have limited the depth of the pit.

Associated finds:

Base of Oxford red/brown colour-coat beaker, probably form C24 (Young 1977, 152, fig. 55, AD 270–400), with a single row of rouletting around the body.
Grey ware jar (fabric 2), form R38 (Young 1977, 219, fig. 80, 1st–4th centuries AD).

Cremation 1006 *(Fig. 2.27)*

Located within a small pit cutting the north-east corner of the burial enclosure 1217 (Fig. 2.12). Fragmentary plough-damaged remains of two vessels were scattered over an area 0.6 m × 0.4 m. Both vessels were presumably buried in the same pit. These remains probably represent a burial pit cutting into the filling of the burial enclosure ditch 1217, with two vessels surviving as fragments in the base of the medieval ploughsoil. Both pots contained ashes, and there were also some ashes which may have come from either or both pots. At least two people are represented, a child and an adolescent or adult. The remains were originally deposited in a shallow pit which stopped at the surface of the gravel. Plough damage occurred during the formation of the open field system but the surviving fragments were ploughed only once or twice before the increasing height of the ridge protected them from further damage.

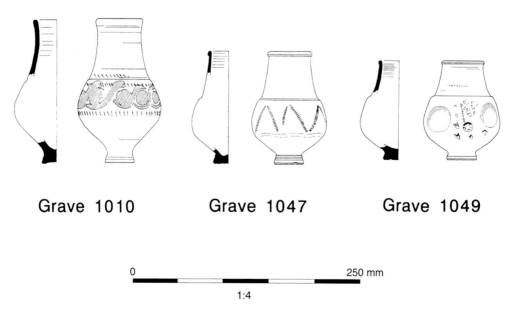

Grave 1010   Grave 1047   Grave 1049

0 ⸺⸺⸺⸺ 250 mm

1:4

Figure 2.23 Pottery beakers from graves 1010, 1047, 1049 (1:4).

Grave 1013

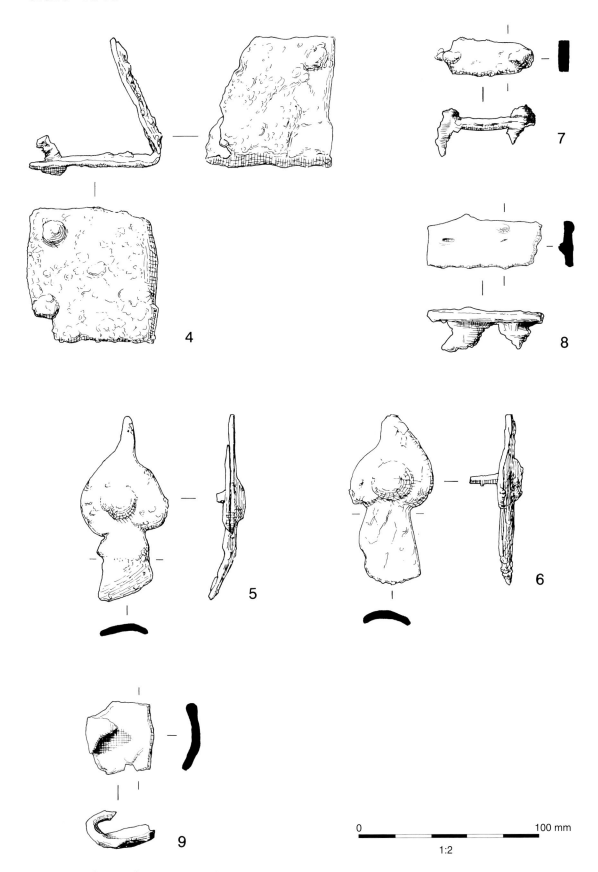

Figure 2.24   Iron fittings from grave 1013.

Grave 1042

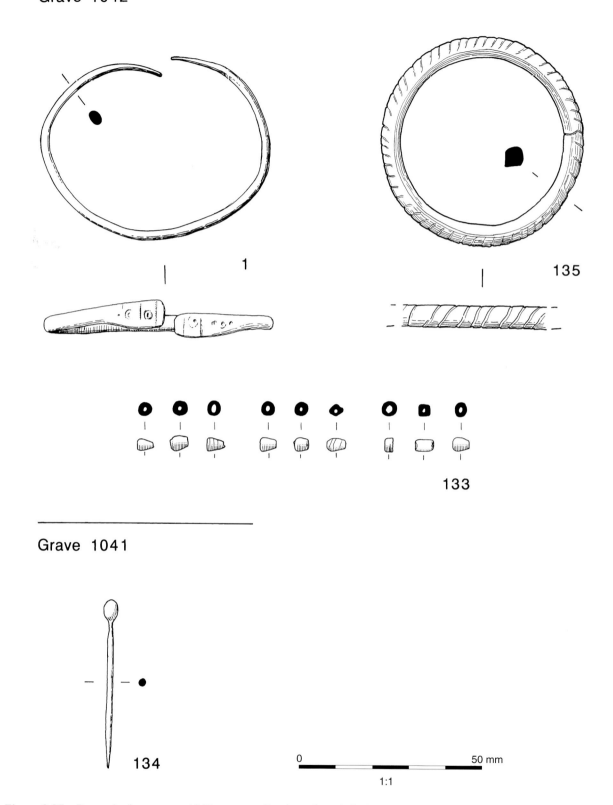

Grave 1041

Figure 2.25   Bone pin from grave 1041; copper alloy bracelet, shale bracelet and selected glass beads from a necklace from grave 1042.

Cremation 1001

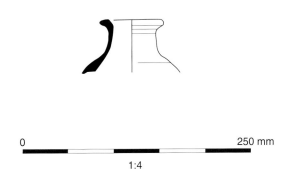

0   250 mm

1:4

Figure 2.26   Pottery beaker from 1001, probable cremation in ploughsoil (1:4).

Associated finds:

Oxford red/brown colour-coat beaker, probably form C23 (compare examples from topsoil and 1007, AD 270–400).
Base of shell-tempered jar (fabric 15).

Cremation 1007 *(Fig. 2.27)*

The central cremation burial within the square enclosure ditch 1217 with which it is presumably contemporary. The enclosure lies midway along this north-south linear cemetery on the western flank (Figs 2.12–13). North-south burials immediately to the south appear to respect the enclosure. The burial comprised a deformed grey ware pottery beaker within a larger grey ware jar placed in a more or less square pit cutting 0.2 m into the gravel. No plough damage. Both vessels contained bones of adults, and cremated bone also occurred in patches within the soil around the grey ware jar. It is possible that only one person is represented, distributed in two pots. A strong nuchal crest on a skull fragment suggests that one or the only person may have been male. Some of the pieces in the second pot were black or grey rather than being completely calcined, suggesting that cremation was not very efficient. The patches in the soil may have been secondary cremations deposited around the vessel, they may be residual from a previous cremation or they may represent the aftermath of the burrowing rodents which had substantially altered the outline of the burial pit, with two small scatters of cremated bone visible on the surface. The two fragmentary nails suggested that this burial may have originally been placed within a wooden casket.

Associated finds:

Oxford red/brown colour-coat beaker, probably form C23 (Young 1977, 152, fig. 55, AD 270–400). The vessel is overfired and distorted. It is possible that this beaker was burnt with the body whose cremated bones surrounded it inside the grey ware jar. The beaker was found intact though with many hairline cracks and fell apart as the cremation urn was excavated.
Grey ware jar (fabric 2). Form R24 as 1004. 1st-4th centuries AD.

11   Round-headed iron nail. Maximum length 29 mm (SF 330). Not illustrated

12   Fragmentary iron nail. Surviving length 25 mm (SF 335). Not illustrated

Cremation 1203 *(Fig. 2.27)*

Located 3.0 m north-west of the burial enclosure 1217 (Figure 2.12). 4th-century shell tempered ware pottery jar containing calcined bones, placed in a circular pit cutting 0.06 m into the gravel. Upper portion of this burial deposit ploughed away with the lower part of the vessel *in situ* but broken. Some calcined bone appeared to have suffered redeposition within an animal burrow 1205 and associated nesting chamber to the east.

Associated finds:

4th-century shell-tempered ware pottery jar. Not illustrated

Cremation 1208 *(Fig. 2.28)*

Located 3.0 m north-west of the burial enclosure 1217 beside cremation burial 1203 (Fig. 2.12). Base of a sub-circular burial pit 0.4 m in diameter cutting 0.10 m into the gravel. The burial deposit had been partly destroyed by ploughing and an animal burrow. The burial pit contained the surviving lower portion of a coarse shell-tempered later 4th-century jar containing calcined bone, including some black and grey pieces which suggested that the cremation was not thorough. The presence of a fragment of bird bone which had survived cremation is of interest: cremated fowls are known in Romano-British cremation deposits and fowl skeletons have also been found in inhumation graves. Much of the cremation deposit had been lost to ploughing. An Oxford product colour-coated beaker which exhibited much wear survived the cremation pyre only to be shattered by ploughing. The beaker did not appear to contain cremated remains. Two iron nails suggested the former presence of some wooden object.

Associated finds:

Oxford red/brown colour-coat beaker, form C24 (Young 1977, 152, fig. 55, AD 270–400).

Shell-tempered jar. See 1001 (topsoil) and 1006.

98   Round-headed iron nail. Maximum length 23 mm (SF 213).
99   Round-headed iron nail. Maximum length 23 mm (SF 333).

Cremation 1218 *(Fig. 2.28)*

Within the enclosure 1217 east of the central burial lay traces of a cremation burial with several sherds of a coarse ware vessel in the base of a rabbit burrow. This appears to have been a burial pit re-excavated by a rabbit leaving only a few sherds of the former burial container. The section continued back as a series of burrows.

Associated finds:

Shell-tempered ware sherds. Not illustrated.

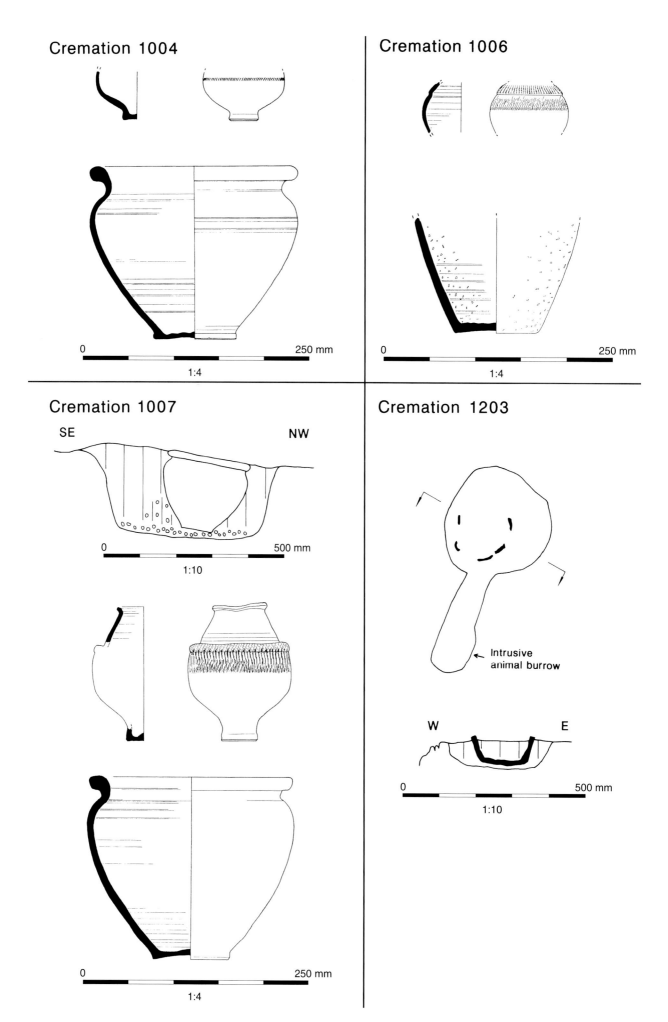

Figure 2.27 Cremation 1004, beaker and grey ware jar; cremation 1006, beaker and coarse jar; cremation 1007, section, deformed grey ware beaker and grey ware jar; cremation 1203, plan (note intrusive animal burrow) and section (pottery at 1:4).

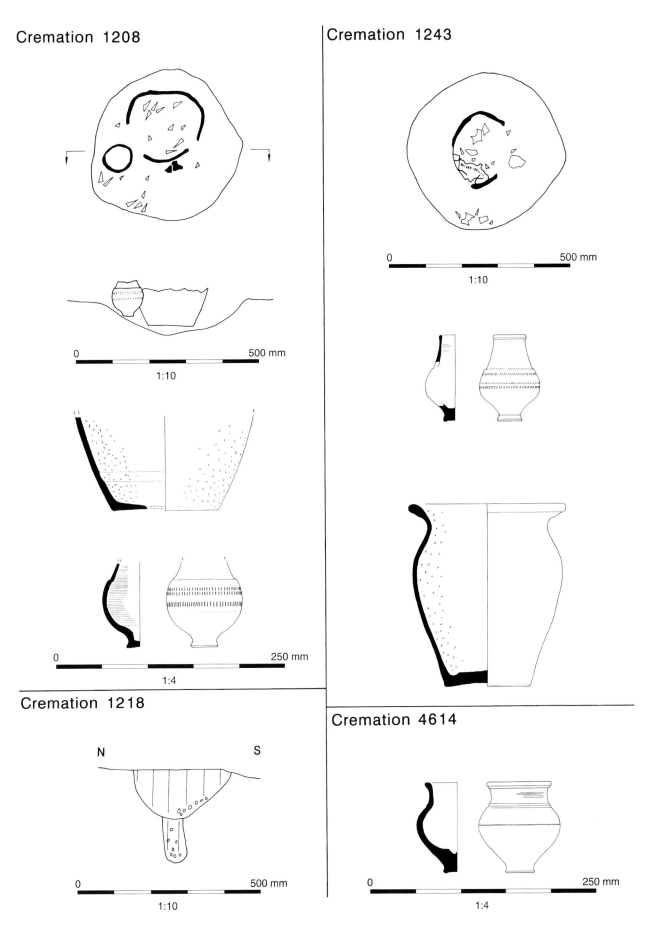

Cremation 1208

Cremation 1243

0   500 mm
1:10

0   500 mm
1:10

0   250 mm
1:4

Cremation 1218

N   S

0   500 mm
1:10

Cremation 4614

0   250 mm
1:4

Figure 2.28   Cremation 1208, plan, section, beaker and coarse ware vessel; cremation 1218, section (note animal burrow); cremation 1243, plan, beaker and coarse ware vessel; cremation 4614, beaker (pottery at 1:4).

Cremation 1233 (Fig. 2.12)

Within the square enclosure 1217 west of the central burial was a pocket of cremated bone and charcoal some 0.03 m deep × 0.10 m in diameter in loam above an animal burrow. No evidence of pottery. The top of the cremation had been ploughed off. The preservation of this portion of the cremation deposit was due to the gradual subsidence of the soil into the animal burrow bringing the base of the deposit to below plough depth.

Cremation 1234 (Fig. 2.12)

Within the square enclosure 1217 against the east side of the central burial 1007 lay a pocket 0.05 m in diameter × 0.05 m deep of calcined bone and charcoal fragments. Like 1233 this is apparently the remains of a cremation deposit without pottery vessels or grave goods. Most of this deposit had been ploughed away.

Cremation 1235 (Fig. 2.12)

A collapsed animal burrow containing pottery fragments and calcined bone suggesting the remains of a plough-damaged cremation and urn transported by burrowing activity from nearby.

Cremation 1243 (Fig. 2.28)

Sub-circular pit 0.4 m in diameter cutting 0.22 m into the gravel. Coarse ware vessel containing calcined bone fragments. Small red colour-coated beaker placed against east side of the vessel. The colour coat was worn away around the girth and lip of the beaker before burial. Both vessels upright. Badly damaged by ploughing.

Associated finds:

Oxford red/brown colour-coated beaker, a miniature form C24 (see Fig. 2.28). Shell-tempered jar (fabric 15). This is the most complete example of the six coarse shell-tempered wheel-thrown vessels associated with cremations. From the published description they appear similar to late Roman vessels from Shakenoak where they are described as 'calcite-gritted' (Brodribb *et al.* 1971, 69 and 73, fig. 37, 660–668) and from Barton Court Farm (Miles 1986, 7:C12, fig. 130).

Cremation 4614 (Fig. 2.28)

An isolated burial pit cutting 0.1 m into the gravel which contained the lower portion of a cremation deposit with ash, charcoal, calcined bone and a 4th-century colour-coated beaker. Two iron nails suggested this burial may have been placed within a wooden box.

Associated finds:

Oxford red/brown colour-coat beaker. In this fabric it is most similar to form C 102.3 but perhaps intermediate between C102 and C101 (Young 1977, 174, fig. 66). Both of these types occur in probable early 4th-century contexts in the Oxfordshire production site at Lower Farm, Nuneham Courtenay (Booth *et al.* 1993). A very close parallel for the form, however, is the grey ware type R24.5 (Young 1977, fig. 78)

130   Fragmentary iron nail. Surviving length 22 mm (SF 1206).
131   Fragmentary iron nail. Surviving length 40 mm (SF 1207).

Chapter 3:   The Anglo-Saxon Settlement, Structural Evidence

By Ellen McAdam

INTRODUCTION

This chapter describes the archaeological evidence for Anglo-Saxon occupation excavated at Barrow Hills between 1983 and 1985. The features are listed in five gazetteers:

1 Post-built structures.
2 Sunken-featured buildings.
3 Anglo-Saxon inhumations.
4 Pits, barrow ditches and miscellaneous contexts.
5 Anglo-Saxon features at Barton Court Farm (published in fiche in Miles 1986).

CONDITIONS OF SURVIVAL

The history of land use on the site has been described in Chapter 1. The soil was light and free-draining (the field was known as 'Dry Piece'), only 0.15–0.30 m thick and prone to leaching and drought. It provided an ideal habitat for burrowing animals but not an ideal environment for crops (the sample of charred grain from the Romano-British pit 411, south-east of barrow 13, was not necessarily grown on site: Moffett 1999, 246). It was probably used for grazing until it was brought under ridge and furrow cultivation in the medieval period. After the Second World War the site was intensively cultivated for cereals, and both medieval and modern ploughing had caused extensive damage to features. The Romano-British and Anglo-Saxon site at Barton Court Farm (Miles 1986), 300 m to the south-west across the Daisy Banks stream, was excavated between 1972 and 1976, and the Anglo-Saxon features are noticeably better preserved than those at Barrow Hills, which had endured an additional decade of deep ploughing. There was some evidence of erosion on the south-east of the site, towards the edge of the second terrace, and the site was crossed by at least two service trenches which disturbed SFBs 33 and 36/37. These were not planned in relation to the archaeological features during the excavation but appear on the magnetometer survey (David 1994, fig. 1; Barclay and Halpin 1999, fig. 2.2). As one might expect on a site which was apparently occupied for over a century, there was also a high level of replacement and repair of structures. All these factors, but particularly the replacement, ploughing and animal disturbance, contributed to a loss of detail and clarity which contrasts sharply with chalk sites such as Cowdery's Down (Millett and James 1983; Alcock and Walsh 1993) and Chalton (Addyman *et al.* 1972; Addyman and Leigh 1973; Walsh 1992, fig. 3). In many cases it is not possible to establish even the original dimensions of the structures with any certainty, and the site can contribute little to the discussion of Anglo-Saxon metrology or building techniques. Fine details of construction and internal fittings have been lost, and although the excavator has stated (Chapter 1) that even small stakeholes penetrated the gravel it would appear, in some areas at least, that this was not the case, and that slighter features did not survive.

The virtual absence of postholes in the 10 m square north-east of SFB 2 is probably the result of a recording error or loss of records, as noted in Chapter 1. The absence of postholes around the outer ditch of barrow 12, on the other hand, may reflect the survival into the Anglo-Saxon period of an external bank now destroyed by ploughing. This was probably relatively slight (Barclay and Halpin 1999, 102).

ORIGINAL EXTENT OF SETTLEMENT

The pits of the sunken-featured buildings showed up clearly as dark rectangles on the aerial photographs (Pl. 1.1, Fig. 1.4), and even the shallowest were visible. It may be possible to detect at least one such rectangle on Plate 1.1 to the south of Audlett Drive, suggesting that the settlement may have continued some distance towards the edge of the gravel terrace. The dark marks visible on this photograph on the north-east side of Audlett Drive, on the other hand, were excavated in 1985 and proved to be tree-throw holes. No further trace of Anglo-Saxon settlement was found in this direction, and the ditches of barrow 1 contained only small quantities of Anglo-Saxon material.

Deposits in the northern ditch of the oval barrow suggest that Anglo-Saxon activity continued some distance to the north, and in 1928 Leeds collected Saxon pottery from pits revealed by gravel extraction to the north of the excavated area (Avery and Brown 1972; see also Fig. 1.3). The marshy area of Daisy Banks seems to have formed the boundary of the activity at Barrow Hills to the west, and there is no aerial photographic or other evidence of activity between Daisy Banks and Barton Court Farm. The area between the Daisy Banks streams produced a possibly Saxon skeleton and Saxon pits containing rubbish which included the burnt remains of what may have been a wattle and daub structure, 5th- to 6th-century pottery and an amethyst bead of 7th-century type (Avery and Brown 1972; see Fig. 1.3). Leeds collected Saxon pottery from gravel pits to the north of the present excavations, although he did not record the presence of sunken-featured buildings like those he had previously excavated at Sutton

Courtenay (Leeds and Harden 1936, fig. 1). The settlement at Barton Court Farm may originally have extended some distance to the west into an area destroyed by 19th-century gravel extraction. The pottery suggests that Anglo-Saxon occupation at Barton Court Farm began slightly earlier than at Barrow Hills and probably also ended earlier, but the use of the same pottery stamps on both sites indicates that they have a strong claim to be considered part of the same community.

The excavated area of Barrow Hills seems therefore to have more or less coincided with the extent of this part of the settlement to the east and west. It probably continued for some distance to the north and south. The density of features is not great in either direction, however. To the south the spread of activity would have been limited by the slope down to the lower terrace, here quite steep. It seems likely that the excavated area of Barrow Hills, together with its sister settlement at Barton Court Farm and the other fragments of evidence noted above, covered most of the original Anglo-Saxon activity in the immediate area, with the possible exception of the area to the north of the present site.

POST-BUILT STRUCTURES

Methodology

The published site plan (Fig. 7.11) gives a misleadingly tidy impression of Anglo-Saxon activity on the site. In addition to the post-built structures and sunken-featured buildings that were recognised in the field, the site plans show high densities of other features, particularly in the areas west of the Romano-British cemetery and around the cluster of buildings at its north end and, to a lesser extent, in the areas between and east of PBS 21 and SFB 43 and around the pond barrow.

One of the first tasks of the second phase of post-excavation was therefore to produce an overall site plan showing all recorded features. A site mosaic of 32 plans was assembled from the 1:50 'C' plans prepared during excavation, and this allowed a working site plan to be produced. At a scale of 1:250 it measured approximately 1.5 × 1.25 m. This in turn formed the basis for Figure 7.11.

Using the working site plan, the site records were systematically re-examined. A key aid to identification was the marked preference displayed by the Anglo-Saxon inhabitants of the site for a north-east to south-west orientation, approximately parallel to the edge of the gravel terrace and the line of the barrow cemetery. A broadly east-west orientation was a common feature of early Anglo-Saxon settlements (Marshall and Marshall 1993, 375–7). This may have been because doorways positioned in the long south-facing walls of sunken-featured buildings or post-built structures, as for example in PBSs 1 and 8, would have captured maximum daylight. The first step was therefore to examine the overall site plan for groups of postholes of the same approximate size, spaced at more or less regular intervals, which appeared to form rectilinear arrangements.

The site records for all the features in the proposed alignments were then checked. Features positively identified as animal burrows were excluded, and some potential structures were eliminated in this way. In many instances, however, it was clear that burrows had disturbed existing postholes, accounting for the irregular shapes of many of the planned features. Selecting only those features which seemed to fit the plan of a proposed structure would have lent a false certainty to the interpretation of groups of features which as excavated and recorded were extremely confusing and difficult to understand. In assembling the 1:100 plans of the structures in the gazetteers, therefore, all the features identified in the site records as probable or possible postholes in the immediate area of the structure have been included.

Some structures have almost certainly not been recognised, and some of the less coherent structures have been retained on the basis of a presumption in favour of the original excavator's observation and interpretation. Although the site records are generally good, there are some problems. In the case of the groups of features identified as PBSs 21 and 22, for example, there are no section drawings and the context records provide only the context number and grid reference. It is therefore impossible to distinguish animal burrows from postholes. In all, 22 post-built structures have now been identified. The 22 possible or probable post-built structures have been divided into rectangular post-built structures, structures whose plans are less clear and are described as ancillary structures, fencelines and structures of uncertain function.

Very few postholes contained finds. Five (PBSs 1, 5, 8, 21 and 22) produced small quantities of Anglo-Saxon pottery: PBS 1 also yielded a reused Roman sherd and the postholes of PBS 6 held two quern fragments. The remaining post-built structures are dated to the Anglo-Saxon period primarily on the grounds of their spatial relationship to the sunken-featured buildings. There was no evidence of the use of post-in-trench construction.

Posthole depths varied considerably within buildings, from shallow, barely visible depressions in the ground to holes up to 0.3 m deep. Depth seemed to be unrelated to post size as indicated by posthole diameter and presumably reflects the use of timbers of uneven length which had to be level with each other at the top. Many slighter postholes have probably been obliterated by ploughing. No evidence for postpipes was recorded (except for the postholes of SFBs 35 and 45). Apart from posthole 1430 of PBS 5, which cut the north-west corner of the Romano-British grave 1013, no stratigraphic relationships were recorded.

Rectangular post-built structures
(Figs 3.1, 3.3–4; Pl. 3.1)

Seven buildings were identified with varying degrees of confidence as free-standing rectangular post-built structures, PBSs 1, 5, 6, 7, 8, 10 and 11. Some or all of these may have been family dwellings, like the 'halls' West records at West Stow (West 1985, 112), or the 'posthole' houses identified at West Heslerton (Powlesland 1999, 22–5), or they may have been barns or byres, or they may have fulfilled a range of functions throughout their lifetimes. As a group they are poorly preserved and incomplete, and chronological or other variations in construction technique cannot be detected. PBS 1 seems to show clear signs of timber replacement (Fig. 3.3: 1512 for 1513 and 1511 for 1510), and the general lack of clarity in the plans may conceal other replacements. Powlesland (pers. comm.) also notes repairs in the post-built structures at West Heslerton.

PBS 8, the best preserved of the structures, was clearly constructed using a double line of posts along each of the long walls. The double-post technique may also have been employed in PBS 7, the worst preserved and least coherent of all the rectangular post-built structures at Barrow Hills. It has been suggested that the double posts held in place the horizontal boards which formed the walls, and that they performed the same function as the raking timbers recognised at Cowdery's Down and Chalton in stabilising the wall plate against the outward thrust of the rafters, but James *et al.* argued that the angle of raking timbers was too steep to act as buttressing, and that their to function was to counter torsion in the wall plate (Hamerow 1993, 8; James *et al.* 1984, 194). In the absence of foundations it seems very probable that these buildings derived their structural integrity from the tie-beam construction of the roof, and the main focus of effort would have been on keeping the posts in place to support the tie-beam rather than countering thrust.

In all the rectangular post-built structures at Barrow Hills, the end walls seem to have been less substantial than the long walls, and they are clearly visible only in PBSs 1 and 8 and at the south end of PBS 5. There is no convincing instance of internal subdivision, and in many cases it is difficult to establish the positions of the doorways. In PBS 1 there seem to have been opposing doorways in the long walls towards the south-west end, between 1512/3 and 1510/1 on the southern side and 1436 and 1437 on the northern. There may also have been a doorway in the south-west end wall between 1619 and 1700, but the plan of this end is confused. There is a clear entrance between 3853/4 and 3841/50 of PBS 8, but there is no equally clear sign of an entrance in the opposite wall. In PBS 11, which probably continued originally some distance to the north-east, there seems to have been an entrance in the southern long wall between 3977 and 3980, which again has no obvious partner on the opposite wall.

There has been much discussion of the metrology of Anglo-Saxon buildings, and the arguments were summarised by Hamerow (1993, 9–10). The post-built structures at Barrow Hills were measured according to the method suggested by Huggins (1991) using a clear plastic ruler to measure the distances between lines drawn as a best fit through the centres of the postholes of the walls. The structures at Barrow Hills are not sufficiently well preserved to make a significant contribution to this debate, but there is some indication that a standard unit of measurement, possibly of 3.5 m, was in use.

The rectangular post-built structures at Barrow Hills are smaller than those at Mucking (Hamerow 1993, 9–10 and fig. 4), where the ten best preserved were on average 10 m in length with an average floor area of 50 m^2, but they fall within the same range as the equally poorly preserved building plans from West Stow (Fig. 3.1; West 1985, 10–13). Figure 3 of James *et al.* (1984, 188) indicates that the majority of buildings in what are defined as Group 1 settlements (those without large, 'high status' buildings) are under 50 m^2 in area. The floor areas for the post-built structures at Barrow Hills range from 24.5–37.5 m^2 in area, and thus fall within the range for early Saxon buildings in the Midland area defined by Marshall and Marshall (1993, 371–2). Marshall and Marshall suggested that 5th-century buildings were small, with clusters at 10 × 5 m and 7 × 3.5 m, and that building sizes tended to increase with time (1993, 374–9 and 390–1), although in the light of the arguments concerning dating evidence reviewed in Chapter 7 this observation should be regarded with caution. Most of the rectangular post-built structures at Barrow Hills fall roughly into the 7 × 3.5 m cluster, although two of the Barton Court Farm structures are larger. PBSs 1 and 5, in the centre of the site, have areas of 24.5 m^2 and *c* 31.5 m^2, while PBS 6 to the south has an area of 37.5 m^2. It is impossible to determine whether these differences in size reflect differences in date, status or function. At the later and supposedly high status sites of Chalton and Cowdery's Down there is a marked distinction between the large halls and the smaller buildings facing three sides of a square in the adjacent compounds (see Table 7.2).

PBSs 1 and 8 reflect the use of a two-square module. PBS 1 is a simple double square, PBS 8 a double square plus door width. Unfortunately, the northern end of the rectangular post-built structure in the central group of buildings, PBS 5, lay in an area of extensive disturbance where few postholes survived, and its original dimensions can only be estimated. If these buildings were dwellings, the use of bilateral symmetry might reflect a division by function, gender, status or generation, or a combination of all four. Two-room one-storey cottages were in widespread use as rural housing in the British Isles well into the 20th century, and their patterns of usage often accommodated these factors.

Ancillary structures (Figs 3.3, 3.5–6)

This category includes PBSs 2–4 (all part of the central group of PBSs 1–5) and PBSs 9, 12 and 13. They were all small, enclosing (as far as their plans can be reconstructed) floor areas of 15 m^2 or less. Their plans are approximately rectilinear. Little can be said about the function of these buildings, which presumably had a variety of domestic, agricultural and craft uses.

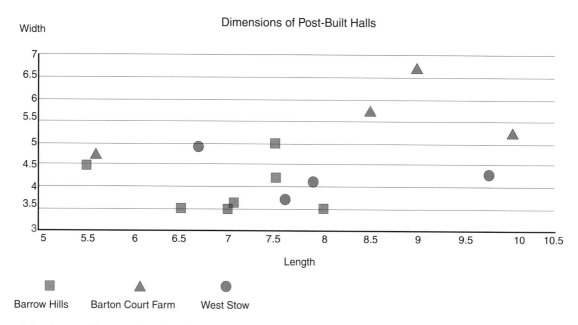

Figure 3.1   Scatter diagram showing dimensions of post-built halls at Barrow Hills, Barton Court Farm and West Stow.

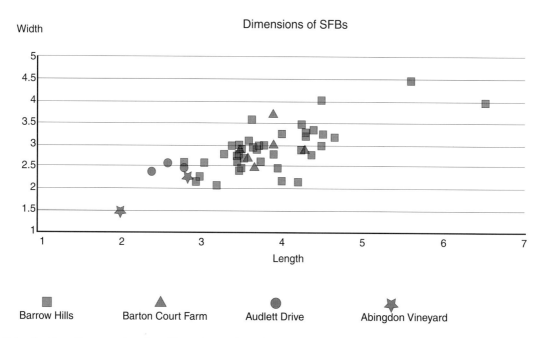

Figure 3.2   Scatter diagram showing dimensions of sunken-featured buildings at Barrow Hills, Barton Court Farm, Audlett Drive and Abingdon Vineyard.

PBS 13 was a roughly D-shaped arrangement of postholes, open on the south-east side (the straight stroke of the D) and situated about 1.3 m north-west of SFB 4 (Fig. 3.6). The superficially similar structure 122 at New Wintles (Chadwick Hawkes and Gray 1969, fig. 1; Gray 1974, 51–5) was in fact a building cut by SFBs 123 and 124, but there is no evidence at Barrow Hills that PBS 13 was part of a larger building cut by SFB 4. It may have been a pen or lean-to associated with SFB 4.

Fencelines (Figs 3.6–8)

PBSs 14, 15, 16, 17, 18, 19 and 20 have been tentatively identified as fencelines. PBS 14 consists of two approximately parallel lines of postholes *c* 3.5 m apart, the northernmost possibly continuing on the same line some distance to the south-west as PBS 15. If these were in fact one fenceline it would have been over 20 m long. There are few traces of Anglo-Saxon activity in this part of the site, apart from SFB 39. It is

68

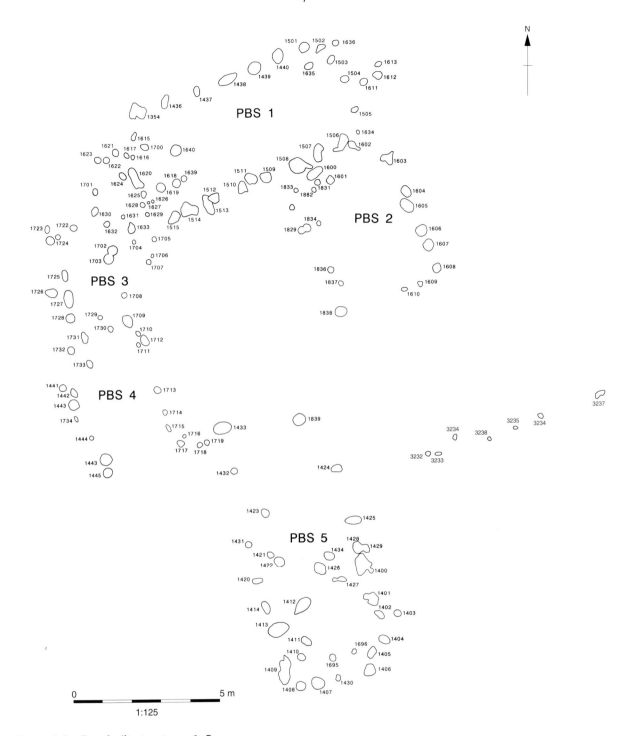

Figure 3.3   Post-built structures 1–5.

possible that PBSs 14–15 represent a simpler and less well-preserved version of PBS 21, which was also situated in an area with few definitely Anglo-Saxon features and is discussed in more detail below. PBS 16, which appears in plan to be a funnel-shaped arrangement of posts, may in fact be two unrelated fragments of fenceline.

It is extremely difficult to distinguish the detail of the structures originally formed by PBSs 19 and 20 (Fig. 3.8), but the overall impression is of two fencelines enclosing two sides of an area of about

18×10 m which contains SFBs 7 and 15. The northernmost fenceline starts with posthole 1784 in the north-east and continues south-west in an approximately straight line for about 18 m to 3117, at which point it turns through a somewhat dog-legged right-angle to continue north-west to 3624. The southern line starts in the north-east at 1744, continues south-west to 3753 and then turns northwards to 3614. Over most of their extent they are 1.5 to 2 m apart, with a funnel-shaped gap between them at the north-east end.

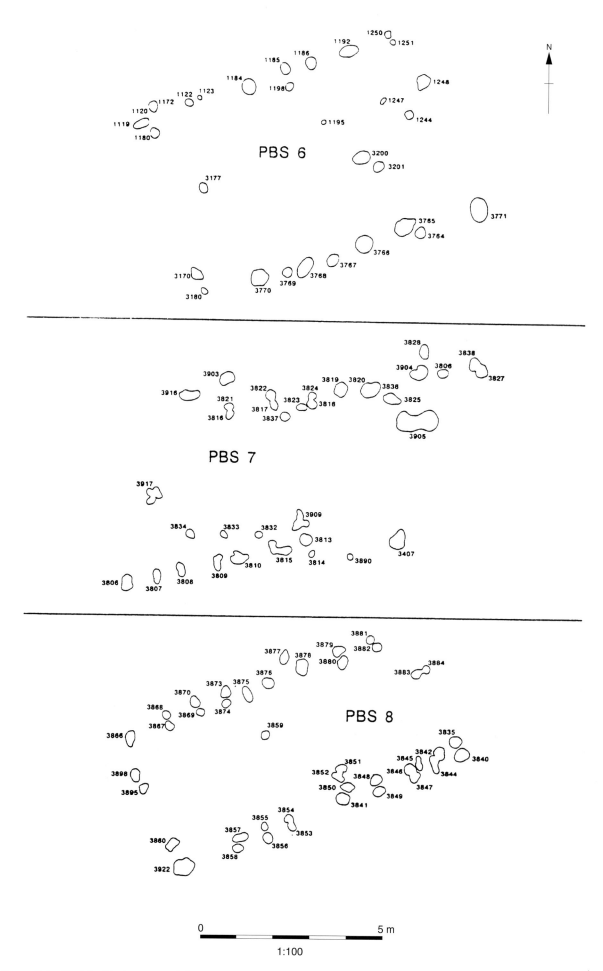

Figure 3.4   Post-built structures 6–8.

Plate 3.1   Looking south across PBS 1 to PBS 5 and the Romano-British cemetery: PBS 2 and SFB 6 on the left.

The most probable interpretation of these two features is that one is a replacement for the other, perhaps of the northern line by the southern one after the construction of SFB 7. There was a posthole structure in this area, but its plan and stratigraphic relationship to SFB 7 cannot be reconstructed. It is worth noting that both phases of the fenceline consisted of two sides at right angles, and there is no trace of a third and fourth side.

The postholes of the southern line in particular seem to be paired (eg 3585/3614, 3625/6, 3584/3621, 3739/40, 1951/2 and the off-line 3589/3613), and the postholes of PBSs 14 and 21 also appear in pairs or groups of three with gaps of from 1.5 to 4 m between groups. The details of Anglo-Saxon fencing techniques can be seen more clearly at Cowdery's Down, where the phase A/B fenceline consisted of alternate closely and more widely spaced pairs of postholes (Millett and James 1983, 202–3 and figs 28 and 30). The closely spaced pairs probably clasped at least one horizontal timber, and the more widely spaced pairs acted as buttresses to panels of wattling. The phase C fenceline at the same site involved three different methods of construction; individual postholes in a closely spaced staggered pattern, paired timbers in the same posthole, and individual postholes cut into the base of a narrow slot (Millett and James 1983, 209 and fig. 38). The widely spaced staggered pairs of posts in the Barrow Hills fences seem to be a hybrid between the phase A/B technique and the first phase C technique, perhaps with uprights clasping panels of wattling; it is possible that there were originally slighter uprights between the more substantial paired timbers. PBS 17, a line of

double postholes to the east of rectangular post-built structure PBS 6 (Fig. 3.7), seems to demonstrate the second phase C technique, in which the paired uprights (in this case *c* 1 m apart) clasped horizontal planks or panels.

Other post-built structures (Figs 3.9–10)

The site records for PBSs 21 and 22 are unusually poor. There are no sections, and the context records give only context number and grid reference. It is clear from the plan that there was extensive animal disturbance in the area, but it is not possible to identify animal burrows. The plan of PBS 22 cannot be reconstructed with any certainty, although an arrangement of parallel lines of postholes may be discernible.

PBS 21 was one of the most interesting and unusual structures to be identified at Barrow Hills. The plan can be broken down into four elements: two parallel north-east/south-west fencelines 30 m long and 8.5 m apart consisting of the widely spaced paired postholes discussed above and two roughly L-shaped posthole structures of approximately similar plan, a small one at the southern end of the fencelines and a larger one at the northern end. One of these structures may have replaced the other.

SUNKEN-FEATURED BUILDINGS

Methodology

The sunken-featured buildings were excavated and planned as discrete features (see Chapter 1, Recording

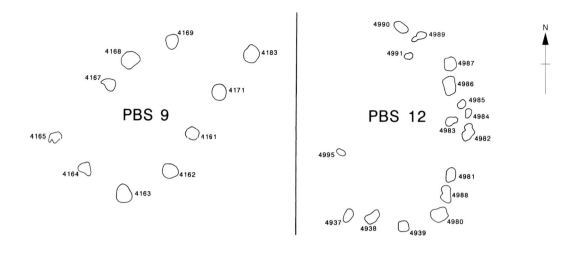

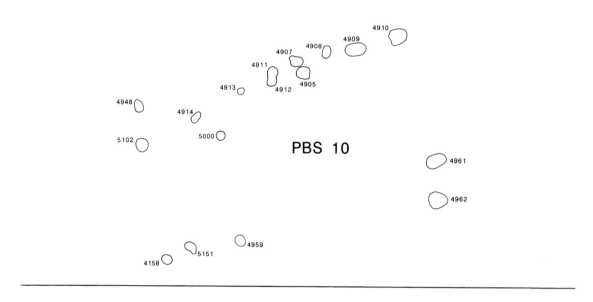

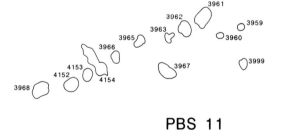

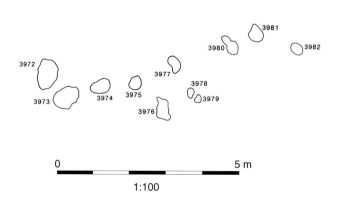

1:100

Figure 3.5   Post-built structures 9–12.

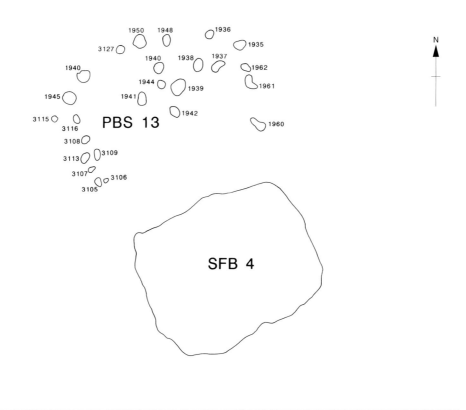

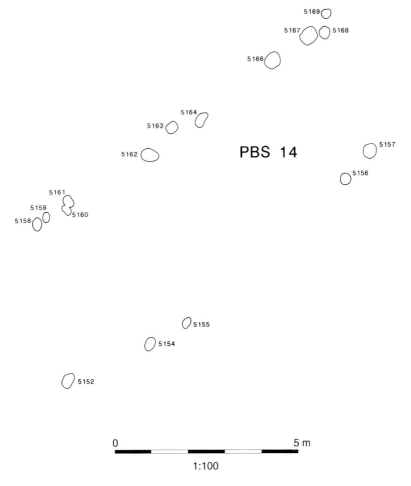

Figure 3.6   Post-built structures 13–14.

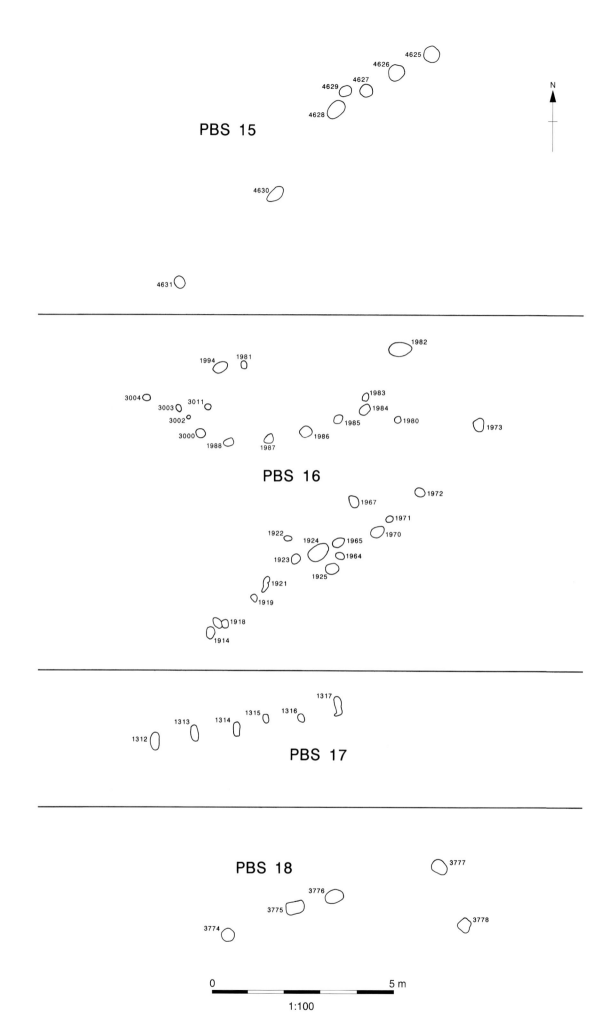

Figure 3.7 Post-built structures 15–18.

system). In the first phase of post-excavation the decision was taken not to publish stratigraphic description, and to treat the finds (apart from those from intercutting features) as a homogeneous group. During the second phase of post-excavation stratigraphic descriptions of each sunken-featured building were incorporated in gazetteer entries and section drawings were prepared for publication wherever possible. In some instances section drawings bore no recognisable relationship to the context and finds records, and these have not been reproduced. They show multiple patches of differently coloured gravel. It is clear from the site records that it was seldom, if ever, possible to excavate the fills of intercutting features separately.

Tipper (2004) has recently produced a comprehensive analysis of all aspects of sunken-featured buildings, their origins, structure, fills and formation processes. Rather than replicating his arguments at length, reference will be made to this volume.

Metrology

Length and width *(Fig. 3.2)*

The sunken-featured buildings are generally sub-rectangular, with straight sides and rounded corners, although some pits are less regular. For those sunken-featured buildings whose full original dimensions are known, surface lengths range from 3 to 6.5 m and widths from 2.1 to 4.45 m, with an average length of 3.89 m and width of 2.92 m. SFBs 4, 12 and 17 were larger than the rest; it has been observed at other sites that there appears to be a general trend towards larger *Grubenhäuser* from the 7th century onwards (Hamerow 1993, 11; Tipper 2004, 66), but Tipper concluded that the size of the pit alone was not a reliable indicator of date. The distribution of length x width is comparable both to other sites in the area and to West Stow (West 1985), Mucking (Hamerow 1993) and West Heslerton (Tipper 2004, tables 15–16), with two clusters, a large one around 3.5 × 2.75 m and a smaller, more diffuse one around 4.5 × 3.5 m These clusters may reflect some functional difference. The base areas of the pits are considerably smaller than the surface areas.

Depth

The average surviving depth of sunken-featured buildings at Barrow Hills is 0.43 m, but would almost certainly originally have been greater, an unknown and probably variable depth of topsoil having been lost. The soil cover at the start of excavation was generally thin, only 0.15–0.30 m, and is likely to have been affected by the medieval ridge and furrow cultivation which ran north-west/south-east across the site (see Bartlett 1999) and by more recent ploughing. SFB 9 in the centre of the oval barrow was almost completely eroded, suggesting that the mound of the oval barrow was standing to a height of perhaps 0.3–0.4 m or more in the

Anglo-Saxon period (Bradley 1992; Pl. 3.2), and the absence of postholes around the outer ditch of barrow 12 may reflect the survival into the Anglo-Saxon period of an external bank now destroyed by ploughing. If so, the bank was probably relatively slight. The surviving central mounds of barrows 12 and 13 may have been high enough to offer some shelter from the prevailing wind to SFBs 23, 24 and 26, and certainly survived long enough, and in a sufficiently impressive form, to give the site its name, the first recorded instance of which occurs in 1547 (Chapter 1, Saxon settlement). There is some evidence of erosion along the south-east edge of the site, where the ground slopes down towards the edge of the Second Terrace. The depth of sunken-featured buildings measured from the top of the gravel to the bottom of the pit ranged from 0 for SFB 9 in the centre of the Neolithic oval barrow to 1.03 for SFB 12. Apart from the three largest SFBs, 4, 12 and 17, there is no clear correlation between size and depth. Some topsoil has been lost, and some parts of the site may have been over-scraped during topsoil removal, but it seems likely that there was originally considerable variation in the depths of sunken-featured buildings.

Typology (Figs 3.2 and 3.11–114)

Thirty-eight out of 45 sunken-featured buildings at Barrow Hills were of two-post type, with a posthole in or near the centre of each short end. This was the predominant type throughout England and on the continent during the migration period (Tipper 2004, 68). There was only one definite example of a three-post sunken-featured building with a central post on the long axis and one possible example (12 and possibly 17). There were two sunken-featured buildings with only one posthole (13 and 26) and two with no postholes (27 and 44), but these probably represent uncompleted or eroded sunken-featured buildings rather than the separate type which has been identified at other sites (West 1985, 113–4). Finally, there was one possible six-post or six-post derivative, SFB 2.

Evidence for construction

Postholes

In most cases the gable postholes were in the centre of the short sides of the pit, although occasionally (for example, SFB 45) they straddled the edge of the pit. In some instances the angle of the gable postholes inclines inwards slightly (eg SFBs 4, 10, 14, 15, 16, 19, 20, 30 and 40). This may reflect the way in which the structure was dismantled at the end of its life, with the posts being pulled down into the pit, rather than a construction technique. In one or two cases (eg SFB 38) the posthole slopes outwards. Postpipes were observed in very few instances, most clearly in the postholes of SFB 35 and 45. The site records are not always informative on the relationship between postholes and pit fill, but in the majority of cases

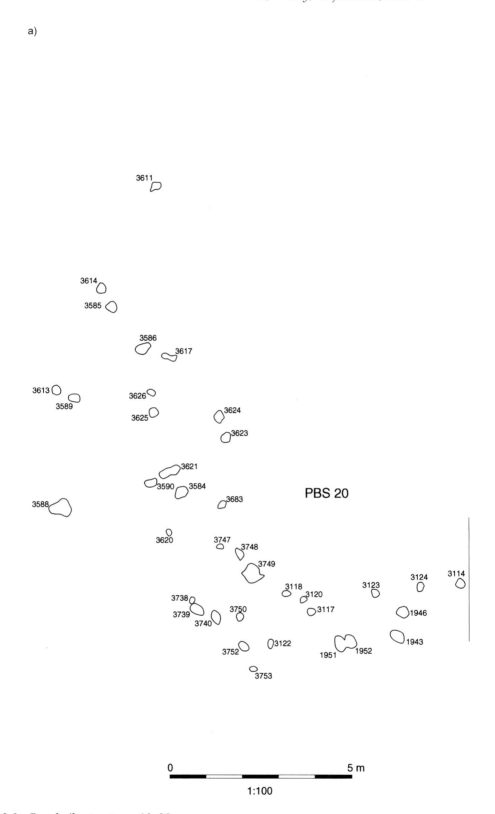

Figure 3.8   Post-built structures 19–20.

in which the relationship could be established with any confidence it seems that the pit fill extended into the postholes, indicating that the posts had been removed before the pit began to fill rather than decaying *in situ*.

There was considerable variation in posthole depths, even within posthole pairs in the same sunken-featured building (eg SFBs 3, 5, 8, 23, 31, 39, 41 and 43). This probably reflects the use of timbers of uneven length which had to be level at the top, but

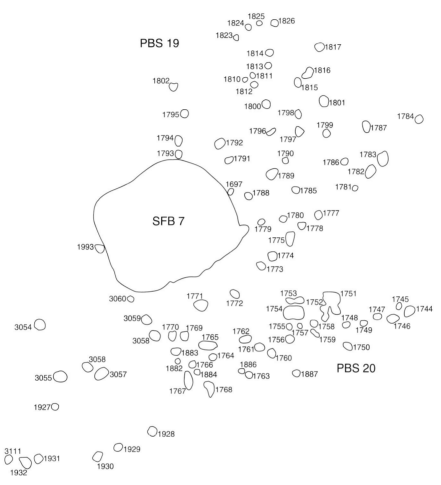

1:100

Figure 3.8   (Cont.)

the extreme shallowness of some postholes suggests that in some cases at least the gable posts were not free-standing and were held in place by other parts of the structure.

Recutting and replacement

Many sunken-featured buildings produced evidence for refurbishment or replacement, and it was not

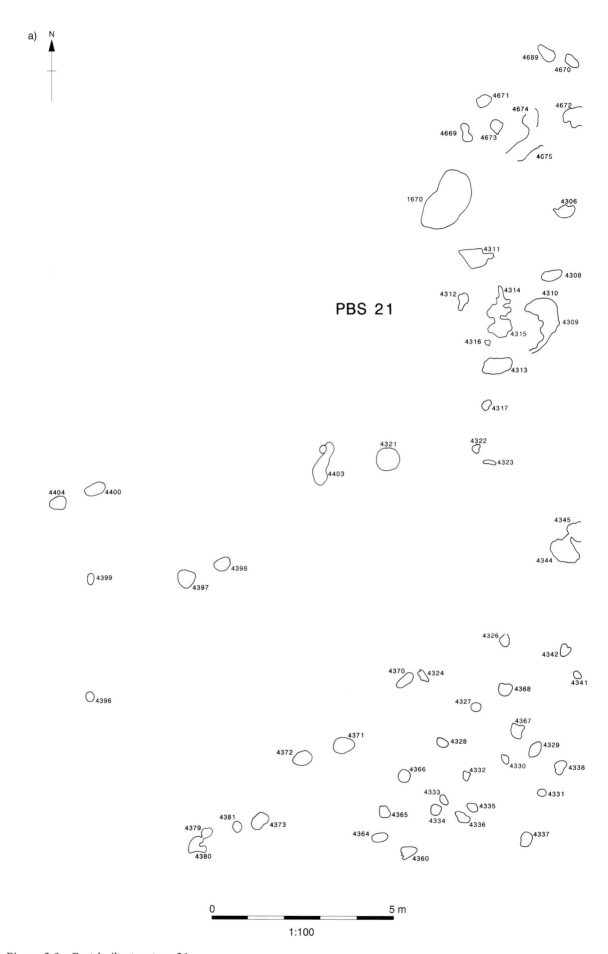

a) N

4689
4670
4671
4674
4672
4669 4673
4075
1670
4306
4311
4308
4312 4314 4310
PBS 21
4309
4315
4316 4313
4317
4321
4322
4403
4323
4404 4400
4345
4344
4398
4399
4397
4326
4342
4370 4324
4341
4368
4327
4396
4367
4371
4328 4329
4372
4330 4338
4366 4332
4333
4331
4381
4365 4335
4379 4373
4334 4336
4364 4337
4380
4360

0   5 m

1:100

Figure 3.9   Post-built structure 21.

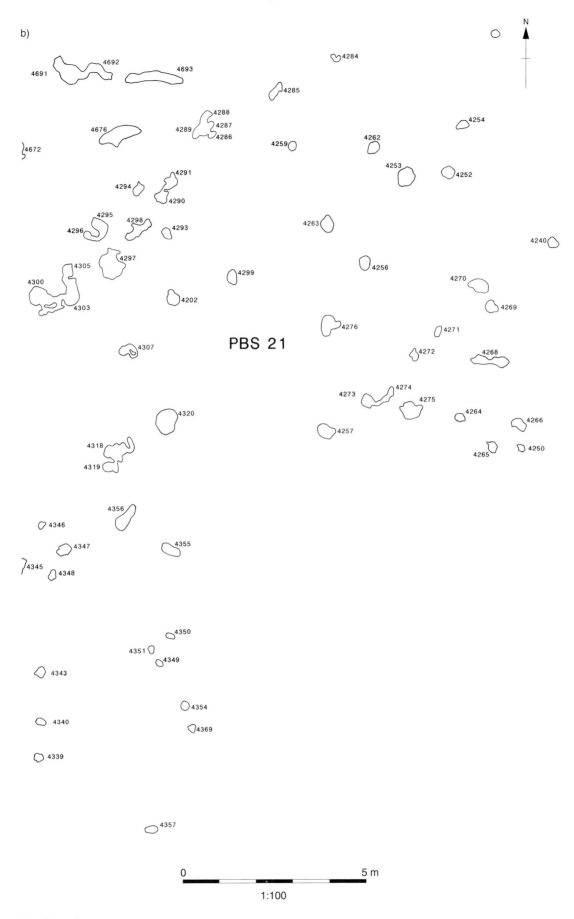

Figure 3.9 (Cont.)

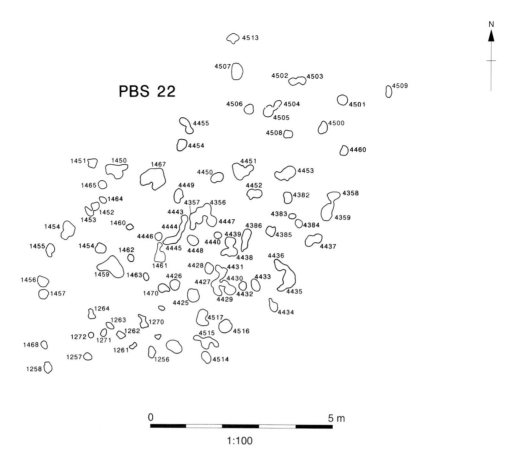

Figure 3.10   Post-built structure 22.

always possible to distinguish between the two processes, or to determine whether there had been a period of disuse before the rebuilding took place. There were possible recut or replacement postholes in

five sunken-featured buildings (1, 2, 3, 8 and 38). In several cases the pit had also been extended or recut (3, 14, 23, 38, 39 and 43), and there were 9 intercutting sunken-featured buildings (17/18, 28/29, 32/33/34,

Plate 3.2   The excavation of the Neolithic oval barrow with SFB 9 in the centre.

and 36/37). The proximity to each other of 20/21/22 and of 30 to 32/33/34 suggests that they too were replacements. This means that around 50% of the sunken-featured buildings were refurbished or replaced in or near the same location. This is broadly comparable to the level of replacement and refurbishment visible in the site plan at West Stow (West 1985, fig. 300), and may imply that their location was significant and that they performed a particular function within the layout of the settlement.

Reconstruction

Sunken-featured buildings have traditionally been envisaged as simple constructions, with two gable posts supporting a ridgepole from which descended a thatched roof (West 1985, 121; Welch 1992, fig. 11; Hamerow 1993, 14). Tipper (2004, 68–74) has discussed the structural role of the gable posts. The fact that some were replaced indicates that they had some function, but some sunken-featured buildings have no postholes, or only one. There is evidence from the experimental reconstructions at West Stow to suggest that they were not essential to the structural integrity of the buildings after they had been erected, since in several cases they had rotted away below ground level without affecting the walls and roof. They may have functioned as scaffolding during the construction of the superstructure, after which the building was self-supporting, the main weight of the roof being borne on purlin-posts (West 1985) or turf walls around the outside of the pit.

Rhizome evidence indicates that the sunken-featured buildings at West Heslerton had turf walls (D Powlesland pers. comm.). R A Chambers, the excavator of Barrow Hills, noted that pits often contained lumps of conglomerated gravel, which he interpreted as evidence that the upcast from the pit had been used to form walls which were then pushed back in when the structure was dismantled. It seems likely that the D-shaped structure north of SFB 4 abutted a wall, and turf seems the most probable building material. Although the site records for several sunken-featured buildings state that daub was present in the fill, only one fragment of daub with impressions of rods and sails is listed in the catalogue of finds, from SFB 28. Hamerow also notes that the use of upcast to form walls is particularly plausible in view of the paucity of daub recovered at Mucking (Hamerow 1993, 11–12).

Use of hut floors

The question of whether sunken-featured buildings had sunken or suspended floors was for many years hotly contested, but in his exhaustive review of the structural evidence Tipper concludes that an interpretation of *Grubenhäuser* as having suspended or cavity floors provides the best fit with most of the archaeological evidence (Tipper 2004, chapters 4 and 9). The data from Barrow Hills would appear to support this. Chambers recorded that there was very little evidence for the use of the base of the pit during the life of the structure, and he concluded that most of the pits at Barrow Hills were covered by plank floors during the lifetime of the building, as West has suggested was the case at West Stow (1985, 116–120). Chambers also observed that there was no evidence of trampling and use of the hut floors while the gable posts were in place and that many pits had struck patches of hard, conglomerated gravel which made the floors and walls extremely uneven (archive notes). In other places the gravel was so loose that without revetment the pit walls would have collapsed upon contact, whereas only minor gravel slumping was recorded. In addition, the pit walls in many cases slope outwards at an oblique angle, so that the area at the base of the pit would have been very restricted. Not all the context records for the sunken-featured buildings refer explicitly to the condition of the floor and sides, but where they do they tend to confirm the excavator's general remarks. The section and profile drawings also show some notably uneven floors with base areas much smaller than the surface area (for example, SFBs 6, 12, 13, 38 and 39).

There is little evidence for pit linings. There were 35 postholes and stakeholes associated with SFB 2, many of them positioned along the south-east side, but their function is obscure. They may have formed a lining for the pit, but there was no evidence for occupation or a floor surface on the base of the hut. At least some of them had gone out of use by the time the pit began to fill. There was a line of limestone and conglomerate lumps on the floor of the pit of SFB 5 parallel to the south-west end, but again these do not seem to have been associated with evidence for the use of the pit floor. There is no evidence for entrances to the pit.

There were occupation layers on the floors of seven of the sunken-featured buildings (SFBs 6, 17/18, 24, 26, 28, 40 and 41). Six of the seven are described as grey, greenish grey or grey brown friable or powdery deposits, usually only a few centimetres thick, containing charcoal flecks and in three cases pottery and animal bone as well. Layers 3–7 of SFB 28 were different, and consisted of a hearth, a layer of clay and several layers of burning on and above the smooth compact gravel which formed a surface on the floor of the pit. The relationship of these layers to the posthole fills is not always clear; in the case of SFB 26 the occupation layer definitely accumulated before the removal of the posts and in the case of 6, 24 and 28 definitely after, with 17/18 and 41 possibly after. The records do not indicate whether there was wear on the pit floor of SFB 26; the intermittent occupation layer 4 may represent debris which has sifted through floorboards, but it contained a substantial weight of pottery, including cross-joins with layer 2. The evidence of these occupation layers is thus inconclusive, but most of them seem to represent the use of the pit floor after the removal of one or more posts, rather than during the lifetime of the structure. The pottery from these layers is not datable.

Existence of floors

West argued on the basis of structural, stratigraphic and finds evidence (in particular the evidence from the burnt hut 15) that the pits of the West Stow sunken-featured buildings had been floored over, and interpreted the primary fills as being for the most part material that had sifted through cracks in the floor boards (1985, 116–121). Powlesland has also stated that most of the sunken-featured buildings at West Heslerton were floored over (1990). Welch, however, challenged West's interpretation of the West Stow evidence, arguing that the plank floor he envisaged rested on the bottom of the pit and that the 'side walls' were in the revetment lining of the pit sides (1992, 21–5). Hamerow also argued for the direct use of hut floors at Mucking (Hamerow 1993, 11).

It has been argued (Welch 1992; Hamerow 1993, 14) that the sunken floor of the hut was used as a work floor to overcome the problems of restricted headroom imposed by the simple gable-post construction, giving the maximum amount of head room for the minimum quantity of raw materials. It is difficult to accept this explanation in the context of Barrow Hills, where it is clear from the mass of postholes covering the site as well as from the evidence of the post-built structures that the inhabitants possessed both ample supplies of timber and sophisticated woodworking skills. It seems improbable in the circumstances that economy of raw materials alone could have prompted the adoption of a building type which offered only a modest increase in head room against a severely restricted floor area and the effort and inconvenience of excavating a sizeable pit, and it seems necessary to seek some other, practical explanation for this form of construction. The balance of evidence suggests that the construction of a suspended floor over the pit was part of a larger ground-level construction which, if the West Stow reconstructions are accurate, could provide spacious accommodation (Tipper 2004, chapter 4).

Function

Many and various functions have been ascribed to sunken-featured buildings and these have been discussed in detail by Tipper (2004, chapter 8). Most have been ascribed on the basis of the material culture found within the pits. However, as we shall see, most of the material found in sunken-featured buildings is the result of tertiary deposition, with no direct relationship to the function of the buildings. The possible functions Tipper considers include dwellings, barns, byres, textile production sheds, stores (particularly grain stores), bake-houses, pottery workshops, loomweight manufactories and craft workshops.

The interpretation of these buildings as weaving sheds has been particularly persistent. Welch (1992, 28) notes 'the frequency with which clay loomweights, spindlewhorls and other items associated with textile production are found in *Grubenhaus* hollows'. He argues that weaving was one of the most important activities practised in them and that one of the functions of the pit was to ensure the damp atmosphere suitable for weaving. However, textile-related artefacts are among the commonest and most widely distributed artefacts on all sites, reflecting the fact that spinning in particular would have been an almost constant activity if a settlement was to be self-sufficient in textiles, and the output of many spinners would have been required to keep one loom intermittently busy. The sets of loomweights at Barton Court Farm (SFB 1190; Miles 1986, 16–17; see below, Gazetteer 5 Anglo-Saxon features at Barton Court Farm) and Sutton Courtenay (House XX; Leeds 1927, 74–5 and fig. 12) seem to have been stored or deposited on strings or sticks, rather than being set up as a loom, and the loomweights in the burnt SFB 15 at West Stow represent either three looms or sets of weights stored separately (West 1985, 23 and 138). This implies that some sunken-featured buildings were used to store or discard weaving equipment, and that weaving may have taken place in them, but not necessarily that all sunken-featured buildings were used for this purpose. One might also question whether dampness has ever been so unusual in Britain as to make it necessary to encourage it artificially.

Powlesland has identified many of the sunken-featured buildings at West Heslerton as grain stores on the basis of large quantities of carbonised grain (1990, 40), although as with the other contents this material does not relate to the primary function of the building. Storage for grain would obviously be an essential part of any farmstead. The following very approximate calculation indicates roughly how much grain could be stored threshed in sacks or baskets in an average 4 × 3 m sunken-featured building, assuming that the floor overlapped the pit edges by 0.5 m in each direction and that the presence of walls allowed an interior height of at least 2 m:

Average length 5 m (5.5 yds).
Average width 4 m (4.4 yds).
Estimated average height: 2 m (2.2 yds).
Therefore interior volume of average sunken-featured building = 53.24 yds^3.
Volume of 1 cwt of threshed wheat = c 1 yd^3.
Therefore storage capacity of average sunken-featured building = c 53.24 cwt.
      = 425.92 st.
      = 5962.88 lb.
      = 95,406.08 oz.
Approximate calorific value of 1 oz of grain = 90 kcal.
Calorific value of 95,406.08 oz = 8,586,547.2 kcal.
If average daily consumption of grain (bread and beer) per adult c 2000 kcal, then 8,586,547.2 kcal = 4293.27 days = 11.76 years.
If average daily consumption of grain (bread and beer) per adult c 3000 kcal, then 8,586,547.2 kcal = 2862.18 days = 7.84 years.

In other words, the average sunken-featured building might have been able to store enough grain to feed about 8 to 12 adults for one year, with an additional requirement for seed corn on top of this. It is perhaps more probable that grain was stored unthreshed, as it was in the later middle ages, but it has not proved possible to locate figures for the volume of unthreshed, hand-harvested grain, which would obviously occupy more space. It is notoriously difficult to establish how people may have occupied a structure of a given size (Millett and James 1983, 249), and hence to arrive at any reliable estimate of the population of a settlement and its possible storage requirements. Crude statistics calculated on the basis of so many occupants per m^2 fail to reflect the constantly changing nature of human populations, and even in periods when documentary records are available historical demography is fraught with difficulty. Jones's model of land use and population and the evidence of the cemetery indicate an adult population for Barton Court Farm of from 5 to 14 adults (see Chapter 2, Romano-British land use and the cemetery location). If the occupants of Barrow Hills were working the same area of land as the Romano-British occupants of Barton Court Farm, these figures suggest that at least two or three sunken-featured buildings per generation would have been needed for grain storage.

The four primary considerations for grain stores are that the walls should be able to withstand the considerable lateral thrust exerted by loose grain (approximately two-thirds of the vertical pressure), that the contents should be both dry and cool (usually achieved by allowing the free circulation of air by the use of a floor supported on low vented walls) and that the structure should be resistant to attacks by pests. It may be that the underfloor space in sunken-featured buildings was designed to improve ventilation and protect against damp, and possibly, if the floor overhung the cavity, to deter rodents.

In the light of what is known of the use of buildings in pre-industrial agricultural societies it seems more than probable that sunken-featured buildings were used for many different purposes, including grain and other food storage, craftworking and accommodation. The apparent existence of two sizes may indicate some functional differentiation. Sunken-featured buildings are rare on chalk sites, where their place was presumably filled by post-built structures.

Tipper has reviewed the distinction in function between post-built structures and sunken-featured buildings (2004, 182–3). At West Stow the excavator described the seven post-built structures as 'halls', focal points for family units, and argued that the sunken-featured buildings formed groups around each hall and performed complementary functions. According to Hamerow there was no evidence for this sort of relationship between individual posthole buildings and sunken-featured buildings at Mucking. At West Heslerton, on the other hand, there is clear spatial differentiation between a zone dominated by posthole buildings, interpreted as housing, and a zone dominated by *Grubenhäuser*, interpreted as a craft and industry area. While not disputing the general interpretation of posthole buildings as dwellings with *Grubenhäuser* forming ancillary buildings on early Anglo-Saxon settlement sites, Tipper

notes that if the reconstruction of *Grubenhäuser* as substantial ground level buildings is correct they would have rivalled some 'halls' in size, and suggests that the rigid functional distinction between the two building types should be reconsidered.

At Barrow Hills there is no clear relationship between the rectangular post-built structures and the sunken-featured buildings. It is difficult not to interpret the sunken-featured buildings in close proximity to post-built structures as related to them, for example SFBs 4–7, 15 and 19 around the cluster of buildings and fencelines in the centre of the site, SFBs 14 and 17/18 near PBS 6 and SFBs 23, 24 and 45 near PBSs 7, 8 and 11. However, there are also rectangular post-built structures with no adjacent sunken-featured buildings, such as PBS 10, and sunken-featured buildings with no adjacent post-built structures, like SFBs 30 and 32–4.

Building lifespans

The lifespan of sunken-featured buildings and timber halls would have depended on the nature and quality of the materials used, especially the timber, and on how carefully the buildings (particularly their roofs) were maintained. This in turn is likely to have been related to their function, since main dwellings tend to be better maintained and less frequently replaced than outhouses, workshops and stores. Estimates vary between 35 years for substantial halls (Hamerow 1993, 90) to 40–50 years, on the assumption that the main hall farmhouse would be rebuilt once every generation (Welch 1992, 29), and 20–25 years for sunken-featured buildings (Welch 1992, 30). The West Stow reconstructions are still in good condition after 20 years and may well exceed this estimate. It seems likely that on well drained soil the lifetime of a substantial, well maintained post-built structure of oak might also have exceeded these estimates, and as will be seen in Chapter 7 there is evidence that this was the case at Barrow Hills.

ANGLO-SAXON INHUMATIONS

Two inhumations datable to the Anglo-Saxon period were found during the 1983–5 excavations. One, Grave 5004 on the south-west side of pond barrow 4866, contained the south-west/north-east inhumation of an adult female over 45 years of age accompanied by a small iron knife, iron buckle and bronze pin of late 6th- or 7th-century type with traces of mineralised cloth (Fig. 3.104). The other, grave 4562, was a much disturbed east-west newborn infant burial in a shallow cut in the bottom of the south side of SFB 32. There were no grave goods.

PITS

Only a few pits could be dated to the Anglo-Saxon period, and these are listed in the gazetteer. They tended to form complexes of shallow, irregular pits and scoops, like 4786 and 4798 near SFB 43 or 414–8 in barrow 13.

ANGLO-SAXON FILLS OF PREHISTORIC BARROW DITCHES

Anglo-Saxon material was found in the ditches of the Neolithic oval barrow, barrows 1, 12, 13, segmented ring ditch 2123 and in the uppermost level of pond barrow 4866. There is also evidence for deliberate levelling of ring ditch 801 in this period. For illustrations see Barclay and Halpin 1999, chapter 4.

Saxon pottery was found in upper fills of the inner (2060) and outer ditches (2061) of the oval barrow, concentrated at the north corner and in the centre of the north-east side of the outer ditch. Very little Saxon material occurred in the remaining ditch sections. These two concentrations may represent deliberate dumping from activity outside the area of the 1983–5 excavations. No other finds or animal bone are recorded from these dumps, but this may be the result of accidental loss.

Barrow 1 was on the east of the excavated area. Layers 2 and 3 produced Anglo-Saxon pottery, animal bone and small finds, including a clay pipe fragment from layer 2. Finds densities were very low and the ditch was not completely excavated.

Layers 1, 2, 3 and 4 of the outer ditch (601) of barrow 12 produced Anglo-Saxon pottery, animal bone and small finds. Layer 1 was topsoil; layers 2 and 3 represent deliberate Anglo-Saxon dumping, with some plough disturbance of layer 2. Layers 2 and 3 both contained post-medieval finds, including a clay pipe fragment from layer 2 and a fragment of post-medieval glass from layer 3. SFB 26 lay between the inner ditch 602 and the more substantial outer ditch 601.

Layers 2 and 3 of the ditch of barrow 13 (401) contained Anglo-Saxon pottery, animal bone and small finds. Plough and animal disturbance extended into layer 4, which produced a clay pipe fragment and a piece of iron bar. A series of intercutting pits 414–8 in the north-west quadrant of the barrow yielded Anglo-Saxon finds, pottery from 414 and a loomweight from 416. The ditch was cut by two SFBs, 23 and 24.

A small amount of Saxon pottery was found in the upper fill of the north-west segment of ring ditch 2123. Just inside the north-east segment was a shallow pit whose fill contained a considerable quantity of ?oak charcoal. This provided a radiocarbon determination of cal 390–600 (1570 ± 50 BP; BM-2705), suggesting that the feature belongs to the period of Anglo-Saxon occupation of the site. A sample of the fill contained a wheat grain and an oat grain (Moffett 1999).

A single Romano-British sherd, a small quantity of Saxon sherds and the almost complete skeleton of a fairly large adult dog (*c* 590 mm shoulder height) were recovered from the uppermost level of pond barrow 4866. The cut of the Anglo-Saxon grave 5004 on the south-west side of pond barrow 4866 was shallow, and the grave may have been inserted in a bank, which was subsequently denuded by ploughing.

Although there were no Anglo-Saxon finds from ring ditch 801, layer 3 of SFB 14 probably represents deliberate backfill of the ditch, either derived from the slighting of a barrow mound or redeposited from the digging of SFBs 17–18 as an attempt to level the ground surface (see Barclay and Halpin 1999).

Gazetteer 1: Post-built Structures

By Richard Chambers and Ellen McAdam

INTRODUCTION

A total of 22 post-built structures were identified at Barrow Hills and are listed in this gazetteer (see site plan, Fig 7.11). The structures were not well preserved and the problems of identification are discussed in the introduction to this chapter. Each entry gives the post-built structure (PBS) number assigned during the second phase of post-excavation, the grid reference of the centre of the feature, Figure number(s), original site plan number (for ease of reference to the archive) and orientation. Wherever appropriate, dimensions are given in the format length x width. The measurements were taken from the 1:50 site plans drawn up after excavation. Each PBS is illustrated in plan at a scale of 1:100. Very few of the postholes of the PBSs contained finds, but details of these have been included under the relevant structure.

PBS 1

Grid reference: SU 51314 98151; Figure 3.3; Site plan: E6 Orientation: ENE/WSW Dimensions: 7.0 m × 3.5 m

Description

PBS 1 was the northernmost and best preserved structure of the group of five PBSs to the north of the Romano-British cemetery (Figs 7.3 and 7.11). The long walls were constructed of *c* seven pairs of substantial, evenly spaced single postholes. The postholes of the end walls were slighter and there are no definite corner posts. Some of the posts appeared to have been replaced and some were affected by animal disturbance. The most probable position for the doors is between postholes 1436 and 1437 on the north side and 1512/3 and 1510/1 on the south side; 1512 may have been a replacement for 1513 and 1511 for 1510. There may also have been a door in the west end between 1619 and 1700. There is a confused arrangement of postholes and stakeholes in this area which may represent another structure.

Finds

Posthole 1440
Reused Roman sherd no. 37 SF 1456 Diameter 90 mm. Almost complete cut down foot ring base in Oxford red/brown colour coated fabric 3. (Not illustrated)

PBS 2

Grid reference: SU 51318 98148; Figure 3.3; Site plan: E6 Orientation: NNW/SSE Dimensions: 4.0 m × 3.5 m

Description

PBS 2 was positioned at right-angles to PBS 1, about 1 m from the east end of the south wall. The east wall was marked by a line of large postholes, but the other walls were less well preserved.

PBS 3

Grid reference: SU 51309 98147; Figure 3.3; Site plan: E6 Orientation: N/S Dimensions: 4.2 m × 1.8 m

Description

PBS 3 was a small, poorly preserved structure approximately 2 m from the west end of PBS 1 and at right-angles to it. Posthole 1722 was the only trace of an end wall. There is a possible doorway between 1702/3 and 1708.

PBS 4

Grid reference: SU 51310 98142; Figure 3.3; Site plan: E6 Orientation: NNW/SSE Dimensions: 3.2 m × 2.7 m

Description

PBS 4 was a small, poorly preserved structure. The east side more or less continued the alignment of the east side of PBS 3, but PBS 4 extended further to the west, close to the north-east end of SFB 5. As with PBS 3, there was no trace of the end walls.

PBS 5

Grid reference: SU 51316 98136; Figure 3.3; Site plan: E6 Orientation: NNE/SSW Dimensions: *c* 9.0 m × 3.5 m

Description

PBS 5 was a poorly preserved structure extending southwards from the south side of the open area bordered by PBSs 1–4. The plan south of postholes 1425 and 1431 is reasonably coherent, with long walls consisting of paired posts and weak corners, although it is confused by rebuilding or another structure at the south end. The north end lies in what appears to have been an area of particularly severe damage, but the large posthole 1433 lines up with the west wall, giving an overall length of about 9 m.

Posthole 1430 cuts the north-west corner of the Romano-British grave 1013, and the south end of the structure is sited over the Romano-British infant burial 1011.

PBS 6

Grid reference: SU 51302 98090; Figure 3.4; Site plan: D/E7 Orientation: NE/SW Dimensions: 7.5 m × 5.0 m

Description

PBS 6 was situated to the east of ring ditch 801. The long walls are reasonably distinct, with several sets of paired postholes, although the postholes of the south wall seem to have been more substantial than those on the north. As usual, there is relatively little trace of the end walls.

Finds

Posthole 1186

413 SF 1182 **Rotary quern** Length 200 mm. Fragment of coarse sandstone conglomerate, red and feldspathic, Upper Old Red Sandstone from Welsh border/ Forest of Dean. (Not illustrated)

Posthole 3765

414 SF 1181 **Rotary quern** Length 75 mm. Fragment of coarse calcareous grit with gastropods, Corallian. (Not illustrated)

PBS 7

Grid reference: SU 51393 98074; Figure 3.4; Site plan: H8 Orientation: ENE/WSW Dimensions: >7.0 m × 3.5 m

Description

There was extensive animal activity in the area of PBS 7 and the plan of this structure or structures is not clear. There seem to be two approximately parallel lines of postholes running ENE-WSW (3816/21 to 3827/38 on the north and 3806–3813 on the south). Several of the postholes on the northern side were double, but the postholes in the southern row were disturbed by animal burrows. There is no sign of end walls and it is not certain that these two lines were related as a structure, although the spacing of 3.5 m between them supports this interpretation.

PBS 8

Grid reference: SU 51388 98083; Figure 3.4; Site plan: H7/8 Orientation: NE/SW Dimensions: 8.0 m × 3.5 m

Description

PBS 8 was the best preserved rectangular post-built structure at Barrow Hills. The long walls were represented by predominantly double postholes, with posts at the south-west and south-east corners. The west end was represented by three small single postholes and the east end by one double posthole.

The most likely position for a doorway was between 3853/4 and 3841/50 on the south side, but there was no obvious gap on the north side.

PBS 9

Grid reference: SU 51322 98062; Figure 3.5; Site plan: E8 Orientation: NE/SW Dimensions: c 5.0 m × 2.5 m

Description

PBS 9 was a small, narrow structure represented by ten postholes which may have formed three sides of an irregular rectangle or some other plan.

PBS 10

Grid reference: SU 51425 98107; Figure 3.5; Site plan: I/J7 Orientation: NE/SW Dimensions: 7.5 m × 4.2 m

Description

PBS 10 was the westernmost post-built structure identified, to the south-east of pond barrow 4866. The plan is not clear. The north-west long wall (5102 to 4910?) was fairly substantial, with at least one double posthole, but the south-east side (4158 to 4961?) was considerably less so.

PBS 11

Grid reference: SU 51375 98080; Figure 3.5; Site plan: H7/8, G7/8 Orientation: NE/SW Dimensions: c 5.5 m × 4.5 m

Description

There was extensive animal activity in the area of PBS 11, with an incoherent mass of postholes and animal burrows at the north-east end. The long walls consisted of mainly single postholes, some of which were paired. If this was originally the full extent of the building then the paired posts include four corner posts. There was little trace of the end walls. There appears to have been a doorway between 3977 and 3980 on the south-east side.

PBS 12

Grid reference: SU 51387 98124; Figure 3.5; Site plan: H6 Orientation: NNE/SSW Dimensions: 4.2 m × 2.5 m

Description

PBS 12 was an irregular structure north-east of barrow 13 consisting of two lines of postholes 4980 to 4987 and 4937 to 4980 approximately at right-angles to each other.

PBS 13

Grid reference: SU 51296 98145; Figure 3.6; Site plan: D6 Orientation: NE/SW Dimensions: 4.7 m × 3.0 m

Description

PBS 13 was an approximately D-shaped structure, open on the south-east side facing SFB 4 and *c* 1.5 m north-west of it.

FENCELINES AND OTHER STRUCTURES

PBS 14

Grid reference: SU 51327 98192; Figure 3.6; Site plan: E/F 5 Orientation: NE/SW Dimensions: 10.0 m × *c* 4 m apart.

Description

PBS 14 consisted of two approximately parallel lines of postholes in the northern part of the site, both discontinuous. The northernmost line is on the same alignment as PBS 15.

PBS 15

Grid reference: SU 51313 98185; Figure 3.7; Site plan: E5 Orientation: NE/SW Dimensions: 9.5 m

Description

PBS 15 is a line of postholes on the same alignment as the north part of PBS 14 but *c* 10 m to the south-west. If these features were part of the same structure, it extended over a distance of 20 m.

PBS 16

Grid reference: SU 51324 98155; Figure 3.7; Site plan: E/F6 Orientation: *c* NE/SW Dimensions: north line 7.0 m south line 9.0 m Distance apart 2.5–6.5 m

Description

PBS 16 was situated immediately to the north-east of PBS1. The structure or structures consisted of two curving lines of postholes which together formed a funnel shape, possibly an animal pen or two unrelated fencelines.

PBS 17

Grid reference: SU 51312 98092; Figure 3.7; Site plan: E7 Orientation: ENE/WSW Dimensions: 5.2 m

Description

PBS 17 consisted of six postholes in a row between PBS 6 and the Romano-British cemetery, possibly a fenceline.

PBS 18

Grid reference: SU 51314 98088; Figure 3.7; Site plan: E7 Orientation: NE/SW Dimensions: 6.0 m

Description

PBS 18 was about 5 m south of and parallel to PBS 17 and consisted of four substantial postholes in a row, possibly a fenceline, with another, 3778, *c* 1.75 m to the south of 3777.

PBS 19

Grid reference: SU 51304 98156; Figure 3.8; Site plan: E6 Orientation: NE/SW Dimensions: *c* 8.0 m × 3.5 m

Description

PBS 19 describes the area of postholes to the north-east of SFB 7. There may have been a structure or structures in this area cutting or cut by SFB 7, or even associated with it, but it is not possible to reconstruct any plan.

PBS 20

Grid reference: SU 51290 98147; Figure 3.8; Site plan: D6 Orientation: ENE/WSW turning to NNW/SSE Dimensions: ENE section 18.0 m NNW section 9.5 m

Description

PBS 20 comprised two approximately parallel lines of postholes 1784–3624 and 1744–3614, aligned WSW for about 15 m before turning at right-angles to run NNW to enclose an area of about 9.5 × 10.0 m to the west and north of SFB 7 which was devoid of postholes. It is not possible to determine whether the two lines were contemporary or one was a replacement for the other.

PBS 21

Grid reference: SU 51350 98120; Figure 3.9; Site plan: F/G 6, F7 Orientation: NE/SW Dimensions: *c* 30 m × 8.5 m

Description

PBS 21 was an area of postholes and animal disturbance which contained one or more structures. The features in this area were drawn in plan but not in section, and only grid references and context numbers were recorded on the context sheets. It is therefore impossible to distinguish postholes from animal burrows and it is difficult to reconstruct the plan or plans with any certainty.

At least four, possibly related, structures can be discerned. There was a northern line 4396 to 4284 which ran NE/SW for over 14 m, and the Bronze Age cremation pit 4321 containing the cremation of a subadult covered by an inverted Collared Urn was approximately on this alignment (Barclay and Halpin 1999, 175–83). A parallel line 4380 to 4318 ran NE/SW for 9 m *c* 5 m to the south. Finally, there were two roughly L-shaped arrangements, one at the southern end of the fencelines and a larger one at the northern end. The plan of the southern arrangement is more distinct. Each appeared to consist of four very approximately parallel rows of NE/SW postholes (tentatively, 4364 to 4342, 4360 to 4341, 4336 to 4329 and 4337 to 4336 in the south, and 4303 to 4259, 4307 to 4252, 4320 to 4253 and 4257 to 4270 in the north). The nature and function of these structures are obscure: they are dated to the Anglo-Saxon period by a small quantity of pottery (see below).

PBS 22

Grid reference: SU 51332 98102; Figure 3.10; Site plan: F7 Orientation: *c* NE/SW Dimensions: *c* 15 m × 5.5 m

Description

This was an area of postholes and animal disturbance to the south-west of PBS 21 which almost certainly concealed the plan of one or more structures. The features in this area were drawn in plan but not in section, and only grid references and context numbers were recorded on the context sheets. As in PBS 21, it is therefore impossible to distinguish postholes from animal burrows and no plan can be reconstructed. There was a single sherd of Anglo-Saxon pottery from one of the postholes.

Pottery

It was impossible to date any of the post-built structures on the basis of the pottery. Few of the buildings produced any pottery, and none any decorated wares. The assemblages were too small to allow even the remotest speculation with regard to chronology. The pottery from the PBSs is summarised below; all other PBSs were aceramic.

Pottery occurrence per post-built structure by weight (in g) per fabric type per structure.

PBS no.	F1	F2	F3	Total wt (g)
1	0	62	2	64
5	0	12	20	32
8	0	0	2	2
21	32	0	32	64
22	0	0	3	3

Gazetteer 2: The Sunken-featured Buildings

By Richard Chambers and Ellen McAdam

INTRODUCTION

A total of 45 *Grubenhäuser* or sunken-featured buildings were recorded at Barrow Hills and are listed in this gazetteer. Each entry gives the sunken-featured building (SFB) number assigned in order of excavation during the first phase of post-excavation, the context number, grid reference of the centre of the feature, Figure number(s), original site plan number (for ease of reference to the archive) and orientation. The descriptions of the sunken-featured buildings are quoted from site context records with only minor editorial changes, and interpretative text, if any, follows the layer descriptions. The site records state that virtually all the sunken-featured buildings had been disturbed by burrowing animals, and disturbance is mentioned only in those cases in which it appeared to be unusually severe.

Four dimensions are given for each sunken-featured building: length at surface, the overall length of the pit as it was first defined; distance between postholes, from centre to centre of the postholes in the ends of the sunken-featured buildings; width at surface; and depth, taken from the top of the natural gravel.

Wherever possible the measurements were taken from the 1:20 plans and sections made on site of the individual features during or soon after excavation. The plans prepared for publication were based on the 1:50 A4 site plans which were drawn up after excavation and slight discrepancies may therefore exist. Each sunken-featured building is illustrated in plan and section at a scale of 1:50. In some cases sections have been lost or are unintelligible, because they cannot be related to the context and finds records. They appear to record all patches of colour variation in the gravel fills. These sunken-featured buildings are illustrated by profiles only.

The gazetteer entries also include a summary and catalogue of the finds and pottery. Objects are referred to by their number in the catalogue prepared during the first phase of post-excavation by John Hedges, which lists all the Anglo-Saxon finds arranged by material and function. A copy of this catalogue is lodged with the archive. The small find number assigned in the field is also given, prefixed by SF. In the illustrations, glass and copper alloy objects are shown at 1:1 and all other materials at 1:2. Pottery is illustrated at 1:3. The finds were catalogued by Barbara Ford and pottery by Paul Blinkhorn.

SFB 1

Context 1005; Grid reference: 51309 98104; Figures 3.11–13; Site plan: E7; Orientation: E/W; Length at surface: 3.05 m; Distance between postholes: 2.70 m; Width: 2.60 m; Depth: 0.4 m

Description

SFB 1 lay on the west edge of the Romano-British cemetery. The pit was slightly irregular on the north side, with an uneven floor and sloping sides. There were three large postholes, 1089 in the centre of the east end, a shallow impression 1056 in the centre of the west end and 1086, which projects beyond the west end. The posthole 1088 in the north-west corner may also have been associated with this structure.

The fill consisted of three layers:

1 medium brown sandy loam with 40% gravel, containing medieval and post-medieval pot and tile.
2 medium grey/brown sandy loam with 10% gravel, containing bone, pottery, burnt limestone, burnt daub and heat-cracked quartzite pebbles.
3 medium brown sandy loam with 60% medium gravel; seems to represent silting from the sides while the pit was open.

Posthole 1086 may have replaced 1056. Since the post pit of 1089 appeared as a different filling from 2 it may have remained in situ while the main layer of pit fill accumulated, but 1086 had clearly contained the same sequence of fills as the pit.

Finds

Ten objects were recovered. These included a hobnail, 242, and a fragment of a flask, 291, both of Roman date. The glass fragment has secondary polishing and has been reused at some later date. There are also a modified complete base and a cut half base of two reused Roman pottery vessels.

Number 158 is a fragment of a very corroded copper alloy pin, the head of which is missing. 192, a fragment of a rod with a hooked terminal, is probably a handle from a bucket or cauldron. An iron handle of this type has been found on a copper alloy cauldron from the Anglo-Saxon cemetery at Morning Thorpe, Grave 200 (Green *et al.* 1987, 87, fig. 356 Ai). A similar complete iron handle was found on a bucket from Grave 27 at Alton, Hampshire (Evison 1988, 78, fig. 31).

Weaving equipment included a fragment of an annular loomweight, 452, a type generally dated to the early Saxon period (Dunning *et al.* 1959, 24), and a bone pin beater, 356, used for separating the warp threads with a warp-weighted loom. Other items of bone include a pig's metapodial which has been pierced, probably for use as a dress fastener. Such toggles are common on sites from the Iron Age through to the medieval period. Part of an antler beam recovered from layer 2 is waste, left over from antler-working.

Layer 1

242 SF 334   **Iron hobnail** Length 20 mm Domed head and rectangular cross-sectioned shank (Not illustrated)

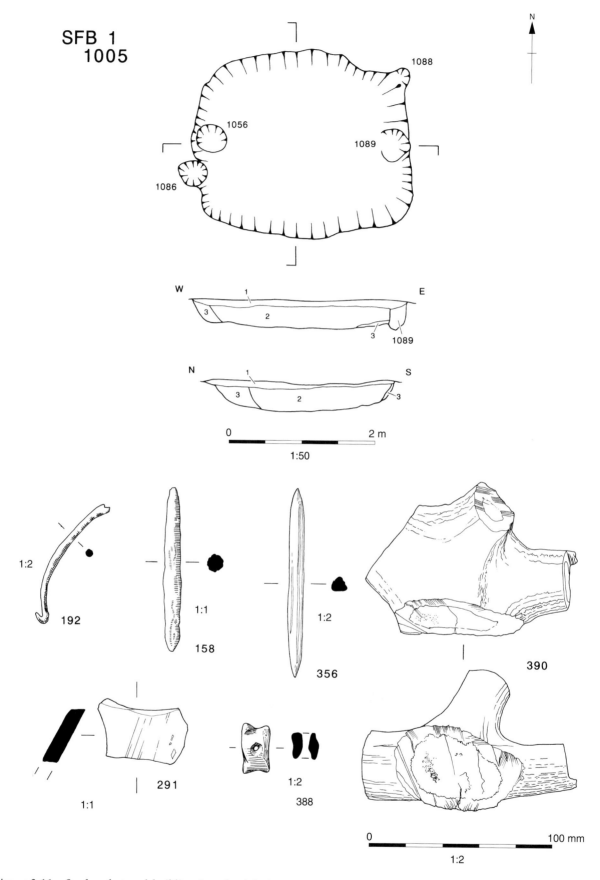

Figure 3.11 Sunken-featured building 1 and artefacts.

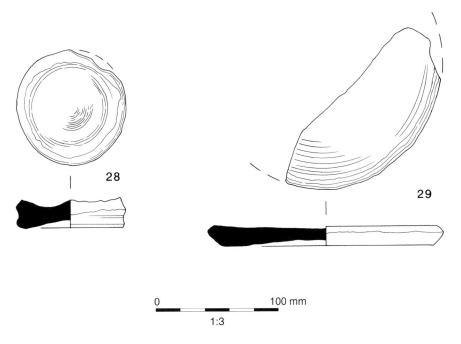

0   100 mm

1:3

Figure 3.12   Sunken-featured building 1 artefacts continued.

192 SF 228   **Iron handle** Length 77 mm. Part of a rod with circular cross-section, turned up at end to form a hooked terminal.

291 SF 329   **Vessel glass** Thickness 4 mm. Pale green transparent fragment. Possibly part of the neck of a flask. One edge has secondary polish extending beyond the true lip of the outer edge. Scratched outer edge. Late Roman.

Layer 2

158 SF 26   **Copper alloy pin** Length 45 mm, diameter 4.5 mm. Pointed at one end, head missing.

356 SF 19   **Bone pin beater** Length 105 mm; diameter 9 mm. Highly polished. Triangular cross-section. Tapers to a point at both ends.

388 SF 1526 **Bone toggle** Length 28 mm, width 16 mm. Astragalus, probably from a sheep? Perforated.

390 SF 230   **Antler waste** Fragment from a beam. Sawn at both ends. Two tines also removed by sawing. Sawn through almost to the edge and then broken off leaving small burrs.

452 SF 341   **Annular fired clay loomweight** Diameter 120 mm. Fragment approx 20% Surface roughly smoothed. Estimated total weight 395.5 g (Not illustrated).

Reused Roman sherd no. 28 SF 1463   Diameter 60 mm. Cut down base in greyware from a small beaker or jar, fabric 2.

Reused Roman sherd no. 29 SF 1453   Diameter 120 mm. Cut down half of a flat greyware base, fabric 4.

Pottery **tpq** *early-mid 6th century?*

Pottery occurrence per layer by fabric type.

Layer/ fabric	F1	F2	F3	F4	F6	% mineral	% chaff	Total wt (g)
1	64	71	240	12	79	67.8	32.2	466
2	364	1362	877	20 g	60 g	47.0	53.0	2683
3	1	0	0	0	0	100	0	1
Total wt (g)	429	1433	1117	32	139			3146
Mean sherd wt	8.8	37.7	20.3	8.0	19.9			

Pottery occurrence per quadrant and layer, all fabrics.

Layer/ quadrant	A	B	C	D	Total wt (g)
1	122	36	171	137	466
2	1590	540	195	358	2683
3	0	0	1	0	1
Total wt (g)	1712	576	367	495	3150
% of total	54.4	18.3	11.6	15.7	

EVE: Jars = 1.60; Bowls = 0.21.

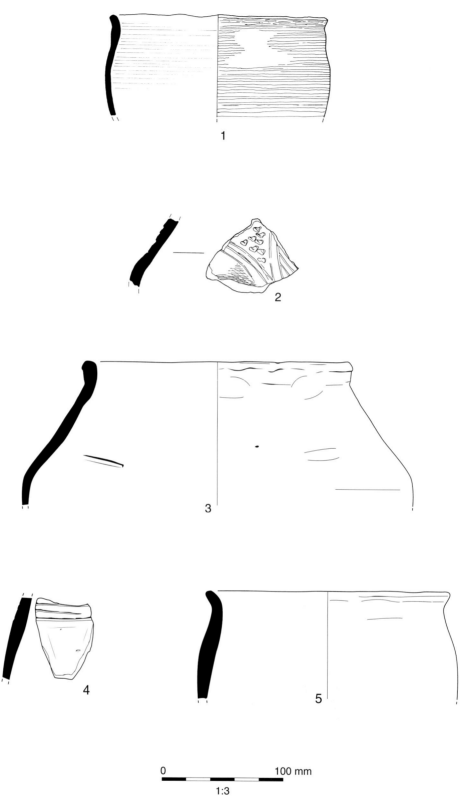

Figure 3.13   Sunken-featured building 1 pottery.

Four incised sherds: (A/1, F3, 16 g; A/2, F6, 16 g; B/2, F1, 20 g; D/1, F3, 6 g).
One sherd, bossed, incised and stabbed, (D/2, F2, 56 g).
One stamped sherd (D/1, F1, 4 g).

Cross fits: A/2 = C/1, A/2 = C/2.

Illustrations

3.13.1   Rim sherd from jar. Black fabric with burnished surfaces.

3.13.2   Bossed and incised sherd. Black fabric with brown outer, both surfaces burnished.

3.13.3   Profile through large shouldered jar. Black fabric with burnished outer surface on upper body.

3.13.4   Incised sherd. Black fabric with burnished surface.

3.13.5   Rim sherd from large jar. Black fabric with brown smoothed surfaces.

The overall decorative scheme of the bossed sherd (Fig. 3.13.2) is not entirely clear, but it appears similar to two vessels from Cambridgeshire (Myres 1977, fig. 295 no. 265 and fig. 310 no. 2712). Myres dates such vessels to the first half of the 6th century.

SFB 2

Context 1053; Grid reference: 51300 98119; Figures 3.14–15; Site plan: D7/E7; Orientation: NE/SW; Length at surface: 3.80 m; Distance between postholes: 3.40 m; Width: 3.02 m; Depth: 0.40 m

Description

SFB 2 was 10.0 m west of the Romano-British cemetery, *c* 20 m north-west of SFB 1. It lay directly under a medieval plough furrow. The pit was rectangular, with main postholes 1081 in the centre of the east end and 1075 (for which 1080 may be a replacement) in the centre of the west end and possible corner posts 1062, 1226, 1077 and 1156. The sides were sloping and irregular. In all, 35 postholes and stakeholes are associated with 1053, many positioned along the south-east side. There was no evidence of occupation or a floor surface on the base of the pit.

The fill consisted of four layers, of which layers 1 to 3 were similar in colour and texture, but the colour lightened progressively towards the base of the feature, the gravel content decreased and the fill became more silty and friable. The fill was stratified and the differences between the layers noticeable. Layer 3 continued into postholes 1075 and 1081, suggesting that the main posts 1081 and 1075 were removed before the pit was backfilled. The fill of some of the 35 postholes and stakeholes was overlain by layers 3 and 4, indicating that they had gone out of use before the pit was filled in. They may represent a pit lining.

1   dark brown sandy loam with 40% gravel, containing bone and pottery.

2   medium dark brown sandy loam with 20% gravel containing pottery, bone and pieces of limestone, burnt limestone and quartzite.

3   medium to light red brown loamy silt with 5% pea gravel, containing pottery and bone.

4   pea gravel.

Finds

Finds included a small plain dome-headed stud, 152, of a type commonly found from Roman through to post-medieval sites, a fragment of an iron nail, 253, and an iron tool 207, possibly part of an awl, for piercing holes in leather. An almost complete awl, still with its antler handle intact, was found in SFB 56 at West Stow (West 1985, 45, fig. 188.1). 375 is a fragment of a pierced pig fibula pin, of a type common on this site.

The glass globular drawn triple bead, 289, is of a type which occurs from the 2nd to the 6th centuries (Boon 1977). A similar bead has been recovered from the cemetery at West Stow (West 1985, 71–74, T15, fig. 275.19).

Layer 1

207 SF 27   **Iron awl** Length 108 mm. Circular in cross-section changing to square cross-section and tapering to a point.

253 SF 151   **Iron nail** Length 30 mm. Shank fragment. (Not illustrated)

Layer 2

152 SF 206   **Copper alloy stud** Diameter 7 mm. Domed head. Broken shank with rectangular cross-section.

375 SF 323   **Bone pin** Length 37 mm. Made from a pig fibula perforated at proximal end, with modified head. Polished. Tip missing.

Layer 3

289 SF 207   **Glass bead** Length 12 mm; Diameter 4.5 mm. Blue, opaque. Cylindrical with three unequal segments along its length. Straight hole. Iridescent.

Pottery **tpq** *5th/6th century?*

Pottery occurrence per layer by fabric type.

Layer/ Fabric	F1	F2	F3	F4	F6	% mineral	% chaff	Total wt (g)
1	72	240	293	15	19	59.5	40.5	639
2	117	965	188	5	38	23.6	76.4	1313
3	0	175	31	0	102	10.1	89.9	308
Total wt (g)	189	1380	512	20	159			2260
Mean sherd wt	7.9	27.1	13.8	5.0	17.7			

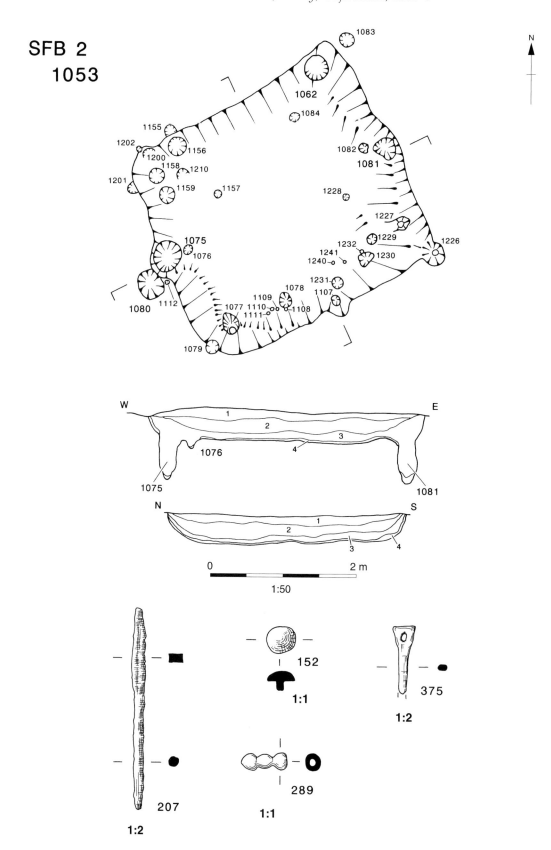

Figure 3.14   Sunken-featured building 2 and artefacts.

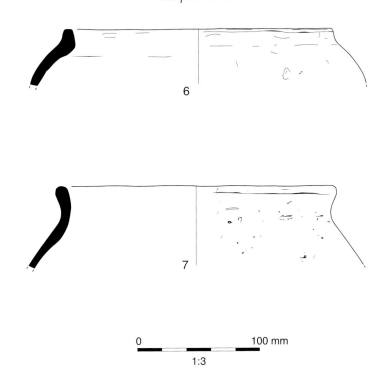

Figure 3.15   *Sunken-featured building 2 pottery.*

Pottery occurrence per quadrant and layer, all fabrics.

Layer/quadrant	A	B	C	D	Total wt (g)
1	320	203	107	9	639
2	486	432	312	83	1313
3	0	217	0	91	308
Total wt (g)	806	852	419	183	2260
% of total	35.7	37.7	18.5	8.1	

EVE: Jars = 0.62; Bowls = 0.04.

Two incised sherds (B/2, F2, 36 g; B/2, F6, 22 g).

Illustrations

3.15.6   Rim sherd from large jar. Black fabric with burnished surfaces.
3.15.7   Light grey fabric with black smoothed surfaces.

SFB 3

Context 1061; Grid reference: 51294 98108; Figures 3.16–17; Site plan: D7 Orientation: NE/SW; Length at surface: 4.0 m; Distance between postholes: 3.10 m; Width: 3.28 m; Depth: 0.72 m.

Description

SFB 3 was *c* 10.0 m south-west of SFB 2, west of the Romano-British cemetery. The pit was an irregular rectangle with a protrusion at the east end and bulging edges. There were two postholes 1282 and 1242 at the east and west ends respectively, possibly compound and/or recut, and the posthole 1516 to the south-west of 1242 may also have been associated with the structure. The sides of the pit were almost vertical. There was no evidence of a floor or occupation surface; the base of the pit was conglomerate and gravel.

1   dark red brown loam with 40% gravel, containing bone, pottery and worked flint.
2   medium grey brown friable loam with 60% gravel containing pottery and bone.
3   light grey buff silt with 80% gravel.
4   pea gravel.

The pit fill continued into the recut of 1242.

Finds

There were two reused Roman pottery vessels, 30 and 31, both cut down bases. 215 is a possible latch lifter used to raise a latch or bolt, although it is unlike Roman latch lifters. It may be a lift key used in conjunction with a tumbler lock like those from Graves 134 and 369 at Morning Thorpe (Green *et al.* 1987, fig. 343.F, 428.Ui). The iron ferrule, 183, is probably the butt from a staff or spear. Another example comes from SFB 11 (see Fig. 3.33, no. 184). Many Anglo-Saxon graves have produced similar iron ferrules in association with spearheads, for example Grave 24, Fonaby, Lincs (Cook 1981, 28, fig. 27) and Abingdon Grave 49 (Leeds and Harden 1936, 40, pl XVIII). An iron fitting, 224, is of uncertain use. 332, a tooth segment from a comb, is similar to the many combs of 5th- to 7th-century date from the site (see for example Fig. 3.23, no. 3.19).

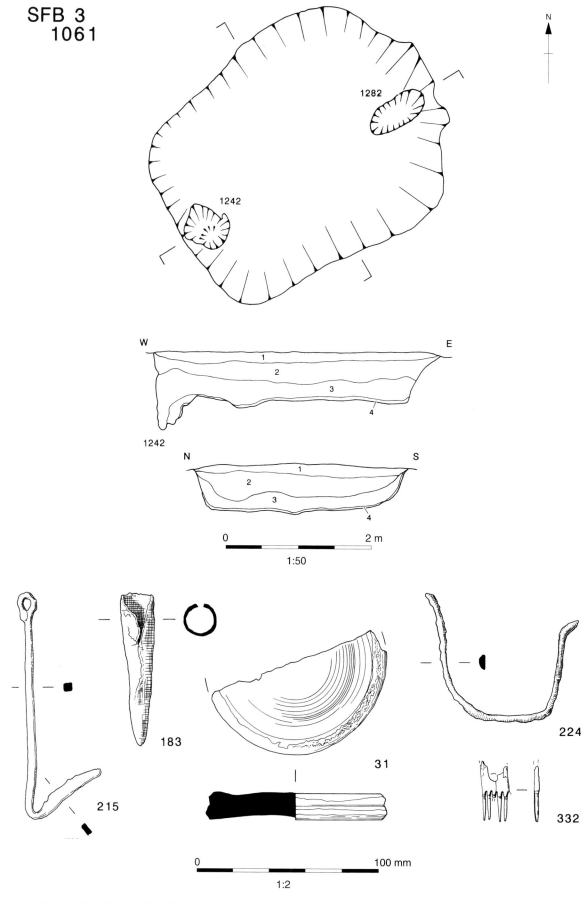

Figure 3.16   Sunken-featured building 3 and artefacts.

There are two deposits of slag. Number 607 is a planoconvex slag which has been furnace-cooled and is probably a 'hearth bottom' from a smith's hearth. Number 608 is in a mostly vitrified state and has been formed by the interaction of the lining of a hearth or furnace with bulk slag.

Layer 1

Reused Roman sherd no. 30 SF 1452 Diameter 45 mm. Cut down half of a foot-ring base of a beaker in Oxford red/brown colour-coated, fabric 3. (Not illustrated).

Layer 2

215 SF 33	**Key/latch lifter** Length 120 mm. Stem has a square cross-section and hooked terminal. The bit is a knifelike projection bent up at an angle of 45°.
183 SF 29	**Iron ferrule** Length 80 mm; max diameter 18 mm. Hollow conical shape made from a rolled sheet with slightly overlapping edges. Closed at pointed end.

Reused Roman sherd no. 31 SF 1455 Diameter 100 mm. Cutdown half of a flat base in greyware, fabric 4.

Layer 3

224 SF 32	**Iron fitting** Length 68 mm. U-shaped, D-sectioned bar with out-splayed ends.
332 SF 219	**Antler comb** Fragment of a tooth segment with 4 teeth per cm. Remains of one rivet hole.

607 SF 1653	**Slag, plano-convex fragment** (not illustrated)
609 SF 1339	**Slag, lining reaction product** (not illustrated)

Pottery tpq *5th/6th century?*

Pottery occurrence per layer by fabric type.

Layer/Fabric	F1	F2	F3	F6	% mineral	% chaff	Total wt (g)
1	122	0	67	15	92.6	7.4	204
2	314	539	47	0	40.1	59.9	900
3	44	126	31	0	37.3	62.7	201
4	116	50	0	11	65.5	34.5	177
Total wt (g)	596	715	145	26			1482
Mean sherd wt	10.3	16.3	9.7	8.7			

Pottery occurrence per quadrant and layer, all fabrics.

Layer/quadrant	A	B	C	D	Total wt (g)
1	30	142	32	0	204
2	188	248	279	185	900
3	20	97	56	28	201
4	0	177	0	0	177
Total wt (g)	238	664	367	213	1482
% of total	16.1	44.7	24.8	14.4	

EVE: Jars = 0.72; Bowls = 0.

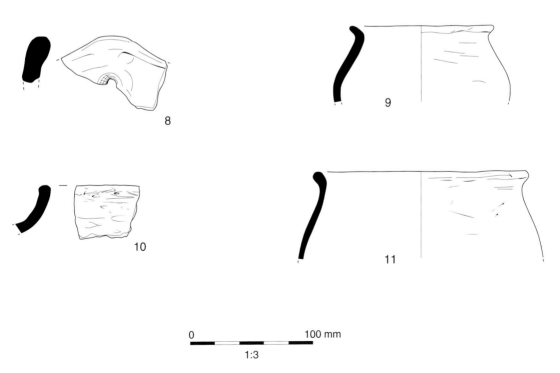

0   100 mm

1:3

Figure 3.17   Sunken-featured building 3 pottery.

One incised sherd (C/2, F1, 5 g).
One rusticated sherd, (D/2, F1, 11 g).
Cross fits: A/2 = A/2 = C/1 = C/2 = C/3 = D/2
(× 2); B/2 = A/2 = C/1 = C/2 = C/3 = D/2.

Illustrations

3.17.8	Upright lug. Black fabric, light brown unfinished surfaces.
3.17.9	Jar rim. Light grey fabric with black burnished surfaces.
3.17.10	Rim from small jar. Black fabric with burnished outer surface.
3.17.11	Rim from large jar. Black fabric with burnished outer surface.

SFB 4

Context 1105; Grid reference: 51298 98140; Figures 3.18–20; Site plan: D6 Orientation: NE/SW; Length at surface: 4.5 m; Distance between postholes: 3.5 m; Width: 4.05 m; Depth: 0.88 m.

Description

SFB 4 lay to the west of the central group of post-built structures, north-west of the Romano-British cemetery. The sub-rectangular pit was larger and deeper than average, with two small postholes, 1355 and 1280, in the centres of the north-east and south-west sides respectively. The sides were vertical. There was no evidence of a floor or occupation surface.

There were five layers of fill over a pit base of hard conglomerate. There were lumps of conglomerate at all levels in the fill and layers 4 and 5 continued into both postholes.

1 medium red brown sandy loam with 40% gravel containing pottery, bone, worked flint and lumps of conglomerate.
2 medium red brown sandy loam with 20% gravel containing pottery, bone and worked flint.
3 medium light red brown loamy silt with 20% gravel.
4 light red brown loamy silt with 80% gravel increasing towards the bottom.
5 intermittent layer of pea gravel on the base and sides of the feature.

PBS 13 was adjacent to the north-west and may have been in association. (Note: the line of the east-west section as indicated on the publication drawing is estimated. It is not possible to establish the actual line of the section, which clearly runs through posthole 1355.)

Finds

Thirteen artefacts were recovered. These included a copper alloy disc fragment, 139, with a series of small circular hammer marks on the underside. 140, the foot and catchplate from a brooch, is probably part of a Roman trumpet brooch, a type which is common in the 1st century but continues well into the 2nd century (Hattatt 1985, 105). The copper alloy mount, 149, is pierced with two rivet holes and is probably a belt fitting.

Number 156, from layer 3, is a large copper alloy nail. Part of the shaft has been twisted towards the tip and the shank is deliberately bent. The head is burred from use but presumably the shaft could only have been partly driven into the wood.

There are fragments of two iron nails, 243 and 248: 248 is probably part of a horseshoe nail. Other iron objects include an iron hook, 223, which is similar to one from a Anglo-Saxon pit at West Stow (West 1985, 57, fig. 232.1). There is also an iron mount, 217, made from a tapering sheet pierced with three holes. This may have been a bucket fitting.

There are two fragments of worked antler. 387 is part of a tine which has been sharpened at one end. The sides have been trimmed and it has been pared down at the other end. It was probably used as a peg. 380, which is a tine with a small section of the beam, shows extensive wear and is probably a tool, possibly used for digging or scraping.

Layer 1

139 SF 101	**Copper alloy disc** Thickness 0.5 mm. Fragment with hammering marks on the reverse. Obverse tinned.
140 SF 247	**Copper alloy brooch** Length 37 mm. Fragment of moulded foot knob and catchplate. The rear of the pin catch is decorated with incised horizontal and diagonal lines. The bow has two incised lines marking the edges.
248 SF 107	**Iron horseshoe nail** Length 33 mm. Part of head missing. Rectangular cross-sectioned shank. (Not illustrated)
387 SF 205	**Antler peg** Length 72 mm Modified tine, pared down towards the tip, now missing. The other end has been shaped to a point.

Layer 2

243 SF 250	**Iron nail** Length 53 mm. Shank fragment with square cross-section. (Not illustrated)
303 SF 341	**Window glass** Max thickness 5.5 mm. Tapering fragment of bottle green translucent bubbled glass. Badly scratched and worn on both sides. Roman. (Not illustrated)
311 SF 1524	**Bone pin** Length 16 mm. Shaft fragment. (Not illustrated)
380 SF 215	**Worked antler** Length 183 mm. Tine and sloping portion of the beam, cut from the beam with signs of wear at the cut end.
624 SF 1406	**Clay pipe** Stem fragment. Post-medieval. (Not illustrated)

Layer 3

149 SF 251	**Copper alloy mount** Length 23 mm; width 9 mm. Rectangular cut sheet with two rivet holes. File marks on underside.

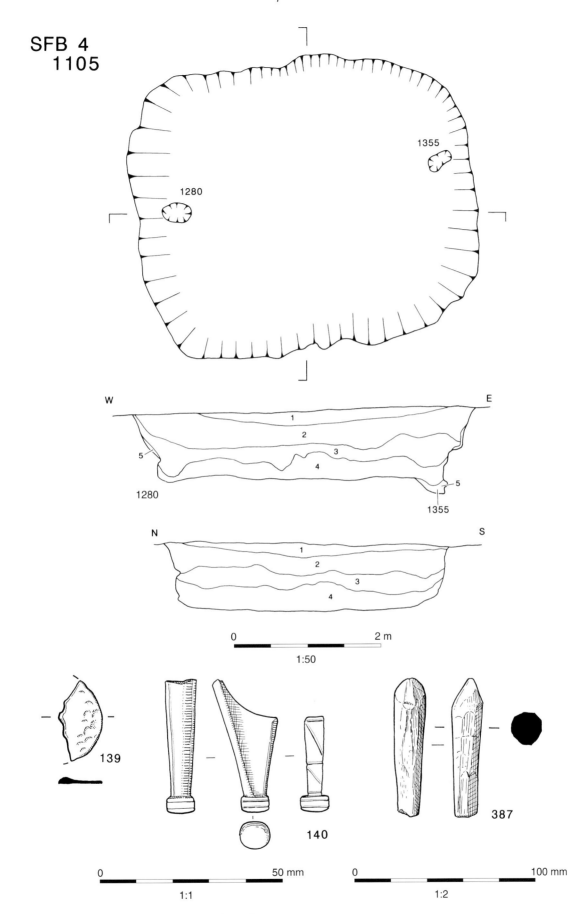

Figure 3.18   Sunken-featured building 4 and artefacts.

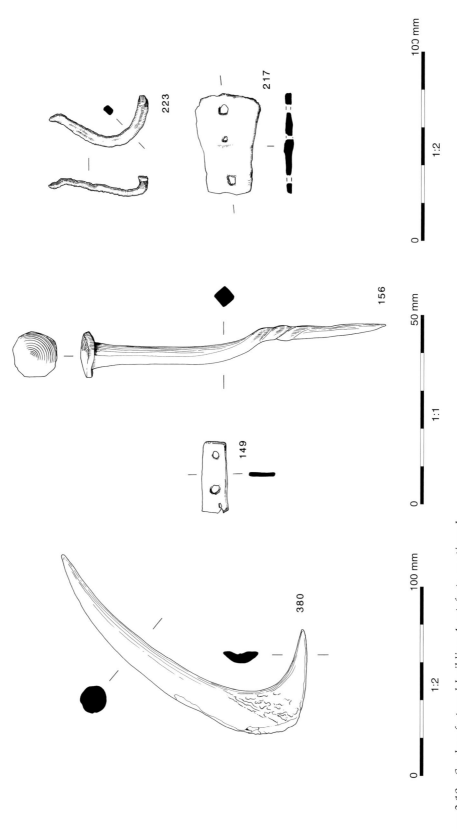

Figure 3.19 *Sunken-featured building 4 artefacts continued.*

156 SF 245   **Copper alloy nail** Length 103 mm; Diameter of head 14 mm. Circular head slightly burred at edges. The shaft has a square cross-section and is bent and twisted near the tip.

223 SF 137   **Iron hook** Length 66 mm. Rectangular cross-sectioned curved rod with both ends curved to form small hooks.

Layer 4

217 SF 246   **Iron mount** Length 23 mm; width 9 mm. Tapering sheet, perforated by three rivet holes down the centre.

Pottery tpq 6th century?

Pottery occurrence per layer by fabric type.

Layer Fabric	F1	F2	F3	F4	F6	% mineral	% chaff	Total wt (g)
1	180	112	22	0	46	56.1	43.9	360
2	270	197	60	2	83	54.2	45.8	612
3	163	44	44	0	90	60.7	39.3	341
4	124	106	9	0	115	37.6	62.4	354
Total wt (g)	738	459	135	2	333			1667
Mean sherd wt	6.4	5.7	6.8	2.0	9.0			

Pottery occurrence per quadrant and layer, all fabrics.

Layer/quadrant	A	B	C	D	Total wt (g)
1	124	53	70	113	360
2	282	35	210	85	612
3	152	73	19	97	341
4	132	29	61	132	354
Total wt (g)	690	190	360	427	1667
% of total	41.4	11.4	21.6	25.6	

EVE: Jars = 0.74; Bowls = 0.

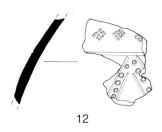

12

0   100 mm

1:3

Figure 3.20   Sunken-featured building 4 pottery.

Six incised sherds, (A/2, F2, 2 g; A/3, F6, 8 g; A/4, F2, 4 g; A/4, F2, 2 g; B/4, F3, 2 g; C/2, F1, 1 g; C/4, F1, 6 g).

Two stamped and incised sherds (C/4, F2, 6 g).

Illustrations

3.20.12   Stamped and incised sherd. Brown fabric with dark grey, smoothed surfaces.

The stamped and incised sherd (Fig. 3.20.12) indicates a *terminus post quem* of the 6th century for the backfill of the feature.

SFB 5

Context 1225; Grid reference: 51306 98140; Figures 3.21–2; Site plan: E6 Orientation: NE/SW; Length at surface: 3.46 m; Distance between postholes: 3.06 m; Width: 2.64 m; Depth: 0.2 m.

Description

SFB 5 was immediately to the west of PBS 4, one of the central group of post-built structures north of the Romano-British cemetery. The pit was shallow and sub-rectangular in plan, with postholes 1356 and 1281 in the centres of the north-east and south-west sides. There was no evidence of occupation debris. The sides were near vertical.

Two layers of fill were recorded. A line of limestone and conglomerate lumps resting on the base of the pit formed a line parallel to the south-west end. Layer 1 extended into both postholes.

1   dark red brown sandy loam with 40% gravel, containing pottery and bone.
2   pea gravel over the hard conglomerate base of the feature.

Finds

The only objects recovered were reused Roman sherds.

Layer 1

Reused Roman sherd no. 32 SF 1467   Diameter 70 mm. Modified foot-ring base in Oxford red/brown colour-coated fabric 3. (Not illustrated)

Posthole 1281

Reused Roman sherd no. 33 SF 1458   Diameter 170 mm. Wedge-shaped cut down fragment of a foot-ring base in Samian ware, fabric 8. (Not illustrated)

Pottery tpq 5th century?

Pottery occurrence per layer by fabric type

Layer/ Fabric	F1	F2	F3	F6	% mineral	% chaff	Total wt (g)
1	360	315	89	290	42.6	57.4	1054
Mean sherd wt (g)	10.0	7.9	8.1	9.7			

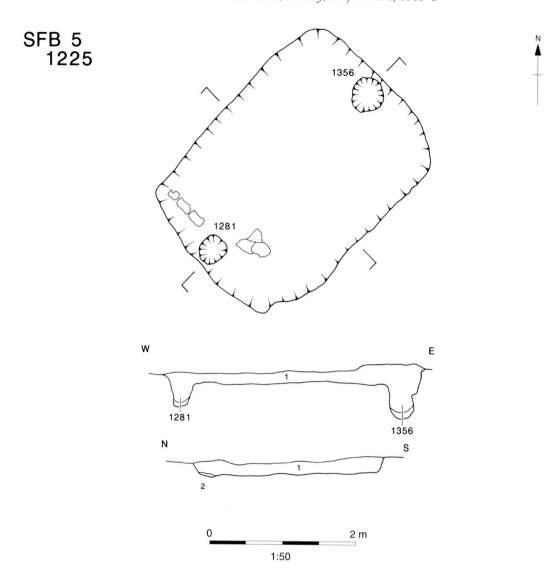

SFB 5
1225

Figure 3.21   Sunken-featured building 5.

Pottery occurrence per quadrant and layer, all fabrics.

Layer/quadrant	A	B	C	D	Total wt (g)
1	350	339	251	114	1054
% of total	33.2	32.2	23.8	10.8	

EVE: Jars = 0.63; Bowls = 0.

One incised sherd, (B/1, F2, 3 g).
Rim from carinated vessel with zig-zag decoration, 8% complete (B/1, F1, 24 g).

Illustrations

3.22.13   Jar rim. Uniform black fabric, both surfaces burnished.
3.22.14   Incised carinated ?jar rim. Uniform black fabric, both surfaces burnished.
3.22.15   Jar rim. Uniform black fabric, both surfaces brown and burnished.

It is highly probable that the carinated vessel with the zig-zag decoration (Fig. 3.22.14) is an early type. There are a number of similar examples in the Myres corpus (1977, fig. 120), and such vessels are said by Myres to be among the earliest Anglo-Saxon vessels found in England (Myres 1977, 23–4). Hamerow (1993, 42–4) has made a case for such vessels still having been in use in the 6th century. In this case, however, no stamped pottery is present, and so the feature may have a *terminus post quem* in the 5th century.

SFB 6

Context 1297; Grid reference: 51323 98144; Figures 3.23–5; Site plan: E6; Orientation: ENE/WSW; Length at surface: 3.74 m; Distance between postholes: 3.3 m; Width: 3.0 m; Depth: 0.66 m.

Description

SFB 6 was one of a group of sunken-featured buildings in the area of the central cluster of post-built structures

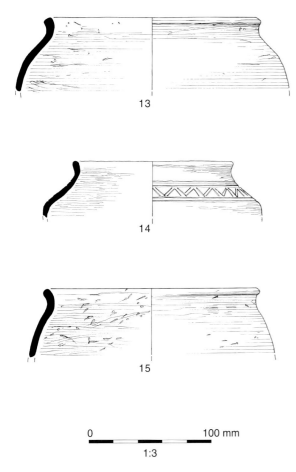

Figure 3.22   *Sunken-featured building 5 pottery.*

north of the Romano-British cemetery. The pit was sub-rectangular with an irregular plan and uneven, sloping sides. The postholes 1517 and 1518 were in the centres of the east and west sides respectively. Eight other postholes or possible postholes around the pit may be associated with SFB 6 and perhaps indicate that it was part of a larger, less archaeologically obvious structure, although there was extensive animal activity within and around the edges of the feature which had disturbed some of the postholes. The base and sides of the pit were loose gravel, with ridges and ledges of hard conglomerate.

1   dark red brown sandy loam with 60% medium gravel.
2   dark red brown loamy silt with 20% medium gravel.
3   medium grey brown loamy silt with 60% medium gravel.
4   dark grey-brown loamy silt containing charcoal flecks, powdery burnt material and much pottery and animal bone: appears to be a midden deposit which accumulated in the feature after abandonment.
5   intermittent pea gravel on the base of the feature, which consisted for the most part of fairly loose gravel, with ridges and ledges of hard conglomerate.

It is not possible to relate the fills of the postholes to the fill of the pit with certainty, but from the context descriptions it seems that the post of posthole 1517 was in place while layers 3 and 4 accumulated on the bottom of the pit, whereas 1518 seems to have begun to fill before 3 and 4 were deposited.

Finds

Fourteen artefacts were recovered, including three iron nails (of which 249 is probably from a horseshoe), an iron strip, 262, and a very worn iron knife, 193, of Böhner's type A, in use during the 5th to 7th centuries (Böhner 1958, 214). There is also a whetstone, 427, which exhibits extensive wear, producing a waisted profile. It is made of a calcareous sandstone which was probably collected locally. There was a small fragment of Roman window glass, 304, and two reused bases of Roman pots, 34 and 35. Number 35 has a scratched lattice on the inside which was applied after reuse. There are two incomplete antler combs. Number 319 is typical of Anglo-Saxon combs of 5th- to 7th-century date. Number 315 is a small fragment decorated with ring and dot motifs, a common feature of Anglo-Saxon combs. Numbers 365 and 308 are bone pins. Number 308 is a dress pin with a very simple head. Bone headless pins of this type are described by Crummy as hairpins. She puts the date of manufacture between the 1st and early 3rd centuries (Crummy 1983, 20–21). Number 365 is a pierced pig fibula pin of a type common at this site.

Layer 1

257 SF 1341   **Iron nail** Length 19 mm. Shank fragment with rectangular cross-section. (Not illustrated)

Layer 2

193 SF 253   **Iron knife** Blade fragment, length 122 mm, width 18 mm, thickness 4.5 mm. Point central to blade. Inclined back, angled back slope and leading edge. (Type A. 1. b). Very worn. Tang length 31 mm. Set just below back, sloping shoulders.

232 SF 233   **Iron nail** Length 46 mm. Shank fragment with square cross-section. (Not illustrated)

249 SF 1355   **Iron horseshoe nail** Length 32 mm. Part of head missing. Rectangular cross-sectioned shank, bent. (Not illustrated)

304 SF 235   **Window glass** Thickness 6 mm. Small fragment of pale green translucent tapering bubbled glass. Abraded and now semiopaque. Roman. (Not illustrated)

Reused Roman sherd no. 34 SF 1464   Diameter 110 mm. Cut down base in greyware, fabric 4. (Not illustrated).

Layer 3

262 SF 324   **Iron strip** Length 58 mm, width 7.5 mm, thickness 2 mm. Rectangular cross-section. Broken at both ends. (Not illustrated)

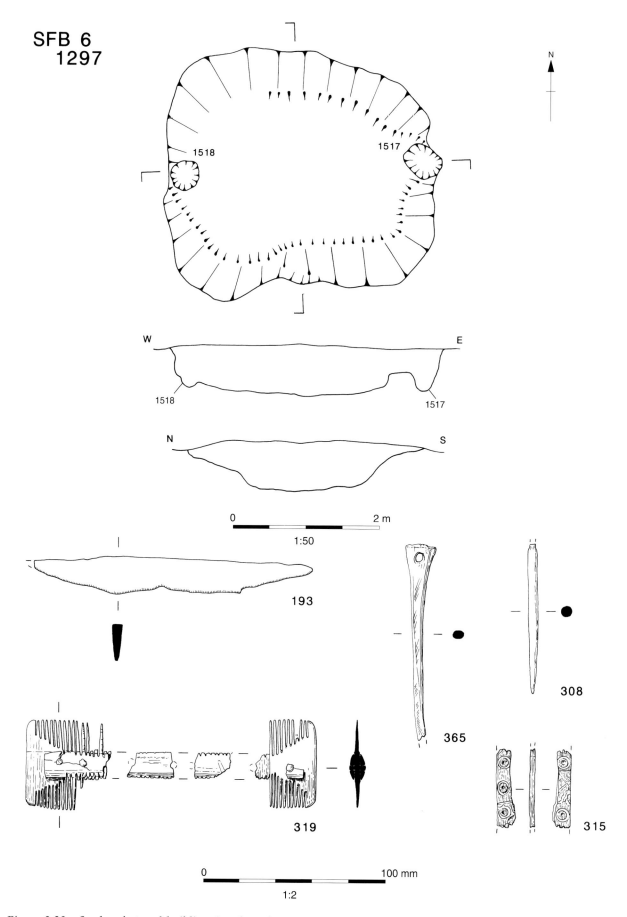

SFB 6
1297

1518   1517

W   E

1518   1517

N   S

0   2 m

1:50

193

365

308

319

315

0   100 mm

1:2

Figure 3.23   Sunken-featured building 6 and artefacts.

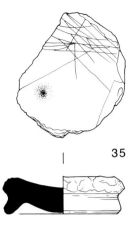

35

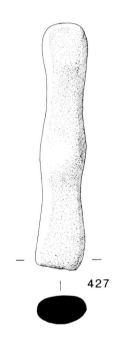

427

0				100 mm

1:2

Figure 3.24 Sunken-featured building 6 artefacts continued.

319 SF 238 **Double-sided composite bone comb** Height 48 mm. Fragments of the same comb from layers 3 and 4. Two rectangular end plates with graduated teeth, plus part of another tooth segment. The teeth average 4 per cm on one side and 5 per cm on the other. The connecting plates have a flat, D-shaped cross-section. Remains of three iron rivets and part of two rivet holes. There are two additional fragments of a connecting plate with the remains of four rivet holes each with iron staining.

365 SF 237 **Bone pin** Length 103 mm. Made from a pig fibula. The proximal end has been trimmed and perforated. Tip missing. Polished.

308 SF 236 **Bone pin** Length 79 mm. Polished shaft with simple waisted head.

377 SF 325 **Bone point** Length 31 mm Shaft fragment. Polished. Head missing. (Not illustrated)

Layer 4

315 SF 340 **Double-sided composite bone comb** Length 41 mm; width 10 mm. Fragment of an end plate with a straight end and rectangular cross-section. Decorated on both sides with ring and dot motifs.

Reused Roman sherd no. 35 SF 1460 Diameter 65 mm. Modified half of a foot-ring base in Oxford red/brown colour-coated fabric 3. Scratched lattice decoration on the inside of the sherd.

427 SF 240 **Whetstone** Length 130 mm. Heavy wear on all four faces, producing a waisted profile. Oval cross-section. Calcareous sandstone. Local Corallian.

Pottery tpq *6th century?*

Pottery occurrence per layer by fabric type.

Layer/Fabric	F1	F2	F3	F6	% mineral	% chaff	Total wt (g)
1	12	27	29	65	30.8	69.2	133
2	273	161	0	83	52.8	47.2	517
3	331	167	220	34	73.3	26.7	752
4	436	613	19	16	42.0	58.0	1084
Total wt (g)	1052	967	268	199			2486
Mean sherd wt	12.2	19.8	19.1	9.4			

Pottery occurrence per quadrant and layer, all fabrics.

Layer/quadrant	A	B	C	D	Total wt (g)
1	10	74	35	14	133
2	87	49	294	87	517
3	33	111	432	176	752
4	230	0	562	292	1084
Total wt (g)	360	234	1323	569	2486
% of total	14.5	9.4	53.2	22.9	

EVE: Jars = 1.06; Bowls = 0.43.

One incised sherd, (B/2, F1, 8 g).
One incised and stamped sherd, (D/2, F2, 45 g).
Other illustrated decorated sherds now missing.

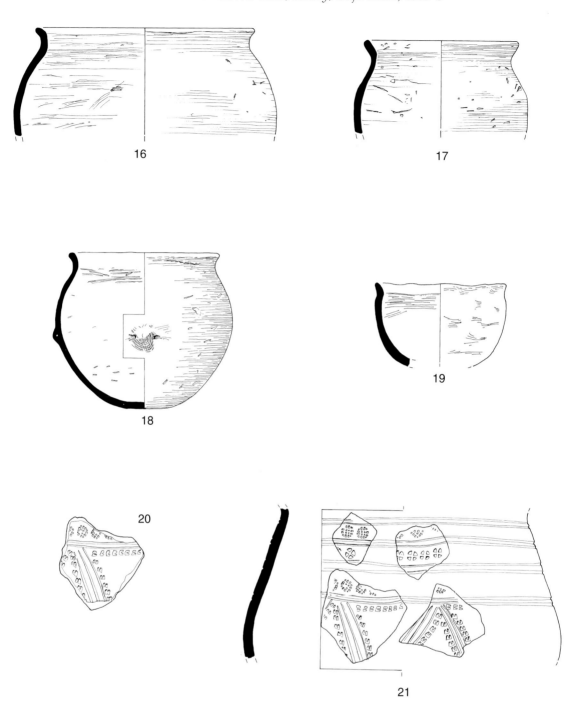

0   100 mm

1:3

Figure 3.25   Sunken-featured building 6 pottery.

Illustrations

3.25.16   Rim sherd from jar. Black fabric, burnished outer surface.

3.25.17   Rim sherd from jar. Black fabric, smoothed surfaces, brown below the waist.

3.25.18   Full profile of lugged jar. Uniform black fabric with burnished surfaces.

3.25.19   Rim from small bowl. Black fabric with burnished surfaces.

3.25.20–1   Incised and stamped sherd. Uniform black fabric, smoothed surfaces.

The stamped sherds (Figs 3.25.20–1) appear typical of those vessels dated by Myres (1977) to the 6th century.

SFB 7

Context 1298; Grid reference: 51300 98154; Figures 3.26–7; Site plan: D6/E6; Orientation: NE/SW; Length at surface: 3.52 m; Distance between postholes: 3.1 m; Width: 2.92 m; Depth: 0.51 m.

Description

SFB 7 lay about 8 m to the north-west of the central group of SFBs and PBSs. The pit was sub-rectangular with two postholes 1300 and 1990 in the centres of the north-east and south-west ends. The external posthole 1993 may be associated with this feature. In places the sides were near vertical but elsewhere they were uneven.

The fill of the pit extended into the postholes.

1 dark grey brown sandy loam with 30% gravel, contained pot and bone and may have been disturbed by ploughing.
2 dark reddish grey brown sandy loam with 15% gravel containing pot, bone and fragments of burnt clay or daub.
3 intermittent layer of redeposited gravel in a matrix of reddish brown sandy loam. This layer probably represents gravel slip from the sides of the feature.

Finds

Only two finds were associated with this SFB: a knife fragment, 203, and a complete reused base of a Roman mortarium, 36.

Layer 1

203 SF 1004 **Iron knife** Length 63 mm. Blade fragment width 11.5 mm, thickness 3 mm. The broken end is squared, possibly filed smooth, blade worn. Tang, length 35 mm central on blade, sloping shoulders, tapering and bent.

Reused Roman sherd no. 36 SF 1462 Diameter 90 mm. Modified foot-ring base of a mortarium in Oxford red/brown colour-coated fabric 3.

Pottery tpq *5th century?*

Pottery occurrence per layer by fabric type.

Layer/ Fabric	F1	F2	F3	F4	F6	F7	% mineral	% chaff	Total wt (g)
1	240	292	4	1	25	0	43.6	56.4	562
2	321	525	170	0	24	5	47.5	52.5	1045
3	0	82	0	0	0	14	14.6	85.4	96
Total wt* (g)	561	899	174	1	49	19			1703
Mean sherd wt	12.7	24.0	18.0	1.0	8.7	9.5			

*some of the pottery from this feature was not assigned a specific quadrant or layer by the excavators

Pottery occurrence per quadrant and layer, all fabrics.

Layer/quadrant	A	B	C	D	Total wt (g)
1	27	278	0	257	562
2	371	93	415	166	1045
3	11	0	85	0	96
Total wt (g)	409	371	500	423	1703
% of total	24.0	21.8	29.4	24.8	

EVE: Jars = 0.95; Bowls = 0.20.

Five incised sherds (A/2, F3, 10 g; C/2, F1, 23 g; C/2, F2, 47 g; D/1, F1, 42 g; D/2, F2, 47 g).
Incised carinated jar rim, 19% complete, (A/2, F1, 33 g).

Illustrations

3.27.22 Rim from decorated carinated jar. Black fabric with burnished surfaces, outer surface brown below the carination.
3.27.23 Upright lug. Dark grey fabric with unfinished surfaces.
3.27.24 Incised bodysherd. Black fabric with burnished surfaces.
3.27.25 Incised bodysherd. Dark grey fabric with black burnished surfaces.
3.27.26 Incised bodysherd. Dark grey fabric with black smoothed surfaces.
3.27.27 Incised bodysherd. Black fabric with burnished surfaces.
3.27.28 Pierced rim from small jar. Black fabric with burnished surfaces.

The decorated vessel (Fig. 3.27.22), with its carinated form, slashing and hanging curves (*hängende Bogen*) has no direct parallels in the corpus, but all the elements are classified by Myres as being characteristically early. The use of *hängende Bogen* in linear schemes is very early in date (Myres 1977, 57–8), and small carinated vessels such as this are said to be amongst the earliest Anglo-Saxon vessels found in England (1977, 17). The use of diagonal linear decoration is also said to be early (1977, 38–40).

SFB 8

Context 2082; Grid reference: 51345 980580; Figures 3.28–9; Site plan: F8; Orientation: ENE/WSW; Length at surface: 3.5 m; Distance between postholes: 3.25 m; Width: 2.5 m; Depth: 0.26 m? (top 50–60 mm of feature removed by shovel).

Description

SFB 8 was situated *c* 15 m south of barrow 601, on the north edge of the 19th-century tree plantation. The pit was sub-rectangular, with postholes 5373 and 5371 at the east-north-east and west-south-west

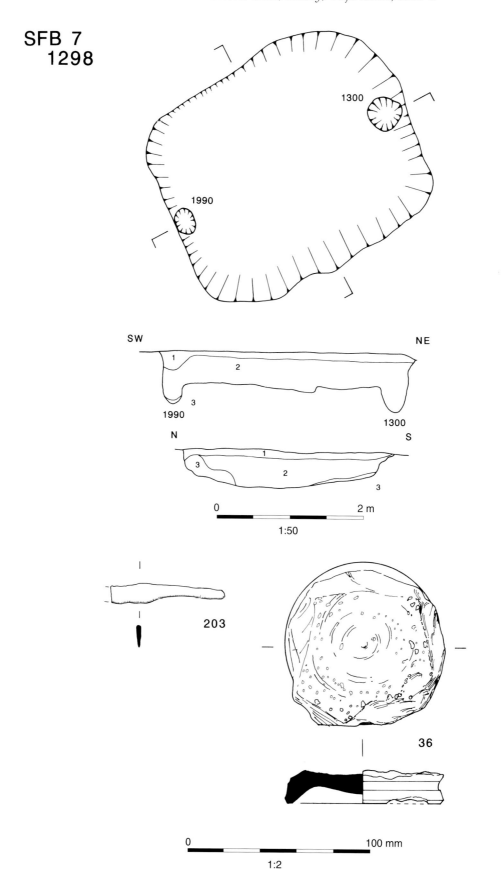

Figure 3.26 Sunken-featured building 7 and artefacts.

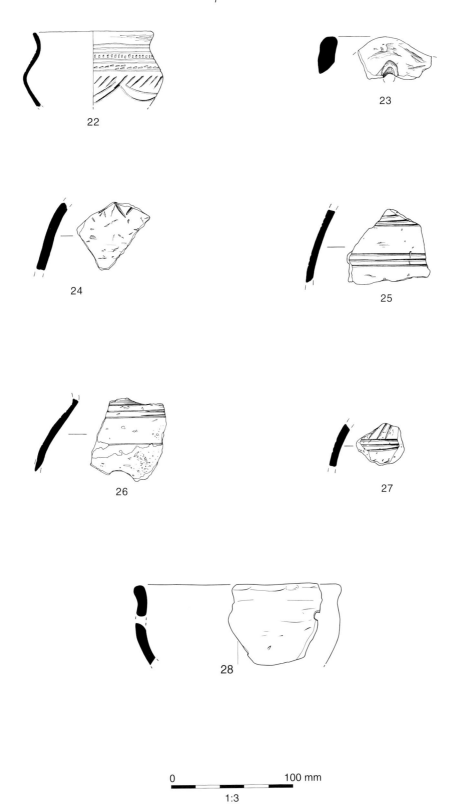

Figure 3.27 Sunken-featured building 7 pottery.

ends; another posthole, 5372, was a possible replacement for 5371. Posthole 5373 extended beyond the pit edge, and had been infilled and redug; it had cut a Neolithic pit and a large number of flint artefacts were found in the fill of SFB 8. The sides were sloping and irregular. The sunken-featured building was cut by pit 2083 of the tree plantation.

There was difficulty in distinguishing the inter-cutting features and the site records are hard to interpret. There seems to have been one layer of fill in SFB 8, a dark reddish brown clayey soil, but there was some mixing with the fills of the tree planting hole 2083 and feature 2084, both of which cut 2082. It was not possible to differentiate between the fills of posthole 5373 and the Neolithic pit, and finds from them were recorded as from 2082/B/2 and 3

and 2082/C/2 and 3. Finds from the posthole 5371 were recorded as 2082/A and D/2.

Finds

Four objects were recovered. Layer 1 was heavily disturbed and contained post-medieval material.

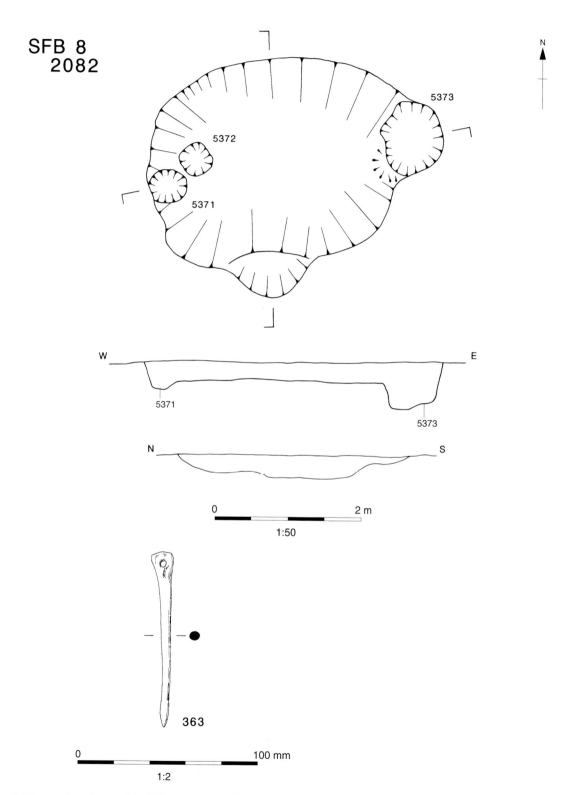

Figure 3.28 Sunken-featured building 8 and artefacts.

Layer 2, however, produced a perforated pig fibula pin of a type common throughout the site.

Layer 1

251 SF 1374   **Iron nail** Length 45 mm. Shank with square cross-section. (Not illustrated)

615 SF 1308   **Glass bottle** Fragment, clear, colourless. 20th-century. (Not illustrated)

620 SF 1393   **Clay pipe** Stem fragment. Post-medieval. (Not illustrated)

Layer 2

363 SF 264   **Bone pin** Length 92 mm. Made from a pig fibula. The proximal end is perforated. Polished.

Pottery tpq 6th century?

Pottery occurrence per layer by fabric type.

Layer/Fabric	F1	F2	F3	% mineral	% chaff	Total wt (g)
1	232	325	212	57.7	42.3	769
2	8	13	0	38.1	61.9	21
Total wt* (g)	247	437	242			790
Mean sherd wt	6.2	14.6	9.7			

*some of the pottery from this feature was not assigned a specific quadrant or layer by the excavators.

Pottery occurrence per quadrant and layer, all fabrics.

Layer/quadrant	A	B	C	D	Total wt (g)
1	85	299	218	167	769
2	10	0	0	11	21
Total wt (g)	95	299	218	178	790
% of total	12.0	37.8	27.6	22.5	

EVE: Jars = 0.52; Bowls = 0.19.

Incised boss, (A/1, F1, 10 g)
Incised boss, (B/1, F3, 2 g)
Incised sherd, (D/1, F3, 4 g).

29

0   100 mm

1:3

Figure 3.29 Sunken-featured building 8 pottery.

Illustrations

3.29.29   Incised and bossed sherd. Black fabric with orange-brown, worn outer surface.

The sherd with the bosses and triangles (Fig. 3.29.29) appears to belong to Myres's 'Long-boss' decorative scheme, typified by closely packed bosses, often delimited by vertical incised lines, which run down most of the length of a vessel's body, often with linear or stamped decoration. Again, there are no exact parallels for this sherd in Myres' corpus, but the use of stamped triangles above incised long-bosses is paralleled (Myres 1977, fig. 261). The style is very similar to that employed by Norwegian potters of the period, and three similar pots are known from the cemetery at Brighthampton in Oxfordshire (Myres 1977, fig. 260, 52–4). Myres indicates that the main *floruit* of this technique was during the first half of the 6th century.

SFB 9

Context 2143; Grid reference: 51247 98196; Figure 3.30; Site plan: B5; Orientation: E/W; Length at surface: *c* 4.2 m; Distance between postholes: *c* 3.70 m.

Description

The site records for this feature are missing. It lay approximately in the centre of the Neolithic oval barrow. The pit was very shallow, with shallow postholes 5375 and 5374 at the east and west ends.

According to the excavator the fill extended into the postholes.

Finds

Only one object was recovered, a fine example of a bone hipped pin with a thistle-like head. This is an uncommon type from Anglo-Saxon contexts. Hipped pins, however, are considered to be of 6th- to 9th-century date (Stevenson 1955, 285–6).

Layer 1

306 SF 295   **Bone pin** Length 37 mm. Thistle head, with thickened hip.

Pottery

Pottery occurrence per layer by fabric type.

Layer/Fabric	F1	F2	F6	F8	% mineral	% chaff	Total wt (g)
1	11	4	47	24	45.3	54.7	86
2	0	0	5	0	0	100	5
Total wt (g)	11	4	52	24			91
Mean sherd wt	5.5	4.0	5.8	12.0			

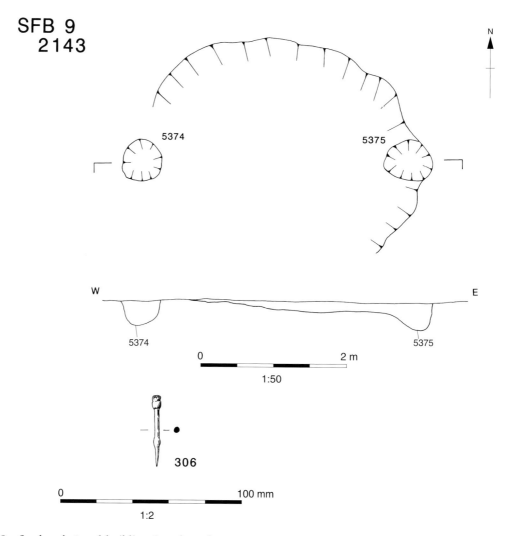

Figure 3.30   Sunken-featured building 9 and artefact.

Pottery occurrence per quadrant and layer, all fabrics.

Layer/ quadrant	A	B	C	D	Total wt (g)
1	29	55	2	0	86
2	5	0	0	0	5
Total wt (g)	34	55	2	0	91
% of total	37.4	60.4	2.2	0	

EVE: Jars = 0.04; Bowls = 0.

No chronologically diagnostic pottery.

SFB 10

Context 3216; Grid reference: 51277 98093; Figures 3.31–2; Site plan: D8; Orientation: ENE/WSW; Length at surface: 3.64 m; Distance between postholes: 3.2 m; Width: 3.58 m; Depth: 0.35 m

Description

SFB 10 was just to the west of ring ditch 801. The pit was almost square in plan, with substantial postholes 3260 and 3286 cut 0.87 m and 0.7 m into the gravel at the east and west ends. The sides were sloping and irregular and the base sloped upwards towards the north.

There were three layers of fill, of which 1 and 2 contained numerous tip lines. The fill of the pit continued into the postholes.

1 medium brown sandy loam with 20–30% gravel containing pot, bone and small finds.
2 fine silty brown loam with gravel varying from almost none to 30%.
3 layer of loam with pea grit and gravel which covered the bottom of the pit and also produced pottery and small finds.

Finds

Five objects were recovered: 150, a copper alloy pin, has a flattened, perforated head; the iron concretion in the hole is probably the remains of an iron suspension ring. This could be a pricker from a toilet set. There is also a perforated pig fibula pin, 366. Number 191 is a

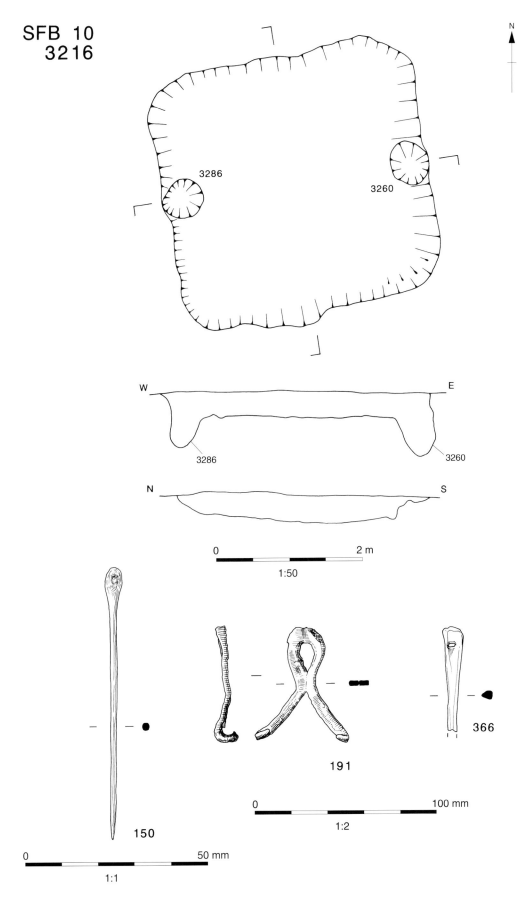

Figure 3.31 Sunken-featured building 10 and artefacts.

looped bucket fitting; the curved and pointed ends would have been driven into the wood to hold it in place. A similar copper alloy fitting occurs on a bucket from the 4th-century find at Saetrang in Norway (Slomann 1959, 56, pl III). An iron nail, 235, with T-shaped head is probably a woodworking nail.

Layer 1

150 SF 1011   **Copper alloy pricker** Length 72 mm. Made from a rolled sheet. The head is hammered flat and pierced. The hole contains iron concretion.

191 SF 1009   **Iron bucket loop fitting** Length 59 mm. Made from a rod with rectangular cross-section bent to form a loop with curved and pointed ends.

420 SF 1012   **Quern** Length 58 mm. Fragment of friable, porous, coarse-grained feldspathic grit, dark grains suggest Old Red Sandstone. Millstone Grit or Old Red Sandstone. (Not illustrated).

Layer 2

366 SF 1176   **Bone pin** Length 54 mm. Made from a polished pig fibula. The proximal end is perforated. Tip missing.

Layer 3

235 SF 1013   **Iron nail** Length 95 mm. T-shaped head. The shank tapers from rectangular to square cross-section. (Not illustrated)

Pottery

Pottery occurrence per layer by fabric type.

Layer/Fabric	F1	F2	F3	F6	% mineral	% chaff	Total wt (g)
1	77	343	10	78	17.1	82.9	508
2	0	227	138	0	37.8	62.2	365
3	0	60	0	0	0	100	60
Total wt (g)	77	630	148	78			933
Mean sherd wt	15.4	15.0	29.6	39.0			

Pottery occurrence per quadrant and layer, all fabrics.

Layer/quadrant	A	B	C	D	Total wt (g)
1	26	98	306	78	508
2	94	3	44	224	365
3	0	0	17	43	60
Total wt (g)	120	101	367	345	933
% of total	12.9	10.8	39.3	37.0	

EVE: Jars = 0.35; Bowls = 0.34.

No chronologically diagnostic pottery.
Cross-fits: C/1 = D/2 (x2).

Illustrations

3.32.30   Rim sherd from lugged vessel. Uniform black fabric with burnished outer surface.

3.32.31   Rim sherd from small lugged vessel. Dark grey fabric with partially smoothed surfaces.

3.32.32   Rim sherd from bowl. Uniform dark grey fabric with partly smoothed outer surface.

SFB 11

Context 3246; Grid reference: 51274 98102; Figures 3.33–4; Site plan: C7; Orientation: NW/SW; Length at surface: 4.3 m; Distance between postholes: 2.9 m; Width: 3.3 m; Depth: 0.35 m.

Description

SFB 11 was about 10 m north-west of ring ditch 801. The pit was sub-rectangular, with postholes 3287 and 3411 in the centre of the north-east end and *c* 1 m from the south-west end respectively. The sides were sloping. There was a large lump of limestone with traces of burning in layer 2.

Three layers were distinguished but the fill was very extensively disturbed by animal burrows, and post-medieval glass and china were found even in layer 3. There were numerous tip lines.

1   reddish brown sandy loam with 10–50% gravel.
2   medium reddish brown sandy loam with 10–50% gravel.

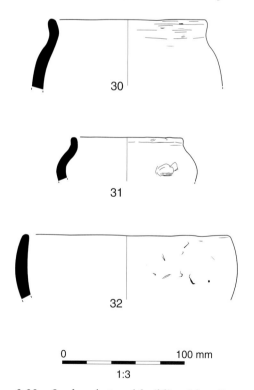

Figure 3.32 Sunken-featured building 10 pottery.

3 dark or reddish brown sandy loam with varying quantities of gravel and pea grit.

Layer 2 appears to have continued into post-hole 3287; 3411 had been disturbed by an animal burrow.

Finds

Six objects were recovered. They included an iron ferrule, 184, similar to that from SFB 3 (see Fig. 3.16, no. 183), the butt from a staff or spear. There was a fragment of waste, 392, from antler-working and a double-sided composite comb, 330, with fine and coarse teeth, a type more common in the Roman period. A complete base from a reused Roman pottery vessel, 39, was also found.

Layer 1

184 SF 1017   **Iron ferrule** Length 78 mm, max. Diameter 23 mm. Hollow, conical in shape. Made from a rolled sheet, closed at the pointed end.

302 SF 1447   **Glass fragment** Bright green translucent glass. Post-medieval. (Not illustrated).

Reused Roman sherd no. 39 SF 1494 Diameter 85 mm. Modified foot-ring base in Oxford red/brown colour-coated fabric 3.

Layer 2

616 SF 1015   **Glass wine bottle** Fragment from the neck. 18th–19th century. (Not illustrated)

330 SF 1277   **Double-sided composite antler comb** Length 36 mm. Part of two teeth segments with fine teeth on one side averaging 8 per cm and coarse teeth on the other averaging 4 per cm. The connecting plates have a D-shaped cross-section. One iron rivet and part of two rivet holes remain.

392 SF 1517   **Antler waste** Discarded burr with tines and beam partly sawn and then broken off. (Not illustrated)

Pottery

Pottery occurrence per layer by fabric type.

Layer/ Fabric	F1	F2	F3	F6	F7	% mineral	% chaff	Total wt (g)
1	614	511	133	0	35	60.5	39.5	1293
2	355	374	104	0	3	55.3	44.7	836
3	7	172	8	23	6	9.7	90.3	216
Total wt (g)	976	1057	245	23	44			2345
Mean sherd wt	13.0	14.5	18.8	11.5	7.3			

Pottery occurrence per quadrant and layer, all fabrics.

Layer/quadrant	A	B	C	D	Total wt (g)
1	197	905	37	158	1293
2	130	125	449	132	836
3	102	0	114	0	216
Total wt (g)	429	1030	600	290	2345
% of total	18.3	43.9	25.6	12.4	

EVE: Jars = 1.40; Bowls = 0.18.

Six incised sherds, (A/1, F1, 4 g; A/2, F3, 7 g; A/3, F3, 8 g; B/1, F2, 34 g; B/2, F3, 34 g; C/2, F1, 28 g).

One rusticated sherd (D/1, F1, 7 g).

Illustrations

3.34.33   Lugged rim sherd. Uniform dark grey fabric with burnished surfaces.

3.34.34   Incised sherd. Uniform dark grey fabric with burnished surfaces.

3.34.35   Uniform black fabric with smoothed and burnished outer surface.

3.34.36   Uniform black fabric with smoothed and burnished surfaces.

SFB 12

Context 3284; Grid reference: 51264 98200; Figures 3.35–7; Site plan: C4/5; Orientation: NE/SW; Length at surface: 5.6 m; Distance between postholes: 4.9 m; Width: 4.45 m; Depth: 1.03 m.

Description

SFB 12 was an unusually large sunken-featured building just to the east of the Neolithic oval barrow. The pit was irregularly sub-rectangular in plan, with three postholes 3802, 3803 and 3804 positioned on the long axis of the pit. The pit base and near-vertical sides were irregular.

The site records for this sunken-featured building are somewhat confused but there seem to have been five fill layers. There were numerous tip lines.

1 disturbed by a rabbit burrow: dark or medium red brown sandy loam with 10%-20% gravel, containing pottery and small finds.
2 medium red brown sandy loam with 40% gravel.
3 medium red brown sandy loam with 60–70% gravel containing many small fragments of daub.
4 gravel slip.
5 red/brown sandy loam with gravel and pea grit.

Finds

SFB 12 produced seven small finds, including two fragments from top stones of rotary querns, 405 and 406. There was a fine example of a highly decorated comb, 312, of a type common in the 5th to 7th centuries. The cross-hatched decoration is similar to that on Saxon combs from Shakenoak (Brodribb *et al.* 1972, fig. 57 and 58). There is also a tooth fragment

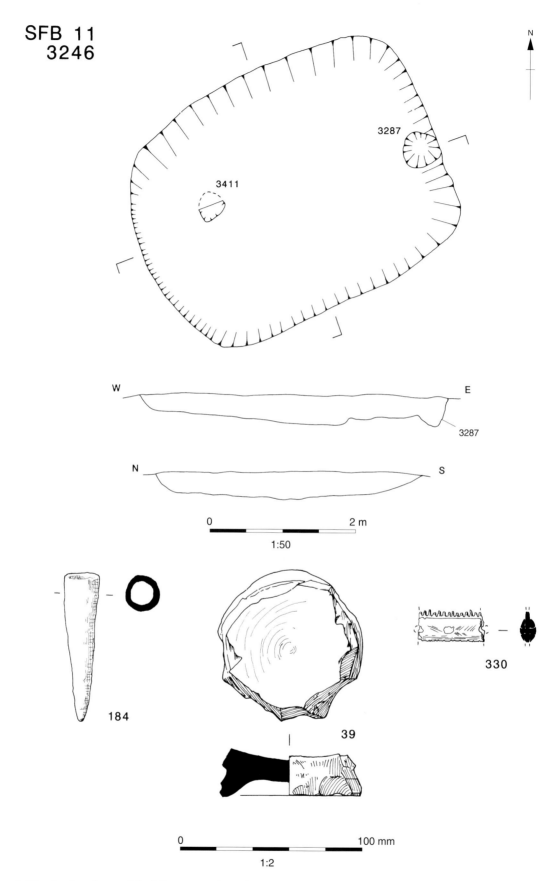

Figure 3.33   Sunken-featured building 11 and artefacts.

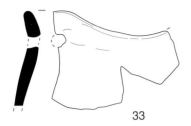

33

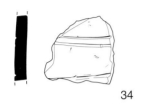

34

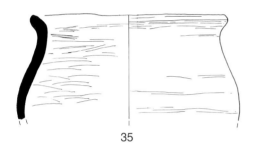

35

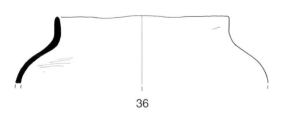

36

0   100 mm

1:3

Figure 3.34   Sunken-featured building 11 pottery.

from another comb, 338. Two small iron pins, 241, an iron woodworking nail, 238, and a complete reused base from a Roman pottery vessel, 40, were also found.

Layer 1

238 SF 1356   **Iron nail** Length 48 mm. The flat square head is a slight expansion of

shank with square cross-section. (Not illustrated)

312 SF 1033   **Double-sided composite antler comb** Length 145 mm, height 57 mm. Plain rectangular end-pieces with graduated teeth, one of which is pierced for suspension. The teeth on one side average 5 per cm and on the other 3 per cm. Six tooth segments. The convex connecting plates have a D-shaped cross-section, with six iron rivets. The teeth cuts on the connecting plates have been incorporated into the decorative scheme. The connecting plates are decorated at the ends with incised crosshatching, with a central panel with incised border containing ring and dot motifs.

Reused Roman sherd no. 40 SF 1488   Diameter 75 mm. Modified foot-ring base in Oxford red/brown colour-coated fabric 3. (Not illustrated)

405 SF 1016   **Rotary quern** Top stone fragment. (Not illustrated)

406 SF 1031   **Rotary quern** Thick top stone fragment. (Not illustrated)

Layer 4

241 SF 1532   **Two iron pins** Lengths 26 mm and 17 mm. Circular cross-sections.

338 SF 1529   **Antler comb tooth** Length 18 mm. (Not illustrated)

Pottery

Pottery occurrence per layer by fabric type.

Layer/Fabric	F1	F2	F3	F4	F6	% mineral	% chaff	Total wt (g)
1	88	132	114	0	361	29.1	70.9	695
2	35	19	20	37	221	27.7	72.3	332
3	0	19	36	0	19	48.7	51.3	74
4	0	0	0	0	16	0	100	16
Total wt (g)	123	170	170	37	617			1117
Mean sherd wt	7.2	11.3	28.3	37.0	19.9			

Pottery occurrence per quadrant and layer, all fabrics.

Layer/quadrant	A	B	C	D	Total wt (g)
1	153	106	164	272	695
2	178	0	134	20	332
3	0	7	67	0	74
4	0	0	0	16	16
Total wt (g)	331	113	365	308	1117
% of total	29.6	10.1	32.7	27.6	

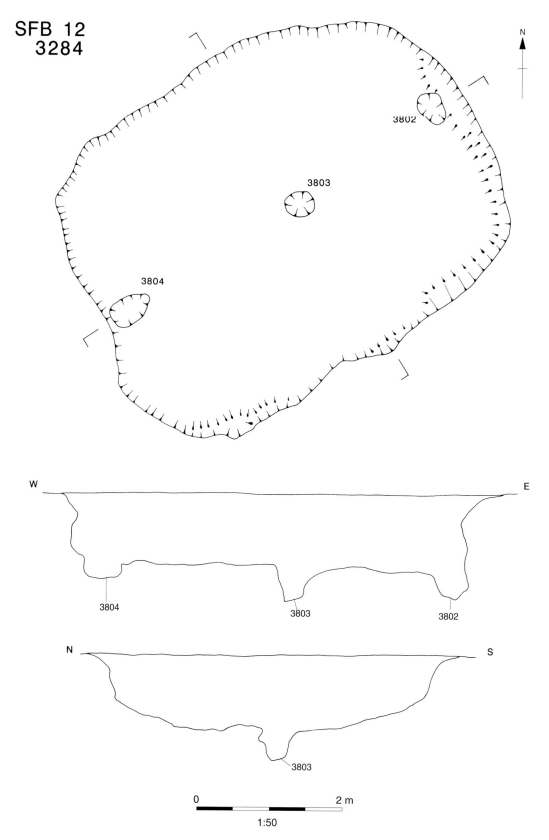

Figure 3.35   Sunken-featured building 12 and artefacts.

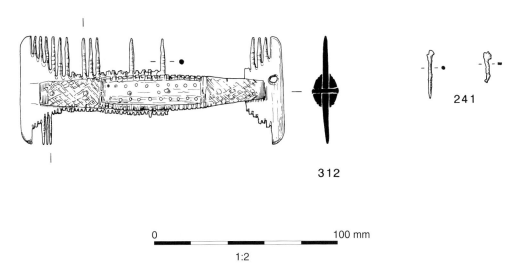

241

312

0 ▬▬▬▬▬▬▬▬▬ 100 mm

1:2

Figure 3.36   Sunken-featured building 12 artefacts continued.

EVE: Jars = 0.44; Bowls = 0.

One rusticated sherd (D/1, F2, 16 g).

Illustrations

3.37.37   Rim sherd from jar. Uniform dark grey fabric, unfinished surfaces.
3.37.38   Base and lower body from small jar. Dark grey fabric, unfinished surfaces.

SFB 13

Context 3285; Grid reference: 51278 98193; Figures 3.38–9; Site plan: D7/D8; Orientation: E/W; Length at surface: *c* 2.8 m; Width: 2.6 m; Depth: 0.43 m.

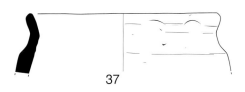

37

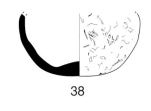

38

0 ▬▬▬▬▬▬▬ 100 mm

1:3

Figure 3.37   Sunken-featured building 12 pottery.

Description

SFB 13 was immediately west of ring ditch 801, between SFBs 10 and 11. There was a posthole, whose number is not recorded, in the centre of the east end. The floor of the pit was irregular and the sides were curving.

Four layers were distinguished; 1–3 contained numerous tip lines.

1 dark grey brown sandy loam with 10% gravel, containing pottery and animal bone.
2 medium red brown sandy loam with 50% medium gravel, containing pottery and animal bone.
3 medium red brown sandy loam with 80% pea gravel.
4 thin layer of redeposited natural gravel.

Finds

Three finds were recovered: 153 is a copper alloy drop handle. Drop handles are common finds on Roman sites and were probably fittings from furniture. Number 153 could have been from a small chest. A number of Roman drop handles from furniture have been found during excavations in Colchester (Crummy 1983, 80, fig. 85). A complete base of a reused Roman pot, 41, came from layer 3.

Layer 1

153 SF 1018   **Copper alloy drop handle** Length 72 mm. Made from a circular cross-sectioned rod. The handle has been filed down to a rectangular cross-section. The terminals remain circular.
301 SF 1442   **Glass wine bottle** Olive green glass. Post-medieval. (Not illustrated)

Layer 3

Reused Roman sherd no. 41 SF 1487   Diameter 80 mm. Cut down base in Oxford red/brown colour-coated fabric 3.

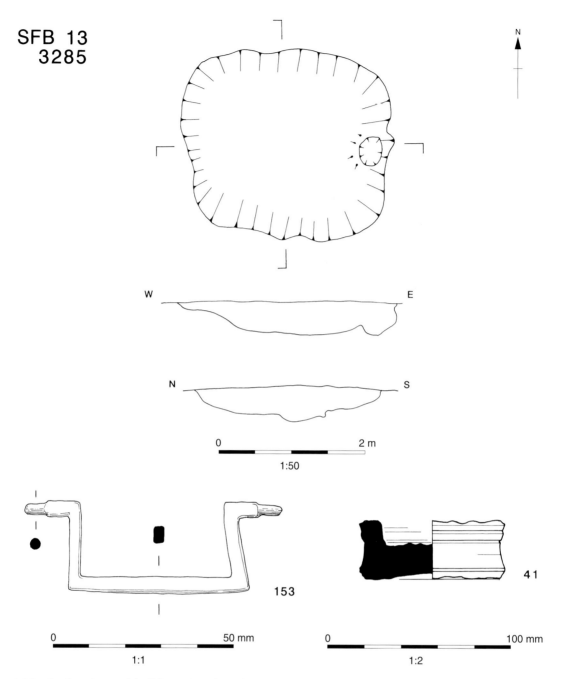

Figure 3.38   Sunken-featured building 13 and artefacts.

Pottery

Pottery occurrence per layer by fabric type.

Layer/ Fabric	F1	F2	F3	F4	% mineral	% chaff	Total wt (g)
1	4	571	6	0	1.7	98.3	581
2	28	0	0	37	100	0	65
Total wt (g)	32	571	6	37			646
Mean sherd wt	8.0	43.9	6.0	7.4			

Pottery occurrence per quadrant and layer, all fabrics.

Layer/quadrant	A	B	C	D	Total wt (g)
1	0	267	307	7	581
2	20	0	0	45	65
Total wt (g)	20	267	307	52	646
% of total	3.1	41.3	47.5	8.0	

EVE: Jars = 0.22; Bowls = 0.05

Cross-fit: B/1 = C/1

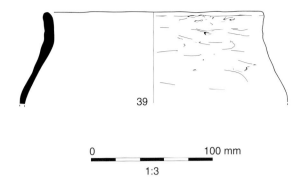

39

0   100 mm

1:3

Figure 3.39   Sunken-featured building 13 pottery.

Illustrations

3.39.39   Rim sherd from small jar. Uniform black fabric, both surfaces burnished.

SFB 14

Context 3288; Grid reference: 51280 98080; Figures 3.40–3; Site plan: D7/D8; Orientation: ENE/WSW; Length at surface: 4.4 m; Distance between postholes: 3.7 m; Width: 3.36 m; Depth: 0.40 m.

Description

SFB 14 was cut into ring ditch 801. The pit was extremely irregular in outline, with substantial postholes 3443 at the east-north-east end, 3444 *c* 0.75 m from 3443 and 3442 at the west-south-west end. 3442 had been recut and may have been paired with either 3444 or 3443; the irregularity of the pit outline may be the result of a radical rebuilding of the structure. The pit bottom was irregular and the sides were curving.

There were three layers in the pit. Spindlewhorl 441, SF 1020, was found at the interface between 2 and pea grit on the bottom of the hut.

1   dark red brown sandy loam with 15% gravel.
2   dark grey brown sandy loam with red and yellow daub and charcoal flecks, containing pottery, bone and small finds.
3   thin layer of medium red brown sandy loam with 50% gravel which represents the fill of the ring ditch.

It is not possible to reconstruct with certainty the relationship of the postholes to the pit fill, but it seems probable that the pit fill continued into the postholes.

Layer 3 probably represents deliberate backfill of the ditch, either derived from the slighting of a barrow mound or redeposited from the digging of SFBs 17–18 as an attempt to level the ground surface (see Barclay and Halpin 1999, chapter 4, ring ditch 801).

Finds

SFB 14 contained a rather mixed group of 15 finds. These included three reused Roman pot bases; 42 and 43 are half bases and the letter R has been incised into the underside of 44 after firing. There was also a single gaming piece, 1473, in an Anglo-Saxon fabric and part of a cornice rim flask, 290, of late Roman date.

Textile equipment included one complete spindlewhorl, 441, and a fragmentary whorl, 468, both in coarse Anglo-Saxon fabrics. 441 came from the interface of layer 2 and pea grit on the base of the sunken-featured building. There are no objects specifically attesting to weaving from this sunken-featured building, but a complete perforated pig's fibula pin and a fragment of an Anglo-Saxon antler comb were found.

A fragment of a knife blade, 199, was recovered in association with part of a whetstone, 430, of probably local stone. Also found were an iron woodworking nail, 228, and fragments of two iron rods, 263 and 264, of unknown function.

Layer 1

228 SF 1354   **Iron nail** Length 79 mm. Circular flat head. Rectangular cross-sectioned shank now bent. (Not illustrated)

263 SF 1229   **Iron rod** Length 120 mm, width 8 mm, thickness 6 mm. Rectangular cross-section, tapering to one end. Both ends broken. (Not illustrated)

360 SF 1046   **Bone pin** Length 105 mm. Made from a pig fibula perforated at the proximal end. Head cut square. Polished.

337 SF 1177   **Antler comb** Length 14 mm. Fragment of an end plate with graduated teeth.

468 SF 1534   **Ceramic spindlewhorl** Fragment with part of central hole. (Not illustrated)

SF 1473   **Ceramic counter** Diameter 22 mm. Made from a body sherd in Anglo-Saxon fabric.

Reused Roman sherd no. 42 SF 1483   Diameter 80 mm. Modified half of a foot-ring base in Oxford red/brown colour-coated fabric 3. (Not illustrated)
Reused Roman sherd no. 43 SF 1479   Diameter 60 mm. Modified half of a foot-ring base in Oxford red/brown colour-coated fabric 3.

Layer 2

170 SF 1049   **Copper alloy sheet** Length 13 mm; thickness 0.5 mm. Fragment. (Not illustrated)

199 SF 1168   **Iron knife** Blade fragment Length 48 mm, width 10.5 mm, thickness 2 mm. Point central to blade, inclined back? angled back slope, angled leading edge (type A/C. 1.b).

264 SF 1027   **Iron rod** Length 95 mm, width 8 mm. Fragment with square cross-section. (Not illustrated)

290 SF 1053   **Glass vessel** Thickness 9 mm. Blue-green translucent fragment of a moulded everted rim, possibly from a flask. Late Roman.

430 SF 1175   **Whetstone** Length 45 mm. Fragment with signs of wear on one face. Square cross-section. Calcareous sandstone. Local Corallian

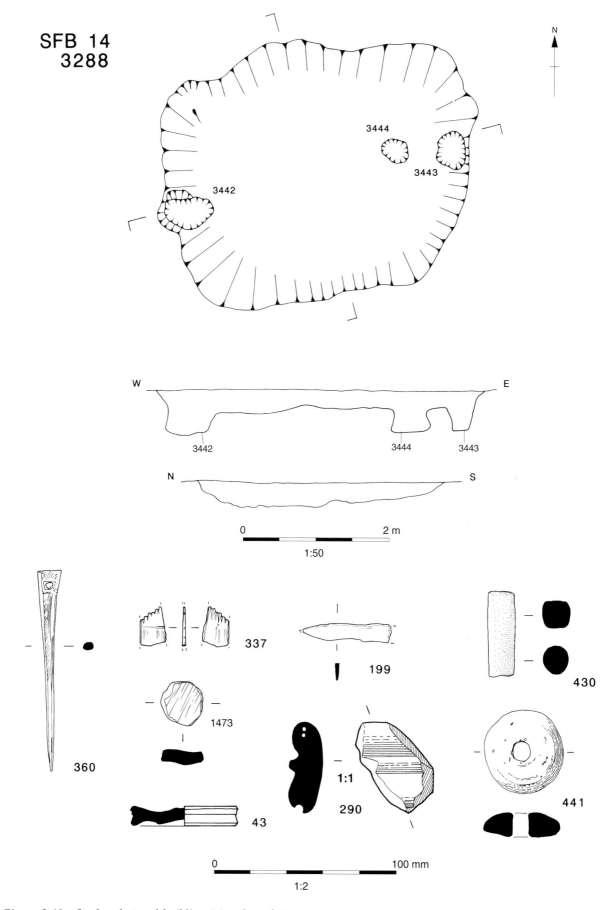

Figure 3.40 Sunken-featured building 14 and artefacts.

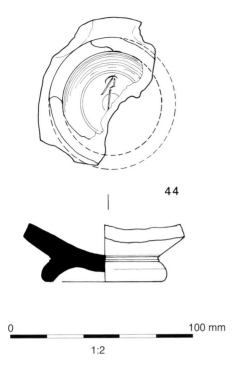

44

|————————|
0   100 mm

1:2

Figure 3.41 Sunken-featured building 14 artefacts continued.

441 SF 1020 Ceramic spindlewhorl Diameter 43 mm. Hemispherical with convex upper and flat lower surface. Diameter of hole 10 mm. Weight 23.03 g.

Reused Roman sherd no. 44 SF 1042 Samian ware bowl. Diameter *c* 80 mm. Cut down half of a base with letter R cut into the underside, fabric 8.

Posthole 3443

Reused Roman sherd no. 49 SF 1499 Diameter 55 mm. Complete cut down foot-ring base in Oxford red/brown colour-coat. (Not illustrated).
Reused Roman sherd no. 50 Diameter 60 mm. Cut down foot-ring base in Oxford red/brown colour coat. (Not illustrated)

Pottery tpq 6th century?

Pottery occurrence per layer by fabric type.

Fabric	F1	F2	F3	F8	% mineral	% chaff	Total wt (g)
1	468	554	400	24	61.7	38.3	1446
2	1016	1668	381	0	45.6	54.4	3065
3	0	6	0	0	0	100	6
Total wt (g)	1484	2228	781	24			4517
Mean sherd wt	16.1	31.8	19.5	24.0			

Pottery occurrence per quadrant and layer, all fabrics.

Layer/quadrant	A	B	C	D	Total wt (g)
1	543	330	220	353	1446
2	1445	195	130	1295	3065
3	0	0	6	0	6
Total wt (g)	1988	525	356	1648	4517
% of total	44.2	11.6	7.9	36.5	

EVE: Jars = 2.52; Bowls = 0.62.

One bossed and incised sherd, (A/1, F8, 24 g).
One incised sherd, (B/2, F1, 18 g).
One stamped sherd (B/2, F1, 15 g).

Cross-fits: A/1 = A/2, A/2 = D/2 (x2), D/1 = D/2 (x2).

Illustrations

3.42.40	Rim sherd from small bowl. Black fabric with smoothed surfaces.
3.42.41	Rim sherd from small bowl. Black fabric with smoothed surfaces.
3.42.42	Rim sherd from small bowl. Black fabric with smoothed surfaces.
3.42.43	Rim sherd from jar. Dark grey fabric with smoothed surfaces.
3.42.44	Rim sherd from pierced vessel. Grey fabric, unfinished surfaces.
3.42.45	Rim sherd from jar. Dark brown fabric with burnished surfaces.
3.42.46	Rim sherd from jar. Black fabric with burnished surfaces.
3.42.47	Rim sherd from jar. Black fabric with burnished surfaces.
3.42.48	Rim sherd from bowl. Black fabric with burnished surfaces.
3.42.49	Rim sherd from jar. Black fabric with burnished surfaces.
3.42.50	Rim sherd from jar. Black fabric with burnished outer surfaces.
3.42.51	Rim sherd from small jar. Black fabric with burnished surfaces.
3.43.52	Rim sherd from large jar. Dark grey fabric with burnished surfaces.
3.43.53	Rim sherd from jar. Light brown fabric with burnished surfaces.
3.43.54	Jar rim. Uniform black fabric, brown patches on burnished outer surface.
3.43.55	Jar rim. Reddish-brown fabric with black, burnished outer surface.
3.43.56	Upright lug. Black fabric with smoothed surfaces.
3.43.57	Incised sherd. Black fabric with smoothed surfaces.
3.43.58	Bossed and incised sherd. Dark brown fabric with smoothed surfaces.
3.43.59	Incised base sherd. Black fabric with smoothed surfaces.

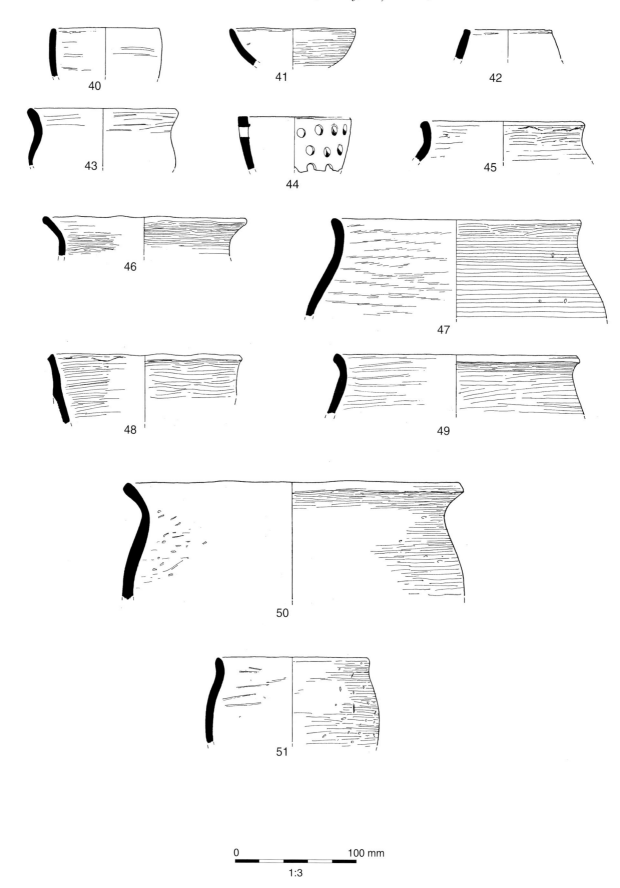

Figure 3.42   Sunken-featured building 14 pottery.

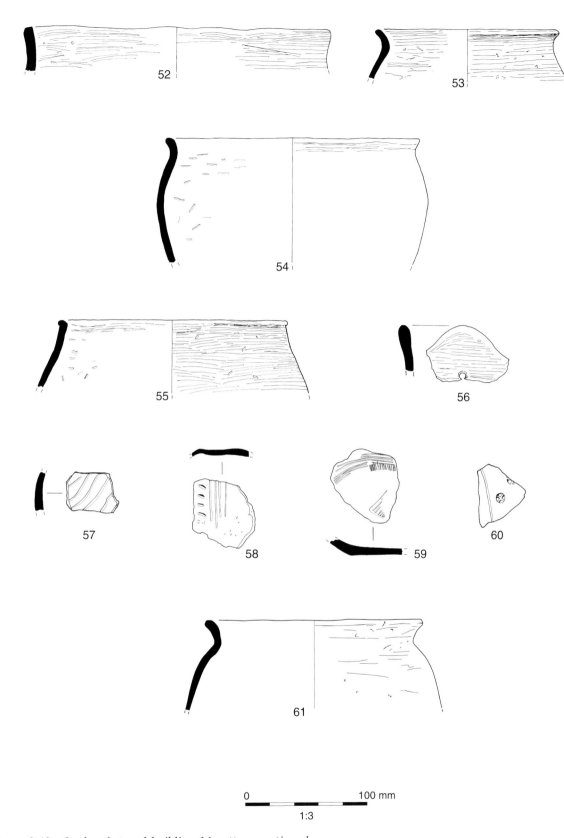

Figure 3.43   Sunken-featured building 14 pottery continued.

3.43.60 Stamped sherd. Dark grey fabric with black burnished surfaces.

3.43.61 Large rim sherd from jar. Black fabric with burnished, brown outer surface.

The decorated pottery from this feature generally comprises small sherds, and is difficult to date. However, Figure 3.43.60 appears to be a fragment of a stamped pendant triangle, and may be a 6th-century type, as is the bossed sherd (Fig. 3.43.58).

SFB 15

Context 3307; Grid reference: 51295 98163; Figures 3.44–5; Site plan: D5; Orientation: NE/SW; Length at surface: 4.36 m; Distance between postholes: 3.8 m; Width: 2.8 m; Depth: 0.4 m.

Description

SFB 15 was approximately 15 m north-west of the central group of sunken-featured buildings and post-built structures. The pit was sub-rectangular in plan with postholes 3447 and 3445 in the centres of the north-east and south-west ends. The sides sloped outwards, with a shelf on the south-east side.

1 dark reddish brown sandy loam with 5–10% gravel.
2 dark reddish brown sandy loam with 20–30% gravel.
3 medium reddish brown sandy loam with 40% gravel which constituted the fill of posthole 3447.

It is not possible to reconstruct with certainty the relationship of the pit fills to the postholes, but it appears that a post remained *in situ* in 3447 while the fills accumulated.

Finds

Only five objects were associated with this SFB. These included a woodworking nail, 237, and a knife, 198, probably of 5th- to 7th-century date. A quern, 415, probably of Old Red Sandstone, and part of a base of a Roman pot, 45, which has been cut into a wedge shape, were also recovered.

Number 324 is a comb, typical of those found on Anglo-Saxon sites. It has been broken in antiquity and repaired with copper alloy rivets. An original iron rivet has been replaced by one of copper alloy and three additional rivets have been used to secure the repair.

Layer 1

198 SF 1022 **Iron knife** Blade length 48 mm, width 17 mm, thickness 2 mm. Point central to blade, inclined back, back slope and leading edge angled, tip missing. (Type A/C. 1. b.). Blade worn. Tang length 20 mm, set just below back, sloping shoulder.

237 SF 1024 **Iron nail** Length 58 mm. The small flat square head is a slight expansion of the square cross-sectioned shank. (Not illustrated)

324 SF 1023 **Double-sided composite bone comb** Length 58 mm, height 48 mm. Two tooth segments. The teeth on both sides average 5 per cm. The connecting plates have D-shaped cross sections and saw marks along both edges. Three iron rivets and four copper alloy rivets remain.

415 SF 1025 **Quern** Length 100 mm. Fragment of reddish-brown feldspathic coarse-grained, probably Old Red Sandstone. (Not illustrated)

Layer 2

Reused Roman sherd no. 45 SF 1497 Diameter 100 mm. Wedge-shaped fragment of a grooved base in Oxford red/brown colour-coated fabric 3.

Pottery tpq 5th century?

Pottery occurrence per layer by fabric type.

Fabric	F1	F2	F3	F6	% mineral	% chaff	Total wt (g)
1	340	1274	128	136	24.9	75.1	1878
2	42	248	118	23	37.1	62.9	431
3	0	27	0	0	0	100	27
Total wt (g)	382	1549	246	159			2336
Mean sherd wt	10.1	17.8	18.9	9.4			

Pottery occurrence per quadrant and layer, all fabrics.

Layer/quadrant	A	B	C	D	Total wt (g)
1	327	552	754	245	1878
2	112	284	0	35	431
3	27	0	0	0	27
Total wt (g)	466	836	754	280	2336
% of total	19.9	35.8	32.3	12.0	

EVE: Jars = 1.12; Bowls = 0.22.

One vessel with multiple collars/finger-grooves, (A/1, A/2, B/1 and D/1, F2, 319 g).
Two incised sherds, (B/1, F1, 3 g; B/2, F2, 3 g).
One pedestal base (B/2, F2, 19 g)
Pierced sherd (B/2, F2, 5 g).

Cross-fits: A/1 = A/2 = B/1 = D/1.

Illustrations

3.45.62 Large jar with finger-grooved shoulders. Uniform dark grey fabric with smoothed outer surface.

3.45.63 Rim from small bowl. Black fabric with burnished surfaces.

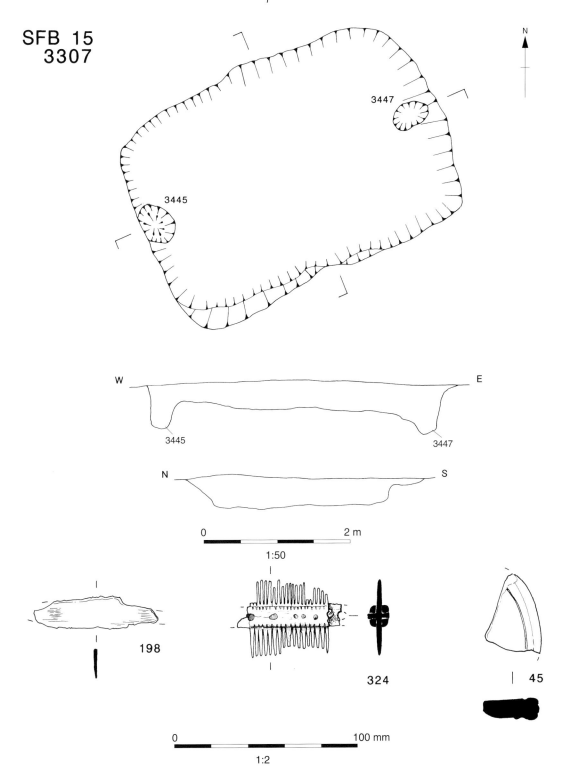

Figure 3.44   Sunken-featured building 15 and artefacts.

3.45.64	Rim from small bowl. Black fabric with burnished surfaces.	3.45.67	Stamped sherd. Dark grey fabric with smoothed surfaces.
3.45.65	Sherd from 'stepped' base. Black fabric, unfinished surfaces.	3.45.68	Incised sherd. Black fabric with burnished surfaces.
3.45.66	Miniature jar. Dark grey fabric with smoothed surfaces.	3.45.69	Incised sherd. Black fabric with burnished surfaces.

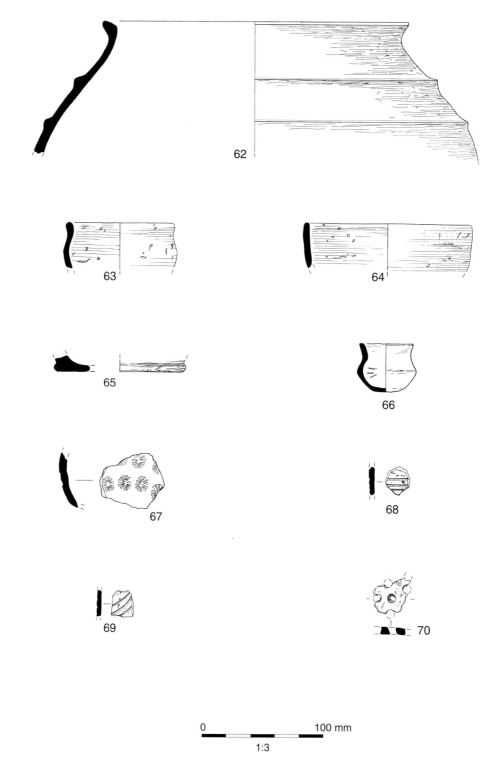

Figure 3.45   Sunken-featured building 15 pottery.

3.45.70   Pierced bodysherd. Dark grey fabric with unfinished surfaces.

The vessel with the finger-grooved shoulders (Fig. 3.45.62) is extremely unusual, and has only one parallel, a carinated bowl from Sussex (Myres 1977, fig. 89, no. 3652). The Barrow Hills vessel is obviously a jar, but it seems highly likely due to be of the same date due to the distinctive nature of the vessel. Support for this date comes from the presence of the small carinated jar in the same feature (Fig. 3.45.66). Such vessels are said by Myres to be characteristically early.

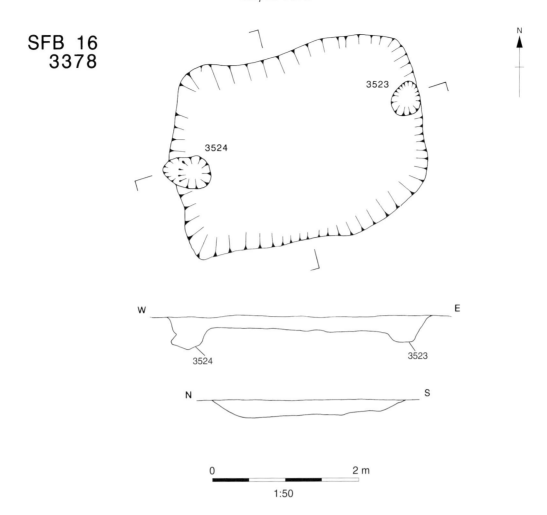

Figure 3.46   Sunken-featured building 16.

SFB 16

Context 3378; Grid reference: 51286 98137; Figures 3.46–7; Site plan: D6; Orientation: ENE/WSW; Length at surface: 3.48 m; Distance between postholes: 3.1 m; Width: 2.44 m; Depth: 0.22 m.

Description

SFB 16 was approximately 20 m to the south-west of the central group of structures. The pit is sub-rectangular in plan with postholes 3523 and 3524 in the centres of the east-north-east and west-south-west sides respectively. The sides sloped out-wards.

Only two layers were distinguished, containing numerous tip lines and animal disturbance. There was 30–40 mm of pea grit and gravel in the bottoms of the postholes.

1   medium brown sandy loam with 10–50% gravel.
2   medium red brown sandy loam with 5–20% gravel.

It is not possible to reconstruct with certainty the relationship of the fill to the postholes.

Finds

There were no finds.

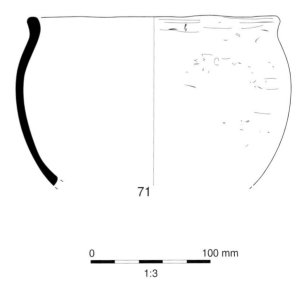

Figure 3.47   Sunken-featured building 16 pottery.

Pottery

Pottery occurrence per layer by fabric type.

Fabric	F1	F2	F3	F6	% mineral	% chaff	Total wt (g)
1	81	349	11	16	20.1	79.9	457
2	28	361	0	8	7.1	92.9	397
Total wt (g)	109	710	11	24			854
Mean sherd wt	0.4	21.5	5.5	12.0			

Pottery occurrence per quadrant and layer, all fabrics.

Layer/quadrant	A	B	C	D	Total wt (g)
1	0	108	349	0	457
2	346	15	0	36	397
Total wt (g)	346	123	349	36	854
% of total	40.5	14.4	40.9	4.2	

EVE: Jars = 0.20; Bowls = 0.

Illustrations

3.47.71   Jar rim. Dark grey fabric with burnished outer surface.

SFBS 17 AND 18 (FIGS 3.48–50)

These two intercutting sunken-featured buildings were excavated together as feature 3441 in six sectors. It is no longer possible to establish the exact lines of the sectors, which were irregular in shape, but they ran in the usual anti-clockwise direction starting from A in the usual position of the south-west quadrant with B adjacent to the east, C next to B in the north-east end of SFB 18 with D in the north-west end, E to the west and finally F in the usual position of quadrant D of SFB 17. The line of the cut could not be distinguished in plan and proved difficult to detect in section. There was therefore considerable mixing between the fills of the two features and it is extremely difficult to reconstruct their relationships, particularly in view of the fact that not all the layers identified in the context records appear in section.

SFB 17

Context 3441; Grid reference: 51295 98096; Site plan: D7/8; Orientation: E/W: Length at surface: *c* 6.5 m; Distance between postholes: 6.2 m; Width: 4.0 m; Depth: 0.56 m.

Description

SFB 17 was unusually large and cut the north-east ditch of ring ditch 801. It cut or was cut by the south-west end of SFB 18. The pit was sub-rectangular in plan with postholes 3797 and 3801 in the centres of the east and west ends. The sides of the pit sloped outwards. The posthole 3796 in the centre was filled by the occupation layer 5 and was probably the south-west posthole of SFB 18, although the possibility that it held a centre post for SFB 17 cannot be completely excluded. A limestone block lay on the base of the pit.

It appears from the context records and sections that SFB 17 contained six main layers of fill:

1 grey brown sandy loam with 50% gravel containing pottery and bone.
2 medium red brown sandy loam with 40% gravel containing pottery, bone, a large piece of limestone, green clay, burnt material and small finds.
3 medium red brown sandy loam with 70% gravel containing pea grit inclusions, pottery, bone, green clay, powdery burnt material, conglomerate and limestone.
4 discontinuous deposits of medium yellow brown sandy silt above and within layer 3.
5 well defined layer of slightly powdery medium grey brown silt containing powdery burnt material and ash, overlying 6.
6 pea gravel and natural gravel overlying the natural soft gravel base of the feature.

SFB 18

Context 3441 Grid reference: 51295 98096; Site plan: D7 Orientation: NE/SW; Length at surface: *c* 4.5 m; Distance between postholes: 4.0 m; Width: > 3.0 m; Depth: *c* 0.5 m.

Description

SFB 18 lay just outside the ditch of ring ditch 801 and cut or was cut by SFB 17. The pit appears to have been the usual sub-rectangular shape, with postholes 3798 and 3796 at the north-east and south-west ends. The pit edges sloped outwards.

1–5 descriptions as 17.
6 yellow brown sand, discontinuous between 2 and 3.
D/7 = C/9 light-medium red brown sandy loam, 50% medium gravel, apparent only around 'upper edge' of sector (labelled as 7 on section, Fig. 3.48).
D/8 = C/10 pea gravel underlying D/7 = C/9.
D9 = C7 natural sand extending into base of 3798, underlying 5.
C/8 redeposited natural gravel stained with topsoil and pea gravel.

The pits of SFBs 17 and 18 were dug to the same approximate depths. There were four postholes in SFBs 17 and 18; 3796, 3797, 3798 and 3801. The nature of the fill of 3801 is not recorded, but it seems clear that it was the west posthole of SFB 17. It seems equally clear that 3798 was the north-east posthole of SFB 18. The records concerning the fill of 3797 are confusing; its position strongly suggests that it was the east posthole of SFB 17, but it is described as having a fill homogeneous with D7 = C9, said to have been part of the primary fill of 18. However, the site records elsewhere state that at times it was extremely difficult to distinguish between layers 2 and 3 of 17 and 9 of 18, and it is possible that layers 3 and 9 have been confused. From its position, it also seems likely that 3796 was originally the south-west posthole of 18. It is filled by layer 5, which from the soil description was probably an occupation layer.

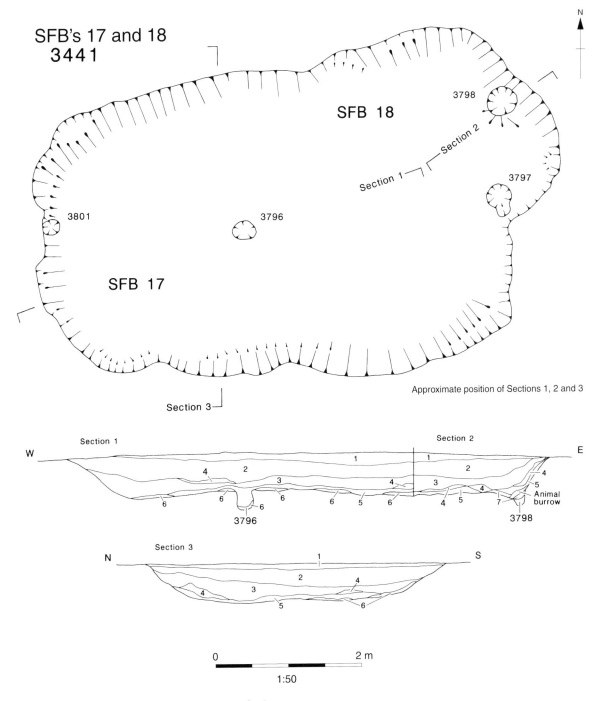

Figure 3.48   Sunken-featured buildings 17 and 18.

Since 5 extends as far as the north-east end of SFB 18, overlying the fill of posthole 3798, but on the section stops *c* 0.6 m short of the south-west end of SFB 17, the balance of probability seems to be that 5 represents an occupation layer in the base of 18 after its posts had been removed and that 18 therefore post-dates 17, possibly reusing its central posthole 3796. The cut could not be identified in the field, although the site records state that C/9 and C/10 appeared to have been cut by other fills. It is possible that they represent slumping from the sides of the pit of SFB 18 after the posts had been removed and before the buildup of occupation layer 5. It is impossible, however, to be certain of the stratigraphic relationship of these two features.

Finds

Eleven finds were associated with SFBs 17 and 18. Textile equipment consisted of a simple bone spindle-whorl, 348, and a very fine example of a pin beater, 343, used to separate the warp threads in conjunction with a warp-weighted loom. It has a number of transverse grooves due to extensive use.

131

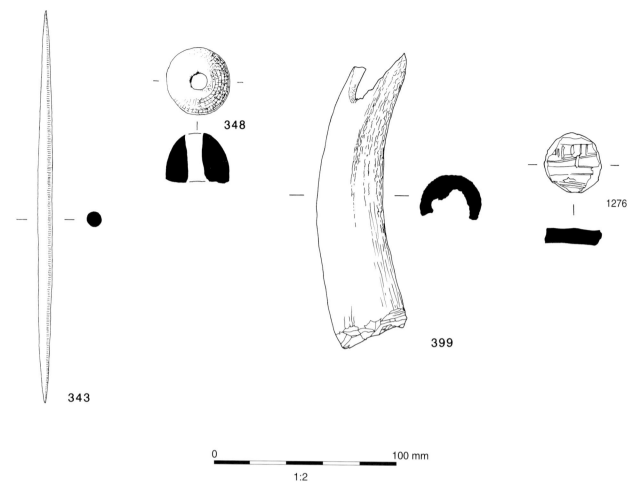

Figure 3.49   Sunken-featured buildings 17 and 18 artefacts.

Part of an antler tine, 399, is a waste product of antler working. There are also a woodworking nail, 229, and a fragment of an iron rod 266.

Three reused bases of Roman vessels were also recovered. 46 is a half base. 47 and 48 have been cut into wedge shapes. There is also a small gaming counter SF 1276 in an Anglo-Saxon fabric. 611 is a fragment of vitrified pottery, which has been subjected to an intense amount of heat over a short time.

Layer 1

266 SF 1026   **Iron rod** Length 55 mm, width 11 mm, thickness 8 mm. Rectangular cross-section, broken at both ends. (Not illustrated)

614 SF 1028   **Copper alloy farthing** Harington farthing. James VI and I 1613–1614. (Not illustrated)

Reused Roman sherd no. 48 SF 1495   Diameter 60 mm. Wedge-shaped fragment of a foot-ring base in Oxford red/brown colour-coated fabric 3. (Not illustrated).

611 SF 1654   **Slag, vitrified sherd** (Not illustrated)

Layer 2

229 SF 1065   **Iron nail** Length 55 mm. Circular flat head, bent shank with square cross-section. (Not illustrated)

343 SF 1066   **Bone pin beater** Length 207 mm. Highly polished shaft tapering to a point at both ends. Transverse grooves down one side.

348 SF 1064   **Bone spindlewhorl** Diameter 35 mm. Hemispherical. Bovine? femur head with central perforation, diameter 9 mm. Weight 11.2 g.

399 SF 1519   **Antler waste** Antler tine, the base has been chopped part way through and then broken off to detach it from the beam.

Reused Roman sherd no. 46 SF 1496   Diameter 90 mm. Modified half of a foot-ring base in Oxford red/brown colour-coated fabric 3. (Not illustrated)

Reused Roman sherd no. 47 SF 1498   Diameter *c* 70 mm. Wedge-shaped fragment of a foot-ring base in Oxford red/brown colour-coated fabric 3. (Not illustrated)

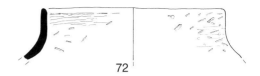

Layer 3

SF 1276   **Ceramic counter** Diameter 30 mm. Made from a body sherd in Anglo-Saxon fabric.

Pottery

Pottery occurrence per layer by fabric type.

Fabric	F1	F2	F3	F4	F6	% mineral	% chaff	Total wt (g)
1	154	28	24	0	20	78.8	21.2	226
2	85	141	83	2	236	31.1	68.9	547
3	137	121	46	2	559	21.4	78.6	865
5	0	0	0	0	45	0	100	45
Total wt* (g)	376	290	153	4	860			1683
Mean sherd wt	8.4	7.4	13.1	2.0	14.3			

*some of the pottery from this feature was not assigned a specific quadrant or layer by the excavators.

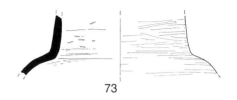

Pottery occurrence per quadrant and layer, all fabrics.

Layer/quadrant	A	B	C	D	E	F	G	Total wt (g)
1*								–
2		28	148	102	111	65	93	0	547
3		168	183	0	159	255	100	0	865
5		38	0	0	0	3	0	4	45
Total wt (g)	234	331	102	270	323	193	4	1457
% of total	16.1	22.7	7.0	18.5	22.2	13.3	0.3	

*Layer 1 was not excavated by quadrant.

EVE: Jars = 0.75; Bowls = 0.

No chronologically diagnostic pottery.

Cross-fit: C/2 = D/2.

Illustrations

3.50.72	Upright jar rim. Black fabric with burnished surfaces.
3.50.73	Neck of jar with upright rim. Black fabric with burnished surfaces.
3.50.74	Jar rim. Black fabric with burnished surfaces.
3.50.75	'Stepped' base sherd. Black fabric with brown unfinished surfaces.

SFB 19

Context 3542; Grid reference: 51279 98154; Figures 3.51–2 Site plan: D6; Orientation: NE/SW; Length at

Figure 3.50 Sunken-featured buildings 17 and 18 pottery.

surface: 3.9 m; Distance between postholes: 3.5 m; Width: 2.8 m; Depth: 0.39 m.

Description

SFB 19 was approximately 25 m north-west of the central group of post-built structures. The pit was an irregular sub-rectangle with postholes 3546 and 3555 at the north-east and south-west ends. The floor of the pit was uneven and the sides sloped outwards.

The fill consisted of three layers:

1. red brown sandy loam with 35% gravel containing bone, pot, slag, daub and charcoal flecks.
2. brown black sandy loam with 25% gravel, flecks of charcoal, dark burnt patches, bone and pot.
3. brown sandy loam with 30% gravel at the sides of the pit.

There was a layer of pea gravel on the bottom of the pit.

It is not possible to relate the fill of the postholes to the fill of the pit with certainty, but from the soil descriptions it seems most likely that the fill of the pit continued into the postholes.

Finds

The five finds from this sunken-featured building include two reused bases of Roman pots. Number 51 is a complete base and 52 a cut half base. There is also a large ceramic fragment of uncertain use, 467. Number 273 is a small fragment of iron wire and 606 is two fragments of slag; both are probably the products of smiths' hearths. The larger fragment has been furnace-cooled and the smaller fragment cooled at a rapid rate.

Layer 1

Reused Roman sherd no. 51 SF 1500 Diameter 60 mm. Modified base sherd in greyware, fabric 4. (Not illustrated)

Reused Roman sherd no. 52 SF 1501 Diameter 90 mm. Half of a flat base in greyware, fabric 4.

606 SF 1338 **Slag, two planoconvex fragments** (Not illustrated)

Layer 2

273 SF 1353 **Iron wire** Length 35 mm Circular cross-section, broken at both ends. (Not illustrated)

467 SF 1588 **Large ceramic fragment** (Not illustrated)

Pottery tpq 6th century?

Pottery occurrence per layer by fabric type.

Layer/ Fabric	F1	F2	F3	F6	% mineral	% chaff	Total wt (g)
1	233	240	113	34	55.8	44.2	620
2	997	543	806	858	56.3	43.7	3204
3	107	20	40	14	81.2	18.8	181
Total wt (g)	1337	803	959	906			4005
Mean sherd wt	13.2	13.0	26.6	45.3			

Pottery occurrence per quadrant and layer, all fabrics.

Layer/quadrant	A	B	C	D	Total wt (g)
1	248	187	128	57	620
2	276	813	611	1504	3204
3	0	85	0	96	181
Total wt (g)	524	1085	739	1657	4005
% of total	13.1	27.1	18.5	41.4	

EVE: Jars 1.97; Bowls = 0.10.

Three incised sherds (A/1, F3, 5 g; A/2, F1, 2 g; C/2, F2, 6 g).
One stamped sherd (B/1, F1, 7 g).
One incised sherd (A/1 and B/1, F2, 121 g, rim sherd 18% complete).
One rusticated sherd (B/2, F1, 2 g).
One combed sherd (A/2, F2, 118 g).

Cross-fits: A/1 = B/1, A/1 = B/2, B/2 = B/3, B/2 = D/2, D/2 = D/3.

Illustrations

3.52.76	Profile of jar. Black fabric with browner, hand-smoothed outer surface.
3.52.77	Rim from incised jar. Black fabric with burnished surfaces.
3.52.78	Rim from large jar. Black fabric with smoothed surfaces.
3.52.79	Rim from large jar. Black fabric with burnished surfaces.
3.52.80	Rim from large jar. Dark grey fabric with brown surfaces.
3.52.81	Rim from small bowl. Black fabric with smoothed surfaces.
3.52.82	Stamped and incised sherd. Dark grey fabric with burnished surfaces.

The stamped and incised sherd (Fig. 3.52.82) is probably of 6th-century date.

SFB 20

Context 3606; Grid reference: 51299 98214; Figures 3.53–4; Site plan: D4; Orientation: NE/SW; Length at surface: 4.3 m; Distance between postholes: 3.6 m; Width: 2.9 m; Depth: 0.57 m.

Description

SFB 20 was one of a group of three sunken-featured buildings (20, 21 and 22) on the north-west edge of the excavated area, *c* 15 m north-east of the Neolithic oval barrow. The pit was sub-rectangular with postholes 3609 and 3695 in the centres of the north-east and south-west sides. The floor of the pit was uneven and the sides sloped outwards.

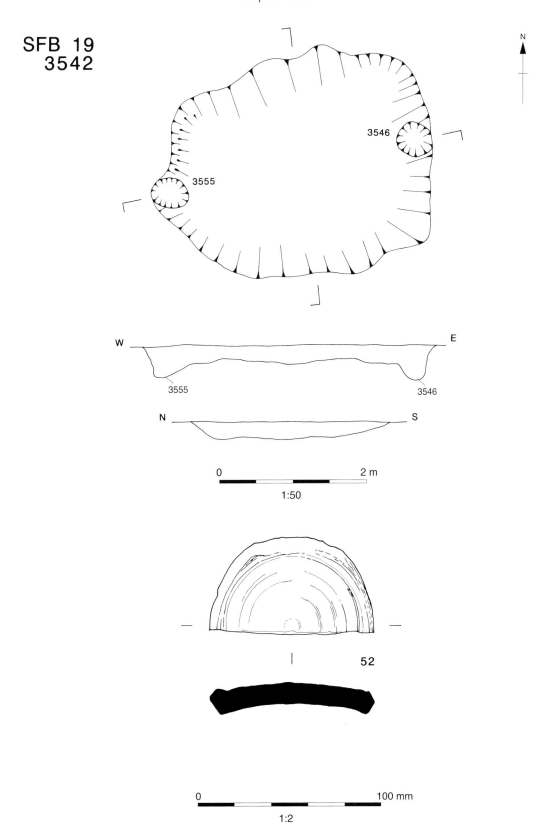

Figure 3.51 Sunken-featured building 19 and artefact.

There were three layers of fill:

1 reddish brown sandy loam with 40% gravel containing small quantities of bone, pot and flint.

2 brown black sandy loam with 25% gravel containing bone, pot, charcoal, daub, green clay and burnt limestone.

3 brown loam with yellow gravel inclusions and increasing quantities of pea grit towards the bottom of the feature.

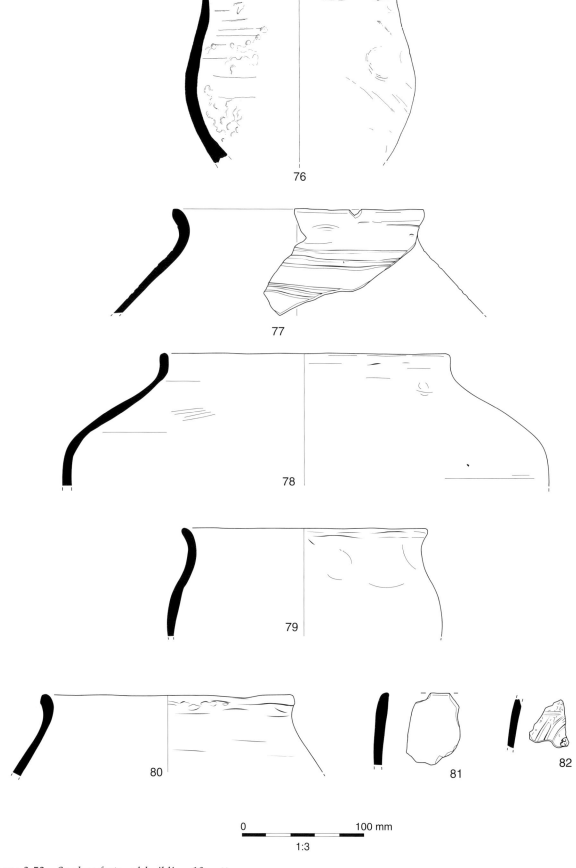

Figure 3.52 Sunken-featured building 19 pottery.

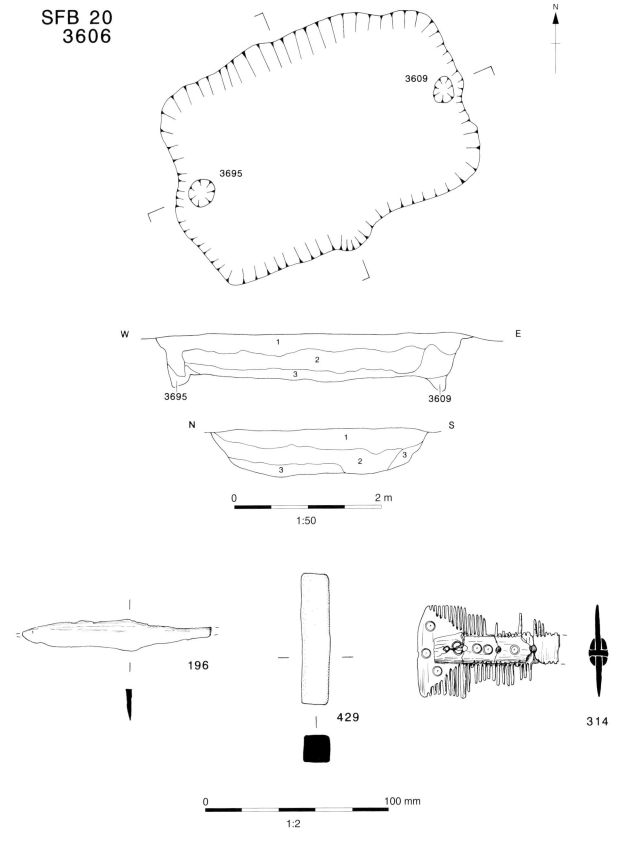

Figure 3.53   Sunken-featured building 20 and artefacts.

Finds

Only four finds were associated with this sunken-featured building. These include an iron knife, 196, of a type common in the 5th to 7th centuries. This has a worn blade and was found in association with a hone, 429, which also shows signs of wear.

Layer 3 produced part of a double-sided composite comb with ring and dot decoration, 314. This is similar to many combs from the site and is typical of Anglo-Saxon combs of 5th- to 7th-century date. An additional tooth, 339, was found in layer 2.

Layer 2

196 SF 1048   **Iron knife** Blade length 60 mm, width 16 mm, thickness 2 mm. Blade point central, inclined back with convex back slope and curved leading edge (Type A.1.c) Worn. Two grooves along one side of the blade. Tang set central to blade, length 44 mm, sloping shoulders

339 SF 1179   **Antler comb tooth** Length 16 mm. Fragment. (Not illustrated)

429 SF 1050   **Whetstone** Length 69 mm Fragment with signs of wear on all faces. Fine grained green-grey sandstone.

Layer 3

314 SF 1047   **Double-sided composite bone comb** Length 79 mm, height 48 mm. Rectangular end plate with graduated teeth. The teeth on one side average 4 per cm and on the other 5 per cm. Remains of four tooth segments. The connecting plates have a flat D-shaped cross-section, with saw marks on both edges. Remains of four iron rivets. The connecting plates and end plates are decorated with simple ring and dot motifs.

Pottery tpq 6th century?

Pottery occurrence per layer by fabric type.

Layer/ Fabric	F1	F2	F3	F6	% mineral	% chaff	Total wt (g)
1	367	215	18	105	54.6	45.4	705
2	221	1097	8	289	14.2	85.8	1615
3	22	334	74	141	16.8	83.2	571
Total wt (g)	610	1646	100	535			2891
Mean sherd wt	14.5	20.1	20.2	16.7			

Pottery occurrence per quadrant and layer, all fabrics.

Layer/quadrant	A	B	C	D	Total wt (g)
1	260	78	367	0	705
2	287	454	346	528	1615
3	383	0	0	188	571
Total wt (g)	930	532	713	716	2891
% of total	32.2	18.4	24.7	24.8	

EVE: Jars = 1.27; Bowls = 0.20.

Two collared sherds (A/1, F3, 8 g; D/2, F2, 28 g). Four incised sherds (A/1, F6, 8 g; A/2, F1, 3 g; A/3, F1, 22 g; D/2, F2, 8 g). One incised and stamped sherd (A/3, F2, 3 g). One incised and bossed sherd (A/3, F2, 87 g). One stamped sherd (D/3, F2, 11 g).

Cross-fits: A/1 = A/2 = D/2, A/2 = C/2.

Illustrations

3.54.83	Jar rim. Uniform black fabric with smoothed and burnished outer surface.
3.54.84	Upper body of jar. Black fabric with smoothed surfaces.
3.54.85	Rim of lugged vessel. Uniform black fabric, burnished outer surface.
3.54.86	Stamped and incised jar. Black fabric with burnished surface.
3.54.87	Stamped and incised jar rim. Black fabric with burnished surfaces.
3.54.88	Incised and stabbed sherd. Black fabric with burnished surfaces.
3.54.89	Finger-grooved sherd. Dark grey fabric with burnished surfaces.
3.54.90	Bodysherd from incised and bossed vessel. Black fabric with burnished outer surface.

The stamped pendant triangle sherd (Fig. 3.54.86) appears typical of those vessels dated by Myres to the 6th century (1977), and this is generally supported by the nature of the other decorated sherds from this feature (3.54.87 and 88).

SFB 21

Context 3607; Grid reference: 51292 98213; Figures 3.55–6; Site plan: D4; Orientation: NE/SW; Length at surface: 3.48 m; Distance between postholes: 3.0 m; Width: 2.8 m; Depth: 0.4 m.

Description

SFB 21 was one of a group of three sunken-featured buildings on the north-west of the excavated area. Its south edge cut or was cut by SFB 22, but the stratigraphic relationship is not clear. It was sub-rectangular in plan with postholes 3677 and 3678 in the centres of the north-east and south-west sides.

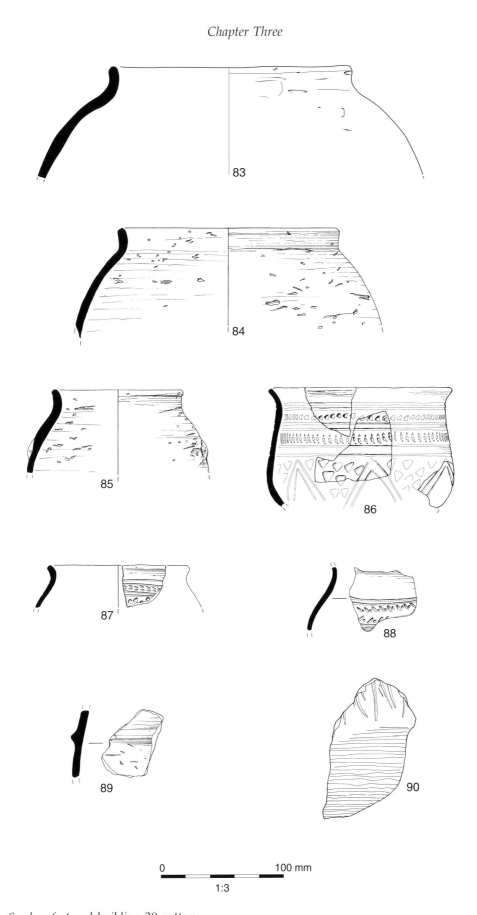

0   100 mm

1:3

Figure 3.54   Sunken-featured building 20 pottery.

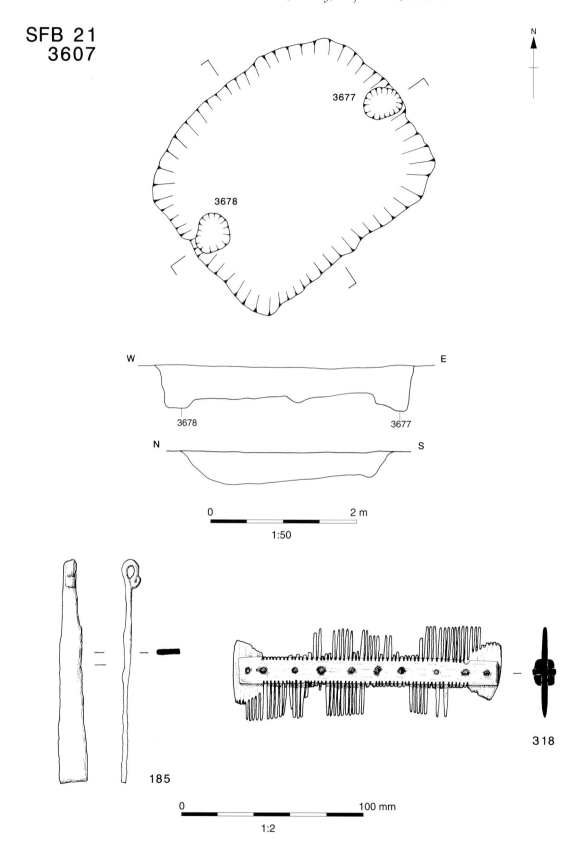

Figure 3.55   *Sunken-featured building 21 and artefacts.*

The floor of the pit was uneven and the sides sloped outwards.

1   medium reddish brown sandy loam with 25–30% gravel.

Finds

Several fragments of copper alloy sheet, catalogued together as 162, were found in this sunken-featured building. There was also part of a padlock key, 185, probably used with a barbed spring padlock. Other barbed spring padlock keys have been found at Shakenoak (Brodribb *et al.* 1972, figs 40, 179, 181 and 186).

The remaining find, the comb 318, is interesting because it is the only one from the site with curved end plates. The teeth start very close to the edge and the connecting plate runs right up to the edge of the comb. The edge of the end plate has been shaved. It appears that this comb has been repaired in antiquity, probably to remove some broken teeth.

Layer 1

162 SF 1051   **Copper alloy sheet** Length 21 mm, width 10 mm, thickness 0.5 mm. Rectangular cut sheet broken across one side. (Not illustrated). Also SF 1051 Copper alloy sheet. Thickness 0.5 mm. Four fragments. (Not illustrated)

185 SF 1045   **Iron padlock key** Length 118 mm. Stem with rectangular cross-section, bit missing. Hooked terminal.

244 SF 1052   **Iron nail** Length 36 mm. Shank fragment with square cross-section. Bent. (Not illustrated)

318 SF 1040   **Double-sided composite antler comb** Length 147 mm, height 49 mm. Curved end plates with graduated teeth starting at the very edge of the comb. Both sides have teeth averaging 5 per cm. The nine tooth segments are connected by plates with flat D-shaped cross-sections. Saw marks on both edges. Remains of ten iron rivets.

Pottery tpq 6th century?

Pottery occurrence per layer by fabric type.

Layer/Fabric	F1	F2	F4	F6	% mineral	% chaff	Total wt (g)
1	51	79	132	1423	10.9	89.1	1686
Mean sherd wt	12.8	8.9	18.9	13.7			

Pottery occurrence per quadrant and layer, all fabrics.

Layer/quadrant	A	B	C	D	Total wt (g)
1	447	245	0	994	1686
% of total	26.5	14.5	0	59.0	

EVE: Jars = 1.05; Bowls = 0.59.

Two incised sherds (D/1, F1, 1 g; D/1, F6, 3 g).
One handled cup/bowl (A/1, F6, 72 g, rim 43% complete).
Full profile of vessel with longitudinal lugs and a pedestal base (D/1, F6, 426 g, rim 23% complete).

Cross-fit: A/1 = B/1.

Illustrations

3.56.91   Near complete lugged jar. Black fabric with smoothed brown outer surface.
3.56.92   Jar rim. Black fabric with burnished outer surface.
3.56.93   Jar rim. Black fabric with smoothed outer surface.
3.56.94   Jar rim. Black fabric, unfinished surfaces.
3.56.95   Small handled cup/bowl. Black fabric with dark brown unfinished surfaces.

The near-complete vessel with the lugs and foot-ring base (Fig. 3.56.91) has a number of parallels from around England (Myres 1977, figs 75–77). Myres suggests that they belong to the 'sixth century or even later' (1977, 10).

SFB 22

Context 3608; Grid reference: 512935 982100; Figures 3.57–8; Site plan: D4; Orientation: ENE/WSW; Length at surface: 3.74 m; Distance between postholes: 3.4 m; Width: 2.64 m; Depth: 0.48 m.

Description

SFB 22 was the southernmost of the group of three sunken-featured buildings on the north-west of the excavated area, *c* 15 m north-east of the Neolithic oval barrow, and may have cut or been cut by SFB 21, although the stratigraphic relationship is not clear. It was irregularly sub-rectangular in plan with postholes 3604 and 3780 in the centres of the north-east and south-west sides. The floor of the pit was uneven and the sides were straight, almost vertical. The east-west section cannot be reconstructed.

Four layers of fill were distinguished. There were extensive rodent burrows in quadrant B. Small quantities of clay were noted in all four layers.

1   red brown sandy loam with green clay and 25% gravel.
2   dark red or grey brown sandy loam with 10% gravel.
3   lens of redeposited gravel within 2.
4   intermittent layer of dark red brown sandy loam with 15% gravel on the uneven bottom of the pit and in the postholes.

Finds

Four finds were recovered. There is a fragment of a bone shaft, 403, which has been polished. This is likely to be part of a pin or pin beater. Number 381 is a fragment from a bone spoon; spoons are comparatively rare finds from Anglo-Saxon sites, but there are a few 6th- and 7th-century examples (MacGregor 1985, 181–3). Number 381 is likely to have a flat spatulate bowl

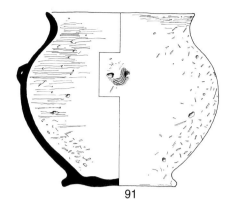

91

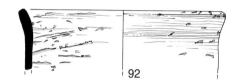

92

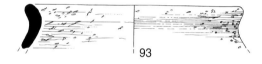

93

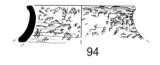

94

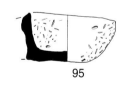

95

0   100 mm

1:3

Figure 3.56   Sunken-featured building 21 pottery.

similar to one from Shakenoak (Brodribb *et al.* 1972, 122, fig. 59.71) and to another from Buckquoy, Orkney (Ritchie 1977, 194, fig. 6.43). Another example with a shovel-shaped spoon and well defined shoulders came from Jarlshof (Hamilton 1956).

There is also a fragment of a rotary quern, 412, and a reused base from a Roman pottery vessel cut into a wedge shape, 55.

Layer 1

403 SF 1169   **Bone pin** Length 33 mm. Cylindrical polished shaft fragment. Broken at both ends. (Not illustrated)

381 SF 1170   **Bone spoon** Length 49 mm. Polished shaft with circular cross-section opening to a flat scoop, now broken.

412 SF 1180   **Rotary quern** Length 145 mm. Fragment, friable coarse grained feldspathic grit, colour close to Old Red Sandstone. ?Old Red Sandstone, ?Millstone Grit. (Not illustrated)

Layer 2

Reused Roman sherd no. 55 SF 1486   Diameter 70 mm. Wedge-shaped modified foot-ring base of a bowl in Oxford red/brown colour-coated fabric 3. (Not illustrated)

Pottery

Pottery occurrence per layer by fabric type.

Layer/Fabric	F1	F2	F3	F4	F6	% mineral	% chaff	Total wt (g)
1	458	279	49	66	234	52.8	47.2	1086
2	92	130	53	45	2	59.0	41.0	322
3	76	54	0	4	6	57.1	42.9	140
4	115	38	5	0	28	64.5	35.5	186
Total wt (g)	741	501	107	115	270			1734
Mean sherd wt	8.7	15.7	6.3	9.6	11.7			

Pottery occurrence per quadrant and layer, all fabrics.

Layer/quadrant	A	B	C	D	Total wt (g)
1	308	0	278	500	1086
2	189	34	99	0	322
3	91	0	49	0	140
4	186	0	0	0	186
Total wt (g)	774	34	426	500	1734
% of total	44.6	2.0	24.6	28.8	

EVE: Jars = 2.25; Bowls = 0.22.

No chronologically diagnostic pottery.

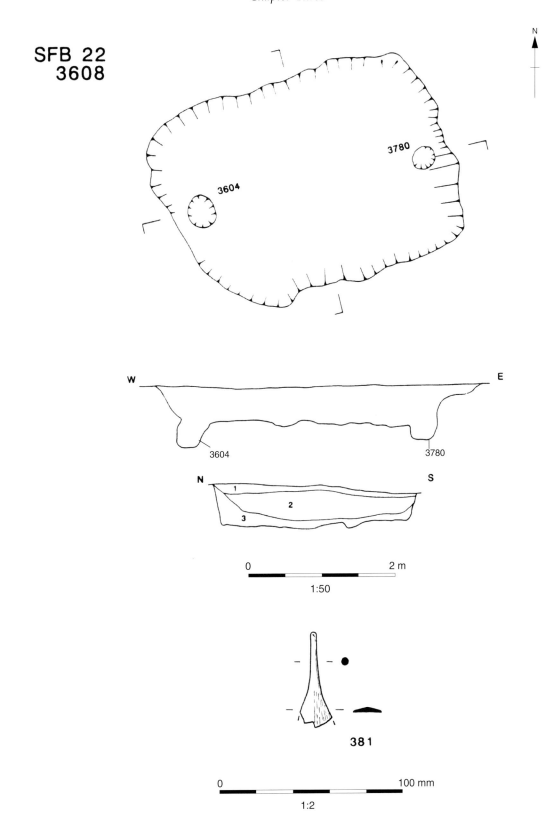

Figure 3.57   Sunken-featured building 22 and artefact.

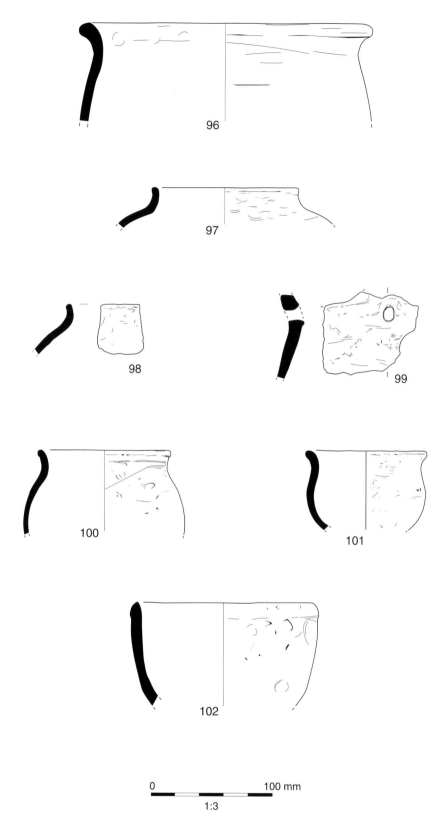

Figure 3.58   Sunken-featured building 22 pottery.

Illustrations

3.58.96	Rim sherd from jar. Black fabric with smoothed brown surfaces.
3.58.97	Rim sherd from jar. Black fabric with burnished surfaces.
3.58.98	Rim sherd from small jar. Black fabric with smoothed surfaces.
3.58.99	Upright lug. Black fabric with unfinished surfaces.
3.58.100	Rim sherd from jar. Black fabric with smoothed and burnished surfaces.
3.58.101	Rim sherd from small jar. Black fabric with burnished surfaces.
3.58.102	Bowl rim. Black fabric with smoothed brown surfaces.

SFB 23

Context 3800; Grid reference: 51378 98087; Figures 3.59–61; Orientation: a) NE/SW b) E/W; Site plan: H7; Length at surface: 4.25 m; Distance between postholes: a) 3.2 m b) 3.5 m; Width: 3.5 m; Depth: 0.3 m.

Description

SFB 23 abuts the south side of barrow 13. It appears to have consisted of two intercutting sunken-featured buidings, or a major rebuild, but the stratigraphic relationships cannot be reconstructed from the site records. The feature as excavated was very irregularly sub-rectangular and contained four postholes which probably represent two pairs. It is not possible to establish which postholes belong together, but from the plan and depths the most probable pairing is one in which pair a) consists of 3991 and 3901 on a north-east/south-west alignment and pair b) of 3993 and 3992 on an east/west alignment. The pit was shallow, with an uneven floor and near-vertical sides.

1 brown loam with 5% gravel.
2 deposit of large fragments of conglomerate and white limestone in the centre of the pit.

Finds

Twelve finds were recovered: 154 and 167 are both copper alloy sheets. Number 154 has been decorated with punched dot motifs and may have been part of a belt fitting. Number 167, which has two rivet holes, is probably part of a strap-end, broken in antiquity and then rolled up into a parcel and saved, probably to put back into the melt.

There are three nails, 226, 239 and 255, two of which are almost complete woodworking nails, and part of the top stone of a quern, 408.

There were a number of articles associated with textile working: a small shale spindlewhorl, 404, and two annular loomweights, 454 and 456, of a type generally thought to be of early Anglo-Saxon date

(Dunning *et al.* 1959, 24). There were also two complete bases of reused Roman pots, 56 and 57.

Number 396 is a fragment of worked antler. It is a quadrant which has been split from a beam. This could be a stage in preparing to make an artefact, possibly part of a comb.

Layer 1

154 SF 1069	**Copper alloy strip**	Length 18 mm, width 16 mm, thickness 0.5 mm. Rectangular cut sheet, broken along one end. Pierced for a rivet now missing. Decorated with a band of punched dots around the perimeter.
226 SF 1070	**Iron nail**	Length 89 mm. Circular flat head, square cross-sectioned shank. Tip missing. (Not illustrated)
239 SF 1171	**Iron nail**	Length 60 mm. The small square flat head is a slight expansion of the square cross-sectioned shank. (Not illustrated)
255 SF 1071	**Iron nail**	Length 44 mm. Shank fragment with square cross-section. (Not illustrated)
404 SF 1068	**Shale spindlewhorl**	Diameter 31 mm. Hemispherical whorl with convex upper and roughly flat lower surface, possibly damaged. Central perforation, diameter 7 mm. Weight 8.14 g.
396 SF 1523	**Worked antler**	Length 59 mm. Part of a tine with saw marks at both ends. The tine was then split longitudinally to form a quadrant.

Layer 2

454 SF 1072	**Annular fired clay loomweight**	Diameter 130 mm. Three fragments, approx. 25%. Estimated weight 747.28 g. (Not illustrated)
456 SF 1080	**Annular fired clay loomweight**	Diameter 160 mm. Two fragments, approx 30%. Roughly smoothed surfaces. Estimated weight 733.5 g. (Not illustrated)
408 SF 1073	**Rotary quern**	Thin top stone. (Not illustrated)

Layer 3

167 SF 1172	**Copper alloy sheet**	Length 42 mm, thickness 0.5 mm. Rectangular cut sheet with two rivet holes. Folded over into a parcel. Lines of solder on the upper surface.

Reused Roman sherd no. 56 SF 1489 Diameter 60 mm. Modified base from a pedestal beaker in greyware, fabric 2.

Reused Roman sherd no. 57 SF 1490 Diameter 50 mm. Modified foot-ring base from a beaker in Oxford red/brown colour-coated fabric 3. (Not illustrated).

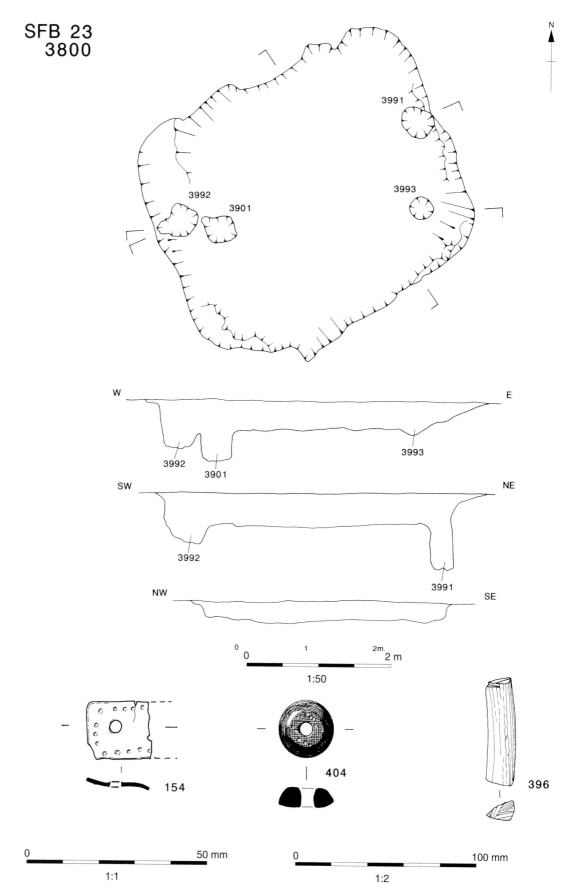

Figure 3.59   *Sunken-featured building 23 and artefacts.*

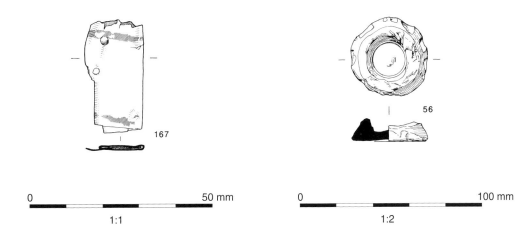

0		50 mm

1:1

Figure 3.60   Sunken-featured building 23 artefacts continued.

Pottery tpq 6th century?

Pottery occurrence per layer by fabric type.

Layer/ Fabric	F1	F2	F3	F4	F6	% mineral	% chaff	Total wt (g)
1	95	63	17	0	0	64.0	36.0	175
2	121	145	59	8	17	53.2	46.8	350
3	22	23	2	0	77	19.4	80.6	124
Total wt (g)	238	231	78	8	94			649
Mean sherd wt	9.5	11.6	15.6	8.0	6.7			

Pottery occurrence per quadrant and layer, all fabrics.

Layer/quadrant	A	B	C	D	Total wt (g)
1	136	111	23	0	270
2	0	45	153	152	350
3	0	76	0	48	124
Total wt (g)	136	232	176	200	744
% of total	18.3	31.2	23.7	26.9	

EVE: Jars = 0.35; Bowls = 0.12.

Two incised sherds, (C/1, F1, 15 g; C/1, F3, 8 g). Stamped sherd (B/1, F2, 22 g).

Cross-fit: Stamped sherd joins pit 414, barrow 13 H/2.

Illustrations

3.61.103   Stamped sherd. Black fabric with burnished surfaces.
3.61.104   Jar rim. Uniform black fabric with brown outer surface below the carination.

The stamped sherd (Fig. 3.61.103) is probably 6th century.

103

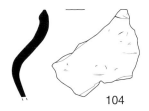

104

0		100 mm

1:3

Figure 3.61   Sunken-featured building 23 pottery.

SFB 24

Context 3805; Grid reference: 51381 98098; Figures 3.62–3; Site plan: H7; Orientation: NNE/SSW; Length at surface: 3.54 m; Distance between postholes: 2.6 m; Width: 2.72 m; Depth: *c* 0.5 m.

Description

SFB 24 was cut into the east side of barrow 13. It was sub-rectangular in plan with two postholes, 3872 and 3871, in the centres of the NNE and SSW sides. The pit bottom was level and the sides sloped outwards.

1   dark brown loam with 10% gravel containing much domestic debris.

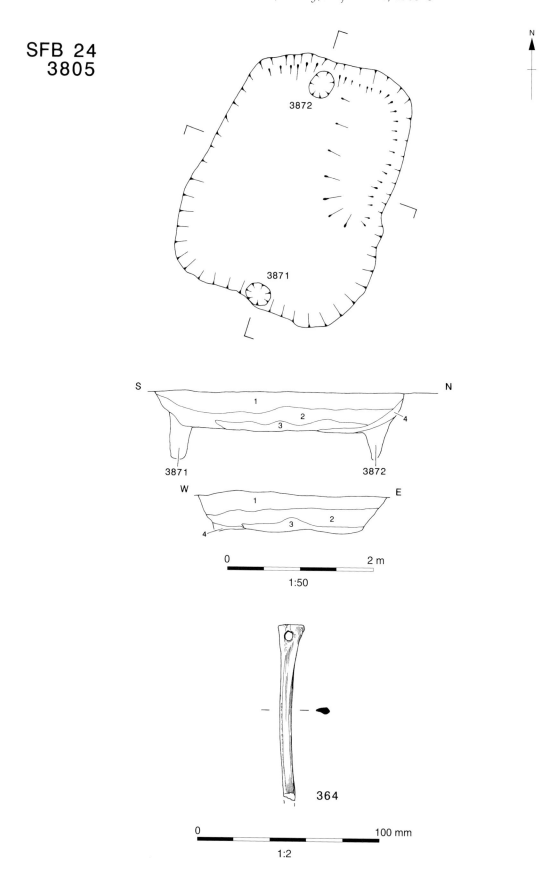

Figure 3.62   Sunken-featured building 24 and artefact.

2 darker grey brown loam with 10% gravel containing some charcoal flecks and domestic debris.
3 grey brown fine friable soft loam with 5% gravel containing large quantities of ash and charcoal, burnt bone and pottery. The sections indicate that this deposit overlay another layer (4 on section), dark brown sandy loam with 5% gravel, which had accumulated at the north edge of the pit.

The two layers of fill within each posthole are described as sandy loams with 20% and 5% gravel and there is no indication that the burnt layer continued into the postholes. It therefore seems most likely that the posts had been withdrawn and the pit had begun to fill before the pit bottom was used as a hearth.

Finds

Seven finds were recovered. Textile equipment includes three annular loomweights, 459, 463 and 464, of a type used with a warp-weighted loom and common in the early Saxon period (Dunning *et al.* 1959, 24), and a possible pin beater, 357. A perforated pig fibula pin, 364, was also found, a very common type at Barrow Hills. Also found were a fragment of a late Roman glass bowl, 295, and a nail fragment, 259.

Layer 1

259 SF 1075 **Iron nail** Length 45 mm. Shank fragment with square cross-section. (Not illustrated)

295 SF 1173 **Glass bowl** Thickness 1.2 mm. Small fragment of pale green heavily bubbled translucent glass. Patches of a dark brown flaky weathering crust. Late Roman. (Not illustrated)

464 SF 1596 **Annular, fired clay loomweight** Length 42 mm. Fragment. (Not illustrated)

Layer 2

459 SF 1076 **Annular, fired clay loomweight** Diameter 140 mm. Fragment approx. 15% with roughly smoothed surfaces. Estimated weight 638.33 g. (Not illustrated)

Layer 3

357 SF 1219 **Bone pin beater?** Length 45 mm, diameter 7 mm. Polished shaft fragment with circular cross-section. (Not illustrated)

364 SF 1074 **Bone pin** Length 92 mm. Made from a pig fibula polished and perforated at the proximal end. The head has been modified. Tip missing.

463 SF 1218 **Annular, fired clay loomweight** Length 57 mm. Fragment. (Not illustrated)

Pottery tpq 6th century?

Pottery occurrence per layer by fabric type.

Layer/Fabric	F1	F2	F3	F4	F6	% mineral	% chaff	Total wt (g)
1	446	1572	334	72	146	33.2	66.8	2570
Mean sherd wt	8.3	17.5	13.4	9.0	10.4			

Pottery occurrence per quadrant and layer, all fabrics.

Layer/quadrant	A	B	C	D	Total wt (g)
1	1342	844	248	131	2565
% of total	52.3	32.9	9.7	5.1	

EVE: Jars = 1.35; Bowls = 0.35.

Seven incised sherds: (A/2, F1, 16 g; A/2, F2, 5 g; B/1, F1, 4 g; B/2, F1, 14 g; B/3, F3, 14 g, jar rim 8% complete; D/1, F1, 15 g; D/2, F6, 17 g).

Six stamped and incised sherds: (A/2, F2, 11 g; B/1, F1, 4 g, B/1, F1, 5 g; B/3, F1, 5 g; D/2, F2, 20 g; D/2, F6, 4 g).

Cross-fits: A/1 = B/3 (x2), A/2 = B/1, B/1 = B/2 = D/2.

Illustrations

3.63.105 Rim sherd from lugged jar. Dark grey fabric with unfinished surfaces.

3.63.106 Rim sherd from incised jar. Black fabric with burnished surfaces.

3.63.107 Rim sherd from small bowl. Black fabric with smoothed surfaces.

3.63.108 Rim sherd from small jar. Black fabric with burnished surfaces.

3.63.109 Lugged bowl. Black fabric with burnished surfaces, turning brown on lower body.

3.63.110 Rim sherd from small jar. Black fabric with burnished surfaces.

3.63.111 Stamped and incised sherd. Uniform dark grey fabric. Surfaces worn.

3.63.112 Incised sherd. Black fabric with burnished surfaces.

3.63.113 Stamped and incised sherd. Uniform dark grey fabric, brown worn outer surface.

3.63.114 Incised sherd. Black fabric with burnished surfaces.

The presence of the stamped and incised sherds (Figs. 3.63.111 and 113) suggests a 6th-century *terminus post quem*.

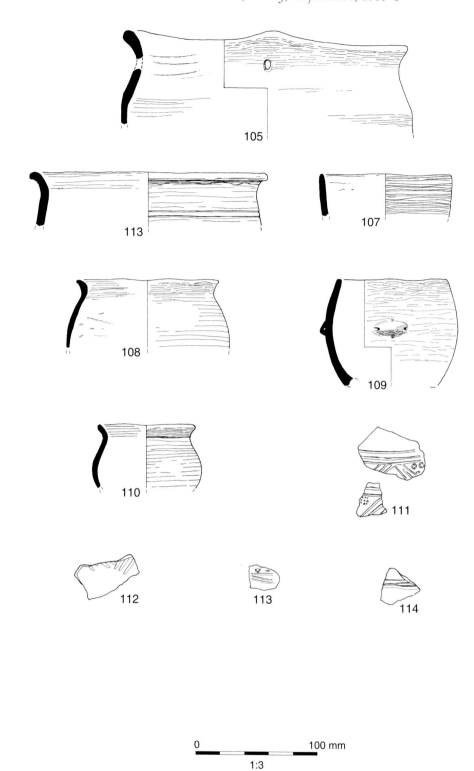

0   100 mm

1:3

Figure 3.63   Sunken-featured building 24 pottery.

SFB 25

Context 3811; Grid reference: 51310 98033; Figures 3.64–5; Site plan: F9; Orientation: NE/SW; Length at surface: >3.95 m; Distance between postholes: 3.5 m; Width: 2.5 m; Depth: 0.11 m.

Description

SFB 25 was in the south of the excavated area, 50 m south-west of the segmented ring ditch. The pit was shallow and irregular and its identification as a sunken-featured building rests mainly on the shape

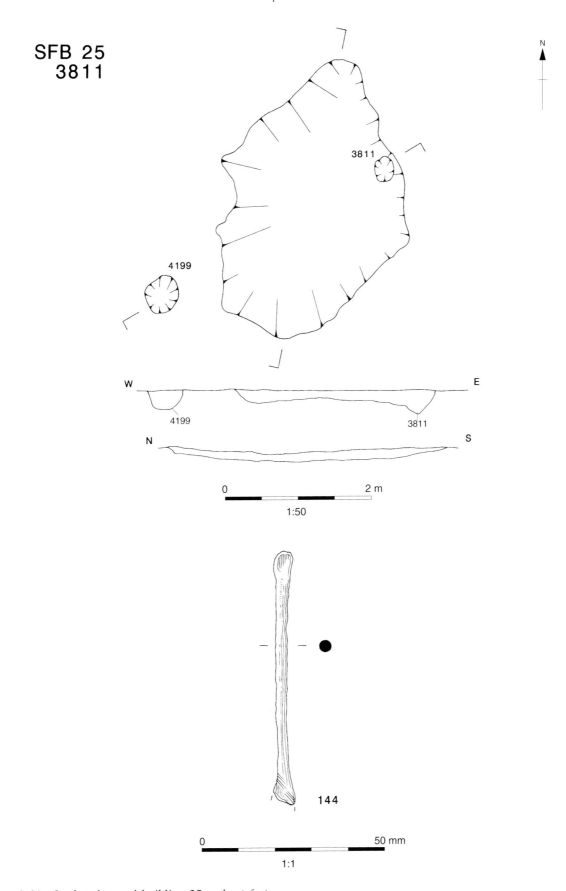

SFB 25
3811

Figure 3.64   Sunken-featured building 25 and artefact.

of the north-east end and the presence of two post-holes, 3811 and 4199, on a north-east/south-west alignment, the former in the centre of the north-east end and the latter slightly to the south-west of the surviving edge of the depression.

1 dark grey brown sandy loam with 15–20% gravel containing flecks of charcoal and sherds of Saxon and Romano-British pot, the latter noticeably abraded.

Finds

Only three objects were found in this sunken-featured building: 144, a toilet spoon, is very corroded and was probably pierced for suspension. Spoons such as this were often features of toilet sets and were used as ear scoops. They are common in female graves in the Upper Thames region in the 5th and 6th centuries (Dickinson 1976, 224). The feature also contained a cut wedge-shaped fragment from the base of a Roman pot, 58, and part of an annular loomweight, 460, of early Saxon type (Dunning *et al.* 1959, 24).

Layer 1

144 SF 1077   **Copper alloy toilet spoon** Length 67 mm. Made from a rolled sheet. There is a spoon-like bowl at one end and the other end has a flattened scoop, now broken. File marks on scoop.

460 SF 1174   **Annular, fired clay loomweight** Length 51 mm. Fragment. (Not illustrated)

Reused Roman sherd no. 58 SF 1503 Diameter 170 mm. Wedge-shaped fragment from a flat base in greyware, fabric 4. (Not illustrated).

Pottery tpq 5th-6th century?

Pottery occurrence by fabric type.

Fabric	F1	F2	F3	F6	% mineral	% chaff	Total wt (g)
	51	11	319	5	95.9	4.1	386
Mean sherd wt	7.3	3.7	39.9	5.0			

*not excavated by quadrant and layer.

EVE: Jars = 0.11; Bowls = 0.02.

One incised sherd (F1, 6 g).

Illustrations

3.65.115   Rim sherd from small jar. Black fabric with smoothed and burnished outer surface.

3.65.116   Incised sherd. Grey fabric with dark brown burnished surfaces.

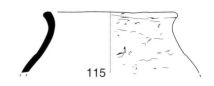

115

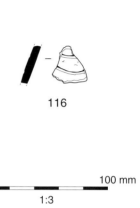

116

0   100 mm

1:3

Figure 3.65   Sunken-featured building 25 pottery.

SFB 26

Context 4001; Grid reference: 51347 98079; Figures 3.66–7; Site plan: F8b; Orientation: ENE/WSW; Length at surface: 3.4 m; Distance between post-holes: not known; Width: 3.0 m; Depth: 0.6 m.

Description

SFB 26 cut the inner southern ditch of barrow 12. The pit was sub-rectangular in plan with posthole 4603 in the centre of the WSW side. The base of the pit was uneven.

Four layers were distinguished. Layers 1–3 contained numerous tip lines and 3, which became greyer towards the bottom, continued into posthole 4603.

1 reddish brown sandy loam with few finds.
2 reddish brown sandy loam with less gravel.
3 grey brown loam with varying amounts of gravel.
4 fine greenish grey loam, possibly representing an occupation deposit contemporary with the use of the sunken-featured building, perhaps debris fallen through floorboards: intermittent over the base of the pit, nowhere more than 60 mm thick.

Finds

Thirteen objects were recovered from the fills of this feature. Textile working equipment consisted of two pin beaters, 351, which was short and cigar-shaped, and 354, which was longer and slimmer and came from the possible occupation layer. There was also a fragment of a biconical spindlewhorl, 446, in the backfill. Found in association with one of the pin beaters, 354, also in the possible occupation debris, were a perforated pig fibula pin, 373, a fragment of a composite comb, 327, of the type common in the

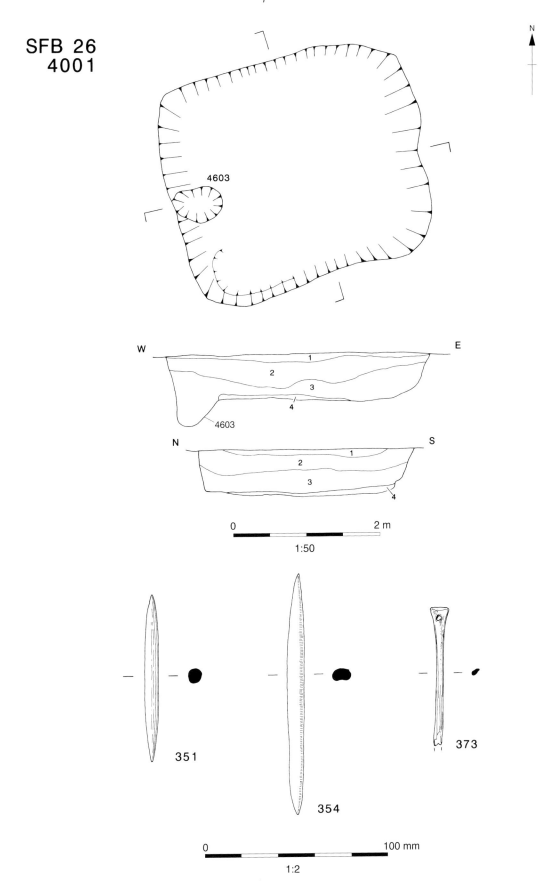

Figure 3.66   Sunken-featured building 26 and artefacts.

5th to 7th centuries, a nail with a T-shaped head, 231, and two ceramic gaming pieces, 1193 in an Anglo-Saxon fabric, and 60 in samian ware. From layer 3 there is a complete base from a reused Roman pot, 59. Two fragments of an abraded tine, 398, which had been sawn and split, are probably waste from antler working.

Layer 1

254 SF 1351 **Iron nail** Length 24 mm. Shank fragment with square cross-section. (Not illustrated)

623 SF 1408 **Clay pipe** Stem fragment. Post-medieval. (Not illustrated)

Layer 2

398 SF 1520 **Antler waste** Fragments of two abraded tines. Probably sawn and split to detach them from the beam. (Not illustrated)

Layer 3

272 SF 1158 **Iron pin** Length 40 mm, diameter 2 mm. Shaft fragment with circular cross-section. (Not illustrated)

351 SF 1085 **Bone pin beater** Length 88 mm, diameter 8 mm. Made from a polished shaft with circular cross-section. Pointed at both ends.

446 SF 1221 **Ceramic spindlewhorl** Fragment of a biconical whorl, approx 25% Estimated weight 20.8 g. (Not illustrated)

Reused Roman sherd no. 59 SF 1491 Diameter 65 mm. Modified foot-ring base in Oxford red/brown colour-coated fabric 3. (Not illustrated)
Reused Roman sherd no. 60 SF 1492. Ceramic counter Diameter 40 mm. Samian ware, fabric 8, burnt. (Not illustrated)

Layer 4

231 SF 1086 **Iron nail** Length 60 mm. T-shaped head, rectangular cross-sectioned shank. (Not illustrated)

327 SF 1192/1222 **Double-sided composite antler comb** Height 42 mm. Tooth segment with teeth averaging 4 per cm on both sides. Half rivet holes at both edges with traces of iron staining. Fragment of a connecting plate with D-shaped cross-section and saw cuts along both edges. One iron rivet and part of two rivet holes remain. (Not illustrated)

354 SF 1092 **Bone pin beater** Length 128 mm, diameter 9 mm. Made from a polished

shaft with oval cross-section. Pointed at both ends.

373 SF 1220 **Bone pin** Length 72 mm. Made from a pig fibula perforated at the proximal end. Tip missing. Polished.

SF 1193 **Ceramic counter** Diameter 34 mm. Modified body sherd in Anglo-Saxon fabric. (Not illustrated)

Pottery tpq 6th century?

Pottery occurrence per layer by fabric type.

Layer/ Fabric	F1	F2	F3	F4	F6	% mineral	% chaff	Total wt (g)
1	167	229	205	3	28	63.1	36.9	632
2	13	159	23	0	19	16.8	83.2	214
3	256	554	1123	0	41	69.9	30.1	1974
4	269	379	388	0	27	61.8	38.2	1063
Total wt (g)	705	1321	1739	3	115			3883
Mean sherd wt	6.4	9.3	25.6	3.0	7.2			

Pottery occurrence per quadrant and layer, all fabrics.

Layer/quadrant	A	B	C	D	Total wt (g)
1	77	126	90	339	632
2	69	0	15	130	214
3	1126	0	139	709	1974
4	151	0	182	730	1063
Total wt (g)	1423	126	426	1908	3883
% of total	36.6	3.2	11.0	49.1	

EVE: Jars = 1.27; Bowls = 0.24.

Four incised sherds (A/1, F1, 15 g; A/1, F2, 8 g; C/1, F3, 19 g; D/3, F1, 2 g).
Two stamped and incised sherds (D/1, F6, 9 g; D/3, F2, 24 g).
Cross-fit: D/2 = C/4 = D/4.

Illustrations

3.67.117 Jar rim. Black fabric with dark brown smoothed surfaces.
3.67.118 Jar rim. Black fabric with brown burnished outer surface.
3.67.119 Jar rim. Black fabric with smoothed and burnished surfaces.
3.67.120 Jar rim. Black fabric with burnished surfaces.

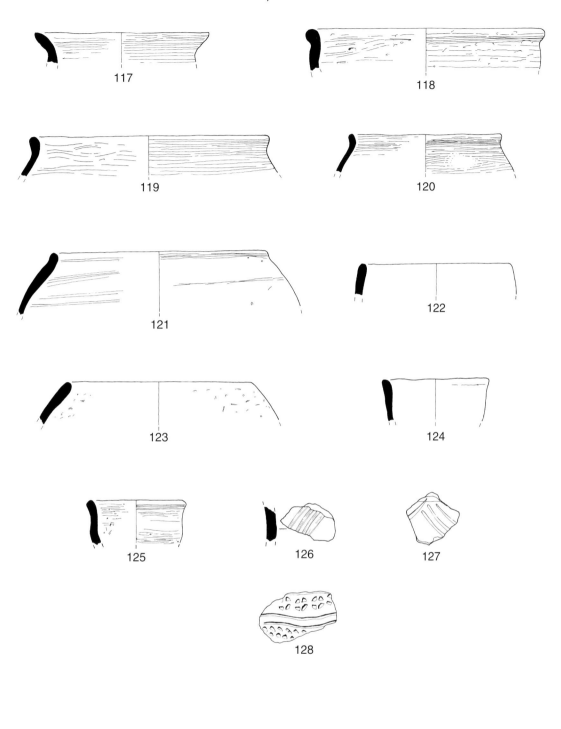

Figure 3.67   Sunken-featured building 26 pottery.

3.67.121	Inturned jar rim. Dark grey fabric with smoothed surfaces.	3.67.123	Inturned bowl rim. Black fabric with smoothed surfaces.
3.67.122	Inturned bowl rim. Black fabric with smoothed surfaces.	3.67.124	Rim sherd from small bowl. Black with smoothed surfaces.

3.67.125 Rim sherd from small jar. Dark reddish-brown fabric with smoothed black outer surface.

3.67.126 Incised sherd. Black fabric with burnished outer surface.

3.67.127 Incised sherd. Black fabric with burnished surfaces.

3.67.128 Stamped and incised sherd. Dark grey fabric with smooth surfaces, outer lightly burnished.

The stamped sherd (Fig. 3.67.128) suggests a 6th-century *terminus post quem* for this group.

SFB 27

Context 4101; Grid reference: 51345 98035; Figure 3.68; Site plan: F9; Orientation: NE/SW; Length at surface: 2.95 m; Distance between postholes: not applicable; Width: 2.2 m; Depth: 0.24 m.

Description

SFB 27 was *c* 35 m south of barrow 12, near the southeast edge of the excavated area. The sub-rectangular plan of the pit suggests a sunken-featured building, although an unusually small one; there were no postholes and the floor slopes markedly upwards towards the west. It is possible that the feature represents the excavation of a sunken-featured building pit which for some reason was never completed.

1 dark brown friable loam with 10% gravel.

Finds

There were no small finds.

Pottery

Pottery occurrence per layer by fabric type.

Layer/Fabric	F1	F3	F6	% mineral	% chaff	Total wt (g)
1	10	57	7	90.5	8.5	74
Mean sherd wt (g)	3.3	57	7			

Pottery occurrence per quadrant and layer, all fabrics.

Layer/quadrant	A	B	C	D	Total wt (g)
1		60	14	0	0	74
% of total		81.1	18.9	0	0	

EVE: Jars = 0; Bowls = 0.

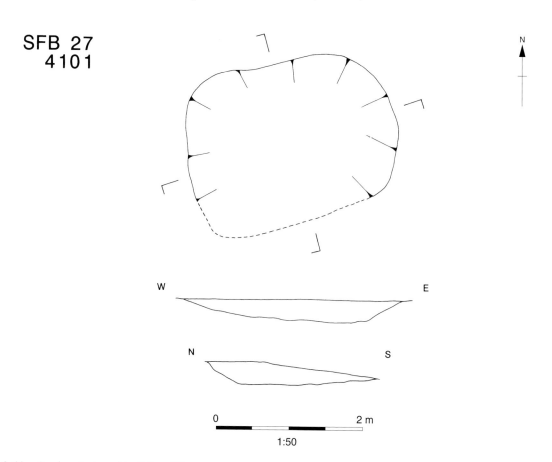

SFB 27
4101

Figure 3.68 Sunken-featured building 27.

156

SFB 28

Context 4198; Grid reference: 51307 98048; Figures 3.69–74; Site plan: E8; Orientation: ENE/WSW; Length at surface: 3.65 m; Distance between post-holes: 2.85 m; Width: 2.95 m; Depth: 0.44 m.

Description

SFB 28, which cut SFB 29, was about 25 m south of the segmented ring ditch. The pit was sub-rectangular, with a slightly irregular south side and postholes 4556 and 4401 in the centres of the ENE and WSW sides. The presence of a cross-join suggests that the finds of the two features were mixed, either during or before excavation.

The context records list up to seven layers:

1 dark greyish brown sandy loam containing charcoal flecks, domestic debris, burnt limestone and patches of greenish soil suggesting decayed faecal matter.
2 dark grey brown fine friable loam with some ash and charcoal flecks and much domestic debris, patches of greenish soil as 1.
3 patchy charcoal spread.
4 charcoal spread below 3 containing circular hearth.
5 charcoal blackening of floor of pit (6).
6 smooth compact gravel forming a surface on the floor of the pit.
7 orange brown loamy clay spread irregularly over the occupation surface of which 3 was part.

Layer 4 continued into posthole 4556 and therefore post-dated its use but did not continue into 4401, which contained medium red brown sandy loam.

Finds

The 21 finds from this SFB are very mixed and include some personal items. Number 142 is part of a cable bracelet, of a type commonly found in the Roman period and similar to examples from Barton Court Farm (Miles 1986, fig. 106.3). Number 143 is a very fine gilded pin with a biconical head and faceted and ribbed decoration which is paralleled by pins found on the continent in the early 5th century (Van Es 1967, 143) and other British pins from 5th-century contexts (Ross 1991, 281–2). Numbers 147 and 157 are both fragments of copper alloy wire. Number 147, with its hooked terminal, is possibly a ring from a toilet set. Number 148 is a thin sheet metal buckle plate which has broken across the pin slot. Number 181 is an iron arrowhead with a leaf-shaped blade, similar to Swanton's class C1 spearheads although much smaller. A similar arrowhead comes from Chinnor I, dated to the later 5th/early 6th century (Dickinson 1976).

There are no items which may be definitely associated with textile production but there are two pig fibula pins; 358 is perforated and of a type common from the site and 378 is unperforated and may have been used as an awl. Numbers 395 and 397 are fragments of antler-working-waste which have been sawn and chopped. Other finds include five bases of reused Roman pots 61–65, four complete and one which is a half circle. Stone artefacts comprise a well worn whetstone, 432. There is also a fragment of a quern, 419.

A slag deposit, 604, was recovered from layer 3. It is furnace-cooled and probably the product of a smith's hearth.

Layer 1

147 SF 1126 **Copper alloy wire** Diameter 1 mm. Fragment bent out at one end.

148 SF 1039 **Copper alloy buckle plate** Length 33 mm, width 12 mm, thickness 0.5 mm. Made from a thin cut sheet broken off at fold, with rectangular slot for pin. Holes for two missing rivets.

157 SF 1090 **Copper alloy wire** Length 78 mm, diameter 1.5 mm. Fragment. (Not illustrated)

143 SF 1094 **Copper alloy pin** Length 114 mm. Biconical head with flat top. Two bands of moulded decoration below the head. Separated by a faceted section with traces of gilding. The shaft has a circular cross-section. Tip missing.

176 SF 1031 **Lead waste** Length 70 mm. (Not illustrated)

181 SF 1128 **Iron arrowhead** Length 64 mm, width of blade 11 mm. Leaf-shaped blade with one angular and one rounded shoulder and a blunt point. The blade is flat. Open socket.

245 SF 1087 **Iron nail** Length 38 mm. Shank fragment with square cross-section. (Not illustrated)

395 SF 1096 **Antler waste** Upper beam and three tines. Lower part of the beam detached by sawing. (Not illustrated)

Reused Roman sherd no. 65 SF 1093 Diameter 50 mm. Modified grooved base of a beaker in greyware, fabric 3. (Not illustrated)

Layer 2

142 SF 1133 **Copper alloy bracelet** Length 39 mm. Formed by twisting two strands of cable around a central core. Broken at both ends.

378 SF 1228 **Bone pin** Length 90 mm. Made from a pig fibula. Polished, broken at tip.

397 SF 1521 **Worked antler** Tine chopped and broken off from the beam. Additional tine removed by sawing and breaking. Partially pared down.

Reused Roman sherd no. 64 SF 1481 Diameter 75 mm. Modified foot-ring base in Oxford red/brown colour-coated fabric 3. (Not illustrated)

432 SF 1101/1231 **Whetstone** Length 97 mm. Signs of wear on all faces. Grooves for sharpening points on one flat face and one

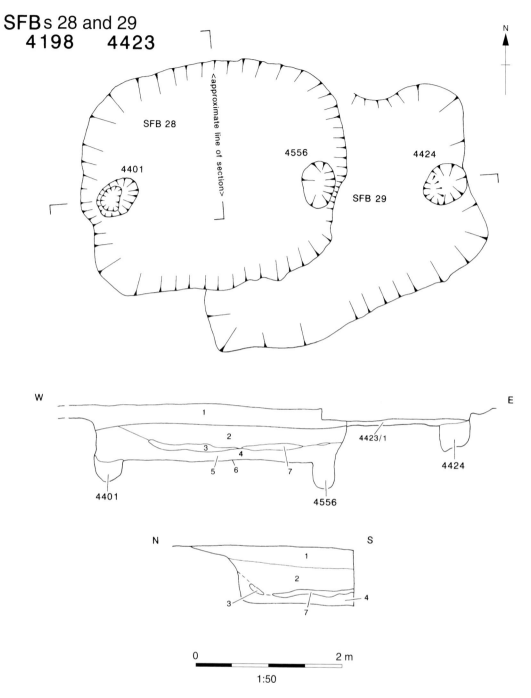

Figure 3.69   Sunken-featured buildings 28 and 29.

edge. Fine grained reddish/brown sandstone with mica similar to Brownstones of the Lower Old Red Sandstone of eg Monmouthshire.

419 SF 1098   **Rotary quern** Length 73 mm. Fragment, reddish-brown, feldspathic coarse grained probably Old Red Sandstone. (Not illustrated)

604 SF 1100   **Slag, plano-convex fragment**. (Not illustrated)

Layer 4

358 SF 1232   **Bone pin** Length 106 mm. Made from a pig fibula perforated at the proximal end and polished.

400 SF 1522   **Antler waste** Part of a tine. The tip has been partially sawn through and then broken off. (Not illustrated)

Reused Roman sherd no. 61 SF 1493   Diameter 100 mm. Semicircular fragment from a foot-ring base

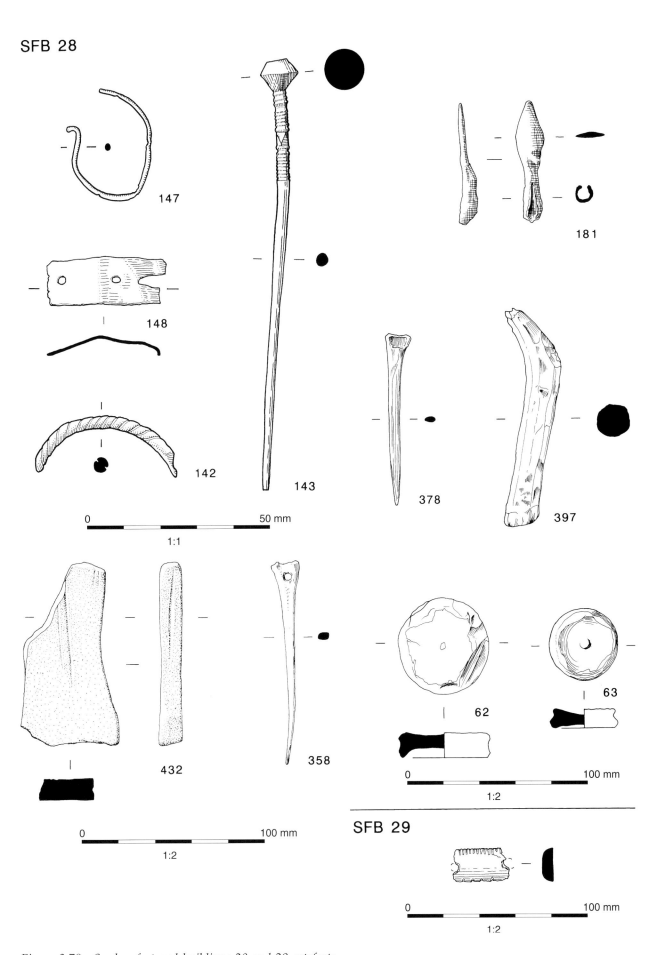

SFB 28

147

148

142

143

181

378

397

432

358

62

63

0   50 mm

1:1

0   100 mm

1:2

0   100 mm

1:2

SFB 29

0   100 mm

1:2

Figure 3.70   Sunken-featured buildings 28 and 29 artefacts.

159

in Oxford red/brown colour-coated fabric 3. (Not illustrated)

Reused Roman sherd no. 62 SF 1129 Diameter 50 mm. Modified foot-ring base in Oxford red/brown colour-coated fabric 3.

Reused Roman sherd no. 63 SF 1134 Diameter 35 mm. Modified foot-ring base in Oxford red/brown colour-coated fabric 3.

Pottery tpq 6th century?

Pottery occurrence per layer by fabric type.

Layer/ Fabric	F1	F2	F3	F4	F5	F6	% mineral	% chaff	Total wt (g)
1	946	837	343	3	8	49	59.5	40.5	2186
2	2627	5242	497	46	0	265	36.5	63.5	8677
3	22	572	36	0	0	48	8.6	91.4	678
4	75	647	55	0	0	0	16.7	83.3	777
7	3	20	5	0	0	0	28.6	71.4	28
Total wt (g)	3673	7318	936	49	8	362			12346
Mean sherd wt	11.8	19.7	13.8	12.3	8.0	21.3			

Pottery occurrence per quadrant and layer, all fabrics.

Layer/ quadrant	A	B	C	D	Total wt (g)
1	1172	0	508	506	2186
2	2414	0	433	5830	8677
3	538	0	0	140	678
4	412	0	115	250	777
7	0	0	28	0	28
Total wt (g)	4536	0	1084	6726	12346
% of total	36.7	0	8.8	54.5	

EVE: Jars = 4.22; Bowls = 1.89.

Five incised sherds (A/1, F1, 5 g; A/2, F1, 15 g; A/2, F2, 8 g; C/2, F2, 19 g; D/1, F1, 3 g).
Three rusticated sherds (C/2, F3, 18 g; D/1, F3, 38 g; D/2, F3, 89 g).
One stabbed sherd, (D/2, F1, 6 g).
One bossed sherd (C/2, F6, 26 g).
Five pierced sherds (A/1, F1, 2 g; A/1, F1, 3 g; C/1, F3, 19 g; C/4, F1, 3 g; D/2, F3, 9 g).
Drilled sherd (D/1, F1, 4 g).
One stamped sherd (A/2, F1, 18 g).

Cross-fits: A/2 = A/3 = D/3, A/2 = D/2, A/3 = A/4, A/4 = D/4.

Illustrations

3.71.129 Rim sherd from large jar. Black fabric with burnished outer surface.

3.71.130 Rim sherd from jar. Black fabric with burnished surfaces, outer body lightly finger-grooved.

3.71.131 Rim from incised vessel. Black fabric with burnished surfaces.

3.71.132 Jar rim. Black fabric with smoothed surfaces.

3.71.133 Rim sherd from small shallow bowl. Black fabric with burnished surfaces.

3.71.134 Rim of large jar. black fabric with burnished surfaces.

3.71.135 Bowl rim. Black fabric with smoothed surfaces.

3.71.136 Rim sherd from carinated jar. Black fabric, burnished surfaces, brown below the carination.

3.71.137 Jar rim. Black fabric with burnished surfaces.

3.71.138 Jar rim. Black fabric with burnished surfaces.

3.72.139 Full profile of jar. Black fabric with burnished surfaces, outer body becoming browner towards base.

3.72.140 Small bowl. Black fabric with burnished surfaces.

3.72.141 Jar rim. Black fabric with smoothed surfaces.

3.72.142 Jar rim. Black fabric with smoothed surfaces.

3.72.143 Jar rim. Black fabric, burnished surfaces, outer surface brown.

3.72.144 Bowl rim. Black fabric with burnished outer surface.

3.72.145 Bowl rim. Black fabric with burnished outer surface.

3.72.146 Bowl rim. Black fabric with dark brown burnished surfaces.

3.72.147 Rim of small bowl. Black fabric with brown burnished outer surface.

3.72.148 Rim sherd from shallow bowl. Black fabric with burnished surfaces.

3.72.149 Rim sherd from small bowl. Black fabric with burnished outer surface.

3.73.150 Lugged rim sherd. Black fabric with unfinished surfaces.

3.73.151 Rim sherd from lugged vessel. Uniform black fabric with unfinished surfaces.

3.73.152 Rim sherd from small bowl. Black fabric with smoothed surfaces.

3.73.153 Rim sherd from small jar. Black fabric with burnished surfaces.

3.73.154 Rim sherd from small bowl. Black fabric with smoothed surfaces.

3.73.155 Upright lug. Black fabric with unfinished surfaces.

3.73.156 Longitudinal lug. Black fabric with burnished surfaces.

3.73.157 Upright lug. Black fabric with smoothed surfaces.

3.73.158 Upright lug. Black fabric with unfinished surfaces.

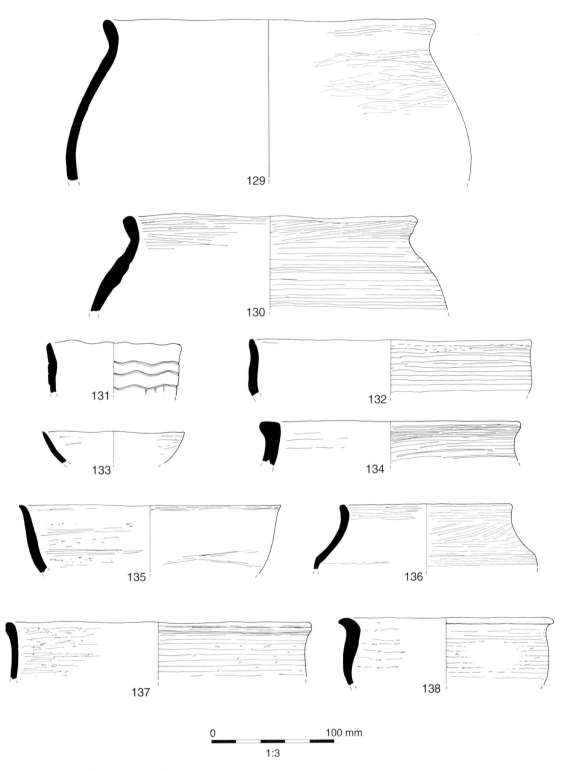

Figure 3.71   Sunken-featured building 28 pottery.

3.73.159	Pierced sherd. Dark grey fabric with unfinished surfaces.	3.74.162	Body sherd from bossed miniature jar. Black fabric with brown unfinished surfaces.
3.74.160	Rusticated base sherd. Black fabric with brown, smoothed outer surface.	3.74.163	Rim sherd from small bowl. Black fabric with brown burnished outer surface.
3.74.161	Rusticated sherd. Uniform black fabric with brown outer surface.		

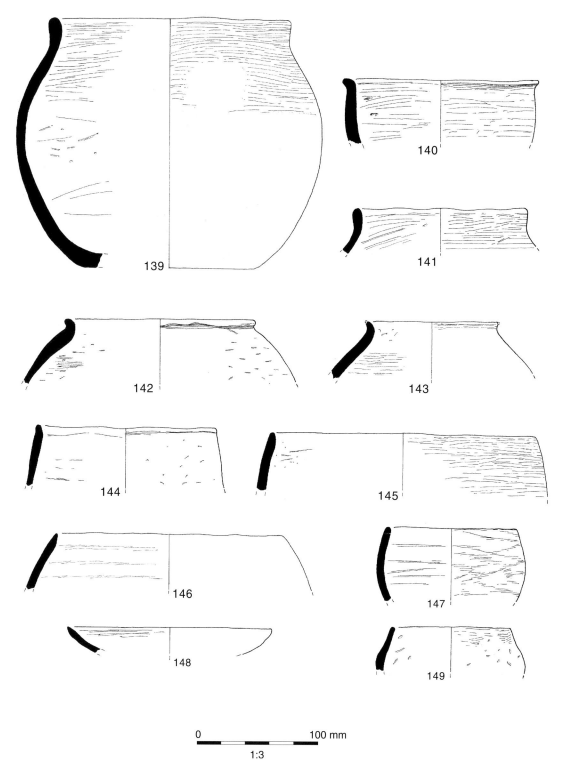

0   100 mm

1:3

Figure 3.72   Sunken-featured building 28 pottery continued.

3.74.164   Jar rim. Grey fabric with reddish-brown surfaces. Outer smoothed.

3.74.165   Pierced sherd. Dark grey fabric with unfinished surfaces.

3.74.166–7   Stamped sherds. Dark grey fabric, black surfaces, outer burnished.

3.74.168   Stamped sherd. Dark grey fabric, black surfaces, outer burnished.

The general date range of the decorated pottery from this sunken-featured building would conventionally be ascribed to the 5th century, and other material

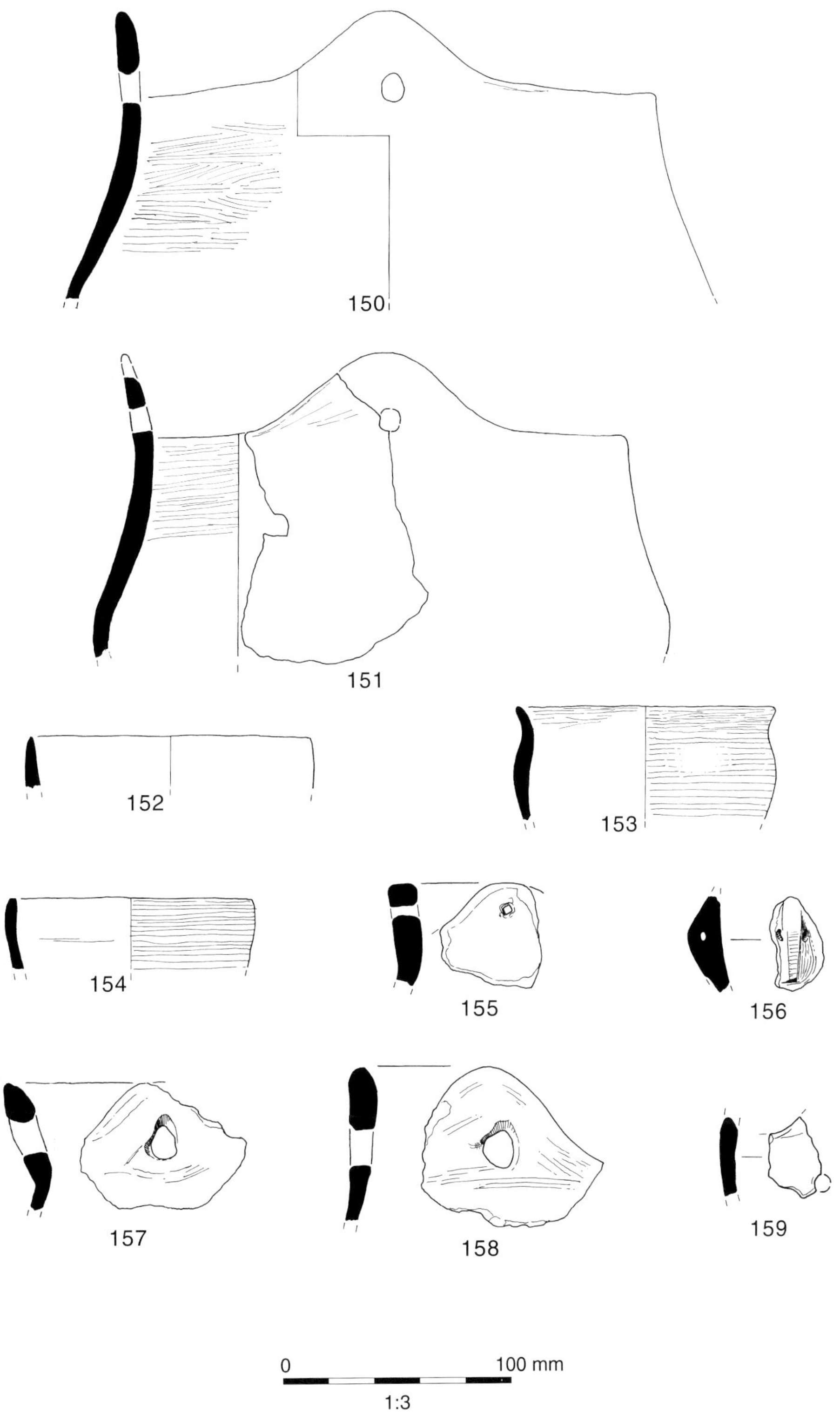

Figure 3.73 Sunken-featured building 28 pottery continued.

present, such as the 5th-century pin and 5th- to 6th-century arrowhead would appear to support this date. However, the structure cuts SFB 29, the backfill of which has a *terminus post quem* in the 6th century. There is also an unstamped sherd which cross-joins with the stamped vessel in SFB 29, and the records indicate that there was mixing of the finds from the two structures, certainly during and possibly before excavation. The bossed sherd from SFB 29 (Fig. 3.74.162) appears to have originated from a sharply carinated vessel, with the bosses located along the carination, possibly similar to those vessels illustrated in Myres (1977, figs 79–81), particularly a vessel from Norfolk (Myres 1977, fig. 79 no. 1792)

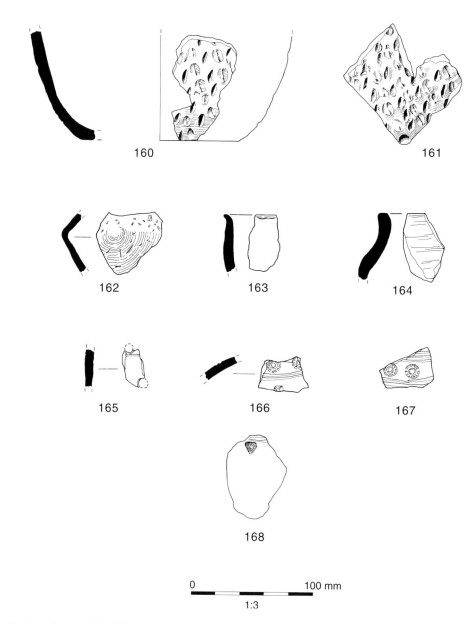

160 161 162 163 164 165 166 167 168

0   100 mm

1:3

Figure 3.74   Sunken-featured building 28 pottery continued.

which is dateable to the 5th century. This is from an upper layer.

SFB 29

Context 4423; Grid reference: 51308 98049; Figures 3.69–70, 75; Site plan: E8; Orientation: NE/SW; Length at surface: 3.95 m; Distance between postholes: not applicable; Width: *c* 2.5 m; Depth: not known.

Description

SFB 29, which was cut by the deeper SFB 28, was about 25 m south of the segmented ring ditch. It appears to have been sub-rectangular in plan, with a posthole 4424 in the centre of the north-east side.

There are no context descriptions in the site records for this sunken-featured building, which

was very shallow, but the cut was recognised in plan from an early stage and the records state that the finds were recovered separately. The pottery records indicate that two layers of fill were identified, although only one is shown on section.

Finds

Only two finds were recovered, a woodworking nail, 236, and a fragment of a connecting plate from a double-sided antler comb, 329, with fine and coarse teeth; this type is more common in the Roman period.

Layer 1

236 SF 1137   **Iron nail** Length 27 mm. Rectangular flat head. Square cross-sectioned shank. (Not illustrated)

329 SF 123 **Double-sided composite antler comb**
Fragment of a connecting plate with saw cuts on both sides. The teeth would have averaged 4 per cm on one side and 10 per cm on the other. Remains of two rivet holes with iron staining.

Pottery tpq 6th century?

Pottery occurrence per layer by fabric type.

Layer/ Fabric	F1	F2	F4	F6	% mineral	% chaff	Total wt (g)
1	146	463	0	0	24.0	76.0	609
2	67	145	7	142	20.5	79.5	361
Total wt (g)	213	608	7	142			970
Mean sherd wt	7.9	16.9	7.0	35.5			

Pottery occurrence per quadrant and layer, all fabrics.

Layer/ quadrant	A	B	C	D	Total wt (g)
1	0	609	0	0	609
2	0	361	0	0	361
Total wt (g)	0	970	0	0	970
% of total	0	100	0	0	

EVE: Jars = 0.76; Bowls = 0.16.

Two incised and stamped sherds (B/2, F2, 4 g; B/2, F6, 142 g).

Illustrations

3.75.169 Stamped rim sherd. Dark grey-brown fabric with smoothed outer surface

3.75.170 Jar rim. Black fabric with smoothed surfaces.

3.75.171 Rim from small bowl. Black fabric with burnished surfaces.

3.75.172 Small lugged jar. Black fabric with smoothed surfaces.

3.75.173 Small lugged bowl/cup. Black fabric with smoothed, abraded surfaces.

3.75.174 Stamped sherd. Grey fabric with darker smoothed surfaces. Outer surface lightly burnished.

3.75.175 Indented base. Black fabric with brown outer surface.

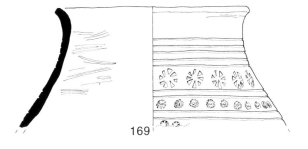

169

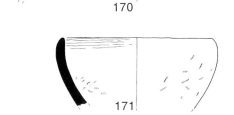

170

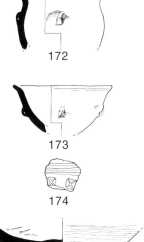

171

172

173

174

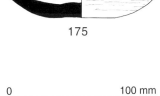

175

0 ____ 100 mm
1:3

Figure 3.75 Sunken-featured building 29 pottery.

The stamped vessel (Fig. 3.75.169) is almost certainly 6th-century in date, and joins with a sherd from SFB 28. There is also another small stamped sherd. It is impossible to ascertain in which of the SFBs the cross-joining vessel was originally stratified.

SFB 30

Context 4472; Grid reference: 51364 98181; Figures 3.76–7; Site plan: G5; Orientation: ENE/WSW;

Length at surface: 3.45 m; Distance between post-holes: 3.0 m; Width: 2.75 m; Depth: 0.46 m

Description

SFB 30 was the northernmost of a group of sunken-featured buildings approximately 40 m west of barrow 1. It was irregularly sub-rectangular in plan with postholes 5365 and 5364 in the centres of the ENE and WSW sides. There was a slight shelf in the south-west corner.

Two fills were distinguished. Layer 2 represented the fill of the feature and layer 1 the fill of a pit dug into it. Layers 1 and 2 were mixed in quadrant A but removed separately elsewhere.

1   dark sandy loam with 30% small pebbles, confined to the centre of the feature.
2   pale yellow and grey brown very sandy loam with 60% gravel.

The fills of the postholes were not recorded and it is not possible to reconstruct with certainty their relationship to layer 2.

Finds

Three finds came from the backfill, a Roman coin 280 dated AD 335 to 341, a fragment of a copper alloy sheet, 172, and an antler double-sided composite comb, 317, of a type common in the 5th to 7th centuries.

Layer 1

280 SF 1161   **Bronze coin** Reverse GLORIA EXER-CITUS (1 standard). Denomination 4. AD 335–341.

172 SF 1130   **Copper alloy sheet** Length 11 mm, thickness 0.5 mm. Fragment. (Not illustrated)

Layer 2

317 SF 1152   **Double-sided composite antler comb** Length 122 mm, height 44 mm. Plain rectangular end plates with graduated teeth. The teeth on both sides average 4 per cm. Five tooth segments connected by plates with a trapezoidal cross section. Eight iron rivets.

Pottery tpq 5th– 6th century?

Pottery occurrence per layer by fabric type.

Layer/ Fabric	F1	F2	F3	F4	F6	% mineral	% chaff	Total wt (g)
1	792	726	684	0	116	63.7	36.3	2318
2	226	183	126	2	0	65.9	34.1	537
Total wt (g)	1018	909	810	2	116			2855
Mean sherd wt	15.0	9.0	21.3	2.0	38.7			

Pottery occurrence per quadrant and layer, all fabrics.

Layer/quadrant	A	B	C	D	Total wt (g)
1	620	439	1065	197	2318
2	0	363	0	174	537
Total wt (g)	620	802	1065	371	2855
% of total	21.7	28.1	37.3	13.0	

EVE: Jars = 1.94; Bowls = 0.64.

Three rusticated sherds (A/1, F1, 98 g; C/1, F1, 16 g; C/1, F3, 11 g).
Two incised sherds (B/1, F2, 5 g; B/2, F2, 8 g).
One 'swallow's nest' lug (B/1, F1, 104 g, jar, rim 22% complete).

Cross-fits: A/1 = B/1 = D/1,   A/1 = C/1,   B/1 = B/2, B/1 = C/1, C/1 = D/2 (x2).

Illustrations

3.77.176	Rim from large jar. Black fabric with burnished surfaces.
3.77.177	Rim from small jar. Black fabric with burnished surfaces
3.77.178	Rim from small jar. Uniform black fabric with burnished surfaces
3.77.179	Rusticated sherd. Black fabric. Non-rusticated areas burnished
3.77.180	'Swallow's nest' lug. Dark reddish-brown fabric with burnished outer surface
3.77.181	Rim sherd from large jar. Dark grey fabric with burnished outer surface
3.77.182	Rim sherd from small bowl. Black fabric with burnished surfaces
3.77.183	Small lugged jar. Black fabric with burnished surfaces.

SFB 31

Context 4550; Grid reference: 51322 98023; Figure 3.78; Site plan: E9; Orientation: NE/SW; Length at surface: not known; Distance between postholes: 2.4 m; Width: not known; Depth: 0.15 m.

Description

SFB 31 was a shallow, irregular pit on the south-east edge of the excavated area, 50 m south of the segmented ring ditch. Only the north-east section of the pit edge was traced successfully; on the north-west the edge was over excavated and to the south the pit seems to have tailed out. There were two postholes, 4590, which was probably originally in the centre of the north-east end, where there was an area of animal burrows, and 4589, which was also rodent-disturbed and was probably near the south-west end. The floor of the pit was very uneven.

There seem to have been two layers:

1   medium brown loam with 20% gravel.
2   sandy brown loam with 15% gravel.

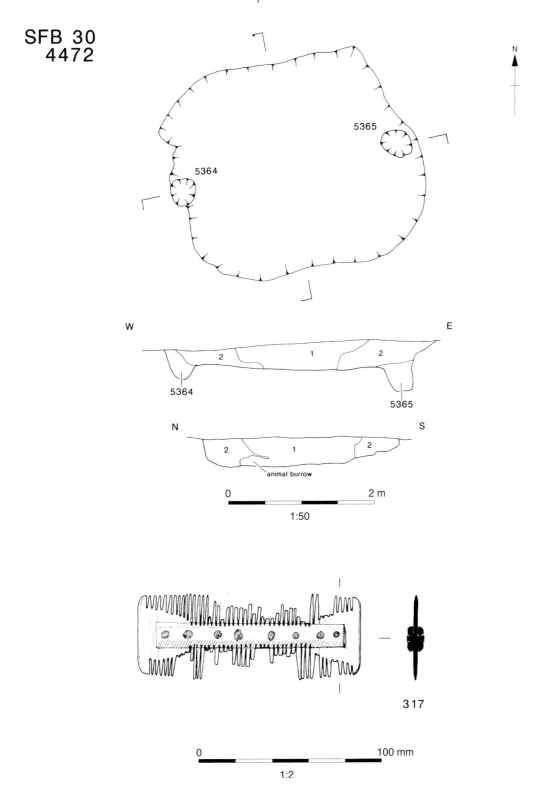

Figure 3.76   Sunken-featured building 30 and artefact.

The fills of the pit appear to have continued into the postholes.

Finds

Five objects were recovered from the backfill. These included a tooth from a heckle for carding wool or flax, 213, and part of a comb of a type common in the 5th to 7th centuries, 323. It has been pierced for suspension, probably from a cord or belt. Layer 1 produced a deposit of slag, 601, which had solidified within a furnace at a high temperature, probably during the process of welding.

167

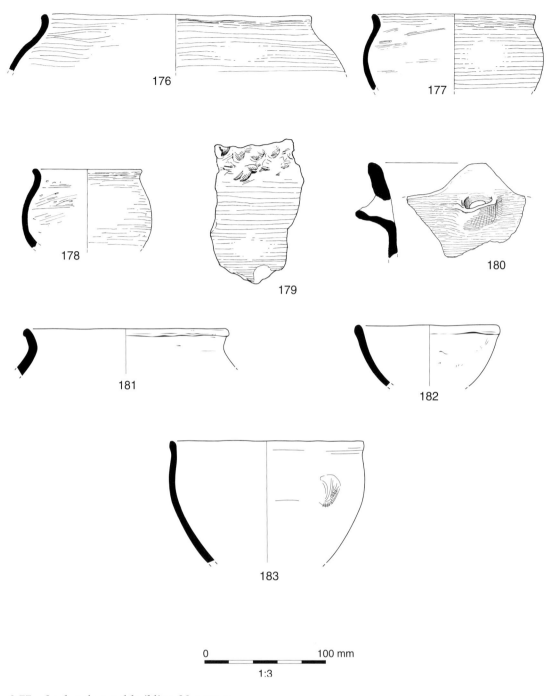

Figure 3.77   Sunken-featured building 30 pottery.

A loomweight fragment was found in posthole 4589.

Layer 1

213 SF 1142   **Iron heckle tooth** Length 42 mm. Circular cross-section, head missing.

260 SF 1163   **Iron strip** Length 19 mm. Rectangular cross-section. (Not illustrated)

622 SF 1409   **Clay pipe** Stem fragment. Post-medieval. (Not illustrated)

601 SF 1335   **Slag, small irregular elongated fragment**. (Not illustrated)

Layer 2

323 SF 1162   **Double-sided composite antler comb** Length 47 mm. Fragment of a rectangular end plate with graduated teeth. Pierced by a hole for suspension; 5 teeth per cm on both sides. Remains of three tooth segments, teeth now missing. The connecting plates have trapezoidal cross-sections and saw cuts along both edges. Remains of three iron rivets and one rivet hole

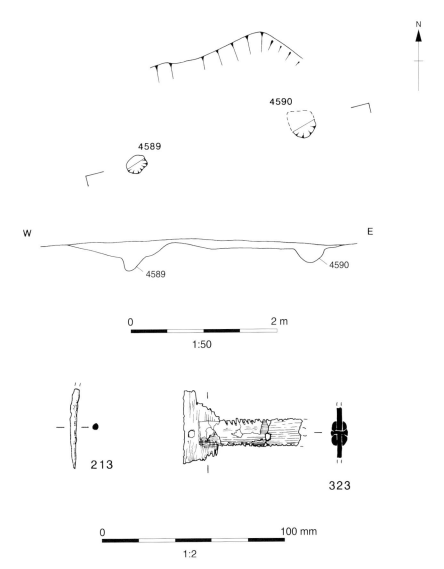

Figure 3.78   Sunken-featured building 31 and artefact.

Posthole 4589

458 SF 1189 **Annular, fired clay loomweight** Diameter 110 mm. Well made from a fine clay with well smoothed surfaces. Fragment approx 25% Estimated weight 471 g. (Not illustrated)

Pottery

Pottery occurrence per layer by fabric type.

Layer/Fabric	F2	% mineral	% chaff	Total wt (g)
1	77	0	100	77
2	55	0	100	55
Total wt (g)	132			132
Mean sherd wt	8.8			

Pottery occurrence per quadrant and layer, all fabrics.

Layer/quadrant	A	B	C	D	Total wt (g)
1	0	47	30	0	77
2	0	0	0	55	55
Total wt (g)	0	47	30	55	132
% of total	0	35.6	22.7	41.7	

EVE: Jars = 0; Bowls = 0

Cross-fits: B/1 = D/2

SFBS 32, 33, 34 (Figs 3.79–81)

As in the intercutting SFBs 17 and 18, the records for these intercutting sunken-featured buildings are somewhat complex and difficult to understand, and

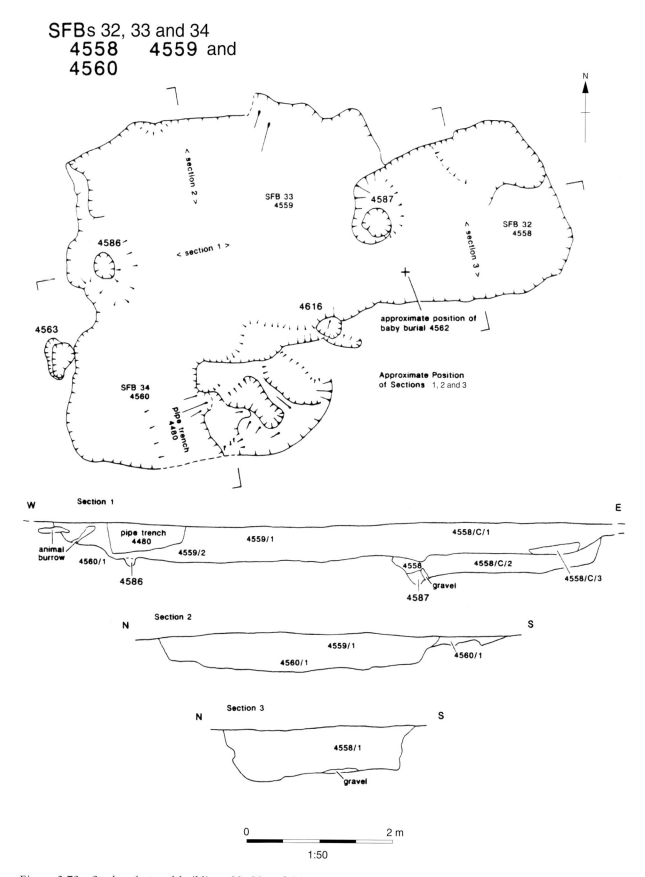

Figure 3.79   Sunken-featured buildings 32, 33 and 34.

the difficulty is compounded by extensive renumbering of contexts. The section in Figure 3.79 indicates the approximate position of layers as far as these can be established. Like 17 and 18, the features were excavated in six sections, A to F. In sections A, C and E two layers were recognised, but there seems to have been very little difference between the two fills. In A the two were taken out together. In B, D and F only a red brown sandy loam with 20% gravel was recorded.

1 red brown sandy loam with 20–25% gravel and in places large quantities of conglomerate.
2 red brown loam with 10–20% gravel.

SFB 32

Context 4558; Grid reference: 51366 98178; Site plan: G5; Orientation: NE/SW; Length at surface: not known; Distance between postholes: not known; Width: 2.1 m; Depth: 0.6 m.

Description

SFB 32 was the easternmost of the three intercutting sunken-featured buildings 32, 33 and 34, *c* 40 m west of barrow 1, and was cut by SFB 33. The pit seems to have had the usual sub-rectangular plan, with a post depression 4588 in the centre of the north-east end. The posthole 4587 seems to have belonged to SFB 33. The infant burial 4562 was cut into the south-west corner of the pit; it lay east/west with the head at the east end.

Finds

There were four objects in the fill; a knife blade fragment, 197, fragments of a possible bone pin, 309, a spindlewhorl, 445, and a gaming piece made from a sherd of Roman pottery, 68.

Layer 1

197 SF 1136 **Iron knife** Blade length 77 mm, thickness 2 mm. Inclined back, straight back slope? Curved leading edge. The cutting edge is very worn (type A/B.1.a). Tang, length 50 mm set just below the back.
309 SF 1165 **Bone pin** Three fragments of polished bone. Head and tip missing. (Not illustrated)
445 SF 1160 **Ceramic spindlewhorl** Diameter 50 mm. Fragment of a biconical whorl with tapering hole. Approx. 35%. Diameter of hole 9 mm. Estimated weight 34.37 g.
68 SF 1159 **Ceramic counter** Diameter 25 mm. Modified body sherd in Oxford red/brown colour-coated fabric 3.

Pottery tpq 5th–6th century?

Pottery occurrence per layer by fabric type.

Layer/Fabric	F1	F2	F3	F6	% mineral	% chaff	Total wt (g)
1	361	374	86	700	29.4	70.6	1521
Mean sherd wt	14.4	10.4	10.8	29.2			

Pottery occurrence per quadrant and layer, all fabrics.

Layer/quadrant	A	B	C	D	E	F	Total wt (g)
1	0	1080	0	325	17	99	1521
% of total	0	71.0	0	21.4	1.1	6.5	

EVE: Jars = 1.26; Bowls = 0.30.

One rusticated sherd (B/1, F3, 37 g).

Cross-fits: B/1 = D/1 (x2).

Illustrations

3.81.184 Rim from lugged jar. Uniform grey fabric with burnished black surfaces
3.81.185 Rusticated sherd. Black fabric with smoothed brown surfaces
3.81.186 Rim sherd from jar. Black fabric, smoothed surfaces, brown outer
3.81.187 Profile of jar. Burnished, with outer surface becoming browner down the body

SFB 33

Context 4559; Grid reference: 51363 98175; Site plan: G5; Orientation: ENE/WSW; Length at surface: 4.3 m; Distance between postholes: 3.75 m; Width: 3.2 m; Depth: 0.41 m

Description

SFB 33 was the westernmost of the three intercutting SFBs 32, 33 and 34, *c* 40 m west of barrow 1, cutting SFBs 32 and 34. It had been disturbed by a pipe trench running north-west/south-east through the centre. The pit was irregularly sub-rectangular in plan, with a fairly level base. The posthole 4587 probably belonged to this feature and would have been in the centre of the ENE end, opposite 4586.

Layer 2 continued into posthole 4586.

Finds

Seven finds were recovered from the backfill. A single tooth, from a heckle for combing wool or flax, 210, and

SFB 32

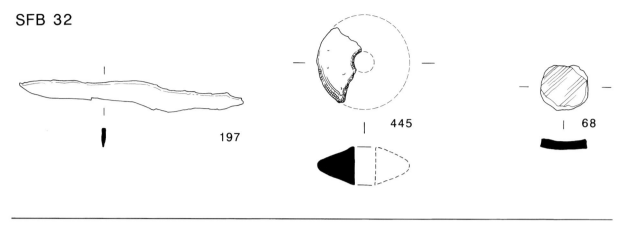

197   445   68

SFB 33

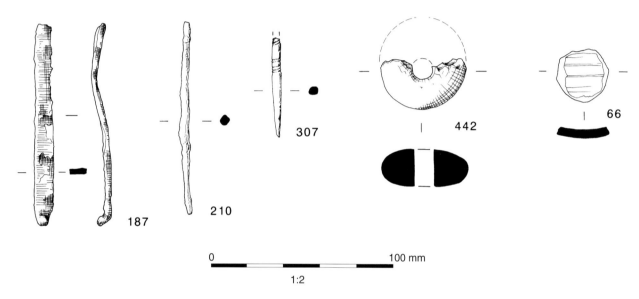

187   210   307   442   66

0   100 mm

1:2

Figure 3.80   Sunken-featured buildings 32 and 33 artefacts.

a fired clay spindlewhorl, 442, were the only textile equipment found. Other finds were a ceramic gaming piece, 66, a decorative bone dress pin, 307, and part of a bottom stone from a quern 409. Number 187 is an iron rod with a upturned end; an object similar to this from Grave 25 at Fonaby, Lincolnshire, has been described as a simple key (Cook 1981, fig. 9.4).

Layer 1

66 SF 1144   **Ceramic counter** Diameter 28 mm. Modified body sherd in Oxfordshire red/brown colour coated fabric 3.

187 SF 1141   **Iron rod?** Length 106 mm. Rectangular cross-section upturned at one end, other end broken.

210 SF 1156   **Iron heckle tooth** Length 102 mm. Circular cross-section, broken at both ends.

252 SF 1139   **Iron nail** Length 33 mm. Shank fragment. (Not illustrated)

307 SF 1153   **Bone pin** Length 52 mm. Highly polished, with oval cross-section. Two

bands of spiral decoration below the head (now missing).

442 SF 1155   **Ceramic spindlewhorl** Diameter 46 mm. Fragment from a biconical whorl. Approx. 55% Diameter of hole 11.5 mm. Estimated weight 42.07 g.

409 SF 1135   **Rotary quern** Fragment of a bottom stone. (Not illustrated)

Pottery

Pottery occurrence per layer by fabric type.

Layer/ Fabric	F1	F2	F3	F6	F7	% mineral	% chaff	Total wt (g)
1	103	52	59	30	14	68.2	31.8	258
Mean sherd wt	4.7	4.7	6.6	4.3	14.0			

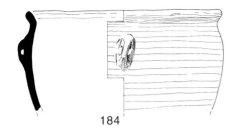

184

185

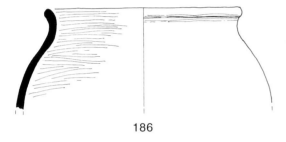

186

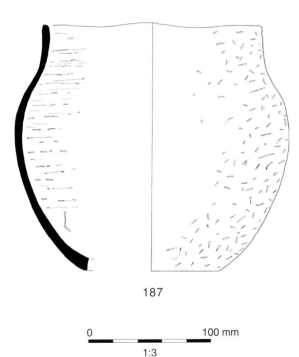

187

0   100 mm

1:3

Figure 3.81   Sunken-featured building 32 pottery.

Pottery occurrence per quadrant and layer, all fabrics.

Layer/ quadrant	A	B	C	D	Total wt (g)
1	0	108	49	101	258
% of total	0	41.9	19.0	39.1	

EVE: Jars = 0.16; Bowls = 0.02

SFB 34

Context 4560; Grid reference: 51367 98175; Site plan: G5; Orientation: E/W; Length at surface: *c* 3.3 m; Distance between postholes: 3.7 m; Width: not known; Depth: 0.32 m

Description

SFB 34 was the southernmost of the three intercutting SFBs 32, 33 and 34, *c* 40 m west of barrow 1, cut by 33. It had been disturbed by a pipe trench running north-west/south-east through the centre. The east end was also disturbed. There was a posthole 4563 just beyond the west side which may have been paired with posthole 4616. The floor of the pit on the east side was cut into conglomerate and therefore irregular.

There seems to have been only one layer of fill, an orange grey sandy loam with 35–40% gravel. The section shows a fragment of conglomerate in the fill.

Finds

The only object recovered is a very small fragment of a glass vessel of uncertain date.

Layer 1

300 SF 1226   **Glass vessel** Thickness 2.8 mm. Very pale green transparent bubbled fragment. Flaky dark brown weathering crust. (Not illustrated)

Pottery

No pottery was separately recorded.

SFB 35

Context 4561; Grid reference: 51330 98066; Figures 3.82–3; Site plan: F8; Orientation: E/W; Length at surface: 3.3 m; Distance between postholes: 2.7 m; Width: 2.8 m Depth: 0.23 m

Description

SFB 35 was *c* 10 m south-west of barrow 12. The pit is irregularly sub-rectangular in plan with postholes 4584 and 4574 in the centres of the east and west sides. Post impressions were visible in both.

There were only two layers of fill:

1   grey brown loam with some gravel, charcoal flecks and domestic debris, found mainly in the middle of the SFB, surrounded by
2   reddish brown loam with 40% gravel, charcoal flecks and domestic debris.

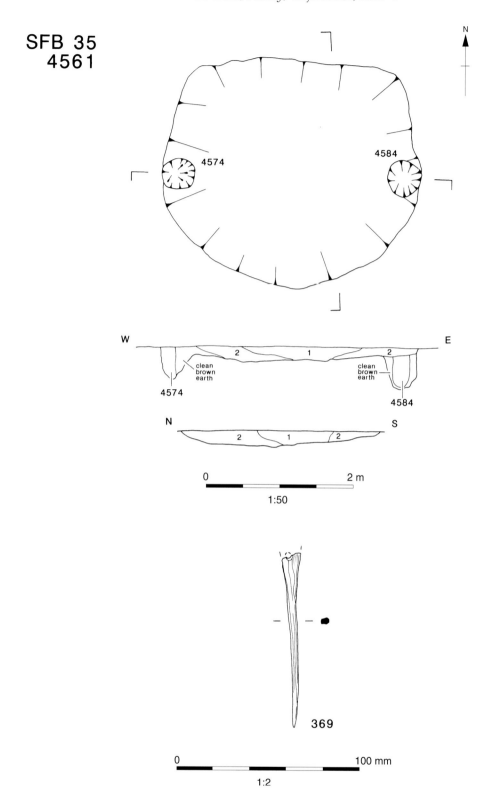

Figure 3.82   Sunken-featured building 35 and artefact.

Finds

Only two finds were recovered: 369, a perforated pig fibula pin of a type common from the site; and a reused base from a Roman pot, 67, which has been cut into a wedge.

Layer 1

369 SF 1227   **Bone pin** Length 91 mm. Made from a pig fibula perforated at the proximal end. Broken across perforation

Reused Roman sherd no. 67 SF 1485 Diameter 140 mm. Wedge-shaped fragment of a flat base of a jar in greyware, fabric 2. (Not illustrated)

Pottery **tpq** *5th century?*

Pottery occurrence per layer by fabric type.

Layer/Fabric	F1	F2	F3	F4	% mineral	% chaff	Total wt (g)
1		6	436	15	91	20.4	79.6	548
2		10	6	0	25	85.4	14.6	41
Total wt (g)	16	442	15	116			589
Mean sherd wt	3.2	8.5	7.5	14.5			

Pottery occurrence per quadrant and layer, all fabrics.

Layer/Quadrant	A	B	C	D	Total wt (g)
1	156	86	37	269	548
2	6	0	0	35	41
Total wt (g)	162	86	37	304	589
% of total	27.5	14.6	6.3	51.6	

EVE: Jars = 0.16; Bowls = 0.02.

Three rusticated sherds (A/1, F4, 13 g; A/1, F4, 6 g; B/1, F4, 6 g).
One finger-grooved and incised sherd, (A/1, F4, 30 g).
One incised sherd (D/1, F4, 12 g).

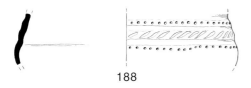

188

189

0 ———— 100 mm

1:3

Figure 3.83 Sunken-featured building 35 pottery.

Illustrations

3.83.188	Finger-grooved and incised sherd. Black fabric with burnished outer surface.
3.83.189	Rusticated sherd. Black fabric with unfinished surfaces.

The finger-grooved and incised sherd (Fig. 3.83.188) from this sunken-featured building appears to be early in date. The sherd has no precise parallels, but simple line-and-dot decoration is generally dated by Myres to the 5th century (1977, 18 and fig. 94).

SFBS 36 AND 37 (FIGS 3.84–6)

These two intercutting sunken-featured buildings were excavated at different times and the site records reveal some confusion.

SFB 36

Context 4572; Grid reference: 51237 98162; Site plan: B5; Orientation: NE/SW; Length at surface: 3.5 m; Distance between postholes: 3.2 m; Width: 3.0 m; Depth: 0.3 m.

Description

SFB 36 was near the western edge of the excavations, *c* 25 m south-west of the Neolithic oval barrow. Its south-west corner cut SFB 37. The line of the southern edge is uncertain (see below), but the pit seems to have been of the usual sub-rectangular form, with postholes 4578 and 4601 in the centres of the north-east and south-west sides. The floor of the pit was uneven.

There was some confusion in the recording and mixing of 4572 and 4598 occurred; all material from 4598/-/1 was included with 4572/B/1. According to the context records the feature was sectioned in January 1984 by a trench across the drainage channel (3610/A) but was not recognised as a sunken-featured building and was allocated a context number, now unknown. Once it had been recognised as a sunken-featured building it was excavated in two parts (A in the east and B in the west), but because of the difficulty in distinguishing soils during excavation the finds were allocated either to:

1 grey brown sandy loam with charcoal flecks and domestic debris, or
2 grey brown sandy loam with patches of cleaner reddish brown loam, charcoal flecks, domestic debris and lumps of chalky head.

Finds

The only finds recovered were fragments of copper alloy sheeting.

Layer 1

163 SF 1185	**Copper alloy strip** Length 45 mm, width 2 mm, thickness 0.5 mm. Three fragments. (Not illustrated)
SF 1186	**Copper alloy sheet** Length 11 mm, width 5 mm, thickness 0.5 mm. Rectangular cut fragment. (Not illustrated)

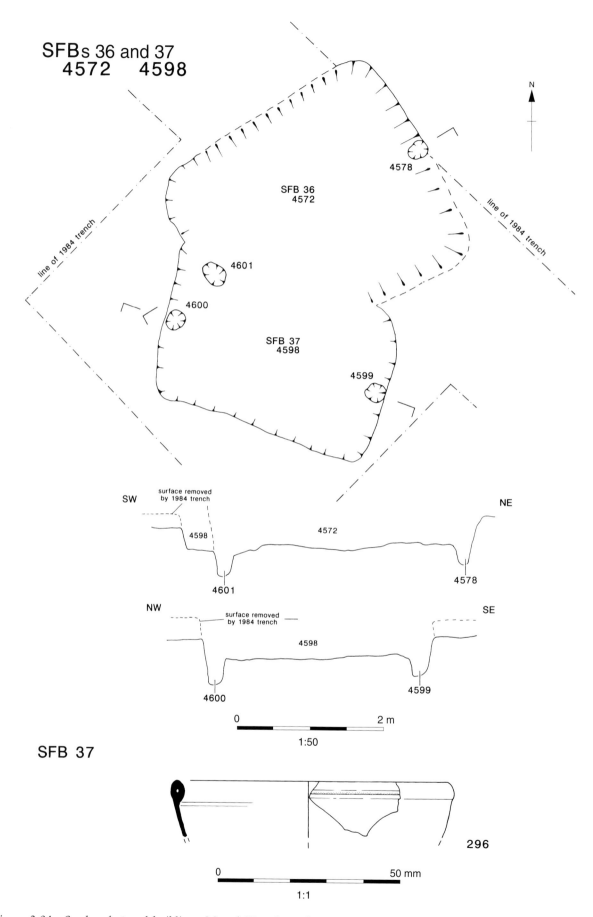

Figure 3.84   Sunken-featured buildings 36 and 37 and artefact.

Pottery tpq *5th–6th century?*

Pottery occurrence per layer by fabric type.

Layer/ Fabric*	F1	F2	F3	% mineral	% chaff	Total wt (g)
1	107	25	59	86.9	13.1	191
2	244	66	111	84.3	15.7	421
Total wt (g)	351	91	170			612
Mean sherd wt	7.6	12.3	8.6			

Pottery occurrence per quadrant and layer, all fabrics.

Layer/Quadrant*	A	B	C	D	Total wt (g)
1	0	191	0	0	191
2	0	421	0	0	421
Total wt (g)	0	612	0	0	612
% of total	0	100	0	0	

*some of the pottery was not ascribed a layer or quadrant by the excavators.

EVE: Jars = 0.38; Bowls = 0.16.

One incised sherd (F1, 15 g).
One pedestal base sherd (B/2, F2, 17 g).
Pierced sherd (F2, 29 g).

Illustrations

3.85.190   Rim sherd from small jar. Black fabric with brown outer surface.

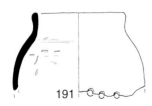

0   100 mm

1:3

Figure 3.85 Sunken-featured building 36 pottery.

3.85.191   Rim from pierced jar. Black fabric with smoothed surfaces.

SFB 37

Context 4598; Grid reference: 51237 98159; Site plan: B5; Orientation: NW/SE; Length at surface: 3.2 m; Distance between postholes: 2.9 m; Width: 2.1 m; Depth: 0.3 m.

Description

SFB 37 was near the western edge of the excavations, *c* 25 m south-west of the Neolithic oval barrow. Its north-west corner was cut by SFB 36. Although its orientation was unique on this site it was the usual sub-rectangular shape, with postholes 4600 and 4599 in the centres of the north-west and south-east sides.

There was some confusion in the recording and mixing of 4572 and 4598 occurred; all material from 4598/-/1 was included with 4572/B/1. A second layer was distinguished as a grey brown soil with charcoal flecks and domestic debris.

Finds

Four finds were recovered. A rim from a glass bowl of Roman date, 296, is very abraded. There are also fragments of a nail, 246, some copper alloy sheets, and a gaming piece, 69, made from the body sherd of a Roman pot.

Layer 2

173 SF 1188   **Copper alloy sheet** Max length 17 mm, thickness 1 mm. Six small irregularly shaped fragments. (Not illustrated)

246 SF 1191   **Iron nail** Length 35 mm. Shank fragment with square cross-section. (Not illustrated)

296 SF 1217   **Glass bowl** Thickness of rim 4 mm. Tubular rim fragment from a bowl in pale green transparent, finely bubbled glass. Worn and abraded on outer surface. Roman.

Reused Roman sherd no. 69 SF 1190 **Ceramic counter.** Diameter 20 mm. Made from a body sherd in Oxford red/brown colour-coated fabric 3. (Not illustrated)

Pottery tpq *6th century?*

Pottery occurrence per layer by fabric type.

Layer/ Fabric	F1	F2	F3	F8	% mineral	% chaff	Total wt (g)
1	55	9	8	0	87.5	12.5	72
2	74	488	16	14	17.6	82.4	592
Total wt (g)	129	497	24	14			664
Mean sherd wt	5.9	33.1	4.8	14.0			

Pottery occurrence per quadrant and layer, all fabrics.

Layer/ Quadrant	A	B	C	D	Total wt (g)
1	0	72	0	0	72
2	592	0	0	0	592
Total wt (g)	592	72	0	0	664
% of total	89.2	10.8	0	0	

EVE: Jars = 0.25; Bowls = 0.

One rusticated sherd, (B/1, F1, 42 g).
Two stamped sherds (A/2, F2, 10 g; B/1, F1, 3 g).

Illustrations

3.86.192	Dark grey fabric with brown core margins, smoothed outer surfaces.
3.86.193	Stepped base sherd. Black fabric with smoothed surfaces.

The stamped sherd (Fig. 3.86.192) suggests a 6th century *terminus post quem*.

SFB 38

Context 4602; Grid reference: 51264 98176; Figures 3.87–8; Orientation: NE/SW; Site plan: C5; Length at surface: 3.6 m; Distance between postholes: 5367–5370 3.15 m and 5367–5366 2.9 m; Width: 3.1 m; Depth: 0.54 m.

Description

SFB 38 was *c* 20 m south-east of the Neolithic oval barrow. The pit was irregularly sub-rectangular in

192

193

0   100 mm

1:3

Figure 3.86 Sunken-featured building 37 pottery.

shape, with three postholes: 5367 in the centre of the north-east side, 5370 in the centre of the south-west side and 5366 a little to the south-east of 5370, perhaps indicating rebuilding.

1 grey sandy loam with 10% gravel.
2 red sandy loam containing pea gravel.

Finds

Several artefacts associated with the manufacture of textiles were recovered from the fill of SFB 38. There are two spindlewhorls, 345 and 347, both of bone, and two pin beaters, used to separate the warp threads on a loom. One of these, 355, is of the short cigar-shaped type, whereas 349 is longer and more slender. Other finds include a perforated pig fibula pin, 370, and a tooth from an antler comb 340.

One unusual find is a modified portion of a lower mandible of a large animal, possibly cattle or a horse, 379, cut to a triangular shape. The back of the tool is very worn and fits well into the hand. It has had extensive use resulting in the breakage of the blade-like edge. It was probably used in a downward motion possibly for scraping hides or as a scoop. Another object of this type was recovered from the Anglo-Saxon settlement at Sutton Courtenay (Leeds 1924, pl XXVIII, fig. 1F). Again, it is made from a lower mandible and has a blade-like edge. However, the Sutton Courtenay tool is somewhat smaller than 379 and could not have been used as a scoop.

A part of an antler beam, 394, with its tines removed, has been discarded from antler-working. Number 600, a piece of slag, also came from this SFB. It is from a furnace and has been subjected to a high temperature, as would be achieved if welding had been taking place.

Layer 1

256 SF 1198	**Iron nail** Length 27 mm. Shank fragment with square cross-section. (Not illustrated)
349 SF 1194	**Bone pin beater** Length 133 mm, diameter 6 mm. Made from a polished shaft with circular cross-section. pointed at both ends.
370 SF 1195	**Bone pin** Length 80 mm. Made from a pig fibula perforated at the proximal end. Broken across perforation. Polished. Tip missing.
340 SF 1196	**Antler comb tooth** Length 18 mm. Fragment. (Not illustrated)
345 SF 1209	**Annular bone spindlewhorl** Diameter 40 mm. Polished with central hole diameter 10 mm. Turned, decorated with shallow concentric circles. Very worn on lower surface and uneven wear on the upper surface. Weight 25.46 g.
355 SF 1201	**Bone pin beater** Length 80 mm, diameter 6 mm. Made from a polished shaft with oval cross-section. Pointed at both ends.

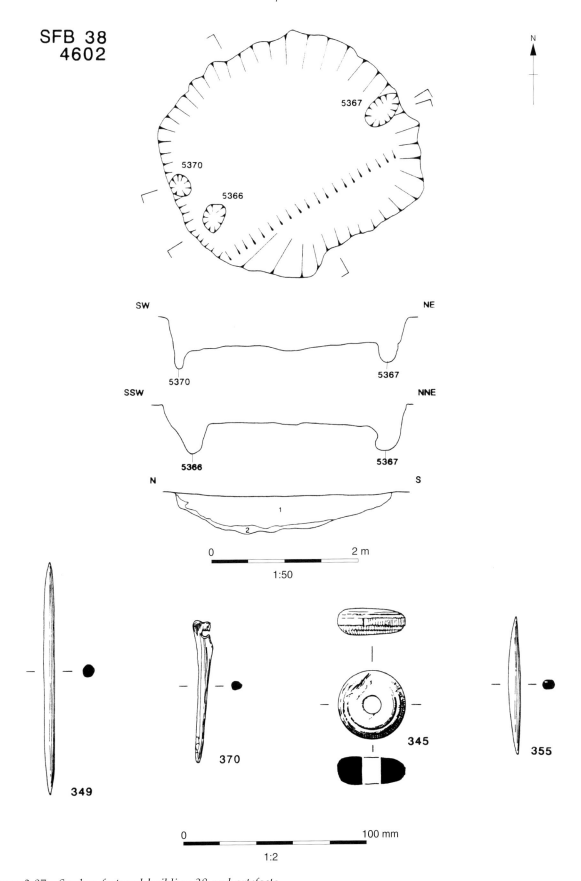

SFB 38
4602

Figure 3.87 Sunken-featured building 38 and artefacts.

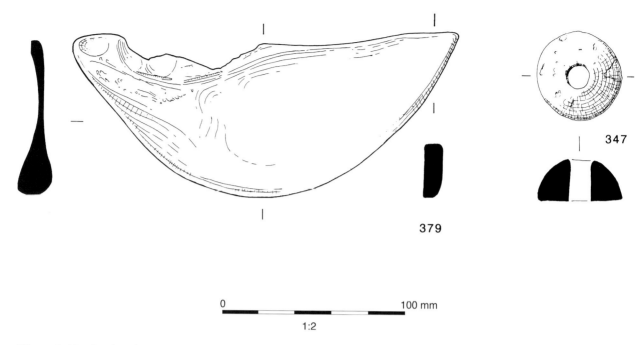

0   100 mm

1:2

Figure 3.88   Sunken-featured building 38 artefacts continued.

379 SF 1210   **Bone scraper** Length 212 mm. Made from a cattle or horse lower mandible. The edge has become highly polished from much wear. The blade edge has been worn to a fine point. Part of the blade is broken off.

394 SF 1516   **Antler waste** Part of the beam and three tines. The tines have been removed by chopping and the rest of the beam has been removed by chopping and splitting. (Not illustrated)

600 SF 1332   **Slag, irregular elongated fragment** (Not illustrated)

Layer 2

347 SF 1203   **Bone spindlewhorl** Diameter 46 mm. Hemispherical with convex upper and flat lower surfaces. Made from a bovine femur head with central perforation diameter 13 mm. Weight 21.07 g.

Pottery tpq 5th/6th century?

Pottery occurrence per layer by fabric type.

Layer/ Fabric	F1	F2	F3	F6	% mineral	% chaff	Total wt (g)
1	522	381	66	211	49.8	50.2	1180
2	447	242	255	134	65.1	34.9	1078
Total wt (g)	969	623	321	345			2258
Mean sherd wt	11.0	13.8	45.9	11.9			

Pottery occurrence per quadrant and layer, all fabrics.

Layer/ Quadrant	A	B	C	D	Total wt (g)
1	521	0	557	102	1180
2	0	1025	0	53	1078
Total wt (g)	521	1025	557	155	2258
% of total	23.1	45.4	24.7	6.9	

EVE: Jars = 1.28; Bowls = 0.05.

Four rusticated sherds (A/1, F2, 18 g; B/2, F2, 175 g; C/1, F2, 19 g; D/1, F6, 1006 g).
One incised sherd (D/2, F1, 10 g).

Illustrations

3.89.194   Base of rusticated vessel. Black fabric with brown outer surface.

3.89.195   Jar rim. Uniform dark grey fabric, smoothed outer surface.

3.89.196   Jar rim. Uniform black fabric. Smoothed surfaces with chaff voids.

3.89.197   Two non-joining incised bodysherds. Uniform dark brown fabric with burnished outer surfaces.

3.89.198   Jar rim. Uniform black fabric with smoothed and lightly burnished surfaces.

SFB 39

Context 4605; Grid reference: 51312 98173; Figures 3.90–91; Site plan: E5; Orientation: NE/SW; Length

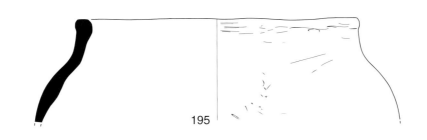

194

195

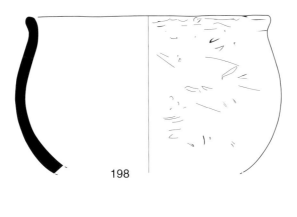

196

197

198

0   100 mm

1:3

Figure 3.89   Sunken-featured building 39 pottery.

at surface: 4.2 m; Distance between postholes: 5369–4615 3.15 m and 5369–5368 3.75 m; Width: 2.2–2.6 m; Depth: 0.46 m.

Description

SFB 39 was *c* 20 m north of the central group of post-built structures. The pit was irregular in outline, as if a sub-rectangular pit with postholes 5369 and 4615 had been extended to the south-west and 4615 replaced by 5368.

Two layers were distinguished, but the feature had been cut into during machining and layer 1 was present only in quadrants B and part of C.

1 red brown loam with 10% gravel.
2 light yellow grey silty loam with 20–40% gravel.

The relationship of the pit fill to the postholes cannot be certainly established, but the pit fill appears to have continued into posthole 4615.

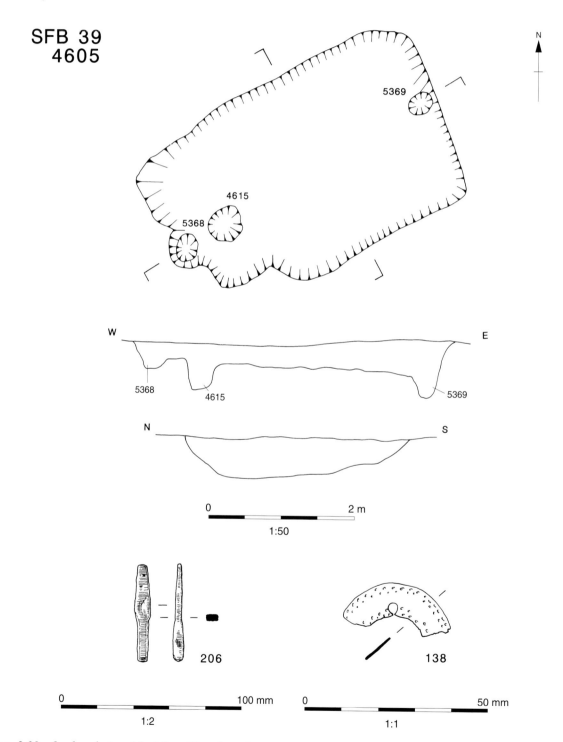

Figure 3.90 Sunken-featured building 39 and artefacts.

Finds

Seven objects were recovered. They include part of a flat annular brooch, 138, with punch dot decoration of narrow 'Anglian' type, which is probably a 6th-century import (Dickinson 1976, 146).

Iron objects consist of part of a rod, 265, and a lanceolate head and shank fragment, 206, probably the head from a drill bit or auger (Manning 1985, 25). There is also a fragment of slag 608, a slag lining reaction product from a hearth which was being run under reducing conditions. It has been subjected to a high temperature for some length of time. Number 367 is a bone point, probably from a pin. Number 70 is a reused Roman pot which has been deliberately cut to form a semicircle.

Layer 1

206 SF 1199   **Iron tool** Length 52 mm. Shank with square cross-section terminating in a flat lanceolate head, tapering to a flat edge.

265 SF 1200   **Iron rod** Length 100 mm. Shank with rectangular cross-section, tapers to a point at one end. Bent. (Not illustrated)

Layer 2

138 SF 1208   **Copper alloy annular brooch** Diameter 34 mm, width 9 mm, thickness 1 mm Fragment of a flat band with a rounded perforation for the loop of the pin. Double row of irregular punched dots around the inner and outer perimeters. Pin missing. (MacGregor and Bolick 1993, no. 35a)

376 SF 1525   **Bone point** Length 27 mm. Polished fragment. (Not illustrated)

Reused Roman sherd no. 70 SF 1482   Diameter 75 mm. Modified half of foot-ring base in Oxford red/brown colour-coated fabric 3. (Not illustrated)

438 SF 1204   **Worked stone** Length 120 mm. Semicircular flat fragment. Corallian lower calcareous grit. (Not illustrated)

608 SF 1202   **Slag, lining reaction product**. (Not illustrated)

Pottery tpq 6th century?

Pottery occurrence per layer by fabric type.

Layer/ Fabric	F1	F2	F3	F6	% mineral	% chaff	Total wt (g)
1	26	129	0	76	11.3	88.7	231
2	606	1243	524	128	45.2	54.8	2501
Total wt (g)	632	1372	524	204			2732
Mean sherd wt	16.2	21.8	174.7	14.6			

Pottery occurrence per quadrant and layer, all fabrics.

Layer/ Quadrant	A	B	C	D	Total wt (g)
1	0	88	143	0	231
2	510	827	368	796	2501
Total wt (g)	510	915	511	796	2732
% of total	18.7	33.5	18.7	29.1	

EVE: Jars = 0.77; Bowls = 0.

Rusticated sherds, (A/2 and D2, F2, 162 g).
Two incised sherds, (B/2, F1, 37 g; D/2, F2, 12 g).
One sherd with runic graffito (B/2, F2, 49 g, rim sherd, 8% complete).

Cross-fit: A/2 = D/2.

Illustrations

3.91.199   Rim sherd from large carinated jar. Grey fabric with black burnished surfaces.

3.91.200   Base sherds from rusticated vessel. Uniform black fabric. Some sooting on outer surface, limescaling on inner.

3.91.201   Rim sherd with runic inscription. Uniform black fabric with smoothed surfaces.

No chronologically diagnostic pottery was noted, but a 6th-century annular brooch fragment was present.

The sherd with the runic inscription (Fig. 3.91.201) is highly unusual, with few parallels. The Myres corpus has examples of cremation urns with runic stamps (eg 1977, pl IIIb) and with single, incised runes, but only one vessel (fig. 369 no. 1437), from Loveden Hill in Lincolnshire, with what can be considered to be a free-hand inscription. The inscription in question appears to make no sense, and has been interpreted as a charm formula (Fennel 1964; Wilson 1992). In the case of the Barrow Hills sherd, it seems likely that the runes were scratched after breakage. If they were scratched on the pot before it was broken, the chances of their still being virtually central on a sherd after breakage would be very low indeed.

Sherds with runic graffiti are very rare, and only one parallel could be found, on an unpublished sherd of samian ware from Deansway in Worcester. I am grateful to Hal Dalwood of the Worcester Archaeology Service for the following information. The sherd was broken after the inscription was added. There are the ends of two separate words, transliterated as -suir and -dis (or -mis). Professor R I Page (Cambridge University) and Dr Elisabeth Okasha (University College, Cork) both examined the sherd. It is agreed that the letters are indeed runes but, unfortunately, without the complete inscription, neither scholar could suggest a possible translation.

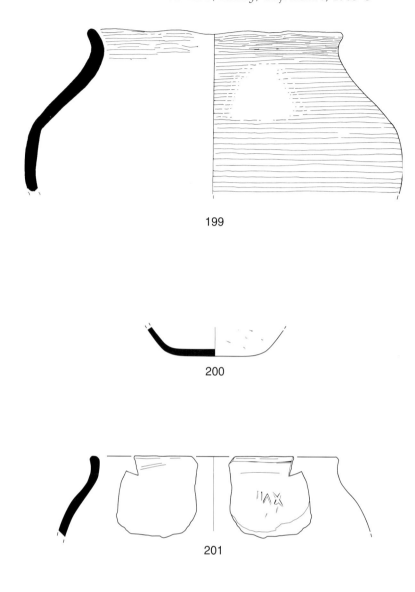

199

200

201

0   100 mm

1:3

Figure 3.91   Sunken-featured building 39 pottery.

Dr Okasha suggested that texts on pots are most likely to be personal names.

The inscription on the Barrow Hills sherd comprises three or four characters, the first of which is not entirely clear, which can be translated as either 'ThIUG', 'RIUG' 'IIUG' or 'HUG' (Elliott 1959, 14–20). None of these are known Anglo-Saxon words, although it is possible that, like the Worcester sherd, they may be a personal name (D Parsons, pers. comm.).

SFB 40

Context 4617; Grid reference: 51280 98174; Figures 3.3.92–4; Site plan: D5; Orientation: NE/SW; Length at surface: 3.7 m; Distance between postholes: 3.4 m; Width: 2.9 m; Depth: 0.4 m.

Description

SFB 40 was *c* 30 m north-west of the central group of post-built structures. The pit was sub-rectangular in plan, with a posthole in the centre of each end; the numbers of the postholes were not recorded.

1   brown loam with 30% gravel, flecks of charcoal and domestic debris, over
2   clean sandy gravel, containing tip lines and possibly representing deliberate backfill.
3   fine grey-brown loose friable loam with some gravel and much ash and domestic debris, intermittent over the base of the pit.

The relationship of the postholes to the fill of the pit is unknown. Layer 3 may represent occupation on the base of the pit.

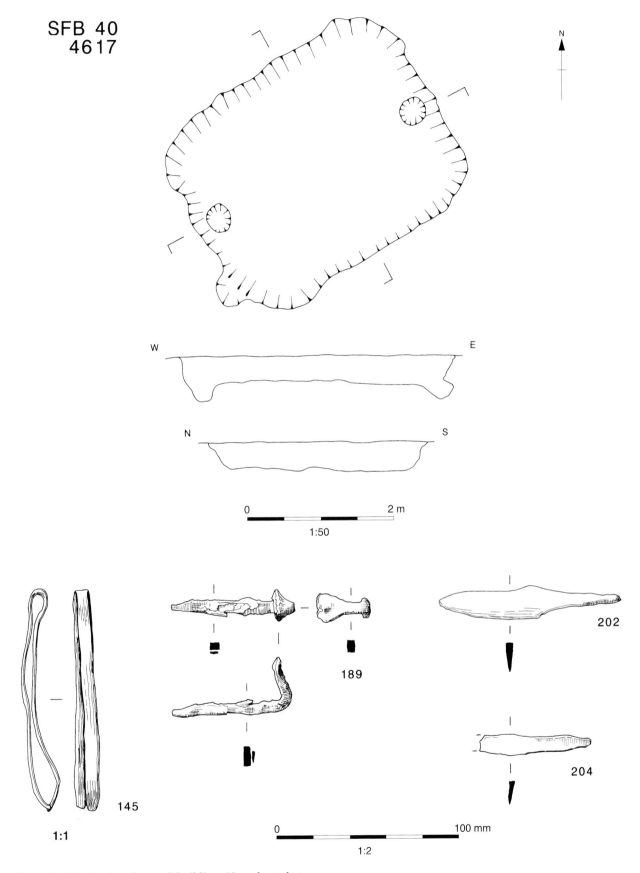

SFB 40
4617

W E

N S

0   2 m

1:50

145

1:1

189

202

204

0   100 mm

1:2

Figure 3.92   Sunken-featured building 40 and artefacts.

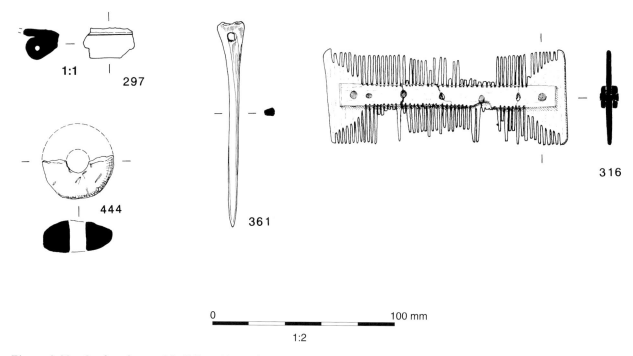

0   100 mm

1:2

Figure 3.93   Sunken-featured building 40 artefacts continued.

Finds

Eight finds were recovered. These included a fragment of a late Roman glass bowl, 297, and a pair of simple tweezers, 145, similar to a pair of tweezers from cremation 2616/1 at Spong Hill (Hills *et al.* 1987, 62, fig. 101). There are two knives: 204 is fragmentary but 202 is of Böhner's type C, which appeared at the beginning of the 7th century (Böhner 1958, 214). There is also a fragment from a barb spring padlock bolt, 189, which is similar to one found in a 4th-century context at Colchester (Crummy 1983, 168, fig. 206.4694). Half of a spindlewhorl of fired clay, 444, a perforated pig fibula pin, 361, of the type common on the site, and a double-sided composite antler comb, 316, of a type common in the 5th to 7th centuries, were also found.

Layer 1

145 SF 1211   **Copper alloy tweezers** Length 58 mm. Made from a narrow strip of sheeting with rounded hammered ends Sheet folded double to make a loop at one end.

189 SF 1215   **Iron barb spring padlock bolt** Length 68 mm. Single spine with double leaf spring. Part of bolt missing.

202 SF 1223   **Iron knife** Blade, length 56 mm, width 17 mm, thickness 3.5 mm. Inclined back with convex back slope and curved leading edge (Type C.1.c) groove along one side of blade. Tip missing. Tang, length 44 mm set just below back. Sloping shoulder.

204 SF 1216   **Iron knife** Blade, length 53 mm, tip missing. Fragment possibly with inclined back. Tang central to blade, sloping shoulders.

297 SF 1230   **Glass bowl** Thickness 9.5 mm. Small fragment of a tubular foot-ring in pale green transparent finely bubbled glass. Late Roman.

361 SF 1224   **Bone pin** Length 108 mm Made from a polished pig fibula perforated at one end. Worn at tip.

Layer 2

316 SF 1225   **Double-sided composite bone comb** Length 133 mm, height 50 mm. Rectangular end plates with graduated teeth. The teeth on both sides average 5 per cm. Six tooth segments connected by plates with rectangular cross-section. Seven iron rivets.

444 SF 1214   **Ceramic spindlewhorl** Diameter 40 mm. Fragment approx 50% of a biconical whorl with tapering hole. Max. diameter of hole 12.5 mm. Estimated weight 11.5 g.

Pottery tpq 6th century?

Pottery occurrence per layer by fabric type.

Layer/ Fabric	F1	F2	F3	F6	F7	% mineral	% chaff	Total wt (g)
1	636	761	220	939	59	35.0	65.0	2615
2	61	212	650	77	0	71.1	28.9	1000
3	7	160	14	226	0	5.2	94.8	407
Total wt (g)	704	1133	884	1242	0			4022
Mean sherd wt	8.1	11.2	30.4	20.7	29.5			

Pottery occurrence per quadrant and layer, all fabrics.

Layer/Quadrant	A	B	C	D	Total wt (g)
1	730	275	338	1272	2615
2	0	572	102	326	1000
3	404	0	3	0	407
Total wt (g)	1134	847	443	1598	4022
% of total	28.2	21.1	11.0	39.7	

EVE: Jars = 2.41; Bowls = 0.22.

Four incised sherds (A/1, F1, 4 g; B/1, F2, 5 g; C/1, F2, 5 g; D/2, F3, 2 g).
Two stamped sherds (A/1, F1, 23 g; B/1, F1, 9 g).
One pedestal base (C/3, F2, 102 g).

Illustrations

3.94.202   Jar rim. Dark grey fabric with smoothed and burnished surfaces.
3.94.203   Stamped and incised jar. Black fabric with burnished surfaces.
3.94.204   Stamped and incised sherd. Dark grey fabric with smoothed and lightly burnished outer surface.
3.94.205   Slashed bodysherd. Dark reddish-brown fabric with black burnished surfaces.
3.94.206   Profile of small jar. Black fabric with smoothed outer surface.

Both the stamped vessels (Figs 3.94.203–4) have pendant triangle arrangements, indicating a 6th-century *terminus post quem.*

SFB 41

Context 4641; Grid reference: 51290 98022; Figures 3.95–6; Site plan: D9; Orientation: NE/SW; Length at surface: 4.5 m; Distance between postholes: 3.8 m; Width: 3.25 m; Depth: 0.4 m.

Description

SFB 41 was *c* 70 m south-west of ring ditch 801 in the southern tip of the excavated area. The pit was sub-rectangular with postholes 4718 and 4659 in the centres of the north-east and south-west sides.

1   dark brown silty loam with 5–10% gravel and occasional charcoal flecks.
2   dark brown loam with 30–40% gravel.
3   reddish brown sandy loam with 30–40% gravel.
4   light grey silt with 30% gravel and charcoal flecks.

The relationships of the postholes to the fill of the pit were not recorded, but from the descriptions of the posthole fills it seems likely that layer 3 continued into 4718 and layer 4 into 4659. Layer 4 may represent occupation debris accumulating on the pit floor after the superstructure had been removed.

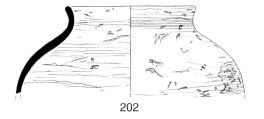
202
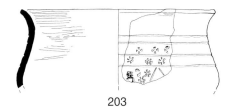
203

204

205
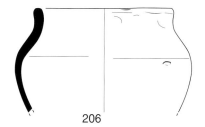
206

0   100 mm
1:3

Figure 3.94   Sunken-featured building 40 pottery.

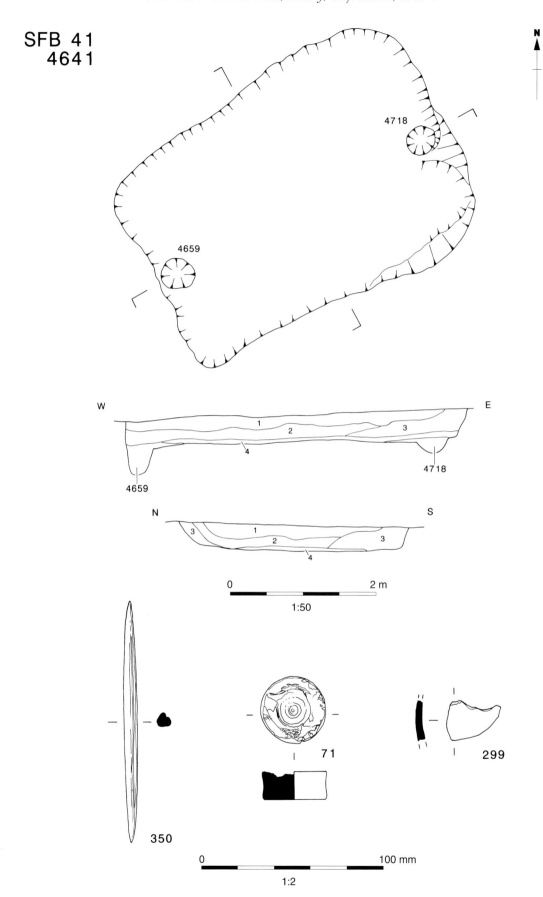

Figure 3.95   Sunken-featured building 41 and artefacts.

Finds

Four objects were recovered. They included a fragment of a beaker, 299, of probable Anglo-Saxon date, a gaming piece, 71, made from the base of a Roman pot, and a bone pin beater, 350, used during weaving to separate the warp threads on a warp-weighted loom.

Layer 1

618 SF 1443   **Wine bottle** Dark green glass. 18th–19th century. (Not illustrated)

350 SF 1236   **Bone pin beater** Length 127 mm, Diameter 7.5 mm. Made from a polished shaft with triangular cross-section. Pointed at both ends.

Layer 2

Reused Roman sherd no. 71 SF 1235 Ceramic counter. Diameter 35 mm. Modified grooved beaker base in Oxford red/brown colour-coated, fabric 3.

Layer 3

299 SF 1444   **Glass vessel** Thickness 4 mm. Translucent green glass fragment with few bubbles. Possibly part of a beaker. Patches of a dark brown weathering crust. Probably Anglo-Saxon.

Pottery tpq 6th century?

Pottery occurrence per layer by fabric type.

Layer/Fabric	F1	F2	F3	F6	% mineral	% chaff	Total wt (g)
1	415	1022	594	293	43.4	56.6	2324
2	401	521	216	42	52.3	47.7	1180
3	119	177	97	81	45.6	54.4	474
Total wt (g)	935	1720	907	416			3978
Mean sherd wt	7.9	14.0	10.9	9.7			

Pottery occurrence per quadrant and layer, all fabrics.

Layer/Quadrant	A	B	C	D	Total wt (g)
1	28	132	1132	1032	2324
2	366	275	0	539	1180
3	274	0	172	28	474
Total wt (g)	668	407	1304	1599	3978
% of total	16.8	10.2	32.8	40.2	

EVE: Jars = 2.04; Bowls = 0.18.

Five incised and stamped sherds (A/2, F1, 5 g; A/2 and A/3 and B/3, F1, 54 g; B/2, F1, 16 g; B/2, F3, 9 g; D/1, F1, 7 g).

Two bossed and incised sherds (A/2, F1, 33 g; A/3, F1, 6 g).

Seven incised sherds (A/2, F2, 10 g; C/1, F1, 6 g; C/1, F1, 45 g; C/3, F1, 4 g; D/1, F2, 17 g; D/2, F2, 32 g; D/2, F3, 35 g).

One rusticated sherd (A/2, F2, 8 g).

Cross-fit: A/2 = A/3 = B/3.

Illustrations

3.96.207	Jar rim sherd. Dark grey fabric with smoothed and burnished surfaces.
3.96.208	Rim sherd from small lugged/bossed jar. Dark grey fabric with unfinished surfaces.
3.96.209	Longitudinal pierced lug. Black fabric with smoothed surfaces.
3.96.210	Incised rim sherd. Reddish-brown fabric with black, smoothed outer surface
3.96.211	Incised sherd. Black fabric with burnished surfaces.
3.96.212	Stamped and incised sherd. Uniform dark grey fabric, smoothed outer surface.
3.96.213	Stamped and incised sherd. Uniform dark grey-brown fabric, smoothed outer surface.
3.96.214	Stamped and incised sherd. Uniform dark grey fabric, smoothed outer surface.
3.96.215	Incised sherd. Black fabric with burnished surfaces.
3.96.216	Incised sherd. Buff fabric with pale orange burnished surfaces.
3.96.217	Bossed and incised sherd. Dark grey fabric with browner burnished surfaces.

This group appears to indicate a 6th-century *terminus post quem*. The bossed sherd (Fig. 3.96.208) appears to be a 'melon-ribbed' type which Myres dates to the later part of the early Anglo-Saxon period. The stamped sherds (Figs. 3.96.212–4) are almost certainly of 6th-century date.

SFB 42

Context 4661; Grid reference: 51265 98073; Figure 3.97; Site plan: C8; Orientation: ENE/WSW; Length at surface: 3.0 m; Distance between postholes: 2.9 m; Width: 2.3 m Depth: 0.24 m.

Description

SFB 42 was *c* 70 m west of the segmented ring ditch on the west edge of the excavated area. The pit was sub-rectangular with posthole 4739 in the centre of the west-south-west side; there was a corresponding shallow depression in the centre of the east-north-east side.

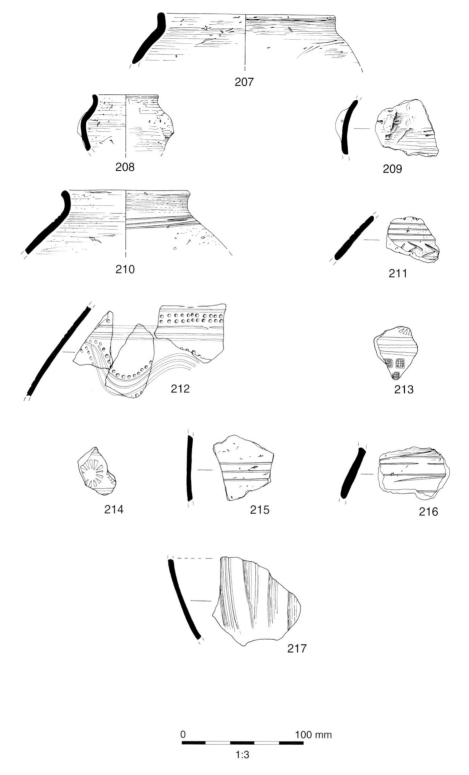

Figure 3.96   Sunken-featured building 41 pottery.

1   orange brown sandy loam with 50–70% gravel.
2   dark brown loam with 40–60% gravel.

The relationship of posthole 4739 to the pit fill was not recorded but from the context description it seems likely that the fill of the pit continued into the posthole.

Finds

Five objects were recovered, including a very worn Roman coin, 274, dated AD 138–161. Two objects definitely associated with textile manufacture are a fragment of an early Saxon annular loomweight, 457,

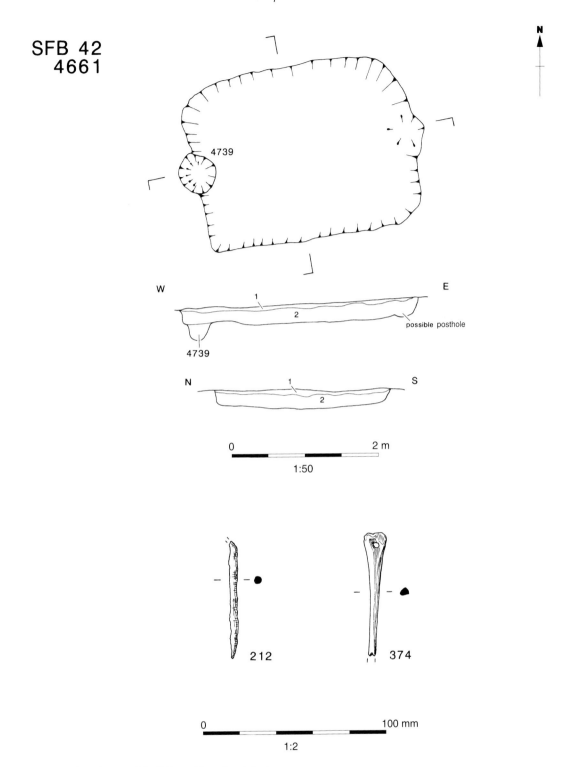

Figure 3.97 Sunken-featured building 42 and artefacts.

and a tooth from a heckle, 212, used for preparing flax and wool before spinning. Two teeth from an antler comb, 341, and a perforated pig fibula pin, 374, of a type common from the site were also found.

Layer 1

274 SF 1246 **Bronze coin** Antoninus Pius. Very worn. AD 138–161. (Not illustrated)

212 SF 1237 **Iron heckle tooth** Length 62 mm. Circular cross-section tapering to a flat point. Other end broken.

341 SF 1527 **Antler comb tooth** Length 8 mm. Two broken teeth. (Not illustrated)

374 SF 1282 **Bone pin** Length 65 mm. Made from a pig fibula perforated at the proximal end. Polished. Tip missing.

457 SF 1244 **Annular, fired clay loomweight** Diameter 90 mm. Two fragments, approx. 22% with roughly smoothed surfaces. Estimated weight 259 g. (Not illustrated)

Pottery **tpq** *5th/6th century?*

Pottery occurrence per layer by fabric type.

Layer/ Fabric	F1	F2	F3	F6	% mineral	% chaff	Total wt (g)
1	105	93	233	13	75.5	24.5	444
2	0	16	3	0	15.8	84.2	19
Total wt (g)	105	109	236	13			463
Mean sherd wt	5.5	9.9	12.4	6.5			

Pottery occurrence per quadrant and layer, all fabrics.

Layer/ Quadrant	A	B	C	D	Total wt (g)
1	37	244	100	63	444
2	0	0	19	0	19
Total wt (g)	37	244	119	63	463
% of total	8.0	52.7	25.7	13.6	

EVE: Jars = 0.41; Bowls = 0.

One incised sherd (A/1, F3, 22 g).

SFB 43

Context 4666; Grid reference: 51338 98162; Figures 3.98–100; Site plan: F5; Orientation: a) ENE/WSW b) E/W; Length at surface: 4.65 m; Distance between postholes: a) 4.1 m b) 3.65 m; Width: 3.2 m; Depth: 0.52 m.

Description

SFB 43 was *c* 20 m north-east of the central group of post-built structures. It almost certainly represented two intercutting sunken-featured buildings, a larger, shallower one aligned east-north-east/west-south-west with postholes 4730 and 4729 which was cut by a smaller, deeper sunken-featured building aligned east-west, with a new posthole 4771 at the east end and the reused and perhaps deepened 4729 at the west end.

The two phases were removed as one and three layers were recorded:

1 orange brown loam with 40% mixed gravel
2 dark grey brown loam with 15% gravel and occasional charcoal flecks.
3 (present in quadrants C and D only) orange brown sandy loam.

It seems probable from the sections and profiles that the fills of the deeper SFB 43b cut the fills of the shallower SFB 43a rather than *vice versa*. The section and posthole descriptions indicate that layer 2 extended into the postholes.

Finds

Eighteen objects were recovered, including a Roman coin, 287, dated AD 364–378, which has been perforated twice, probably for suspension. Roman coins are the most common metal pendants on necklets in the Upper Thames region and are occasionally found in bags within graves (Dickinson 1976, 213, 239).

Two knives were recovered, 194 and 200. They are of Böhner's type A, in common use from the 5th to 7th centuries (Böhner 1958, 214). A well used whetstone, 435, of a type of Old Red Sandstone found in the Monmouthshire area, was also found. There were two fragments of quernstones, 411 and 418, one in a local shelly limestone and the other in Upper Old Red Sandstone of a type found around the Forest of Dean.

The only artefact specifically associated with textile manufacture is a fragment of a spindlewhorl, 443. However, there is a pierced pig fibula pin, 359, of the type common to the site, which may have been used in textile production. There is also a fragment of an antler comb, 334, which has been drilled for suspension. There are two other antler objects, 382 and 384; both are utilised tines. The point of 382 has been sharpened and it has been pierced for suspension, probably for use as a peg. The tip of 384 has been removed and it has been hollowed at one end. There has been an attempt to hollow out the other end but this was abandoned. It was probably intended for use as a handle. A fragment of worked bone, 386, is broken at both ends but one end has been pared down.

Number 221, an iron rod with two looped terminals one of which is broken, is similar to objects described as links from snaffle bits. Another similar object, 220, comes from the Anglo-Saxon fill of barrow 12. Two-linked snaffle bits were used in Britain in the Iron Age and throughout the Roman period (Manning 1985, 66), and other examples have been found on the Anglo-Saxon site at Shakenoak (Brodribb *et al.* 1972, fig. 39, 168–170).

There are two gaming pieces, 72 and 74, both made from sherds of Roman pots. Number 73 is a modified complete base of a Roman mortarium.

Layer 1

221 SF 1248 **Iron hook** Length 72 mm. Rod with square cross-section curved at one end to form an open-ended loop. Other end bent but now broken.
267 SF 1241 **Iron strip** Length 60 mm, width 9 mm, thickness 6 mm. Rectangular cross-section. (Not illustrated)
359 SF 1249 **Bone pin** Length 99 mm. Made from a pig fibula perforated at the proximal end. Polished.

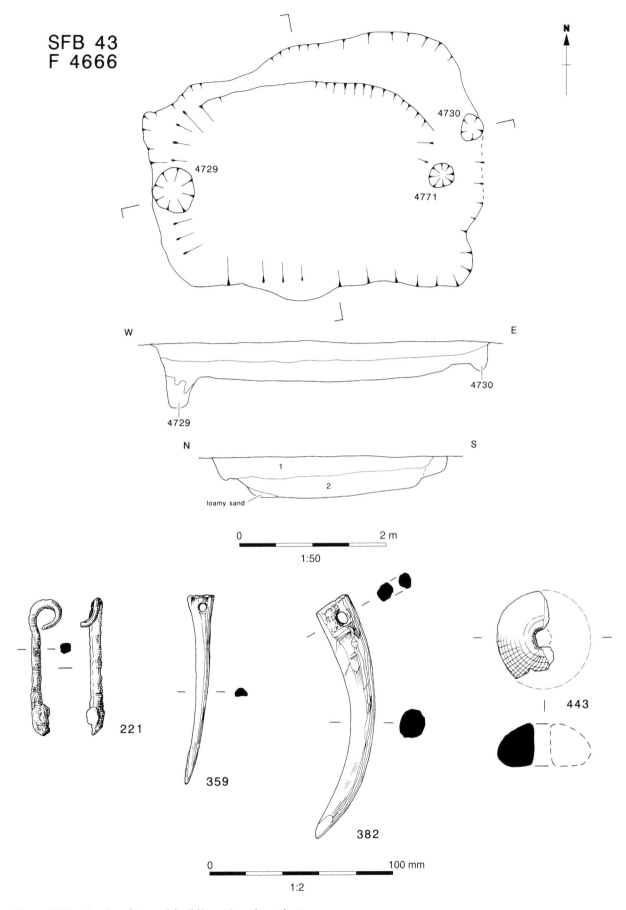

SFB 43
F 4666

Figure 3.98 Sunken-featured building 43 and artefacts.

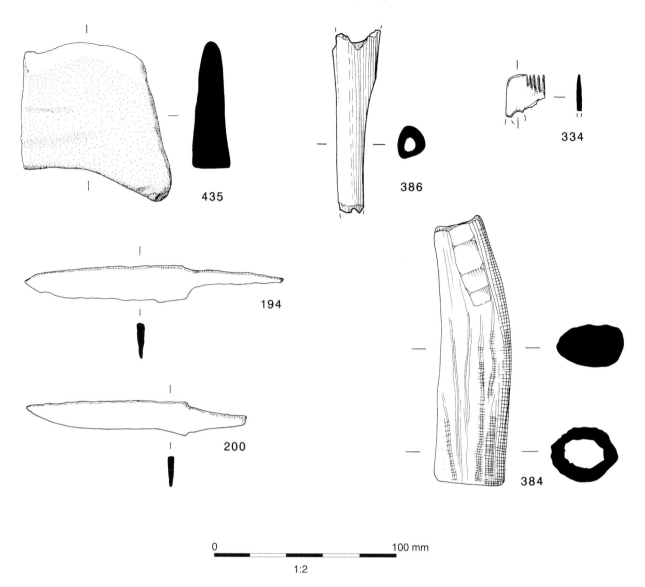

0   100 mm

1:2

Figure 3.99   Sunken-featured building 43 artefacts continued.

382 SF 1239 **Antler peg** Length 130 mm. Tine which has been pared down and polished. The tip has been sharpened. It has been sawn from the beam, split part way down and perforated.

443 SF 1278 **Ceramic spindlewhorl** Diameter 50 mm. Fragment of a hemispherical whorl with convex upper and flat lower surfaces approx. 32%. Tapering hole, max diameter of hole 11.5 mm. Estimated weight 84.34 g.

Reused Roman sherd no. 72 SF 1238 Ceramic counter Diameter 20 mm. Made from a body sherd in greyware, fabric 2. (Not illustrated)

Reused Roman sherd no. 73 SF 1480 Diameter 60 mm. Modified foot-ring base of a mortarium in Oxford red/brown colour-coated fabric 3. (Not illustrated)

435 SF 1243 **Whetstone** Length 110 mm. Fragment of a flat worked stone. Signs of wear on all faces. Fine-grained reddish brown sandstone with mica, similar to Brownstones of the Lower Old Red Sandstone of eg Monmouthshire.

439 SF 1245 **Worked stone** Length 104 mm. Rectangular flat fragment. Reddish-brown, feldspathic, coarse-grained, probably Old Red Sandstone. (Not illustrated)

411 SF 1247 **Rotary quern** Length 72 mm. Fragment of coarse-grained sandstone conglomerate, red and feldspathic. ?Upper Old Red Sandstone from Welsh Borders/Forest of Dean. (Not illustrated)

386 SF 1528 **Worked bone** Length 99 mm, width 30 mm. Broken at both ends. One end has been pared down.

418 SF 1242 **Rotary quern** Length 108 mm. Fragment of shelly limestone, local Corallian. (Not illustrated)

Layer 2

287 SF 1252   **Bronze coin** Gratian. Reverse, GLOR-IA NOVI SAECULI. Minted at Arles. Denomination 3. AD 364–378 Perforated twice. (Not illustrated)

194 SF 1253   **Iron knife** Blade, Length 89 mm, Width 18 mm, Thickness 4 mm. Blade point central, inclined back, angled back slope and curved leading edge The cutting edge is worn (type A.1.b). Tang, length 55 mm, set just below blade back, sloping shoulders, bent.

200 SF 1255   **Iron knife** Blade, Length 89 mm, Width 17 mm, Thickness 2.5 mm. The blade point is central, inclined back with angled back slope and curved leading edge. Groove along one side of the blade. The cutting edge is worn (type A.2.b). Tang, length 33 mm, set just below back, sloping shoulders.

334 SF 1250   **Antler comb** Length 21 mm. Fragment from a rectangular end plate with graduated teeth and part of a hole for suspension.

Reused Roman sherd no. 74 SF 1251 Ceramic counter. Diameter 40 mm. Modified base of a beaker in Oxford red/brown colour-coated fabric 3. (Not illustrated)

Layer 3

384 SF 1254   **Worked antler** Length 140 mm. Tine, the tip and beam detached by sawing. The tip has been slightly pared down on one face and is partly hollowed. The beam end is hollow.

Posthole 4729

Decorated body sherd.

Pottery tpq 5th century?

Pottery occurrence per layer by fabric type.

Layer/ Fabric	F1	F2	F3	F4	F5	F6	F7	% mineral	% chaff	Total wt (g)
1	2330	571	1423	20	51	52	6	86.0	14.0	4453
2	246	297	841	13	8	0	0	78.9	21.1	1405
Total wt (g)	2576	868	2264	33	59	52	6			5858
Mean sherd wt	38.4	24.1	17.2	8.3	8.4	13.0	6.0			

Pottery occurrence per quadrant and layer, all fabrics.

Layer/Quadrant	A	B	C	D	Total wt (g)
1	2891	214	941	407	4453
2	0	813	0	592	1405
Total wt (g)	2891	1027	941	999	5858
% of total	49.4	17.5	16.1	17.1	

EVE: Jars = 2.87; Bowls = 0.16.

Two sherds, line-and-dot decoration (D/2, F1, 14 g, B/1, F1, 4 g).
Two pedestal base sherds (C/1, F1, 17 g; C/1, F1, 40 g).
One near-complete globular jar (A/1, F1, 1867 g, rim 91% complete).

Illustrations

3.100.218   Line-and-dot decorated sherd. Uniform black fabric. Highly burnished outer surface.

3.100.219   Rim sherd from large jar. Black fabric with burnished outer surface.

3.100.220   Rim sherd from small jar. Black fabric with smoothed surfaces.

3.100.221   Rim sherd from bowl. Black fabric with unfinished surfaces.

3.100.222   Rim sherd from small bowl. Black fabric with smoothed surfaces.

3.100.223   Pedestal base. Dark grey fabric with smoothed surfaces.

3.100.224   Pedestal base. Dark grey fabric with dark brown surfaces.

3.100.225   Near complete jar. Black fabric with smoothed and lightly burnished surfaces.

The sherds with line-and-dot decoration (Fig. 3.100.218) are probably early in date. The upper layers of the feature are contaminated, and a sherd of late medieval Cistercian ware was also present, but the larger line-and-dot sherd is from the lower layer of the fill, and the features therefore have a *terminus post quem* of the 5th century.

SFB 44

Context 4773; Grid reference: 51260 98122; Figure 3.101; Site plan: C6; Orientation: not known – possibly NE/SW; Length at surface: >2.75 m; Distance between postholes: not known; Width: >2.1 m; Depth: 0.14 m.

Description

SFB 44 was *c* 35 m north-west of ring ditch 801, 50 m west of the Romano-British cemetery. The feature appears to represent the bottom of a denuded sunken-featured building, better preserved on the east than

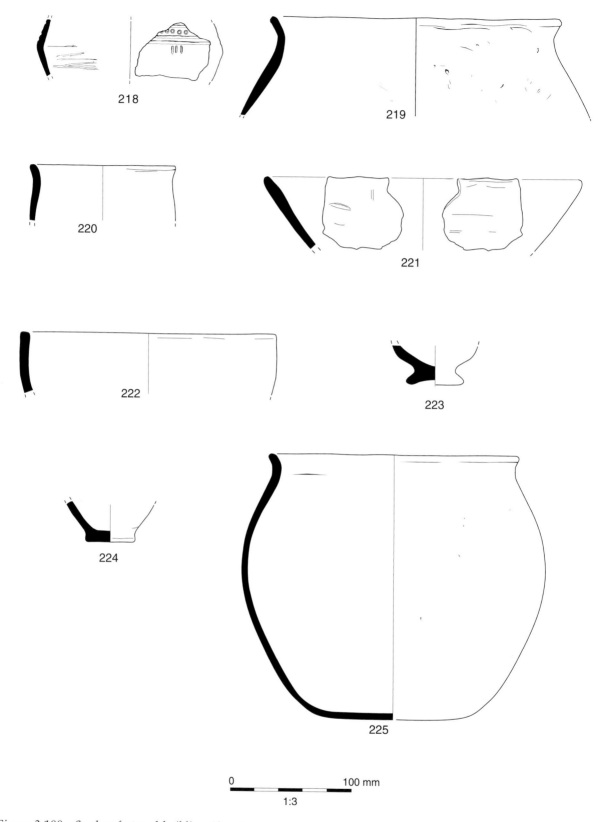

Figure 3.100   Sunken-featured building 43 pottery.

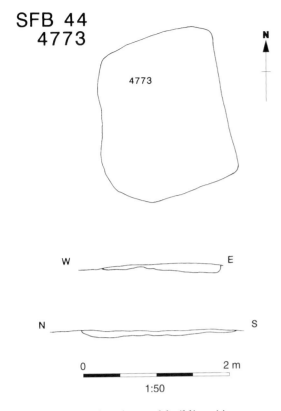

SFB 44
4773

4773

W————E

N————S

0 ————— 2 m

1:50

Figure 3.101   Sunken-featured building 44.

on the west side. No postholes survived and the fill consisted of dark grey brown loam with 30% gravel.

Finds

There were no finds.

Pottery

Pottery occurrence per layer by fabric type.

Layer/ Fabric*	F1	F2	F3	F7	% mineral	% chaff	Total wt (g)
1	76	76	6	4	53.1	46.9	162
Mean sherd wt	10.9	12.7	6	4			

Pottery occurrence per quadrant, all fabrics.

Quadrant*	A	B	C	D	Total wt (g)
Total wt (g)	9	50	103	0	162
% of total	5.6	30.9	63.6	0	

* some of the pottery from this feature was not ascribed a layer by the excavators.

EVE: Jars = 0.05; Bowls = 0.

No chronologically diagnostic pottery.

SFB 45

Context 4865; Grid reference: 51401 98086; Figures 3.102–3; Site plan: I7; Orientation: ENE/WSW; Length at surface: 4.0 m; Distance between post-holes: 3.6 m; Width: 2.2 m; Depth: 0.44 m.

Description

SFB 45 was *c* 20 m south-east of barrow 13. The pit was neatly sub-rectangular, with well defined corners and postholes 4876 and 4875 projecting slightly beyond the centres of the east-north-east and west-south-west ends.

Six layers were recorded, although they were excavated as three:

1 dark brown grey loam with stones and gravel.
2 dark brown grey clayey loam with stones and gravel. These layers were removed together and finds labelled as layer 1.
3 sandy brown loam with gravel. (Finds from this layer were labelled as layer 2).
4 dark brown silty loam with flecks of charcoal and gravel.
5 very dark brown silty loam with gravel, lumps of greenish yellow clay and many charcoal flecks. (Finds from layers 4 and 5 were labelled as layer 3).
8 dark brown grey clay loam with 10% gravel which filled a small pit cut into the centre of the feature; the pit contained a cattle skull and was sealed by 1.

According to the section the posts remained *in situ* while the pit filled.

Finds

Four finds were recovered, including a nail shank, 268, and a fragmentary fitting, 225, similar to one from SFB 3 (224). The two remaining finds are both connected with the manufacture of textiles. Number 344 is a spindlewhorl and 353 a pin beater used for separating warp threads on a warp-weighted loom.

Layer 1

353 SF 1280   **Bone pin beater** Length 77 mm, diameter 8 mm. Polished shaft with circular cross-section. Pointed at both ends.

Layer 2

225 SF 1263   **Iron fitting** Length 70 mm. Bent rod with V-shaped cross-section and arms of unequal length. (Not illustrated)

268 SF 1262   **Iron nail** Length 55 mm. Shank with rectangular cross-section. (Not illustrated)

Layer 3

344 SF 1264   **Bone spindlewhorl** Diameter 32 mm. Hemispherical with flattened top and bottom and convex sides. Made from a large femur head, polished with central hole diameter 9 mm. Turned. Decorated with shallow concentric circles, worn on the base. Weight 29.08 g.

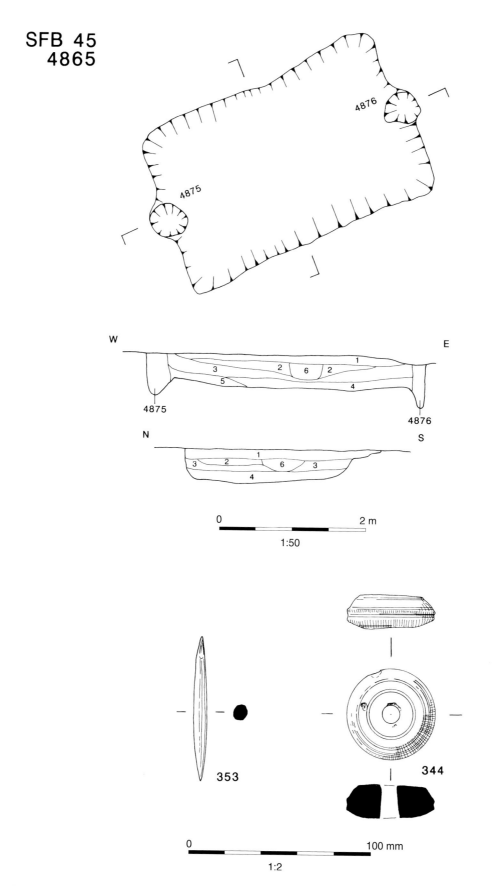

Figure 3.102   *Sunken-featured building 45 and artefacts.*

Pottery tpq *6th century*

Pottery occurrence per layer by fabric type.

Layer/ Fabric	F1	F2	F3	F5	F6	F7	% mineral	% chaff	Total wt (g)
1	192	539	328	38	9	44	52.3	47.7	1150
2	86	222	184	0	0	1	55.0	45.0	493
3	7	170	677	0	366	4	56.2	43.8	1224
4	0	23	37	0	0	0	61.7	38.3	60
8	0	13	30	0	0	15	77.6	22.4	58
Total wt (g)	285	967	1256	38	375	64			2985
Mean sherd wt	7.7	17.6	16.7	38.0	187.5	8.0			

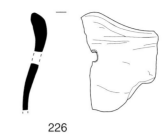

226

227

Pottery occurrence per quadrant and layer, all fabrics.

Layer/ quadrant	A	B	C	D	Total wt (g)
1	587	6	373	184	1150
2	122	29	71	271	493
3	383	515	0	329	1227
4	0	43	0	17	60
8	0	45	0	13	58
Total wt (g)	1092	638	444	814	2988
% of total	36.5	21.4	14.9	27.2	

228

0   100 mm

1:3

EVE: Jars = 0.60; Bowls = 0.63.

One sherd, stabbed pendant triangles (A/1, F2, 145 g).
One incised sherd (A/2, F1, 5 g).
One rusticated sherd (D/3, F3,19 g).

Cross-fits: A/2 = A/3 = B/3 = B/4 = C/1, A/3 = D/3, B/3 = D/4.

Figure 3.103   Sunken-featured building 45 pottery.

Illustrations

3.103.226   Upright lug. Dark grey fabric with smoothed surfaces.
3.103.227   Bowl rim. Black fabric with burnished surfaces.
3.103.228   Jar rim. Black fabric with smoothed and burnished surfaces.

The stamped sherds indicate a *terminus post quem* in the 6th century.

Gazetteer 3: Anglo-Saxon Inhumations

By Ellen McAdam

GRAVE 5004

Grid ref.: 51408 98110; Figure 3.104

Grave 5004 was on the south-west side of pond barrow 4866. The cut was shallow and may have been inserted in a bank which was subsequently denuded by ploughing. It contained the SW/NE inhumation of an adult female over 45 years of age in a sub-rectangular pit 1.63 m × 0.77 m × 0.22 m deep.

The upper level of the pond barrow contained a single Romano-British sherd, Anglo-Saxon sherds and the almost complete skeleton of a dog.

Good preservation, head south-west 266° on left side facing north; trunk on back, left hand over left pelvis, right arm straight with hand by knees, legs flexed.

Small iron knife (201) by left hip, small iron buckle at waist (180) and bronze pin (141) with traces of mineralised cloth at the throat.

Finds

Grave 5004 contained three artefacts. A copper alloy pin, 141, with a flat perforated head is of a late 6th- to early 7th-century type. Other examples have come from a late 6th- or 7th-century context at Colchester (Crummy 1988, 6, fig. 2.3) and West Stow (West 1985, fig. 266.6, fig. 246.3). An iron buckle, 180, has a simple D-shaped frame and a knife, 201, is of Böhner's type A in use from the 5th to the 7th centuries (Böhner 1958, 214).

141 SF 1266   **Copper alloy pin** Length 57 mm. Made from a wire with circular cross-section. One end has been flattened and filed to form a flat circular head which has been perforated. Diameter of hole 1.5 mm.

180 SF 1267   **Iron buckle** Length 27 mm. Single sided D-shaped frame with circular cross-section. Iron pin. Mineralised textile in top of pin.

201 SF 1265   **Iron knife** Fragmentary blade width 14 mm, thickness 2 mm. Blade point central, straight back, convex back slope, angled leading edge. (Type A.2.c). Tang length 30 mm, set just below blade back, sloping shoulders.

GRAVE 4562

Newborn infant inhumation burial, disturbed by an animal burrow. The infant lay in a shallow cut 0.4 × 0.2 × 0.1 m in the bottom of the south side of SFB 32 (4558), oriented east-west. The backfill over the burial consisted of sand from the side of the sunken-featured building cut mixed with gravelly loam. Skull at east end of grave, much of body missing. No grave goods.

Anglo-Saxon Grave 5004

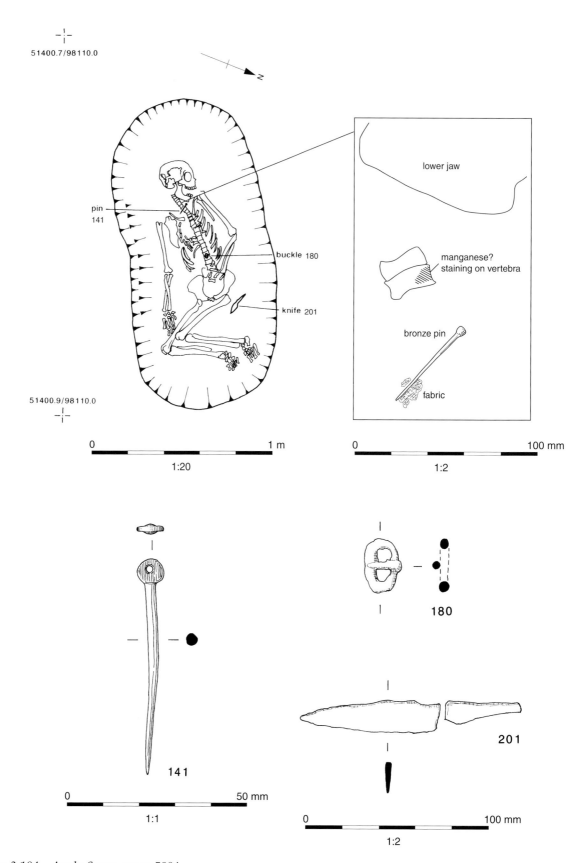

Figure 3.104   *Anglo-Saxon grave 5004.*

Gazetteer 4: Anglo-Saxon Finds from Pits, Barrow Ditches and Miscellaneous Contexts

By Ellen McAdam

PITS

3297 Grid reference: 51275 98122; Site plan: C6c; Length: 1.26 m; Width: 0.97 m; Depth: 0.36 m

Oval pit *c* 15 m south-west of SFB 19
576 SF 1601 **< 100 g fired clay**. (Not illustrated)

3519 Grid reference: 51264 98159; Figure 3.106; Site plan: C6c; Length: 2.2 m; Width: 1.8 m; Depth: 0.13 m

Shallow irregular scoop *c* 15 m north-west of SFB 19.

433 SF 1037	**Whetstone** Length 85 mm. Fragment with very heavy wear on all four faces giving a waisted profile. Fine grained reddish-brown sandstone with mica. Similar to Brownstones, Lower Old Red Sandstone from eg Monmouthshire.

3551 Grid reference: 51267 98148; Site plan: C6c; Length: 3.56 m; Width: 1.5 m; Depth: 0.58 m

Irregular pit *c* 15 m south-west of SFB 19.

Reused Roman sherd no. 53 SF 1502 Diameter 50 mm. Fragment of a cut down foot-ring base in Oxford red/brown colour-coated fabric 3. (Not illustrated)

3578 Grid reference: 512470 98148; Site plan: D4c; Length: 1.75 m; Width: 1.2 m; Depth: 0.36 m

Oval pit *c* 2 m north of SFBs 20 and 21. Produced Anglo-Saxon pottery and reused Roman sherd.

Reused Roman sherd no. 54 SF 1484 Diameter 70 mm. Complete cut down foot-ring base in Oxford red/brown colour-coated fabric 3. (Not illustrated)

4664 Grid reference: 51290 98025; Site plan: D9c; Length: 1.1 m; Width: 0.8 m; Depth: 0.26 m

Pit 0.75 m north of SFB 41.

3.107.261	Jar with *hängende Bogen* decoration. Dark brown fabric with smoothed and burnished surfaces.

4798 Grid reference: 51341 98159; Site plan: F6c; Length: 1.43 m; Width: 1.3 m; Depth: 0.32 m

Approximately circular pit on west side of complex of scoops 4786, 0.6 m south-east of SFB 43.

368 SF 1279	**Bone pin** Length 90 mm. Made from a pig fibula, polished. Broken across perforation. Tip missing. (Not illustrated)

4829 Grid reference: 51349 98159; Figure 3.106; Site plan: F6c, G6c; Length: 1.75 m; Width: 1.6 m; Depth: 0.42 m

Pit *c* 10 m east-south-east of SFB 43.

331 SF 1261	**Double-sided composite antler comb** Width 30 mm. Two fragments of a tooth segment with teeth averaging 5 per cm on one side and 9 per cm on the other. (Not illustrated)
449 SF 1662	**Annular, fired clay loomweight** Diameter 120 mm. Fragment approx. 35% Estimated weight 425.06 g.
450 SF 1259	**Annular, fired clay loomweight** Diameter 120 mm. Fragment approx. 48% Estimated weight 281.3 g.

ANGLO-SAXON FILLS OF PREHISTORIC BARROW DITCHES

Neolithic oval barrow

Contexts 2004 (ploughsoil from clearance over and around the barrow), 1926 (relic stream course to the south-west), upper fills of inner (2060) and outer (2061) ditches Grid ref.: 51244 98195 Figures 3.105 and 108 (relic stream course), 3.109 (outer barrow ditch), 3.110 (inner barrow ditch) (Bradley 1992, 127–43; Barclay and Halpin 1999, 19–28).

SFB 9 was cut into the centre of the oval barrow and damaged the north-east end of the barrow grave. The pit was shallow to the point of non-existence, and Bradley has argued from this that a barrow mound at least 0.22 m high (probably more; see Chapter 3, Depths) was still standing when the SFB was constructed (1992, 133). SFB 12 was immediately to the east of the east corner of the barrow.

Saxon pottery was found in 2004, ploughsoil from clearance over and around the barrow, and 1926, said to be a relic stream course to the south-west of the barrow, as well as in the upper fills of the inner (2060) and outer ditches (2061) of the oval barrow. It was concentrated at the north corner (ditch sections 2061/J and Z and 2060/Z) and in the centre of the north-east side of the outer ditch (2061/K and D).

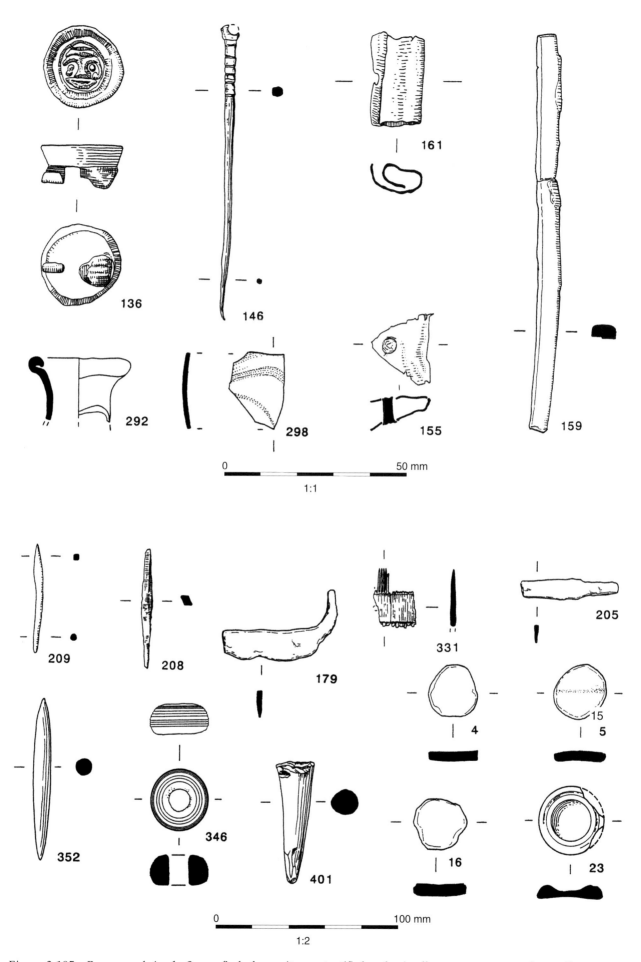

Figure 3.105 Roman and Anglo-Saxon finds from pits, unstratified and miscellaneous contexts and topsoil.

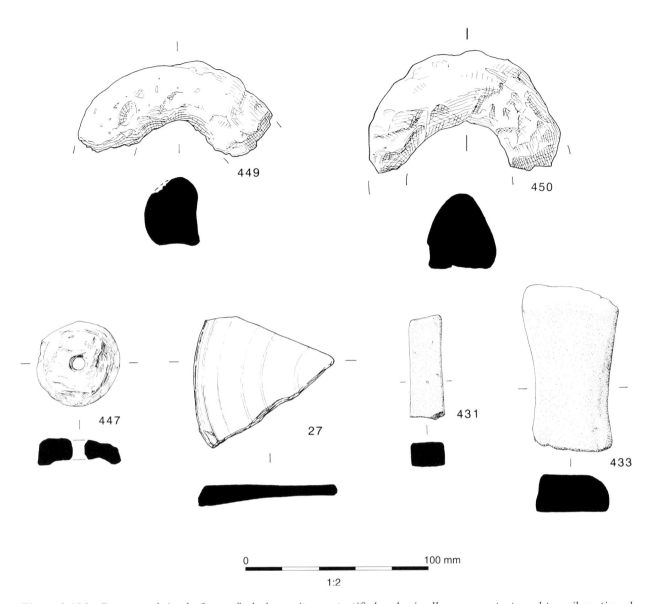

449

450

447

27

431

433

0   100 mm
          1:2

Figure 3.106   Roman and Anglo-Saxon finds from pits, unstratified and miscellaneous contexts and topsoil continued.

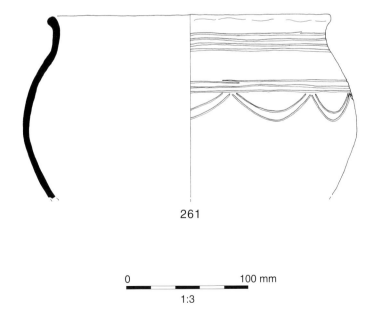

261

0   100 mm
          1:3

Figure 3.107   Pit 4664 pottery.

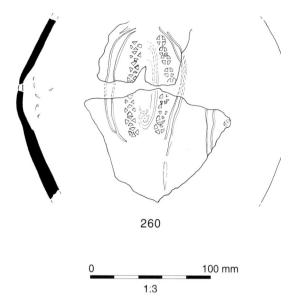

260

0 _____ 100 mm
1:3

Figure 3.108   Relic stream course pottery.

Very little Saxon material occurred in the remaining ditch sections. These two concentrations may represent deliberate dumping into the stable hollows of the barrow ditches, possibly from occupation outside the area of the 1983–5 excavations, since neither is

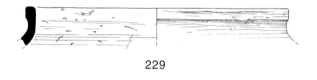

229

230

231

0 _____ 100 mm
1:3

Figure 3.109   Oval barrow outer ditch pottery.

immediately next to the two sunken-featured buildings in the area. There were no small finds from these dumps, and apparently little animal bone.

Relic stream course

Context 1926.

Finds

401 SF 1530   **Worked antler** Length 62 mm. Hacked off tine with pared down point. Figure 3.105.

Pottery

3.108.260   **Bossed and stamped vessel**. Grey fabric, surfaces slightly abraded.

Pottery (outer ditch 2061) tpq 5th/6th century

Pottery occurrence by weight (in g) per fabric type per excavated segment.

Context	F1	F2	F3	F6	Total wt (g)	% feature assemblage
2061/C	0	2	0	0	2	0.2
2061/D	15	74	0	0	89	6.9
2061/E	0	14	0	0	14	1.1
2061/H	3	0	0	0	3	0.2
2061/I	64	25	11	21	121	9.4
2061/J	10	441	0	0	451	35.0
2061/K	21	0	0	0	21	1.6
2061/L	0	18	0	0	18	1.4
2061/N	0	8	0	0	8	0.6
2061/P	4	0	0	0	4	0.3
2061/Q	16	3	0	0	19	1.5
2061/V	0	41	0	0	41	3.2
2061/Z	0	499	0	0	499	38.7
Total wt (g)	133	1125	11	21	1290	
%		10.3	87.2	0.9	1.6	
Mean sherd wt		4.9	14.2	5.5	7.0	

EVE: Jars = 0.49; Bowls = 0.

One incised sherd (Q/1, F1, 11 g).
One rusticated sherd (Z/1, F1, 37 g).
Pierced sherd (I/1, F3, 8 g).

Cross-fits: J/1 = Z/1 (x4).

Illustrations

3.109.229   Rim sherd. Dark grey fabric with smooth dark brown outer surface.
3.109.230   Rusticated sherd. Black fabric with dark brown outer surface.
3.109.231   Stamped sherd. Dark grey fabric with smooth black outer surface.

Pottery (inner ditch 2060)

Pottery occurrence by weight (in g) per excavated segment per fabric type.

Context	F1	F2	F3	F6	Total wt (g)	% feature assemblage
2060/A	9	0	0	0	9	10.2
2060/I	0	41	0	0	41	46.6
2060/L	8	0	0	0	8	9.1
2060/Z	4	26	0	0	30	34
Total wt (g)	21	67	0	0	88	
%		23.9	76.1	0	0	
Mean sherd wt	7.0	22.3	0	0		

EVE: Jars = 0.05; Bowls = 0.

Illustrations

3.110.232   Jar rim, uniform dark grey fabric.

No chronologically diagnostic pottery.

BARROW 1

Context 1; Grid ref.: 51419 98190; Figures 3.111 and 3.113 (Barclay and Halpin 1999, 141–8).

Barrow 1 was on the east of the excavated area next to Wick Hall Drive, at the south-west end of the linear group of barrows. Layers 2 and 3 produced Anglo-Saxon pottery, animal bone and small finds, including a clay pipe fragment from layer 2. These layers probably represent deliberate Anglo-Saxon dumping into the open barrow ditches, with plough disturbance in layer 2. The density of finds was very low and the ditch was not fully excavated.

Finds

Six small finds were recovered. These included two Roman coins, 284 and 285, both of mid 4th-century date, a fragment of worked bone 385, a reused half base of a Roman pot, 2, a ceramic gaming piece, 3, and 621, a clay pipe fragment.

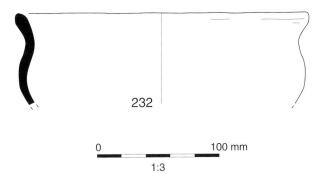

232

0   100 mm

1:3

Figure 3.110 Oval barrow inner ditch pottery.

Layer 2

621 SF 1514   **Clay pipe fragment**. (Not illustrated)
285 SF 503   **Bronze coin** Obverse GLORIA ROMANORUM. Minted Trier? Denomination 3. AD 364-378 (Not illustrated)
385 SF 1657   **Worked bone** Length 91 mm. Fragment of a tibia. Broken at both ends. One end has been pared down.

Reused Roman sherd no. 2 SF 1477 Diameter 50 mm. Modified half base of a beaker in Oxford fine white ware, fabric 11. (Not illustrated)

Layer 3

Reused Roman sherd no. 3 SF 1468 Diameter 25 mm. Made from a modified body sherd in grey ware fabric 2.

284 SF 504   **Bronze coin** Imitation. Constantius. Reverse FEL TEMP REPARATIO. Mint illegal. Denomination 4. c 348–360. (Not illustrated)

Pottery tpq 6th century

Pottery occurrence by weight (in g) per fabric type per excavated segment.

Context	F1	F2	F3	F6	Total wt (g)	% feature assemblage
1/B	0	1	0	0	1	0.4
1/D	0	0	2	0	2	0.7
1/E	114	0	0	0	114	41.9
1/F	1	11	0	0	12	4.4
1/G	2	0	0	0	2	0.7
1/H	0	0	0	6	6	2.2
1/J	0	73	0	42	115	42.3
1/K	0	0	20	0	20	7.3
Total wt (g)	117	85	22	48	272	
%		43.0	31.3	8.1	17.6	
Mean sherd wt		4.2	21.3	11.0	6.0	

EVE: Jars = 0.37; Bowls = 0.

Two stamped sherds (E/2 and E/3, F1, 78 g; J/3, F2, 1 g).
Incised sherds, (J/3, F6, 12 g; 31 g).

Cross fits: E/2 = E/3.

Illustrations

3.113.233   Stamped sherd. Black fabric with burnished surfaces.
3.113.234   Stamped sherd. Black fabric with burnished surfaces.

The stamped and incised sherds suggest a *terminus post quem* of the 6th century.

Barrow 1

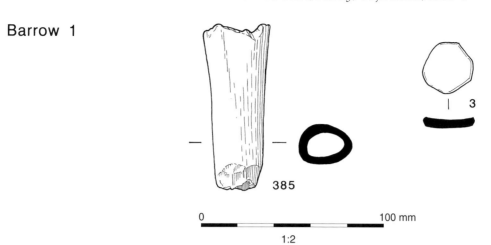

Barrow 12

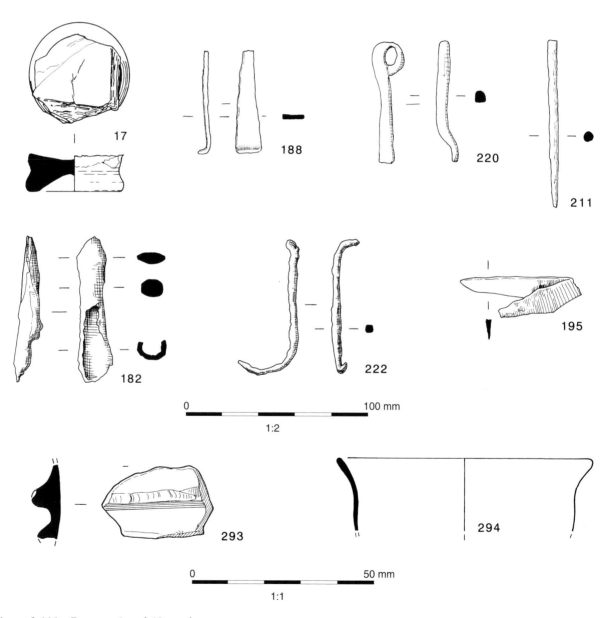

Figure 3.111   Barrows 1 and 12 artefacts.

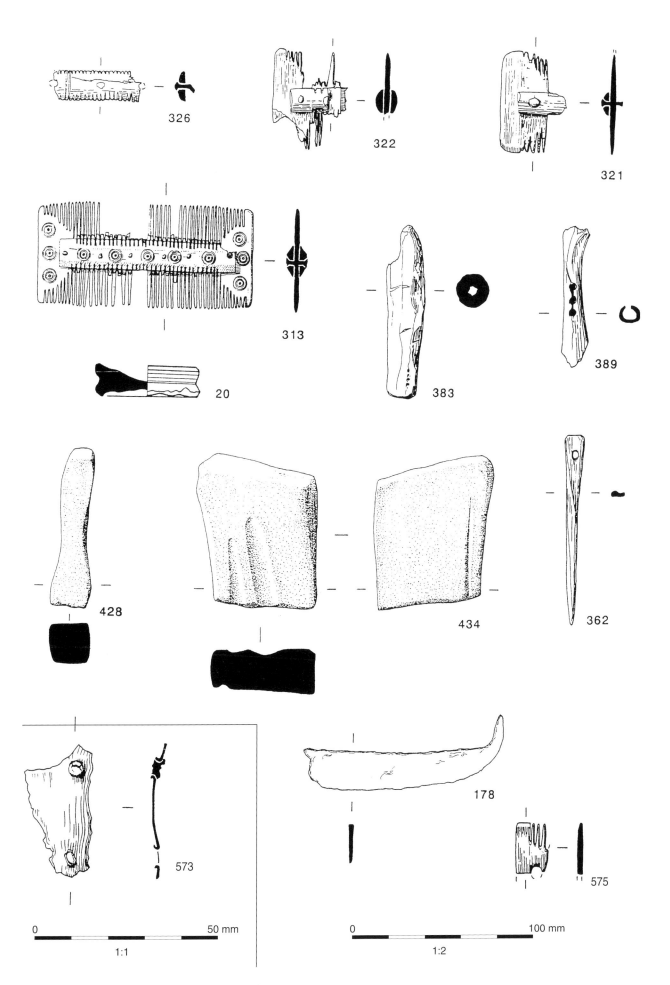

326

322

321

313

389

383

20

428

434

362

573

178

575

0   50 mm

1:1

0   100 mm

1:2

Figure 3.112   Barrow 12 artefacts continued.

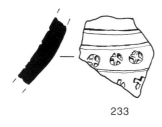

233

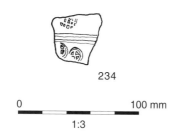

234

0   100 mm

1:3

Figure 3.113   Barrow 1 pottery.

BARROW 12

Context 601 (outer ditch); Grid ref.: 51346 98086; Figures 3.111–2, 3.114; (Barclay and Halpin 1999, 97–111)

Layers 1, 2, 3 and 4 of the outer ditch of barrow 12 produced Anglo-Saxon pottery, animal bone and small finds. Layer 1 was topsoil; layers 2 and 3 represent deliberate Anglo-Saxon dumping, with some plough disturbance of layer 2. Layers 2 and 3 both contained post-medieval finds, including a clay pipe fragment from layer 2 and a fragment of post-medieval glass from layer 3. SFB 26 was constructed between the inner ditch 602 and the more substantial outer ditch 601.

Finds

Forty small finds were recovered. These include three Roman coins: 275, which is very worn, is 3rd-century, 282 is dated to 330–335 and 283 is dated to AD 348–360. There are also fragments of a late Roman bottle, 293, and bowl, 294. There are six fragments of reused Roman pots. Numbers 18 and 19 are complete circles; 20 is a half base; and 19, 21 and 22 are all wedge-shaped pieces. Number 182, a spearhead, is too fragmentary to discern its type. Number 220, a rod with two looped terminals, one of which is broken, is similar to objects described as links from snaffle bits. It is similar to 221 from SFB 44. The complete looped terminal is very worn. Other examples have been found at the Anglo-Saxon site at Shakenoak (Brodribb *et al.* 1972, fig. 39, 168170). Number 212 is another hook-like object with hooks at both ends which are at 90° to each other. It is of unknown function. Number 188 is part of the stem and bit of a barb spring padlock key, similar to examples from Baldock (Manning *et al.* 1986, fig. 68, 559–561).

Number 195 is a knife of Böhner's type A, a type used from the 5th to the 7th centuries (Böhner 1958,

214). There is also a bladed object, 178, which Grainger has identified as a razor, and which he tentatively dates to the 7th–8th centuries. Another possible razor, 179, was found in possible posthole 3835. Although razors are common from Anglian cemeteries such as Spong Hill (Hills *et al.* 1987, figs 98 and 99), the form varies considerably from the Barrow Hills examples. The examples from Barrow Hills are squared off and do not have the looped tangs common on the Anglian types. There are, as yet, no published parallels to these objects from the Upper Thames region.

Two whetstones were also recovered. Number 428 is of Calcareous sandstone, probably of local origin. Number 434 is probably Old Red Sandstone or ?Millstone Grit. Number 428 has had extensive wear, producing a waisted profile. Number 434 has three point or needle sharpening grooves. There are also six fragments of quernstones: 416, 417, 422, 423, 424, and 425.

Evidence for textile manufacture is limited. There is a single iron tooth, 211, from a heckle, used for carding wool or flax fibres prior to spinning. Associated finds are three perforated pig fibula pins 362, 367, and 371. These may have been used for mesh knitting or looped needle netting or in association with a loom. There are fragments of five combs. They are all double sided composite combs, typical of the 5th to 7th centuries. Number 313 is a fine example with well executed ring-and-dot decoration. Number 326 is decorated with two transverse grooves. The remaining combs 321, 322 and 575 are all plain. 383 is a handle made from an antler tine which has been trimmed. The socket at one end was broken in antiquity and a new socket has been formed at the other end. Number 393 is a fragment of a beam which has had the tines removed by sawing. It has been discarded from antler working.

Unstratified

282 SF 564,
601/0   **Bronze coin** Obverse Vrbs Roma. Reverse wolf and twins TRP. Mint Trier. Denomination 4. AD 330–335. (Not illustrated)

Reused Roman sherd no. 18 SF 1476 Diameter 100 mm. Modified foot-ring base in Oxford red/brown colour-coated fabric 3. (Not illustrated)

Layer 1

Reused Roman sherd no. 17 SF 1457 Diameter 55 mm. Modified foot-ring beaker base in Oxford red/brown colour-coated fabric 3.

Layer 2

625 SF 1505   **Clay pipe fragment**. (Not illustrated)
283 SF 564   **Bronze coin** Constans. Obverse DN CONSTANS PF AVG. Reverse FEL TEMP REPARATIO (fh). Mint illegal. Denomination 4. AD 348–360 (Not illustrated)

182 SF 554 **Iron spearhead** Length 77 mm. Fragmentary blade and open-ended socket.

188 SF 657 **Iron barrel padlock key?** Length 53 mm, width 14 mm. Part of a flat stem and fragment of bit.

220 SF 550 **Iron snaffle bit** Length 64 mm. Rod with square cross-section curved round to form a loop at one end. The other end was also curved but now broken.

211 SF 578 **Iron heckle tooth** Length 90 mm, diameter 4.5 mm. Circular cross-section. The head has a slight lip.

222 SF 577 **Iron hook** Length 74 mm. Made from a rod with a square cross-section. Curved at one end to form a hook and bent at the other.

195 SF 548 **Iron knife** Blade length 82 mm, width 14 mm, thickness 3 mm, blade point central, inclined back, convex back slope, leading edge curved. Groove down one side of the blade. Cutting edge worn. Bent. (Type A.1.c). Tang length 31 mm, set just below blade back, sloping shoulders.

269 SF 1426 **Iron rod** Length 60 mm, thickness 6 mm. Fragment with square cross-section. (Not illustrated)

293 SF 663 **Glass bottle** Green heavily bubbled, transparent fragment with the remains of two parallel strengthening ribs. One rib is fractured along most of its surviving length. Late Roman.

294 SF 576 **Glass bowl** Diameter 70 mm. Everted rim and part of the wall from a straight sided bowl. Pale green translucent glass with patches of a dark brown weathering crust. Late Roman.

326 SF 553 **Double-sided composite bone comb** Length 46 mm. Fragment from a connecting plate with D-shaped cross-section. Saw cuts along both edges and decorated with two transverse parallel incised lines. Remains of one iron rivet and two rivet holes.

322 SF 583 **Double-sided composite antler comb** Height 51 mm. Rectangular end plate with graduated teeth, 4 per cm on one side and 5 per cm on the other. The connecting plates have D-shaped cross-sections and saw cuts along both edges. Two iron rivets remain and also a detached tooth segment.

321 SF 582 **Double-sided composite antler comb** Height 54 mm. Rectangular end plate with graduated teeth. The teeth average 5 per cm. The connecting plate has a D-shaped cross-section. One iron rivet and part of a rivet hole remain. Also four fragments of a tooth segment.

313 SF 551 **Double-sided composite antler comb** Height 54 mm. Rectangular end plates with graduated teeth. Each end plate is decorated with three ring-and-dot motifs with central perforations. Six tooth segments with teeth averaging 5 per cm on both sides. The connecting plates have trapezoidal cross-sections and saw cuts along both edges and are held by six iron rivets. Each connecting plate is decorated with five ring-and-dot motifs.

367 SF 547 **Bone pin** Length 104 mm. Made from a pig fibula. Broken across perforation, tip missing. (Not illustrated)

362 SF 580 **Bone pin** Length 99 mm. Made from a pig fibula. Head modified and pierced. Polished.

371 SF 644 **Bone pin** Length 60 mm. Made from a pig fibula. Broken across perforation. Tip missing. (Not illustrated)

310 SF 579 **Bone shaft** Fragment broken at both ends. (Not illustrated)

383 SF 586 **Antler handle** Length 91 mm, width 36 mm. Made from a tine, trimmed down and socketed at both ends.

389 SF 1531 **Worked bone** Length 74 mm. Part of a tibia broken at both ends. The central shaft is pierced with three holes. Diameter of holes 4 mm.

Reused Roman sherd no. 19 SF 1459 Diameter 65 mm. Wedge-shaped cut down fragment of a foot-ring base in Oxford red/brown colour-coated fabric 3. (Not illustrated)

Reused Roman sherd no. 20 SF 1457 Diameter *c* 55 mm. Semicircular cut down body sherd in coarse greyware fabric 5. (Not illustrated)

Reused Roman sherd no. 22 SF 1478 Diameter *c* 130 mm. Wedge-shaped fragment of a base in greyware fabric 2. (Not illustrated)

416 SF 587 **Quern** Length 120 mm. Fragment of friable, porous, coarse grained feldspathic grit, colour near range for Old Red Sandstone. ?Old Red Sandstone or ?Millstone Grit. (Not illustrated)

417 SF 645 **Quern** Length 52 mm. Fragment of reddish-brown, feldspathic coarse grained sandstone. Probably Old Red Sandstone. (Not illustrated)

424 SF 658 **Quern fragment?** Length 47 mm. Calcareous and highly ferruginous coarse grit with fossil bivalves, Faringdon Lower Greensand. (Not illustrated)

425 SF 1533 **Quern fragments?** Length 47 mm. Coarse grit with cement of iron ore, Shotover? (Cumnor?) and calcareous grit, Corallian? (Not illustrated)

428 SF 584 **Whetstone** Length 82 mm. Complete. Square cross-section. Extensive wear on all four sides producing a waisted profile. Calcareous sandstone. Local Corallian.

434 SF 585 **Whetstone** Length 99 mm. Rectangular cross-section, traces of wear on the

broader faces. Two wide grooves on one of the broader faces. The other broad face has a single deep groove containing traces of iron concretion. Coarse porous pink quartz grit with feldspar, ?Old Red Sandstone or ?Millstone Grit.

Layer 3

275 SF 574 **Bronze Sestertius, very worn** AD 200–300. (Not illustrated)

SF 573 **Copper alloy sheet** Length 33 mm. Fragmentary. Pierced with holes for two rivets. One copper alloy rivet survives.

178 SF 571 **Iron razor** Length 108 mm. Straight blade back and curved blade with squared off end. The tang is set at almost 90° to the blade.

SF 575 **Antler comb** Fragment from a rectangular end plate with graduated teeth. Part of a hole for suspension.

393 SF 1660 **Antler waste** Part of a beam, two tines removed by sawing. Chop marks at the base of the beam. (Not illustrated)

Reused Roman sherd no. 21 SF 1450 Diameter 90 mm. Wedge-shaped fragment of a foot-ring base in Oxford red/brown colour-coated fabric 3. (Not illustrated)

422 SF 558 **Quern fragment?** Length 108 mm. Coarse grit with highly ferruginous matrix. Shotover? (Cumnor?). (Not illustrated)

423 SF 560 **Quern fragment?** Length 100 mm. Coarse grit with highly ferruginous matrix. Shotover? (Cumnor?). (Not illustrated)

617 SF 1290 **Post-medieval glass.** (Not illustrated)

Pottery tpq 6th century?

EVE: Jars = 5.78; Bowls = 1.97.

Eighteen incised sherds (C/1, F1, 3 g; D/3, F1, 17 g; G/2, F3, 5 g; H/1, F2, 4 g; H/3, F2, 5 g; I/2, F1, 22 g; I/2, F2, 16 g; I/2, F2, 6 g; J/2, F1, 3 g; J/2, F1, 13 g; J/2, F1, 5 g; J/2, F2, 17 g; J/2, F3, 36 g; J/2, F3, 10 g; K/2, F1, 61 g; L/2, F2, 17 g; N/2, F2, 30 g; N/3, F3, 18 g).
One incised and stabbed sherd (I/2 and J/2, F3, 98 g).
One incised and stabbed bossed sherd (J/2, F3, 145 g).
One incised, stamped and bossed sherd (J/2, F3, 38 g).
One stabbed sherd (J/2, F7, 3 g).
Two rusticated sherds (J/2, F2, 10 g; J/2, F2, 16 g).
Three pierced sherds (D/3, F1, 3 g; N/2, F2, 3 g; N/4, F1, 13 g).

Illustrations

3.114.235 Pierced sherd. Dark grey fabric with unfinished surfaces.

Pottery occurrence by weight (in g) per fabric type per excavated segment.

Context	F1	F2	F3	F4	F6	F7	Total wt (g)	% feature assemblage
601/A	8	18	22	0	0	0	48	0.3
601/B	0	2	3	0	14	0	19	0.1
601/C	63	129	199	0	0	0	391	2.2
601/D	77	40	191	0	13	0	321	1.8
601/E	35	124	86	3	0	7	255	1.4
601/F	5	93	49	0	0	0	147	0.8
601/G	15	63	5	0	0	0	83	0.5
601/H	152	277	62	0	124	0	615	3.4
601/I	5174	1091	1061	0	220	0	7546	42.2
601/J	1000	1206	547	6	220	13	2992	16.7
601/K	217	311	113	8	461	0	1110	6.2
601/L	595	212	305	9	98	0	1219	6.8
601/M	687	245	411	0	189	0	1532	8.6
601/N	140	345	618	0	272	14	1389	7.8
601/O	20	48	0	0	20	3	91	0.5
601/P	45	44	34	0	0	0	123	0.7
Total wt (g)	8233	4248	3706	26	1631	37	17881	
%		46.0	23.8	20.7	0.1	9.1	0.2	
Mean sherd wt	17.3	10.7	17.2	6.5	10.6	6.1		

3.114.236 Jar rim. Dark brown fabric with smoothed outer surface.
3.114.237 Bowl rim. Uniform black fabric with smoothed outer surface.
3.114.238 Jar rim. Uniform black fabric with smoothed outer surface.
3.114.239 Rim sherd from small bowl. Uniform black fabric with orange-brown surfaces.
3.114.240 'Stepped' base. Uniform dark grey fabric with smoothed surfaces.
3.114.241 Stabbed and incised sherd. Uniform black fabric with smoothed surfaces.
3.114.242 Bossed and incised vessel. Black fabric with burnished brown outer surface.
3.114.243 Incised sherd. Uniform black fabric with burnished outer surface.
3.114.244 Incised sherd. Uniform black fabric with burnished outer surface.
3.114.245 Jar rim. Uniform black fabric with smoothed outer surfaces.
3.114.246 Jar rim. Uniform black fabric with smoothed outer surfaces.
3.114.247 Jar rim. Uniform black fabric with smoothed outer surfaces.
3.114.248 Stabbed and bossed sherd. Dark grey fabric with smoothed surfaces.
3.114.249 Incised sherd. Black fabric with burnished brown outer surface.

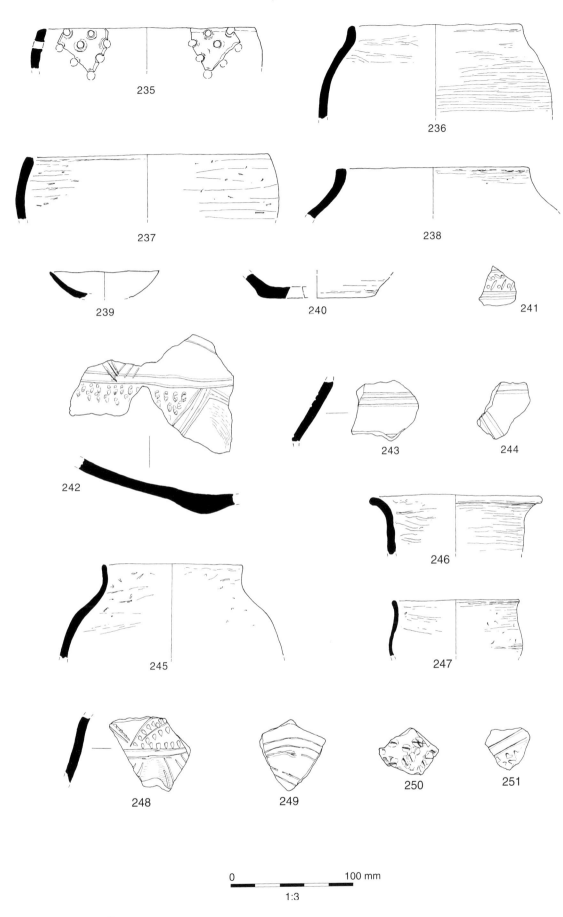

Figure 3.114   Barrow 12 pottery.

3.114.250 Rusticated sherd. Black fabric with brown outer surface.

3.114.251 Stamped and incised sherd. Black fabric with smoothed brown outer surface.

The decorated sherds indicate a firm 6th-century *terminus post quem* for the backfilling of this feature.

BARROW 13

Contexts 401 (ditch) and 414–8 (inter-cutting pits); Grid ref.: 51371 98098; Figures 3.115–6, 3.117 (pit 414) (Barclay and Halpin 1999, 111–5).

Barrow 13 was north-east of barrow 12. The ditch 401 was cut by two sunken-featured buildings, 23 and 24, and layers 2 and 3 contained Anglo-Saxon pottery, animal bone and small finds, probably representing deliberate dumping. Disturbance extended into layer 4, which produced a clay pipe fragment and a piece of iron bar. A series of inter-cutting pits 414–8 in the north-west quadrant of the barrow yielded Anglo-Saxon finds, pottery from 414 and a loomweight from 416.

Finds

Thirty-five finds were recovered from the upper fills. These included five Roman coins 271, 279, 281, 286, and 288. Their dates range between AD 321 and 378. Number 288 has been pierced for suspension as has a further coin, 287, from SFB 44 probably for use as a pendant. An applied disc brooch, 137, is similar to those from Grave 75 Long Wittenham and Grave 19 Standlake I and is probably of mid 5th- to mid 6th-century date (Dickinson 1976, 191). Other personal items include a pyramid stud 151 and 160, a perforated and broken sheet, which could be the remains of a belt fitting.

Number 190 is a fragment of a horseshoe of pre-Conquest type (Clark 1986). It is similar to one from a 9th-century context at Winchester (Goodall 1990, 1055, fig. 340, 939). Number 186 is a rectangular sectioned rod with an up-turned end. Objects such as these when found in graves are often interpreted as simple keys, such as those from Grave 25, Fonaby, Lincolnshire (Cook 1981, fig. 9.4). There is also a single woodworking nail (SF 1423).

Textile equipment consisted of five fragmentary loomweights 448, 452, 455, 461 and 451. They are all of the early Saxon annular type and appear to have been dumped into the barrow ditch. Other loomweights have been found in SFB 25, which cut the ditch and SFB 24 to the south. A worked stone, 436, is probably also a weight but it is considerably heavier than those of fired clay. Number 372, a perforated pig fibula pin, is of the type common from the site which may have been used in association with a loom or for open mesh knitting or netting. Only one fragmentary comb was recovered, 336. It has a very wide solid zone and additional perforation similar to examples from Lankhills (Clarke 1979, fig. 31) and is of a type common from the second half of the 4th century onwards (MacGregor 1985, 92). Number 342 is a very

fragmentary piece of antler with a notch towards one end. Number 391 is part of an antler beam which has had the tines sawn off. It is waste from antler working.

There are eight reused bases from Roman pots: 6, 7 and 14 are complete circles. Numbers 8, 9, 10, 11 and 12 are all wedges. There are also two counters, 5 and 13, which are probably gaming pieces.

Layer 2

137 SF 568 **Copper alloy applied disc brooch** Diameter 36 mm. Composite construction with a sheet metal backplate and an applied disc on the obverse, notched around the edge. Inserted fastenings, both missing. (MacGregor and Bolick 1993, no. 58)

279 SF 563 **Bronze coin** Constantius. Obverse DN CONSTANTIUS NOB C. Reverse GLORIA EXERCITUS (2 standards). Mint illegal. Denomination 4. AD 330–335. (Not illustrated)

281 SF 610 **Bronze coin** Obverse Constantinopolis. Reverse victory on a prow PLG. Mint Lyons. Denomination 4. AD 330–335. (Not illustrated)

286 SF 566 **Bronze coin** Obverse GLORIA NOVI SAECULI. Minted at Arles. Denomination 3. AD 364–378. (Not illustrated)

160 SF 565 **Copper alloy sheet** Length 41 mm. Rectangular cut sheet broken across one end. The other end is pierced with two rivet holes, now broken across both holes. One of the longer edges has two rectangular cut notches.

151 SF 561 **Copper alloy stud** Diameter 15 mm. Pyramid-shaped stud with circular cross-sectioned shank, most now missing.

174 SF 562 **Lead waste**. (Not illustrated)

190 SF 615 **Iron horseshoe**. Width 26 mm. Fragment of one arm with two rectangular nail holes and part of a third. Two nails with T-shaped heads and clenched shanks are still in place.

SF 1423 **Iron nail** Length 69 mm. Circular flat head, square cross-sectioned shank. (Not illustrated)

372 SF 625 **Bone pin** Length 74 mm. Made from a pig fibula. Broken across perforation. Tip missing. Polished.

336 SF 616 **Double-sided composite antler comb**. Length 35 mm. Fragment of a rectangular end plate with fragments of teeth on both sides. One rivet hole in the centre and two decorative holes close to the edge.

448 SF 614 **Ceramic loomweight**. Diameter 70 mm. Made from a fragment of modified Roman tile, pierced off-centre. The edges have been ground. Diameter of hole 12 mm. Weight 180.27 g.

Barrow 13

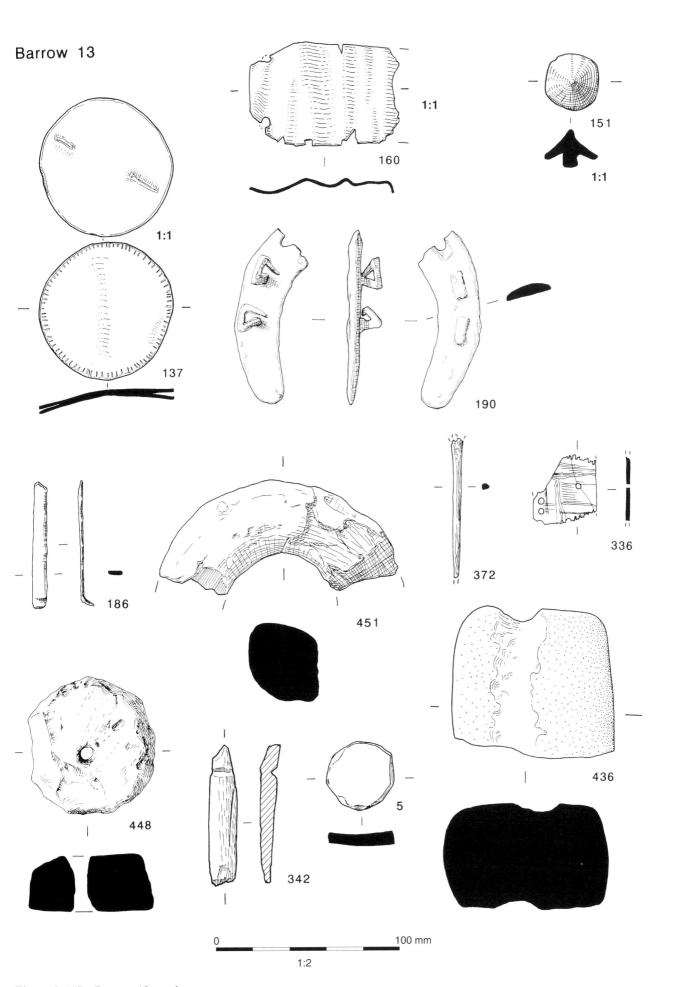

1:1 160

1:1 151

1:1

1:1 137

190

186

451

372

336

448

342

5

436

0 100 mm

1:2

Figure 3.115 Barrow 13 artefacts.

451 SF 629   **Annular, fired clay loomweight**. Diameter 140 mm. Fragment approx. 40% with roughly smoothed surfaces. Estimated weight 450 g.

452 SF 626   **Annular fired clay loomweight**. Diameter 130 mm. Fragment approx. 25% Estimated weight 425.32 g. (Not illustrated)

455 SF 659   **Annular, fired clay loomweight** Diameter 120 mm. Fragment approx. 22% Estimated weight 395.18 g. (Not illustrated)

461 SF 646   **Annular, fired clay loomweight** Length 57 mm. Fragment. (Not illustrated)

Reused Roman sherd no. 5 SF 1475 Diameter 35 mm. Made from a body sherd in Oxford red/brown colour-coated fabric 3.

Reused Roman sherd no. 6 SF 1651 Diameter 100 mm. Base of a jug or large flagon in Oxford red/brown colour-coated fabric 3. (Not illustrated)

Reused Roman sherd no. 7 SF 1470 Diameter 50 mm. Modified base of a thick walled beaker in Oxford red/brown colour-coated fabric 3. (Not illustrated)

Reused Roman sherd no. 8 SF 1474 Diameter 80 mm. Wedge-shaped cut down flat base in Oxford red/brown colour-coated fabric 3. (Not illustrated)

Reused Roman sherd no. 9 SF 1471 Diameter 70 mm. Wedge-shaped cut down foot-ring base of a mortarium in Oxford red/brown colour-coated fabric 3. (Not illustrated)

Reused Roman sherd no. 10 SF 1454 Diameter 110 mm. Wedge-shaped cut down fragment of a foot-ring base in Oxford red/brown colour-coated fabric 3. (Not illustrated)

Reused Roman sherd no. 11 SF 1469 Diameter 60 mm. Wedge-shaped cut down fragment of a foot-ring base in greyware, fabric 4. (Not illustrated)

Reused Roman sherd no. 12 SF 1650 Diameter 50 mm Wedge- shaped cut down fragment of a beaker base in Oxford red/brown colour-coated fabric 3. (Not illustrated)

Reused Roman sherd no. 13 SF 594 Diameter 60 mm Made from a flat base in greyware fabric 4. The edges have been ground smooth. (Not illustrated)

421 SF 628   **Quern fragment** Length 80 mm (Not illustrated)

426 SF 634   **Quern fragment?** Length 57 mm Fragment of coarse grit with highly ferruginous matrix, Shotover? (Cumnor?) (Not illustrated)

436 SF 592   **Stone weight** Length 91 mm, width 79 mm thickness 56 mm Fragment with pecked central groove.

Layer 3

271 SF 607   **Bronze coin** Constantine I. Obverse CONSTANTINUS AVG. Reverse BEATA TRANQUILLITAS. PTR.

Minted at Trier. Denomination 3. AD 321–323.

288 SF 572   **Bronze coin** Reverse GLORIA NOVI SAECVLI. Minted in Arles. Denomination 3. AD 364–378. Perforated.

342 SF 618   **Worked antler** Length 73 mm, width 14 mm Fragment of a tine with a notch towards one end.

391 SF 1661   **Antler waste** Length 80 mm Part of beam, two tines and part of beam sawn off. (Not illustrated)

Reused Roman sherd no. 14 SF 1466 Diameter 45 mm. Modified foot-ring base in fine greyware fabric 9. (Not illustrated)

469 SF 623   **Ceramic?** Fragment of an object with large perforation. (Not illustrated)

Layer 4

186 SF 612   **Iron rod** Length 67 mm. Rectangular cross-section, very short arm with rounded tip.

619 SF 1510   **Clay pipe fragment** Post-medieval. (Not illustrated)

Pottery tpq 6th century?

Pottery occurrence by weight (in g) per fabric type per excavated segment.

Context	F1	F2	F3	F4	F6	F7	Total wt (g)	% feature assemblage
401/A	0	8	12	0	108	0	128	1.8
401/B	37	9	0	0	102	0	148	2.0
401/C	66	114	0	0	35	0	215	3.0
401/D	4	0	0	0	0	0	4	0.1
401/E	165	25	22	0	63	3	278	3.8
401/F	29	21	69	0	43	0	162	2.2
401/G	39	56	19	0	26	0	140	1.9
401/H	394	285	44	0	283	23	1029	14.2
401/I	45	40	19	0	0	7	111	1.5
401/J	39	51	19	0	0	0	109	1.5
401/K	824	252	201	6	245	0	1528	21.0
401/L	203	54	115	3	53	95	523	7.2
401/M	9	0	2	0	0	0	11	0.2
401/N	27	80	93	0	101	0	301	4.1
401/O	497	758	312	6	228	0	1801	24.8
401/P	120	472	49	0	142	0	783	10.8
Total wt (g)	2498	2225	976	15	1429	128	7271	
%		34.4	30.6	13.4	0.2	19.7	1.8	
Mean sherd wt		9.0	11.6	10.6	2.5	11.6	25.6	

EVE: Jars = 3.92; Bowls = 1.41.

Three incised sherds, (H/2, F1, 215 g; H/2, F1, 4 g; P/2, F2, 19 g, rim sherd, 13% complete).

One stamped, incised and carinated sherd (O/2, F1, 8 g).

Three stamped sherds, (H/2, F2, 22 g; O/2, F2, 8 g; P/2, F3, 2 g).

One complete miniature lugged vessel (No cut number, layer 2, 78 g, rim 100% complete).

One swallow's nest lug L/3, F6, 53 g, rim sherd, 14% complete).

Three pierced sherds (A/2, F3, 6 g, rim sherd, 18% complete; K/2, F2, 32 g, rim sherd, 3% complete; P/2, F3, 9 g, rim sherd, 6% complete).

Foot-ring base (F/3, F3, 23 g).

Pedestal base (J/2, F6, 19 g).

Illustrations

3.116.252   Miniature lugged vessel. Rough, orange-brown fabric, unfinished surfaces.

3.116.253   'Swallow's nest' lug, black fabric with dark brown unfinished surfaces.

3.116.254   Rim from pierced vessel. Dark grey fabric, unfinished surfaces.

3.116.255   Stamped and incised sherd from ?carinated vessel. Uniform black fabric, smoothed surfaces.

3.116.256   Incised sherd. Black fabric with smoothed burnished surfaces.

The stamped sherds indicate a *terminus post quem* of the 6th century. The carinated sherd (Fig. 3.116.255) may be earlier, but is so small that it is impossible to date with any accuracy, and the presence of stamps on the piece suggest a later date.

PITS 414 AND 416

Pit 414

Pottery

3.117.257   Stamped sherd. Black fabric with burnished surfaces.

3.117.258   Stamped sherd. Black fabric with burnished surfaces.

3.117/259   Stamped sherd. Black fabric with burnished surfaces.

Pits 414–416 were the only features from this group to produce any pottery. Pit 414 produced small sherds of stamped pottery and no other decorated wares, indicating a *terminus post quem* of the 6th century for both features.

Pit 416

462 SF 619   **Annular, fired clay loomweight** Length 67 mm. Fragment with roughly smoothed surfaces. (Not illustrated)

SEGMENTED RING DITCH 2123

Grid ref.: 51316 98078.

252

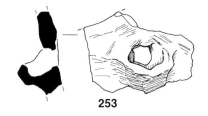

253

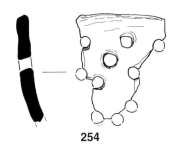

254

255

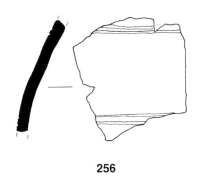

256

0   100 mm

1:3

Figure 3.116   Barrow 13 pottery.

PIT 2142 Grid ref.: 51317 98080. (Barclay and Halpin 1999, 44–6)

A small amount of Saxon pottery was found in the upper fill (2113 and 2080) of the north-west segment 2122 of the segmented ring ditch 2123. Just inside the north-east segment, 2155, was a shallow pit 2142

257

258

259

0   100 mm

1:3

Figure 3.117   Pit 414 pottery.

whose fill, 2135, contained a considerable quantity of ?oak charcoal. This provided a radiocarbon determination of cal 390–600 (1570 ± 50 BP; BM-2705), suggesting that the feature belongs to the period of Anglo-Saxon occupation of the site. A sample of the fill contained a wheat grain and an oat grain (Moffett 1999, 246).

POND BARROW 4866

Grid ref.: 51409 98110 (Barclay and Halpin 1999, 115–128); Site plan I7.

A single Romano-British sherd, a small quantity of Saxon sherds and the almost complete skeleton of a fairly large adult dog (*c* 590 mm shoulder height) were recovered from the uppermost level of pond barrow 4866.

Finds

Reused Roman sherd no. 75 SF 1268, 4866/B/1 Diameter 55 mm. Complete cut down foot-ring base in greyware, fabric 9. (Not illustrated)

Pottery

Pottery occurrence by weight (in g) per excavated segment.

Context	F1	F2	F3	F6	Total wt (g)	% feature assemblage
4866/A	8	15	0	0	23	25.6
4866/B	3	10	17	9	39	43.3
4866/D	7	4	3	14	28	31.1
Total wt (g)	18	29	20	23	90	
%	20.0	32.2	22.2	25.6		
Mean sherd wt	3.6	4.1	10.0	7.6		

No chronologically diagnostic pottery.

ROMAN AND ANGLO-SAXON FINDS FROM MISCELLANEOUS FEATURES

3610/1 Grid ref.: 51265 98186; Figure 3.105

Section across 8 m silt spread, 0.1 m deep, running NW/SE.

208 SF 1043   **Iron awl** Length 63 mm. Awl tapering to both ends. Circular cross-section at one end, square cross-section at the other.

3835 Grid ref.: 51392 98082; Figure 3.105

Possible posthole in area of PBS 11.

179 SF 1078   **Iron razor** Length 60 mm, width 16 mm, blade thickness 3 mm. The blade back is straight and the blade is worn and fragmentary and the end is missing. The curved tang is set almost at 90° to the blade.

4459 Probable posthole

Reused Roman sherd no. 66 SF 1144 Ceramic counter. Diameter 28 mm. Modified body sherd in Oxford red/brown colour-coated fabric 3. (Not illustrated)

2164, 2165, 2166 Grid ref.: 51254 98199; Figure 3.105

Fills of posthole cutting inside edge of inner ditch of oval barrow. Contained Saxon pottery and find.

352 SF 296   **Bone pin beater** Length 85 mm, diameter 9 mm. Cigar-shaped polished shaft with circular cross-section. Pointed at both ends

ROMAN AND ANGLO-SAXON FINDS FROM UNSTRATIFIED CONTEXTS AND TOPSOIL

136 Figure 3.105 SF 545   **Copper alloy button brooch** Diameter 22 mm. Single hinge plate with deposit of

iron corrosion; catch-plate. Annular rim enclosing anthropomorphic face-mask with horizontal lines forming helmet; well defined nose and mouth. All within a plain border. (MacGregor and Bolick 1993, no. 11, 1988.47).

276 SF 1234 **Bronze coin** House of Constantine. Reverse BEATA TRANQUILLITAS VOTIS XX. Denomination 3. Very worn. AD 320–325. (Not illustrated)
278 SF 569. **Bronze coin** Helena. Obverse FL HELENA AUGUSTA. Obverse SECVRITAS REIPUBLICE STRE. Mint Trier. Denomination 3. AD 325–330. (Not illustrated)

146 Figure 3.105 SF 607 **Copper alloy pin** Length 76 mm. Made from a drawn wire hammered below the head to give a rectangular cross-section tapering to an oval cross -section towards the tip. The head has been flattened to an oval and pierced. Broken across hole. Decorated below head with incised lines on all four faces.
161 Figure 3.105 SF 1030 **Copper alloy buckle plate?** Width 22 mm, thickness 0.5 mm. Rectangular cut sheet broken off at one end across a perforation. Rolled, traces of gilding.
155 Figure 3.105 SF 16 **Copper alloy repair fitting** Length 15 mm. Made from a cut sheet folded over and secured by a tubular copper alloy rivet.
159 Figure 3.105 SF 1257 **Copper alloy strip** Length 102 mm. Rectangular cross-section. Broken at both ends.
205 Figure 3.105 SF 661 **Iron knife** Blade length 33 mm, width 10 mm, thickness 2 mm. Straight back, angled back slope. Tip missing. (Type ?.2.b). Tang length 20 mm, set just below blade back, angled shoulders.
209 Figure 3.105 SF 1283 **Iron awl** Length 58 mm. Diamond-shaped cross-section pointed at both ends.
431 Figure 3.106 SF 1281 **Whetstone** Length 55 mm. Fragment with rectangular cross-section, broken at both ends. Signs of wear on one of the broader faces. Calcareous sandstone, local Corallian.
447 Figure 3.106 SF 643 **Ceramic spindlewhorl** Diameter 46 mm. Made from a modified and perforated beaker base in Oxford red/brown colour-coated fabric 3. The edges have been ground. Diameter of hole 10 mm. Weight 25.64 g.

3900 Grid ref.: 51307 98048; Topsoil in area of SFB 28

292 Figure 3.105 SF 1151 **Glass bottle** Diameter at rim 28 mm. Pale green semi-transparent bubbled glass with rolled rim. Patches of a dark brown weathering crust.

UNSTRATIFIED/PIPE TRENCH

298 Figure 3.105 SF 1441, 4480 **Glass vessel** Translucent brown fragment, possibly from a bowl. Outer surface has swathes of white opalescent decoration which may have originally formed an arcaded pattern. Tapering thickness. Anglo-Saxon.

1001 TOPSOIL

305 SF 1436 **Window glass** Thickness 6 mm. Fragment of pale green transparent glass. Roman. (Not illustrated)

346 Figure 3.105 SF 1 **Bone spindlewhorl** Diameter 32 mm. Annular, made from the head of a femur. Turned, the upper surface is decorated with shallow incised circles. Uneven wear on the lower surface. Weight 11.21 g.

REUSED ROMAN SHERDS FROM TOPSOIL

Reused Roman sherd no. 4 SF 1472 Figure 3.105 Diameter 25 mm. Made from a body sherd in greyware, fabric 2.
Reused Roman sherd no. 15 SF 1652 Figure 3.105 Diameter 25 mm. Made from a body sherd in greyware, fabric 6.
Reused Roman sherd no. 16 SF 1465 Figure 3.105 Diameter 25 mm. Made from a body sherd in greyware fabric 4.
Reused Roman sherd no. 23 SF 1448 Figure 3.105 Diameter 35 mm. Made from a beaker base which has been cut down and ground. In Oxford red/brown colour-coated fabric 3.
Reused Roman sherd no. 24 SF 1648 Diameter 70 mm. Wedge-shaped fragment of a foot-ring base on Oxford red/brown colour-coated fabric 3. (Not illustrated)
Reused Roman sherd no. 25 SF 1649 Diameter c 80 mm. Wedge-shaped fragment of a foot-ring base in Oxford red/brown colour-coated fabric 3. (Not illustrated)
Reused Roman sherd no. 26 SF 1649 Diameter c 80 mm. Wedge-shaped fragment of a foot-ring base in Oxford red/brown colour-coated fabric 3. (Not illustrated)
Reused Roman sherd no. 27 SF 1449 Figure 3.106 Diameter 140 mm. Wedge-shaped cut down flat base fragment in greyware, fabric 2.
Reused Roman sherd no. 38 SF 1504 Diameter 75 mm. Complete flat base in greyware, fabric 2. (Not illustrated)

OTHER ANGLO-SAXON FEATURES IN THE AREA OF BARROW HILLS (FIG. 1.3)

CAUSEWAYED ENCLOSURE

Grid ref.: 511 983 (Avery and Brown 1972, 66–81; Leeds and Harden 1936, fig.1)
1905: possibly Saxon extended male skeleton found in north of area between Daisy Banks streams, next to the Radley Road.
1928: Saxon pottery collected by Leeds from pits revealed by gravel extraction on east side of Daisy Banks, just north of the area of the 1983–5 excavations.
1963: Salvage excavation in advance of housing in the area of the Neolithic causewayed enclosure recovered evidence for two Saxon pits containing rubbish deposits, including the burnt remains of a

structure, possibly of wattle and daub. Finds included 5th- to 6th-century pottery, a Roman coin pierced for stringing, a bone comb, a shale spindlewhorl, a bone pin beater and an amethyst bead of a possibly 7th-century type.

BARROW 2

Grid ref.: 5148 9322 (Parrington 1977, 37, 39 and 41 and figs 1, 4 and 7).

Secondary inhumation burial in layer 3 of ditch section 3 (north-west quadrant) of individual aged 17–19 with a 7th-century iron knife near left hip. Supine, north/south, head south and tilted east. Right arm across stomach with hand on left hip, left arm flexed with hand near right shoulder. Two wormian bones.

BARROW 5

Grid ref.: 5160 9929 (Williams 1948, 9–11 and fig. 4)

Two skeletons were discovered during gravel extraction on the north-west side of the barrow. They were inserted into the mound and therefore secondary, possibly Anglo-Saxon. One was of an adult male 1.69 m in height. All but one leg bone of the other was lost.

BARROW 16

Grid ref.: 5195 9842 (Leeds 1938, 33–4 and fig. 8)

Saxon sherds were recorded from the south-west quadrant of the ditch of barrow 16 at a depth of 2'6".

Gazetteer 5: Anglo-Saxon Features at Barton Court Farm

By David Miles

INTRODUCTION

The wording and layout of this section closely reflect the original fiche publication, and all figure numbers refer to the original report (Miles 1986). For an overall plan of the Anglo-Saxon features at Barton Court Farm see Figure 7.2.

SUNKEN HUTS

Seven sunken huts or *Grubenhäuser* were found during the excavation. One, 188, was dug into the south-west angle of the Iron Age enclosure ditch 27 m west of the villa building (Miles 1986, fig. 78). The rest were spread along the edge of the gravel terrace to the south of the main farmyard enclosure ditch, within the area of the last phase of Romano-British enclosures. These six huts were all found on the strip of gravel about 30 m wide between the main villa complex and the wetter soils of the terrace slope. It is likely that evidence of further Saxon occupation to the W was destroyed when the 19th-century gravel pits were dug.

SFB 188 Figure 64; Orientation: E/W?

Length at surface: *c* 3.3 m; Distance between postholes: -; Width: 2.9 m; Depth: 0.5 m.

Description

This, the first Saxon sunken hut to be found in the 1972 season of excavation, was not satisfactorily excavated. The hut had been partially dug into the top of the Iron Age enclosure ditch and was not visible to the excavators on the surface. The hut was first noticed when a section was being dug across the Iron Age ditch, by which time the west end of the sunken hut had been removed, including the posthole that probably existed there.

The sunken hut was an irregular sub-rectangular shape. The fill of the hut was a uniform layer of brown, gravelly loam. The hut had a flat bottom and steeply sloping sides except on the east, where the gravel had been eroded to form a shelf. The posthole at the east end was 0.4 m deeper than the hut floor.

Finds

A whetstone (38), a perforated bronze plate (39), 2 bone pin fragments (40, 62), piece of glass (41).

SFB 952 Figure 64; Orientation: ENE/WSW

Length at surface: 3.5 m; Distance between postholes: 3.0 m; Width: 2.9 m; Depth: 0.25 m.

Description

This hut lay 2 m south of the main east-west Romano-British farmyard ditch (Fig. 83). It had a uniform brown gravelly loam fill. There was a centrally placed posthole at each end of the hut, 0.55 m deeper than the base of the hut. Two postholes close to its north edge and two off the west end could have supported a structure spanning the sunken feature.

This sunken hut sat within a rectangular arrangement of postholes, PBS C, which indicated a larger timber structure. The sunken feature was off-centre to the rectangular structure, lying very close to the north wall. The post building probably impinged on the Romano-British ditch, which contained Saxon pottery, implying that it was constructed at a late phase in the Saxon phase of occupation. The pottery in the sunken feature was consistent with a 5th-century date. The evidence is not conclusive but, on balance, it points to a timber-framed building having been constructed on the site of an earlier sunken hut.

Finds

Two bone pin beaters (823, 525), iron objects (524, 561), lead loomweight (526), iron knife (527), bone comb (528) (562), shale fragment (641), two iron rings (643, 666).

SFB 1023 Figure 64; Orientation: ENE/WSW

Length at surface: 3.9 m; Distance between postholes: 3.6 m; Width: 3.7 m; Depth: 0.57 m.

Description

This was the only hut inside the late Romano-British south-east paddock. It had a flat floor and a centrally placed posthole at each end a further 0.30 m deep. There were traces of five stakeholes in an irregular line along the central long axis of the hut floor. A stratum of natural gravel resulted in a shelf forming around the wall of the sunken hut. The erosion below this shelf contributed to the lower loamy gravel fill of the sunken area. Above this was a dark-brown sandy loam which had seemed to have been deposited after the hut had gone.

Finds

All the finds were from layer 1 except 555–7, two needles and the lead loomweight, which were in layer 2: pottery spindlewhorl (537), iron object (540), lead fragment (541), iron object (542), slag (543), iron object (544), iron buckle (546), bronze object (547), bronze object (548), perforated oyster shell (549), iron object (550), worked bone fragment (551), lead fragment (552), bone comb fragments (553–4), bronze needle (555), bone needle (556), lead loomweight (557), bone ring fragment (565), bone needle (568), bone pin beater (569), decorated bronze fragment (570), bone (571), clay loomweight fragments (575), bone needle (576), coprolite (577), bone tool (578), coprolite (579), iron pin (669).

SFB 1026 Figure 64; Orientation: NE/SW

Length at surface: 3.6 m; Distance between postholes: 3.4 m; Width: 2.7 m; Depth: 0.3 m.

Description

This sunken hut lay just over 1 m west of the latest Romano-British paddock ditch (Fig. 87). On the ground this ditch curved to the south-east and the hut was tucked in close to it. It is not impossible that the ditch curved to avoid the existing hut, but on the whole it is most likely that the ditch pre-existed the hut.

The hut was of rectangular shape with two postholes centrally placed in the narrow ends; unusually, the postholes projected out from the sides of the hut. The east posthole was 0.25 m deeper than the floor of the hut, but the west one was only about the same depth. In three of the corners shallow hollows indicated the existence of slight corner posts.

The floor of the hut was flat and there was a linear cluster of Corallian ragstone aligned between the two postholes. The fill of the hut was a uniform brown sandy loam. Most of the stones were not directly on the gravel floor of the hut but sat 10–20 mm above it. Two stones at the west end were actually on the gravel floor, at right-angles to one another, with a bone comb (637) in the angle.

Finds

Perforated oyster shell (549), iron buckle (626), bone object (634), bone comb (637), iron buckle (657).

SFB 1178 Figure 65, 85; Orientation: ENE/WSW

Length at surface: 4.3 m; Distance between postholes: 3.4 m; Width: 2.9 m; Depth: 0.4 m.

Description

A sub-rectangular hut with a flat base and gently sloping sides. The centrally placed postholes in each end are 0.3 and 0.4 m deep. A slab of limestone 0.4 × 0.3 m in size lay just above the base of the hut at its centre. The uniform fill of the hut consisted of a dark brown sandy loam. The finds included a fragment of glass slag.

Finds

Clay spindlewhorl (612), iron pin (613), worked tooth (614), bronze sheet (616), glass bead (617), glass slag (618), coin, AD 364–78 (564).

SFB 1181 Figure 65, 85; Orientation: NE/SW

Length at surface: 3.9 m; Distance between postholes: 3.4 m; Width: 3.0 m; Depth: 0.6 m.

Description

Less than 2 m to the south-east of hut 1178 and on the same axis lay hut 1181. The base was flat and the sides sloping. The postholes at each narrow end were relatively slight; the one at the west end was dug into the sloping wall of the hut about 0.2 m and the other was dug a similar depth into the base. There was a shallow depression just to the south of the centre of the hut floor, possibly indicating a third post in this position. The fill was a uniform brown sandy loam with a few fragments of stone in the central area 0.2 m from the base. The fill also included a horse skull.

Finds

Bone handle (586), glass fragment (609), bronze bracelet (611), coins, AD 351–3 (585), coins, AD 388–92 (608).

SFB 1190 Figure 65, 85; Orientation: ENE/WSW

Length at surface: 3.67 m; Distance between postholes: 3.2 m; Width: 2.5 m; Depth: 0.4 m.

Description

The sunken hut was cut into the shallow Romano-British ditch 1175 at a time when this feature had become filled with loam. The two postholes were cut 0.6 m below the level of the hut base. The fill was a uniform dark-brown sandy loam.

Thirteen lead loomweights were found on the base of the hut. Ten of them were in a row lying one over the next as if they had been threaded together on a cord. Three others were found to the south-west as well as fragments of clay loomweights.

Finds

Lead loomweights (587–598, 622), bone comb fragment (601), shale bracelet fragment (602), clay loomweights (603, 623), bone plaque (604), coal (605).

POST-BUILT STRUCTURES

The site was carefully excavated with potential timber structures in mind. The whole site was trowelled over several times and the gravel surface was sprayed with water; particular attention was paid to areas apparently empty of features. In this way postholes were found which were not visible in the early stages of excavation. Most of the postholes were shallow and devoid of any datable material so that their allocation to a particular period contains an element of supposition. The following are believed to belong to the Saxon phase of occupation.

PBS A Figure 82; Orientation: NNW-SSE; Dimensions: 9 × 6.7 m

Description

A rectangular building aligned between the farmhouse enclosure ditch and the main farmyard boundary ditch; it overlay a straight shallow slot 611, which could not be accurately dated. The north side was well defined by four substantial and two lesser postholes. The position of the south end was less certain; two postholes, 627 and 653, probably indicated the south corners, but the south cross-wall was less pronounced than the north. This may be because the postholes supporting the end wall were not load-bearing, did not need to penetrate so deeply, and were therefore eroded by ploughing. The east side of the structure was indicated by a line of six postholes of varying spacing. The two southern-most, 654 and 653, were 2.4 m apart, possibly the position of a doorway near the south-east corner.

The west side of structure A was defined by a line of five postholes and to the east of these a second line of four postholes. This wall, possibly of planking, may have been supported by posts on both sides. These postholes were irregularly spaced though a central entrance may have existed between 629 and 630. The postholes varied in size: 654 was one of the larger ones (about 0.5 m diameter × 0.23 m deep), while others were about 0.3 m diameter × 0.15 m deep. All had U-shaped profiles, no obvious post voids or packing, and a brown sandy loam fill.

Dating

Of the 21 postholes forming the structure, only six contained any cultural material – a total of 19 sherds of Iron Age and Romano-British pottery, some identifiable as worn 4th-century AD types. These sherds indicated that the structure must have belonged to the late Roman period or later. The dark soil within the postholes, characteristic of the later settlements, also supports a date in the late Roman or post-Roman period. The orientation and position of the structure respected the Romano-British farmyard ditches, and it is possible that it was an agricultural building contemporary with the villa phase of settlement. On the other hand, the buildings positively dated to that phase had either stone foundations or stone-packed postholes. Structure A bears a much closer resemblance to the posthole structures on the site which produced Saxon material.

PBS B Figure 82; Orientation: E-W; Dimensions: approx. 4.2 × 3.5 m

Description

A rectangular arrangement of postholes parallel to the main Romano-British farmyard ditch and 1.3 m S of it. The west end had been removed by the 19th-century quarry so its length was uncertain.

The seven postholes varied in size between 0.22 and 0.4 m diameter and between 0.06 and 0.12 m deep. All contained the same brown sandy loam fill as structure A. Only one posthole, 665, contained a sherd of pottery of late Romano-British type. The structure had no related floor levels.

PBS C Figure 83; Orientation: E-W; Dimensions: 10 × 5.2 m

Description

A rectangular structure just south of the main villa farmyard boundary ditch. The sunken hut 952 lay within the area enclosed by the postholes. The north side of structure C was made up of a single, slightly irregular line of eight postholes. These averaged 0.3 m in diameter and 0.1 m in depth, with a brown sandy loam fill. The south side was formed of paired postholes, possibly one line replacing the other or alternatively providing support for a plank wall between interior and exterior supports. No trace of the end walls survived, presumably because the posts were not load-bearing. The postholes were on average 0.9 m apart. A slightly larger gap between postholes 947 and 970, centrally placed in the south side, might indicate an entrance.

At the west end of the south side there were two stone-packed postholes, 987 and 973, 1.5 m apart. These were of a very different character to the rest and it might be suggested that they were the door-posts of structure C. Neither feature contained any datable material; they were slightly off the general alignment of structure C; three postholes lie between the two and a fourth 1024, cut 973. It is probable that these two postholes were earlier than structure C and most likely belonged to the late Romano-British period. If so, they may indicate the entrance to a structure which has otherwise left no trace.

Dating

Posthole 852 produced a coin (Cat No. 76) datable to AD 364–78. Seven postholes contained a total of eleven sherds of pottery and one fragment of tile; these included two sherds of Oxfordshire ware. Posthole 963 contained two sherds of Saxon pottery.

Although structure C was aligned on the same axis as the late Romano-British farmyard boundary ditch, at its east end posthole 912 almost impinged on the Romano-British ditches. The top of the Romano-British ditch 853 was carefully examined for postholes. No convincing ones were found, but as the fills of the postholes and the ditch were almost identical, the failure to locate postholes within the upper fill of the ditch was not regarded as significant. On the whole, the positions of structure C and the line of postholes to the south suggest that the building was constructed when the ditch was more or less completely infilled. Structure C seems to fit best in a secondary Saxon phase, later than SFB 952 which lay within it.

PBS D Figure 86 Orientation: E/W;
Dimensions: 5 m × ?

Description

When the modern hedge line was removed in this area it was found that the habit of ploughing a double furrow on each side of the hedge had created a hollow in the surface of the gravel. On the east side of the hedge a rectangular but apparently incomplete arrangement of postholes was found; the west side of this structure had probably been eroded by the plough.

Thirty-four postholes were found, all but two to the east of the hedge line. To the south-east of the main complex of postholes was a shallow oval hollow 6 m long and 2.5 m wide with fragments of limestone and Corallian ragstone lying on its floor. This may represent a working hollow or a spot worn by animal activity, or most likely an entrance in the corner of the Saxon enclosure. The postholes to the north-west of the hollow, 1030, 1031 etc, are thought to have been part of the Saxon fenceline. The rectangle bounded by postholes 1231 in the north-west, 1060 in the north-east, 1034 in the south-east, and 1037 in the south-west may outline a building lying close to the fence.

These postholes indicate a structure 5 m wide, almost the same as structure C, and of uncertain length, with a possible entrance on the east side. The postholes averaged 0.3 m diameter and 0.2 m in depth and had a brown sandy loam fill. Only two postholes contained any cultural material: 1037 had a sherd of Romano-British greyware and 1165 two sherd of red colour-coated Oxfordshire ware.

PBSs E and F Figure 80; Orientation: N-S and E-W;
Dimensions: 5.7 × 8.5 m: 5.6 × 4.7 m

Description

An irregular but more or less rectangular complex of 27 postholes was found 27 m east of the villa building. These averaged 0.30 m in diameter and 0.20 m in depth with a brown sandy loam fill.

The postholes appear to have formed a rectangle aligned alongside a Romano-British ditch. Other postholes indicate a possible second structure, F, partially 'overlying' structure E. If there were two structures on this site, their relationship cannot be defined. The postholes in both were of similar character and the two structures can only be defined in terms of layout. It is not impossible that all belong to a single construction.

Dating

The postholes of structure E contained a total of 18 sherds of red colour-coated Oxfordshire ware of late 3rd- or 4th-century date. The similarity of the structure to the others dated to the Saxon period and the proximity to the late Romano-British ditch, suggesting that at the time of construction the ditch was infilled, makes a Saxon date likely for structures E and F.

PBS G Figure 84; Orientation: E-W;
Dimensions: 6.5 m long

Description

A line of 11 postholes 6.5 m long ran east-west in the north-east corner of the latest Romano-British paddock. These lay parallel to the main Romano-British farmyard boundary ditch and about 4.5 m south of it. Several of the postholes, (eg 1079 and 1080) were paired as in the south wall of structure C.

The postholes were between 0.2 and 0.4 m diameter and about 0.1 m deep. These may have represented one wall of a building which otherwise has left no trace, or alternatively a length of fencing.

One of the postholes, 1082, contained a coin (Cat No. 69) dating to AD 364–78, and also an iron nail (563). Postholes 1082, 1085, 1088 and 1089 contained a total of nine sherds, including four of Romano-British greyware, one of Oxfordshire red colour-coated ware, one Romano-British shell-gritted ware, and two of Saxon grass-tempered fabric. One posthole, 1084, contained two sherds of Neolithic pottery. In other respects it was similar to the postholes in the row; in particular it had a brown sandy loam fill.

PBS H Figure 85; Orientation: N-S; Dimensions:
3.6 × 2.7 m

Description

A rectangular structure made up of ten postholes. The east side had four postholes, 1208 and 1211–13, 0.8 m apart, and both the north and south sides had three postholes 1 m apart. The lack of postholes on the west side suggested that this small structure was an open-sided lean-to. This interpretation was supported by the location of an intermittent line of six postholes running south from the south-east corner of structure H.

The postholes of structure H were all between 0.4 and 0.5 diameter and between 0.15 and 0.25 m deep; their fill was brown sandy loam. The postholes of the presumed fenceline, 1210, 1255, 1201–1204, were about 0.4 m diameter and only 0.1 m deep. The line of postholes was visible in a tongue of gravel which projected into the heavier clay soil of the terrace slope (see Fig. 85). It is possible that similar slight features might not have been seen if they had been cut into this more difficult subsoil.

Dating

A coin (Cat No. 38) was found in the south-east posthole, 1208, of structure H dating to AD 337–41. The same feature also produced four sherds of Saxon pottery fabric 1 and three sherds of Saxon fabric 3. Postholes 1209 and 1214 each contained a single sherd of Saxon pottery (fabric 1); 1219 had two sherds of Saxon fabric 1, two sherds of Romano-British grey ware, and two sherds of Romano-British shell-gritted pottery. None of the posts in the proposed fenceline contained any datable material.

THE FENCED ENCLOSURE

A line of 17 postholes was traced for 24 m running in a curving line NW-SE between the Romano-British well 950 and the corn-drying area (Fig. 83). At the north end posthole 940 was 2 m south of the edge of the trench: the line may have continued beyond this point into the unexcavated area. Posthole 957 formed the south-east corner of the fenced enclosure; the line of postholes then turned and ran south-west for 27 m crossing the late Romano-British paddock ditch 993. At the south-west corner, by posthole 1003, was a hollowed area 994, which may have resulted from wear of the surface at an entrance into the paddock. The fenceline then ran for approximately 10 m to the north-west alongside structure D. Beyond this point the gravel surface had been eroded by modern ploughing and, as already explained (see p. 224), postholes tended to disappear. Alternatively, posthole 1049 was level with the north-west corner of structure D and the fence may have stopped at this point.

On the east side the postholes were regularly spaced *c* 0.7 m apart, similar in size, 0.5 m diameter and about 0.2 m deep. The fill in all of them was a brown sandy loam. Context 919 had a distinct postmould visible in it 0.2 m in diameter, centrally placed in the posthole.

The south side of the enclosure was less regular, with the spacing becoming more erratic and the traces of the postholes slighter. On the west side the line of the fence was less certain as it ran close to structure D. In this area the postholes were shallow and close together.

Dating

Three of the postholes on the east side, 941, 946, and 947, contained eight Romano-British sherds, all grey wares except one sherd of red colour-coated Oxfordshire ware. 947 also contained a sherd of Saxon fabric 1. On the south side 959 produced a single sherd of grass-tempered Saxon pottery and 1003 two sherds of Saxon fabric 1.

If, as the pottery and the character of the postholes suggest, the fenced enclosure belonged to the Saxon period, it must have been constructed across the late Romano-British paddock ditches 870 and 993. Both these ditches were excavated carefully with the possibility of locating postholes cut into their filling, but no convincing ones were found. As explained above, the fills of all these features were so similar that the failure to find postholes within the ditches is not a convincing argument in the dating of the fenceline, and does not preclude a Saxon date.

WELL 1083 Figures 88, 66

A cutting across the line of the east side of the late Romano-British paddock revealed a dark brown layer of waterlogged material containing a dense concentration of Corallian ragstone about 0.3 m from the ground surface. After the layer of tumbled stones had been removed, it could be seen that a circular wicker- and stone-lined well had been inserted into the bottom of the ditch, apparently while the ditch was still open.

The well consisted of a hole 1 m deep, the bottom of which was about 1.45 m from the ground surface. The hole was lined with wicker work of hazel, oak, and willow withies with a maximum diameter of 1.2 m and surviving to a height of 0.8 m. Horizontal wattles were woven between oak and hazel uprights between 0.21 and 0.25 m apart. Unfortunately, before the wicker lining could be accurately drawn, the sides of the well fell in under the pressure of incoming water.

Above the wicker lining there was a crude retaining wall of Corallian ragstone, the upper courses of which had fallen into the well. The fill of the well consisted principally of a mixed deposit of stone, silt, yellow clay, and waterlogged organic material. It was excavated in three spits of about 0.3 m each. It appeared that the well had silted up gradually, eventually becoming little more than a shallow puddle with watercress growing in it and colonised by water beetles. When the well was fully excavated it filled with water to a depth of 1.0 m.

THE SAXON BURIALS AND THEIR GRAVE GOODS
by P D C Brown

Four inhumations of the pagan Saxon period were excavated, two within the late Romano-British farmhouse and two in the late Romano-British Building 2. The skeletal details are reported on in the section on human burials (4:D10) by Mary Harman.

GRAVE 258 Figures 67, 79

Largely incomplete post-cranial skeleton of an adult male, possibly a young man, in Room 5 of the farmhouse. Supine, head to south. Damaged by ploughing.

Grave goods Figure 68

1   (60) Fragment of iron knife, lying on left radius close to right hand.
2   (57) Fragment of iron knife point lying on right-hand edge of grave (possibly intrusive).
3   (55) A 3rd-century Antoninianus (*c* AD 268–70; Cat No.13), found to the left of where the skull should have been, possibly deliberately placed with the body; originally in the mouth?

GRAVE 271 FIGURES 67, 79

Fragmentary remains of an adult female with a newborn infant; damaged by ploughing. Inserted into room 4 of the late Romano-British farmhouse. Female supine with head to south; child lay by her right side, head to north.

Grave goods Figure 68

1 (87) Beads in fragments at head end. Parts of three amber beads, roughly rounded but angular. Dimensions 17, 17, and 15 mm. Part of a sub-spherical crystal bead, uneven surface. Length 16 mm. Fragment of a spherical (haematite?) pebble; would be ideal as a bead though not enough survives to show whether it was pierced or not. Diameter *c* 16 mm.
2 (86) Cast bronze ring, regular in shape, circular cross-section. Diameter 25–29 mm. Found in the area of the left ribs.
3 (88) Coin (Cat No. 10). Illegible sestertius of *c* 230–48. Close to the head and possibly deliberately placed with the body.

Comment

Disturbed and presumably incomplete. The cast bronze ring could be from a purse/amulet group. The combination of amber and crystal beads suggest a 6th-century date.

GRAVE 807 Figures 8, 67

Female aged between 18 and 23 years; supine, head to south-west and accompanied by a newborn infant. Inserted in building 2.

Grave goods Figure 69

1 (353–7) Five amber beads and a fragment of a sixth; found near the infant.

Three together:
L: 12 mm; D: 5/11 mm; flat angular.
L: 10 mm; D: 6/10 mm; angular.
L: 10 mm; D: 8/11 mm; rounded.

Two together:
L: 9 mm; D: 6 × 10 mm; rounded.
L: 9 mm; D: 7 × 10 mm; rounded.

2 (420) Cast bronze ornament, adapted for use as a brooch. The casting was originally like a fish, but the head and tail have been removed so that it is not symmetrical, and could be thought of as an animal viewed from above. The back is flat; originally a stud projected from the centre of the back, but this was removed and only its scar remains. Traces of solder on the two ends show where brooch fittings were attached. The front of the object is curved, reflecting the shape of the fish's body. The surface was gilded, but gilding remains only in the hollows of the triangular punch marks surrounding the body and vestigial fins, and in the triple engraved lines. The triangular punch seems almost flat-headed, but was perhaps originally three-spotted. Neck and tail junctions are marked by a raised moulding beyond which the ends are broken off. Present dimensions: L: 61 mm; W: 27 mm; Th: 2 mm.

3 (359) Small iron buckle with fragmentary tongue and plate. From left shoulder. L: 34 mm; W: 24 mm. Maximum strap width 14 mm.
4 (358) Iron knife. L: 142 mm; W: 18 mm.
5 (348) Point of iron pin, flaking surface; from shoulder area. D: 2–3 mm.
(360) Shaft or iron pin with folded crookhead. L: 50 mm.
Although these pieces do not join, they could well be from the same object. Overall length would be 110 mm.
6 (361) Bone comb, double-sided, conventional construction (7 iron rivets). Plain flat bar with plain ends, a single hole through each end. Found by lower right leg.
L: 144 mm; W: 54 mm. This comb is discussed with other combs from the site (5:E8).

Comment

The unusual brooch is discussed separately below; the iron pin in connection with the bronze pins in the next grave; and the comb below (5:F2–4). The assemblage seems substantially complete, though presumably there were originally two brooches.

Date

6th century, second half.

GRAVE 820 Figures 81, 67

Female aged 30–35 years. Inserted in building 2. Body supine with head to north. Grave goods slightly disturbed.

Grave goods Figure 70

1 (412) 24 amber beads, smoothed, most approximately rounded. D: 6–11 mm; one larger: 16 mm. Scattered over ribs, mostly on left side.
2 (413) Cast bronze saucer brooch, gilt surface; seven pointed spiral coils; short catch-plate, two pin lugs; rusting iron pin preserves traces of thread, chiefly a single coarse S-spin thread. D: 46 mm.
3 (409) Two bronze pins on a wire ring. Made of solid metal, and rounded perhaps by hammering in a grooved block resulting in a certain amount of lapping over of the edges of the metal, and in places, in its breaking off. Ends of plain, flattened, and rounded shapes. One pin is stained with iron rust. Both pins were bent while buried. Original L: 125 mm and 128 mm. Found overlying left side of chest.
4 (416) Flat iron ring, buckle, covered on one face with a plain sheet of silver. Incomplete, total shape uncertain and not necessarily circular. No trace of rivets or other fastenings. Slight traces of textile preserved by rust on both sides of ring suggest it may have been attached with a cord.

D: 32 mm; W: *c* 9 mm; Th: 2 mm. Found overlying centre of chest.

5 (299) A pair of bronze ornaments, appliques, in S-shape: an animal with head twisted backwards. The head-cum-neck and hindquarters are chip-carved and gilt; the body is flat, and covered with a thin plate of silver. At the back are two rivets, showing that the pieces were attached permanently rather than being movable. The two pieces are identical; the animals face the same way rather than in opposite directions. L: 32 mm; rivet length: 3–4 mm.

6 (410) Penannular ring of bronze, made by folding up a piece of a late Romano-British cogged-edge bracelet. D: 17 mm Found outside right thigh. Perhaps a chance inclusion in the grave.

7 (414–5) Two bronze rivets with flat, circular silver-plated heads. D: 15 mm; L. of rivet 4.5 mm D: 10 mm; L. of rivet 7 mm. Found overlying centre of chest.

8 (411) Small iron buckle, in fragments. Iron pin, no plate. W: 27 mm; max. strap width 17 mm. Not illustrated.

Comment

Although the skeleton is substantially complete, the grave goods seem to have been disturbed, and it is reasonable to assume that a brooch has been lost.

The bronze pins in this grave and the iron pin in the preceding grave can be matched elsewhere. They are commonly found on one or other side of the chest, suggesting that they were carried attached below one of the brooches; other local examples are Abingdon B60, B61, and B66, (Leeds and Harden 1936), and Harwell 9 (Ashmolean Museum).

The unusual appliqué and silver-plated rivets congregate in the centre of the chest. The nearby buckle suggest that they may have been decoration for a belt, though the buckle itself is very plain, unless the curious silver-plated ring was used somewhere to embellish it.

Date

6th century, mid-second half.

Chapter 4:   Anglo-Saxon Pottery

By Paul Blinkhorn

INTRODUCTION

The Barrow Hills Anglo-Saxon pottery assemblage, comprising 9131 sherds with a total weight of 127.62 kg, is one of the largest ever recovered from an early Anglo-Saxon site in England: of the other large assemblages from Oxfordshire, only Eynsham Abbey (Blinkhorn 2003) and Barton Court Farm (Miles 1986) can be said to be comparable, but neither is as large. Eynsham Abbey produced 6248 sherds of early/middle Saxon pottery (53.3 kg) of which 3221 (24.5 kg) were redeposited in later features. The mean sherd weight of the Barrow Hills assemblage is some 60% greater than that of the Eynsham group, indicating a somewhat better level of preservation which is perhaps unsurprising due to the lack of later activity at the former site. The Barton Court Farm assemblage weighed 33.49 kg (sherd count unknown). On a national scale there are few sites of the period in England which have comparable pottery assemblages, with perhaps the only larger published examples being West Stow in Suffolk (West 1985) and Mucking, Essex (Hamerow 1993), which produced 53,570 sherds (weight unknown) and *c* 32,000 sherds (weight unknown) respectively. However, both of those sites produced Ipswich ware, indicating that they continued in use into the middle Saxon period. They were therefore longer-lived than Barrow Hills, which appears to have begun in the 5th century and fallen out of use in the 7th century.

The early Saxon pottery of Oxfordshire has come in for some scrutiny in the last few decades. Mellor (1994, 36–7) noted how numerous sites of 5th- and 6th-century date have been recognised in the county, and how chaff-tempered pottery is the commonest type found in association with them. The middle Saxon period is more problematic, and she notes that there was, and still is, no evidence of an identifiable middle Saxon ceramic tradition, with the recognition of assemblages of such date entirely reliant upon the presence of regional imports such as Ipswich ware and Maxey ware. Since her work was published, Ipswich ware has been recognised at sites such as Eynsham and Yarnton, but these sites have also produced very strong evidence to indicate that the people in those areas stopped making pottery for a considerable part of the 8th century, and perhaps also during the 9th century (Blinkhorn 2003; 2004). However, Mellor has also noted that there is some evidence that there was a revival (or perhaps even a continuation) of the handmade pottery tradition in Oxfordshire in the 9th or 10th century. Such pottery has been found in association with St Neots ware in places such as Dorchester, Benson and North Stoke

(Mellor 1994, 36). The quantities of pottery involved make it very difficult to dismiss the material as residual, although the possibility remains.

Thus, it is possible that activity at Barrow Hills continued into the middle Saxon period, but the overall weight of evidence makes this unlikely. There are certainly no middle Saxon imports, regional or continental, and with the increasing numbers of finds of Ipswich ware in the area, it might be expected that the material would have occurred at Barrow Hills if the settlement was still active in the 8th century. Status does not appear to be an issue; although Eynsham Abbey was a nationally important religious settlement, and thus a magnet for trade, the same cannot be said of Yarnton at that time. Also, at Radley, there is nothing in the other finds evidence to suggest that the site continued in use beyond the early 7th century (Chapter 5).

The basic data for all the analyses carried out below is listed in the research archive, as follows:

Mean sherd weight per SFB.
Pottery occurrence by fabric type per SFB, expressed as a
    percentage of the total weight of pottery per SFB.
Fabric occurrence versus distance of SFB from southern and
    western extremities of the site.
Pottery occurrence by vessel type, all sunken-featured buildings,
    all fabrics.
Stamped pottery – number of sherds per structure by motif type.
Lug occurrence by number of vessels per type per SFB.

RECORDING METHODOLOGY

The Anglo-Saxon pottery assemblage from Barrow Hills comprised 9131 sherds weighing 127.62 kg. The estimated vessel equivalent (EVE), by measurement of rim sherd length, was 71.55. The pottery was initially bulk-sorted and recorded using dBase IV software. The material from each context was recorded by number and weight of sherds per fabric type, with featureless body sherds of the same fabric counted, weighed and recorded as one database entry. Feature sherds such as rims, bases and lugs were individually recorded, with individual codes used for the various types. Decorated sherds were treated similarly. In the case of the rim sherds, the form, diameter in mm and percentage remaining of the original complete circumference were all recorded. The terminology used is that of the Medieval Pottery Research Group's *Guide to the classification of medieval ceramic forms* (MPRG 1998). All the statistical analyses were carried out using a dBase package written by the author, which interrogated the original or subsidiary databases, with some of the final calculations made with an electronic calculator.

All analyses were carried out to the minimum standards suggested by Orton (1998–9, 135–7).

The various methods of recording pottery, and the arguments concerning which method is the most useful, have received some consideration (eg Orton 1975, 1982; Rice 1987, 290–3), with Hamerow's (1993, 22–3) summary of past work and discussion of the quantification of the Anglo-Saxon pottery from Mucking in Essex being of particular relevance.

Sherd count, perhaps the commonest method of recording pottery, is also the least accurate. Used alone, the method can take no account of fragmentation, and provides a poor representation of the amount of pottery involved. One sherd can be a whole pot or a fragment the size of a pinhead. A sherd count should always be carried out, however, as it can be very useful in conjunction with weight or rim percentage for assessing fragmentation, and some statistical analyses, such as the chi-squared test, can only be carried out using sherd number (Orton 1998–99, 136).

Weight is a much better method of expressing the amount of pottery present. The weight of a piece of pottery never changes, despite the effects of post-depositional disturbance, or even damage during excavation. The disadvantage of the method is that sherds from large vessels, or those with thick walls, can appear over-represented, as their very robustness leads to better resistance to breakage, and thus sherds tend to be larger. Vessels such as Roman amphorae are perhaps the best example of this.

One of the best methods of quantifying pottery is by estimated vessel equivalent, calculated by summing the percentage present of all rim sherds, then dividing by 100 to obtain a number which gives a ratio of vessel use at the site. In reality, the number of vessels which were in use would have been considerably larger than the figure obtained by this method, but the figures produced are probably the least distorted in terms of allowing analysis and comparison within and between assemblages, and an accurate representation of patterns of pottery consumption. Hamerow (1993, 23) has noted that early Anglo-Saxon pottery is too irregular to allow rim diameters and, by inference, the percentage present, to be calculated with accuracy. This appears a little extreme; although handmade pottery is not as symmetrical as wheel-thrown, hand-made vessels are rarely so irregular in shape as to make measurement impossible. The only real disadvantage of this method is that large assemblages are required to allow meaningful analyses to be undertaken.

A final method of quantification, and one used for the analysis of the pottery from Mucking (Hamerow 1993), is that of sherd group. This is done by grouping together all the sherds which the analyst considers to be from the same vessel. This is a highly unsatisfactory method of quantifying Anglo-Saxon pottery. The colour, texture and fabric of handmade pottery vary considerably over a complete vessel, and the author has found cross-fits between sherds considered by other analysts to be of different fabrics, and hence different vessels. It is also an extremely time consuming method of analysis, and beyond the scope of projects such as this. Conversely, many sherds, with their similar range of colours and fabrics, could appear to be from the same vessel, but are in reality from different ones. Only decorated Anglo-Saxon pottery is suited to this form of quantification, as the decorative schemes of individual vessels tend to be distinctive, and finding two exactly the same is very rare.

The methods of quantification used for the analysis of the Barrow Hills assemblage are therefore sherd number, sherd count and estimated vessel equivalent. Wherever possible, the last method has been used for comparative analysis, but as many of the individual sunken-featured building assemblages are too small to permit this, sherd weight was also used. In some cases, however, sherd count had to be used, particularly when using comparative statistics.

Fabric analysis

Each sherd was examined using a x20 binocular microscope, and assigned one of eight fabric categories, based on the broad characteristics of the main inclusion type(s). A small number of sherds were also subjected to thin-section analysis by Alan Vince in 1985, during the first stage of the analysis of the pottery by Sheila Raven. This report may be found in the archive but Vince's report will be referred to here.

The fabric groups are as follows:

F1: *Fine quartz.* Moderate to dense sub-angular quartz up to 0.5 mm. Occasionally rare calcareous material of the same size and shape. 3238 sherds, 37,133 g, EVE = 25.84.

F2: *Quartz and chaff.* Sparse to moderate sub-rounded quartz up to 2 mm, sparse to moderate chaff voids. 3235 sherds, 49,974 g, EVE = 24.99.

F3: *Coarse quartz.* Moderate to dense sub-rounded quartz up to 3 mm. Occasionally rare calcareous material of the same size. 1480 sherds, 24,646 g, EVE = 11.12.

F4: *Calcareous quartz.* Sparse to moderate sub-rounded calcareous material up to 1 mm. Sparse sub-rounded quartz up to 0.5 mm. Sparse chaff voids and fine silver mica. 80 sherds, 791 g, EVE = 0.92.

F5: *Ironstone.* Sparse to moderate rounded red ironstone up to 3 mm. Sparse quartz up to 0.5 mm, rare flint up to 5 mm. 9 sherds, 105 g, EVE = 0.14.

F6: *Chaff,* no other visible inclusions. 1046 sherds, 14479 g, EVE = 8.33.

F7: *Oolitic limestone.* Moderate to dense subangular oolitic limestone up to 2 mm, rare sub-rounded quartz and red ironstone up to 0.5 mm. 36 sherds, 418 g, EVE = 0.17.

F8: *Sandstone.* Sparse to moderate sub-angular calcite-cemented sandstone fragments up to 3 mm, moderate to dense subangular 'free' quartz grains up to 0.5 mm, occasionally rare calcite fragments up to 1 mm. 4 sherds, 62 g, EVE = 0.04.

The nature of the handmade pottery of the Anglo-Saxon period suggests that more refined categorisation is of questionable validity, as natural variations in the mineralogical composition of the source clay, when combined with the methods of manufacture of the pottery itself, can result in the creation of over-complex fabric groupings which are, at best, unhelpful

(Blinkhorn 1997). The chaff-tempered fabrics were perhaps the most problematic. Chaff, unlike minerals, does not occur naturally in clay, and must have been added by the potter. It rapidly became clear during analysis that there was enormous variation in the amount of chaff present in a sherd, with the issue further complicated if mineral inclusions were also present. This pattern was also noted at Barton Court Farm (Miles 1986, fiche 7), strongly suggesting that chaff was added to a clay mix by a potter on an instinctive basis, that is until the clay mix 'felt right'. This seems to have been the case with the addition of quartz sand temper to middle Saxon Ipswich ware (Blinkhorn in press a), and there are numerous examples from the ethnographic record of similar practices (eg Rice 1987, 122). It therefore seems likely that this was also the case with the Barrow Hills pottery. Vince (unpublished) noted that many of the thin-sectioned sherds had 'chaff... present in most fabrics in proportions which have no obvious relationship to the material inclusions'. Consequently, in this report, the sherds were assigned to a fabric group on the basis of the main inclusions.

Quartz- and/or chaff-tempered fabrics dominate, with calcareous fabrics forming very much the minor component of the assemblage. This is very similar to the range of frequency of fabric types identified at the sister settlement at Barton Court Farm (Miles 1986, fiche 7). At that site, however, quartz-tempered fabrics were even more dominant, comprising 76% of the assemblage by weight, with chaff-tempered wares making up only 20% of the assemblage. Calcareous wares were similarly scarce, with only around 4% of the assemblage consisting of such material. As with Barrow Hills, there was a great deal of variation in the amounts of each fabric type found in individual sunken-featured building hollows, although the sand-tempered fabrics were always in the majority.

This range of fabric types is typical of the early Saxon pottery from sites from the area in and around Abingdon, but there are differences when compared with material from the rest of the county. Calcareous fabrics are generally rare. Like Barrow Hills and Barton Court Farm, excavations at the Spring Road cemetery in Abingdon produced only one sherd (12 g) out of 328 (5955 g) early and/or early/middle Saxon examples with noticeable calcareous material in the fabric, including two fairly large groups from sunken-featured buildings (Blinkhorn in prep). A similar picture was noted at the Oxford Science Park site, where out of a total of 900 sherds of early Saxon pottery (18,174 g) only 19 (307 g) had calcareous fabrics (Blinkhorn 2001). At Audlett Drive, Abingdon, a total of 6.6 kg of early Saxon pottery was dominated by quartz and chaff fabrics, with only 2% of the assemblage comprising calcareous wares (Underwood-Keevill 1992, 67–74).

Elsewhere in the county, this is not the case. The range of fabric types at Eynsham Abbey, while overlapping with those from Barrow Hills, showed some fairly significant differences in occurrence

(Blinkhorn 2003). Quartz and/or chaff-tempered fabrics made up a significant proportion of the assemblage (42.6% and 12.6% by weight respectively), but a significant portion of the assemblage (44.7% by weight) consisted of limestone-tempered wares, of which 22.1% (by weight) were of oolitic type. This contrasts with the Barrow Hills assemblage, which contained only 0.3% (by weight) oolitic limestone and 0.6% other limestone fabrics. Similarly, chaff-tempered fabrics were considerably commoner at Barrow Hills, making up 50.5% (by weight) of the assemblage. There were also differences in iron-rich fabrics; at Eynsham they were 5.7% (by weight), at Barrow Hills less than 0.1%.

Of the 380 sherds of early Anglo-Saxon material from excavations at the Beech House Hotel at Dorchester-on-Thames, 14% of the pottery (by sherd count) had limestone or shell temper (Berisford 1981, 39–40). The site was also notable for the relatively low occurrence of chaff-tempered wares (6% by sherd count).

Clay sources

The range of pottery types to some extent reflects the geology in the vicinity of the site, but there is evidence to suggest that the clay sources exploited were not on the site itself.

The oolitic wares may have originated at one or more of several sources. For example, Mellor (1994, 44) has argued that several later pottery types with similar petrologies are known from at least two wide areas of the Cotswolds, and also in Buckinghamshire and Northamptonshire, although more recent work has indicated that the latter is likely to have originated somewhere in the vicinity of Peterborough (Blinkhorn in press b). However, calcareous gravel is known from the Second Terrace in Oxfordshire, and the detrital clays of the north of the county have a similar composition (Mellor 1994, 44). By contrast, Berisford (1981, 40) noted that sites to the south-east of Oxford produced a high proportion of vessels with fine sand temper. She suggested that this might be due to the local geology, which consists of Kimmeridge and Gault clay on greensands. Vince (unpublished) has suggested that the oolitic wares are probably tempered with the local Second Terrace sands, as they are identical in composition to the late Saxon Oxford fabric OXAC ('Cotswolds-type ware', Mellor 1994).

This has implications for the nature of pottery production and consumption at the site. Barrow Hills is located at the intersection of gravel and clay, and it would therefore appear that all the materials needed for potting were at hand. The traditional picture of early Anglo-Saxon pottery production is that most of it was made as and when required, at or very near the point of consumption, with perhaps only the more elaborate decorated funerary pottery being made by semi-professional, itinerant potters (cf Myres 1977, 12). There is some evidence of pottery production from early Anglo-Saxon settlements, such as the clay dump and stamp dies from West Stow (West 1985, 58). However, more recent work has revealed some evidence to suggest that in certain areas of England there was at least partly formalised production and trade in what can be considered domestic pottery. Alan Vince and David Williams (pers. comm.) have made a strong case for pottery from the Charnwood Forest area of Leicestershire having been traded as far south as London. It is therefore possible that we are seeing something similar, albeit on a smaller scale, for the Abingdon area. Vince (unpublished) concluded that most if not all of the sand-tempered fabrics at Barrow Hills were derived from the Lower Greensand, the nearest outcrop being to the north of the settlement, at Bagley Wood. However, he also noted that there are other outcrops in the area, for example at Nuneham and Culham, as well as further to the south and north-east at the foot of the Chiltern scarp. These outcrops are petrologically indistinguishable, and Vince suggested Bagley Wood as the clay source simply because it was the nearest to the site.

The ironstone-tempered sherds are likely to have come from a distant source. Vince noted that the sherds also contained disaggregated ooliths and fossiliferous limestone, indicating that they may have come from Wiltshire or Northamptonshire, although it was possible that there were localized deposits of such material in the Corallian beds of Oxfordshire. The sandstone-tempered pottery was from a fluvio-glacial source, with similar material known from Gloucestershire, Worcestershire and Warwickshire.

It has been suggested in the past that some early Anglo-Saxon pottery fabrics may be dateable, with potters favouring certain clay sources at certain times. This was almost certainly was not the case at Barrow Hills.

Chronological and spatial analysis: methodology

Early Anglo-Saxon pottery is still dated on the basis of the scheme devised by Myres (1977), which is largely dependant on the presence and style of decorated pottery, and also vessel form. However, in recent years it has become obvious that at least some areas of Myres's chronological scheme are in need of revision (Hamerow 1993, 42–4; Blinkhorn 1997).

In terms of vessel form, Myres divided jar types into five main groups, but 'each of these main groups merges imperceptibly into the others, and a number of the urns... could be placed in a different group' (1977, 2). In addition, the bodies of hand-made pots are often asymmetrical, making it difficult to classify the form of a vessel. As Myres wrote, 'This is particularly true of those ... pieces whose profile differs markedly from one side to another.... For this reason, it would be misleading to treat these broad groupings as sharply demarcated or mutually exclusive... which might imply a more rigid typological classification than is in fact possible' (ibid.). Consequently, vessel form is rarely used in

this report as a chronological marker, the exceptions being two distinctive forms, the sharply carinated bowl forms *(Schalenurnen)*, which appear to be early in date, and high-necked 'Frankish' forms, which appear to belong to the 7th century.

Decorated pottery appears to be more reliable as a chronological marker, although this too needs to be treated with a degree of caution. 'It is not possible to classify the decorated pottery according to any rigid system. The most that can be attempted is to group the designs according to the use made in them of certain basic elements ... The aim in doing so is not primarily to produce categories that have a distinc-tive (chronological) significance' and also that 'some schemes were certainly long-lived, especially the sim-plest ones' (Myres 1977, 12). However, Hamerow's analysis of the Mucking pottery produced evidence for some reliable chronological trends in decorated Anglo-Saxon pottery; stamping became commoner as a decorative technique from the 5th to the 7th century, but decoration in general became less common during the same period (Hamerow 1993, figs 37 and 39).

In addition, Julian Richards (1987) has shown that the form and decoration of cremation pottery, which appears to have the same range as the decorated pottery found in domestic contexts, was directly related to the age, gender and social status of the contained individuals. How this relates to the use of such pottery in domestic contexts is unclear, but Richards showed convincingly that the choice of decoration and form of cremation urns was not merely determined by fashion.

The style of the decorated pottery present is therefore the primary source of evidence for the date of the site. Some features contained very little, others none, but the dates should be treated with caution. In addition to the problems of Myres's scheme, the nature of the deposits must be taken into account. The sunken-featured buildings which produced most of the pottery from the site were almost cer-tainly deliberately back-filled with domestic refuse, as were the barrow ditches. The source of this material is highly likely to have been middens, and it is impossible to know which, if any, of the pots relate to the building in which they were found. The presence of sherd joins between barrow 13, pit 414 and SFBs 7 (each with a 5th-century *tpq*) and 23 (6th-century *tpq*) indicates how dangerous it is to assume that the material in a feature relates to its use, or that a small number of decorated sherds can safely be used to date a whole assemblage. If material is being tranported across the site for deliberate backfilling, we must question whether it is safe to assume that all the material in a feature comes from one source and what functional and chronological relationship the individual items in the assemblage had to each other. The extent to which the contents of any feature can be regarded as a discrete group must be doubtful.

The fact that very few complete or near-complete vessels were recovered supports the contention that the material was the product of secondary or tertiary deposition. The duration of the initial deposition before it was used to backfill the hollows of the sunken-featured buildings is unknown. All the pottery dates must thus be regarded as *termini post quem*, in which the *post* is a period of unknown duration.

Many of the assemblages produced small sherds with traces of linear decoration. These are largely undatable, except to within the 5th or 6th centuries. Features which produced such sherds and no other chronologically diagnostic pottery could be dated to the 5th/6th century, although as most sherds are very small, and given the already secondary nature of the deposited pottery, the pottery groups which produced them could easily be later. Consequently, sunken-featured buildings which produced only decorated pottery of this type have been omitted from the spatial analysis.

Features which produced no decorated pottery may be of 7th-century date, but in many cases the assemblage size was too small for this to be stated with confidence. It is possible that the sunken-featured buildings with the least pottery may be the latest in date. Analysis of the pottery from the early to middle Saxon settlements at Eynsham Abbey and Yarnton in Oxfordshire (Blinkhorn 2003; 2004) suggested that hand-built pottery ceased to be used at those sites during the early years of the 8th century. If this ceramic hiatus was not merely limited to those sites, but was a regional phenomenon, then it may be that the same ceramic use-pattern was in place at Barrow Hills, and that the sunken-featured buildings that produced small quantities of pottery with no decorated wares could date to the later 7th or even the 8th century. Consequently, sunken-featured buildings without datable pottery are omitted from most analyses. It is, however, worth pointing out that the pot densities in these features are not unusually low, with the exception of SFB 12 in the north of the site, one of the largest sunken-featured buildings.

Fabric: chronological trends

Past studies of the early Anglo-Saxon pottery fabrics at sites in the Abingdon area (Brown 1972; Berisford 1981; Underwood-Keevill 1992) and others from further afield (Hamerow 1993) have suggested that some early Anglo-Saxon pottery fabrics may be chronologically diagnostic. Other studies (Blinkhorn 1997) argue that the amounts of different fabric types at a site of this date are a reflection of the size of different social groups with different traditions of pottery manufacture within a settlement, and also of how the size of the social groups, or the nature of their practices, may have changed over time. The evidence from Barrow Hills provides an opportunity to examine these ideas.

Early Anglo-Saxon pottery was recovered from Radley Road, Abingdon, some 100 m to the north-west of the Neolithic oval barrow at Barrow Hills, during excavation of a Neolithic causewayed en-

closure in 1963 (Avery and Brown 1972), and from gravel pits in the immediate vicinity by E T Leeds in 1928 (Leeds and Harden 1936). These features were almost certainly part of the Barrow Hills settlement (Fig. 1.3), as was Barton Court Farm on the other side of the Daisy Banks stream. Brown (1972) analysed both groups of pottery, and also considered the cremation urns from the Anglo-Saxon cemetery to the south of Abingdon (Myres 1968) and domestic pottery from a settlement at Dorchester. He suggested that chaff-tempering generally was not used for decorated vessels until the 6th century, and that since there were no chaff-tempered domestic vessels dating to the 5th century at these sites, chaff-tempering must have been an early 6th-century introduction to the Abingdon area. However, all the pottery from the Abingdon cemetery was decorated, and the other groups examined were small.

Berisford (1981, 40) highlighted the lack of chaff-tempered pottery at the Beech House Hotel site in Dorchester, and while noting that chaff-tempered pottery tended to increase 'in popularity' through time in the Upper Thames region, did not claim that the lack of it at the Dorchester site was a feature of chronology. She also stated that calcitic wares tended to decrease through time.

Underwood-Keevill's (1992) analysis of the pottery from Audlett Drive, Abingdon, less than 2 km to the south-west of Barrow Hills, noted that there was relatively little chaff-tempered pottery from the site, despite the fact that the assemblage appeared generally to be of 6th- to 7th-century date.

Hamerow's (1993) analysis of the Mucking pottery showed that by the latest phase of the site, chaff-tempered pottery was overwhelmingly the commonest fabric type in use. The Barrow Hills assemblage provides limited support for Berisford's idea that calcitic wares are early, but the quantities involved are so small that the results can hardly be regarded as conclusive.

When Brown's ideas with regard to chronology and functionality are examined, the Barrow Hills assemblage indicates that chaff-tempered clays were used for the manufacture of 5th-century decorated vessels, although rarely. SFB 15 produced a collared vessel in F2, although almost all the other decorated 5th-century pottery from the site was made from sandy clays: SFB 5 produced a carinated incised vessel in F1, as did SFB 7, and SFB 43 yielded a sherd with line-and-dot decoration in F1. The exception was a finger-grooved and stabbed sherd in F4 from SFB 35.

The data in Table 4.1 suggest that chaff-tempering was not a 6th-century introduction at Barrow Hills. Chaff-tempered fabrics F2 and F6 comprise 30.6% (by EVE) of the assemblage with a *tpq* of the 5th century. The material may have become more common with time. Chaff-tempered wares make up 50.7% (by EVE) of groups with a 6th-century *tpq*. This also appears to have been the case at Barton Court Farm. A total of 36% of the pottery from SFB 1023 at Barton Court Farm was chaff-tempered,

Table 4.1   Pottery occurrence in the SFBs by EVE, major fabrics only, expressed as a percentage of the total assemblage.

TPQ	% F1	% F2	% F3	%F6	Phase Total
5thC	47.5	28.3	22.0	2.3	6.19
6thC	34.1	41.5	15.2	9.2	29.47
					35.66

Table 4.2   Mean sherd weight per major fabric type (g).

Tpq	F1	F2	F3	F6
5thC	20.3	16.2	16.7	9.7
6thC	10.2	17.3	18.7	17.2

Table 4.3   Mean vessel rim diameters (in mm), all dated SFBs, per major fabric type.

Tpq	F1	F2	F3	F6
5thC	161.9	174.4	171.5	170.0
6thC	170.8	172.0	182.8	159.6

despite the fact that the feature produced a range of vessels of 5th-century date (Miles 1986, fiche 7).

In addition, despite the fact that chaff-tempered wares comprise a minor component of the total assemblage with a 5th-century *tpq*, in some cases most of the pottery from an individual feature with such a date consists of such fabrics. For example, 57.4% of the ceramic from SFB 5 is chaff-tempered, and the material dominates in all layers of SFB 7, with 85.4% of the pottery in the lowest deposit in the feature (layer 3) being chaff-tempered. Chaff-tempered wares form most of the assemblage in SFBs 15 and 35, although in SFB 43 mineral-tempered pottery dominated heavily. In many cases, chaff-tempered pottery is in the majority in the lowest deposits of the sunken-featured buildings irrespective of their *tpq* (eg SFB 2). Given the evidence that these features were backfilled deliberately with midden material in a single operation the significance of this is hard to assess. Mineral-tempered pottery does, in some cases, form the majority of the assemblage from sunken-featured buildings with a *tpq* in the 6th century, such as SFB 26.

It seems, however, that there are grounds to suspect that chaff-tempered fabrics may have been even more widely used in the 6th century that the bare data suggest. Analysis of the mean sherd weights of the pottery from the sunken-featured buildings (Table 4.2) suggests that F2 and F3 slightly increase their mean sherd weight through time, while F1 declines sharply and F6 shows a large increase. This might suggest that a greater part of the later F1 assemblages are residual, but other factors, such as vessels in this fabric becoming generally smaller, and therefore breaking into smaller pieces, could be the cause. However, the mean rim diameters of F1 jars actually increased between features with a 5th-century and 6th-century *tpq* (Table 4.3), despite the mean sherd weight showing a large fall. This suggests that the 6th-century F1 assemblage has a large component of very small sherds from fairly large vessels. Conversely, in the 6th century, the mean rim diameter of F6 declines sharply, but the mean sherd weight increases significantly, indicating that much of the F6 assemblage in the features with a 6th-century *tpq* comprises large pieces of small vessels. It would therefore seem that there is a considerable residual element to the F1 fabric in the 6th-century *tpq* features.

Unfortunately, there is no reliable way of dividing a group of early Anglo-Saxon pottery into residual and contemporary elements. The data in Table 4.2 suggest strongly that much of the F1 pottery in features with a 6th-century *tpq* is residual, but not all the sherds are small and abraded, and the material was obviously still in use up to the time of backfilling (for example, large rim sherds in fabric 1 occurred in SFBs 14 and 19). Thus it can be seen that while it is probably true that chaff-tempered pottery increased as a proportion of the assemblage over time, the presence of large amounts of chaff-tempered pottery in a feature cannot be used as an indicator of late date. Some features with a 5th-century *tpq* produced pottery assemblages dominated by chaff-tempered wares. Similarly, the presence of large amounts of mineral-tempered pottery cannot be taken as evidence of an early date; again, as noted, some features with a 6th-century *tpq* produced mainly mineral-tempered pottery. It would seem therefore that in the case of the Barrow Hills assemblage, although chaff-tempered wares probably become commoner with time, the use of Anglo-Saxon pottery fabrics as a chronological marker is not feasible.

SPATIAL ANALYSIS

Quantitative analysis

A total of 90,354 g of pottery (6220 sherds, EVE = 52.16) was recovered from the sunken-featured buildings, with the mean weight per sunken-featured building being 2008 g. Generally, the sunken-featured buildings on the western and southern edges of the excavation (SFBs 8, 10, 13, 14, 23, 24, 25, 26, 27, 28 (mixed with 29), 31, 35, 36, 37, 41, 42) produced relatively little pottery, with most producing less than 1000 g. The exceptions were SFBs 14, 24, 26, 28/29, 41, and 45, which each produced well over 2500 g, with SFB 28/29 producing the largest assemblage on the site, some 12,346 g of pottery. Most of the sunken-featured buildings in the central area produced well over

1000 g of pottery, with many producing assemblages in the range 2500 to 6000 g. The only exception to this was SFB 16, which yielded just 854 g. When pot and bone densities are plotted, however, no clear distribution patterns emerge (Fig. 7.1).

It is possible that the sunken-featured buildings with the least pottery may be the latest in date. Certainly, at Eynsham Abbey, the 'aceramic' period features were notable for their low mean sherd weight and the lack of cross fits. To investigate this at Barrow Hills, the mean sherd weight of the sunken-featured building assemblages was calculated. In the first instance, the relationship between the size of an assemblage from a sunken-featured building and the mean sherd weight of that assemblage was examined.

The mean sherd weight for pottery from the sunken-featured building hollows was 14.5 g. The mean sherd weight for each sunken-featured building was calculated, and while there was a great deal of variation (range 5.2–28 g), there was no obvious spatial pattern to the distribution; sunken-featured buildings with a large mean sherd weight were apparently as randomly scattered as those with a small value. It is worth noting, however, that the largest sunken-featured building, SFB 12, produced an exceptionally low pot density.

The relationship between assemblage size and mean sherd weight was plotted, and some basic correlation statistics carried out, ie the calculation of the correlation coefficient, *r* (Drennan 1996, 216). The value for the Barrow Hills sunken-featured buildings was 0.31. This suggested that there was little significant correlation between assemblage size and mean sherd weight, or in other words that large sunken-featured building assemblages were no more 'primary' than the smaller ones, and that large assemblages were scarcely more likely to contain large sherds than small ones, and vice versa.

Fabric distribution

Previous work at the Anglo-Saxon settlement at Mucking, Essex (Hamerow 1993) indicated that there was a nucleated distribution of some of the different fabric types in use at the settlement. This possibility was investigated for the Barrow Hills site, and while there were some broad trends, the results suggest that they were not significant, except perhaps during the early life of the site.

The sunken-featured buildings with around 50% or greater of chaff-tempered fabric 6 tended to be located in the northern half of the site (SFBs 9, 12, 21 and 32), with the exception of SFB 17/18. Those with between *c* 20% – 50% F6 (SFBs 4, 5, 19 and 40) were located in or near the central cluster of buildings. The sunken-featured buildings with less than 20% F6 showed no pattern, being located all across the site, including the northern area.

Of the other major fabrics, F1 does not comprise more than 50% of any sunken-featured building assemblage, and shows no obvious spatial pattern-

ing. The chaff and quartz fabric F2 occurs in fairly large quantities right across the site, with sunken-featured buildings with greater than 50% of this ware occurring in all areas. Those sunken-featured buildings with greater than *c* 40% of F3 (SFBs 26, 27, 45), the coarse quartz fabric, are mostly the southern area of the site, apart from SFB 43 to the west of the central cluster. Many of the sunken-featured buildings on the western edge of the site have a very low (<10%) proportion of F3, but sunken-featured buildings in the other areas of the site, including the southern area, also fall into this category. None of the minor wares show any significant distribution.

To test these distributions, the proportion of each of the major fabric types (F1, F2, F3, F6) was compared with the distance of each sunken-featured building from both the southern and western extremities of the site (Table 4.4), and the correlation coefficient, *r*, calculated. While there is a slight tendency for lower proportions of F2 and F3 to occur in the northerly sunken-featured buildings, and hence slightly more F1 and F6 in the same areas, the results cannot be considered to be significant. In addition, while the more easterly sunken-featured buildings tend to have slightly more F3, this again cannot be seen as significant.

Thus, the spatial nucleation of some fabric types seen at Mucking does not occur at Barrow Hills. This does not, however, take chronology into account. It is possible that pottery use at the site changed over time, and so the assemblages were again examined, with the sunken-featured buildings divided into phases on the basis of the decorated pottery.

The analysis centres on the main fabric types, F1, F2, F3 and F6. Previous work at the early and middle Saxon settlement at North Raunds, Northants (Blinkhorn in press c) showed that it was possible to demonstrate that there were nucleated fabric distributions around the site by grouping the pottery according to the manufacturing method used, although the long life of the Raunds site and a lack of refined chronology meant that only two phase groups, early (5th to 7th century) and middle Saxon (8th to 9th century), could be compared. The uncertain chronology of the Barrow Hills material, coupled with the fact that there is no definite

Table 4.4 Correlation coefficient (r) values between fabric proportion and SFB.

Direction	Fabric	R
N	F1	0.26
N	F2	-0.38
N	F3	-0.28
N	F4	0.47
E	F1	-0.13
E	F2	-0.06
E	F3	0.29
E	F4	-0.08

Table 4.5   SFBs with 5th-century tpqs.

SFB	Distance north (m)	Distance east (m)	Sand-tempered %	Chaff-tempered %
35	53.6	112.1	25.0	75.0
5	125.7	88.6	42.6	57.4
7	139.3	82.1	43.1	56.9
43	146.4	119.3	82.7	17.3
15	147.8	77.1	85.2	14.8

Table 4.6   Central SFBs with a 5th-century tpq.

SFB	F1	F2	F3	F6
5	36	41	11	30
7	49	41	17	7
15	38	87	13	17
43	67	36	132	4
Total	190	205	173	58

Table 4.7   Southern SFBs with a 5th-century tpq.

SFB	F1	F2	F3	F6
35	5	52	2	0

evidence for middle Saxon occupation at this site, meant that there was no guarantee that this would be the case here.

With this in mind, a parallel methodology was used for the Barrow Hills pottery. The different fabric types were grouped together in two categories: chaff temper (F2, quartz and chaff, and F6, chaff with no other inclusions) and sand (F1 and F3). The correlation coefficient, r, was calculated for the distance north of the sunken-featured building from the most southerly point of the site versus the fabric group, and also for the distance east of the sunken-featured building from the most westerly point of the site *versus* the fabric group. This was carried out for each of the *tpq* groups.

For this group, the correlation coefficient, r, produced a value of 0.77 for distance north versus mineral-tempered pottery, and a value of -0.78 for the chaff-tempered pottery. This shows that there was a fairly strong correlation between site location and pottery use; the further north the sunken-featured building, the greater the proportion of sand-tempered pottery (Table 4.5).

During the analysis stage, it was noted that there seemed to be differences in vessel size between those sunken-featured buildings south of the prehistoric barrows and a central/northern group, comprising those sunken-featured buildings in the central cluster of buildings at the north end of the Romano-British cemetery and those to the north of them. This suggested some difference between the two groups of buildings. Thus, to further investigate any spatial patterning in fabric type, the sunken-featured buildings were grouped into southern and central/northern groups. The data were examined utilizing the chi-squared test (eg Drennan 1996, 187–92). For this, the total number of sherds of each fabric type from the sunken-featured buildings in each of the two clusters was summed, to give the total number of sherds of each fabric type for each cluster.

The totals for 'mineral-' and 'chaff'-tempered wares were combined for each group, and the resulting data formed the basis of the chi-squared test. This produced a value of 46.35 (1 d. f.), with a confidence level considerably greater than 99.9%, indicating that there is a significant difference in the make-up of the two pottery assemblages. The level of 'difference' between two populations which have produced a chi-squared value can be expressed by the calculation of Cramer's V, which produces a value of between 0 and 1, where 0 indicates that there is no difference between the two groups, and 1 indicates that they are as different as it is possible to be. In this case, $V = 0.26$, indicating there is some difference, but that the argument is weak, probably due to the relatively small amounts of pottery present and the small number of features involved.

For features with a 6th-century *tpq*, differences in fabric use across the site are less apparent. Calculation of r produces a value of -0.43 for mineral-tempered pottery and distance north, indicating that the more northerly sunken-featured buildings tend to favour more chaff-tempered pottery. It is probable that some of the pottery in sunken-featured buildings with a 6th-century *tpq* was residual 5th-century material, which would weaken the correlation.

Table 4.8   Proportions of sand- and chaff-tempered wares by distance north and east.

SFB	Distance north (m)	Distance E (m)	Sand-tempered %	Chaff-tempered %
41	10.0	74.3	46.8	53.7
25	21.4	92.9	60.1	39.2
29	35.7	98.6	22.0	78.0
28	36.4	88.6	37.4	62.2
8	45.7	128.6	57.2	42.8
26	65.7	130	63.0	37.0
45	72.8	185.7	51.5	34.6
23	73.6	161.4	42.5	56.4
14	74.3	65.7	50.2	49.3
24	82.8	165.7	30.2	67.0
1	91.4	91.4	51.0	49.9
4	126.4	80.0	52.3	47.5
6	130.0	104.9	53.1	46.9
19	140.0	61.4	57.3	42.6
37	145.7	19.3	23.0	74.8
39	157.1	95.0	42.3	57.7
40	158.6	61.4	40.3	59.6
20	198.6	81.4	24.6	75.4

Table 4.9   Central/northern group, 6th-century tpq.

SFB	F1	F2	F3	F6
1	49	38	55	7
4	116	81	20	37
6	86	49	14	21
19	101	62	36	20
20	42	82	5	32
37	22	15	5	0
39	39	63	3	14
40	87	101	29	60
Total	542	491	167	191

Table 4.10   Southern group, 6th-century tpq.

SFB	F1	F2	F3	F6
8	40	30	25	0
14	92	71	40	0
23	25	22	5	15
24	54	90	25	14
25	7	4	8	1
26	112	143	68	16
28	311	371	68	17
29	213	608	0	142
41	119	123	86	43
45	37	55	75	2
Total	1010	1599	400	250

The data for the 6th-century were again subjected to the chi-squared test (using sherd count), with the sunken-featured buildings broken down into a southern and a central group.

The pottery assemblages were again amalgamated into the two fabric groups, and analysis produced a chi-squared value of 37.4 (1 d. f.), with $V = 0.09$. The relationship is even weaker than for the sunken-featured buildings with a 5th-century *tpq*. There is also the problem of residuality. In addition to the fragmentation evidence, it should be noted that a sherd of an early to mid 5th-century carinated bossed vessel was noted in the upper layers of SFB 28, once again throwing doubt on our ability to date an entire assemblage by one or two diagnostic sherds (Fig. 3.74.162).

The nature of the pottery deposition in the barrow ditches was investigated. Of these, barrows 12 and 13 had by far the largest assemblages, and thus were likely to be the most reliable. It appears probable that these features were back-filled during the 6th century, and that as with the sunken-featured buildings, secondary domestic refuse was used. The location of the monuments might have suggested that the northern half of each ditch was back-filled with refuse from the central area, and the southern half with material from the southern area. However, the presence of sherd joins between SFB 7,

the northern ditch of barrow 12 and SFBs 23 and 24 casts doubt on this (see below, Cross-fits). Each barrow ditch was divided into 'northern segments' and 'southern segments', with the pottery occurrence shown in Tables 4.11–4.14.

In both cases, the proportions of the different fabric types in the northern and southern halves of the barrow ditches show the same general trend. In the case of barrow 12, the northern half of the ditch produced 43.4% sandy fabrics and 56.6% chaff-tempered fabric, while the southern half produced 69.2% sandy fabrics and 30.8% chaff-tempered fabrics. For barrow 13, the northern half yielded 39.9% sandy and 60.1% chaff and the southern half 58.4% sandy and 41.5% chaff, However, comparing the sherd totals for the northern and southern halves of barrow 12 by chi-squared returns a value of 7.54 (3 d.f., $0.1 > p > 0.05$, $V = 0.08$), which suggests that, statistically, support for the argument that the two sherd populations are different in character is very weak. This is likely to be due to the difference in the sherd quantities; the northern half of the barrow produced only 90 sherds of pottery, whereas the

Table 4.11   Pottery occurrence by weight (in g) per excavated segment, barrow 12, northern segments.

Context	F1	F2	F3	F6	Total Wt	% feature assemblage
601/A	8	18	22	0	48	0.3
601/B	0	2	3	14	19	0.1
601/E	35	124	86	0	245	1.4
601/F	5	93	49	0	147	0.8
601/G	15	63	5	0	83	0.5
601/O	20	48	0	20	88	0.5
601/P	45	44	34	0	123	0.7
Total	128	392	199	34	753	4.3
% group	17.0	52.1	26.4	4.5		

Table 4.12   Pottery occurrence by weight (in g) per excavated segment, barrow 12, southern segments.

Context	F1	F2	F3	F6	Total Wt	% feature assemblage
601/C	63	129	199	108	128	1.8
601/D	77	40	191	102	148	2.0
601/H	152	277	62	63	275	3.8
601/I	5174	1091	1061	43	162	2.2
601/J	1000	1206	547	26	140	1.9
601/K	217	311	113	101	301	4.1
601/L	595	212	305	228	1795	24.8
601/M	687	245	411	142	783	10.8
Total Wt	7965	3511	2889	813	3732	51.4
% group	50.8	22.4	18.4	21.8		

Table 4.13 Pottery occurrence by weight (in g) per excavated segment, barrow 13, northern segments.

Contexts	F1	F2	F3	F6	Total Wt	% feature assemblage
401/A	0	8	12	108	128	1.8
401/B	37	9	0	102	148	2.0
401/E	165	25	22	63	275	3.8
401/F	29	21	69	43	162	2.2
401/G	39	56	19	26	140	1.9
401/N	27	80	93	101	301	4.1
401/O	497	758	312	228	1795	24.8
401/P	120	472	49	142	783	10.8
Total	914	1429	576	813	3732	51.4
% group	24.5	38.3	15.4	21.8		

Table 4.14 Pottery occurrence by weight (in g) per excavated segment, barrow 13, southern segments.

Context	F1	F2	F3	F6	Total Wt	% feature assemblage
401/C	66	114	0	35	215	3.0
401/D	4	0	0	0	4	0.1
401/H	394	285	44	283	1006	13.7
401/I	45	40	19	0	104	1.5
401/J	39	51	19	0	109	1.5
401/K	824	252	201	245	1522	21.3
401/L	203	54	115	53	425	7.2
401/M	9	0	2	0	11	0.2
Total	1584	796	400	616	3396	48.5
% group	46.6	23.4	11.8	18.1		

southern half yielded 1151 (87.9% of the ditch assemblage by weight, 92.7% by sherd count). For barrow 13, the same exercise yielded a chi-squared value of 232.1 (3 d.f., $p > 0.01$, $V = 0.58$), which provides much stronger support for the argument than for barrow 12. The proportions of pot and bone by volume in barrows 12 and 13 are discussed in Chapter 7. Finally, the outer ditch of the Neolithic oval barrow, on the north edge of the settlement produced 111 sherds of pottery, of which 74% (by count) were chaff-tempered fabrics.

There is therefore some slight suggestion that chaff-tempered fabrics were used more frequently than sand-tempered wares in the areas generating the fills of the central area of the site during the 6th century, but the statistical arguments are weak, and the argument cannot be advanced with conviction.

Vessel use

The Anglo-Saxon pottery from Barrow Hills occurred in two basic vessel forms, jars and bowls. The

Table 4.15 Vessel occurrence in SFBs, all fabrics.

Tpq	Jars	Bowls	Total EVE
5thC	90.8%	9.2%	6.30
6thC	80.7%	19.3%	28.87
Total EVE	29.03	6.14	35.17

distribution of these around the site was given some consideration in an effort to identify different use areas at the site. The data are presented in Table 4.15.

The data in Table 4.15 suggest that for the site as a whole there may have been a decline in the consumption of jars from the 5th to the 6th century. They comprise 90.8% of the assemblage for the 5th-century *tpq* group, but only 80.7% for the 6th-century group. However, subjecting the data to a chi-squared test indicates that this difference is not statistically significant (chi-squared = 0.39 with 1 d.f., $p < 0.5$).

5th-century* tpq *group (Tables 4.5–7)

There appear to be no significant differences in terms of vessel use in different areas of the site for the 5th-century *tpq* group, although the sample is small and all but SFB 35 are in the central cluster. Calculation of the correlation coefficient for the data shown in Table 4.16 using distance east and percentage of jars gives a value for *r* of 0.18.

For the 6th-century *tpq* group, the situation is different. The value for *r* was again calculated, for the same parameters (distance east versus % of jars), and this time the value was -0.77. This is quite a strong correlation, and indicates a distinct drop-off in the presence of jars in the eastern sunken-featured buildings of this group.

This, like the fabric analysis, indicates a change in vessel-use practice at the site over time. What this may mean is another matter. Vessel use in the early Anglo-Saxon period is far from understood. The limited range of vessels may mean that there was a limited range of uses for pottery, or that the few forms in use had a multiplicity of purposes, as was the case in the early medieval period (Blinkhorn 1999). Social factors or functional differentiation between areas of the site may also have been a consideration.

Table 4.16 Percentage of vessel forms versus distance east, 5th-century tpq.

SFB	E	Jars %	Bowls %	Total EVE
7	82.1	82.6	27.4	1.15
15	77.1	83.6	16.4	1.34
43	119.3	94.5	5.5	2.92
5	88.6	100	0	0.63
35	112.1	100	0	0.15

Vessel size

Generally, archaeologists have given very little consideration to ceramic vessel capacity, despite the fact that the parameter has the potential to enhance considerably the understanding of pottery assemblages (see Woodward and Blinkhorn 1997 and Blinkhorn 1999 for further discussion). One of the main handicaps to such analyses is the lack of reconstructable or whole vessels from archaeological sites, particularly early Anglo-Saxon settlements such as this, where the nature of pottery deposition means that most assemblages are often tertiary and partial. However, the work cited has shown that it is possible to show a correlation in pottery between rim diameter and vessel capacity for other periods. The rim diameters of the pottery from Barrow Hills were therefore collated, with the intention of identifying spatial variation. It seems likely from examination of the fragmentary remains of the pots that any variation is due to vessel size rather than form, as the vast majority of sherds showed little evidence of any great variation from fairly simple globular forms. Thus, any spatial clustering of rim diameter size could be taken as evidence of areas of differential vessel use within the settlement. Even if these differences were due to form rather than size, then any clustering could still be taken to be significant; the form of early Anglo-Saxon pottery certainly was important in a funerary context, and the same is likely to have been true in a domestic context (Blinkhorn 1997).

Jars

The pottery was divided into two groups, based on location; the results are presented in Table 4.18. The raw data appear significant, and are worthy of discussion. Generally, there is little difference in the mean size of jar rim diameters in use at the site between the 5th- and 6th-century *tpq* groups. However, there is a difference in the size of vessels found in these groups in different areas of the settlement.

5th-century tpq

The raw data suggest that a different pottery use regime was in place, with the southern SFB 35 generally producing larger pots than the central/northern group. This was examined statistically, using Student's t-test (Drennan 1996, 155–8). The resulting value of t was 1.33 (52 d.f., .2 > p > .1). This suggests that there is between 80–90% confidence that this difference is real, although the sample is very small.

6th-century tpq (Tables 4.17, 4.19)

The sunken-featured buildings were again divided into two groups, with those on or to the south of the

Table 4.17 Percentage of vessel forms versus distance east, 6th-century tpq.

SFB	Location	E	Jars %	Bowls %	Total *EVE*
37	W	19.3	100	0	0.25
19	Centre	61.4	95.1	4.9	2.07
40	Centre	61.4	91.6	8.4	2.63
14	W	65.7	80.3	19.7	3.14
41	S	74.3	91.9	8.1	2.22
4	Centre	80	100	0	0.74
20	N	81.4	86.4	13.6	1.47
28	S	88.6	70.9	29.1	5.95
1	Centre-S	91.4	92.0	8.0	1.74
25	S	92.9	84.6	15.4	0.13
39	Centre-E	95	100	0	0.77
29	S	98.6	82.6	17.4	0.92
6	Centre	104.9	71.1	28.9	1.49
8	SE	128.6	73.2	26.8	0.71
26	SE	130	86.4	13.6	1.47
23	SE	161.4	74.5	25.5	0.47
24	SE	165.7	75.0	25.0	1.4
45	SE	185.7	48.8	51.2	1.23

Table 4.18 Jars.

Feature type	No. rim sherds	Mean diameter (mm)	Standard deviation (mm)
5th –century *tpq*			
All SFBs	54	166.9	53.33
Central/northern group (4 features)	52	164.81	52.7
Southern group (1 feature)	2	220	56.6
6th-century *tpq*			
All SFBs	318	171.92	47.8 min
Central/northern group	133	159.77	39.9
Southern group	190	180.21	51.0

settlement area (SFBs 8, 14, 23, 24, 25, 28/9, 41, 45) being classed as 'southern', and those in the centre or north (SFBs 1, 4, 6, 19, 20, 39, 40) being regarded as 'central/northern'. Comparison using Student's t this time produced a value of 3.85 (323 d.f., 0.001 < p). This can be said, simply, to mean that there is greater than 99.9% confidence that the differences in vessel size use in the two groups is real and that the areas from which the fills of the southern features derived were using larger vessels.

This difference seems to be unrelated to fabric. When the entire assemblage is considered, irrespective of location, the mean rim diameter of the sand-tempered jars is 176.7 mm, while that of the chaff-tempered types was 175.7 mm. Both groups also had similar standard deviations (50.5 mm and 49.8 mm), further suggesting that there was little difference in

Table 4.19   Bowls.

Feature type	No. rim sherds	Mean diameter (mm)	Standard deviation (mm)
6th-century *tpq*			
All SFBs	69	150.72	47.2
Central/northern group	10	136.0	32.4
Southern group	59	153.2	49.0

the size range of the two different fabric groups. This is confirmed by the plot of the different vessel sizes shown in Figures 4.1a and 4.1b.

The results of the statistical analysis of the vessel sizes for the two sunken-featured building clusters defined for each period show that there were differences in vessel use between the areas producing the fills of the central/northern and southern sunken-featured buildings for the 6th-century *tpq* group. This cannot be said with confidence for the 5th-century group. Traditional statistical analyses tend to use the 95% confidence level as significant; results above that can be regarded as significant, those below it indicate that any observed differences are simply the result of the vagaries of sampling. Using this approach, the *t*-value obtained for the 5th-century *tpq* group with a null hypothesis 'is the apparent difference in the size of vessels noted in the two sunken-featured building groups simply due to the vagaries of sampling?' suggests that this is indeed the case. Thus, despite the apparent difference in the data, it cannot be said with confidence

A

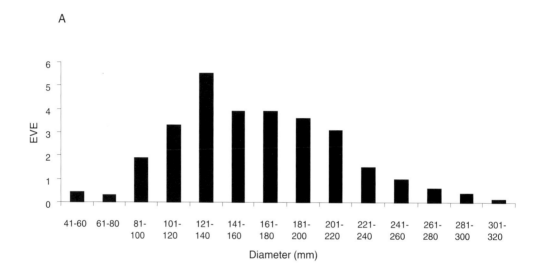

B

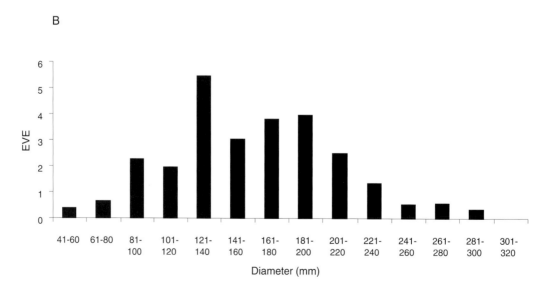

Figure 4.1   (A) Rim diameter of jars, sand-tempered fabrics, by MNV per diameter category, sand-tempered fabrics; (B) Rim diameter of jars, sand tempered fabrics, by MNV per diameter category, chaff-tempered fabrics.

that there were differences in vessel use between the two areas. Drennan (1996, 162–3) has suggested that a less Draconian approach to the assessment of significance levels is required for archaeological data, and proposed a more 'graded' approach, Using his method (Drennan 1996, table 11.3), the *t*-value for the 5th-century group, which is very close to the 80% significance level, suggests that is likely that the apparent difference in the vessel sizes in the two clusters is the result of the vagaries of sampling rather than being a real difference.

Bowls

Considerably fewer bowls than jars were noted, to such an extent that analysis of those from the 5th-century *tpq* group would have produced results which were all but meaningless. However, the assemblages from the 6th-century *tpq* group were somewhat larger, and so the vessels were analysed in the same way as the jars.

6th-century tpq group (Table 4.19)

These data immediately suggest two major differences in the occurrence of bowls in the two areas of the site. In the central/northern area, bowls were far less common (7.0% of the vessel assemblage) than in the southern area (23.7% of the vessel assemblage), and those in use in the central/northern area were considerably smaller than those in the southern area.

As with the jars, this suggests that the function of pottery finding its way into sunken-featured buildings in the central/northern area was different from that finding its way into those in the southern area. Bowls appear less frequently than jars in the central/northern area, and those that were in use were smaller and had a far more restricted size-range than those in the south. This may suggest some differentiation in function between the two areas of the site. Small bowls may represent individual consumption, and could have been used for a variety of functions, ranging from drinking to serving individual portions of food. Whatever the case, nearly all the possible uses would probably have been related to food/drink consumption rather than processing or preparation. The fact that so few large pottery bowls were found in the central/northern area might suggest that they were less in use in this area. This will be discussed in relation to site formation processes and other evidence in Chapter 7. It is likely that more perishable or recyclable materials such as wood, metal and glass were also used, with the type of material doubtless related to the wealth and rank of the user.

In the southern group, bowls show a similar pattern to jars. Vessels are larger than in the central/northern area, and are also present in greater proportions. Large bowls could have had many uses, but these are perhaps more likely to have related to the storage, processing and preparation of foodstuffs rather than consumption. In later periods,

such vessels had a wide range of roles in the preparation of foodstuffs, with such uses as milk-skimmers, mixing bowls and flour or meal measures in bakeries.

Decoration (Tables 4.20–4.25)

In a small community... it would appear that (cremation) urns were carefully manufactured with a particular 'client' in mind, according to a culturally controlled set of symbolic rules... The form and decoration of the cremation vessels nay have been a simple 'mirror' refection of the deceased ... or may have been deliberately controlled and manipulated, both in the working out of social tensions, and in the reinforcement of social solidarity and group cohesion (Richards 1987, 206)

The main methods of surface enhancement for the Barrow Hills pottery, burnishing and smoothing aside, were incised decoration, stamping, plastic decoration (mainly in the form of collars), and applied or impressed bosses, with the techniques noted in all possible combinations.

The role of decorated pottery in early Anglo-Saxon society is still something of an enigma. Julian Richards's (1987) study of the use of such pottery in funerary contexts as cremation urns has shown that there were statistically significant correlations between certain forms and styles of decoration and age/gender. There is no evidence for this in a settlement context, for the simple reason that the pots cannot be directly related to individuals. Decorated pottery is also far less common in non-funerary contexts, usually comprising around 3–4% (by sherd count) of large assemblages from sites such as West Stow or Mucking (West 1985; Hamerow 1993). The Barrow Hills assemblage appears to be no different. Of the 9,131 sherds of Anglo-Saxon pottery, only 335 were decorated, some 3.7% of the assemblage.

Hamerow's work at Mucking showed that there was some nucleated spatial distribution of the decorated pottery at the site, particularly the carinated bowls, or *Schalenurnen*, which were largely restricted to the southern area, whereas bossed vessels occurred all over the site. There was also some evidence of correlation between fabric type and form and decoration. For example, only one of

Table 4.20 Decorated pottery, all periods, by decoration type and fabric group, expressed in number of sherds.

Decoration	Sand-tempered	Chaff-tempered	Total
Incised only	118	80	198
Stamped only	4	4	8
Incised and Stamped	60	49	109
Bossed, Stamped, Incised	2	3	5
Bossed and Incised	1	5	6
Bossed	0	1	1
Collared	6	2	8
Total	191	144	335

Table 4.21 Occurrence of decorated pottery by type, 6th-century tpqs, *by number of sherds.*

	Incised only	Stamped only	Incised + Stamped	Bossed, Stamped + Incised	Bossed + Incised	Bossed	Collared	Total
Central/northern	25	2	9	1	0	0	0	37
Southern	44	2	30	0	5	1	2	84

Table 4.22 Decorated sherds in central and southern groups.

	Incised	Stamped	Bossed	Total
Central	25	11	1	37
Southern	44	32	8	84

the *Schalenurnen* at Mucking was in a chaff-tempered fabric, whereas bossed pottery was made from both sand- and chaff-tempered clays (Hamerow 1993, 56). With these facts in mind, the Barrow Hills pottery was analysed, with the vessels again divided into two fabric 'groups', sand temper and chaff temper.

The data in Table 4.20 indicate that there is little evidence of major trends in the relationship between fabric and decoration type. Slightly more sherds occur in sand-tempered fabrics, but sand-tempered fabrics form a greater proportion of the site assemblage, and so this cannot be regarded as greatly significant. The bossed vessels and the collared examples have some bias, but the assemblages are so small that is also difficult to suggest that the data are particularly meaningful.

In an attempt to clarify the picture, the decorated pottery from the sunken-featured buildings was examined, with the structures divided into two groups, southern and central/northern, as above. During the analysis, fabric type was noted, but it appears to have no relationship to the decoration type, and is thus ignored. The data are shown in Table 4.21.

These data highlight several features worthy of comment. There are more decorated sherds from the southern sunken-featured buildings than from those in the central area. This suggests that their fills derive from areas where decorated pottery was more commonly used than in the sources for the central group. Stamped pottery also appears more in the southern sunken-featured buildings, as does bossed

pottery, with only a single bossed vessel occurring in the central/northern area. It should be noted that two large sherds from a bossed vessel were noted in a relic stream course to the south-west of the oval barrow. The existence of this feature was recorded and it was assigned a context number, but no context record can be found. Because of this uncertainty, the vessels have been omitted from the following analyses.

To assess whether the two groups are significant, they were subjected to a chi-squared test. Due to the small assemblage size, the groups were amalgamated into three classes: incised only, stamped (with or without incised decoration) and bossed (all bossed categories + collared): (Table 4.22)

Comparison of these groups gives a chi-squared value of 3.13 (3 d.f., $0.5 < p < 0.8$), indicating that the differences between the two assemblages are not significant, and that the apparent differences are likely to be the results of the vagaries of sampling.

To confirm this, the decorated pottery from the ditches of barrows 1, 12 and 13 was tested in a similar way, with the assemblages separated into northern and southern segments as with the fabric analysis. Tables 4.23–4 present the data.

This produces a chi-squared value of 17.46 (3.d.f, $p > .999$), which is, superficially, a highly significant result. However, calculation of Cramer's V gives a value of 0.5, which suggests that the result is not especially strong, and that the apparent differences may again be simply due to the vagaries of sampling, probably due to the small sample size.

In an attempt to overcome the problem of sample size, a new dataset was created, comprising two groups. Group A, the decorated pottery from the northern segments of the barrows and the central/ northern sunken-featured buildings with 6th-century *tpqs*, and group B, the decorated pottery from the southern segments of the barrows and the southern 6th-century *tpq* group (Table 4.25). This was also subjected to a chi-squared test, producing a value of

Table 4.23 Occurrence of decorated pottery by type, Barrows 1, 12 and 13, by number of sherds.

	Incised only	Stamped only	Incised + Stamped	Bossed, Stamped + Incised	Bossed + Incised	Bossed	Collared	Total
Northern segments	3	2	11	0	0	0	0	16
Southern segments	40	2	11	2	0	0	0	55

Table 4.24   Decorated sherds from northern and southern segments of barrow ditches.

	Incised	Stamped	Bossed	Total
Northern segments	3	13	0	16
Southern segments	40	13	2	55

Table 4.25   Decorated pottery, 6th-century tpqs.

	Incised	Stamped	Bossed	Total
Group A	28	24	1	53
Group B	84	45	10	139

4.07 (3d.f, $0.5 < p < 0.8$), suggesting that the result is not significant.

It would therefore appear either that there was little significant spatial difference in the use and disposal of decorated pottery at the site or that the site formation processes have obscured it. It is known that such material had a highly important social role when used as cremation containers, but we do not know what role the material played in a domestic context. If it did have a role in signalling identity, then at Barrow Hills the social information it conveyed is unclear. The distribution of the material does not take the same form as the vessel size data, which may suggest that vessel size relates to the practical functions of different parts of the site rather than social status. Only one bossed pottery vessel occurs in the central area, but no statistical conclusions can be drawn from this, as the amount of bossed pottery present is simply too small. If the data were reduced further to two classes, stamped and/or incised versus all bossed vessels, the resulting chi-squared value would still suggest there is no great significance, and the argument would also be very weak (chi-squared = 2.01, 1d.f., $0.8 > p > 0.9$, $V = 010$).

Spatial distribution of stamp motifs

Richards (1987) discussed the significance of the stamp motifs used on early Anglo-Saxon pottery. He noted that while some designs had an overtly pagan symbolism (swastikas, 'wyrms', runics), others appeared to have little obvious significance, although they could be paralleled on prehistoric rock-art, indicating that they had a long currency. Richards's study was entirely concerned with pottery used as cremation containers, and while he argued that there was some evidence of stamping having a symbolic meaning in that context, it is not known whether this meaning was the same for pottery used in the domestic context, or indeed if it had any meaning at all.

The stamped pottery at Barrow Hills exhibited a somewhat limited range of motif types, with by far the commonest being a simple cross motif, some-times cut into a circular die-head. Simple stabbed decoration, not made with a carved die, but perhaps with any convenient tool or even domestic debris, was the next commonest, followed by wheel motifs, that is a circular stamp with a motif of a cross with eight or more arms. Finally, small numbers of annular 'ring-and-dot' motifs, grids (multiple lines crossing at right-angles) and S-shaped 'wyrm' stamps were also present.

In an attempt to try and identify any significance that these stamps may have had, their distribution around the site was analysed, and although the results were far from conclusive, some general trends were identified.

The majority of the stabbed sherds occurred in the barrow ditches or southern sunken-featured buildings. Two sherds of this type were noted in the central area, one in SFB 6 and the other in SFB 1. Wheel stamps showed a similar distribution, mainly occurring in the barrow ditches and southern sunken-featured buildings, with only two from the central/northern area. The same is true of grid stamps. Cross stamps mainly occurred in the barrow ditches and the central sunken-featured buildings, although three were noted from the southern group. Of the three 'wyrm' stamps, three occurred in the ditches of barrow 13 and the oval barrow, with just a single example from the central area, from SFB 7; however, this joined the sherds from barrow 13. Two of the ring stamps occurred in the central area, while the other was in a southern sunken-featured building.

It is difficult, with such small populations, to read any great significance into these results. Relatively large numbers of stamped sherds occurred in the barrow ditches, but this is most probably due to the size of the assemblages. Barrow 13 produced 7128 g of pottery and barrow 12 produced 17,818 g. As the latter is the largest feature-specific assemblage from the site, and the former one of the largest, this would therefore suggest that the large number of stamped sherds is not evidence of any specific depositional practice. This is illustrated by the relatively large number of stamped sherds that occurred in SFB 28/29, which produced by far the largest assemblage of pottery from the entire site, but was unfortunately mixed during excavation.

Lugged, rusticated, pierced and footring-base pottery

Anglo-Saxon pottery has a number of attributes other than decoration which can be regarded as enhancing the functional efficiency of the pot, but also have the potential to have been transmitters of social information. In the case of the Barrow Hills pottery, the parameters in question are lugs, piercing, rustication and foot-ring bases. Three basic types of lug were noted: upright (attached to the top of the rim of a vessel), longitudinal (attached to the body of a vessel), or 'swallow's nest', which are upright lugs with an exterior pocket (see Figs 3.17.8, 3.73.156, 3.77.180). There seems to be little difference in the functional efficiency of the three types (other than the fact that the swallow's nest type would offer protection to an inflammable suspension mechanism if the vessel was held over a fire), and so there is the possibility that the selection of lug position on a vessel may have been culturally influenced (Blinkhorn 1997). Thus, any pattern in the distribution of the lugged pottery around the site may offer an insight into the social structure of the settlement.

Rustication, the repeated 'pinching' of the surface of a vessel to provide a rough finish, is another technique which is generally regarded as functional, but has the potential to offer social information. It is often described as having been done to make the pot easier to grip, although there are several problems with this argument, not least the fact that the technique appears entirely limited to squat, wide-mouthed vessel forms (see Blinkhorn 1997 for a fuller argument). In a cremation context, such forms are strongly associated with female burials (Richards 1987), and thus what we may in fact be seeing in the domestic context is a pottery type which is strongly female-linked.

Vessels with multiple piercing over most of the body are regularly found in small quantities at Anglo-Saxon settlement sites. These have, in the past, been interpreted as having being placed on fires to allow the warming of iron wool-combs (Jones 1975), although this interpretation appears doubtful when the size of the pots and the combs in question are considered. Many other interpretations seem possible, particularly fire-pots, vessels used for the transportation around the site of hot embers for fire-lighting. They could also have functioned as colanders, or as cheese-presses. Whatever their use, they appear to be a highly specialised vessel, and their distribution will also be examined.

Finally, foot-ring base pottery should be considered. Such attributes are rare on early Anglo-Saxon pottery, and appear to be mainly associated with two particular vessel types, the highly decorated bossed vessels which Myres defined as *Buckelurnen* (1977, 31–3), or vessels with longitudinal body-mounted lugs (1977, 34–6). Not all lugged pottery has foot-ring bases, but a considerable proportion of pots with such bases has such lugs. There is a functional argument for their presence in that they allow the vessels to stand on a flat surface such as a table, but this is contradicted by the fact they have lugs, which suggests that they were intended for suspension over a fire. Foot-ring bases would have been considerably more prone to thermal shock fracture than rounded bases. Thus, they were less functionally efficient than pots without foot-rings. The distribution of these pots will be considered in a similar manner to the other types discussed above.

The lugged pottery shows no clear distribution. Only two swallow's nest lugs were noted, so their distribution is of little use, but the other two types are found in features all over the site, and sometimes in the same structure. This suggests that there was no spatial discrimination in their use.

The pierced pottery tends to occur in southern sunken-featured buildings, although two sherds were noted from the central area, in SFBs 15 and 16. The picture is similar for the rusticated wares. They occur in both areas of the site. Only two sherds came from the heart of the central area, from SFBs 19 and 39. The foot-ring pottery favoured the central area. No sherds were found in the southern sunken-featured buildings but a single sherd was noted from barrow 13 itself, and also from SFB 18, which cut the north-east side of ring ditch 801, and SFB 21, at the northern edge of the site.

The most obvious aspect of the distribution of the various feature sherds around the site is that there appears to be no clear-cut nucleation as there was, for example, with some of the decorated pottery types at Mucking or with the vessel sizes at Barrow Hills. All the different sherd types occurred in both central and southern sunken-featured buildings, and in some of the barrow ditches. This suggests that if any of the pottery types under consideration here had any sort of social significance, the consumers of the material did not use it in restricted areas of the site. Similarly, if the vessels were purely functional, then they were also used all over the site, and not in specific areas, or else site formation processes were redistributing it. This appears to contradict the evidence of the vessel size analysis. In the case of the pierced pottery, we may be looking at a multi-functional type; if they were used as fire-pots, then it would be expected that they occur all over the site. Some of the post-built structures are likely to have had hearths, and these would have had to be lit from time to time. The biggest number of finds of this particular sherd-type came from SFB 28/29, SFB 35 and the barrow ditches. If this area of the site was where most of the preparation and processing of food took place, and if as has been suggested in the past these vessels were used as cheese-presses or strainers, then it is perhaps no surprise that a large number of them occurred in this area.

In the case of the rusticated pottery, the picture is perhaps less clear. We do not know exactly what role these vessels played in early Anglo-Saxon society, so that interpreting their distribution is necessarily a little difficult. Most sherds came from the edges of the central area, and few from the central cluster of buildings or the southern sunken-featured buildings. This may indicate that the sunken-featured buildings on the periphery of the central area were filled with material at least partly derived from an activity in which rusticated pottery played a part. If, has been suggested, they were only used by women, this distribution may mark out an area where female-linked activity such as textile production or dairying took place.

The lack of foot-ring pottery in the southern features may suggest that this material may have had a role in broadcasting social information, or may have had a formalized function, such as only being used on certain occasions in a specific context. However, as only ten of these were noted from the whole site, it is difficult to pursue the argument with much confidence.

Further spatial analysis

The groups of structures within the settlement may have formed discrete clusters of post-built halls and associated sunken-featured buildings within the two broad 'central' and 'southern' areas of the site, as appears to have been the case at other sites, such as West Stow (West 1985). These groups were defined as follows:

Inner group: SFBs 4, 5, 6, 7, 15, 16, 19.
South-east group: barrows 12 and 13, pits 414–416, SFBs 23, 24, 26, 45.
Middle (S) SFBs: 1, 2, 3, 10, 11, 13, 14, 17/18.
Middle (N) SFBs 36, 37, 38, 39, 40, 43.
Outer (N): oval barrow, SFBs 9, 12, 20, 21, 22.
Outer (E) barrow 1, SFB 30, 32, 33, 34.
Outer (S) SFBs 8, 25, 28, 29, 35, 41, 42.

In most cases, the size of the assemblages meant that the only worthwhile analyses concerned fabric occurrence, vessel type and vessel size (Tables 4.26–27).

i) Inner group versus south-east group

When the fabric occurrences in the inner group and the south-east group were compared, the chi-squared value, based on number of sherds per fabric group, was 4.15 (1 d.f., $0.95 < p < 0.99$), with a Cramer's V value of 0.03. This would suggest that while there may be some difference in the fabric proportions in the two groups, the argument was too weak to be regarded as significant. In the case of the vessel proportions, the inner group yielded a far smaller proportion of bowls (12.5%) than the south-east group (26.3%). With regard to vessel size, the two groups show the same basic pattern as the internal and peripheral groups. In the case of the inner group, the mean jar diameter is 156.4 mm (90 rims, standard deviation = 43.9 mm), with the south-east group having a mean jar diameter of 183.8 mm (204 rims, standard deviation = 50.0 mm). The jars in the south-east group are generally much larger than those in the inner group. The bowls show the same pattern; the mean diameter for those in the inner group is 131.4 mm (7 rim sherds, standard deviation = 76.5 mm, whereas those in the south-east group have a mean diameter of 157.6 mm (52 rim sherds, standard deviation = 52.86 mm). When tested statistically, using Student's t test, the returned value for the jars is 4.50 (292 d.f., $p > 0.001$), whereas that for the bowls is 1.17 (57d.f., $.5 > p > .8$) indicating that the difference between the jar sizes for the two groups is highly significant, but not for the bowls. In the case of the bowls, this is probably due to the small number of such vessels which occurred in the inner group.

ii) Others

The data for the sub-clusters very much mirror the general trends for the central and southern groups. There is no real pattern to the fabric distribution, other than perhaps the relatively large number of sherds of chaff-tempered pottery from the outer (northern) group around (and including) the oval barrow. Comparing this to the pottery from the nearest cluster, middle (northern), using the chi-squared test, returns a value of 105.8 (1d.f., $p > 0.001$, $V = 0.26$). This indicates that there is a definite, statistically significant difference between the fabric occurrence in the two groups, although it is rather weak when the sizes of the assemblages are considered. Large sherd populations like this one can give slightly misleading results, in that they can produce very large chi-squared values even when the difference between the groups under consideration is not that large (C Orton, pers. comm.). It would appear therefore that although the outer (northern) group has a fabric composition which is statistically,

Table 4.26 *Fabric comparison, middle and outer groups.*

Group	No. Sandy	No. Chaff	Total
Mid (S) SFBs	536	454	990
Mid (N) SFBs	571	378	949
Outer (N)	216	423	639
Outer (E)	200	194	394
Outer (S)	738	695	1433
Total	2261	2144	4405

Table 4.27 *Vessel size comparison, middle and outer groups.*

Group	No. Jars	Mean diameter (mm)	Standard Deviation (mm)	No. Bowls	Mean diameter (mm)	Standard Deviation (mm)
Mid (S) SFBs	105	185.4	50.2	19	141.6	32.9
Mid (N) SFBs	92	167.8	46.7	10	132.0	32.9
Outer (N)	69	167.4	49.0	6	120.0	29.0
Outer (E)	47	168.3	51.9	11	143.6	45.2
Outer (S)	121	181.1	50.8	37	158.9	50.8
Total	434			83		

245

significantly different to that of the nearest sunken-featured building cluster, the difference is not that great when the size of the assemblages is taken into consideration, and cannot be taken as an indication that the pottery use in this area of the site was different to anywhere else.

The vessel size analysis very closely mirrors the data for the central and southern groups. The two (middle (southern) and outer (southern)) groups have a larger mean rim diameter for jars than the other groups. The picture is not as clear-cut with the bowls, although those from the southern part of the site have a larger mean diameter than most of the groups in the central area.

CROSS-FITS

Many of the sunken-featured buildings and barrow ditches had internal cross-fits, which are noted in the Gazetteers in Chapter 3. The following cross-fits were noted between features:

Barrow 13, 401/H/2 = 3805/A/2, SFB 24 (x2).
Barrow 13, 401/O/2 = Pit 414 = SFB 7, 1298/A/2 = SFB 7, 1298/A/2 SFB 7 = SFB 23, 3800/A/1, (x4).
SFB 28, 4198/C/1 = SFB 29, 4423/13/2 (the records indicate that the fills of these features were mixed during excavation).

SUMMARY OF RESULTS

Chaff-tempered fabrics increase from the 5th-century *tpq* group to the 6th-century group, although the increase is not of an order which suggests that it is significant.

Large sunken-featured building assemblages were generally as fragmented as small ones.

The distribution of pottery fabrics around the site showed no significant concentrations.

There is little significant change in the proportions of jars and bowls in use between the 5th- and 6th-century *tpq* groups.

There appear to be no significant differences in terms of vessel use in different areas of the site for the 5th-century *tpq* group. For the 6th-century group, there is a significant fall-off in the use of jars in the sunken-featured buildings in the area of barrows 12 and 13.

Overall, the mean size of vessels does not change significantly from the 5th- to the 6th-century groups. However, for the 6th-century *tpq* group, the vessels found in the central area were significantly smaller than those found on the south of the site. Bowls were also less common in the central area than in the southern features, although the sample is a small one.

The decorated pottery demonstrated broad trends, although due to the small populations involved, none were statistically significant.

Bossed vessels occurred mainly in southern features.

Stabbed sherds occurred mainly in southern features and the barrow ditches.

Wheel-stamps occurred mainly in southern features and the barrow ditches.

Cross-stamps occurred mainly in central features and the barrow ditches.

Lugged pottery did not show any significant distribution.

Pierced pottery tended to occur in southern features.

Foot-ring bases occurred mainly in the central area of the site.

Rusticated pottery occurred mainly on the fringes of the central area and on the southern side of the site.

DISCUSSION AND CONCLUSIONS

The evidence from Barrow Hills shows that during the 6th century, there is a definite, statistically significant difference in the size of vessels finding their way into features in different areas of the site. This may provide evidence for social organisation on site.

Numerous anthropological works have shown that the size of pot can be related to function. Generally, although by no means universally, small pots are used by individuals for the consumption of food or the preparation of food for themselves alone, whereas larger ones are used for storage or cooking meals for large numbers of people. Other uses are known, but these are the most common. Thus, the pattern of pottery consumption at Barrow Hills suggests that, by the 6th century and as far as jars were concerned, the material finding its way into features in the central area of the site came from an area that was primarily concerned with food consumption, and not preparation and/or storage, with material associated with those actions being found in the southern part of the site. The large jars found in the southern sunken-featured buildings (but not those in the area of barrows 12 and 13) could have had several functions: storage vessels, water jars or cooking pottery for communal meals. Additionally, bowls found in the southern area were larger than those found in the centre, which also suggests food preparation and storage rather than consumption. In the central area, the greater number of smaller jars and bowls indicates a greater emphasis on the consumption of food and drink by individuals.

The distribution of the different fabric types around the site was also considered. The statistical arguments are somewhat weak due to a combination of 'contamination' by residual pottery and widely differing sherd populations. There is a very faint suggestion that there were differences in the fabric types favoured in the central and southern areas of the site. It has been suggested in the past (Blinkhorn 1993; 1997) that Anglo-Saxon pottery fabrics are indicators of social identity. Thus, if more chaff-tempered pottery were found in the central area of the site it might reflect the fact that those in the central area had a different social identity to those occupying the buildings on the southern part of the site. Although most of the material from the sunken-featured buildings represents tertiary deposits it may be that the pottery, like the animal bone, includes a component that was directly and locally discarded into the open, disused pits, and reflects household consumption, the remains of kitchen and table waste rather than larger-scale food processing. However, no other aspects of the pottery reflect this difference. The functional features of the pottery, such as lug position and rustication, which could also be regarded as social indicators, do not have any strongly nucleated distributions. It is possible that if decorative or functional features of pottery had social meaning this had largely been lost by the later 6th century. This might tie in with Moreland's idea (2000) that the later 6th century saw the rise of the concept of Anglo-Saxon identity, and thus a more homogeneous identity would produce a more homogeneous material culture. Equally, however, we may be dealing with a small, family-based farming settlement with few marked distinctions in status.

Chapter 5: The Finds from the Settlement Site

By Barbara Ford

PERSONAL ORNAMENTS

Brooches

by Anne Dodd

There are four brooches from the Anglo-Saxon settlement. Two are fragmentary, but a fine example of a complete button brooch (136, Fig. 3.105) was recovered from topsoil. It is of copper alloy, with a rim diameter of 22 mm, and the iron pin is aligned across the face. The decoration, which is fairly well executed, consists of a single field of a human mask, surrounded by a plain border inside the rim. The representation of the human face is stylised, with the eyebrows, nose and cheeks combined in a single element. The eyes are small and round and the nose is flaring; the helmet is represented by two lines, and the mouth by a single large bar with an indentation.

The Barrow Hills example does not fit readily into any of the classes proposed by Avent and Evison (1982), but is most closely comparable with their class Ei; it shares the saucer-shaped profile of this group, and all class E brooches are characterised by a stylised representation of the human face. Avent and Evison noted only three examples of Class Ei, all of which were found at Mucking, Essex (Grave 99, 22.1 and 2; Grave 690); related types in class Eii are noted from Alton, Hants (Grave 37, 3.3 and 4), and Vierville, Manche (Grave 77) and in class Eiii from Alfriston, Sussex (Grave 62). Down and Welch (1990, 97) have noted a further example from Apple Down, Sussex (unstratified 583), which they associate with class Eii. No other examples of class E brooches are currently known from the Upper Thames valley, but Avent and Evison have noted links between Mucking and Upper Thames valley brooches in classes I and J (1982, 86–7, figs 8 and 9).

The early dating of button brooches proposed by Avent and Evison remains controversial; however, they have placed class Ei comparatively late in their chronology, dating the group from the late 5th century into the early 6th century (1982, fig. 13). This would not conflict with the general date-range for the type supported by Dickinson (forthcoming; Dodd 1995) and Welch (Down and Welch 1990, 97; Welch 1985).

A moulded fragment of a foot knob and catchplate from a Roman brooch, probably a trumpet brooch, came from layer 1 in SFB 4 (140, Fig. 3.18). Trumpet brooches appeared just before the middle of the 1st century and lasted until the late 2nd century (Hattatt 1985, 105).

An applied disc brooch was recovered from an Anglo-Saxon fill of barrow 13 (137, Fig. 3.115). Both the upper foil and the backplate are made from sheet copper alloy, and were probably soldered together; the backplate has two rectangular slots to take the inserted fastenings, both of which are missing. The applied disc has simple nicked decoration around the perimeter, which reproduces a design found on simple cast disc brooches in the Upper Thames Valley.

Applied disc brooches are a comparatively rare class of hybrid brooch, characterised by a flat copper alloy sheet backplate and an upper disc ornamented like a simple disc brooch. Dickinson noted only four examples from the Upper Thames Valley, and suggested that production might have been limited to defined types. A design of nicked edges and concentric circles occurred on a pair of brooches from Long Wittenham I (Grave 75), and a pair decorated with concentric circles alone were recovered at Berinsfield, Wally Corner (Grave 125). Other examples noted by Dickinson, from East Shefford and the Avon valley incorporate bull's-eyes and raised and repoussé studs (Dickinson 1976, Vol 1, 190–192). More recently, further examples have been recovered at Alveston (Meaney 1964, 263) and a pair with undecorated fronts occurred in grave 146 at Lechlade, Butler's Field (Ager, forthcoming). A possible base of an applied disc brooch was also found in ditch 233 at West Stow (West 1985, fig. 229.24).

Distribution of this type, with a few exceptions, seems to be concentrated in the Upper Thames and Avon Valleys. Dickinson (1976) has postulated, because of their affinity with true disc brooches, that they were contemporary in production and use, and places the chief period of use between AD 450 and 550. The pair at Lechlade were found in a grave dated broadly to the 6th century. However, the examples from Alveston are from late 6th-century graves, and detailed examination has led the excavator to conclude that these particular brooches had a very long life, each one having gone through a series of repairs before deposition. They are therefore likely to be of an earlier date than the graves (W J Ford, pers. comm.).

A small fragment of an annular brooch was recovered from the backfill of SFB 39 (138, Fig. 3.90). It belongs to the class of annular brooches with flat-sectioned hoops made from sheet metal. Although the ratio of hoop width to overall diameter cannot be assessed from this fragment, the hoop is relatively narrow, and perhaps finds its closest local parallel with a brooch from Filkins 4, which has similar punched-dot decoration (see Dickinson 1976, 146, pl 42e). Annular brooches are comparatively rare in the Upper Thames Valley, and Dickinson considers brooches of this narrow 'Anglian' type to be imports from Anglian areas during the 6th century.

Bracelet

A single bracelet fragment was found in layer 2 of SFB 28 (142, Fig. 3.70). It was formed by twisting two lengths of cable around a central core, a common Roman type. Two twisted cable bracelets were found at West Stow, one in Building 7 and another in SFB 15 (West 1985, fig. 21B.7 and fig. 72.2). Another came from the upper fill of a Romano-British well at Barton Court Farm (Miles 1986, fig. 106.3).

Buckles and belt equipment

Very few items of belt equipment were found. A single iron D-shaped buckle, 180, was found in the Anglo-Saxon inhumation 5004 (Fig. 3.104). There are two studs, 152 from SFB 2 (Fig. 3.14) and 151 from the fill of barrow 13 (Fig. 3.115), which may have been from belts. Number 149, from SFB 4 (Fig. 3.19), is a perforated plain mount, and this and the mount 154 with punched dot decoration from SFB 23 (Fig. 3.59) could have been belt stiffeners. Number 167 from SFB 23 (Fig. 3.60), 148 from SFB 28 (Fig. 3.70), 160 from the fill of barrow ditch 13 (Fig. 3.115) and 161, which is unstratified (Fig. 3.105), are all probably parts of strap-end buckles or buckle plates. They are all made of simple copper alloy sheets. Number 167 has traces of solder and 161 has traces of gilding. Both these items have been broken in antiquity and rolled up into parcels, probably so that the copper alloy could be melted down and reused.

Toilet items

The most common toilet items from Anglo-Saxon graves are tweezers, picks and scoops, often found in sets on a ring for suspension from a belt, although they may occur individually. With the exception of tweezers, all the toilet items from cemeteries in the Upper Thames region are found in female graves (Dickinson 1976, 220). One of each of these items was recovered from the settlement at Barrow Hills. A pair of tweezers, 145, came from the fill of SFB 40 (Fig. 3.92). They are of a very simple form, made from a strip of copper alloy folded over to form a ring at one end, probably for suspension. Similar plain tweezers have been found in Cremation 2616/1 at Spong Hill (Hills *et al.* 1987, 62, fig. 101) and at Droxford (Aldsworth 1979, fig. 34.33). A single copper alloy scoop with a broken spatulate end, 144, was found in SFB 25 (Fig. 3.64). It is not certain if this item was made for suspension; the small scooped end is very corroded and may be pierced. A similar plain scoop was found in Grave 5 at Abingdon (Leeds and Harden 1936, 32). The majority of ear scoops from Anglo-Saxon cemeteries in the Upper Thames region

belong to the 5th or early 6th centuries, but there are later examples (Dickinson 1976, 224).

Object 150 from SFB 10 was probably a pick (Fig. 3.31), although it is difficult to distinguish single picks from pins, which can be of very similar form. Number 150 has a very small head which has been flattened and pierced. The hole is covered with iron concretion, probably the remains of an iron suspension ring. There was a single pick suspended on a loop from cremation 28 at Abingdon I and another from Grave 60 (Leeds and Harden 1936, 17, pl III; pl XII). Number 146 is an unstratified pin which has been broken across its perforation and has incised lines below the head (Fig. 3.105); it also may be a pick, although decorated picks are rare. A small wire loop from SFB 28, 147, with one hooked and one broken terminal, may be a loop from an individual toilet item or a set (Fig. 3.70).

Dress pins

Seamus Ross has undertaken a study of pins from Anglo-Saxon contexts and, where possible, his typology has been followed (Ross 1991). Number 143 from SFB 28 is a large pin of Ross's type V with a sharply carinated flattened biconical head and a length greater than 90 mm (Fig. 3.70). The tapering shaft is decorated with incised rings with a central faceted section, which has been gilded. Ross dates these pins to the last third of the 5th century. Other examples from this group come from Brighthampton, Oxfordshire (Grave 18: Ashmolean Museum 1966.50) and Alton, Hants. (Evison 1988, Grave 35). However, none of the examples in his group have flattened heads like 143. Pins with biconical heads and ribbed and faceted upper shafts are common from sites in north-western Europe at the beginning of the 5th century. A similar example has been found at Wijster in Holland and Van Es cites a number of further parallels with ribbed and faceted decoration below the head from Cuyk, Maas near Maren, and Rossum, all in Holland (Van Es 1967, 143, fig. 69.42, fig. 70.1,2 and 3). Other pins with flattened biconical heads have been found at excavations in both Southampton and York (Ross 1991, 282–8), but these have smaller heads and appear to be of a type common during the 7th and 8th centuries (Ross's type LXVIII).

Pin 306, from SFB 9 (Fig. 3.30), is a small bone pin with a thistle head and hipped shaft. Pins of this type are uncommon from Anglo-Saxon contexts. There are three copper alloy examples belonging to Ross's type XXXVIII from Castle Bytham, Lincs., Bawsey (Norfolk) and Dover (Ross 1991, 222; Evison 1987, fig. 62.160). Ross considers this to be a 7th-century type, but evidence is limited. Short bone hipped pins with a ball-like head have been found at Little Wilbraham (Lethbridge 1931, fig. 3.2) and Sarre, Kent (Payne 1892), and these have been dated to the 6th or 7th centuries (MacGregor 1985, 117). Stevenson (1955, 285–6) states that pins with hipped shafts span the 6th to 9th centuries. They are usually identified as dress pins used in loosely woven garments (Oakley 1979, 308). A shaft from a bone pin, 307, was found in the backfill of SFB 33 (Fig. 3.80). It has two bands of lathe-turned spiral decoration on the shaft, but the head is missing.

Pin 141, from the Anglo-Saxon inhumation 5004, has a disc head with an off-centre perforation (Fig. 3.104). A wire ring would have passed through the hole, but this is now missing. Number 141 has a tapering undecorated shaft and is very similar to early 7th-century examples from West Stow (West 1985, fig. 266.6, fig. 246.3). On another example from Dover the ring is still in place (Evison 1987, fig. 48.101.1). One from Colchester comes from a context dated to the late 6th or 7th centuries (Crummy 1988, 6, fig. 2.3). Other examples from the Upper Thames region come from Standlake Down (Ashmolean Museum 1921.1114) and Abingdon Grave 106, with incised ornament on the shank (Leeds and Harden 1936, 51–2). Ross dates this type to the late 6th or early 7th centuries (Ross 1991, 370).

Combs

Fragments of 23 combs were recovered. Where enough of the comb remains, it can be seen that they are all double-sided composite combs made of antler. The combs fall into three groups.

The majority of the combs form a very homogeneous group with elongated outlines and rectangular end plates with graduated teeth, a standard type in the Anglo-Saxon period. All except one of the combs have rectangular straight-sided connecting plates. The exception is 312, from layer 2 in SFB 12 (Fig. 3.36), which has a convex outline. There are slight differences in the cross-sections of the connecting plates. The majority are D-shaped with both flat and more bulbous cross-sections. There are also examples with trapezoidal sections and one with a rectangular section, all of which can be paralleled on other Anglo-Saxon sites.

The teeth were cut after the blanks had been riveted together, resulting in saw marks cut into the connecting plates. On the comb already mentioned from SFB 12, 312, these saw marks have been incorporated into the decorative scheme. The majority of the combs have teeth cut on both sides of almost the same size, either 4 or 5 per cm, sometimes with a slight variation between the two sides. However, there are two combs, 312 from SFB 12 (Fig. 3.36) and 330 from SFB 11 (Fig. 3.33), which have a combination of three and six and four and eight teeth per cm respectively. Although there is a variation in teeth size on each side of these combs, neither could be described as having fine teeth like those on earlier Roman combs.

Five of the combs are decorated. Number 314 from SFB 20 (Fig. 3.53), 315 from SFB 6 (Fig. 3.23) and 313 from the ditch fill of barrow 12 (Fig. 3.112) have been decorated with simple ring- and-dot motifs. Decoration on 314 and 315 consists of a dot and single ring. Number 313 has a central dot and two rings.

The central dots on the end plates have been perforated. Number 312 from SFB 12 is a more highly decorated example, with additional incised lines and cross-hatching. Cross-hatching was a common decorative motif on Anglo-Saxon combs and several examples can be seen on combs from Shakenoak (Brodribb *et al.* 1972).

The second group is made up of two comb fragments: 329 from SFB 29 (Fig. 3.70) and 331 (Fig. 3.105) which was unstratified. Unfortunately, not enough of these combs survives to allow them to be classified, but they both have a set of fine teeth and a set of coarse teeth. Number 329 averages 4 and 10 teeth per cm and 333 averages 5 and 9 teeth per cm. Both combs have a set of very finely cut teeth, a feature not normally noted on Anglo-Saxon combs but common on combs of the Roman period.

The third group consists of a single end plate fragment from the fill of the ditch of barrow 12, 321 (Fig. 3.117). This has a very wide solid zone, and as well as having a rivet hole has two additional perforations. Combs with decorative profiling of the end plates are common from the second half of the 4th century onwards (MacGregor 1985, 92), and two combs with similar perforated end plates have come from graves 333 and 402 at Lankhills, dated AD 390–410 (Clarke 1979, fig. 31.316 and 521).

HORSE EQUIPMENT

A single horseshoe, 190, was found in the Anglo-Saxon fill of the ditch of barrow 13 (Fig. 3.115). Horseshoes are rare from pre-Conquest sites. The webb or section is usually wide but made of a much thinner bar iron than that of the later types, the widths of the arms generally being between 20–30 mm (Goodall 1990, 1055). The nail holes, which are usually three on each side, have circular holes and rectangular countersinkings. The edges, as on 190, are usually smooth or slightly wavy (Clark 1986); 190 is of this early type. It has two clenched nails still in place. Nails with fiddle heads are usually used with this type of horseshoe but, as with 190, they are generally worn to a T-shape. Two more horseshoe nails were recovered from SFB 4 (248) and SFB 6 (249), but both have damaged heads. There was a 9th-century example of this type of horseshoe from Winchester (Goodall 1990, 1055, fig. 340.3939) and several 9th- to 10th-century examples were found at Thetford (Rogerson and Dallas 1984, 104, fig. 142).

Two iron objects, 220 from the Anglo-Saxon fill of the ditch of barrow 12 (Fig. 3.111) and 221 from SFB 43 (Fig. 3.98), are possibly parts of bridle bits. They are short rods with loops at each end. On both examples the second loop has broken. The loops are set in different planes, at right-angles to each other. Complete links of this type are often identified as parts of two-link snaffle bits, although positive identification of fragments is more difficult (Manning 1985, 66). Two-link snaffle bits were in use in the Iron Age; they were very popular throughout the Roman period (Manning 1985, 66) and continued to be used in the medieval period (LMMC 1940, 81, fig. 19b.II). A group of links from snaffle bits from Shakenoak have been discussed and a number of further parallels cited (Brodribb *et al.* 1972, fig. 39, 167–70).

WEAPONRY

A possible arrowhead, 181, was recovered from the fill of SFB 28 (Fig. 3.70). It has a tiny leaf-shaped blade and a split socket. It is too small to be included in Swanton's Class C1 (Swanton 1974, fig. 2a). Arrowheads are unusual finds from Anglo-Saxon sites, although four were found at the settlement site at West Stow (West 1985, fig. 241.1–4). There is another example from the Upper Thames from Chinnor I which is of the same type and length as 181 (Dickinson 1976). Four probable spear or arrowhead fragments were recorded from the Anglo-Saxon settlement at Mucking (Hamerow 1993, 69, fig. 83.3, 89.3, 116.7). Number 182 (Fig. 3.111), from the Anglo-Saxon fill of the ditch of barrow 12, is fragmentary and may have been a spearhead, although it is not possible to discern the original blade shape. Two simple conical iron ferrules were recovered from SFB 3, 183 (Fig. 3.16), and SFB 11, 184 (Fig. 3.33). These are common finds on Anglo-Saxon sites with examples from Abingdon (Leeds and Harden 1936) and West Stow (West 1985, fig. 241.12–15). They could have been put to a number of uses such as shoeing the ends of sticks or spears. Many examples have been found in graves in association with spearheads, for example in Grave 24, Fonaby, Lincs., (Cook 1981, 26–28, fig. 27) and Abingdon Grave 49 (Leeds and Harden 1936, 40, pl XVIII).

DOMESTIC EQUIPMENT

Lock and keys

Part of a barb spring padlock bolt 189 was recovered from SFB 40 (Fig. 3.92). It is similar to a more corroded example found in a mid to late 4th-century context at Colchester (Crummy 1981, 168, fig. 206.4694). The number of leaf springs could be varied on such padlocks and 189 has a double leaf spring set in different planes. The padlock would have been opened by drawing or pushing a padlock key along the springs, compressing them and thereby ejecting the bolt. Number 185 from SFB 21 (Fig. 3.55) is the handle of a key used with this type of lock and 188 from the Anglo-Saxon fill of barrow 12 is the simple bit and part of the stem from a barb spring padlock key (Fig. 3.111). The rods with bent-up ends recovered from SFB 33, 187 (Fig. 3.80), and the fill of barrow ditch 13, 186 (Fig. 3.115), could also be simple keys, but identification is extremely tentative. Simple objects like these are more positively identified as keys when found in graves, for example in Grave 25, Fonaby, Lincs. (Cook 1981,

fig. 9.4). An unusual object from SFB 3, 215 (Fig. 3.16), could possibly be a latch lifter or a lift key from a tumbler lock. Keys for such locks were often T-or L-shaped. Although no precise parallels can be found for 215, there are similar keys from Graves 134 and 369 at Morning Thorpe, Norfolk (Green *et al.* 1987, fig. 343.F and 428.Ui).

Vessels

Although no wooden vessels survive from the site, four items which were probably fittings from buckets were found. Number 192, part of an iron handle, was recovered from SFB 1 (Fig. 3.11). It is similar to a complete handle seen on a bucket in Grave 27 at Alton, Hampshire (Evison 1988, 78, fig. 31). It could also be a handle from a cauldron, like that seen on a copper alloy cauldron from Grave 200, Morning Thorpe (Green *et al.* 1987, 87, fig. 356.Ai). Number 191 from SFB 10 is a bucket loop fitting (Fig. 3.31). It has pointed tips for driving into the wood and would have been used to attach the handle. A copper alloy bucket loop fitting of the same form was found with a set of wooden buckets in the 4th-century Saetrang find in Norway (Slomann 1959, 56, Pl III). Anglo-Saxon buckets found in graves often had strap-end loops to attach the handles. 217 from SFB 4 could possibly be a fragment of one these (Fig. 3.19).

Number 155, which was unstratified, is characteristic of copper alloy repair fittings for wooden vessels (Fig. 3.105). They are small U-sectioned sheets which are fastened with rivets, and often still have remains of wood adhering, as in examples from Grave 34 at Spong Hill (Hills *et al.* 1984, 84, fig. 90.34). Two further examples of repair pieces came from *Grubenhäuser* 63 and 81 at Mucking (Hamerow 1993, 60 figs 121.1, 132.2).

Iron implements

Tools

There are very few objects which can be specifically identified as tools and no large tools survive from the site. There are three iron awls. Two are unstratified, 208 and 209 (Fig. 3.105). The third, 207, came from SFB 2 (Fig. 3.14). They are all of the same type, with diamond or square cross-sectioned tangs and circular cross-sectioned points, the most common type in the Roman period (Manning 1985, 40). A complete awl from West Stow SFB 56 (West 1985, fig. 188.1) is of the same type, with its antler handle still in place. Two from York still have wooden handles (MacGregor 1978, fig. 26). Other examples from Anglo-Saxon contexts were found at Shakenoak (Brodribb *et al.* 1972, fig. 52.315), Mucking (Hamerow 1993, 69, figs 132.3, 153.2) and at the Middle Saxon smelting site at Ramsbury, Wiltshire (Haslem *et al.* 1980, fig. 21, 9–13). Awls would have had many uses, particularly for piercing hides in leatherworking.

Number 206 from SFB 39 is a lanceolate terminal from a tool, probably part of a drill bit (Fig. 3.90). Drill bit heads are readily identifiable and the flattened form of 206 is often found on spoon bits and augers (Manning 1985, 25, fig. 5); a complete spoon bit from York has a similar flat lanceolate head (MacGregor 1978, fig. 26.7). Drill bits must have been used on articles from the site, for example to drill the holes in the bone spindlewhorls and the suspension holes in combs.

Knives

Thirteen knives (193–205) were recovered, ten in the fills of SFBs. SFBs 6, 7, 14, 15, 20 and 32 each contained one knife (Figs 3.23, 3.26, 3.40, 3.44, 3.53, 3.80) and SFBs 40 and 43 each contained two knives (Figs 3.92 and 3.99). Another knife came from the Anglo-Saxon inhumation 5004 (Fig. 3.104) and one was found in the Anglo-Saxon fill of barrow ditch 12 (Fig. 3.111). The remaining knife was unstratified (Fig. 3.105). The knives in SFBs 6, 14, 20 and 43 were found in association with whetstones.

Discussion of the knives and razors (Tables 5.1–2) by Guy Grainger

The iron knives (193–205) from Barrow Hills have been described according to the typology devised for the knives from the Anglo-Saxon cemetery at Finglesham, Kent (Grainger 2006) which was, in turn, a subdivision of the classes distinguished by Böhner for the 5th- to 7th-century knives of the Trier region (Böhner 1958, 214). The forms encountered at Barrow Hills are listed in Table 5.1.

Böhner concluded that, in the Trier region, Class A was in use from the 5th to 7th centuries and Class B, an important type in the 5th to 6th centuries, went out of use in the 7th century. Class C appeared only at the beginning of the 7th century but it was the major 7th-century form. Hawkes has pointed out that Böhner's classification and dating appear to be valid for early Anglo-Saxon examples (1973, 199) and this seems to be borne out by the recent evaluations of the knives from Finglesham, Kent, and Kingsworthy, Hampshire (Grainger 2006; unpublished).

Although the numbers involved at Barrow Hills are small the trend is clear – Class A appears to be the major form while there is just one certain example of Class C, and inclined backs (Type 1) dominate with just three examples of straight backs (Type 2) and no raised backs (Types 3 and 4). The Barrow Hills distribution is therefore very similar to the Kingsworthy sample, but noticeably different from the Finglesham group of knives.

The Barrow Hills knives cannot indicate whether settlement commenced in the 5th- or 6th-century but as a group they appear to be a chiefly 5th- to 6th-century assemblage. The single certain Class C knife (202, SFB 40, Fig. 3.92) suggests that deposition continued up to the beginning of the 7th century, but

Table 5.1 Distribution of major knife forms at Barrow Hills, Kingsworthy and Finglesham.

Site/class	Type (no. of examples)						Total
	1	1/2	2	3	4	?	
Barrow Hills							
Class A	4		2				6
Class C	1						1
Class ?	5		1				6
Total	10		3				13
Kingsworthy							
Class A	21		7				28
Class B	1		5				6
Class C	3		2				5
Class ?	4	1				2	7
Total	29	1	14			2	46
Finglesham							
Class A	1		17	2	1		21
Class B	1		9	1			11
Class C	3		47	8	16		74
Class ?	1		9			5	15
Total	6		82	11	17	5	121

Table 5.2 Distribution of knife forms.

Class	Type 1 (inclined back)				Type 2 (straight back)	
	a	b	c	?	b	c
A		193, 194	195, 196		200	201
A/B	197					
A/C		198, 199				
C			202			
?					203, 204	205

with the absence of further examples, the site probably did not remain in use long after *c* AD 600.

Razors

Although the razors (178 from the ditch of barrow 12, Fig. 3.112, and 179 from a possible Saxon posthole, Fig. 3.105) differ somewhat in length, they are of the same basic form, sharing slightly convex blade edges with short angled leading edges and a squared blade end. In addition the slightly concave or inclined back appears to terminate in each case in a small projection at the blade end, while the tang curves sharply upwards.

Although razors occur commonly in the Anglo-Saxon (Anglian) cremation cemeteries of the 5th to 6th centuries in England, the burials from Spong Hill, Norfolk (Hills 1977; Hills and Penn 1980), Caistor-by-Norwich and Markshall, Norfolk (Myres and Green 1973), and Thurmaston, Leicestershire (Williams 1983) failed to provide a convincing parallel. No razors were recognised by the excavators at the 5th- to 7th-century Anglo-Saxon village at West Stow, Suffolk, and while it is possible that some of the very small 'knives' were in fact used as razors (eg West 1985, fig. 240.11 and 28), there is nothing that resembles the Barrow Hills razors.

Slight upward-curving tangs are seen on a number of folding knives of 7th- to 8th-century date from the Alamannic cemetery at Reichenhall, Switzerland (Schneider 1983, 235–239). Stein, considering grave finds of the late 7th to 8th centuries in Germany, notes that folding knives (*Klappmesser*) are often called razors because of their similar form, although folding knives differ from simple razors in occasionally being found in female graves (Stein 1967, 37). The Barrow Hills examples are undoubtedly simple razors, as radiographs indicate that they lack the rivet holes that are a feature of the folding knives. The squared ends of the Barrow Hills razors do not seem to be a common feature of these continental 7th- to 8th-century knives though they are apparently matched by one folding knife, from Wiestock, Germany, grave 17 (Stein 1967, 300, fig. 39). The Wiestock example also has a small projection at the junction of the blade end and back, and an upcurved tang, though of a somewhat different type to the Barrow Hill razors.

The upcurved tang appears to be a very long-lived characteristic, being visible through the iron supporting plates of a folding knife (no. 1639) and on a single loose bone supporting plate of a razor (no. 2340), from Portchester Castle, Hampshire, both of late 18th- or early 19th-century date (Garratt 1994, 122 and fig. 36, no. 49).

It therefore seems most unlikely that the Barrow Hills razors are of 5th- to 6th-century date, but they may well be of 7th- to 8th-century date. However, the possibility that they could be later, perhaps even of medieval or postmedieval date, cannot be ruled out.

Nails

Twenty-eight iron nails were recovered from the site. Number 242 from SFB 1 is a Roman hobnail. Numbers 247 from SFB 6 and 248 from SFB 4 are horseshoe nails. Fifteen are shank fragments. The remaining ten can be grouped into three types:
Type 1 T-shaped heads with shanks of square or rectangular cross-section. (3 examples)
Type 2 Circular flat heads with shank of square or rectangular cross-section. (5 examples)
Type 3 Small flat heads which are a slight expansion of the square cross-sectioned shank. (2 examples)

They are all woodworking nails and are similar to types which occur in the Roman (Manning 1985, 63, types 1, 3, and 5) and medieval periods (Goodall 1980, types 1, 3, and 6). Woodworking nails were

found in SFBs 12, 14, 15, 17/18, 23, 26, and 29. There were no concentrations in any of the buildings and none came from occupation layers.

TEXTILE EQUIPMENT

There are several categories of artefacts used in the various stages of textile manufacture. Before wool can be spun, it must be combed and carded to remove tangles and dirt. This makes the fibres lie smooth and parallel before they are spun into yarn and was often undertaken with objects known as wool carding combs and heckles. These were T-shaped implements with rows of iron teeth set in wood, probably strengthened with iron. Individual teeth, which are probably from heckles, have been found in SFB 31 (213, Fig. 3.78), SFB 33 (210, Fig. 3.80) and SFB 42 (212, Fig. 3.97), and in the Anglo-Saxon fill of barrow 12 (211, Fig. 3.111). Heckle teeth have been found at other Anglo-Saxon sites at Shakenoak, Oxfordshire (Brodribb *et al.* 1972, 134), and at West Stow (West 1985, 124). Some examples from West Stow had traces of wood and replaced wool fibres attached (Crowfoot 1985, 70). A complete heckle has been found at the middle Saxon site at Wicken Bonhunt (West 1985, 124). Heckles were also used to remove seeds and split fibres during the preparation of flax before spinning. Although no flax remains were found at Barrow Hills, there is evidence of flax at Barton Court Farm (Jones and Robinson 1986, 9:E13).

The production of enough yarn for even one garment requires many hours of hand spinning, and it is not surprising to find that spinning was taking place at the site. Thread is produced by using the rotating spindle, weighted by the whorl, to draw out and twist the prepared wool. Spindles would probably have been made of wood or iron, like the one from Sutton Courtenay (Leeds 1924, pl XXII). No spindles survive from this site, although it is possible that some of the fragmentary iron rods could be parts of spindles.

Thirteen spindlewhorls were found. Two are unstratified (447, Fig. 3.106; 346, Fig. 3.105), nine were single finds in the backfills of SFBs 14 (441, Fig. 3.40), 17/18 (348, Fig. 3.49), 23 (404, Fig. 3.59), 26 (446, not illustrated), 32 (445, Fig. 3.80), 33 (442, Fig. 3.80), 40 (444, Fig. 3.93), 43 (443, Fig. 3.98) and 45 (344, Fig. 3.102), and two came from the backfill of SFB 38 (345 and 347, Figs 3.87–8). Of the five bone whorls, two were made from unmodified femur heads, 347 and 348. Number 344, a hemispherical whorl, and 346, an annular whorl, are also made from femur heads which have been lathe-turned and decorated with shallow concentric grooves. Number 345, an annular whorl also of bone, is very dense and heavy and is unlikely to have been made from a femur head. All the bone whorls except 347 and 348 are very worn on the undersides and have had extensive use.

There are six whorls of fired clay: 441 is complete and the remaining five are fragmentary (442–446).

Two are hemispherical and three are biconical in form. All are in a coarse Anglo-Saxon fabric. Of the remaining two spindlewhorls, one is a disc-shaped whorl made from a base sherd of a Roman pot and the other is a hemispherical whorl of shale. Five disc-shaped spindlewhorls of shale were recovered from the Anglo-Saxon settlement at Mucking (Hamerow 1993, 65).

All the whorls have been weighed and, where they are incomplete, the total weight has been estimated. The whorls fall into three groups: 8–12 g, 21–39 g and a single exceptional whorl weighing 54 g. The smallest group is considerably below the average weight of 20–30 g for whorls alone quoted by Wild (1988, 25). It is difficult to relate the size of whorl to the type of thread being spun, as much depends on the diameter and length of the fibres as well as the skill of the spinner. However, it would seem probable that the lighter whorls were being used to spin finer threads and the heaviest whorl, 443, could have been used for stronger, coarser yarns or for plying threads together. Spindlewhorls are common finds from Anglo-Saxon settlement sites, with a good group from Sutton Courtenay (Leeds 1924, pl XXVIII fig. 1; pl XXIX fig. 1). Over 80 were found at West Stow (West 1985, 139). The relatively small number found at Barrow Hills may reflect the use of different materials. Spindles with integral whorls turned from a single piece of wood are still in use in Europe and the Near East and would not survive in the archaeological record (see Wild 1988, 25; 1970, 32–3).

The discovery of loomweights and pin beaters suggests that weaving was being undertaken at the site. Loomweights were used with the warp-weighted loom, where the vertical warp threads were put under tension by attaching weights to their ends. Seventeen loomweights were recovered. One was found in each of the backfills of SFBs 1 (452), 25 (460), 31 (458) and 42 (457), two in the backfill of SFB 23 (454 and 456) and three from SFB 24 (459, 463 and 464). A further five were found in the Anglo-Saxon fills of barrow 13 close to SFBs 23 and 24 (448, 451, Fig. 3.115; 452, 455, 461 – not illustrated), one in the fill of pit 416 in the north-west quadrant of barrow 13 (462, not illustrated), and two were from pit 4829 (449 and 450, Fig. 3.106). All the weights are of the same annular form, a type which made an early appearance in Anglo-Saxon England (MacGregor 1982). All except one of the weights have been roughly made in a coarse tempered fabric. There has been a rough attempt to smooth the exteriors. Only one weight, 458 (not illustrated) from a posthole of SFB 31, has been made in a finer fabric which has been well finished. Groups of loomweights have been found at Sutton Courtenay (Leeds 1924, 19, pl XXVI fig. 3) and over 60 examples were found in a large sunken-featured building at Upton, Northants, dating to the 6th or early 7th century (Jackson *et al.* 1969, 210). Thirteen lead loomweights and fragments of clay loomweights were found on the floor of SFB 1190 at Barton Court Farm (Miles 1986; see Chapter 3, Gazetteer 5). Twenty-two sunken-featured buildings

at West Stow contained loomweights (West 1985, 138), and over 106 loomweights of which 88 were identified as of annular type were found at Mucking (Hamerow 1993, 66).

Where enough of a loomweight has survived it has been weighed and its total weight estimated. These weights range between 259 and 747 grammes and their diameters range between 90 and 160 mm. A fragment of Roman tile, 448, was recovered from the Anglo-Saxon fill of the ditch of barrow 13 (Fig. 3.115). It has been chipped into a circle and perforated off-centre. It may be a loomweight but its size and weight (diameter 70 mm, weight 180.27 g) fall well outside the range of the fired clay weights. A fragment of a stone weight, 436, from the fill of barrow 13 (Fig. 3.115) may also be a loomweight but it weighs much more than those in fired clay. Although the group of loomweights from Barrow Hills is too small for further statistical analysis all weights and diameters fall within the ranges noted in the analysis of a large group of loomweights from the Anglo-Saxon settlement at Mucking (Hamerow 1993, figs 44 and 46).

Nine pin beaters were recovered. One was found in each of SFBs 1 (356, Fig. 3.11), 17/18 (343, Fig. 3.49), 41 (350, Fig. 3.95), and 45 (353, Fig. 3.102), two in each of SFBs 26 (351 and 354, Fig. 3.66) and 38 (349 and 355, Fig. 3.87), and one was from a posthole cutting the inner ditch of the oval barrow (352, Fig. 3.105). A fragment of a possible pin beater was found in SFB 24 (357). Pin beaters are shafts of bone which have been carved to a point at both ends and are typical of the early Saxon period, with groups from the Anglo-Saxon settlements at West Stow and Sutton Courtenay (West 1985; Leeds 1924, pl XXIX fig. 1). They were used with the warp-weighted loom to separate the warp threads when the shed was being changed (Hoffmann 1964). In most cases they have been highly polished, presumably to aid use and to prevent snagging on the threads. The points are not always the same; some have finer and some more rounded ends. The pin beaters from Barrow Hills fall into two main groups. Three have been classified as Type 1, long and slender with lengths ranging from 127 to 132 mm. They have sharp points at both ends and taper fairly evenly from the centre. Examples of this type came from SFBs 26, 38 and 41. Type 2 pin beaters are small and cigar-shaped. They range in length from 77–105 mm and taper towards the ends into fatter, squatter and more blunted points. Examples of this type were found in SFBs 1, 26, 38 and 45, and one was unstratified. An exceptional beater from SFB 17/18 is of the same basic shape as those of Type 1, but is nearly twice as long as any of the other examples. Five of the pin beaters were single finds but SFBs 26 and 38 each contained two pin beaters, one each of Types 1 and 2. It seems likely that pin beaters of Types 1 and 2 had slightly differing functions and may have been used with different types of cloth.

The presence of loomweights and pin beaters in the backfill of sunken-featured buildings is not an indication that weaving was taking place in those particular buildings, but suggests that weaving was taking place at the site, although the small number of loomweights and spindlewhorls found from the site contrasts markedly with the large quantities found at the settlement site at West Stow (West 1985). This quantity of loomweights could conceivably have been used on a single loom. The largest concentration on the site is six, in the fill of the ditch of barrow 13 and an adjacent pit. SFB 24, which abuts the ditch of barrow 13, and SFB 23, which is adjacent to barrow 13, contained three and two weights respectively. The finds in the ditch of barrow 13 are general rubbish.

Pins/needles

There are 21 bone pins/needles made from modified pigs' fibulae. They have triangular heads and all except one example are pierced. Twelve sunken-featured buildings contained one such object in their backfills: 2 (375, Fig. 3.11), 6 (365, Fig. 3.23), 8 (363, Fig. 3.28), 10 (366, Fig. 3.31), 14 (360, Fig. 3.40), 24 (364, Fig. 3.62), 26 (373, Fig. 3.66), 35 (369, Fig. 3.82), 38 (370, Fig. 3.87), 40 (361, Fig. 3.93), 42 (374, Fig. 3.97), and 43 (359, Fig. 3.98). SFB 28 yielded two, one perforated and one unperforated (358 and 378, Fig. 3.70). SFBs 6 and 39 produced bone points which could be from the same type of pin (377 and 376). Three were found in the Anglo-Saxon fill of barrow 12 (362, Fig. 3.112, 367, 371) and one in the Anglo-Saxon fill of barrow 13 (372, Fig. 3.115), and the remaining pin, 368, is from pit 4798, near SFB 43 (not illustrated).

Pins of this type are commonly found on settlement sites and are often associated with other finds used in the manufacture of textiles. Their function is uncertain but it seems likely that they could be used for a number of purposes. Although it is agreed that they are too coarse to be used as needles in ordinary sewing (Ambrosiani 1981, 135–6), it has been suggested that 'tools like these are used for auxiliary textile techniques such as netting and looped needle netting practised in the North from the Bronze Age onwards' (Hald 1950, 461–2). They could also have been used for making stockings or shrouds by mesh knitting, a method practised until knitting was discovered (Lindstrom 1976, 275; Knock 1976, 12). Another use has been suggested by Marta Hoffman, who describes how in the Faroes exactly similar needles were placed at the selvage edge of the cloth on the loom and held the cords which were used to fasten the edges of the woven cloth to the uprights in order to maintain an even width (Hoffmann 1964, 145–6; Rogerson and Dallas 1984, 167). At Barrow Hills, however, only four of these pins were found in sunken-featured buildings in association with other weaving equipment and only five in association with spindlewhorls. There is also evidence that such pins were used as dress fasteners. MacGregor suggests that the perforations may have had a retaining cord passed through them

(MacGregor 1985, 121). Two such pins were recovered near the neck of the occupant of Grave 61 at Wakerley (Adams 1983, 54–55, fig. 55.1–2), and unperforated examples such as 378 could have been used as awls. These pins, which first appear in the pre-Roman Iron Age (MacGregor 1985), are used throughout the Anglo-Saxon period; there were 37 examples from the settlement site at West Stow (West 1985, 125). However, the type is long-lived, and examples have been found in 9th- to 10th-century contexts at Thetford (Rogerson and Dallas 1984, 167) and 9th- to 12th-century contexts at Lincoln (Mann 1982, fig. 6.45, 49 and 50).

The presence of associated artefacts from the site is evidence that different stages of textile manufacture were being undertaken. Wool was being combed and spinning was taking place. There is no concentration in the distribution of spindlewhorls throughout the site, with one and sometimes two occurring in the fills of a sunken-featured building. Only one, from SFB 14, is possibly associated with an occupation layer. Spinning is a fairly simple activity and one which would probably have been undertaken by members of every household. The lack of loomweights from the site would suggest that weaving was not a major occupation, although the quantity of associated textile equipment, such as pin beaters and pig fibula pins/needles, is greater and the distribution much wider. It is probable that such small implements were more easily lost and that items such as loomweights were only discarded when broken. It is possible, however, that looms were shared and were moved around from building to building, as has been suggested at West Stow (West 1985). Twenty-three sunken-featured buildings contained textile equipment. These are fairly well distributed amongst the sunken-featured buildings in the southern half of the site, although SFBs 32, 33, 34, 38, 39, 40 and 43 in the northern half also have textile equipment in their fills. There are, however, two definite groups of sunken-featured buildings which did not contain any artefacts associated with textile manufacture. They are SFBs 9, 12, 20, 21, 22 in the far north of the site and 4, 5, 7, 15, 16 and 19 to the north-west of the cemetery.

Antler working

Nine fragments of antler-working waste were found. All are from red deer. There were single fragments in the backfills of SFBs 1 (390, Fig. 3.11), 11 (392), 17/18 (399, Fig. 3.49), 26 (398) and 38 (394), two fragments in SFB 28 (395 and 400), and a single fragment in each of the Anglo-Saxon fills of barrow ditches 12 and 13 (393 and 391). All these pieces are left over from the operation of detaching sections of the beam for antler working. They include tines, burrs and crowns and they are probably debris from comb-making. Apart from utilised tines, combs are the only antler artefacts from the site. Segments of beams would have been used to make the teeth and connecting plates after first removing the crown, lower tines and the burr. At Barrow Hills this was done in a number of ways. Saws were used on several of the pieces. On 392 the tines have been removed by sawing and the saw marks show that the antler was rotated so that the blade did not become embedded. When it had been sawn part way from four sides it was snapped off. The tines on 390 have also been removed by sawing, but in this case the saw has been taken right through almost to the edge and the last segment has been broken off. Number 391 shows how the saw has been used in two directions until the cuts met in the centre. The fragment 400 has been partly sawn through and then broken off. Other pieces, including 394, have had tines removed by partly chopping and then snapping them in two. Fragment 396 from SFB 23 (Fig. 3.59) is a quadrant from a beam which has been sawn and then longitudinally split. Ulbricht has published a schematic representation of the methods of cutting up and using antler and demonstrates that such quadrants could be utilised for making the teeth segments of combs (Ulbricht 1978). No fragments of partially made combs were found in the current excavations, but in 1968 a bone roughout, probably from a comb, was recovered from the site (Ashmolean Museum 1968.328). A series of antler points, pegs and handles made from modified tines were also found. Number 383 from the fill of barrow 12 (Fig. 3.112) is part of a tine which has been shaved and pierced at both ends; it is almost certainly a handle and was possibly broken in antiquity and reused by hollowing out the other end. Number 384 from SFB 43 (Fig. 3.99) is another section of a tine; the ends have been removed by sawing, the larger end has been hollowed out and the narrow end has been partly hollowed out and shaved on one side. It is not certain whether this object was ever put to use, possibly as a handle, or whether it is unfinished. Number 397 from SFB 28 (Fig. 3.70), 382 from SFB 43 (Fig. 3.98) and 387 from SFB 4 (Fig. 3.18) are all shaved tines. 387 and 382 have sharpened points and 382 has been pierced. Two pierced antler tines were found at Shakenoak (Brodribb *et al.* 1972, fig. 60.73 and 75). Number 401 from the relic stream course (Fig. 3.105) is the tip of a tine which has had its end sharpened. These modified tines could have been put to a number of uses. A group found at York includes many with sharpened tips. MacGregor has suggested they could have been used for pegging out hides during tanning (1982, 100, fig. 53), but they could also have been put to a number of other uses, such as pegging timbers, and their exact function must remain uncertain. Number 380 from SFB 4 (Fig. 3.19) is a tine and part of the beam. It has extensive wear and is likely to have been used as a tool, possibly for scraping or digging.

REUSED ROMAN POTTERY (TABLE 5.3)

Counters and roughouts

By far the largest group of artefacts from the site consists of fragments of reused Roman pots which have been deliberately shaped into circles, half circles and wedges. Seventy-five examples were found. In addition, three counters in Anglo-Saxon fabrics were recovered and these have been included for the purposes of this discussion.

These objects could be divided into seven groups:

1 Small round counters with ground edges. (21)
2 Circular flat base roughouts with chipped edges. (4)
3 Circular roughouts of foot ring bases with chipped edges. (20)
4 Cut half circles from flat bases. (5)
5 Rough half circles of foot ring bases. (7)
6 Cut wedge-shaped fragments from flat bases. (6)
7 Rough wedge-shaped fragments of foot ring bases. (15)

Type 1 counters have been made principally from the body sherds of vessels which have been chipped or clipped to shape. The edges have then been ground down, possibly by rubbing on a whetstone or coarse surface.

The counters of types 2 and 3 are pot bases from which the walls have been roughly chipped off. No attempt has been made to smooth the broken edges. Types 4 and 6 have straight cut edges but the walls have again been roughly removed. Types 5 and 7 have been roughly fashioned to the appropriate shape. These sherds are not the result of accidental breakage and certainly had some use, possibly as gaming pieces and tokens, weights, household objects and for craft processes.

Games and tokens

Counters of type 1 are small and fairly uniform in size and they are likely to have been used as gaming pieces. Types 2 to 7 vary considerably in size. The complete bases, types 2 and 3, could conceivably be roughouts for gaming pieces, but they are much larger in diameter and are nearly all fragments of bases, whereas the counters of type 1 are all body sherds. Since they were fairly large they may not have been used in board games, but they could have formed part of some other type of game, for example one involving throwing, or a game that needed pieces of different value, hence the different shapes. Alternatively, they could have been used as reckoning counters, with different values according to shape.

Weights

It is possible that the counters may have been used as weights. All the pieces were weighed to see if there were any correlations and groupings within the different shapes and categories. The pieces weighed from 4 to 174 grammes. There were a number of small groupings but these seemed to be more a reflection

Table 5.3   Reused Roman pottery.

No	Context	Feature	Original	Dia (mm)	Fabric
1	u/s		cc beaker base (spindle whorl)	45	3
2	1/H/2	barrow 1	gw beaker base	50	11
3	1/C/3	barrow 1	body sherd	25	2
4	400	ploughsoil	body sherd	25	6
5	401/C/2	barrow 13	body sherd	35	3
6	401/H/2	barrow 13	base of jug or large flagon C8?	100	3
7	401/H/2	barrow 13	base of thick walled beaker	50	3
8	401/H/2	barrow 13	cut down grooved base	80	3
9	401/I/2	barrow 13	cut down foot ring base (Mort)	70	3
10	401/K/2	barrow 13	cut down foot ring base	110	3
11	401/M/2	barrow 13	cut down foot ring base	60	4
12	401/O/2	barrow 13	cut down grooved base (beaker)	50	3
13	401/P/2	barrow 13	cut down flat base	60	4
14	401/P/3	barrow 13	cut down foot ring base	45	9
15	600	ploughsoil	gw body sherd	25	6
16	600	ploughsoil	gw body sherd	25	4
17	601/A/1	barrow 12	cut down foot ring base	55	3
18	601/C/US	barrow 12	cut down foot ring base	100	3
19	601/I/2	barrow 12	cut down foot ring base	65	3
20	601/L/2	barrow 12	body sherd	c 80	5
21	601/L/3	barrow 12	cut down foot ring base	90	3
22	601/M/2	barrow 12	cut down flat base	c 130	2
23	1001	topsoil	cut down flat beaker base	35	3
24	1001	topsoil	cut down foot ring base	70	3
25	1001	topsoil	cut down foot ring base	c 80	3
26	1001	topsoil	cut down foot ring base	c 80	3
27	1001	topsoil	cut down flat (wedge shape) base	140	2
28	1005/A/2	SFB 1	cut down flat base	60	2
29	1005/C/2	SFB 1	cut down foot ring base	120	4
30	1061/A/1	SFB 3	cut down foot ring base	45	3
31	1061/D/2	SFB 3	cut down flat base	100	4
32	1225/B/1	SFB 5	cut down foot ring base	70	3
33	1281	PH SFB 5	cut down foot ring base	?170	8
34	1297/B/2	SFB 6	cut down flat base	110	4
35	1297/D/4	SFB 6	cut down foot ring base	65	3
36	1298/A/1	SFB 7	cut down foot ring base (Mort)	90	3
37	1440	PH PBS 1	cut down foot ring base	90	3
38	2065	topsoil	cut down flat base	75	2
39	3246/D/1	SFB 11	cut down foot ring base	85	3
40	3284/B/1	SFB 12	cut down foot ring base	75	3
41	3285/A/3	SFB 13	cut down grooved base (C8?)	80	3
42	3288	SFB 14	cut down foot ring base	80	3
43	3288/A/1	SFB 14	cut down foot ring base	60	9
44	3288/B/2	SFB 14	cut down foot ring base	c 80	8
45	3307/B/2	SFB 15	cut down grooved base	100	3
46	3341/B/2	SFB 17	cut down foot ring base	c 90	3
47	3441/D/2	SFB 17	cut down foot ring base	c 70	3
48	3441/-/1	SFB 17	cut down foot ring base	60	3
49	3443/B/1	PH of SFB 14	cut down foot ring base	55	3
50	3443/B/1	PH of SFB 14	cut down foot ring base	60	3
51	3542/A/1	SFB 19	cut down foot ring base	60	4
52	3542/C/1	SFB 19	cut down flat base	90	4
53	3551	AS pit	cut down foot ring base	50	3
54	3578/B/2	AS pit	cut down foot ring base	70	3
55	3608/C/2	SFB 22	cut down foot ring base	c 70	3
56	3800/B/3	SFB 23	cut down pedestal base	60	2
57	3800/D/3	SFB 23	cut down foot ring base	50	3

Table 5.3   (Continued)

No	Context	Feature	Original	D (mm)	Fabric
58	3811	SFB 25	cut down wedge shaped flat base	170	4
59	4001/A/3	SFB 26	cut down foot ring base	65	3
60	4001/C/3	SFB 26	body sherd (burnt)	40	8
61	4198/A/4	SFB 28	cut down foot ring base	c 100	3
62	4198/A/4	SFB 28	cut down foot ring base	50	3
63	4198/A/4	SFB 28	cut down foot ring base (beaker)	35	3
64	4198/C/2	SFB 28	cut down foot ring base	75	3
65	4198/D/1	SFB 28	cut down grooved base (bowl)	50	3
66	4459/C/1	PPH	body sherd	25	3
67	4561/D/1	SFB 35	cut down flat (wedge) base	140	2
68	4558/D/1	SFB 32	body sherd	25	3
69	4598/B/2	SFB 37	body sherd	20	3
70	4605/D/2	SFB 39	cut down foot ring base	75	3
71	4641/A/2	SFB 41	cut down grooved base (beaker)	35	3
72	4666/A/1	SFB 43	body sherd	20	2
73	4666/B/1	SFB 43	cut down foot ring base (Mort)	60	3
74	4666/B/2	SFB 43	cut down beaker base	40	3
75	4866/B/1	pond barrow	cut down foot ring base	55	9

of the types of pot utilised rather than of any attempt to cut the pieces to uniform weights. The foot ring wedges of type 7 were the only group with consistent weights. It has been concluded, therefore, that they were unlikely to have been used as weights. Nina Crummy arrived at a similar conclusion in her analysis of pottery roundels from Roman Colchester (Crummy 1983, 93).

Household uses

Complete bases, where they occur, have often been interpreted as pot lids, for example those from Sutton Courtenay (Leeds 1924, pl XXVI, fig. 1). It is difficult to see how those with foot ring bases could have operated in this way. Crummy, in her extensive discussion of counters from Roman Colchester, cites another theory, that complete bases could have been used as pot stands (Crummy 1981, 93–94; Addyman and Priestley 1977, 139). This is plausible, as the examples from Sutton Courtenay were found in association with hearths (Leeds 1924, 179). Those from Barrow Hills with foot ring bases would have been fairly stable, but this interpretation does not explain the examples that have been deliberately cut into half circles and wedges.

Craft processes

It is possible that the counters could have been used in some craft process that was taking place on the site. Complete bases may have been roughouts for spindlewhorls. There is, however, only one spindlewhorl made from a perforated potsherd from the site, the inhabitants preferring those of bone and fired clay.

Reused pottery pieces were found in 24 sunken-featured buildings. The only significant association with any other category of finds was that 11 of these sunken-featured buildings also contained textile equipment, but not every sunken-featured building whose fills contained textile equipment produced reused potsherds. For a discussion of the selection and retention of unworked Romano-British sherds see Chapter 2, Roman pottery.

Other groups of rough counters like these have been found at the Anglo-Saxon settlement site at Sutton Courtenay (Leeds 1924, pl XXVI, fig. 1). Although theories can be put forward for their use, it is most likely that they had several functions and their exact use will remain a subject of speculation.

SLAG
by Chris Salter

Introduction

The amount of metalworking slag recovered during this excavation (archive catalogue nos 599–613) was extremely small (925 g in all). This immediately suggests a number of possibilities:

a)   the amount of metalworking that took place on the site was very limited.

b)   the bulk of the slag produced was deposited in areas outside the excavation area and has therefore not been recovered.

c)   the slags found were samples scattered from a more important metalworking site situated outside the area of the excavation.

d)   most of the metal-working activity was iron-forging, the evidence for which can be difficult to recover, as it mainly consists of small flakes of friable hammer-scale.

All the metalworking debris examined was of a type consistent with the processing of iron, although the presence of some slags containing partially dissolved silica grains did suggest the possibility that some non-ferrous metalworking might have taken place on the site. At Hengistbury Head, the presence of such silica grains proved to be an indication that the slags were produced during the processing of copper-based alloys (Salter 1987). However, the examination of polished sections of these silica containing slags proved that they were generated during ironworking, as only metallic iron inclusions were observed, rather than the mixed sulphide and copper-rich inclusions noted at Hengistbury Head. There was also a sample of pottery that had been subjected to a short intense period of heating sufficient to vitrify only a thin surface layer of the sherd.

Detailed description of the samples

Group 1 – Small irregular elongate slags FSI

(archive catalogue nos 599–601, SFBs 36, 38, 31; lab. nos OX701, 705, 708)

This group of physically complete slag flows all had surfaces that felt rough to the touch and rounded or lobate external morphologies. The surface textures and shapes would seem to indicate that these slags were rather viscous, and thus were likely to have solidified within the furnace. This conclusion was confirmed by the scale of the phase distribution seen in the internal microstructure. Thus, it would seem that the furnace temperature was only a little above the melting point of these slags. As the compositions of these slags appears to be in the fayalite-wustite region of the wustite-silica-anorthite phase diagram, it is likely either that these slags were formed in the cooler part of the hearth, or that the furnace was being operated at relatively low temperatures probably in the range 1050–1100°C.

The operating temperature of a smithing hearth during normal forging operations would be between 500 and 950°C. These temperatures would not be sufficiently high to develop any of the types of slag seen in this collection. The debris characteristic of forging operations is a mixture of fragmented fuel and particles of hammer-scale, together with clinker which is formed immediately in front of the tuyère where the temperatures are higher. Usually, the characteristic hammer-scale is only recovered by the sorting of flotation residues produced when floor material has been treated to recover charcoal or carbonised seeds.

If welding operations were to be carried out the hearth temperature would have had to be raised into the range between 1150 and 1300°C for short periods. The duration of these periods at elevated temperatures would be determined by the thickness of the metal to be welded, as the time taken to raise the metal to welding temperature increases rapidly with thickness of section. This in turn would determine the thickness of oxide layer formed on the surface of the metal. This oxide layer reacts with the flux used during welding and fuel ash to form slag. However, if the artefacts being constructed were only small, for example sickles or spearheads,

then only small amounts of welding slags could be formed. Such slags would have the characteristic of those seen in this group of slags.

Group 2 – Slag flows FS

(archive catalogue nos 602–603, SFBs 44, 1; lab. nos OX703, 712)

There are some differences between the external and internal morphologies of these two samples, but they were placed in the same class as they were probably formed by the same process and seem to have solidified at a moderate rate. Although there is some evidence of chilling at both the top and bottom margins of sample 602, it is clear that the majority of the heat loss was from the lower surface of the slag. This, together with the general scale of phase distribution, suggests that this slag solidified within a furnace.

Sample 603 was slightly different, in that there was evidence that the upper surface of the flow had collapsed. This could have been caused by contraction of the liquid slag once a thin surface layer had solidified. However, the internal structure of this slag shows that the cooling rate had increased markedly part way through the solidification process. Therefore, it is more likely that the slag was removed from the furnace when a thin crust of slag had formed on the upper surface, and some of the liquid slag escaped leaving the collapsed and decanted surface structure seen.

Although these samples are more massive than the slags of group 1 (125 g and approximately 200 g against an average of 40 g for Group 1 slags), they are not on the scale one might expect if they had been directly associated with iron smelting. Therefore, it is likely that these slags are also the result of some type of welding operation, the nature of which is discussed more fully below.

Group 3 – The plano-convex slags PC

(archive catalogue nos 604–607, SFBs 28, 36, 19, 3; lab. nos OX 700, 706, 710, 717)

The plano-convex slags I have defined as those slags with a roughly circular oval plan and a plano-convex cross-section, although the upper planar surface may be slightly concave. Such slags are not free running and hence are often vesicular and inhomogeneous. These slags may also be described by the more general term 'hearth bottoms' by other authors as they are thought to be produced in the smith's hearth rather than the smelting furnace (see Discussion). The majority of the slags described below seem to have solidified within the hearth or furnace, rather than having been raked out while in the semi-solid state.

604   A furnace-cooled, inhomogeneous small PC with partially dissolved silica grains in a wustite poor matrix.

605   A small plano-convex-shaped piece of slag with an unusually high density. This sample contained inclusions of claystone,

and hammer-scale as well as silica inclusions. Furnace-cooled.

606   i) A small fragment of the edge of a plano-convex-shaped slag sample. This sample showed evidence of having been cooled at a relatively rapid rate.
ii) A larger fragment of a plano-convex-shaped slag, with a large amount of rust and metallic iron on the upper surface. Furnace cooled.

607   A fragment of a relatively massive plano-convex-shaped slag with the composition varying from layer to layer. The uppermost layer contained a number of relatively unreacted but rounded silica grains. Furnace cooled.

Group 4 – The slag-lining reaction products

(archive catalogue nos 608–609, SFBs 39, 3; lab. nos OX702, 711)

This type of slag is formed by the interaction of the highly vitrified lining of the hearth or furnace with the bulk slag and fluxing materials such as fuel ash or hammer-scale. The thickness of this type of material, together with the composition and phases present can give a good indication of the length of time, temperature, and reducing potential of the hearth. Unfortunately, the determination of such parameters is a rather lengthy and expensive process and it was not possible to carry out the required experiments in this case. As a result the amount of information obtained is rather more limited.

608   The bulk of this sample was in a vitrified state, although a few areas did contain some non-glassy phases. It would appear that this sample had been at a high temperature for a considerable period, as the vitrification was more than 31 mm. It would also seem that the hearth was being run under reducing conditions as samples of metallic iron were found in the surface of the slag. Preliminary analysis showed that this iron had a very high phosphorus content of between 2.5 and 2.8 weight percent. This metal is of a totally different type from that analysed in 601, which had a normal low phosphorus content but a relatively high level of nickel.

609   This sample had not been subjected to the same prolonged period at high temperatures as the previous sample. Although the bulk of this sample was in a glassy state, the silica grains had not fully reacted with the glass, nor had some of the fragments of magnetite scale (hammer-scale). However, the thickness of the sample showed that this sample had been heated for a very considerable time, but at lower temperatures and under more oxidizing conditions.

Group 5 – Miscellaneous

(archive catalogue nos 610–611, barrow 1 and SFB 17/18)

The group contains two small samples which do not fit into any of the above classes.

610   A small fragment of black slag. The internal micro-structure was homogeneous, consisting of a fine scale binary eutectic of olivine and wustite growing in a dendritic manner, with the later development of a ternary eutectic of olivine, wustite, and 'glass'. However, some of the pores showed 'decanted' crystal growth, suggesting that some of the molten slag had flowed out of the sample before the solidification was complete. In all, the sample shows all the signs of having come from a tap slag, although there were no other samples of tap slag within this collection.

611   Initially, it looked as if this sample consisted of a splash of slag adhering to a pottery sherd. On sectioning, however, it

was clear that it was the pottery itself which had become vitrified. The depth of the zone of vitrification was very small, 1.5 mm in all, which would indicate that the sherd suffered a short but intense period of heating over a relatively restricted area. There were no metal splashes or other evidence which could provide further evidence of the use to which it was being put.

Discussion and conclusions

This is a small collection of slag weighing less than one kilogram, and as such is typical of many non-specialised settlements of all iron-using periods. Often such collections mainly consist of low density fuel ash slags (FAS) but unusually there are none in this case. The samples of Group 1 are consistent with being produced in the blacksmith's hearth during the welding operations necessary to produce small-to medium-sized objects. Each individual piece of slag was the result of a single heating of the hearth, but more than one artefact could have been produced or repaired in the course of this single heating.

The amount of slag produced during ironworking operations is a function of the amount of metal processed, as the major chemical component of these slags is the oxides of iron which come from the oxide scale shed from the metal as it is being heated in the hearth, or by the accidental burning of the metal caused by overheating. The amount of iron oxide entering the hearth will be a function of the hearth temperature, the smith's skill, and the shape of the artefact. The thickness of the scale formed depends on the maximum temperature of the metal and the length of time at that temperature. A thick piece of iron will take longer to reach the required tempera-ture than a thinner sample, and hence the oxide layer formed will be thicker. Normally, the thickness of hammer-scale varies between 0.05 and 2 mm. Thinner forms of hammer-scale tend to be generated during welding. A large proportion of the scale generated would be deposited on the working floor, especially around the anvil. At Maiden Castle, as much as 50 g of scale was found in each litre of charcoal-rich floor material sampled (Salter 1991). However, if we assume that 20 percent of the scale of average thickness 0.2 mm ends up in the hearth to form slag, then the 18 to 30 g of iron oxide contained in each of the samples of class 3 represents the processing of between 1.6 and 2.6 square metres of iron surface. This surface area is equivalent to the production of between 10 and 15 medium-sized knives by a skilled smith, or rather less by an unskilled smith.

The samples in Group 2 (slag flows), in theory, could be produced either by the smelting process or by higher temperature smithing operations. How-ever, considering the very small amount of slag found on site, it is very much more likely that these slags are the debris from the welding together of a number of larger pieces of iron. A third possibility is that the slag could have been produced during the conversion of a raw bloom of iron to a malleable iron billet. A bloom is the initial product of the iron-smelting furnace, consisting of a mixture of metallic iron and smelting slag. The slag content of a bloom makes the iron unforgeable at normal forging temperatures, less than 1000° C. Thus the bloom needs to be forged at very high temperatures to remove the majority of this slag. It is certain that the larger plano-convex slags (Group 3) originated in this manner, although slags similar to the smaller examples of the plano-convex type have been produced by the overheating of iron in coal- and coke-fuelled hearths during experiments carried out by the author.

It is unfortunate that such a small fragment of slag sample 610 was recovered, as its internal structure suggests that it was a tap slag, and therefore the result of an iron-smelting operation. A larger sample would be required to confirm this classification.

All the slags were associated with ironworking processes. The scale of the ironworking activity was extremely limited. The scale of the smithing activity would suggest the production and repair of artefacts for domestic use. The metallic iron inclusions within the slags show that more than one source of iron was being used. The evidence from the Group 4 material suggests that some of this iron was transported to the site in the form of blooms rather than scrap artefacts or billet (iron bars). It is unlikely that such blooms would have been transported more than a few kilometres from the original smelting site, unless there was some factor such as a fuel shortage which made the movement of bloom necessary before conversion to a billet. In all, there was evidence to suggest that there had been between 10 and 13 episodes of ironworking in the vicinity of the site. It is difficult to estimate how much iron passed through the site as the ratio of slag produced to metal processed is heavily dependent on the skill of the smith and form of the initial stock and final artefact. However, if it is assumed that the activity was carried out by a semi-skilled part-time black-smith, the probable amount of metal involved was between 2 and 10 kg.

Chapter 6: The Environmental Evidence

FAUNAL REMAINS
by Lyn Barnetson

Introduction

Although Barrow Hills was a multiperiod site, by far the greatest part of the faunal sample was domestic refuse derived from Anglo-Saxon occupation between the 5th and 7th centuries AD. The assemblage comprised 27,644 fragments of animal bones and teeth, excluding worked bone and antler, and weighed slightly in excess of 265 kg, of which *c* 233 kg (15,006 fragments) were identifiable to bone and species. Most of the material was recovered from specifically Anglo-Saxon contexts, predominantly sunken-featured buildings, postholes and pits, but the occupants had also utilised several prehistoric features as dumping grounds and approximately one third (31.4% by fragments, 39.0% by weight) of the total sample was derived from ditches associated with Neolithic and Bronze Age barrows.

As no other Anglo-Saxon deposits of this size have been recovered from the Upper Thames Valley, Barrow Hills provided a unique opportunity to assess the animal husbandry of a period better known from the Saxon settlements of East Anglia and southern England.

Methodology

The total weight of bone in each of the sunken-featured building quadrants and ditch sections was recorded before amalgamation by level, and the weight of identified and non-identifiable fragments was noted for each level in every feature. The range of species and fragment counts is shown in Table 6.1, which excludes the artefacts and sieved material, much of which was identifiable to order but not to species. Most of the problems associated with determination of minimum number of individuals (MNI) have been discussed in the archaeozoological literature and need not be repeated here (see Grayson 1984; Klein and Cruz-Uribe 1984; Gautier 1983). At Barrow Hills the standard practice of deriving minimum numbers from the most commonly occurring element of left or right side was employed for each bone in each level in all features. As it is conceivable that parts of the same animal may have become incorporated in more than one feature/level, thus rendering the amalgamated estimates from individual deposits of little value, the MNI for the sunken-featured buildings was ultimately derived from the most commonly occurring element overall.

In deposits with a high degree of fragmentation, or with very few fragments, it was clear that the MNI derived from the most commonly occurring element did not reflect the actual number of individuals present. Similarly, in some deposits with intact bones, particularly mandibles with teeth *in situ*, elements on left and right sides were obviously unpaired. In all such cases visual assessment was carried out to determine the MNI represented by that bone with the default taken as pair-positive and figures thus derived are shown bracketed alongside all standard MNI estimates in Table 6.2. It must be emphasised, however, that these figures apply solely to individual contexts and cannot be amalgamated for overall site assessment.

Skeletal element frequency (SEF) and age profiles were based on fragment counts and observed differences in profiles were checked for validity using the Kolmogorov-Smirnov statistical test, recommended by Klein and Cruz-Uribe (1984) for its usefulness in two-sample testing of skeletal part representation.

Dimensions were recorded for all bones sufficiently intact to yield valid measurements and the nomenclature follows that of von den Driesch (1976). The biometrical data are available in the archive. Withers heights were derived from long bones using factors given by Fock (1966) and Matolcsi (1970) for cattle and by Teichert (1975) for sheep and pig, and the results are shown in Tables 6.5–7.

Taphonomy general: macrofauna

Due to plough damage and reuse of features, bone preservation was not uniform throughout, but many fragments from the barrow ditches and larger sunken-featured buildings were in extremely good condition, with signs of weathering generally confined to the uppermost levels. Bones in the ditch of barrow 1 were quite noticeably pitted and weathered compared to those in the ditches of barrows 12 and 13. Degree of erosion, at best a subjective judgment and not quantifiable, was noted during preliminary sorting to be greater in barrow 12 than barrow 13 and the condition of bones in the basal level of barrow 13 was markedly variable, with both eroded and well preserved bones found in close association. One possible interpretation is that level 3 (the lowest level) was exposed long enough to become considerably weathered before the next layer (level 2) accumulated, and furthermore some contamination of levels 2 and 3 had clearly taken place. Whether the ditch assemblages are primary or secondary disposal cannot be determined with certainty (Chapter 7, Site formation processes). A similar situation occurred in several sunken-featured buildings where bones of the same animals were found in separate levels and preservation within levels was not uniform.

Table 6.1 Range of species and fragment numbers, excluding sieved material and artefacts. Percentage of species in each assemblage and in the total site assemblage, where greater than 1%, is shown in brackets.

Feature	Cattle	Sheep	Goat	Pig	Deer		Horse	Carn.		Bird		Fish	Rodent	Lago.	Insect	Amphib.	Total
					Red	Roe		Dog	Other	Dom	Wild						
Ditches 1,401,601	2333 (59.2)	1003 (25.5)	5	388 (9.8)	35	27	56 (1.4)	19	14	42 (1.1)	3	–	3	7	1	2	3938
4866	137 (65.5)	32 (15.3)	1	15 (7.2)	2	–	–	*22	–	–	–	–	–	–	–	–	209
SFBs	4425 (44.6)	4081 (41.2)	22	737 (7.4)	45	16	59	9	17	285 (2.9)	7	20	47	16	4	*122	9912
Postholes etc.	415 (58.1)	259 (36.3)	–	40 (5.6)	–	–	–	–	–	–	–	–	–	–	–	–	714
TOTAL	**7310 (49.5)**	**5375 (36.4)**	**28**	**1180 (8.0)**	**82**	**43**	**115**	**50**	**31**	**327 (2.2)**	**10**	**20**	**50**	**23**	**5**	**124**	**14773**

*=contains whole skeleton.

Abbreviations for Figs 6.4–6.6 and 6.8–6.10
L = left; R = right; P = proximal; d = distal; a = acetabulum.
Cr = cranium; Max = maxilla; Md = mandible; Hc = horncore;
Vc = cervical vertebrae (including atlas and axis); Vtl = thoracic and lumbar vertebrae; Co = costae; S = scapula; H = humerus, R = radius, U = ulna, Mc = metacarpal (McI-V for species with 5 metacarpi); It = innominate; F = femur; T = tibia; Fb = fibula; A = astragalus; Ca = calcaneum; Mt = metatarsal (MtI-V for species with 5 metatarsi; PhI-III = 1st to 3rd phalanges).

MNI=minimum number of individuals.
SEF=skeletal element frequency.

A list of abbreviations used in recording has been placed with the archive.

Table 6.2   MNI estimates for the three main domestic species based on most frequently occurring element of left or right side with visual assessment in square brackets.

Species	Deposit/Level	Bone and derived MNI						
		R	It	T	A	Ca	Mt	Md
Cattle	1/2	1[1]	1[1]	1[1]	1[1]	0	2[2]	1[1]
	1/3	2[2]	1[1]	2[4]	1[2]	1[1]	2[2]	1[1]
	401/2	11[13]	8[9]	13[15]	11[11]	13[13]	7[9]	10[14]
	401/3	7[7]	2[2]	2[2]	0	1[3]	3[3]	1[1]
	601/2	4[6]	2[2]	5[6]	7[9]	3[5]	10[11]	2[2]
	601/3	3[3]	3[4]	2[3]	2[2]	1[1]	2[3]	2[2]
	SFBs	16	34	13	15	20	13	33
Sheep	1/2	1[1]	1[1]	1[1]	0	0	2[2]	1[1]
	1/3	2[2]	1[1]	1[1]	0	1[1]	1[1]	2[2]
	401/2	12[14]	8[8]	16[16]	0	3[3]	2[6]	14[21]
	401/3	2[3]	2[2]	2[3]	0	0	2[2]	2[2]
	601/2	13[13]	1[1]	8[8]	0	1[1]	2[7]	12[13]
	601/3	2[2]	1[1]	3[3]	0	0	2[2]	1[2]
	SFBs	37	24	41	5	6	15	62
Pig	1/2	1[1]	1[1]	1[1]	0	1[1]	0	0
	1/3	1[1]	1[1]	0	1[1]	0	0	1[2]
	401/2	2[3]	2[2]	6[9]	0	3[3]	2[2]	7[10]
	401/3	0	1[1]	1[1]	0	0	0	1[1]
	601/2	3[4]	2[3]	1[3]	0	0	0	5[7]
	601/3	2[2]	1[1]	1[1]	0	0	0	2[2]
	SFBs	4	6	6	2	3	2	27

R = Radius; It = Innominate; T = Tibia; A = Astragalus;
Ca = Calcaneum; Mt = Metarsal; Md = Mandible.

Table 6.3   Cattle and sheep rib fragment distribution in the ditch and SFB assemblages.

Species	Fragment type	Ditch No.	(%)	SFBs No.	(%)
Cattle	Vertebral ends	89	(23.4)	256	(21.6)
	Sternal ends	291	(76.6)	928	(78.4)
TOTAL		**380**	**(100)**	**1184**	**(100)**
Sheep	Vertebral ends	49	(31.6)	581	(38.8)
	Sternal ends	106	(68.4)	917	(61.2)
TOTAL		**155**	**(100)**	**1498**	**(100)**

Surprisingly few fragments showed signs of burning or scorching, though small concentrations of burnt material were found in the centre of the site, notably in SFBs 6 and 39. Very little in the way of hearth residues found its way into the ditch dumps. There is no evidence that bone had been allowed to accumulate within buildings in use and the suggestion that old structures were refilled with rubbish was borne out by the nature of the remains.

In the absence of detailed chronological relationships between those Saxon features yielding the larger quantities of bone, the possibility of recognising any change in husbandry practice through time was doubtful and the faunal remains had to be studied as a single horizon. However, as the accumulation had occurred within a 150- to 200-year period, it could be argued that radical changes in husbandry would have been unlikely. By the same token, major changes in site function, which one hopes would be observable outwith the faunal evidence, would be reflected in the composition of the sunken-featured buildings dumps. The overall uniformity of skeletal element frequencies and age profiles of the main domesticates does not indicate any shift in emphasis and slight differences in species distribution and skeletal element frequency are attributable to differential preservation and carcass disposal. The stratification within sunken-featured buildings, apart from the uppermost and basal layers, did not appear to be critical as far as the faunal remains were concerned and although every layer was examined separately, each feature was regarded as a single entity in the final analysis.

In three instances (SFBs 32, 33 and 34; 36 and 37; 29 and 28) where the sunken-featured buildings cut each other, the 'earlier' buildings unfortunately contained samples of less than a hundred fragments and could not be compared reliably with later deposits. The range of species was consistently greater in the larger, overlying deposits and the only other noticeable difference was a higher proportion of sheep fragments in two of the intercutting features (32, 33 and 34; 36 and 37). The site records indicate that 'earlier' and 'later' deposits were

Excavations at Barrow Hills, Radley, Oxfordshire, 1983–5

Table 6.4 Vertebral fragments of sheep and cattle in the ditches and SFBs showing percentage of each type of vertebra.

Vertebra	Ditch				SFBs				N.A.D.		
	Cattle frags	%	Sheep frags	%	Cattle frags	%	Sheep frags	%	Cattle No.	%	Sheep No.
Cervical	80	(34.5)	10	(23.8)	78	(22.7)	47	(20.4)	7	(22.6)	7
Thoracic	99	(42.7)	16	(38.1)	154	(44.9)	98	(42.4)	13	(41.9)	13
Lumbar/Sacral	53	(22.8)	16	(38.1)	111	(32.4)	86	(42.4)	11	(35.5)	10–11
TOTAL	**232**	**(100%)**	**42**	**(100%)**	**343**	**(100%)**	**231**	**(100%)**	**31**	**(100%)**	**31**

N.A.D. = normal anatomical distribution.

Table 6.5 Cattle withers' heights. (* = ditch, M = male, F = female)

Bone	Sex on basis of Bd	Matolcsi		Fock's		Fock's Mean	
		F (6.05	M 6.33)	F (6.00	M 6.25)	F (6.125	M 5.45)
Metacarpus	F*	1.092		1.083		1.106	
	F*	1.130		1.121		1.144	
	F*	1.132		1.123		1.146	
	F	1.131		1.122		1.146	
	F	1.161		1.151		1.175	
	F	1.115		1.118		1.142	
	F	1.130		1.121		1.144	
	M*	1.201		1.186		1.163	
	M	1.193		1.178		1.154	
	M	1.238		1.222		1.198	
	M	1.167		1.153		1.129	
	M	1.151		1.136		1.113	
		(5.28	5.62)	(5.35	5.55)		
Metatarsus	F	1.083		1.097		1.118	
	F	1.087		1.101		1.122	
	F	1.025		1.039		1.058	
	M	1.157		1.143		1.123	

Table 6.6 Sheep withers' heights. (* = ditch).

Bone	Teichert's factor	Height at withers in metres.						
Radius	4.02	*0.538	0.545	0.568	0.590	0.589	0.665	
Femur	3.53	0.556						
Tibia	3.01	0.640						
Metacarpus	4.89	0.532	0.626	0.606	0.647	0.638	0.585	0.551
Metatarsus	4.54	0.604	0.564	0.589	0.548	0.551	0.572	0.562
		0.606	0.674	0.561				
Calcaneume	11.4	*0.580	0.645*	0.617	0.646	0.654	0.595	

Table 6.7 Pig withers' heights.

Bone	Teichert's factor	Height at withers in metres
Tibia	3.92	0.788
Metacarpus IV	10.53	0.751
Astragalus	17.5	0.637, 0.673, 0.689

not consistently separated during excavation and any difference cannot be regarded as reliable.

The total weight of bone in each quadrant of the sunken-featured buildings and all sections of the ditch deposits was noted prior to amalgamation of fragments by level, and the total number of fragments and weight of identified and unidentified bone in the feature levels was recorded during sorting. It is interesting to note that in terms of weight only 12% of the assemblage was unidentifiable compared to 46% in terms of fragment numbers. The explanation lies in the nature of the unidentifiable material, which comprised mainly bone splinters and small fragments, many measuring less than 10 square millimetres.

Although the weight method cannot be used for estimating relative proportions of species, overall weight distribution can be used for gross comparison of deposits containing similar bone frequencies. At Barrow Hills, the close correlation between total weight of bone and weight of identified bone made this exercise worthwhile and there was some evidence to suggest that the greatest sunken-featured buildings accumulations were concentrated in the south-western area. Within sunken-featured buildings the heavier samples were generally found in adjacent quadrants, showing where bone had been tipped or swept in with natural slippage and erosion spreading out smaller fragments to the other quadrants (Figs 6.2 and 7.1). In only a few features were the heavier samples in opposing quadrants, 4, 7, 16, 19, 22 and 39, indicating perhaps that an attempt had been made to even out the dumping process, either chronologically by filling one half before the other, or by dumping from opposite ends at the same time (see Chapter 7, Site formation processes).

The undulating profile of the weight distribution of bone in the ditch sections, most pronounced in barrow 13, has all the appearance of dumping at regular intervals with little natural erosion to level out the deposits (Fig. 6.3). The weight of bone in each section by layer shows the same uneven distribution in all three barrow ditches. Barrow 1 contained few bones in comparison to 13 and 12 and the bones bore signs of greater erosion. As this feature lay on the periphery of the extant site, it was conceivably used last as a dumping ground.

All the material, however, bore the mark of domestic refuse and virtually all the larger bones of cattle had been broken up and the epiphyseal ends damaged prior to deposition, resulting in fewer age and stature observations than one might have hoped for from a sample of this size. Apart from clear signs of butchery in the form of actual cut-marks, it was obvious that most of the bones had also been coarsely smashed or chopped. Despite the fairly wide range of species represented, the overall predominance of cattle, sheep and pig (93% of the total fragment count) confirms the homesteading nature of this site, which exhibits little evidence, in the faunal record at least, of exploitation of wild resources.

Cattle, sheep and goat

As shown in Table 6.1, cattle and sheep dominate the assemblage with cattle outnumbering sheep in terms of fragments though not in minimum numbers. A higher degree of fragmentation of the bovine skeleton and consequent bias in MNI estimates must to a great extent account for this. Apart from small posthole deposits, all the features contained fragments of both cattle and sheep and although in 16 out of 45 sunken-featured buildings sheep outnumbered cattle, only 3 of these deposits did so by more than 50 fragments. Features 20, 21, and 45 were alone in yielding high percentages of sheep compared to cattle, 77%, 85% and 67% respectively. As 45 was some distance from 20 and 21, which were practically adjacent, this is more likely to be a reflection of intrasite activity than of a temporal shift in husbandry practice.

Despite the fact that goat bones are not always distinguishable from sheep, the small number identified as goat at Barrow Hills is probably a fair indication of this species' overall status. The easily recognised elements were noticeably lacking and although fragmentation must result in an over-estimate of the quantity of sheep at the expense of goat, the evidence here indicates that goats had a relatively minor role among the domesticates.

Pig

Pig bones accounted for less than 10% of the overall fragment count but were present in all the ditch and sunken-featured buildings deposits except one, 32. None of the animals were wild and judging by the sporadic distribution of foetal or neonate bones, pigs must have been bred and consumed on site.

Horse

The 115 equid bones and teeth were almost equally divided between the barrow ditch and sunken-featured building deposits. Although no bones were recovered in articulation there were instances of paired bones in the same location and a few bore cut-marks.

Deer

Bones, teeth and antlers of both red and roe deer occurred throughout the site, and although the samples

Mandibular regions

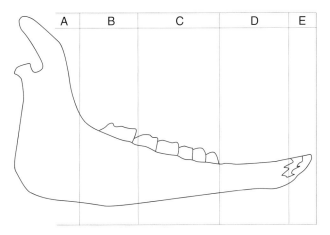

Figure 6.1 Diagram of mandibular regions A, B, C, D, E.

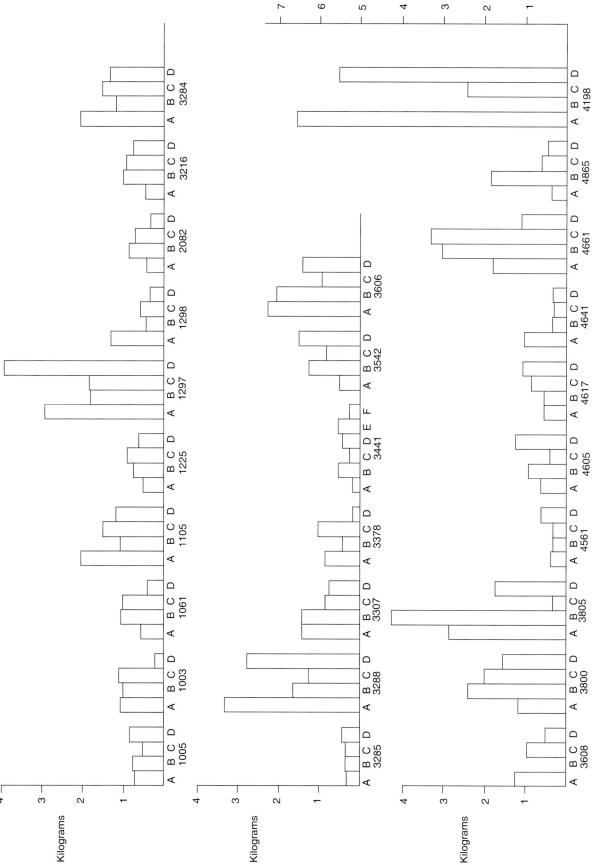

Figure 6.2   Weight distribution in kilograms of animal bone in the major SFBs.

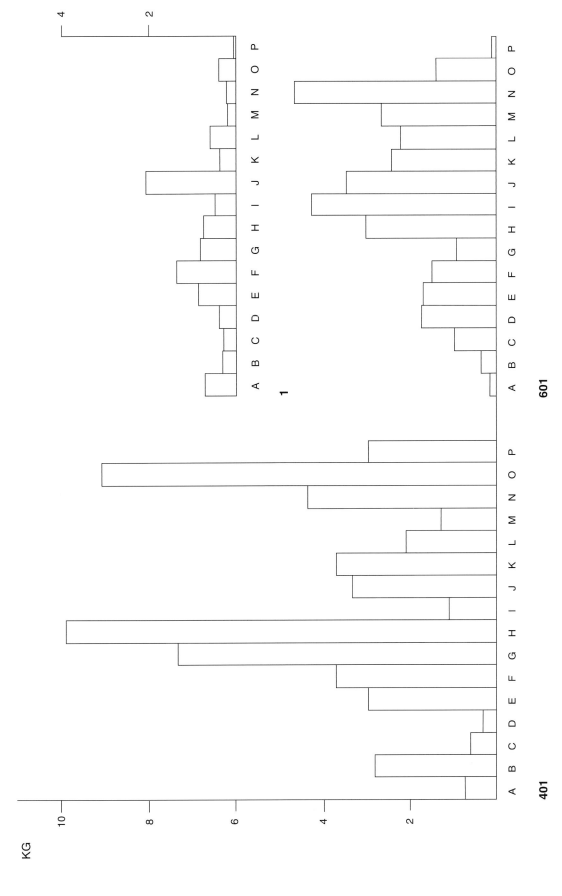

Figure 6.3   Weight distribution in kilograms of animal bone in the ditch sections of Barrow 1 (context 1), Barrow 13 (context 401) and Barrow 12 (context 601).

were small there were roughly twice as many red deer bones in the ditch dumps as in the sunken-featured buildings. Of the 50 fragments of antler identified, just over half were cut/sawn or worked, and apart from one fragment each in the ditches of barrows 12 and 13 all the worked antler was found in the sunken-featured buildings. There were only two recognisably cast antlers in the sample but as the majority of fragments were beam and tine sections it was impossible to ascertain how much shed antler had been utilised. It seems likely that antler from hunted deer was used on an *ad hoc* basis and there was no deliberate collecting of cast red deer antler.

Carnivores

The majority of carnivore bones were identified as dog and included the almost complete skeleton of a fairly large adult (*c* 590 mm shoulder height) from the uppermost level of pond barrow 4866. Although various bones of dog, fox and cat (totalling 19, 3 and 6 respectively) were recovered from barrow 13, there was only one isolated fox mandible in barrow 12. None of the bones in the sunken-featured buildings were in articulation and virtually all were single bones or loose teeth. Dogs obviously scavenged around the middens as evidenced by the ubiquitous gnaw-marks and must have contributed greatly to the taphonomic loss of small bones and epiphyseal ends.

Two fragments were identified as badger and polecat.

Lagomorphs

Both rabbit and hare bones were present in small numbers throughout the site and several features contained well preserved quantities of rabbit bones which were obviously intrusive. No rabbit bones have been found in secure association with pre-Norman deposits and as Barrow Hills was a site greatly disturbed by rabbit activity, only those bones found in lower levels were closely examined for evidence that they might be contemporaneous with the assemblage. There were, however, no signs of burning or cutmarks on any of the lagomorph bones and the rabbits must postdate the Anglo-Saxon occupation.

Birds

Apart from several bones of common Passeriforms, most of which looked fresh and intact, all the birds were domestic fowl, goose and duck, though the last was found in only three features, barrow 12, feature 613 (which also produced eight undiagnostic Anglo-Saxon sherds) and SFB 12. A few bones of both fowl and goose bore tiny cut marks around the furcula and coracoid. One tibiotarsus exhibited thickening of the compacta (medullary bone) associated with egg laying and three fragments of eggshell were recovered from SFB 26. A single fragment of eggshell was found in the sieved sample SFB 16, D/2.

Taphonomy general: microfauna

Owing to excellent preservation and careful excavation most of the smaller bones of birds, rodents, moles and amphibians were recovered during hand trowelling. The total weight of bone in the sieved samples from Saxon contexts was *c* 530 g, roughly one third by weight of the total sieved material from the site. Fragments recovered from the sieves ranged in size from crumbs *c* 1 mm in length to pieces just over 500 mm, for example an intact bovine caudal vertebra in SFB 12. Of the 1193 fragments found in the Saxon sieved deposits, approximately 222 were identifiable to bone and species, the majority of which are cattle, sheep and rodent. The remainder comprised chips of compacta and trabecular bone, some of which could be assigned to species on the basis of size and several pieces of which were clearly recognisable as rodent, amphibian and bird though not identifiable to species.

Insectivores and rodents

Many of these bones were recovered by sieving but a substantial proportion was not identifiable to species. Those found during hand trowelling were in very good condition and posed few problems in identification. Voles (*Arvicola terrestris*) were predominant and the few moles (*Talpa europaea*) may have been intrusive. Field vole (*Microtus agrestis*) and wood mouse (*Apodemus sylvaticus*) were also present but few in number.

Amphibians

The common frog (*Rana temporaria*) was found in many deposits throughout the site but only two bones were recovered from barrow 12 and amphibians were absent from the other ditch dumps of barrow 1, barrow 13 and pond barrow 4866. A large assemblage of fragments was found in SFB 30, apparently the crushed remains of a single frog.

Fish

Some 22 fragments of fish bone were found. These did not form part of the present study, but both pike and eel were tentatively identified.

Environment

The range of species on any site practising animal husbandry may provide few real clues to local environment and a low incidence of non-domesticates can indicate minimal exploitation of wild resources as much as lack of suitable habitat. Though both prefer woodland, red and roe deer can be found in a variety of habitats and their presence on site here in relatively small numbers suggests either limited availability or casual exploitation. The number of deer bones is in proportion to the finds of antler and the two examples of cast antler are both roe. Virtually all the antler is worked/cut, but the quantities involved do not indicate importation as a raw material on any scale.

Although microfauna are more sensitive indicators of environment they are by nature, though not exclusively, incidental visitors and it is not always possible to tie their remains securely to the archaeological context. The presence of *Rana* sp. and *Arvicola terrestris* at Barrow Hills merely confirms the proximity of a waterway such the stream which ran down the west side of the site, but few settlements are established far from a source of water. *Arvicola* has been found on several prehistoric settlements and may have had closer associations with man than previously imagined. Furthermore, it is known to be less aquatic in some regions of Britain, exhibiting behaviour more commonly associated with the European species such as burrowing into pasture. There was no way of confirming *Arvicola*'s contemporaneity with the Saxon fauna and as the settlement was relatively short-lived, *Arvicola* could have colonised the area at any time from the 7th century AD onwards.

The countryside around the settlement must have included sufficient pasture for the not insubstantial herds of cattle and sheep kept at Barrow Hills and some cover for deer in the form of woodland or scrub, though it is unlikely there were extensive forests in the area. It is the absence of species – no wild pigs and little game – which has greater implications here. The virtual absence of aquatic birds and low incidence of fish bones does suggest infrequent exploitation of freshwater resources despite the proximity of the River Thames.

Skeletal element frequency (sef)

The initial assumption that the assemblages in the barrow ditches and sunken-featured buildings were derived from a single population did not rule out the possibility that the faunal composition of these two areas would differ. During preliminary examination, therefore, the barrow ditches (1, 12 and 13) and sunken-featured buildings (all sunken-featured buildings and associated pits and postholes) were sorted as separate entities. There was no evidence to suggest that the two assemblages were derived from different horizons, nor was there any indication from the skeletal element frequency that either comprised material derived exclusively from a specialised activity. In the absence of evidence to the contrary, differences in the SEF patterns and age profiles were attributed to differential preservation and the spatial, as opposed to temporal, use of the site.

Cattle and sheep

Cattle were predominant in terms of fragment count (Table 6.1) and must have made the greatest contribution to the general economy. The relatively large samples in barrows 12 and 13 allowed MNI estimates to be made for the principal bones but the nature of the sunken-featured building deposits rendered such calculations difficult. Many of the

latter contained remains of cattle and sheep which could have been derived from at least one or two individuals of either species in terms of non-duplication of bones. It was not certain, however, whether these bones were in fact derived from one or many different animals of roughly the same age and stature. On the whole, the sunken-featured building deposits are remarkably uniform, each containing a variety of skeletal elements seldom representing more than four individuals of any one species.

It was clear that the rubbish in the disused buildings and pits, though primarily food residues, was not exclusively so. The inclusion of waste material, namely lower legs and feet, suggested on-site butchery and use of carcass secondary products such as horns, hides, fat and marrow, but a proportion of the less meaty parts has been lost. Although the ditch dumps seemed possible candidates for such butchery waste, the relative percentages of principal skeletal elements of the three main domesticates, cattle, sheep and pig, did not show a significantly higher proportion of waste in the barrow ditches.

One striking aspect of the distribution pattern was the high number of sheep fragments (approximately 81% of the sheep fragment count) found in the sunken-featured buildings. This contrasted with cattle and pig where the ratio of sunken-featured buildings to ditch fragments was 2:1 for both species. Part of the reason lies in the disproportionately high number of sheep ribs identified in the sunken-featured buildings, where 42% of the sheep sample is rib, though the ratio of vertebral to sternal ends is much the same in either assemblage (Table 6.3).

The relative SEF for cattle in the barrow ditches is shown in rank order, with each bone represented as a percentage of the most commonly occurring element on the left or right side (Fig. 6.4). The sunken-featured buildings profile is shown alongside ranked in the same order for comparison. The sheep and pig profiles are shown in Figures 6.5 and 6.6. In order to compensate for the swamping effect of rib fragments these profiles were drawn again for sheep and cattle using the number of vertebral ends of ribs rather than total rib count.

When bones were grouped according to high and low meat-yielding areas of the carcass (Fig. 6.7), using fragment counts, the difference between ditch and sunken-featured buildings deposits was most noticeable in the sheep profiles. The dominance of backbone elements in the sunken-featured buildings is not echoed in the barrow ditches but otherwise the profiles are quite similar. The cattle profiles for the two assemblages are also quite similar.

The most obvious differences between the cattle and sheep profiles lie in the areas of the head and backbone. Although there were noticeably fewer sheep heads than cattle in the sunken-featured buildings, the relative percentages of cranial fragments in the barrow ditches were almost equal – 23.6% ovine and 24.3% bovine. Sheep heads were certainly

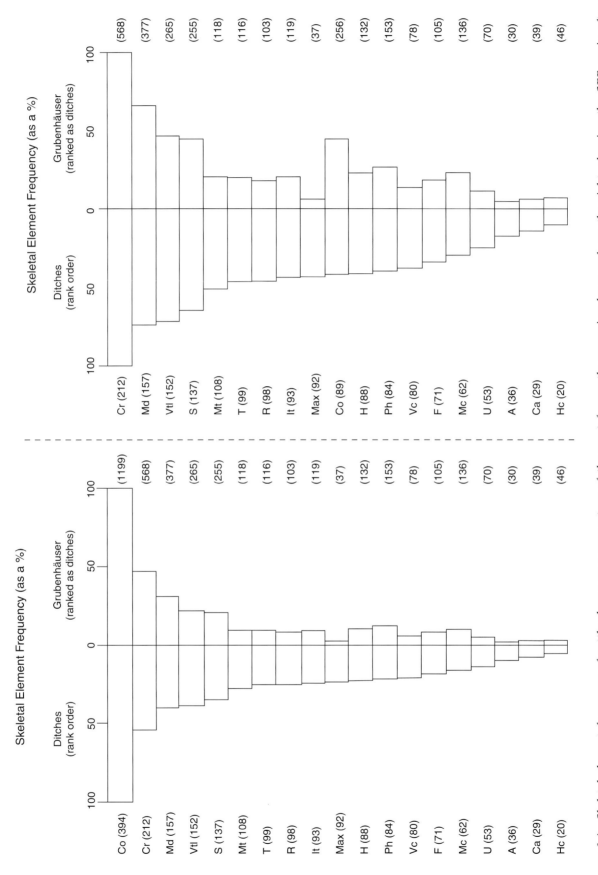

Figure 6.4 Skeletal element frequency of cattle shown as a percentage of the most frequently occurring bone and, on the right, showing the SEF again after rib total adjusted to include vertebral ends only. Fragment numbers are shown in brackets.

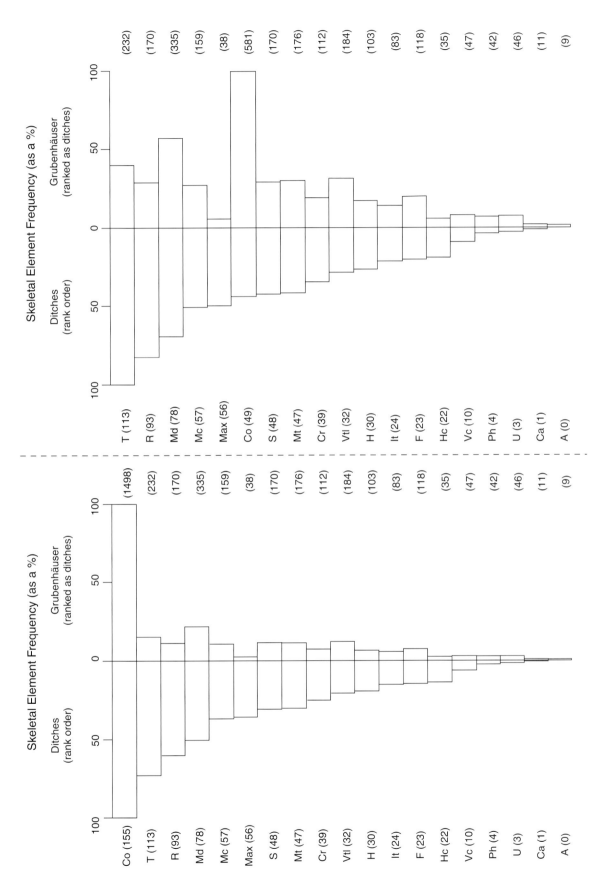

Figure 6.5 Skeletal element frequency of sheep shown as a percentage of the most frequently occurring bone and, on the right, showing the SEF again after rib total adjusted to include vertebral ends only. Fragment numbers are shown in brackets.

Skeletal Element Frequency (as a %)

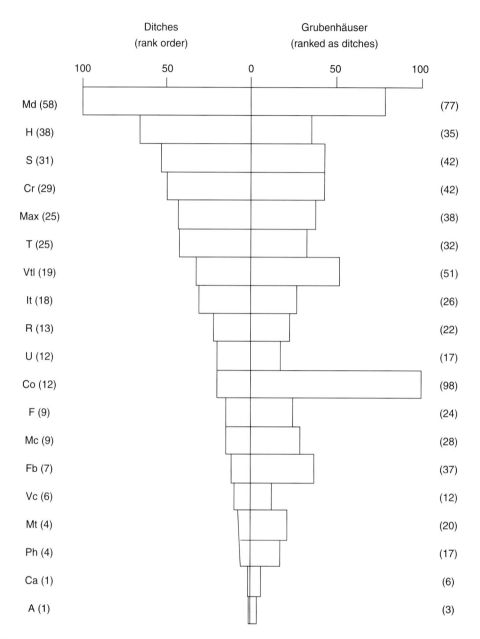

Figure 6.6   Skeletal element frequency of pig shown as a percentage of the most frequently occurring bone. Fragment numbers are shown in brackets.

utilised, as shown by the fairly substantial numbers of mandibles and horn-cores on site. Once the horns had been chopped off and the lower jaws removed, the heads could have been boiled for brawn, resulting in fewer fragments. The horn-cores of both species were more numerous in the sunken-featured buildings than in the barrow ditches, and although approximately one in three of the intact cores ended up in the barrow ditches, the fragment ratio was nearer 2:3. Of the five caprine horn-cores, only one was found in the ditch assemblage (in barrow 12, level 3 – a sub-adult core).

Sheep ribs were relatively more frequent than cattle in the sunken-featured buildings and there was a higher percentage of sheep ribs here than in the barrow ditches. The former is most probably a reflection of small carcass preparation, in which the meat along the backbone can be cooked more economically on the bone and discarded as part of the kitchen/meal debris. In the bovine carcass this high-meat area is more easily boned out. During these calculations cervical (neck) vertebrae were excluded from the high meat-yielding group of the backbone but were not included in the low meat category of the

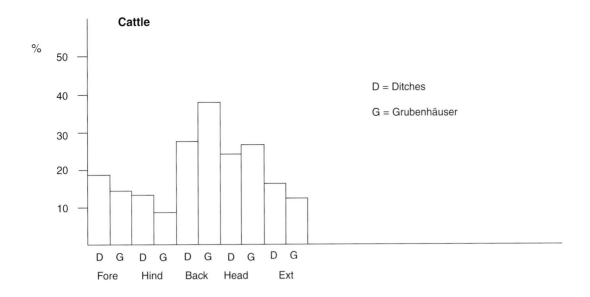

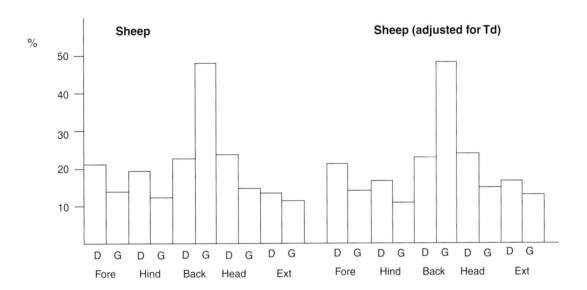

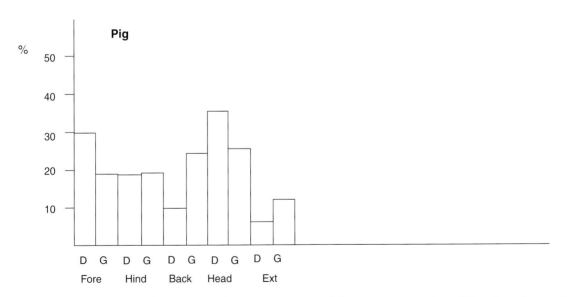

Figure 6.7   Cattle, sheep and pig bones grouped as carcass parts and shown as a percentage of the relevant assemblage. (FORE = scapula, humerus, radius and ulna; HIND = innominate, femur, tibia [and fibula of pig only]; BACK = costae and thoracic and lumbar/sacral vertebrae; HEAD = cranium, maxilla, mandible [and horn cores of cattle and sheep]; EXT = metacarpal, metatarsal, astragalus, calcaneum and phalanges.)

head, as it is clear that some crania in the assemblage were utilised for by-products and the point at which neck vertebrae were discarded cannot be predicted.

On the whole, there was little difference in the frequency of cattle and sheep vertebrae but quite marked deviation in the percentages of different types of vertebrae in the barrow ditches (Table 6.4). The latter is clearly the effect of small sample bias as only 42 sheep vertebrae were recovered from the barrow ditches compared to 232 cattle vertebrae. The proportion of sternal to vertebral ends of ribs was the same in either assemblage but there was a significant difference between the two species. Bovine sternal fragments outnumbered vertebral ends by more than 3:1 whereas in sheep the ratio was 2:1 in the barrow ditches and 3:2 in the sunken-featured buildings. Once again this must be a reflection of butchery and differential preservation. Whereas a number of sheep ribs were found relatively intact there were no complete cattle ribs. One would expect a lower percentage of vertebral ends overall, as the lower half, particularly of bovine rib blades, is often trimmed and cut more than once during carcass preparation and even complete examples are prone to breakage after deposition.

The relative percentages of hind limb fragments were also noticeably different between the two species, but this is probably a reflection of grouping bias. Although both sheep and cattle tibiae were counted as high meat bones, the distal tibia of the mutton carcass may be discarded as part of the low meat hock joint. Readjustment of the figures to include tibiae (that is, intact distal ends only) within the low meat category of the extremities resulted in almost identical sheep and cattle profiles. When the same exercise was carried out on the sunken-featured buildings material, the result was the same, with both species hind limb and waste categories becoming almost identical.

Metapodia and phalanges were noticeably low (in terms of relative percentages and against the norm) for both cattle and sheep in both the barrow ditches and sunken-featured buildings. These bones have little food value and some may have been left attached to hides/fleeces and discarded off-site. The tiny bones of the sheep foot and lower leg joints were virtually absent from the barrow ditches although metapodia were better represented on the whole than those of cattle. Universal evidence of carnivore gnawing shows that dogs and possibly foxes were scavenging on the normal domestic debris, and this must to some extent account for the loss of epiphyseal ends and butchery waste. A few tiny fragments reminiscent of carnivore-defaecated bone were recovered from SFB 4 and SFB 6 but no dog coprolites were found in the faunal sample.

Pig

Pig carcass preparation differs from that of sheep and cattle principally in the ratio of offal, which can affect the SEF pattern. In pigs the skin, head, feet and tail are traditionally included as part of the edible meat carcass and therefore do not form secondary or waste products. Pigs' trotters and pigs' heads, even in unimproved or primitive stock, have considerable meat value. The pig profile (Fig. 6.6) shows that the sunken-featured buildings did yield a higher percentage of lower leg bones and feet than the ditch assemblages, but a slightly higher percentage of head fragments ended up in the barrow ditches. However, the principal component of the 'head' category was mandibular, generally considered to be waste, which accounted for 18% of the total pig assemblage in the barrow ditches and 12% in the sunken-featured buildings.

The frequency of upper fore-limbs in the barrow ditches, principally scapulae and humeri, is of interest. Admittedly the samples are small but the ratio of fused to unfused scapulae and humeri is much higher here than in the sunken-featured buildings. Either the unfused epiphyses did not have a high survival rate in the ditch dumps or perhaps more of the older animals ended up here.

A considerably greater proportion of pig ribs and vertebrae was recovered from the sunken-featured buildings than the barrow ditches, but the samples are small.

Horse, deer and domestic birds

As the sample sizes for these species are relatively small in comparison to the domesticates discussed above, skeletal element frequency results are less informative, but nevertheless reveal some interesting patterns.

Similar numbers of equid bones were found in both the barrow ditches and sunken-featured buildings, and of the latter only one, SFB 30, yielded paired elements, that is, a left and right scapula fragment from the same animal. The finds in the sunken-featured buildings were generally in the form of fragments, seldom from more than two or three different bones of the skeleton. There is some evidence in the form of actual cut-marks to indicate that horse carcasses were butchered. The right parietal of a horse cranium recovered from SFB 1 had clearly been cut/sliced across near to the occipital and six other bones bore signs of slicing or chopping, though whether this was dismemberment before 'burial' or actual butchery for food is not clear. There were a few paired elements in the barrow ditches, but two distal scapulae in barrow 13, layer 2, came from two different animals, as did the left and right astragali in barrow 12, layer 2. Scapulae, innominates, metapodia, phalanges and tarsals dominated the equid assemblage and the taphonomic loss would appear to be great. The humerus, ulna, tibia, mandibles and backbone are under represented, and although limb bones can be difficult to distinguish from cattle when fragmented, these bones would need to have been thoroughly smashed to bias recognition to this extent. It is conceivable that long bones and jaws were broken up deliberately and that only the small compact bones, metapodials and the sturdier parts of the shoulder and hip girdle have survived intact.

Excluding antler, 29 red deer bones were recovered from the barrow ditches, and on the basis of non-duplication of elements these could have been derived from two individuals. Almost half this number of bones were found in the sunken-featured buildings, all as isolated elements apart from three bones, possibly from the same individual, identified in the upper level of SFB 24. The roe deer sample, 33 bones in all, was divided almost equally between the two assemblages. Within the sunken-featured buildings red and roe deer seemed to be mutually exclusive and only SFBs 8 and 37 contained bones of both species (one bone of each in either case). All cut-marks were confined to the antlers and there were no obvious signs of skinning or butchery. The sunken-featured buildings yielded most of the antler (66%), which was predominantly of red deer; just over half of it was cut or worked. Roe antler, presumably less prized as a raw material, accounted for 20% of the overall sample and virtually all of it was found in the ditch deposits.

The edible domestic birds (*Gallus* sp. and *Anser* sp.) were largely confined to the sunken-featured building dumps where 87.3% of these bones were found. The similarity in the relative percentages of species in the two types of deposit is of interest, although admittedly the ditch sample is extremely small (n = 40): 32.5% goose and 67.5% fowl in the barrow ditches compared to 34.9% goose and 65.1% fowl in the sunken-featured buildings (Table 6.8). It is likely that each household killed and plucked birds for the table within sight of the kitchen so the fact that virtually all the skeleton elements of chickens and geese were found in these deposits may indicate that direct discard into the open pits of disused sunken-featured buildings was taking place. It also suggests, however, that the barrow ditch dumps may comprise less kitchen debris than the SEF pattern for the larger animals indicates.

Other species

As stated earlier, the rabbit and hare bones are considered to be intrusive and do not form part of the Anglo-Saxon assemblage.

Signs of carnivore activity are widespread and gnaw marks occurred in virtually every deposit. Barrow 13 yielded the remains of a number of carnivores, predominantly domestic dog of which at least two individuals are represented. Approximately 13 bones and a single tooth of dog were recovered from the sunken-featured buildings, generally as isolated elements, but one almost complete skeleton lay in the upper level of pond barrow 4866.

Most of the microfauna (rodents, moles and amphibians) were found in the sunken-featured buildings, as were all of the fish remains.

Table 6.8 Fragment numbers of principal bones of domestic fowl and goose, excluding one incomplete skeleton of immature domestic fowl. (25 bones)

Bone	Ditch Fowl	Goose	SFBs Fowl	Goose
Cranium	0	0	0	1
Mandible	0	2	1	3
Vertebrae	0	0	0	6
Costae	0	0	0	5
Scapula	6	1	8	5
Coracoid	1	0	7	4
Furcula	1	1	3	4
Sternum	1	1	5	8
Humerus	2	3	12	13
Radius	4	2	17	6
Ulna	1	0	14	7
Carpometacarpus	2	0	2	1
Pelvic girdle	0	0	7	2
Femur	4	1	12	3
Tibiotarsus	1	2	33	4
Fibula	1	0	5	0
Tarsometatarsus	3	0	14	3
TOTAL	27	13	140	75

Age

Age at death was estimated by the standard method of observed state of epiphyseal fusion of long bones and eruption and wear of teeth. No microscopic or radiographic examination was carried out.

Owing to damage during butchery and post-depositional decay, long bone epiphyses are seldom a satisfactory medium for establishing age profiles. Watson (1978), succinctly expounding the problems of epiphyseal ageing, noted sample error, differential destruction and variability in fusion age as the main factors to be considered. Ante- and post-depositional destruction obviously affect SEF patterns and *ipso facto* age profiles, explaining perhaps some of the differences between the two Barrow Hills assemblages. Furthermore, the number of 'ageable' epiphyses was not large and accounts for some of the anomalies in the sheep ditch assemblage. Variability in fusion age is not yet sufficiently documented to allow definitive age analysis of any of the domestic species in archaeological contexts; thus the default is established fusion dates for recent livestock. Figures quoted in agricultural documents of the preceding centuries, considered to be more applicable to archaeological material, are now seriously questioned. Nor is variability limited to post-cranial ageing, although current techniques employing crown heights and incremental growth layers can be used to cross-check age estimated from tooth eruption.

Cattle, sheep and pig

Skeletal age

Bones of very young animals are not included in the profiles. These occurred in small numbers, apart from pig, of which 64 bones were identified in the sunken-featured buildings. Fewer neonate bones of all three species were found in the ditch assemblage. As very young lambs and calves would not have been culled for the table, their absence here is probably confirmation of the food residue nature of the remains. Natural losses may have been discarded in the fields and were probably devoured by scavengers. Certainly there is extensive evidence for carnivore activity on site in the form of gnaw-marks. Piglets, however, are traditionally culled young and as pig litters generally provide a surplus there are sound economic reasons for deliberate slaughter at an early age. It is extremely unlikely that neonate pigs were consumed and their bones may represent the directly discarded sweepings from pens which would not be found to the same extent in the barrow ditches.

The cattle epiphyseal age patterns for barrow ditches and sunken-featured buildings are broadly similar though the percentage of late-fusing fused bones in the barrow ditches is slightly higher (Fig. 6.8). It must be emphasised that the ditch sample is rather small but it appears that more kitchen/meal residues have become incorporated in the sunken-featured buildings than in the barrow ditches. Unfortunately, the number of late-fusing epiphyses of sheep is negligible in the barrow ditches, where the profile fluctuates dramatically, and cannot be used with any confidence (Fig. 6.9). There is, however, some indication that a higher percentage of the earlier-fusing epiphyses appear in the sunken-featured buildings in unfused state than in the barrow ditches, which translates either as a case for differential preservation or for intra-site activity.

The pig profiles (Fig. 6.10) for both types of deposit are remarkably similar, though once again there are indications that a higher percentage of unfused epiphyses are incorporated in the sunken-featured buildings. Differential destruction, either before or after deposition, has obliterated all traces of pig proximal humeri in the sunken-featured buildings and proximal femora and tibiae in the barrow ditches. Virtually all the late-fusing bones of pig are unfused, which has a definite bearing on their survival rate in the ground. Of course much depends on the length of time rubbish was exposed in between episodes of dumping. On a purely subjective basis, as discussed under general taphonomy, barrows 12 and 13 seem to have better preservation that most sunken-featured buildings, and one would expect unfused epiphyses to have a better chance of survival in the barrow ditches.

In percentage terms, therefore, there seems to be a slight emphasis on younger animals in the sunken-featured buildings. The late-fusing bones in the sunken-featured buildings were present in equal numbers of fused and unfused for cattle but showed a marked difference in sheep, where two-thirds were unfused. Unfortunately, there were only six late-fusing epiphyses of sheep in the barrow ditches, too small a sample from which to draw conclusions.

Taken in combination with the SEF data one might speculate that animals culled for meat were butchered and consumed on an *ad hoc* basis within the settlement, but that older animals, kept primarily as breeding stock and for by-products such as milk and fleeces, were butchered separately, with the hides and horns being removed for preparation elsewhere and the long bones broken up for marrow and fat rendering. Thus the general butchery residues have accumulated in the barrow ditches and more specifically 'table' refuse has become incorporated in the sunken-featured buildings.

Dental age

As Grigson (1982) points out in her summary of ageing data for cattle, more information is available for the age of eruption of incisors than cheek teeth, and yet it is frequently the cheek teeth which survive in archaeological contexts. Barrow Hills was no exception and all the incisors recovered were loose teeth. Those few mandibles which retained some cheek teeth were assigned an age in months using Silver's (1969) figures for 19th-century cattle, semi-wild hill sheep and 18th-century pigs. Figures for the last are considered unreliable as indicators of age (see Bull and Payne 1982) but may be regarded as relative, not absolute, age groups. Few jaw bones had more than three cheek teeth *in situ* and many retained only the third molar. For this reason, wear stages (after Grant 1975) were assigned to third molars only.

Figure 6.11 shows the age at death pattern for cattle, sheep and pig based on most frequent left or right mandible in the barrow ditches and sunken-featured buildings. A large number of mandibles had to be excluded as the age at death could not be narrowed to one specific age group. The ditch assemblage comprises few young animals and the apparently high percentage of calves in the 6–18 month group is partly due to small sample bias (n=2). Young and prime sheep are better represented in the sunken-featured buildings than in the barrow ditches, where the sample is dominated by the mandibles of older animals.

This pattern is repeated for the pigs; a higher percentage of prime animals appear in the sunken-featured buildings. None of the mature animals, in either type of deposit, was old and none of the third molars showed wear beyond stage 'c', light wear only.

Other species

The sample sizes for horse and deer were too small for age profile analysis. All the equid bones belonged to mature individuals and apart from two deciduous loose teeth, all the teeth were permanent molars and premolars.

With the exception of a single red deer proximal femur, all bones of deer were fused and no deciduous dentition, either *in situ* or loose, was identified.

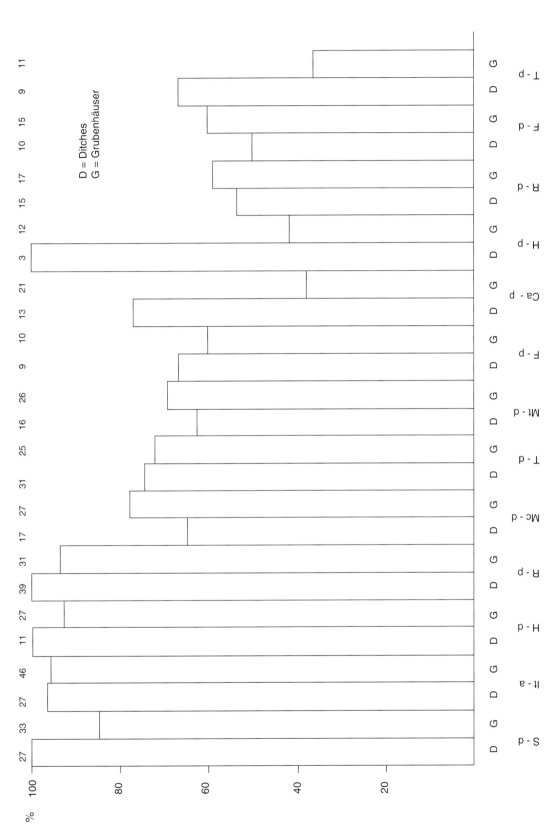

Figure 6.8 Epiphyseal fusion of cattle showing percentage fused for each epiphysis in approximate fusion sequence. Total number of epiphyses (fused, fusing and unfused) is given at the top.

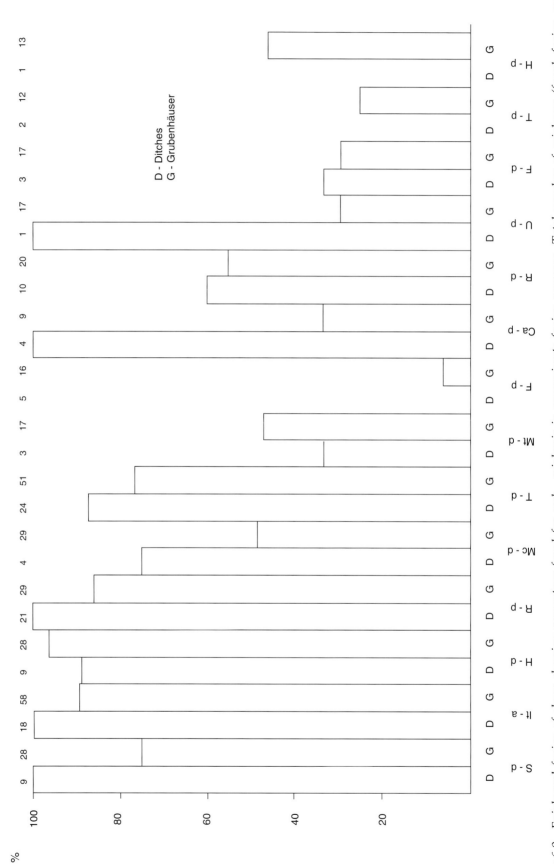

Figure 6.9 Epiphyseal fusion of sheep showing percentage fused for each epiphysis in approximate fusion sequence. Total number of epiphyses (fused, fusing and unfused) is given at the top.

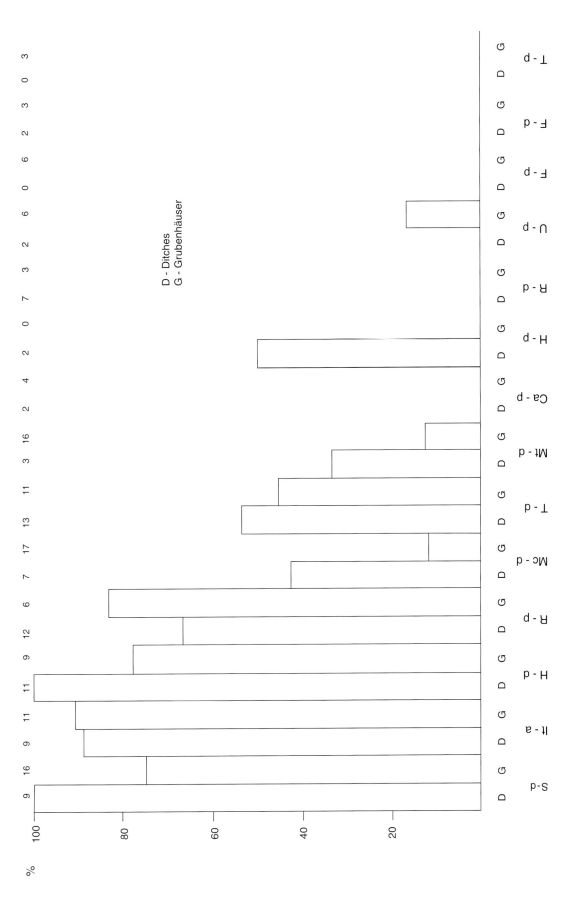

Figure 6.10 Epiphyseal fusion of pig showing percentage fused for each epiphysis in approximate fusion sequence. Total number of epiphyses (fused, fusing and unfused) is given at the top.

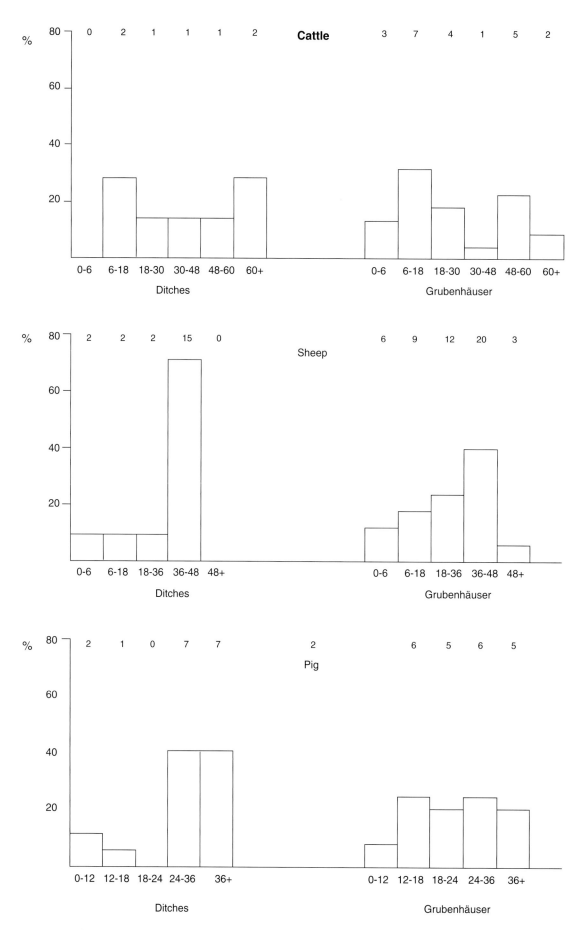

Figure 6.11   Cattle, sheep and pig dental age showing the number of mandibles (L or R) in each age group as a percentage of the total number of 'aged' mandibles in each assemblage.

Several unfused bones of immature chickens were found in sunken-featured buildings but none of the goose bones were identified as young.

Metrical analysis (sex and stature)

Sexual dimorphism in cattle and sheep is determinable on purely morphogenic grounds in innominates (pelves), crania and horncores. However, at Barrow Hills only horncores survive relatively intact; although there is no evidence that horns were imported to the site horn can be a tradable commodity, and no assessment of herd structure in archaeological contexts can be based on the evidence of horncores alone. It is generally accepted that the bones of ungulates reflect sexual dimorphism in their dimensions, but despite repeated efforts by researchers over the years there is as yet no satisfactory way to isolate castrates. Trimodality in single dimension plots is usually interpreted as representing three groups, namely females, castrated males and entire males and the use of indicators to define clusters, pioneered by students of the University of Munich in the 1950s and 60s (see for example Schneider 1958; Polloth 1959; Dürr 1961; Pfund 1961; Mennerich 1968) has been applied with varying degrees of success to metapodia, horncore bases and astragali. The possible presence of neutered females is generally dismissed as this has never been part of bovine husbandry practice, though it may have been for pigs.

Cattle

Metapodia are by far the most sensitive indicators of sexual dimorphism in cattle. Howard (1963) proved that separation of bulls and cows was possible using maximum distal breadth and smallest diaphyseal breadth of the metacarpal but Grigson (1982) has cast doubt on the separation of castrates by this method. Fock (1966) demonstrated that metacarpal indices may be used to differentiate between bulls and cows within specific populations but showed that there was variation in these indices between breeds. Although metapodia gave low fragment counts at Barrow Hills, partly because of minimal butchery, they did provide the greatest number of measurable epiphyses. Similarly, substantial numbers of distal tibiae and proximal and distal radii were sufficiently intact to yield valid measurements (data in archive, list 1). The single dimension plots gave variable results, principally owing to sample size, but similar distribution patterns emerged for those bones where samples were greater than ten.

One of the major problems in deciding where castrates lie on single dimension plots is due to the uncertainty of overlap. Although ox bones are not as massive as those of bulls, they can be longer and, if used as draught animals, certain bones may be broader. The problem is compounded by the fact that young oxen not used for traction would generally be slaughtered for meat in preference to young heifers. Regardless of whether milk was an important component of the diet, the most important yield from a female animal is the calf she produces in her second (or third) year. Early farmers would seldom have risked slaughter of heifers before this critical age was reached unless the animals were obviously unsuitable for breeding. Therefore, if more oxen than heifers are killed before epiphyses are fused, then the dimension plots will skew to the left, a pattern relatively familiar on many early sites.

The astragalus has been used by Ijzereef (1981) and Bartosiewicz (1984), following work done by Noddle (1973), to estimate live weights from the volume (GL x Bd x Dl) of the bone but the underlying assumption is that volume will also separate bulls, oxen and cows. At Barrow Hills, observation of single dimension distribution of the greatest length and distal breadth gave no clear separation, apart from two or three large animals which are either entire males or anomalies (for example, old draught animals or different stock). What did emerge, however, were indications that slightly more of the longer and broader astragali had become incorporated in the sunken-featured buildings and this was echoed in the plot of volume against breadth (Fig. 6.12).

Nor is the evidence of the horncores (morphogenic and metric) unequivocal. Studies of sexual dimorphism exhibited by horncores (for example Armitage 1982; Armitage and Clutton-Brock 1976) have shown that within specific populations observed differences in shape of core correlated with the metrical analysis may be used to differentiate cows, oxen and bulls. However, the authors have pointed out that there is chronological, spatial and genetic-dependent variability, so that rules applied to one faunal assemblage do not necessarily apply to all. At Barrow Hills it was difficult to group those cores which had lost their tips, but apart from two very small cores (less than 130 mm in length) the remainder could be assigned to a medium-sized group (outer length 150–210 mm) in which there was noticeable variation in size and shape of base circumference and thickness of outer wall. Most of the cores were visibly egg-shaped at the base and although several appeared to be more oval, 'flattened', the thinness of the outer wall was more reminiscent of castrates than bulls.

On the basis of high base circumference and low index (LD/GD x 100), the cores in SFBs 6 and 19 and barrow 13 were from bulls. The two smallest cores in the assemblage (from SFB 6) apparently belong to a bull and a cow and there was some evidence that the 'bull' was not fully mature – hence the low base circumference. Of the medium-sized group, only 11 specimens were sufficiently intact to allow measurement of the base circumference and diameter. The oblique chopping on several other cores rendered measurement impossible but sex was tentatively assigned on the basis of shape and robusticity. Those which could be plotted

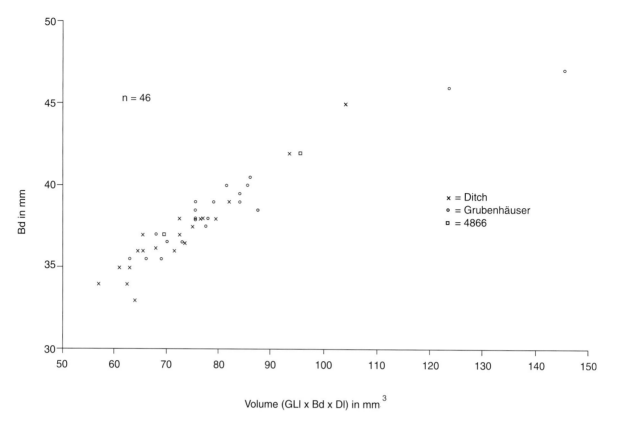

Figure 6.12   Scattergram showing cattle astragalus volumes plotted against distal breadth.

yielded a small group of castrates and the three bulls mentioned above. One massive core in SFB 28 (level 1) was judged to be male but exact measurement was impossible owing to the oblique chopping angle. Measurement at the point of the chop-mark gave a high index value which would place this specimen with the castrates. Level 2 of the same feature yielded a large astragalus and robust metacarpal which may belong to the same animal.

The length of the lower third molar is thought to show no clear sexual dimorphism and the 21 measurable specimens at Barrow Hills are indeed tightly grouped around the mean (range 31.00 – 37.00 mm, x[chi] = 33.6, s.d. = 1.49, v = 2.2).

Stature

Using Matalocsi and Fock's factors, cattle withers heights were estimated from 12 metacarpi and 4 metatarsi (Table 6.5). The metapodia whose distal breadths formed the largest group in the single dimension plots were designated 'female' and their withers' heights estimated using factors for cows. Those forming the smaller group were designated male and assessed accordingly. Withers heights using the mean of Fock's factors for cows and bulls were also derived from these 16 metapodia in order to compare the results with those obtained by this method for the Saxon Hamwih cattle.

Comparison of single dimension ranges and withers' heights showed that the Barrow Hills cattle were slightly larger than their Iron Age predecessors but not far outside the range for Romano-British stock. Epiphyseal dimensions are very similar to those from North Elmham (Noddle 1980) but the range of metapodial lengths is more restricted at Barrow Hills and the mean considerably less, although Noddle does point out that the Period I cattle (middle Saxon) are on the whole larger than one might expect. The range of metapodial withers' heights was again more restricted at Barrow Hills in comparison to Hamwih and the mean heights, though only a few centimetres different, were consistently smaller for the Barrow Hills animals.

Sheep

Single dimension distribution of the epiphyses of principal long bones gave little indication of bimodality, but as with the cattle the range of measurements in the sunken-featured buildings was greater and the number of 'larger' epiphyses was also greater than in the barrow ditches (data in archive, list 2). Fairly tight clusters in the distal breadth of metapodia showed no differentiation between the sexes but using O'Connor's (1982) index EntD/DistB, eight of the metacarpi could be assigned as one male and seven females.

This was in marked contrast to the horncores which were predominantly those of rams. As ram's horn is generally accepted as more suitable for horn-working it is conceivable that these horncores

284

represent the residue of such an industry. There were no polled crania at Barrow Hills, which accords with the findings at Saxon Southampton and North Elmham, but the lack of ewe and wether cores is puzzling. One of the male cores was decidedly slimmer and less robust than the others but the sample was too small to allow meaningful comparison of horn dimensions. The three smallest cores were all immature but two of these had already acquired the triangular cross-section of the male and were decidedly robust in appearance. The third was immature and could not be sexed. It is conceivable that only the males were horned and as the growth and conformation of wethers' horns is dependent on age at castration, it is possible that these may be indistinguishable from those of entire males. If only rams' horns were considered suitable as raw material for horn-working, unsuitable cores of wethers (and ewes if horned) may have been discarded with the metapodia and phalanges.

Stature

Withers heights were derived from 8 metacarpi and 11 metatarsi which gave mean heights of 0.598 and 0.585 m respectively (Table 6.6). Although not significantly different from Hamwih or North Elmham, the Barrow Hills sheep are slightly smaller. They are not much larger than Iron Age and Romano-British sheep in the area. Withers heights derived from other long bones gave a mean value of 0.602 m but it was clear that the calcanea gave consistently high values. The mean for the long bones alone (radius, femur and tibia) was 0.586 m.

Pig

Represented by few bones and fewer fused epiphyses, evidence for sexual dimorphism in pigs was scarce. Thirteen intact and in-wear lower third molars had dimensions below those of wild pigs, greatest value 34.5 mm and mean value 29.9 mm (archive list 3). The smallest tooth, 25.5 mm, was fully in wear and not from an immature animal.

Stature

Withers heights were derived from two intact bones, a tibia and metacarpus (IV) from SFB 24, giving heights of 0.788 m and 0.751 m respectively using Teichert's factors (1975). The former lies beyond the range established for the Hamwih pigs (which reach 0.778 m) and despite the great length of this bone, its other dimensions are not the largest of the Barrow Hills assemblage (*cf* distal breadth). Although von den Driesch and Boessneck (1973) concluded that Teichert's factors for metapodia gave withers heights which were too large, it is possible that the tibia and metacarpus here belong to the same large animal. Shoulder heights derived from astragali and calcanea

are generally unsatisfactory but three values were obtained from pig astragali of 0.637, 0.673 and 0.689 m (Table 6.7).

Other species

All dimensions of horse, deer and dog are included in archive but the samples are too small to show sexual dimorphism.

Butchery

Cattle

Although cattle bones were noticeably more chopped up in the ditch deposits, actual cut-marks were more in evidence in the sunken-featured buildings. The highest recorded instances of butchery were found on high-frequency bones such as scapulae, innominates, vertebrae, costae and crania (including mandibles and horncores) and correspondingly fewer instances were recorded on low-frequency bones such as radii, femora and metapodia. Only one of the 66 astragali was cut and no cuts were observed on calcanea or phalanges.

The cranium

There were no clues to indicate how the animals had been killed and the few relatively intact frontal bones bore no sign of pole-axing. Most of the cuts on crania were clearly the result of butchery, not slaughter, and if skulls were being broken open to extract brain, pole-axing or clubbing damage will have been lost. There were a few examples of medial cleavage of the cranium and transverse chopping across the frontal region. Of the different methods of felling an ox, clubbing alone results in damage to the bony skeleton, and although it is possible to inflict cut-marks using other methods (severing of the main blood vessels), blade penetration to such a depth is unlikely in large carcasses. Decapitation, either before or after skinning, is attested on early British sites by the presence of chopped occipital condyles and split atlas and axis vertebrae. Only one occipital condyle at Barrow Hills showed any sign of cutting, in the form of thin, parallel marks made by a fine blade rather than a coarse chopping tool. Three atlas vertebrae were indeed chopped in two but in a cranio-caudal, not medio-lateral, direction. This form of splitting is not uncommon on Iron Age and Romano-British sites and is often confined to cervical vertebrae.

Besides brain, cattle heads offer edible cheek meat and tongue, the removal of which often leaves traces in the form of scraping and chopping marks on the jawbones. Many mandibles displayed deep cuts and chop marks, all concentrated around the coronoid and condylar processes and the angle of the ascending ramus, which were probably inflicted in detaching the lower jaws from the cranium. Only one mandible was cut at the symphysis but as union at this point is relatively weak, separation of the lower jaw seldom requires much effort and possibly this was an older animal where fusion was more advanced. Little nicks and shallow cuts on hyoid bones, often considered evidence for tongue removal, were recorded in six cases. Most of these, however, were on the stylohyoid in the region of the stylohyoid angle and may not relate directly to tongue removal. The carotid artery passes close to this region of the hyoid and there is possibly a connection between cuts on this bone and sticking (bleeding a carcass).

Of the 63 horncores, including core fragments and frontal bones with traces of core, 21 bore cut-marks. In virtually all cases, the cuts had been inflicted in an effort to remove the horn/core completely. Although many cores had lost their tips, they remained otherwise intact. To lessen the danger of splintering the worker may have gripped the horn and used it to pivot the skull while chopping at the base. This method, not to mention the left- or right-handedness of the cutter, would in some measure explain the apparent randomness of cutting angle noted on many sites including Barrow Hills.

Three specimens (of which two were paired) were hacked at the base but remained attached to fairly large fragments of cranium. Only one specimen, in SFB 39, was broken open along the dorsal surface revealing the inner cavities all the way to the tip. At the base, it had been sliced at a very oblique angle, starting almost half-way along the ventral surface, and although there were slight indications that a similar slicing action had opened part of the dorsal surface, it appears that the remainder of the core broke open and was not cut along its length.

Only one of the six juvenile specimens showed positive signs of cutting where the posterior surface had been sliced off by a blow delivered along the same axis as the core itself. The slice had not detached cleanly and splinters of bone were left near the base of the core at the deepest point of the cut. The purpose of the blow is not clear for it was angled in such a way that it could neither have removed the horn/core nor split the frontal. This was possibly a mis-hit aimed at the occipital region to detach the cranium from the vertebral column. Two of the immature cores bore tiny subtriangular punch marks, possibly gnaw marks, near the base. Dogs can demolish horn, especially if it is fresh or retains any smell of the animal.

The cores of several mature animals were completely free of cut-marks and although it is difficult to gauge the quality of the original horn, these specimens appear to be no worse, and indeed in the case of the cranium in SFB 45 considerably better, than the cores which were hacked off. Horns may have been detached simply to facilitate butchery of the head, but those few examples of chopped cores still attached to crania indicate that the horn sheath itself was in some cases the object of attention. Horn-working was either a casual occupation or an activity which changed in importance through time.

The post-cranial skeleton

Butchery marks are usually concentrated in the high-meat areas of the bovine carcass around the upper limbs and backbone. At Barrow Hills, both scapulae and innominates claimed the highest number of cut-marks, the former with cuts mainly around the spine and on the blade surfaces, and the latter with chop marks on the shaft of the ilium, ischium and pubis. With a certain amount of skill, meat can be cleanly stripped from around the scapula (bladebone) leaving the bone relatively intact though in archaeological contexts whole scapulae seldom survive and mostly distal ends are recovered. Many such pieces were found in the two assemblages with the glenoid cavity and coronoid process coarsely chopped off, though few were actually cut in the region of the neck. The innominate of pelvis (aitchbone) straddles the carcass at a high-meat area and has to be split to facilitate dressing out.

In modern slaughterhouses the carcass is split longitudinally through the axis of the spinal column at an early stage in the butchery process but mid-line cutting does not appear to have been a universal practice in Britain before the medieval period. It is easier to cut to one side of the column and bone out as required than to split the vertebral column into equal halves. There was virtually no evidence of mid-line splitting at Barrow Hills and it seems likely that an animal was butchered where it lay, with joints and cuts removed from either side. Vertebrae were generally chopped medio-laterally and by far the most frequent cut was trimming of the transverse processes of the lumbar vertebrae, 22 instances of which were recorded. As these spines protrude into dense areas of muscle it would seem that the spinal column was indeed being boned out and the processes were probably detached with the meat.

Apart from meat and fat, the carcass would have been a valuable source of offal, including liver, kidney, heart, tripe and pancreas. Minimal butchery is necessary to remove viscera but the process is made easier once the rib cage is opened out by splitting the sternum. One fragment of sternal cartilage was indeed cut. The highest number of cuts were noted on ribs, mainly transverse cuts on the dorsal surface (cranio-caudal direction across the rib blade) showing where meat had been stripped out. Some ribs were sliced through, generally on the sternal half (the less meaty end). There was no obvious scraping on any of the rib blades and the rib heads, though seldom preserved intact, showed no cut-marks at all.

The lower legs and feet are not meatless but would generally be regarded as waste, suitable for boiling. Both radii and tibiae, though bearing few actual cuts, were broken at mid-shaft and presumably had been discarded with the metapodia and phalanges. One metatarsal in pit 4829 bore deep chopping marks at the mid-diaphysis but most of the other signs of butchery on metapodia were confined to the distal end where feet had been severed or the skin released. Only one of the 66 astragali was cut and although more than half the 68 calcanea were broken, there was no consistent pattern of breakage and no cuts were visible. It suggests that these two major bones of the hock joint were discarded in articulation with the distal tibia. At earlier (Iron Age and Romano-British) and later (medieval) sites, the calcaneum is frequently broken at the distal end and the astragalus, occasionally split into two medio-laterally, often has fine cut-marks. Obviously preparation of this joint was different at Barrow Hills but whether this practice was specific to the region or to the Anglo-Saxons is not clear.

Sheep

The difference in butchery technique occasioned by size of carcass is often reflected in the frequency, type and location of cut-marks. In contrast to the bovine sample, where over 200 cuts were recorded, only 60 butchery marks were observed on sheep bones. This count does not include the seven butchered goat bones, all of which are horncores.

The cranium

Excluding horncores, there were only three instances of cranial butchery, namely, deep cuts on an occipital running in an anterio-posterior direction, a single, fine cut running across the ventral aspect of left and right occipital condyles and small score marks on the stylohyoid angle of a hyoid bone. Fifteen horncores showed signs of hacking and chopping generally at the base although one tip was cut, and a large core hacked at the base was also nicked half-way along the posterior surface. Most were mature males, whose large, curled horns could have provided good material for horn-working, but several were either immature rams or ewes whose horns would have been very small. Presumably the latter were cut to facilitate butchery or cooking as it is more economical to boil a sheep's head whole (minus jaws and horns). A skin can easily be removed over small horns but in the case of larger animals it would have been necessary to chop off the entire core.

The post-cranial skeleton

Only a handful of limb bones bear cut-marks, although once again the bones in the ditches appeared to have been more systematically chopped up. Two diaphyses (distal halves) of a humerus(?) and tibia, were whittled at the upper end in a manner reminiscent of bone-working rather than butchery, and although the cuts are very coarse these were not included in the butchery count. A series of deep gouges on the side of a humerus diaphysis, SFB 23, was exactly paralleled on a cattle radius in SFB 14 and has more the aspect of random chopping than standard butchery.

Of all the vertebrae, the lumbar transverse processes bear most cut-marks, generally in the form of thin, knife-like cuts on the process itself. Whereas in cattle the process was often sheared off at its base close to the actual body of the vertebra, in sheep the process was usually 'scored' at the mid-point and not detached. The ribs bear transverse cuts, similar to those on bovine ribs, but there were more instances of diagonally placed cuts and, unlike the bovine examples, often multiple cuts running in parallel. Several ribs were cut at the head and articulation.

Skinning need not result in cut-marks on any of the bones but these, if present, should take the form of shallow knife scoring around metapodia and on the compact bones of the lower leg joints. In view of the smallness of the sample, the absence of such traces on metapodia is not conclusive. One metapodial, the only one to exhibit cut-marks, was chopped around the proximal epiphysis and could be an example of preliminary bone-working.

Pig

In keeping with their low fragment count, pig bones had few butchery marks, but as most animals were killed for the table before reaching maturity their unfused bones may not have survived. It is easier to dress out a younger carcass, which requires less chopping, and it is conceivable that small pigs were roasted whole after gutting and cleaning, so that relatively fewer cuts would have been necessary. Although there is no way of determining whether pork was cured, large sections of carcass may have been salted down after minimal butchery.

Other species

The only goat bones to be cut were horncores, seven in all from sunken-featured building deposits. The base of a right core attached to a frontal/occipital fragment in SFB 7 was deeply cut on the medial surface close to the cranium and the frontal had been medially cleft. The first blow must have split the skull into left and right halves and the right horn was then dealt at least two blows on the medial surface close to the base. The lateral surface of the core was not cut but coarsely splintered where it had presumably been broken outwards along with the horn sheath which may have acted as a lever.

Seven horse bones were cut, including a metatarsal chopped mid-diaphysis and a lumbar vertebra with the processes trimmed and cut. There is some debate concerning whether horses in post-Bronze Age Britain were in fact eaten. Bones with cut-marks indicate some form of butchery but whether the flesh was eaten or the bones simply boiled for fat cannot be determined. The Barrow Hills ponies were not merely being skinned and some utilisation of the carcass is indicated by the cut-marks on a scapula, innominate, lumbar and vertebra and cranium.

One roe deer rib was nicked at the head but apart from slicing of antlers there were no other cut-marks associated with deer bones.

Several bones of domestic fowl bore tiny, very shallow cuts and nicks, either as a result of preparation or possibly even of carving when cooked.

Pathology and anomalies

The greatest problem in interpreting pathological conditions in archaic faunal assemblages is the absence of comparative material. Few animals today, and this applies particularly to livestock, are kept alive long enough to exhibit gross manifestation of disease on the skeleton. Early diagnosis and treatment (or slaughter) prevents the development of those lesions commonly found in archaeological contexts. Furthermore, the early age at which most livestock are culled today limits the occurrence of age-related conditions, and certain forms of stress-induced abnormality (for example of the sort found on plough oxen) have disappeared altogether from western Europe. Levels of nutrition, practicalities of stock-keeping (penning, hobbling) and general husbandry practice (castration, de-horning, breeding strategy) all have some bearing on the general health of the herd or flock.

Bone abnormalities in the Barrow Hills assemblage were loosely grouped according to type, with dental pathology treated under a separate heading. Six broad categories were defined but it must be said that these are not mutually exclusive and are used simply as a means of organising the data:

(a) trauma = callus formation
(b) arthropathy = eburnation, grooving, bone remodelling
(c) exostosis
(d) remodelling = abnormal bone growth
(e) genetic abnormality
(f) miscellaneous = origin of condition not known

Cattle

Most of the conditions observed were confined to the post-cranial skeleton, with 16 skeletal, as opposed to only 5 dental, abnormalities recorded. Almost half the conditions were type (e) and half of these were found in the same sunken-featured building. They comprised phalangeal fistulae, or natural clefts in the articular surfaces, asymmetrical vertebral foramina and perforations at the acetabular rim of innominates. The latter has been noted at other Saxon sites (for example, Bourdillon and Coy 1980) and takes the form of a notch, hole or slit near the acetabular rim. The origins of this phenomenon are not known and it is generally classed as a genetic abnormality. In some respects it is similar to the scapular notch of the human skeleton which may be absent, shallow, deep or manifest itself as an actual perforation. There is some evidence to suggest that bovine perforated innominates encompass imperfect union of pelvic bones and in these instances may reflect nutritional or age-related disorders. The three Barrow Hills examples were indeed formed at the point of union of innominate bones at the acetabular rim. Two were notches, between the ilium and pubis in SFB 43 layer

1 and between the ilium and ischium in SFB 43 layer 2; one was a complete perforation between the ilium and ischium of a fully mature animal in SFB 1. SFB 43 also yielded a first phalanx exhibiting a small fistula on the distal articular surface. Another phalanx in the same layer of this sunken-featured building had an elliptical hole on the palmar surface at the point of attachment of the interdigital ligament, which is presumably a stress-induced condition and neither genetic nor, strictly speaking, pathological.

The concentration of genetic anomalies in SFB 43 is interesting in that the perforated innominates were not paired and thus belong to different but related animals. Coincidentally, level 1 also yielded several ovicaprid tibiae which were noted as longer and more robust than any others in the Barrow Hills assemblage. It is therefore tempting to suggest that SFB 43 contained livestock which were not wholly 'native'.

Barrow 13, level 2 yielded a bovine distal meta-tarsal and first phalanx with classic arthritis, but apart from an acetabulum exhibiting eburnation in SFB 14 there were no other signs of arthropathy among the cattle.

Classed as a type (a) condition but really a type (f) anomaly was the scapula in SFB 32, layer 1. A small, almond-shaped callus(?) had formed on the medial surface of a bovine/equine scapula and become detached after excavation, leaving a patch of light-coloured bone underneath. The bone surface around the area of the detached flake was perfectly normal and the original injury must have healed completely just prior to the animal's death. The callus flake was presumably in the process of being shed.

Dental anomalies comprised teeth with 'frilled' roots, periodontal disease and absence of the posterior or 5th cusp of the mandibular third molar. The latter, a genetic trait, has been reported in other Saxon material (see, for example Noddle 1980). No satisfactory explanation for 'frilled' roots has been recognised by the archaeozoological community though most have opted for an age-related origin. As the condition is normally noted on loose teeth or in mandibles where the alveolar bone is broken to reveal roots there is no way of knowing the true extent of this condition in archaeological material.

Sheep

Only four instances of post-cranial anomaly were noted in the sheep assemblage and three of these were of type (a), exhibiting callus formation, namely ribs in deposits SFBs 3 and 33, and an ilium shaft in SFB 21.

A small fragment of left frontal bone in SFB 27, layer 2, showed anomalous horn growth. No cores remained *in situ* but it was clear that this animal had carried two separate horns on the same side. Bifurcation is a genetic anomaly and may occur in a variety of forms affecting horn formation. Noddle (pl CXVIII, 1980) shows an interesting and unusual example of core bifurcation at the Saxon site of North Elmham. The core growths on the Barrow Hills specimen were obviously small and very close together. Without the right half of the cranium there is no way of knowing whether there was bilateral symmetry and it is possible that this is not a four-horned sheep but a mutation which threw a double horn on one side.

Thirteen mandibles and two maxillae exhibited abnormalities consisting of abscesses/periodontal disease, tooth impaction and crowding and 'frilling' of roots. None of these conditions is at all unusual and the incidence at Barrow Hills is no higher than that of other Saxon sites.

Four specimens showed tooth crowding, a consequence of domestication that may be found in several species, most commonly pig and dog. Type (a) conditions were noted on two bones in separate features, a tibia and fibula in SFB 38 layer 2 and barrow 12 layer 2 respectively. The latter exhibited a healed fracture and the former exostosis and possible fusion of the fibula or spicule formation. A severe inflammatory condition had affected a pig mandible in barrow 13, layer 2 but the precise cause of the condition was not established. In some ways reminiscent of cattle 'lumpy jaw' (actinomycosis) a large cavity had formed at the roots of the third molar where the mandible was visibly swollen. A small, distorted fragment of third molar root remained *in situ* but had been pushed sideways under the second molar. Although the remaining molars were firmly rooted and the surrounding alveolar bone appeared to be normal there were signs that the condition had affected other parts of the mandible in the form of patches of roughened, porous bone.

Other species

Type (c) lesions were found on two equid bones (one indicative of spavin) and a type (b) condition was noted on the posterior articular surface of a lumbar vertebra.

A slightly more unusual case of remodelling due to injury was noted on the antler of a young roe deer in barrow 12, level 2. The frontal bone retained both antlers *in situ* but the right one had been broken during growth leaving a stump about *c* 20 mm long, the upper end of which resembled a second burr.

An ulna of domestic fowl in the lowest level of SFB 6 showed some distortion of the distal end, presumably the result of trauma. Type (a) conditions are most commonly noted on bird wing and leg bones, which are prone to injury.

Conclusions

In any faunal assemblage, the predictable differences in skeletal part representation stem from butchery procedure (large as opposed to small carcasses) and carcass utilisation (as meat or materials). At Barrow Hills it was presumed that whole carcass representation should be expected. The skeletal element frequencies for the main domesticates did show a high proportion of the meatier parts of the carcass, limbs and back, in both ditches and sunken-featured buildings, with low-meat waste forming a minor component of both assemblages. The taphonomic loss in the sunken-featured buildings may be quite high in view of the ubiquitous carnivore gnaw-marks. On the basis of skeletal part representation alone, both barrow ditches and sunken-featured buildings were repositories for food residues as well as butchery/utility waste. The skeletal element frequencies of the main domesticates (cattle, sheep, pig, fowl and goose) and distribution pattern of horse and deer bones and antler, suggest that the sunken-featured buildings deposits comprise predominantly domestic refuse associated with everyday living. Kitchen scraps, raw materials and artefact residues are virtually absent from the large barrow ditch dumps which contain most of the normal butchery refuse.

The age profiles largely confirm the conclusion drawn from the skeletal element analysis, that the assemblages in the sunken-featured buildings comprise mostly domestic debris, with fewer younger animals and correspondingly more of the older animals ending up in the ditch dumps. Though somewhat unsatisfactory, the metric analysis points to general homogeneity of the domestic populations. There are very slight indications that the barrow ditches contain a higher proportion of the larger cattle than do the sunken-featured buildings but the samples are rather small. If this pattern is a true reflection of the original economy, then beef was the major component of the diet and the occupants of Barrow Hills were systematically butchering cattle for both meat and by-products. This pattern is similar to that of other Saxon sites, for example Hamwih, where the cattle bones were highly fragmented and the majority of immature cattle mandibles belonged to males.

Sheep were probably valued as much for their milk and fleeces as their meat, and bones of the older wool-bearing and breeding stock have ended up in the barrow ditches. The smaller mutton carcass was obviously prepared differently, and as one would expect, the bones of the upper limbs were not subjected to the same degree of boning out and chopping for secondary products. Although horns were detached in the same manner as with cattle, this exercise may have served the dual function of providing horn as a raw material and of allowing the head to be more easily cooked. At the nearby Iron Age settlement at Ashville, Wilson (1978) noted that sheep horn cores were broken but not chopped. However, most of the extant cores appeared to belong to ewes and it is possible that their small horns were unsuitable for horn-working. Certainly chopped cores have been reported from British Iron Age sites and there is some evidence from southern Scotland to suggest that male cores were not only preferred but possibly imported (Barnetson forthcoming). The Barrow Hills specimens were similar to those at North Elmham and appear to be predominantly male. There is little positive evidence of skinning but the virtual absence of phalanges and caudal vertebrae, noted also for cattle, may indicate that sheepskins were removed with feet and tails left temporarily *in situ.*

The apparent good health of the livestock and small number of natural losses, accepting of course that the taphonomic loss at Barrow Hills may be quite high, argues for good pasture and careful husbandry. This contrasts with earlier sites in the region, and indeed in other parts of Britain, where a slightly higher incidence of pathological conditions has been recorded. However, the Barrow Hills animals are significantly larger than their Iron Age predecessors although the sheep are demonstrably not as large as those at other Saxon sites. Whether this reflects different planes of nutrition or regional stock differences can only be answered by further excavation of Anglo-Saxon sites in the region. Besides providing some clues to the economy and husbandry of Saxon settlements in the Upper Thames Valley, Barrow Hills prompts more questions than it answers. If another Saxon assemblage is found in the area, comparison of butchering practices and livestock stature in particular should prove to be extremely valuable.

CHARRED CEREALS AND OTHER PLANT REMAINS (Fig. 6.13)
by Lisa Moffett

The present state of archaeobotanical research shows a considerable gap in our knowledge of cultivated plants and associated weed floras for the early and middle Saxon periods (Greig 1983, tables 1–3) which partly reflects an archaeological gap in the number of sites known and investigated.

What little information is available is thought to suggest that there may have been a substantial change in arable crops and husbandry between the Romano-British and Saxon periods, but when these changes took place, over what period of time and how different regions were affected are all questions that have as yet been little investigated.

The most typical cereal crops of the Romano-British period were spelt and six-row hulled barley, with emmer, the main Iron Age wheat, persisting in a few areas (Jones 1981), and occasional finds of rye (eg Helbaek 1952). A change in cereal species is seen in the post-Roman drying kilns at Poundbury, which produced oats and club wheat in addition to six-row barley, but not spelt and emmer (Monk 1981). In the Brecklands of East Anglia, one of the Saxon agricultural changes seems to have been a shift towards the cultivation of rye (Murphy 1983). In the Upper Thames Valley, barley and bread wheat came from Bishop's Court, Dorchester (Robinson 1981). Generally, spelt seems to be replaced by the free-threshing bread/club wheat and especially towards the later

Saxon period there is evidence for the increasing cultivation of rye and oats, though this was probably subject to considerable regional variation. There is some evidence that spelt cultivation may have continued locally in some areas. Spelt was found in a 5th-century structure at West Stow in East Anglia (Murphy 1985) and even in 9th-century contexts at Gloucester (Green 1979).

Thus, the charred plant remains from the early Saxon settlement at Barrow Hills were considered to be of interest for two reasons in particular: the site is one of only a few early Saxon rural sites where plant remains have been recovered, and the absence of Roman occupation meant that it was less likely that the charred plant remains would include any residual Romano-British material.

Usually, the simplest change in arable husbandry to detect is a change in crop species, but this cannot be done reliably if there is contamination from earlier periods. The Saxon settlement at Barrow Hills is near a Romano-British cemetery and cannot be entirely above suspicion of contamination by redeposited material from this period. However, the settlement seems to have avoided disturbing the cemetery, and residual plant remains from this source seem much less likely than from an area containing occupation material.

There was also prehistoric activity at Barrow Hills, and there were slight indications of redeposited material from this phase, mentioned below. The difficulties encountered and the assumptions one must make in disentangling the threads of origin of redeposited material highlight the need for extreme wariness in looking at residual contexts from multiperiod sites. It is all too easy to be led into circular arguments, especially since usually the only way to identify a crop species as contamination from a different phase is to make assumptions about when the crop was cultivated and when it went out of use – the very questions which in this case were being investigated.

Methods

The samples for charred plant remains were taken from the upper filling of a Bronze Age barrow ditch, which had been used as a Saxon midden, and from the sunken-featured buildings. There was also one sample from an undated, but possibly prehistoric, pit. This, however, proved to be very poor in charred remains, producing only two uninformative seeds of a bedstraw (*Galium* sp.). None of the features had *in situ* burning. Most of the soil samples were about 10 litres in volume (sample volumes are given in Tables 6.9–10) but a few ranged from just under a litre to over 26 litres. For ease of comparison the approximate number of items per litre of soil (excluding wood charcoal fragments) was computed for each sample, and these figures are also given in the tables. The samples were processed by bucket flotation using a 500 micron mesh sieve. The flots were sorted by a biotechnician using a low power binocular microscope. Final identifications were done using a Wild M5 microscope and with reference to modern

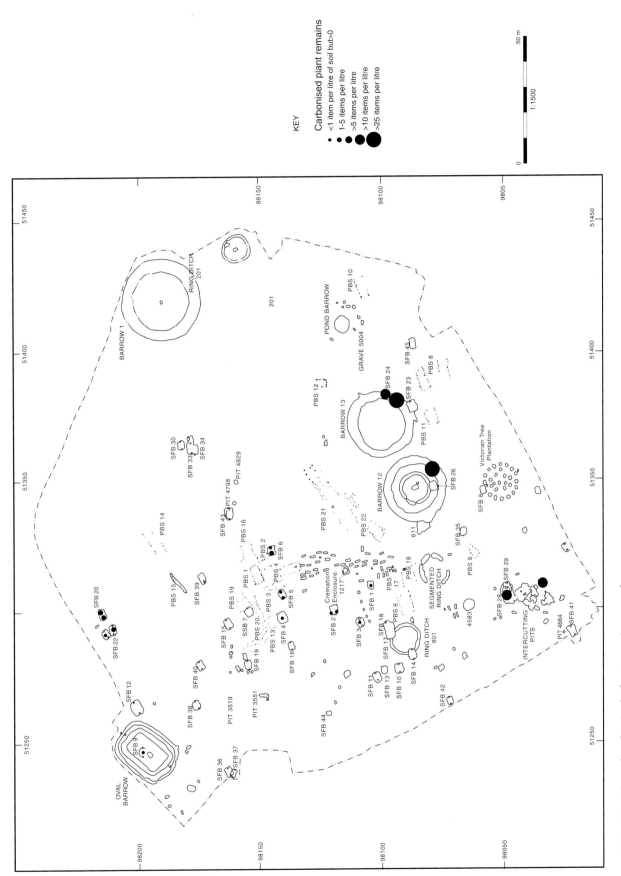

Figure 6.13   Location of carbonised plant remains samples.

Table 6.9 Charred plant remains from Saxon features.

Charred plant remains from SFBs

Context	SFB 1 1005/D/2	SFB 2 1053/B/2	SFB 3 1053/D/2	SFB 3 1061/A/2	SFB 4 1105/B/4	SFB 9 2143/B
Sample size (litres)	15	10	10	11	10	10
Items per litre	<1	<1	<1	<1	<1	<1
Crops						
Triticum aestivum grains	–	–	–	1cf.	–	–
Triticum sp. free-threshing grains	–	1	–	–	–	–
Triticum sp. rachises	–	–	–	1	–	–
Triticum sp. grains	1	–	2	–	–	–
Hordeum sativum hulled grains	1	–	2	–	–	1
H. sativum indet. grains	–	–	1	–	–	–
Cereal indet. grains	3	1	–	1	1	–
Other plants						
Eleocharis palustris/ uniglumis	1	–	–	–	–	–
Unidentified	2	–	1	–	1	–

Context	SFB 5 1225/B/1	SFB 5 1225/D/1	SFB 6 1297/B/4	SFB 6 1297/D/4	SFB 20 3606/D/3	SFB 20 3606/B/2
Sample size (litres)	12	11	10	10	10	10
Items per litres	<1	<1	2	<1	2	1
Crops						
Triticum aestivum s.l. grains	–	–	1	–	1	1
Triticum sp. grains	–	1	2	–	1	1
Hordeum sativum hulled grains	–	–	4	2	3	4
H. sativum indet. grains	–	3	3	–	1	1
Avena sp. grains	–	1	–	–	–	–
Cereal indet. grains	–	4	6	3	11	4
Other plants						
Chenopodium sp.	–	–	–	1	–	–
Polygonaceae indet.	1	–	–	–	–	–
Eleocharis palustris/ uniglumis	–	–	–	–	–	1
Unidentified	–	1	4	–	1	1

Context	SFB 21 3607/D/1	SFB 22 3608/L/2	SFB 24 3805/B/3	SFB 24 3805/D/3	SFB 25 3811/D/1	SFB 28 4198/D/2
Sample size (litres)	10	10	1.5	1.5	2.5	10
Items per litre	<1	1.5	14	44	8	20

Crops	1	2	3	4	5	6
Triticum dicoccum glume bases	1	–	–	–	–	–
T. dicoccum/spelta grains	1	1	1	–	–	–
T. aestivum s.l. rachises	1	–	–	–	–	–
T. aestivum s.l. grains	3	1	1	1	–	–
Triticum sp. grains	5	1	1	–	–	–
Triticum/Secale grains	6	1	1	–	–	–
Hordeum sativum hulled grains	7	–	1	3	2	–
H. sativum indet. grains	7	–	–	6	6	–
Avena sp. grains	–	1	–	–	1	–
Cereal indet. grains	–	1	1	–	5	2
Vicia faba var. *minor*	–	–	–	–	1cf.	–
Other plants						
Thlaspi arvense	1	–	–	–	–	–
Stellaria media type	1	3	1	–	–	–
Chenopodium sp.	19	1	12	1	–	–
Small seeded *Leguminosae*	6	1	3	2	–	–
Vicia/Lathyrus	2	1	3	–	–	–
Sanguisorba officinalis	1	–	–	–	–	–
Polygonum aviculare agg.	9	1	1	–	–	–
Polygonum convolvulus	2	1	1	–	–	–
Rumex sp.	42	–	3	3	–	–
Urtica urens	–	1	1	–	–	–
Lysimachia/Anagallis	4	–	1	–	–	–
Cuscuta sp.	1	–	–	–	–	–
Euphrasia/Odontites	–	–	–	–	–	–
Mentha sp.	1	13	1cf.	–	–	–
Labiatae indet.	1	–	–	–	–	–
Plantago lanceolata type	1	–	1cf.	–	–	–
Valerianella dentata	–	1	–	–	–	–
Sherardia arvensis	1	1	–	–	–	–
Galium palustre agg.	3	–	3	–	–	–
Galium aparine	3	–	–	–	–	–
Anthemis cotula	6	–	–	–	–	–
Compositae indet.	1	–	–	–	–	–
Eleocharis palustris/uniglumis	4	3	3	–	–	–
Carex cf. *Panicea*	1	–	1	–	–	–
Carex sp.	2	–	–	1	–	–
Poa annua	1	–	–	–	–	–
Phleum pratense	–	–	–	–	–	–
Large Gramineae indet.	5	1	1	–	–	–
Small Gramineae indet.	4	2	3	1	–	–
Unidentified (mostly internal parts of seeds)	49	3	26	4	–	1
No charred remains						

SFB 11/B/2

SFB 8/D/1

293

comparative material. Preservation tended to be rather poor and identification was sometimes difficult. The samples from SFBs 24 and 28 in particular had large numbers of items which appeared to be fragments of internal seed/fruit parts, but which could not be further identified.

In addition to the samples given in the tables, 15 one litre samples from the other sunken-featured buildings were processed and their flots quickly examined by the biotechnician. None of these control samples contained more than a single cereal grain or a significant amount of weeds or chaff (M Robinson pers. comm.). The control samples confirm the general low density of charred remains on the site. Location of all the samples and the relative concentrations of remains can be seen in Figure 6.13.

Crops

The crops present were bread wheat (*Triticum aestivum* s.l. – intended to include all free-threshing hexaploid wheats but not spelt), six-row hulled barley (*Hordeum vulgare*) and, possibly, oat (*Avena* sp.). It was not possible to tell if the oats were wild or cultivated, as the diagnostic lemma bases had not survived. The wild oat species, *Avena fatua* and *A. ludoviciana* are aggressive invaders of crop fields. Cultivated oats are one of the crops whose early history of cultivation in Britain is not very well investigated, partly because of the difficulty of separating the cultivated species from the wild ones. There was also a glume base of emmer

(*Triticum dicoccum*), and unidentified glume wheat (*T. dicoccum/spelta*), but these are thought to be residual from the prehistoric, as there is at present no evidence to indicate that emmer cultivation continued beyond the end of the Roman period in southern Britain. A poorly preserved field bean (cf *Vicia faba* var. *minuta*) was also found in one of the samples.

Other plants

Other species found include some weeds of arable and disturbed ground, such as knotgrass (*Polygonum aviculare* agg.), fat hen (*Chenopodium* sp.), black bindweed (*Polygonum convolvulus*), dock (*Rumex* sp.), field pennycress (*Thlaspi arvense*), small nettle (*Urtica urens*), cleavers (*Galium aparine*), field madder (*Sherardia arvensis*) and stinking mayweed (*Anthemis cotula*). Spikerush (*Eleocharis palustris/uniglumis*) is also present. This plant grows on ground that is at least seasonally waterlogged, but could conceivably still be associated with the cereals. Spikerush is often found with charred cereal assemblages and may have grown as a weed in poorly drained arable land (Jones 1978). It is too small a plant to have been gathered deliberately for thatch, bedding or other materials, but could have been included inadvertently with other plants collected for these purposes.

There are a few grassland plants present. Some annual grassland species such as clover (*Trifolium* sp.) can grow as crop weeds, especially if the agricultural

Table 6.10   Charred plant remains from barrow ditch and an undated pit.

	Charred plant remains from Saxon deposits in barrow ditch and undated pit, probably prehistoric		
Context	barrow 12 601/5/2	barrow 12 601/5/3	undated pit
Sample size (litres)	28.5	0.75	10
No. of items per litre	< 1	37	< 1
Crops			
Triticum dicoccum/spelta glume bases	–	1	–
T. aestivum s.l. grains	1	–	–
Triticum sp. grains	5	–	–
Hordeum sativum 6-row rachises	–	2(lax)	–
H. sativum hulled grains	–	1	–
H. sativum indet. grains	1	1	–
Avena sp. awn frags.	–	3	–
Cereal indet. grains	8	2	–
Other plants			
Polygala sp.	–	1	–
Trifolium sp.	–	2cf.	–
Polygonum aviculare agg.	–	1	–
Galium sp.	–	–	2
Eleocharis palustris/uniglumis	–	1cf.	–
Small Graminae indet.	–	5	–
Gramineae indet. culm nodes	–	1	–
Unidentified	1	7	–

regime includes fallowing (J Greig pers. comm.). However, some of the samples had perennial grassland species such as great burnet (*Sanguisorba officinalis*) and milkwort (*Polygala* sp.). The presence of these perennial plants is more likely indicative of permanent grassland and suggests that part of the charred assemblage was not derived from arable activities. There is also an element of a wet ground flora, including carnation grass (*Carex* cf. *panicea*), marsh bedstraw (*Galium palustre* agg.), the spikerush, and could also include mint (*Mentha* sp.), as most mint species prefer damp ground.

Dodder (*Cuscuta* sp.) is an interesting find. Common dodder (*Cuscuta epithymum*) is often parasitic on gorse and heather, both plants which are unlikely to have been growing nearby. Great dodder (*Cuscuta europaea*) is found on nettles, as well as other plants (Clapham *et al.* 1987), and could have been parasitising nettles growing on disturbed ground on or near the site. *Cuscuta epilinum* parasitises flax. Although no flax remains were found at Barrow Hills, flax was found in the immediate vicinity at Barton Court Farm (Jones and Robinson 1986) and a few miles away at Mount Farm (Lambrick forthcoming). It is therefore possible that the presence of dodder indicates that flax was also present at Barrow Hills.

Discussion

The mainly rather low numbers of plant remains make it difficult to attempt much interpretation of the assemblages. Chaff remains are few, so the use of chaff for fuel does not seem to be indicated. The absence of chaff also probably indicates that the cereal grains had already been threshed and winnowed before charring. The grains may have become charred during parching prior to grinding the grain to flour. Alternatively, minor spillages may simply have been swept into a fire along with other domestic rubbish. The arable weeds may have come to the site with the cereals, but some of them could also have been growing on the site itself in disturbed habitats.

SFBs 24 and 28 produced the largest amount of charred remains. Cereal grains, however, were a relatively small percentage of the assemblage in both cases. The ratio of weeds and other seeds (including unidentified seeds) to cereal grains was roughly 5:1 for SFB 24 and 6:1 for SFB 28. The greatest variety of plants came from SFB 28, including great burnet, dodder and some of the wet ground plants, while SFB 24 produced the mint. This high ratio of seeds, and particularly those of grassland and wet ground, may represent the remains of bedding, thatch, flooring, hay, or a combination of these.

Conclusions

The aim of looking at Saxon crop remains uncontaminated by residual Roman remains was probably realised, although there appears to be some contamination from the prehistoric phase. The small range of crops represented in these samples may not be the full range of crops utilised, due to preservational biases. Some of the plants found are unusual in a charred assemblage as they are rarely exposed to fire and thus their seeds are not often found.

A paucity of data from early rural Saxon sites points to a need for much further investigation. We do not yet have much idea of what to expect from such sites, and until basic questions are answered it will not be possible to address more sophisticated research issues.

Chapter 7:   The Anglo-Saxon Settlement

By Ellen McAdam

SITE LOCATION (FIGS 7.1–2)

As we saw in Chapter 1, Barrow Hills lay on a patch of free-draining soil on the Second Gravel Terrace, 1.5 km north of the right bank of the river Thames near Abingdon. In addition to the Anglo-Saxon features, the site contained the prehistoric monuments that gave the site its name and a Romano-British cemetery. On the west the site is bounded by the marshy stream known as Daisy Banks, and to the south the ground drops sharply by a couple of metres to the First Terrace. There are no natural boundaries to the east, and northwards the ground slopes upwards gently.

Why did the Anglo-Saxons choose this site for their settlement? It has been suggested (D Miles, pers. comm.) that the selection of both Barton Court Farm and Barrow Hills was the result of environmental determinism, exploiting the settlement potential of free-draining soils of marginal agricultural importance. It seems likely, however, that the previous associations of the landscape and the continuing existence of a network of trackways also influenced the choice of location, and this will be explored in more detail below.

ORIGINAL EXTENT

The excavations of 1983–5 exposed an area of approximately 3.5 ha. The sunken-featured buildings show up clearly in aerial photographs and may have continued southwards beyond the boundaries of the excavation towards the edge of the gravel terrace (Chapter 3, Original extent of settlement). However, the excavation came quite close to the terrace edge, and it is unlikely that many features were missed. The dark rectangles visible on the north-east side of Audlett Drive, which look like sunken-featured buildings on aerial photographs (Pl. 1.1), were excavated in 1985 and discovered to be tree-throw holes. There were no Saxon finds in this area and relatively little material from the ditches of barrow 1, so it seems probable that the limit of this part of the settlement has been reached here. Saxon activity definitely continued to the north, however (Fig. 1.3), and it is impossible to be certain how dense this was or how far it extended.

Although Daisy Banks forms a natural boundary on the west there is a good case for regarding the Anglo-Saxon occupation at Barton Court Farm, 300 m to the south-west, as part of the same community as Barrow Hills. The distance between the two is only slightly greater than the distance from one side of the excavated area of Barrow Hills to the other. They overlap in date, and there are very close links between the two sites in terms of fabric and stamp types; the large rosette stamp on a sherd from SFB 41 was undoubtedly made from the same die as one from Barton Court Farm (S Raven,

archive report). They apparently lay on a network of trackways which may have continued in use from the Romano-British into the Saxon period. There was no sign of activity in the ground between the sites, although the Saxon activity at Barton Court Farm may originally have extended some distance to the west, nor is there any cropmark evidence for another site in the immediate vicinity. It seems likely that Barton Court Farm and Barrow Hills together represent most of the evidence for this settlement.

DATE

The pottery and most of the finds from Barrow Hills date the site to the 5th and 6th centuries. None of the finds need be dated later than the early 7th-century: there is, for example, only one 7th-century knife (see Chapter 5, Knives and razors). Occupation at Barton Court Farm may have begun slightly earlier in the 5th century and continued into the 6th century, but did not continue for as long as Barrow Hills (S Raven, archive report, discussion). Settlement at Barton Court Farm may have ended before the northern part of that site was used for burials, which date to the 6th or mid to second half of the 6th century. Avery and Brown (1972) found an amethyst bead of 7th-century type in the area to the north-west of the site, and the burial on the south side of the pond barrow is dated to the late 6th to early 7th century. Blinkhorn has suggested in Chapter 4 that pottery stopped being made in the 7th century, and that features with a low concentration of finds may be late. The fact that larger sunken-featured buildings have been thought to be later (see Chapter 3, Metrology, length and width), and that the large SFB 12 has a low pottery density, appears to support this. However, sunken-featured buildings with low pottery densities also include those with sherds dated to the 5th, 5th to 6th and 6th centuries as well as those with no datable sherds. Sunken-featured buildings in the latter category also produced the same range of non-ceramic finds as other features. The argument that a combination of low pottery density and absence of datable sherds indicates lateness may be correct, but it is difficult to see how it can be proved. The site may have continued in use after the early 7th century, but since the later finds are so few in number this seems unlikely. It is therefore possible to state with some certainty that occupation began at the site in the 5th century and continued during the 6th, but did not extend far into the 7th century.

SITE FORMATION PROCESSES

It is much more difficult to pronounce with any conviction on the date of any particular feature or group of features. In order to model the phasing and

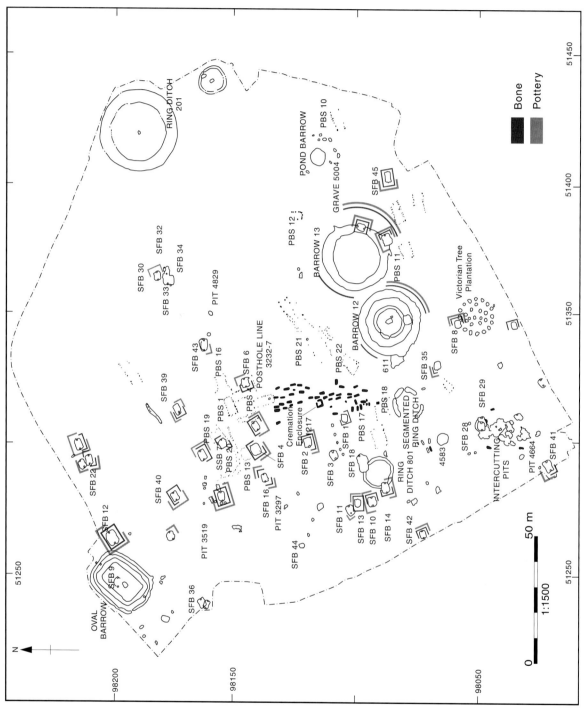

Figure 7.1   SFB quadrants and ditch sections containing highest proportions of bone and pottery by volume.

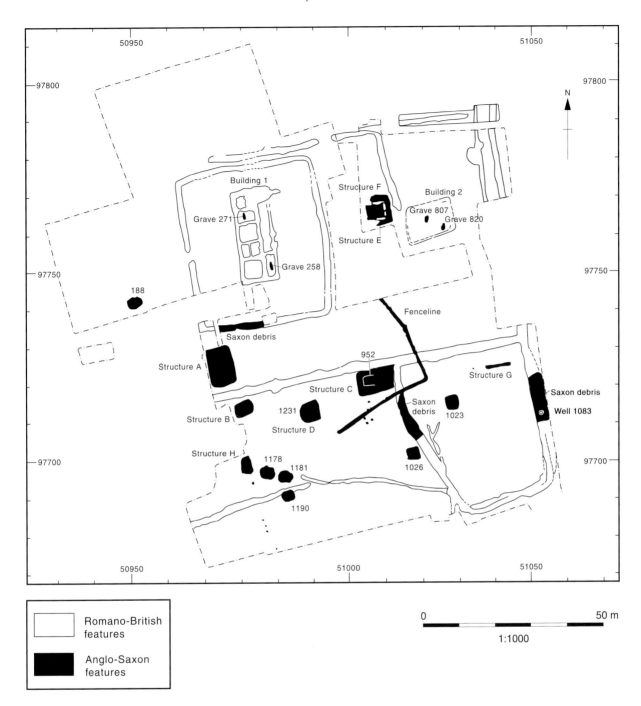

Figure 7.2   Barton Court Farm.

development of the Anglo-Saxon settlement, it is necessary to understand the processes by which the deposits were formed. As we have seen in Chapter 3, only one of the sunken-featured buildings, SFB 26, contained an occupation layer that might have built up during the lifetime of the superstructure. However, the quantity of pottery involved and the presence of cross-joins between layers 4 and 2 cast doubt on whether this layer could be the result of material sifting through floorboards, as has been suggested at other sites such as West Stow. Another six contained deposits that appeared to represent the use of the pit floor after the building had been dismantled. It seems that the

sunken-featured buildings at Barrow Hills did not contain primary fills contemporary with the life of the building.

Most of the sunken-featured buildings contained two or three layers of fill, typically reddish brown and containing large quantities of material including small finds, pottery, ash, fired clay and animal bone, with increasing quantities of gravel towards the bottom of the pit and increasing numbers of medieval and post-medieval finds towards the top. These fills were recorded as containing numerous tip lines and patches of gravel, and had been extensively disturbed by burrowing animals.

The excavator of Barrow Hills believed that in most instances the pits had been deliberately and rapidly backfilled following demolition of the superstructure and removal of the gable posts. Post-pipes were recorded in only two instances, SFBs 35 and 45, and in most cases where it was possible to establish the relationship between the fill of the pit and the fills of the postholes it was clear that the pit fills extended into the postholes. There was little sign of any erosion of the pit sides, and the fill included large lumps of conglomerated gravel, which the excavator suggested represented the material originally excavated from the pit and used to form the walls. The presence of a newborn infant burial on the base of SFB 32 may be further support for the suggestion that the pits were backfilled rapidly in one operation. The fact that several sunken-featured buildings were cut through earlier pits indicates that the fills must have been relatively dense and hard-packed, as otherwise the sides of the recut pits would have tended to collapse. There is no evidence for this happening.

Tipper has examined the nature of *Grubenhäuser* fills at Mucking, West Stow and West Heslerton in detail (2004, chapter 5). He describes a general interpretive sequence to explain the character of the tripartite fills in which the three fills derived from different sources:

1 a large component of the lowest fill derived from the super-structure of the building, although it could also have contained material dumped from elsewhere.
2 the middle fill was made up of spoil redeposited from surface heaps and other pits.
3 the upper fill was the result of gradual accumulation and the deposition of material from surface heaps.

There is some evidence that this model partially accounts for the Barrow Hills fills, with their increasing quantities of gravel towards the bottom. However, the presence of sherd and bone joins between all three fills in some sunken-featured buildings at Barrow Hills and other sites suggests that these tripartite fills were not discrete stratigraphic events but may represent some form of natural soil sorting after deposition. It would appear that rather than filling gradually the pits were backfilled deliberately in one event with material from elsewhere, combined with material from turf walls, with contamination from ploughing and burrowing animals increasing towards the top of the fill.

THE DISTRIBUTION OF BONE AND POTTERY IN SUNKEN-FEATURED BUILDINGS AND BARROW DITCHES (TABLE 7.1)

The Anglo-Saxon contexts at Barrow Hills produced 127.62 kg of pottery and 265 kg of animal bone. Nearly 70% of the pottery and 60% of the bone derived from the sunken-featured buildings, and 20% and 31% respectively from the ditches of barrows 12 and 13. Within these overall figures,

however, there are considerable variations in distribution.

The pottery and animal bone from the Anglo-Saxon features was recorded by quadrant or ditch segment and layer. In order to try to establish a clearer picture of how the deposits found their way into the sunken-featured buildings and barrow ditches, densities of pottery and bone were plotted by quadrant and ditch segment for signs of patterning in the way in which material was dumped in the pits (Fig. 7.1). This follows the observation by Barnetson that heavier samples were generally found in adjacent quadrants, and only rarely in opposing quadrants (Chapter 6, Taphonomy general: macrofauna). This implies that the pits were filled from one direction. Details of weights and densities are given in Appendix 1.

Certain features were excluded from this analysis. It was clear that it had not been possible to separate the fills of the intercutting sunken-featured buildings during excavation, and the figures from these features could not be used. The density of finds in barrow 1 was very much lower than in barrows 12 and 13, and it was not completely excavated, making comparison impossible. It is not clear from the archive whether the Neolithic oval barrow ditches produced no animal bone or whether it was lost after excavation. This analysis has therefore focused on non-intercutting sunken-featured buildings and barrows 12 and 13.

Figure 7.1 shows the quadrants and ditch segments containing the highest proportions of bone and pottery by volume. On the whole, the pottery in the sunken-featured buildings seems to be entering from the same direction as the bone, and there are only a few instances (for example SFBs 6, 39, 41 and 45) where the pottery appeared to be dumped in from a different direction. It may be inferred from this that the bone and pottery usually entered together from a single source rather than deriving from separate activities. This in turn supports the suggestion that these features are being deliberately backfilled in a single operation from a single source of material, rather than being allowed to fill up slowly as a result of numerous incidents of

Table 7.1 Barrows 12 and 13, weight of animal bone and no. of sherds by quadrant.

Barrow 12

	NE	SE	SW	NW	Total
Bone	4.2 k	11.9 k	7.4 k	8 k	31.5 k
Sherds	48	632	325	202	1208

Barrow 13

	NE	SE	SW	NW	Total
Bone	17.8 k	14.5 k	8.45 k	16.4 k	57.15 k
Sherds	87	128	266	234	716

small-scale dumping and erosion. It appears that the inhabitants of the site gathered their waste into general middens, and that these were used, among other things, for the rapid backfilling of the pits left open when sunken-featured buildings went out of use. A large open pit in a working agricultural settlement would have been a danger to people and animals, so it is hardly surprising that they were infilled quickly. The same would have applied to the barrow ditches. A number of sunken-featured buildings contained no bone (SFBs 11, 21, 26, 30, 38), but all contained pottery. There is no evidence to suggest that the features in a given part of the site were being consistently filled from one direction, either from the nearest hall or from the east side of the site, where given the prevailing south-westerly wind one might expect middens to have been sited. However, even if the material were being brought in from one part of the site there would probably have been obstacles now invisible to us that would have determined the line of approach to the feature. The existence of sherd joins between SFBs 7, 23, 24, pit 414 and barrow 13 shows that the fills of features separated by considerable distances could contain material from the same source.

The densities of bone and pottery in the sunken-featured buildings vary widely. Bone ranges from 0 kg/m^3 as noted above to 5.63 kg/m^3 in SFB 42, with a mean of 1.16 kg/m^3, and pottery from 0.04 kg/m^3 to 1.66 kg/m^3, with a mean of 0.26 kg/m^3. Sherd densities range from 2 to 68 m^3, with a mean of 34 m^3. The proportion of bone to pottery varies from 0 to 9, with a mean of 2.6. No spatial patterning can be detected, either by area of the site or supposed date of contents. The fact that SFB 12, the largest sunken featured building and therefore possibly of late date, has the lowest pottery density has already been noted.

The proportion of bone to pottery in the ditches of barrows 12 and 13 is much lower (it should be noted that the calculated volumes of the barrow ditches are only approximations, and do not take into account irregularities in the profiles: the result is that the volumes are overstated and the densities understated). Densities of bone ranged from 0.02 kg/m^3 to 0.42 kg/m^3 in the ditch segments of barrow 12, and from 0.09 kg/m^3 to 1.74 kg/m^3 in barrow 13, and pottery ranged from 0.004 kg/m^3 to 0.48 kg/m^3 in barrow 12 and 0.001 kg/m^3 to 0.21 kg/m^3 in barrow 13. Sherd densities ranged from 0.9 to 24.8 in barrow 12 and 0.6 to 30 in barrow 13. In terms of direction of fill, the greatest densities of both pottery and bone are clearly to be found on the south-east quadrant of barrow 12, and this is also the case for barrow 13, although here the densities on the opposite, north-western quadrant are lower, but still relatively high.

In terms of the contents, we have already noted that there are sherd joins between different quadrants and layers of some sunken-featured buildings, and between ditch segments of barrow 13, pit 414 and SFBs 23, 24 and 7. Barnetson also observed that in several sunken-featured buildings bones of the same animals were found in separate levels, and that preservation within levels was not uniform (see Chapter 5). The bones in barrow 12 were more eroded than those in barrow 13, where preservation within layer 3 was again not uniform. Bones from barrow 1 were noticeably more weathered than those in barrows 12 and 13, perhaps because, being on the periphery of the settlement, it was filled last.

The animal bone evidence indicates that both types of feature contain food residues as well as butchery waste, although there are more hearth and artefact residues (including antler), kitchen scraps and raw materials in the sunken-featured buildings, and the barrow ditches contain more older animals. There is also some evidence from the pottery of variations in the proportions of different vessel types or fabrics (Chapter 4, Summary of results), although statistically most of the evidence for these differences is weak. There were fewer jars from sunken-featured buildings in the area of barrows 12 and 13, and jars tended to be larger in the southern area of the site. Bowls were less common and smaller in the central and northern part of the site than in the southern part. Blinkhorn has suggested that this implies an emphasis on food production or processing in the south of the site, and consumption in the central area. It seems that the sources of the fills in different parts and/or periods of the site varied in composition, but as the location of these sources is unknown and the phasing problematic it is difficult to interpret this variation.

There is little direct evidence for surface dumps or middens on early Anglo-Saxon sites, but given the truncation of occupation surfaces this is not surprising. It is possible that inhabitants seized the chance of an open pit in the area to dump household rubbish directly, saving themselves the trouble of carting it to the midden, and that this may account for the differences between some of the sunken-featured buildings and the barrow ditches. However, very few complete or near-complete vessels were recovered, and the material is highly fragmented. Only a small proportion of the original vessels was deposited in the sunken-featured buildings and barrow ditches, suggesting that they were rarely used for primary rubbish disposal. The balance of evidence would seem to indicate that sunken-featured buildings and barrow ditches were deliberately backfilled in one operation, primarily with material that had previously been collected together elsewhere, plus their turf walls, and the fact that so much material is missing may point to the use of midden material for off-site manuring (Tipper 2004, 157–9). The contents of the sunken-featured buildings are thus neither primary, related to the period of their use, nor secondary, deriving from material collected in the immediate area and dumped in them immediately after disuse (although parts of the fills may be of this type), but tertiary, consisting of material that had been gathered together in another location over an unknown period of time and then transported over an unknown distance (SFB 7 and

SFB 23, which share a cross-join, are 100 m apart) to backfill the empty pit.

PHASING

If material was collected into middens and left for unknown periods of time before being used to fill features, it is difficult to see how individual sherds or finds can be used to date features, since all that datable finds provide is a *terminus post quem* in which the *post* represents a period of unknown duration. There is no guarantee that the rest of the assemblage from the feature is of the same date; it may all be earlier, or it may all be later. This is demonstrated most clearly by the sherd joins between SFB 7, assigned a 5th-century *tpq* on the basis of Figure 3.27.22, and barrow 13, assigned a 6th-century *tpq*. Two features containing parts of the same vessel need not be of the same date; but equally the apparently earlier feature may share the same *tpq* as the later one. This assumes, of course, that the pottery dating is reliable. The joins between SFBs 23 and 24 and the barrow ditch presumably reflect the incorporation in the sunken-featured building fills of material dug out of the ditch to form the pit, introducing a further complexity.

The fact that SFBs 5, 7, 15, 35 and 43 are assigned 5th-century *tpq*s and that SFBs 1, 4, 6, 8, 9, 14, 19, 20, 23, 24, 25, 28/9, 37, 39, 40, 41 and 45 are assigned 6th-century *tpq*s therefore indicates only the general date of the site, as noted above. It tells us virtually nothing about the date of the individual features or the phasing of the site.

There is, however, other evidence on which to base a tentative phasing of the site. There are some stratigraphic relationships. SFBs 23, 24 and 26 postdate the backfilling of the ditches of barrows 12 and 13 (it seems unlikely that SFB 26 would have been constructed while the ditch was open), and this may imply that the nearby post-built structures also postdate this event. The other post-built structures are undatable. The central group of post-built structures at the north end of the Romano-British cemetery may have continued in use throughout the life of the settlement, as PBS 1 shows clear signs of timber replacement and the lack of clarity in other plans may reflect a high rate of refurbishment and repair. Within the central group, one of the fencelines of PBS 20 was probably a replacement for the other, and SFB 7 may have replaced PBS 19, or *vice versa*. One of the structures in PBS 21 may also have replaced the other. The high level of replacement of sunken-featured buildings was observed in Chapter 3; around 50% were recut or replaced in or near the same location, sometimes more than once. The number of sunken-featured buildings in use on the site at one time over the century and a half of its use was therefore probably quite small, although impossible to quantify more precisely.

Occupation at Barton Court Farm may have begun in the first half of the 5th century, slightly earlier than Barrow Hills (S Raven, archive report). The

presence of adult burials at Barton Court Farm and in the pond barrow may indicate the dates by which these parts of the site had gone out of use, since it is unusual to find intact adult burials in close proximity to settlements.

In the light of this evidence, it is possible to suggest a limited phasing of some events at the site, as follows:

1   Anglo-Saxon settlement begins at Barton Court Farm (5th century).
2   Anglo-Saxon settlement begins at Barrow Hills (5th century).
3   The central cluster of buildings north of the Romano-British cemetery is constructed (5th or 6th century).
4   Replacement of one line of PBS 20 by another: replacement of one building of PBS 21 by another (5th or 6th century).
5   The ditches of barrows 12 and 13 are deliberately infilled: replacement of SFB 7/PBS 19 (6th century).
6   SFBs 23, 24 and 26 are constructed, and by implication PBSs 7, 8 and 11 (6th century: after 5).
7   Barton Court Farm no longer used for settlement (6th century).
8   Barton Court Farm is used for burials (6th century to mid to second half of the 6th century).
9   Grave 5004 inserted south of pond barrow (late 6th to early 7th century).
10   Knife in SFB 40 discarded (7th century).
11   Barrow Hills no longer used for settlement (7th century).

The relationship between the infilling of the barrow ditches and the creation of SFBs 23, 24 and 26 is definite, but the distance in time between the rest, and the order in which most of them happened, is relatively vague. We can say with some assurance that 8 is later than 1, 11 than 2 and so on, but not definitely that 8 is later than 7 or in what order 3, 4 and 5 took place. The sunken-featured buildings around the central cluster of buildings include four out of five of those with a 5th-century *tpq*, and the hypothesis that these substantial structures in their commanding position were among the first constructed at the site is a seductive one. However, in view of what we know about site formation processes this cannot be proved.

SITE LAYOUT

The Romano-British cemetery

The Romano-British cemetery and its relationship to the settlement at Barton Court Farm have been discussed above (Chapter 2, Romano-British land use and the cemetery location). To be available and selected for burial, the site was probably not under cultivation, but used as grazing. There is cropmark evidence for a trackway leading north-east along the edge of the terrace towards the Daisy Banks stream and Barrow Hills, and it is likely that this met an approximately north-south trackway leading to the smaller contemporary settlement at Ford's Field on the floodplain (Fig. 1.3). The most convenient route for such a track would have been east of the marshy banks of the stream and west of the still substantial ditches of barrows 12 and 13, possibly along the edge of the villa estate boundary postulated by Jones (1986, 38–42; Fig. 2.14). It seems probable that the cemetery was laid out along the north-south trackway. The boundary may have persisted: John Rocque's map of 1761 shows the boundary between the parishes of Radley and Abingdon running down the east side of Daisy Banks and southwards to the Thames, and this seems to coincide with the borough boundary fixed by a charter of incorporation for Abingdon in 1556 (Miles 1986, 53). A parallel for this location and alignment can be found at Stanton Harcourt (McGavin 1980).

The burial groups identified in the Romano-British cemetery display traits that may indicate that they represent the successive use of the cemetery by the same family group or groups. Over the two phases of the cemetery's use there was a considerable decline in population, from 13–14 adults per generation to 5–6. Jones (1986) devised a series of models for the population and organisation of the Barton Court Farm estate, and although there is no direct correlation between this cemetery and the proposed models, the figures for phase 1 are broadly compatible with his model C, which he considered the most convincing. It therefore seems highly probable that this was the cemetery for Barton Court Farm, and possibly for the smaller settlement at Ford's Field as well.

The Anglo-Saxon settlement (Figs 7.1, 7.3–5)

It has been suggested (P Blinkhorn, pers. comm.) that the presence of the prehistoric barrows was a determining feature in the choice and use of this location for settlement by the Anglo-Saxons. The major earthworks were certainly still visible: the ditches of barrows 1, 12 and 13 were approximately 0.9, 0.7 and 0.6 m deep respectively, and the fact that there were still visible mounds is indicated by the insertion of the now eroded SFB 9 into the Neolithic oval barrow. If the feature was the same depth as other sunken-featured buildings the barrow was probably still standing to a height of 0.3–0.4 m at the time. Williams has written of the ritual appropriation of the past in connection with the reuse of prehistoric and Roman monuments as early Anglo-Saxon burial sites (1997), and there are isolated Anglo-Saxon burials in the prehistoric monuments of Barrow Hills, although the location of the main cemetery is not known (Chapter 3, Gazetteers 3 and 4). As far as the settlement is concerned, however, it is hard to detect any respect for ritual connections with the past. Rather, the Anglo-Saxon inhabitants seem to have set to work deliberately to reduce the nuisance of having large negative features in their settlement, backfilling barrows 1, 12 and 13 with midden material, slighting ring ditch 801 and inserting sunken-featured buildings into the oval barrow and barrow 12. This is not so much monument reuse as monument abuse, and suggests no very great reverence for the ancient dead.

The position is different in relation to the Romano-British cemetery. The group of structures PBSs 1–5 is situated at the north end of the Romano-British cemetery. One posthole of PBS 5 just clips the north edge of one grave, and its south end overlies an infant burial. These are the only instances in which Anglo-Saxon features disturbed the Romano-British graves, although there is intensive Anglo-Saxon activity to the west and south-east of the cemetery. This suggests that the graves were still marked in some way, perhaps by mounds, and that the Anglo-Saxon occupants both recognised and respected them throughout the life of the settlement.

Settlement plan

The overall site plan in Figure 7.11 gives a misleadingly tidy picture of the distribution of activity at Barrow Hills. It shows three main areas of rectangular post-built structures and sunken-featured buildings: the area of PBSs 1–5, 13, 19 and 20, at the northern end of the Romano-British cemetery; the area around PBS 6 between ring ditch 801 and the south end of the cemetery; and the area south and south-east of barrow 13, with PBSs 7, 8 and 11. PBSs 21 and 22 west of the cemetery and north of barrows 12 and 13 appear to be non-domestic structures, and on the whole the area east of the cemetery, between PBS 21 and SFB 6, is relatively free from activity.

There are also post-built structures, sunken-featured buildings and occasional pits at intervals across the rest of the site. What this small-scale plan cannot show, however, is the mass of undated postholes, stakeholes and animal burrows recorded in some areas of the site and visible on the site mosaic (CD ROM). These are densest in the area west of the cemetery and east of a line drawn northwards from SFB 11, bounded on the south by PBS 6 and on the north by the central group of buildings. All the site records for this area were checked, but it was not possible to identify more post-built structures: the impression is of intense, long-term activity and frequent replacement of small temporary structures in this area. There is no direct evidence for the date of these features, but it seems most probable that the majority are Anglo-Saxon. The impression derived from the site mosaic, therefore, is of an intense area of settlement activity west and north of the cemetery, with identifiable structures at the north and south ends connected by a mass of indecipherable 'noise', and another, less busy, focus to the south-east of barrow 13.

The central cluster

As we have already seen, the dating and phasing of individual features are problematic. The most coherent group of buildings are those at the northern end of the cemetery (Figs 7.3 and 7.11). Four post-built structures, PBSs 1–4, face onto three sides of an open area approximately 7 m square, and the short end wall of PBS 5 abuts the south-east side of the open area. SFBs 5 and 6 are arranged more or less symmetrically to the west and east of the south end of the open area. It is not possible to determine

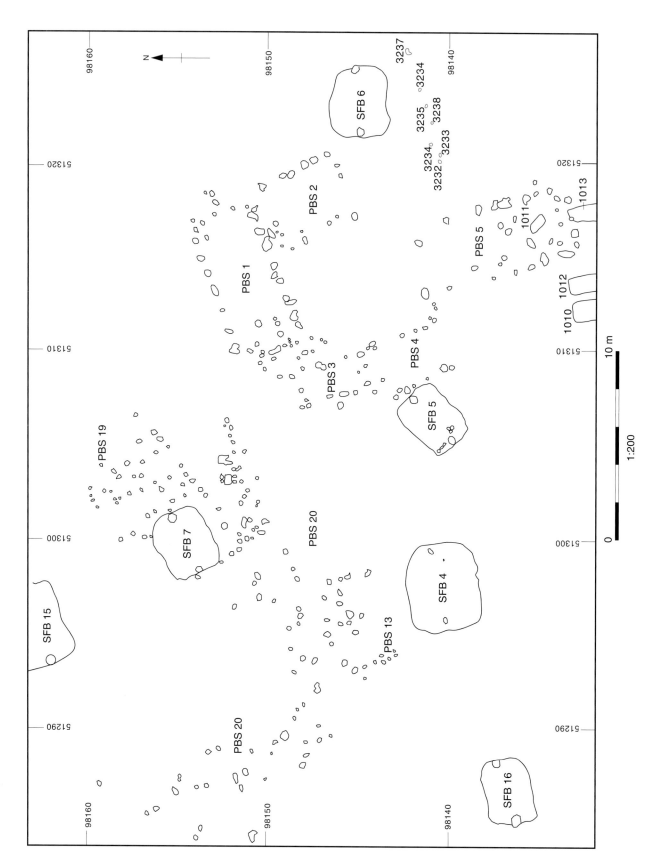

Figure 7.3   Detail of central building group.

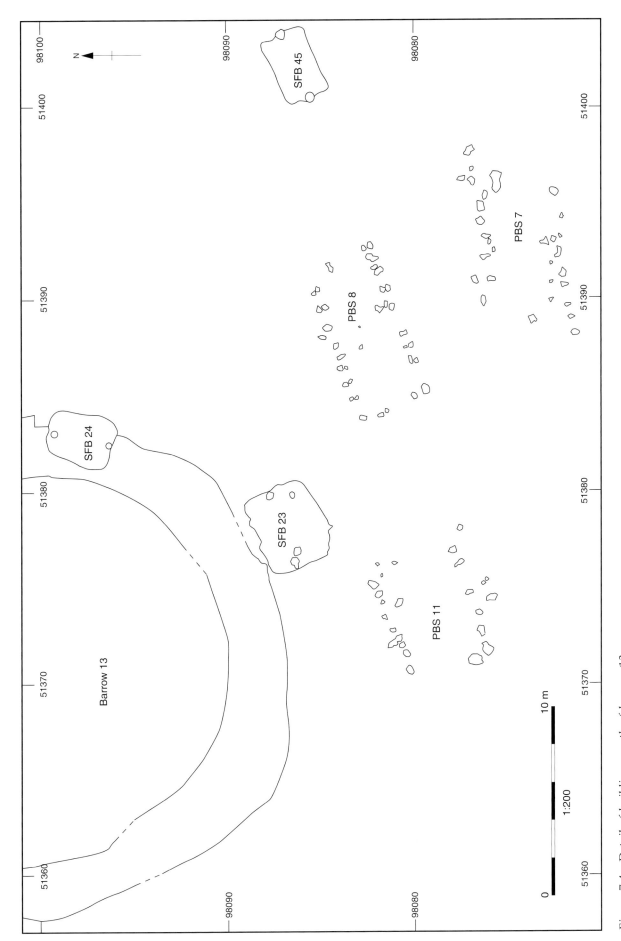

Figure 7.4   Detail of buildings south of barrow 13.

305

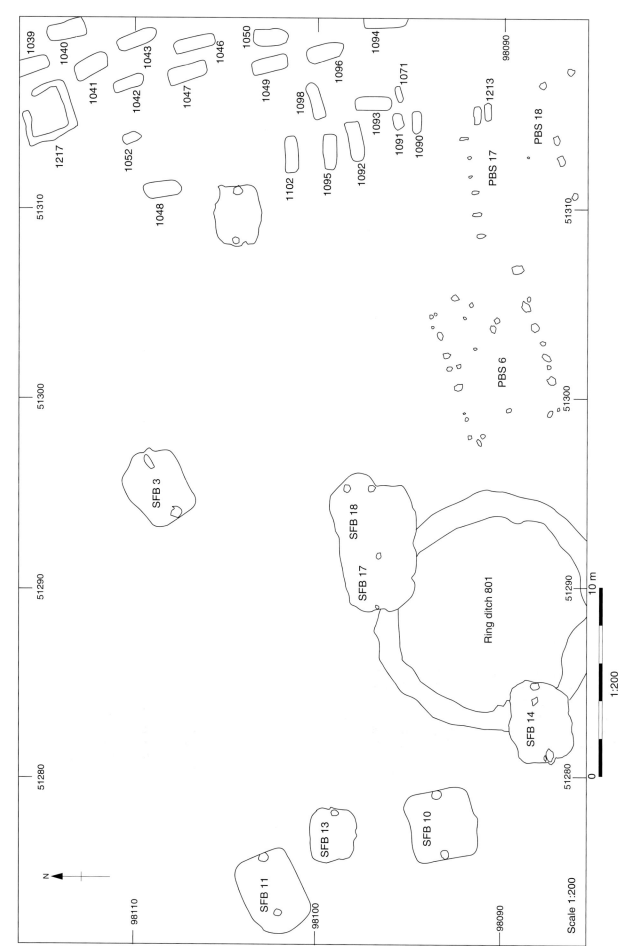

Figure 7.5 Detail of buildings in area of ring ditch 801.

which of these structures were in use at one time. SFB 5 and PBS 4 can scarcely have coexisted, and PBS 2 and SFB 6 would also have been a tight fit: timber structures may have replaced sunken-featured buildings, or *vice versa*. The line of postholes 3232–8 running north-east/south-west some 6 m south of PBS 2 may represent a fragment of fenceline enclosing the central buildings and open area (see Fig. 7.3 and site mosaic).

Roughly 4 m to the north-west of PBS 1 the double fenceline PBS 20 begins, enclosing the south-east and south-west sides of an area *c* 9.5 × 10 m. This is somewhat bigger than the area enclosed by the two-sided fenceline at Barton Court Farm, which also enclosed a post-built structure and sunken-featured building. It may be that instead of seeing these structures as rectangles with two sides missing we should interpret them as triangular animal pens, the third side being closed by moveable hurdles. On the north-eastern side of the enclosed space were SFB 15 and SFB 7, which may have replaced or been replaced by a structure represented by the mass of postholes PBS 19, the plan of which cannot be reconstructed. This may have coincided with the replacement of one fenceline by the other. To the south of the south-east side of PBS 20 was PBS 13, just to the north of and possibly abutting SFB 4. SFB 16 was about 4 m to the south-west of SFB 4 and SFB 19 was just over 2 m to the south-west of the northernmost end of PBS 20. To the north-east of PBS 1 was PBS 16, a possible funnel-shaped structure or the remains of two fencelines.

Three of the sunken-featured buildings in this area, SFBs 5, 7 and 15, produced 5th-century sherds. Although these provide only *termini post quem*, and we have already questioned the reliability of this evidence for dating, the high level of replacement and the density of features in the area suggest that these structures were long-lived. Welch (1992, 29–30) suggested that timber halls would have been rebuilt once a generation when a son inherited the estate from his father, or approximately every 40 to 50 years, and Hamerow estimated the life of a timber hall at Mucking as 35 years (1993, 90). However, a well built and maintained oak building on free-draining soil could last much longer than this, and there is no *a priori* reason why this central cluster of buildings should not have lasted throughout the 150 or so years of the settlement's existence.

This cluster of buildings would have commanded a clear view southwards across the Romano-British cemetery towards the river, west of the surviving mounds of barrows 12 and 13 and conveniently located for the water source of Daisy Banks. The choice of this location suggests that grazing had kept the site open. In 1998, 13 years after the end of excavation, the ground around the edges of the housing development that now covers Barrow Hills was covered by a thick, almost impenetrable tangle of hawthorn, elder and brambles. If the vegetation had regenerated to this extent between Romano-British and Anglo-Saxon use of the site it would have obscured the Romano-British burial

mounds and probably the prehistoric features as well. The fact that the early Anglo-Saxon occupants were able to locate their structures where they did suggests that the ground was still being grazed. The continuing existence of the old north-south trackway on which we have suggested that the cemetery was aligned may have been a factor in their choice, with the central cluster and PBS 6 being ideally positioned to overlook traffic.

Other structural groups

There is no way of knowing which if any of the remaining post-built structures were contemporary with the central cluster or each other. As already noted, PBS 6 forms the southern boundary of an area of dense activity, in which SFBs 1, 3, 10, 11, 13, 14 and 17/18 and PBSs 17 and 18 are recognisable among the remains of many more ephemeral structures.

Activity over the rest of the site is much less intense. If rectangular post-built structures PBSs 7, 8 and 11 to the south and south-east of barrow 13 were contemporary with SFBs 23, 24 and 45 they post-dated the filling of the barrow ditch. This group might have formed a replacement for the structures at Barton Court Farm when they went out of use at some time in the 6th century, but there is no direct evidence for this. The other rectangular post-built structure, PBS 10, is some distance to the east of this group and has no associated sunken-featured buildings.

PBSs 21 and 22 occupy an area of the site to the east of the cemetery with no sunken-featured buildings and relatively little posthole activity. They are larger than the rectangular post-built structures and may have had some craft or agricultural function; PBS 21 seems to represent the replacement of one building by another of similar plan. The prevailing wind at Barrow Hills is from the south-west, so this would have been a suitable area for malodorous processes. The rest of the site consists of isolated features, or groups of intercutting or replaced SFBs.

BARTON COURT FARM

The Anglo-Saxon occupation at Barton Court Farm is some 300 m south-west of Barrow Hills (Miles 1986: Figs 1.3, 2.14 and 7.2). The late 4th-century Romano-British farmhouse was deliberately dismantled, probably in the early 5th century by local Romano-British inhabitants who needed its stone to contruct another building elsewhere, and the cellar was backfilled. Occupation on the site may have continued in the two-roomed 'cottage', Building 2 (Fig. 7.2). This building contained a coin hoard that indicated it was still standing in the second quarter to the 5th century (Miles 1986, 14).

The evidence for Anglo-Saxon occupation at Barton Court Farm consisted of seven sunken-featured buildings, eight groups of postholes, several fencelines, a pit, a wicker-lined well in a Romano-British ditch, four (possibly five) human burials and Saxon material in Romano-British ditches. These features are not phased in any way. It is likely that further Saxon features to the west were destroyed when the 19th-century gravel pits were dug.

Of the groups of postholes, A and C had reasonably coherent plans (Fig. 7.2). Structure A was aligned approximately north/south between the villa enclosure ditch and the southern paddock boundary. It was approximately the same length as PBS 5 at Barrow Hills, 9 m, but at 6.7 m it was considerably wider. There was a possible door in the east wall. Structure C was oriented east/west in the angle of two Romano-British paddock ditches, and at 10 × 5.2 m was close to a double square in plan. It probably overlay the sunken-featured building 953, which contained 5th-century pottery, and possibly the paddock ditches, now silted up and filled with Saxon debris (Miles 1986, 16–19).

It may therefore have lain within and been contemporary with the fenceline which ran north-west/south-east and then turned more or less at right-angles to the south-west. Near the south-western end was a hollowed area containing settlement debris and a stone spread, possibly an entrance, and more postholes may have run north-west from the hollow, alongside Structure D, to form the west side of an enclosure approximately 25 m square. The fenceline crossed the latest Romano-British paddock ditch, which contained Anglo-Saxon material deep in its fill, and it therefore seems likely that this enclosure belongs to a late phase of the Anglo-Saxon occupation here. The relationship of Structure C, sunken-featured building 953 and the right-angled fenceline resembles the arrangement of SFB 7, PBS 19 and the fenceline PBS 20 at Barrow Hills. A second fenceline ran southwards from Structure H, west of the sunken-featured building 1178, down the terrace slope and apparently out of the excavated area.

The seven sunken-featured buildings were similar to those at Barrow Hills, ranging from 3.5 to 4.3 m in length, 2.5 to 3.7 m in width and 0.25 to 0.6 m in depth, oriented roughly east/west. All were of two-post type except 1181, where a shallow depression just to the south of the centre of the hut floor indicated a possible third post.

However unreliable the dating of early Anglo-Saxon pottery, it would appear that the gap between Romano-British and Anglo-Saxon occupation at Barton Court Farm was a short one.

SITE FUNCTION

Although at around 3.5 ha Barrow Hills was a large area excavation, it was not a large settlement. The central cluster of buildings and its adjacent fenced enclosure, with their visible replacement and refurbishment, may have continued in use throughout the life of the site. In addition to this central group, the settlement consisted of five possible rectangular post-built houses plus the structures at Barton Court

Farm. As we have seen, there was a good deal of replacement and recutting (approximately 50%, comparable to West Stow) among the sunken-featured buildings, and it is suggested that PBSs 20 and 21 also represent the replacement of one structure by another. Some of the rectangular post-built structures may also have been replacements for earlier buildings. There is no way of knowing how many of these buildings were in use at one time, but if the replacement rate of the rectangular post-built structures was similar to that of sunken-featured buildings the domestic element of the settlement at any one time over the 150 years of its life may have consisted of parts of the central cluster of buildings plus two or three post-built houses and their associated sunken-featured buildings. This is not a large number of buildings. The strong impression is that this is a single farmstead with a variety of structural types each of which fulfilled one or more of a range of functions during its life.

If we are correct in assuming that the settlement did not continue much further to the north, and that Barton Court Farm and Barrow Hills represent most of the evidence for early Anglo-Saxon settlement in this area, it seems doubtful whether it can be accurately described as shifting in the sense in which the word has previously been applied to early Anglo-Saxon settlement. It has been suggested that the incoherent layout and uniformly small buildings at Mucking reflect the stress and disorder of the migration (Hamerow 1993, 89–90 and 314). The scattered layout of these settlements has been described as less orderly and coherent than their continental counterparts, even 'second-rate in comparison' (Hamerow 1995, 15). Their lack of enclosures, obvious grain storage and communal facilities is explained as the result of the social and economic fragmentation that attended the post-migration period (Hamerow 1995, 16): this changes during the 7th century, when larger, more imposing and better planned layouts appear at some settlements such as Cowdery's Down (Millett and James 1983).

Hamerow has described Mucking as a shifting settlement, with movement across the landscape occurring gradually, one or two farmsteads at a time, although she describes the underlying causes of shift as 'elusive' (1993, 86). She suggests a lifespan for ground-level buildings of 35 years on the basis of structural and stratigraphic evidence from Wijster (1993, 90–2). Welch is more explicit about the process, describing how 'replacement timber halls and *Grubenhäuser* were constructed on open farmland by each generation, the old halls being abandoned as soon as the new ones were ready to move into and any reusable timber extracted from them....' (1992, 32).

Some writers have argued that there is evidence from sites such as Yeavering and Cowdery's Down for buildings being dismantled before they fell into disrepair. There is evidence for the replacement of one building by another, for example at Cowdery's Down (Millett and James 1983). However, there is no archaeological evidence either for the presence and duration of a gap in occupation, or for the absence of such a gap between the two phases, or indeed for the state of repair of the superstructure of the building that was replaced. It is also argued that evidence for the repair of buildings is relatively rare on Anglo-Saxon settlements, but Barrow Hills, West Stow and West Heslerton have all produced evidence of repairs and refurbishments. It is possible that buildings may have been replaced or renewed for social reasons, and that buildings were sometimes abandoned as dwellings on the death of the occupier and new ones built by his heirs. It is less easy to accept that this was the invariable practice across the whole area of Anglo-Saxon occupation during what has been described as a period of stress and disorder, or that perfectly serviceable old buildings were demolished every generation, rather than being reused, possibly for a different function.

Powlesland has recently questioned the view of scattered, shifting early settlements in the context of the settlement at West Heslerton, where he argues that the scale and organisation of the early phases indicate a sophisticated and cohesive society, with no more mobility than one would expect from a normal process of building replacement (Powlesland 1999, 26). The evidence is less clear, but this also appears to be true at Barrow Hills. As we have seen above in the section on phasing, there is limited evidence of some movement within the settlement, but no clear chronological patterning. It seems highly probable there was some movement over 150 years. However, with only seven rectangular post-built structures from Barrow Hills plus two from Barton Court Farm over a total settlement area of not much over 4.5 ha the term 'shifting' seems excessive. Indeed, the consistent replacement of buildings on or near the same site, and the dense activity west of the cemetery compared with the complete absence of such activity to the east, would rather seem to indicate a relatively stable and organised layout in which buildings or areas of the site fulfilled a particular function or range of functions that was maintained over time.

The lack of clarity in the site plan is thus more apparent than real, the result of a combination of circumstances including plough damage and rodent disturbance, the construction over a century and a half of occupation of temporary structures, the repair, refurbishment and replacement of more permanent ones and the lack of dating and phasing evidence.

PARALLELS

At Barrow Hills, the post-built structure PBS 5 lies end-on to a square area around three sides of which are grouped post-built structures 1–4. These structures may have been enclosed by a fence (Fig. 7.3), in which case the northern end of PBS 5 would have lain within the enclosure. It can be argued that the closest parallels for this layout are to be found not at

West Stow or Mucking but at the Wessex chalk sites of Cowdery's Down and Chalton, usually dated to the late 6th to 7th centuries (Table 7.2). Although there are differences in building and settlement size, preservation and feature type (but see Tipper 2004, 24) between Barrow Hills and these two sites, there are also striking similarities between the layout of the central cluster of buildings at Barrow Hills and buildings at these sites.

Cowdery's Down (Figs 7.6–7)

At Cowdery's Down the arrangement of a hall end-on to a fenced enclosure appears in the earliest phase, Period 4A, although in this case the enclosure contains only one building. The large rectangular post-built structure A1 oriented approximately north-east/south-west lay on the south-west side of a square fenced enclosure containing the single post-built structure A3 (Fig. 7.7; Millet and James 1983, fig. 27). Most of A1 was outside the enclosure, with a square annex inside it; there was no door from the annex into the enclosure. A1 had opposing door-ways in the long sides marked by substantial doorposts, doors in the east and west ends and a partition 2 m from the east end. Another enclosure of approximately the same size containing post-built structure A2 was attached to the north side of the first enclosure. Some of the structures of Period 4A continued in use into 4B, including hall A1 and the enclosures. Period 4C, however, was marked by a major change in both the layout of the buildings and of the structural types, in particular the replacement of single post construction by post-in-trench, and it is in this phase that the arrangement of several buildings around an open space within the enclosure appears. A new fence enclosed C7, C8 and a partially excavated building, which were arranged around the north, east and south sides of an open area. West of this enclosure, with a common eastern boundary, was another enclosure which contained a similar grouping of three buildings around an open space, and west again were six further buildings assigned to Period 4C on the grounds of their post-in-trench construction (Fig. 7.6). These included C12, the largest structure excavated, which was placed centrally on the ridge and axially end-on to the structures in the enclosures. This phase also included the only two sunken-featured buildings excavated on the site. At the end of Period 4C the settlement was destroyed by fire.

Constructional details were unusually well preserved in the chalk subsoil of Cowdery's Down and this has permitted detailed reconstructions of the timber buildings, particularly of C12, to be drawn up. The excavators believed that the consistent arrangement of buildings within enclosures throughout the life of the settlement represented more than an agricultural function, perhaps a division into social units, with the major focal buildings near but outside the enclosures being seen as communal, even belonging to the 'chief'. It is argued that the size and

Table 7.2 Comparison of central group at Barrow Hills with Chalton and Cowdery's Down.

Site and phase	Enclosure	Main hall	L side	Top	R Side	Comments
Barrow Hills	PBS 20 c 9.5 × 10 m	PBS 5 c 9 × 3.5 m	PBS 3 4.6 × 1.8 m PBS 4 3.2 × 2.7 m	PBS 1 7 × 3.5 m	PBS 2 4 × 3.5 m	c 22 × 15 m? Estimate of enclosure size includes SFBs 5 & 6
Chalton Phase B	B4 23 × 17 m	B1 12.7 × 6.25 m	B5 7 × 4.6 m	B6 4.9 × 3.7 m	B7 7.8 × 4.4 m	Open side of square not facing main building Chalton dated late 6th – early 8th
Chalton Phase AZ	AZ4 28 × 24 m	AZ1 13.8 × 6.7 m	AZ? c 8 × 5 m	AZ3 6.5 × c 4.7 m	AZ2 7.4 × 4 m	Post-in-trench
Cowdery's Down Phase A	25 × 25 m	A1 12.5 × 6 m + annexe 4 × 4.25 m	–	A3 c 13 × 4.3 m	–	7th century
Cowdery's Down Phase C	36 × 37 m	C12 22 × 8.75 m	–	C7 14.4 × 7.3 m	C8 14 × 7 m	Post-in-trench

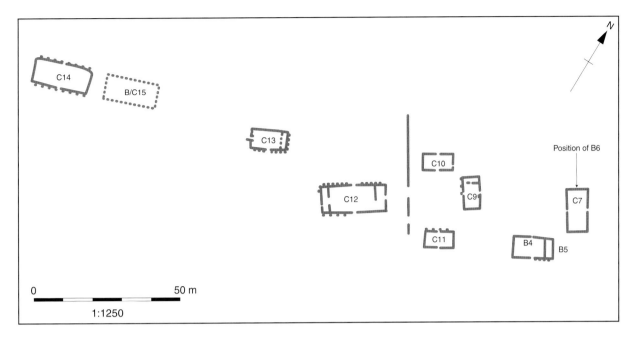

Figure 7.6   Cowdery's Down: Period 4C buildings (after Millett and James 1983).

elaboration of the buildings suggests that Cowdery's Down was a high-status site.

Chalton (Figs 7.8–9)

Like Cowdery's Down, Chalton is dated to the 6th to 7th centuries AD by the pottery, but since only four sunken-featured buildings were found on the site dating evidence was not plentiful (Fig. 7.8; Addyman *et al.* 1972, 13–32; Addyman and Leigh 1973, 1–25, fig. 3; Welch 1992, fig. 3). Four phases of occupation were distinguished. There was a gradual move from single post to post-in-trench construction, and building size increased with time.

Phase C, the earliest phase, consisted of one rectangular building of posthole construction, measuring 7.4 × 4.4 m and oriented north-east/south-west. The walls were of single posts with strong corners, substantial end walls and a door in the centre of the east side. The arrangement of buildings around three sides of an open space appeared for the first time in Phase B, but the relationship of the building B1 to the enclosure and its buildings was not the same as at Cowdery's Down (Addyman and Leigh 1973, fig. 3). Seven structures were distinguished in Phase B, all of single post construction. The largest, B1, was oriented north-west/south-east, with central doorways in the long sides flanked by double posts and a possible door in the west end wall. To the west of B1 were a smaller rectangular structure on the same orientation and a small almost square building with a door on the south side, flanked by substantial posts. To the east of B1 was a fenced enclosure containing three buildings arranged around three sides of a space open to the south.

The fenced enclosure continued in use into Phase A, the period to which most of the excavated structures were assigned. B1 was replaced by two large post-in-trench buildings, A1 and A2, on the same orientation but much larger. About 1 m to the west of A2 was a smaller building, A3, with a door in the centre of its east wall opposite the west door of A2. Some 8 m to the west of A1–3 were three smaller structures, two of which were approximately square. To the east of A1, the fenced enclosure and the arrangement of three single-post buildings continued, although one of the buildings of Phase B was replaced. The replacement may have been prompted by the construction near the fenceline of building A10, oriented north-east/south-west. A10 was unusual, with a wall of post-in-trench construction surrounded by substantial buttressing posts and very stout doorposts, and the excavators suggested that it had some communal function. A10 was joined by a fenceline to the large building A11, oriented north-west/south-east. East of the fenceline was another grouping of three smaller buildings around a space, this time open to the east and possibly related to A11. The site layout in Phase A thus consists of two (or more) parallel north-west/south-east lines of buildings running across the ridge, with A10 and the fenceline forming the east side of a 'village green' between A1–2 and A11. More buildings to the south and west of A11 were also recorded.

The latest phase, Phase AZ, included another example of the combination of large east-west hall and fenced enclosure with smaller buildings arranged around three sides of an open space. AZ1 was oriented north-west/south-east, of post-in-trench construction with opposing doors and an

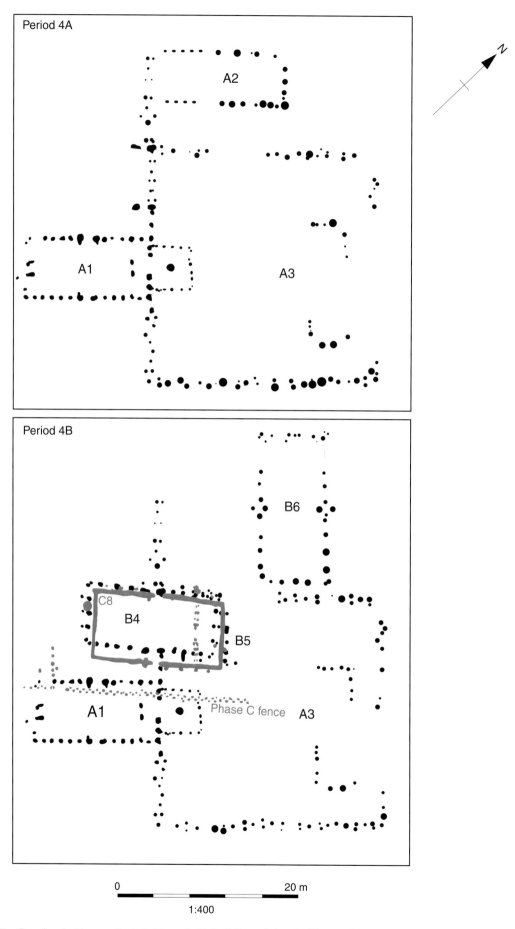

Figure 7.7 *Cowdery's Down: Period 4A and 4B buildings (after Millett and James 1983).*

internal partition at the east end. Its east door opened into the enclosure bounded by fenceline AZ4, within which were three smaller buildings.

Discussion

There are obvious differences between these sites and Barrow Hills, not least in the size of the buildings (Table 7.2). Some of the rectangular post-built structures at Barrow Hills may have been barns or byres rather than dwellings. However, there is a tendency, as noted in Chapter 3, for Anglo-Saxon buildings to get bigger with time, and at approximately 9 by 3.5 m and 7 by 3.5 m PBSs 5 and 1 are respectable sizes for early structures. The size of the later structures, particularly at Cowdery's Down, may reflect higher status or greater affluence (not

necessarily the same thing). There is nothing to suggest that Barrow Hills is anything more than a farm. Some of the buildings round the open space at Barrow Hills are contiguous, whereas those on the chalk sites are always free-standing. There appears to be no stratigraphic evidence at any of these sites to indicate whether the buildings within the enclosure were contemporary or successive. What does appear to remain constant, however, is the relationship of the buildings to each other. The arrangement of buildings facing three sides of an open space within an enclosure with a long building end-on is consistent enough to suggest that it performed some socio-economic function. At Cowdery's Down there is a gate in the fenced enclosure on either side of building A1, which also has a door in the centre of each of its long sides (Millett and James 1983, fig. 30).

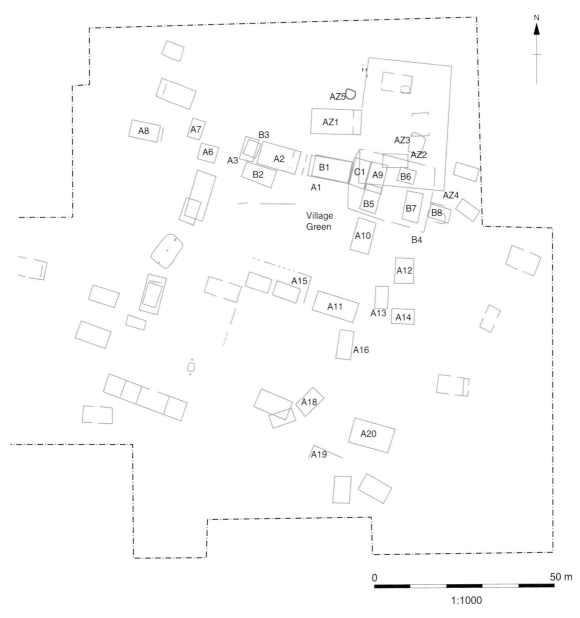

Figure 7.8   Chalton: Plan of major Saxon features (after Addyman and Leigh 1973 and Champion 1978).

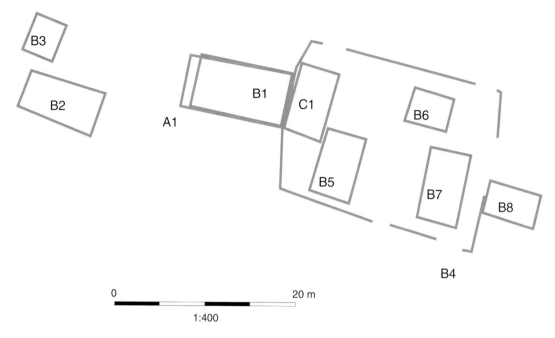

Figure 7.9 Chalton: Phases C And B (after Addyman and Leigh 1973 and Champion 1978).

This suggests that one of the functions of the long building was to observe and control access to the enclosure. At Barrow Hills, it would also have overlooked the trackway, if this was still in use, while the cluster as a whole was in a commanding position looking southwards towards the river. The Thames would have been navigable upstream at least as far as Oxford and a major route for waterborne traffic of all kinds.

Within the enclosure, the sizes and internal arrangements of the buildings vary, but the most usual arrangement is long side on to the open space, with opposing doors in the centre of the long sides or one door opening onto the open space. At Cowdery's Down the end-on hall is consistently east-west, with the enclosed buildings around the north, south and east of the open area, but at Chalton there is more variation, with at least one north-south hall end-on to buildings around the north, east and west sides of the open space as at Barrow Hills. From the surviving details of the buildings within the enclosures at Cowdery's Down it seems likely that some at least of them were dwellings, but some may also have been used for storage of valuable stock and materials. What was the relationship between the end-on buildings and the buildings within the enclosures? Whatever the answer, it seems to have been a feature of Anglo-Saxon society for longer than was hitherto thought, but it is perhaps not surprising to find an earlier, smaller and less elaborated form of the layout known from the Wessex chalk sites. Barrow Hills is, after all, on the right or Wessex bank of the Thames.

ECONOMY

The finds evidence from Barrow Hills and Barton Court Farm suggests a largely self-sufficient agricul-

tural economy, thrifty enough to collect and reuse Roman items such as sherds and fragments of copper alloy but generating enough surplus to afford the brooches and other personal ornaments found in the graves at Barton Court Farm. From the faunal remains, cattle made the greatest contribution to the economy. Beef was the major component of the meat diet, and the inhabitants were systematically butchering cattle for meat and by-products. Sheep were the next most important domesticate, probably kept for milk and wool as much as meat. Pig bones represented less than 10% of the overall fragment count. Together, these three species made up 93% of the total fragment count, and there is little evidence for the exploitation of wild species. This contrasts with the faunal evidence from Barton Court Farm, where sheep were the most numerous species, followed by pig and then cattle. There is considerable variation in the representation of species in individual features across Barrow Hills, so the apparent difference between Barrow Hills and Barton Court Farm may reflect the nature of the deposition process rather than a genuine difference in diet.

Among the plant remains were bread wheat, six-row hulled barley and possibly oat, and one poorly preserved field bean was found. Other plant remains included plants of permanent grassland and of wet ground, perhaps the remains of bedding, thatch, flooring, hay or a combination of these. This complements the evidence from the Anglo-Saxon well at Barton Court Farm, where six-row barley was also found. There was a slight rise in tree pollen from the Roman period, but the same open grassland was probably still present. The absence of stinking mayweed, common in the Roman samples, could reflect the abandonment of the low-lying arable, but flax was abundant, a plant best suited to damp ground.

314

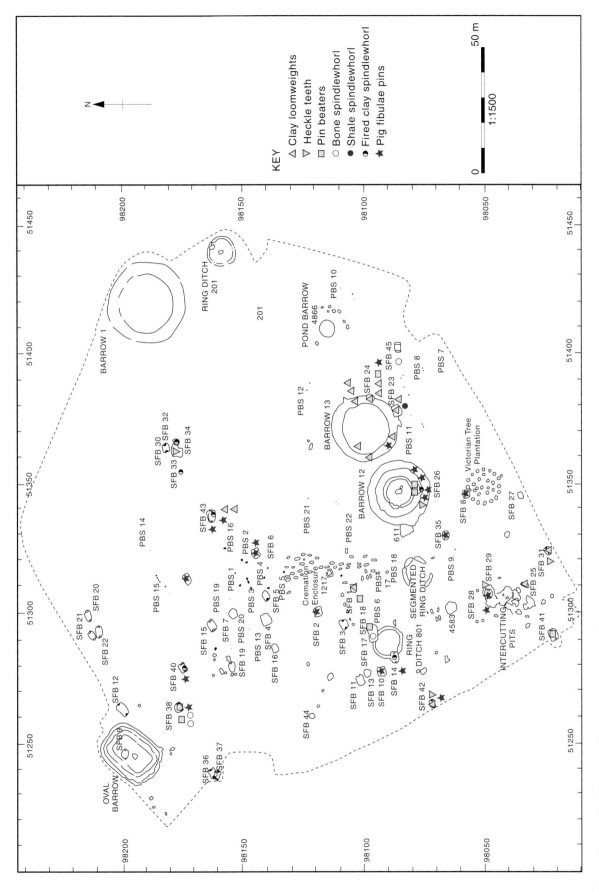

Figure 7.10 Distribution of spinning and weaving equipment.

In order to survive in a pre-industrial subsistence economy a vast range of processes have to be carried out on the raw materials of agriculture, only some of which will leave any trace in the archaeological record. Working by analogy with figures for 19th-century farms, Jones (1986) modelled the numbers of adults required to farm differing combinations of land units at Barton Court Farm. His preferred model was Model C, farming land units 2 and 3 (Fig. 2.14.) with eight working adults, plus an additional five workers brought in at harvest. It is probable, however, that the late 19th-century account on which he based his calculations dealt with primarily male occupations, and overlooked traditional female tasks such as food preparation, cleaning, childcare and textile production. The fact that so many sunken-featured buildings and other structures were rebuilt or replaced in the same or nearly the same position suggests that many of them played a fixed role in the working life of the settlement, and that the functions carried out in and around them remained stable over time.

Strenuous efforts have been made to identify patterns in the finds evidence, but in the light of what we know of the site formation processes it is difficult to advance a coherent interpretation. For the pottery, most of the differences in the distributions are not statistically significant. There are fewer jars in the south-eastern sunken-featured buildings, but they are larger, and bowls are less common and smaller in the central/northern sunken-featured buildings that in the south-eastern area. There are some differences in the distribution of animal bone between barrow ditches and sunken-featured buildings, with more kitchen waste apparently finding its way into the latter, perhaps through direct dumping. Almost all the edible domestic fowl came from sunken-featured buildings. Conversely, the barrow ditches apparently contained more butchery waste, lending weight to the possible interpretation of PBSs 21 and 22 as processing structures of some kind. Analysis of the other finds categories reveals no sign of spatial patterning. There was a notable absence of textile-related items, with the exception of two pig fibulae from SFB 6, in the sunken-featured buildings in the immediate vicinity of the central cluster (Fig. 7.10). This might reflect a difference in function or status, it might reflect a sampling accident (these features happened to be filled with material that did not contain such finds) or it might reflect a difference in date (these features were filled from a dump created at a time when this activity was not taking place).

Cattle and sheep were probably driven home at night to secure fenced enclosures, and this may have been the function of the right-angled fenceline at Barton Court Farm and of PBS 20 at Barrow Hills (cf the second enclosure with its single building in phase 4A at Cowdery's Down). The enclosures surrounding the building groups may also have had this function. Cattle would have required byres for overwintering and storage for fodder, and sheep (and shepherds) need lambing sheds. The structures associated with the various fencelines, and some of

Table 7.3   *Summary of Anglo-Saxon and possibly Anglo-Saxon burials in and around Barrow Hills/Barton Court Farm.*

Location	Burial	Date
Barrow Hills		
Grave 5004 on SW side of pond barrow 4866	Adult female >45 with iron knife and buckle and bronze pin	late 6th–7th century
Grave 4562 in SFB 32	Newborn	phase 3
Barton Court Farm		
Grave 258 in room 5 of farmhouse	Adult male with fragments of 2 iron knives and Roman coin	Anglo-Saxon
Grave 271 in room 4 of farmhouse	Adult female and newborn with amber and crystal beads, bronze ring and Roman coin	6th century
Grave 807 in building 2	Female 18–23 and newborn with amber beads, fish brooch, iron knife, iron buckle, iron pins and bone comb	
Grave 820 in building 2	Female 30–35 with amber beads, saucer brooch, bronze pin set, buckles, S-shaped animal ornaments, silver-plated rivets and ring	mid to 2nd half of 6th century
Grave 1171 inserted into a Roman gully in the SE paddock	Adult male over 40	
Barrow Hills area		
Barrow 2	Individual 17–19 with knife	7th century
Barrow 5	Adult male + adult	Possibly Anglo-Saxon
In N of area between Daisy Bank streams	Adult male	Found in 1905, possibly Anglo-Saxon

the structures in the right-angled arrangements at Barton Court Farm and Barrow Hills, may have fulfilled these functions. Slaughtering, leather production and various other processes associated with preparing and preserving animal products tend to smell unpleasant, and are usually carried out off-site or some distance down-wind of settlements. It is possible that the structures PBS 21 and 22 were associated with such processes.

The use of sunken-featured buildings as grain stores has been discussed in Chapter 3, but they no doubt fulfilled other purposes. The preparation of milk products in particular requires scrupulous cleanliness in order to avoid serious food poisoning, and was traditionally carried out in separate premises from other food production. Brewing also, which would have been an important source not merely of entertainment but of the vitamin B complex, requires attention to hygiene, preferably in its own premises. Water for drinking, cooking and washing would have had to be fetched either from wells sunk along the edge of Daisy Banks, like the wicker-line well at Barton Court Farm, or from springs along the edge of the terrace, and stored on site. Fuel from the nearest woods would also have needed storage.

The settlement was almost certainly self-sufficient in the linen and woollen textiles used in clothing, bedding, food preparation, cleaning and furnishing. The labour this implies is reflected in the prevalence of textile-related finds (Fig. 7.10). There are concentrations of loomweights in SFB 1190 at Barton Court Farm and in the area of barrow 13 at Barrow Hills, suggesting that loomweights were deposited as sets or part sets in a way that prevented them from being widely dispersed after deposition, perhaps tied together on strings or rods. There are relatively few loomweights from the rest of Barrow Hills, and none from the central cluster of buildings, which as we have seen produced very few textile-related finds in general. In the light of what is known about how material found its way into fills we must be cautious in interpreting this, but West observed at West Stow that whereas 'spinning seems to have been a universal practice in the settlement, weaving was predominantly the practice of only two of the [hall] groups' (1985, 138–9). The fact that there are only two concentrations of loomweights from the lifetime of Barrow Hills and Barton Court Farm may reflect some degree of specialisation, or perhaps that the community was too small to need more than one or two looms. Spinning would have been an almost constant occupation for women and girls; it takes a great deal of hand-spun yarn to weave a yard of cloth. Other craft activities including antler-working, iron-working and potting were also practised, and were presumably supplemented by others that have left no archaeological trace, such as woodworking and basket-making.

BURIALS (Fig. 1.3 and Table 7.3)

There were seven burials datable to the Anglo-Saxon period in or near the Barrow Hills/Barton Court Farm settlement and another four which may have been Anglo-Saxon but were not accompanied by grave goods; two at Barrow Hills, five at Barton Court Farm, two inserted into barrow 5 and one in barrow 2 and one in the area between the Daisy Bank streams. Burial in cemeteries seems to have been the preferred rite in the Anglo-Saxon period, although the age distribution in cemeteries suggests that newborns and infants could be treated differently. At West Stow, in addition to two possible adult burials within the area of the settlement, fragments of two adults and not less than four infants under one year old were found in layer 2 and the sunken-featured buildings (West 1985, 58–9), suggesting that in some cases infants were disposed of in such a way that their remains were easily disturbed and became incorporated into the general settlement debris. At Barrow Hills the only unaccompanied burial of a newborn was in the bottom of SFB 32, and it has been argued that this may have been chosen as a site for burial because the hut was about to be deliberately backfilled. It seems probable that the selection of pond barrow 4866 and the Romano-British buildings at Barton Court Farm for burial means that there was no longer any domestic activity in these areas.

There seems no reason to doubt that the stray burials in and around the area of the settlement are those of its former inhabitants, prompting the question of why, in a society that seems to have preferred burial in cemeteries, these individuals should have been buried more or less in isolation. It is possible that there was something in the circumstances of their deaths which made it necessary to exclude them from the normal funerary practice, but equally there may have been purely practical reasons for disposing of them in this way. The location of the cemetery which served the settlement is not known, and it is conceivable that it was some distance away, perhaps in Abingdon itself, or that it was situated in some other way which made it periodically inaccessible, for example in severe weather, or at busy times like harvest. The choice of the barrows and old Romano-British farm buildings may have been an attempt to find resting places with some associations of sanctity for those who could not, for whatever reason, be laid alongside their kin. Unfortunately, in the absence of the cemetery it is difficult to arrive at any convincing model for the population of the settlement.

Appendix 1: Pottery and Bone Proportions per m^3

Proportions are given in the order bone weight (kg); pottery weight (kg); sherds

SUNKEN-FEATURED BUILDINGS

1: .92, .99, 59
2: .74, .49, 31
3: .37, .15, 14
4: .38, .10, 14
5: 1.5, .57, 68
6: 1.4, .33, 24
7: .49, .32, 20
8: .99, .34, 42
10: .66, .20, 7
11: 0, .47, 18
12: .25, .04, 2
13: .48, .20, 10
14: 1.54, .76, 42
15: .92, .47, 35
16: 1.35, .45, 26
19: .95, .94, 48
20: .95, .40, 27
21: 0, .43, 40
22: .58, .36, 38
23: 1.51, 1.6, 21

24: 1.92, .53, 43
26: 0, .63, 62
30: 0, .65, 40
35: .81, .27, 26
38: 0, .37, 28
39: .39, .58, 21
40: .77, .93, 63
41: .33, .63, 63
42: 5.63, .27, 33
43: 0, .75, 38
45: .84, .77, 53

BARROW 12

North-east segments (E, F, G): 0.39, .1, 50
North-west segments (D, N, O, P, A): 1, .27, 23
South-east segments (B, H, I, J, C): 1.26, .99, 41
South-west segments (K, L, M): .57, .3, 29

BARROW 13

North-east segments (A, E, F, G, B): 1.82, .09, 31
North-west segments (N, O, P): 2.05, .35, 33
South-east segments (H, I, J): 2.19, .21, 43
South-west segments (C, K, L, M, D): 1.07, .32, 39

Bibliography

Abingdon and District Archaeological Society, 1973 Notes on Corporation Farm, *Council Brit Archaeol Group 9 Newsletter* **3**, 40

Adams, B, 1983 Anglo-Saxon cemetery at Wakerley, Northamptonshire: the excavation, discussion of the cemetery, its contents and context, Unpublished M Phil thesis Birkbeck College, University of London

Addyman, P V and Leigh, D, 1973 The Anglo-Saxon village at Chalton, Hampshire: second interim report. *Medieval Archaeol* **17**, 1–26

Addyman, P V, Leigh, D and Hughes, M J, 1972 Anglo-Saxon houses at Chalton, Hants. *Medieval Archaeol* **16**, 13–32

Addyman, P V and Priestley, J, 1977 Baile Hill, York, *Archaeol J* **134**, 115–56

Ager, B, forthcoming Disc brooches, in Boyle *et al.* forthcoming

Ainslie, R, 1991 Notes on work at Abingdon Bath Street, *South Midlands Archaeol* **21**, 110–11

Akerman, J Y, 1865 Notes in *Proc Soc Antiq*, 2nd ser iii, 145, 202–3

Alcock, N W, and Walsh, D, 1993 Architecture at Cowdery's Down: a reconsideration, *Archaeol J* **150**, 403–9

Aldsworth, F, 1979 Droxford Anglo-Saxon cemetery, Soberton, Hampshire, *Proc Hampshire Field Club and Archaeol Soc* **35**, 93–182

Algar, D J, 1961 Winterbourne Down: Roman cemetery, *Wiltshire Archaeol Mag* **58** 1961–3, 470

Allen, T G, 1990a Abingdon, *Current Archaeology* **121**, 24–7

Allen, T G, 1990b Notes on Abingdon Vineyard, *South Midlands Archaeol* **20**, 73–8

Allen, T G, 1991 Notes on Abingdon Vineyard, *South Midlands Archaeol* **21**, 97–8

Allen, T G and Kamash, Z, forthcoming Excavations at Spring Road Municipal Cemetery, Abingdon, Oxfordshire, 1990–2000, Oxford Archaeology, Thames Valley Landscapes Monograph

Ambrosiani, K, 1981 Viking age combs, comb making and comb makers: in light of the finds from Birka and Ribe, Stockholm, *Studies in Archaeology* **2**, Stockholm

Ancient Monuments Laboratory, 1983 Radley, Oxon.: magnetometer survey 1983, Internal report of the A M L

Armitage, P, 1982 A system for ageing and sexing the horncores of cattle from British post-medieval sites (with special reference to unimproved British longhorn cattle), in *Ageing and sexing of animal bones from archaeological sites* in (eds R Wilson, C Grigson and S Payne), Brit Archaeol Rep British Series **109**, 91–108, Oxford

Armitage, P and Clutton-Brock, J, 1976 A system for classification and description of horn cores of cattle from archaeological sites, *J Archaeol Sci* **3**, 329–348

Arnold, C J, 1988 *An archaeology of the early Anglo-Saxon kingdoms*, London

Atkinson, R J C, 1952–3 Excavations in Barrow Hills Field, Radley, Berks, 1944–5, *Oxoniensia* **17/18**, 32–5

Avent, R and Evison, V I, 1982 Ango-Saxon button brooches, *Archaeologia* **107**, 77–124

Avery, M and Brown, D, 1972 Saxon features at Abingdon, *Oxoniensia* **37**, 66–81

Barclay, A and Halpin, C, 1999 *Excavations at Barrow Hills, Radley, Oxfordshire. Volume 1. The Neolithic and Bronze Age monument complex*, Thames Valley Landscapes Monograph No. **11**, Oxford Archaeol Unit, Oxford

Barnetson, L P D, forthcoming The faunal remains from the Broxmouth hillfort, East Lothian, in P Hill, *Excavation of the Iron Age hillfort at Broxmouth, East Lothian*

Bartlett, A, 1999 Geophysical survey, in A Barclay and C Halpin, 1999, 11–14

Bartosiewicz, L, 1984 Reconstruction of prehistoric cattle represented by astragali in a Bronze Age "sacrificial pit", in *Animals and archaeology: husbandry in Europe Vol. 4* (eds C Grigson and J Clutton-Brock), BAR Int Ser **227**, 67–80, Oxford

Benson, D, and Miles, D, 1974 *The Upper Thames Valley: an archaeological survey of the river gravels* Oxfordshire Archaeological Unit Survey no. **2**, Oxford

Berisford, F, 1981 The Anglo-Saxon pottery, in Excavations at Beech House Hotel, Dorchester-on-Thames 1972 (T Rowley and L Brown), *Oxoniensia* **46**, 39–43

Blinkhorn, P W, forthcoming The post-Roman pottery, in Allen and Kamash forthcoming

Blinkhorn, P W, in press a *The Ipswich Ware project: ceramics, trade and society in Middle Saxon England*, Medieval Pottery Res Group Monog

Blinkhorn, P W, in press b The post-Roman pottery in Excavations at Warmington, Northants (I Meadows), *Northamptonshire Archaeol*

Blinkhorn, P W, in press c The post-Roman pottery, in *Excavations at North Raunds, Northamptonshire* (M Audouy), English Heritage Monograph Ser, London

Blinkhorn, P W, 1993 Early and Middle Saxon Pottery from Pennyland and Hartigans, in R J Williams, *Pennyland and Hartigans. Two Iron Age and Saxon sites in Milton Keynes* Bucks Archaeol Soc Mono Ser **4**, 246–64, Aylesbury

Blinkhorn, P W, 1997 Habitus, social identity and Anglo-Saxon pottery, in C G Cumberpatch and P W Blinkhorn (eds) 1997, 113–24

Blinkhorn, P W, 1999 The trials of being a utensil: vessel use at the medieval hamlet of West Cotton, Northamptonshire, *Medieval Ceramics* **22–23**, 37–46

Blinkhorn, P W, 2001 The Anglo-Saxon pottery, in Excavations at the Oxford Science Park, Littlemore, Oxfordshire (J Moore), *Oxoniensia* **66**, 189–197

Blinkhorn, P W, 2003 The pottery, in *Ælfric's Abbey: excavations at Eynsham Abbey, Oxfordshire 1989–1992* (A Hardy, A Dodd and G D Keevill), Oxford Archaeology Thames Valley Landscapes Monograph **16**, 159–206, Oxford

Blinkhorn, P W, 2004 Pottery, in *Yarnton: Saxon and Medieval Settlement and Landscape, Results of Excavations 1990–96* (G Hey), Oxford Archaeology Thames Valley Landscapes Monograph **20**, 267–274, Oxford

Böhner, K, 1958 *Die fränkischen Altertümer des Trierer Landes*, Römisch-Germanische Kommission: Germanische Denkmäler der Volkerwanderungszeit, Serie B, Bd 1, Berlin

Bond, C J, 1979 The reconstruction of the medieval landscape; the estates of Abingdon Abbey, *Landscape history* **1**, 59–75

Boon, G C, 1977 Gold-in-glass beads from the ancient world, *Britannia* **8**, 193–207

Booth, P, 1995 Roman pottery, in *Two Oxfordshire Anglo-Saxon cemeteries: Berinsfield and Didcot* (A Boyle, A Dodd, D Miles and A Mudd), Thames Valley Landscapes Monograph No. **8**, Oxford Archaeol Unit, Oxford, 16–26.

Booth, P, 1997 *Asthall, Oxfordshire, excavations in a Roman 'small town', 1992*, Thames Valley Landscapes Monograph No. **9**, Oxford Archaeol Unit, Oxford

Booth, P, Boyle, A and Keevill, G, 1993 A Romano-British kiln site at Lower Farm, Nuneham Courtenay, and other sites on the Didcot to Oxford and Wootton to Abingdon water mains, Oxfordshire, *Oxoniensia* **58**, 87–217

Booth, P, Evans, J and Hiller, J, 2001 *Excavations in the extramural settlement of Roman Alchester, Oxfordshire, 1991*, Oxford Archaeology Mono **1**, Oxford

Bourdillon, J, and Coy, J, 1980 The animal bones in P Holdsworth, *Excavations at Melbourne Street, Southampton, 1971–76*, CBA Res Rep **33**, 79–137, London

Boyle, A, 2001 The human skeletal assemblage, in Booth *et al*. 2001, 385–394, Oxford

Boyle, A, forthcoming Human bone in Hey *et al*.

Boyle, A, unpublished Human bone from Crowmarsh, unpublished report

Boyle, A, Clarke, D, Miles, D and Palmer, S, forthcoming *The Anglo-Saxon Cemetery at Butler's Field, Lechlade, Gloucestershire. Volume 2: Discussion and Synthesis*, Oxford Archaeology Thames Valley Landscapes Monograph

Bradley, R, 1992 The excavation of an oval barrow beside the Abingdon causewayed enclosure, Oxfordshire, *Proc Prehist Soc* **58**, 127–142

Brodribb, A C C, Hands, A R and Walker, D R, 1971 *Excavations at Shakenoak Farm, near Wilcote, Oxfordshire Part II: Sites B and H*, Oxford

Brodribb, A C C, Hands, A R and Walker, D R, 1972 *Excavations at Shakenoak Farm, near Wilcote, Oxfordshire Part III: Site F*, Oxford

Brothwell, D R, 1981 *Digging up bones*, London

Brown, D, 1972 Discussion of the finds, in Avery and Brown 1972, 78–81

Bull, G and Payne, S, 1982 Tooth eruption and epiphyseal fusion in pigs and wild boar, in *Ageing and sexing of animal bones from archaeological sites* (eds R Wilson, C Grigson and S Payne), BAR Brit Ser **109**, 55–71, Oxford

Case, H J, 1982 Cassington 1950–2: Late Neolithic pits and the Big Enclosure, in *Settlement patterns in the Oxford region; excavations at the Abingdon causewayed enclosure and other sites* (eds H J Case and A W R Whittle), CBA Res Rep **44**, 118–151, London

Chadwick Hawkes, S, and Gray, M, 1969 Preliminary note on the early Anglo-Saxon settlement at New Wintles Farm, Eynsham, *Oxoniensia* **34**, 1–4

Chambers, R A, 1976 A Romano-British settlement at Curbridge, *Oxoniensia* **41**, 38–55

Chambers, R A, 1978 Two radiocarbon dates from the Romano-British cemetery and settlement at Curbridge, Oxon., *Oxoniensia* **43**, 252

Chambers, R A, 1980 Note on Abingdon School *Council Brit Archaeol Group 9 Newsletter* **10**, 167

Chambers, R A, 1986 Romano-British burials from Wroxton, Oxon., *Oxoniensia* **51**, 37–44

Chambers, R A, 1987 The late and sub-Roman cemetery at Queensford Farm, Dorchester-on-Thames, Oxon., *Oxoniensia* **52**, 35–70

Champion, T C, 1978 Strategies for sampling an Anglo-Saxon settlement: a retrospective view of Chalton, in Cherry *et al*. 1978, 207–225

Cherry, J, Gamble, C and Shennan, S (eds), 1978 *Sampling in contemporary British archaeology*, BAR Int Ser **50**, 207–25, Oxford

Clapham, A R, Tutin, T G and Moore, D M, 1987 *Flora of the British Isles*, 3rd ed, Cambridge University Press

Clark, J, 1986 *Medieval horseshoes*, Finds Research Group, 700–1700, Datasheet **4**

Clarke, C M, 1996 Excavations at Cold Harbour Farm, Crowmarsh, *South Midlands Archaeol* **26**, 71–76

Clarke, G, 1979 *The Roman cemetery at Lankhills*, Winchester Studies **3**, Oxford

Collis, J, 1977 Owslebury (Hants.) and the problems of burial in the Roman world, in *Burial in the Roman world* (ed. R Reece), CBA Res Rep **22**, 26–34, London

Cook, A M, 1981 *The Anglo-Saxon cemetery at Fonaby, Lincolnshire*, Occ papers in Lincolnshire Hist Archaeol **6**, Sleaford

Crowfoot, E, 1985 The textiles, in West 1985, 69–70

Crummy, P, 1981 Aspects of Anglo-Saxon and Norman Colchester, CBA Res Rep **39**, Colchester Archaeol Rep **1**, London

Crummy, N, 1983 *The Roman small finds from excavations in Colchester*, Colchester Archaeol Rep **2**

Crummy, N, 1988 *The post-Roman small finds from excavations in Colchester 1971–85*, Colchester Archaeol Rep **5**

Cumberpatch, C G, and Blinkhorn, P W, (eds), 1997 *Not so much a pot, more a way of life*, Oxbow Monograph **83**, Oxford

David, A, 1994 The role of geophysical survey in early medieval archaeology in *Anglo-Saxon studies in archaeology and history 7* (eds William Filmer-Sankey and David Griffiths), 1–25, Oxford

Dickinson, T M, 1976 The Anglo-Saxon burial sites of the Upper Thames region and their bearing upon the history of Wessex circa 400–700, Unpublished DPhil thesis, University of Oxford

Dickinson, T, M, forthcoming The saucer brooches, in Boyle *et al.* forthcoming

Dodd, A, 1995 The brooches in *Two Anglo-Saxon cemeteries: Wally Corner, Berinsfield and Didcot Power Station* (A Boyle, A Dodd, D Miles and A Mudd), Oxford Archaeological Unit Thames Valley Landscapes Monograph **8**, 75–86, Oxford

Down, A and Welch, M, 1990 A*pple Down and the Mardens*, Chichester Excavations, **7**, Chichester

Drennan, R D, 1996 *Statistics for archaeologists*, Plenum

Dunning, G C, Hurst, J G, Myres, J N L and Tischler, F, 1959 Anglo-Saxon pottery: a symposium, *Medieval Archaeol* **3**, 1–78

Dürr, G, 1961 *Neue Funde des Rindes aus dem keltischen Oppidum von Manching*, Studien an vor-und frühgeschichtlichen Tierresten Bayerns **12**, Munich

Elliott, R W V, 1959 *Runes: an introduction*, Manchester

Evison, V I, 1987 *Dover, the Buckland Anglo-Saxon cemetery* HBMC Rep **3**, London

Evison, V I, 1988 *An Anglo-Saxon cemetery at Alton, Hampshire,* Hants. Field Club and Archaeol Soc Monograph **4**, Gloucester

Fennel, K R, 1964 The Anglo-Saxon cemetery at Loveden Hill (Hough-on-the-Hill) Lincolnshire and its significance in relation to the Dark Age settlement of the East Midlands, Unpublished PhD Thesis, University of Nottingham

Ferembach, D, Stloukal, M, and Schwidetzky I, 1980 Recommendations for age and sex diagnosis of skeletons, *J Human Evolution* **9**, 517–49

Fock, J, 1966 Metrische Untersuchungen an Metapodien einiger europäischer Rinderassen, Unpublished dissertation of the Institut für Palaeoanatomie, University of Munich

Fulford, M G 1975 *New Forest Roman pottery manufacture and distribution with a corpus of the pottery types*, BAR Brit Ser **17**, Oxford

Garrett, B, 1994, The small finds, in *Excavations at Portchester Castle. Vol. 5: Post Medieval 1609–1819* (B Cunliffe and B Garratt), Soc of Antiq of London Research Report **52**, 98–129, London

Gautier, A, 1984 How do I count you, let me count the ways? Problems of archaeozoological quantification, in *Animals in archaeology: husbandry in Europe Vol. 4* (eds C Grigson and J Clutton-Brock), BAR Int Ser **227**, 237–51, Oxford

Gelling, M, 1974 *The place-names of Berkshire* Vol. 2, English Place-name Society **50**, Cambridge

Goodall, I H, 1980 Ironwork in medieval Britain: an archaeological study, Unpublished PhD thesis, University of Cardiff

Goodall, I H, 1990 Horseshoes, in M Biddle, *Object and economy in medieval Winchester, Vol ii, Winchester Studies 7ii, artefacts from medieval Winchester,* 1054–67, Oxford

Grainger, G, 2006 The knives, in Hawkes and Grainger 2006

Grainger, G, unpublished The knives from the Anglo-Saxon cemetery at Worthy Park, Kingsworthy, near Winchester, Report in site archive

Grant, A, 1975 The animal bones, in B W Cunliffe, *Excavations at Portchester Castle* Vol. 1:, Soc Antiq London Res Rep **32**, 378-408 London

Gray, M, 1974 The Saxon settlement at New Wintles, Eynsham, Oxon., in *Anglo-Saxon settlement and landscape* (ed T R Rowley), BAR Brit Ser **6**, 51–55, Oxford

Gray, M, 1977 Northfield Farm, Long Wittenham, *Oxoniensia* **42**, 1–29

Grayson, D K, 1984 *Quantitative zooarchaeology*, London

Green, B, Rogerson, A, and White, S, 1987 *The Anglo-Saxon cemetery at Morning Thorpe, Norfolk*, EAA Rep **7**, Gressenhall

Green, F, 1979 Plant remains, in C Heighway, A Garrod and A Vince (eds), Excavations at 1 Westgate Street, Gloucester, *Medieval Archaeol* **23**, 186–207

Greig, J, 1983 Plant foods in the past: a review of the evidence from Northern Europe, *J Plant Foods* **5**, 179–214

Grigson, C, 1982 Sex and age determination of some bones and teeth of domestic cattle, in *Ageing and sexing of animal bones from archaeological sites* (eds R Wilson, C Grigson and S Payne), BAR Brit Ser **109**, 91–108, Oxford

Hald, M, 1950 *Olddanske tekstiler* Copenhagen

Halpin, C, 1982 Notes on Abingdon, the former MG car factory site, *Council Brit Archaeol Group 9 Newsletter* **12**, 138–9

Hamerow, H F, 1993 *Excavations at Mucking Volume 2: the Anglo-Saxon settlement*, English Heritage Archaeol Rep **22**, London

Hamerow, H F, 1995 Shaping settlements: early medieval communities in northwest Europe, in *Europe between late antiquity and the middle ages* (eds J Bintliffe and H Hamerow), BAR Int Ser **617**, 8–37, Oxford

Hamilton, J R C, 1956 *Excavations at Jarlshof, Shetland* Edinburgh

Harman, M, Molleson, T I and Price, J L, 1981 Burials, bodies and beheadings, *Bull Brit Mus (Nat Hist)* **35**, 145–187

Haslam, J, Biek, L, and Tylecote, R F, 1980 A middle Saxon iron smelting site at Ramsbury, Wiltshire, *Medieval Archaeol* **24**, 1–68

Hattatt, R, 1985 *Iron Age and Roman brooches a second selection of brooches from the author's collection*, Oxford

Hawkes, S C and Grainger, G, 2006 *The Anglo-Saxon Cemetery at Finglesham, Kent,* Oxford University School of Archaeology Monograph **64**, Oxford

Heighway, C M, 1980 Roman cemeteries in Gloucester district, *Trans Bristol Gloucestershire Archaeol Soc* **98**, 57–72

Helbaek, H, 1952 Early crops in southern England, *Proc Prehist Soc* **18**, 194–227

Hey, G, *et al.* in prep Yarnton: Iron Age and Roman Settlement and Landscapes. Results of Excavations 1989–1998, Oxford Archaeology Thames Valley Landscapes Monograph

Hills, C, 1977 *The Anglo-Saxon cemetery at Spong Hill, North Elmham, Part I*, EAA Rep **6**, Gressenhall

Hills, C, Penn, K and Rickett, R, 1984 *The Anglo-Saxon cemetery at Spong Hill, North Elmham. Part III: catalogue of the inhumations* EAA Rep **21**, Gressenhall

Hills, C, Penn, K and Rickett, R, 1987 *The Anglo-Saxon cemetery at Spong Hill, North Elmham. Part IV: catalogue of the cremations* EAA Rep **34**, Gressenhall

Hoffmann, M, 1964 The warp-weighted loom: studies in the history and technology of an ancient implement, *Studia Norvegica* **14**

Hood, S and Walton, H, 1948 A Romano-British cremating place and burial ground on Roden Downs, Compton, Berkshire, *Trans Newbury District Field Club* **9** No. 1, 10–62

Howard, M M, 1963 The metrical determination of the metapodials and skulls of cattle, in *Man and cattle* (eds A Mourant and F Zeuner), Royal Anthropol Inst Occ Pap **18**, 91–100, London

Huggins, P J, 1991 Anglo-Saxon timber building measurements: recent results, *Medieval Archaeol* **35**, 6–28

Ijzereef, G F, 1981 Bronze Age animal bones from Bovenkarspel: the excavation at Het Valkje, *Nederlandse Oudheden* **10**

Jackson, D, Harding, D and Myres, J N L, 1969 The Iron Age and Anglo-Saxon site at Upton, Northants, *Antiq J* **49**, 202–21

James, S, Marshall, A and Millett, M, 1984 An early medieval building tradition, *Archaeol J* **141**, 182–215

Jones, G, Thomas, R and Wallis, J, 1980 Notes on work at Radley Thrupp Farm, *Council Brit Archaeol Group 9 Newsletter* **10**, 184

Jones, M, 1978 The plant remains, in *The excavation of an Iron Age settlement, Bronze Age ring-ditches and Roman features at Ashville Trading Estate, Abingdon (Oxfordshire) 1974–76* (M Parrington), CBA Res Rep **28**, 93–110, London

Jones, M, 1981 The development of crop husbandry, in *The environment of man: the Iron Age to the Anglo-Saxon period* (eds M Jones and G Dimbleby), BAR Brit Ser **87**, 95–127, Oxford

Jones, M, 1986 Towards a model of the villa estate, in Miles 1986, 38–42, London

Jones, M and Robinson, M, 1986 The crop plants, in Miles 1986, fiche 9:E10-9: E14, London

Jones, M U, 1975 Wool-comb warmers from Mucking, Essex, *Antiq J* **55**, 411–13

Jones, M U and W T, 1975 The crop-mark sites at Mucking, Essex, England, in *Recent archaeological excavations in Europe* (ed R L S Bruce-Mitford), 133–87, London

Keevill, G D and Parsons, M, 1991 Notes on Abingdon Adult Training Centre, *South Midlands Archaeol* **21**, 92

Keevill, G D, 1992 An Anglo-Saxon site at Audlett Drive, Abingdon, Oxfordshire, *Oxoniensia* **57**, 55–79

Klein, R G and Cruz-Uribe, K, 1984 *The analysis of animal bones from archaeological sites*, Chicago

Knock, J, 1976 Skefning *Skalk* **1976:2**, Århus

Lambrick, G, forthcoming *A study in change: early prehistoric to Saxon life and ritual at Mount Farm, (Berinsfield) Dorchester-on-Thames, Oxon.*, Oxford Archaeology Occasional Paper

Lambrick, G, 1992 Alluvial archaeology of the Upper Thames basin 1971–1991: a review, in *Alluvial archaeology in Britain* (eds S Needham and M G Macklin), Oxbow Mono **27**, 209–26, Oxford

Lambrick, G and Allen, T, 2004 *Gravelly Guy, Stanton Harcourt, Oxfordshire. The development of a prehistoric and Romano-British community*, Thames Valley Landscapes Monograph **21**, Oxford

Leeds, E T, 1924 A Saxon village near Sutton Courtenay, Berks., *Archaeologia* **73**, 146–192

Leeds, E T, 1927 A Saxon village at Sutton Courtenay, Berks., *Archaeologia* **76**, 12–80

Leeds, E T, 1938 Further excavations in Barrow Hills Field, Radley, Berks., *Oxoniensia* **3**, 33–4

Leeds, E T, 1947 A Saxon village at Sutton Courtenay, Berks., *Archaeologia* **92**, 79–93

Leeds, E T and Harden, D, 1936 *The Anglo-Saxon cemetery at Abingdon, Berkshire*, Oxford

Lethbridge, T, 1931 *Recent excavations in Anglo-Saxon cemeteries in Cambridgeshire and Suffolk*, Cambridge Antiquarian Society Quarto Publications New Series 5, Burwell

Lindstrom, M, 1976 Nalar av ben, horn och brons. Uppgravt forflutet for PK-banken I Lund. Archaeologica Lundensia, *Investigationes de antiquitatibus urbis Lundas VII*, Malmo

London Museum, 1940 *Medieval catalogue* London Museum Catalogue **7**, London

McGavin, N, 1980 A Roman cemetery and trackway at Stanton Harcourt, *Oxoniensia* **14**, 112–23

MacGregor, A, 1978 Industry and commerce in Anglo-Scandinavian York, in R A Hall (ed.), *Viking Age York and the North*, CBA Res Rep **27**, 34–57, London

MacGregor, A, 1982 Anglo-Scandinavian finds from Lloyds Bank, Pavement and other sites, in *The archaeology of York* **17**, (P V Addyman), CBA, 67–174, London

MacGregor, A, 1985 *Bone, antler, ivory and horn: the archaeology of skeletal material since the Roman period*, London

MacGregor, A and Bolick, E, 1993 *A summary catalogue of the Anglo-Saxon collections: non-ferrous metals*, Ashmolean Museum, Oxford

Mann, J E, 1982 *Early medieval finds from Flaxengate: objects of antler, bone, stone, horn, ivory, amber and jet*, The archaeology of Lincoln Vol XIV-1, Lincoln

Manning, W H, 1985 *Catalogue of the Romano-British iron tools, fittings and weapons in the British Museum*, London

Manning, W H and Scott, I R, 1986 Iron objects, in Stead and Rigby 1986, 145–62

Marshall, A and Marshall, G, 1993 Differentiation, change and continuity in Anglo-Saxon buildings, *Archaeol J* **150**, 366–402

Matolcsi, J, 1970 *Historische Erforschung der Korpergrosse des Rindes auf Grund von ungarischem*

Knochenmaterial, Zeitschrift für Tierzuchtung und Zuchtungsbiologie **87**, Heft 2, 89–137

May, T, 1916 *The pottery found at Silchester*, Reading

Meaney, A, 1964 *A gazetteer of early Anglo-Saxon burial sites*, London

Mellor, M, 1994 Oxford pottery: a synthesis of middle and late Saxon, medieval and early post-medieval pottery in the Oxford Region, *Oxoniensia* **59**, 17–217

Medieval Pottery Research Group, 1998 *Guide to the classification of medieval ceramic forms* MPRG Occ Paper **1**

Mennerich, G, 1968 Romerzeitliche Tierknochen aus Drei Fundorten des Niederrheingebiets, Unpublished dissertation of the Institut für Palaeoanatomie, University of Munich

Miles, A E W, 1962 Assessment of the ages of a population of Anglo-Saxons from their dentitions, *Proc Royal Soc Medicine* **55**, 881–6

Miles, D, 1973 Notes on discoveries at Radley Gooseacre Farm, *CBA Group 9 Newsletter* **3**, 23–6

Miles, D, (ed), 1986 *Archaeology at Barton Court Farm, Abingdon, Oxon*, Council Brit Archaeol Res Rep **50**, London

Miles, D, Palmer, S, Smith, A, and Jones, G, forthcoming *Iron Age and Roman Settlement in the Upper Thames Valley, Excavations at Claydon Pike and other sites within the Cotswold Water Park*, Oxford Archaeology, Thames Valley Landscape Monograph No. **26**, Oxford

Millett, M and James, S, 1983 Excavations at Cowdery's Down, Basingstoke, Hampshire 1978–81, *Archaeol J* **140**, 151–279

Moffett, L, 1999 The prehistoric use of plant resources in Barclay and Halpin 1999, 243–7

Monk, M, 1981 Post-Roman drying kilns and the problem of function: a preliminary statement, in *Irish Antiquity: Essays and studies presented to Professor M.J. O'Kelly* (ed. D O' Corrain) 216–30, Cork

Murphy, P, 1983 Iron Age to late Saxon land use in the Breckland, in *Integrating the subsistence economy* (ed M Jones), BAR Int Ser **181**, 177–209, Oxford

Murphy, P, 1985 The cereals and crop weeds, in *West Stow, the Anglo-Saxon village Vol. 1* (S E West), EAA **24**

Moreland, J, 2000 Ethnicity, power and the English, in *Social identity in early medieval Britain and Ireland* (eds B Frazer and A Tyrell), Leicester

Mudd, A, 1995 The excavation of a Late Bronze/Early Iron Age site at Eight Acre Farm, Radley, *Oxoniensia* **60**, 21–65

Myres, J N L, 1968 The Anglo-Saxon cemetery, in The early history of Abingdon, Berkshire, and its Abbey (M Biddle, H T Lambrick and J N L Myres), *Medieval Archaeol* **12**, 35–41

Myres, J N L, 1977 *A corpus of Anglo-Saxon pottery of the pagan period*, Cambridge

Myres, J N L and Green, B, 1973 *The Anglo-Saxon cemeteries of Caistor-by-Norwich and Markshall, Norfolk, 1973*, Res Rep Comm Soc Antiq London **30**, London

Noddle, B, 1973 Determination of the body weight of cattle from bone measurements, in J Matolcsi (ed), *Domestikationforschung und Geschichte der Haustiere*, 377–389, Budapest

Noddle, B, 1980 The animal bones, in *Excavations in North Elmham Park 1967–72* (P Wade-Martins), EAA **9**, 375–409

Oakley, G E, 1979 The worked bone, in J H Williams, *St Peter's Street Northampton. Excavations 1973–6*, 308–18, Northampton

O'Connor, T, 1982 *Animal bones from Flaxengate, Lincoln c 870–1500*, The archaeology of Lincoln, Vol. **18–1**, London

Office of Population Censuses and Surveys, 1991 *The 1981 census*, Manchester, MIMAS

Orton, C, 1975 Quantitative pottery studies: some progress, problems and prospects, *Science and Archaeology* **16**, 30–5

Orton, C, 1982 Computer simulation experiments to assess the performance of measures of quantities of pottery, *World Archaeol* **14(1)**, 1–19

Orton, C, 1998–9 Minimum standards in statistics and sampling, *Medieval Ceramics* **22–23**, 135–8

Parrington, M 1977 Excavations in Barrow Hills Field, Radley, Oxon 1976, *Oxoniensia* **42**, 30–41

Hawkes, S C, 1973 The dating and significance of the burials in the Polhill Cemetery, in *Excavations in West Kent 1960–1970* (B Philp), 2nd Research Report in the Kent Series, 186–201, Dover

Parrington, M, 1978 *The excavation of an Iron Age settlement, Bronze Age ring-ditches and Roman features at Ashville Trading Estate, Abingdon (Oxfordshire) 1974–76*, CBA Res Rep **28**, London

Payne, G, 1892, Catalogue of the Kent Archaeological Society's collections at Maidstone, *Archaeol Cantiana* **19**, 4–38

Pfund, D, 1961 *Neue Funde von Schaf und Ziege aus dem keltischen Oppidum von Manching*, Studien an vor und fruhgeschichtlichen Tierresten Bayerns **11**, Munich

Philpott, R, 1991 *Burial practices in Roman Britain AD 43–410*, BAR Brit Ser **219**, Oxford

Plouviez, J, 1985 The late Romano-British pottery, in S West, *West Stow the Anglo-Saxon village*, EAA **24**, 82–85, Gressenhall

Polloth, K, 1959 *Die Schafe und Ziegen des La Tène-Oppidums Manching*, Studien an vor und fruhgeschichtlichen Tierresten Bayerns **6**, Munich

Powlesland, D, 1990 An interim report on the Anglo-Saxon village at West Heslerton, North Yorkshire, *Medieval Settlement Research Group Annual Report* 5, 36–40

Powlesland, D, 1999 West Heslerton settlement mobility: a case of static development, in *Early Deira. Archaeological studies of the East Riding in the fourth to ninth centuries AD* (eds H Geake and J Kenny), 19–26, Oxford

Rice, P M, 1987 *Pottery analysis: a sourcebook*, Chicago

Richards, J D, 1987 *The significance of the form and decoration of Anglo-Saxon Cremation Urns*, BAR Brit Ser **166**, Oxford

Ritchie, A, 1977 Excavation of Pictish and Viking Age farmsteads at Buckquoy, Orkney, *Proc Soc Antiq Scot* **108**, 174–227

Robinson, M, 1981 The Iron Age to early Saxon environment of the Upper Thames terraces, in *The environment of man: the Iron Age to the Anglo-Saxon period* (eds M Jones and G Dimbleby), BAR Brit Ser **87**, 251–86, Oxford

Robinson, M, 1986 Waterlogged plant and invertebrate evidence, in *Archaeology at Barton Court Farm, Abingdon, Oxon.* (ed D Miles), CBA Res Rep **50**, fiche 9:C1-E7, London

Robinson, M, 1992 Environment, archaeology and alluvium on the river gravels of the south Midlands, in *Alluvial archaeology in Britain* (eds S Needham and M G Macklin), Oxbow Mono **27**, 197–208, Oxford

Rogerson, A and Dallas, C, 1984 *Excavations at Thetford 1948–59 and 1973–80*, EAA **22**, Gressenhall

Ross, S, 1991 Dress pins from Anglo-Saxon England: their production and typo-chronological development, Unpublished D Phil thesis, University of Oxford

Rowley, T and Brown, L, 1981 Excavations at Beech House Hotel, Dorchester-on-Thames 1972, *Oxoniensia* **46**, 1–55

Salter, C, 1987 Ferrous metallurgy and other slags, in *Hengistbury Head Dorset, 1: The prehistoric and Roman settlement, 3500 BC–AD 500* (B Cunliffe), Oxford University Committee Archaeol Monograph **13**, 197–205, Oxford

Salter, C, 1991 Ferrous metalworking evidence, in *Maiden Castle: excavations and field survey 1985–6* (N M Sharples), English Heritage Archaeol Rep **19**, 165–70, London

Schneider, F, 1958 *Die Rinder des La Tene-Oppidums Manching*, Studien an vor und fruhgeschichtlichen Tierresten Bayerns **5**, Munich

Schneider, J E, 1983 Rasiermesser des 7./8. Jahrhunderts, *Helvetia Archaeologica* **14**, 235–40

Silver, I A, 1969 The ageing of domestic animals, in *Science in archaeology* (eds D Brothwell and E Higgs), 281–302, London

Slomann, W, 1959 *Saetrangfunnet Hiemlig Fradision og Fremmede Innslag*, Norske Oldfunn **9**

Spickett, G P, 1975 Peachcroft Farm, Radley, Oxfordshire, *CBA Group 9 Newsletter* **5**, 14–16

Stead, I M and Rigby, V, 1986 *Baldock: the excavation of a Roman and pre-Roman settlement, 1968–72*, Britannia Monogr Ser **7**

Stein, F, 1967, *Adelsgräber des achten Jahrhunderts in Deutschland*, Germanischer Denkmäler der Völkerwanderungszeit. Serie A, Band IX, Berlin

Stevenson, R B K, 1955 Pins and the chronology of brochs, *Proc Soc Antiq Scot* **21**, 282–94

Swanton, M J, 1974 *A corpus of pagan Anglo-Saxon spear-types*, BAR Brit Ser **7**, Oxford

Teichert, M, 1975 Osteometrische Untersuchungen zur Berechnung der Widerristhöhe bei Schafen, in *Archaeozoological studies* (ed A Clason), Groningen

Thomas, C, 1981 *Christianity in Roman Britain to AD 500*, London

Timby, J, 1996 The pottery, in The Roman and early Anglo-Saxon settlements at Wantage, Oxfordshire, Excavations at Mill Street, 1993–4 (N Holbrook and A Thomas), *Oxoniensia* **61**, 131–147

Tipper, J, 2004 *The Grubenhaus in Anglo-Saxon England: an analysis and interpretation of the evidence from a most distinctive building type*, The Landscape Research Centre, Yedingham, North Yorkshire

Ulbricht, W A, 1978 *Die Geweihverarbeitung in Haithabu*, Die Ausgrabungen in Haithabu **7**

Underwood-Keevill, C, 1992 The pottery, in Keevill 1992, 67–74

van Es, W A, 1967 Wijster: a native village beyond the imperial frontier, 150–425 AD, *Palaeohistoria* **11**, Groningen

VCH 1906 *Victoria County History of Berkshire, Volume I*

Vince, A G, unpublished Barrow Hills: the petrology of the Saxon pottery, unpublished report

von den Driesch, A, 1976 A guide to the measurement of animal bones from archaeological sites, *Peabody Museum Bulletin* No. **1**

von den Driesch, A and Boessneck, J, 1973 Kritische Anmerkungen zur Widerristhöheberechnung aus Längenmassen vor und frühgeschichtlicher Tierknochen, *Saugetierkundliche Mitteilungen* **22**, 325–48

Wallis, J, 1981a Radley: Abingdon peripheral road, *CBA Group 9 Newsletter* **11**, 132–4 and fig. 36

Wallis, J, 1981b Radley: Thrupp Farm, *CBA Group 9 Newsletter* **11**, 134–7

Watson, J P N, 1978 The interpretation of epiphyseal fusion data, in *Research problems in zooarchaeology* (eds D Brothwell, K D, Thomas and J Clutton-Brock), Inst Archaeol London Occasional Paper **3**, 97–102, London

Watt, R J, 1979 Evidence of decapitation, in *Pre-Roman and Roman Winchester Part II. The Roman cemetery at Lankhills* (G Clarke), Winchester Studies **3**, 342–44, Oxford

Watts, D J, 1989 Infant burials and Romano-British Christianity, *Arch J* **146**, 372–383

Welch, M, 1985 Button brooches, clasp buttons and facemasks, *Medieval Archaeol* **29**, 142–5

Welch, M, 1992 *Anglo-Saxon England*, English Heritage, London

Wells, C, 1960 A study of cremation, *Antiquity* **34**, 29–37

West, S E, 1985 *West Stow. The Anglo-Saxon village*, EAA **24**, Ipswich

Wild, J P, 1970 *Textile manufacture in the northern Roman provinces*, Cambridge

Wild, J P, 1988 *Textiles in archaeology*, Princes Risborough

Williams, P W, 1983 *An Anglo-Saxon cremation cemetery at Thurmaston, Leicestershire*, Leicestershire Museums Art Galleries and Records Series, Archaeological Report No. **8**, Leicester

Williams, A, 1948 Excavations in Barrow Hills Field, Radley Berkshire 1944, *Oxoniensia* **13**, 1–17

Williams, H, 1997 Ancient landscapes and the dead: the reuse of prehistoric and Roman monuments as

Early Anglo-Saxon burial sites, *Medieval Archaeol* **41**, 1–32

Wilson, B, 1991 Abingdon, *South Midlands Archaeol* **21**, 109–10

Wilson, B and Wallis, J, 1991 Prehistoric activity, early Roman building, tenement yards and gardens behind Twickenham House, Abingdon, *Oxoniensia* **56**, 1–15

Wilson, D R, 1970 Roman Britain in 1969: I. Sites explored, *Britannia* **1**, 268–305

Wilson, D R, 1972 Roman Britain in 1971: I. Sites explored, *Britannia* **3**, 298–351

Wilson, D, 1980 Abingdon, Boxhill *CBA Group 9 Newsletter* **10**, 167

Wilson, D, 1992 *Anglo-Saxon paganism*, London

Wilson, R, 1978 The animal bones, in *The excavation of an Iron Age settlement, Bronze Age ring-ditches and Roman features at Ashville Trading Estate, Abingdon (Oxfordshire) 1974-6* (M Parrington), CBA Res Rep **28**, 108–139, London

Witkin, A, 2006 Human bones, in Prehistoric and Roman Activity and a Civil War Ditch: Excavations at the Chemistry Research Building, 2–4 South Parks Road, Oxford, *Oxoniensia* **70**, 181–185

Woodward, A, and Blinkhorn, P W, 1997 Size is important: Iron Age vessel capacities in central and southern England, in Cumberpatch and Blinkhorn (eds) 1997, 153–62

Young, C J, 1977 *Oxfordshire Roman pottery*, BAR Brit Ser **43**, London

Index

339

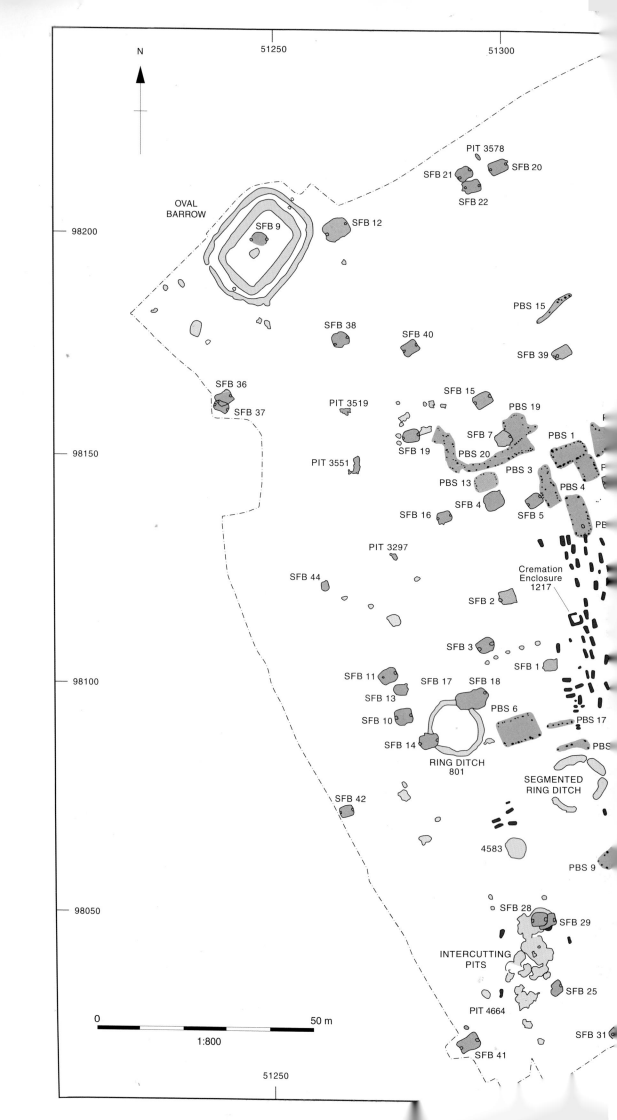